Praise for *A Developer's Guide to SQL Server 2005*

"I come from a T-SQL background, so when I first laid my eyes on SQL Server 2005, I was shocked—and then, I was scared! I didn't have a CLR or XML background and suddenly had an urgent need to learn it. SQL Server 2005 is too big of a release to learn from the books online. Fortunately, now there is a book for developers who need to go from SQL Server 2000 to SQL Server 2005 and to do it as painlessly as possible. Basically, it's one-stop shopping for serious developers who have to get up to speed quickly. I'll keep this one on my desk—not on my bookshelf. Well done, Bob and Dan!"

—Dr. Tom Moreau
SQL Server MVP and Monthly Columnist
SQL Server Professional, Brockman Moreau Consulting Inc.

"A SQL book truly for developers, from two authorities on the subject. I'll be turning to this book first when I need to understand a component of SQL Server 2005."

—Matt Milner
Instructor
Pluralsight

"An excellent book for those of us who need to get up to speed on what's new in SQL Server 2005. The authors made sure this book includes the final information for the release version of the product. Most other books out now are based on beta versions. It covers key areas from XML and SQLCLR to Notification Services. Although the wide variety of information is great, my favorite part was the advice given on when to use what, and how performance is affected."

—Laura Blood
Senior Software Developer
Blue Note Computing, Inc.

"SQL Server 2005 is a massive release with a large number of new features. Many of these features were designed to make SQL Server a great application development platform. This book provides comprehensive information about the SQL Server features of most interest to application developers. The lucid text

D1504850

and wealth of examples will give a developer a clear understanding of how to use SQL Server 2005 to a whole new class of database applications. It should be on every SQL Server developer's bookshelf."

"While there will be a lot of good books on SQL Server 2005 development, when people refer to the 'bible,' they'll be talking about this book."

"SQL Server 2005 is loaded with new features and getting a good overview is essential to understand how you can benefit from SQL Server 2005's features as a developer. Bob and Dan's book goes beyond enumerating the new SQL Server 2005 features, and will provide you with lots of good examples. They did a good job striking a balance between overview and substance."

A Developer's Guide
to SQL Server 2005

Microsoft .NET Development Series

John Montgomery, *Series Advisor*
Don Box, *Series Advisor*
Martin Heller, *Series Editor*

The **Microsoft .NET Development Series** is supported and developed by the leaders and experts of Microsoft development technologies including Microsoft architects and DevelopMentor instructors. The books in this series provide a core resource of information and understanding every developer needs in order to write effective applications and managed code. Learn from the leaders how to maximize your use of the .NET Framework and its programming languages.

Titles in the Series

Brad Abrams, *.NET Framework Standard Library Annotated Reference Volume 1: Base Class Library and Extended Numerics Library*, 0-321-15489-4

Brad Abrams and Tamara Abrams, *.NET Framework Standard Library Annotated Reference, Volume 2: Networking Library, Reflection Library, and XML Library*, 0-321-19445-4

Keith Ballinger, *.NET Web Services: Architecture and Implementation*, 0-321-11359-4

Bob Beauchemin, Niels Berglund, Dan Sullivan, *A First Look at SQL Server 2005 for Developers*, 0-321-18059-3

Don Box with Chris Sells, *Essential .NET, Volume 1: The Common Language Runtime*, 0-201-73411-7

Keith Brown, *The .NET Developer's Guide to Windows Security*, 0-321-22835-9

Eric Carter and Eric Lippert, *Visual Studio Tools for Office: Using C# with Excel, Word, Outlook, and InfoPath*, 0-321-33488-4

Eric Carter and Eric Lippert, *Visual Studio Tools for Office: Using Visual Basic 2005 with Excel, Word, Outlook, and InfoPath*, 0-321-41175-7

Mahesh Chand, *Graphics Programming with GDI+*, 0-321-16077-0

Krzysztof Cwalina and Brad Abrams, *Framework Design Guidelines: Conventions, Idioms, and Patterns for Reusable .NET Libraries*, 0-321-24675-6

Anders Hejlsberg, Scott Wiltamuth, Peter Golde, *The C# Programming Language*, 0-321-15491-6

Alex Homer, Dave Sussman, Mark Fussell, *ADO.NET and System.Xml v. 2.0—The Beta Version*, 0-321-24712-4

Alex Homer, Dave Sussman, Rob Howard, *ASP.NET v. 2.0—The Beta Version*, 0-321-25727-8

James S. Miller and Susann Ragsdale, *The Common Language Infrastructure Annotated Standard*, 0-321-15493-2

Christian Nagel, *Enterprise Services with the .NET Framework: Developing Distributed Business Solutions with .NET Enterprise Services*, 0-321-24673-X

Brian Noyes, *Data Binding with Windows Forms 2.0: Programming Smart Client Data Applications with .NET*, 0-321-26892-X

Fritz Onion, *Essential ASP.NET with Examples in C#*, 0-201-76040-1

Fritz Onion, *Essential ASP.NET with Examples in Visual Basic .NET*, 0-201-76039-8

Ted Pattison and Dr. Joe Hummel, *Building Applications and Components with Visual Basic .NET*, 0-201-73495-8

Dr. Neil Roodyn, *eXtreme .NET: Introducing eXtreme Programming Techniques to .NET Developers*, 0-321-30363-6

Chris Sells, *Windows Forms Programming in C#*, 0-321-11620-8

Chris Sells and Justin Gehtland, *Windows Forms Programming in Visual Basic .NET*, 0-321-12519-3

Paul Vick, *The Visual Basic .NET Programming Language*, 0-321-16951-4

Damien Watkins, Mark Hammond, Brad Abrams, *Programming in the .NET Environment*, 0-201-77018-0

Shawn Wildermuth, *Pragmatic ADO.NET: Data Access for the Internet World*, 0-201-74568-2

Paul Yao and David Durant, *.NET Compact Framework Programming with C#*, 0-321-17403-8

Paul Yao and David Durant, *.NET Compact Framework Programming with Visual Basic .NET*, 0-321-17404-6

For more information go to www.awprofessional.com/msdotnetseries/

A Developer's Guide to SQL Server 2005

- Bob Beauchemin
- Dan Sullivan

✦Addison-Wesley

Upper Saddle River, NJ • Boston • Indianapolis • San Francisco
New York • Toronto • Montreal • London • Munich • Paris
Madrid • Capetown • Sydney • Tokyo • Singapore • Mexico City

Many of the designations used by manufacturers and sellers to distinguish their products are claimed as trademarks. Where those designations appear in this book, and the publisher was aware of a trademark claim, the designations have been printed with initial capital letters or in all capitals.

The .NET logo is either a registered trademark or trademark of Microsoft Corporation in the United States and/or other countries and is used under license from Microsoft.

The authors and publisher have taken care in the preparation of this book, but make no expressed or implied warranty of any kind and assume no responsibility for errors or omissions. No liability is assumed for incidental or consequential damages in connection with or arising out of the use of the information or programs contained herein.

The publisher offers excellent discounts on this book when ordered in quantity for bulk purchases or special sales, which may include electronic versions and/or custom covers and content particular to your business, training goals, marketing focus, and branding interests. For more information, please contact:

U.S. Corporate and Government Sales
(800) 382-3419
corpsales@pearsontechgroup.com

For sales outside the United States, please contact:

International Sales
international@pearsoned.com

 This Book Is Safari Enabled

The Safari® Enabled icon on the cover of your favorite technology book means the book is available through Safari Bookshelf. When you buy this book, you get free access to the online edition for 45 days.

Safari Bookshelf is an electronic reference library that lets you easily search thousands of technical books, find code samples, download chapters, and access technical information whenever and wherever you need it.

To gain 45-day Safari Enabled access to this book:

- Go to http://www.awprofessional.com/safarienabled
- Complete the brief registration form
- Enter the coupon code 81D6-VTRC-813R-SQC1-W2SD

If you have difficulty registering on Safari Bookshelf or accessing the online edition, please e-mail customer-service@safaribooksonline.com.

Visit us on the Web: www.awprofessional.com

Library of Congress Cataloging-in-Publication Data

Beauchemin, Bob.
  A developer's guide to SQL server 2005 / Bob Beauchemin, Dan Sullivan.
    p. cm.
  Includes bibliographical references and index.
  ISBN 0-321-38218-8 (pbk. : alk. paper)
  1. SQL server. 2. Client/server computing. 3. Relational databases. I.
Sullivan, Dan. II. Title.

  QA76.9.C55B425 2006
  005.2'768—dc22

                                                                2006003470

ISBN 0-321-38218-8

Text printed in the United States at Courier in Stoughton, Massachusetts.
First printing, May 2006

To Mary, who just smiles now when I say,
"I'm almost done, just one more book. . . ."
—*BB*

▪

To Alberta who continues to be
a rock of support, patience, and love.
—*DS*

▪

Contents at a Glance

Contents

Figures

Tables

Foreword

by Roger Wolter

AS I SAID IN THE foreword to *A First Look at SQL Server 2005 for Developers,* I have been a Bob Beauchemin fan for the past seven years. Bob is one of the few people I know who not only knows a lot about database programming, but also is very good at teaching other people to be great database programmers. Bob wrote the book on ADO programming and has many years of experience teaching database programming classes and giving presentations at conferences and seminars.

In addition to reviewing several chapters of this book multiple times as they were changed to keep pace with changes to the beta content, I sat in on several classes that Bob and Dan taught about SQL Server 2005 programming. They both have a unique talent for simplifying complex topics and explaining them in a way that is relevant to developers. This talent is obvious in the content of this book, and I highly recommend it to anyone who wants to learn how to take advantage of the new features of SQL Server 2005 in his or her applications.

About three years ago, I sat for a couple of hours at a Starbucks in Seattle with Bob to talk about the Service Broker chapter of this book. In those three years, this book has gone through countless reviews and rewrites, until now, it's the most authoritative book about SQL Server 2005 programming available. Many people on the SQL Server development team have provided input and reviewed many of the chapters several times. I have been involved in various ways throughout this process, so I'm very excited to see the RTM version of this book reach completion.

The thing that makes this book truly unique is that Bob and Dan taught SQL Server 2005 programming to several hundred developers in the Microsoft Ascend and TAP programs while they were writing the book, so the content of the book is heavily influenced by what real developers found useful and the questions they asked. There's no better way to learn a new technology than trying to explain it to someone else, so after teaching this material many times all over the world, Dan and Bob have a deep understanding of what developers need to know and how best to explain it to them. This is evident in both the clear, lucid text and the excellent sample code included in this book. Examples are the key elements in any programming book, and the examples in this book are exceptionally clear and relevant.

SQL Server 2005 is the most feature-rich version of SQL Server ever released, and many of the most significant features were developer oriented, so a book on the developer features of SQL Server 2005 is critical. Dan and Bob do an excellent job of explaining the most significant new developer-centric features and how to use them to improve your database applications. I was heavily involved in the Service Broker chapter, so naturally I think it's the best one, but the sections on XML and CLR integration are also very good. These three features together make SQL Server 2005 a serious contender as an application platform for data-intensive applications. Understanding these new technologies is a key part of being a successful SQL Server 2005 developer, and this book is an excellent place to start learning.

I wish you luck as you embark on your journey into the next generation of database development and hope that you enjoy this book as much as I have.

Roger Wolter
Solutions Architect
SQL Server Team
Microsoft Corporation
Redmond, Washington
January 2006

Foreword

by Gert E. R. Drapers

THE SQL SERVER landscape has changed dramatically over the years. When I started working on SQL Server in 1988, while still at Ashton-Tate, all we had were the base RDBMS-level functionality inherited from Sybase, no real extensibility, some arcane tools like ISQL and BCP, and a single database access API named DB-Library. You had to write your applications in C, squeeze all memory out of your MS-DOS based client to be able to load the network stack, and enable named pipes so you could communicate with the Intel 80286–based PC running OS/2 with LAN Manager and the Ashton-Tate/Microsoft SQL Server 1.0. Twenty-two TPC-B transactions per minute later, we proved that you could build client-server–based database applications on top of a PC platform. In reality, it would take many more years before the environment was ready to host real customer applications.

In 1996, I moved to Redmond, Washington, to join the SQL Server development team. As Lead Software Design Engineer in Test for the Storage Engine, I was responsible for tasks that included the validation of the on-disk conversion from 2K to 8K pages. The new page format was just one of many architectural changes that drove the SQL Server 7 release. Changes ranged from row-level locking, which triggered a different logging and recovery scheme, to the brand-new query processor. These were just a few of the key aspects that laid the foundation for SQL Server as we know it today.

While working on SQL Server 7, we were very cautious not to make too big a leap between SQL Server 6.x and SQL Server 7. We tried to keep the DBA and developer experience as stable as possible. Granted, data access APIs came and went—DAO, RDO, ADO, OLE-DB, ODBC, and ADO.NET—but from a server perspective, we kept the changes to a minimum. The amount of new syntax in the form of Data Definition Language (DDL) and Data Manipulation Language (DML) and the number of new data types were pretty limited.

SQL Server 2000 introduced limited XML support, which for many set-based purists was a real shock or maybe even an insult, depending on their point of view. This was just the tip of the iceberg waiting to be revealed by the introduction of SQL Server 2005, however. The changes between SQL Server 6.x and 7 or 2000 were small compared with the huge new feature set of SQL Server 2005.

SQL Server 2005 expands in almost every possible dimension: server-side extensibility through the SQL-CLR integration; support for queue-based and message-based constructs and operations in the form of Service Broker; first-class XML integration as a storage object, but also through query extensions in the form of XQuery; and new T-SQL constructs like exception handling, common table expressions, output clauses, and new data types. On the client programming side, the list is analogous, because a lot of the new server-side features have corresponding supporting infrastructure to make them accessible to the developer.

All this new, changed, and enhanced functionality is great but yields one very important question: Which technology do we use, when, where, how, and why? What is the appropriate use of SQL-CLR, XML, Service Broker, Web Service endpoints, and so on? These and many more questions are the ones you will—or should—ask yourself when designing and/or implementing SQL Server 2005–based applications.

This is exactly why this book will be playing such a crucial role in building new systems that leverage SQL Server 2005. Not only does it provide you the overview that every (database) developer and even DBA should understand on how to leverage the new developer-oriented features and functionality, but it also provides you much-needed guidance in decisions like T-SQL versus SQL-CLR usage, how to leverage message-based processing, and how best to use XML inside the server.

Most important, this book has already proved itself. When this book first appeared during the beta stages of the project, it quickly became the de facto standard for developers who needed to educate themselves on SQL Server 2005. Bob and Dan have done a great job of updating the book—incorporating user feedback and reflecting the many changes between the first book and the final release of the product. The many samples do a great job of explaining the usage models and hidden aspects behind the features. Last but not least, many colleagues at Microsoft helped by reviewing the content to ensure its correctness and completeness so that you can use it as *the* guideline for designing and implementing your SQL Server–based systems.

Bottom line, this truly is *A Developer's Guide to SQL Server 2005*, providing you the knowledge, examples, and use cases to make the SQL Server 2005 implementation really happen!

Gert E. R. Drapers
Development Manager
Visual Studio Team System
Microsoft Corporation
Redmond, Washington
January 2006

Preface

Bob Beauchemin

Wow. I can't believe it's been almost two years since I was writing the preface for our first book, *A First Look at SQL Server 2005 for Developers.* Those two years, and the two years before, have been a whirlwind of working with the SQL Server product, including teaching, consulting, writing, and conferences. I still haven't stopped to catch my breath. SQL Server 2005 was officially launched in September 2005. And we've been working on enhancements to the *First Look* book since it was published in mid-2004. As with any book on a beta version of a product, the product itself changed after the book was published. In fact, one of the first changes was a feature cut that came two weeks after the book shipped. Keeping up has been a high-energy endeavor, because since beta 2, there were an order of magnitude more additions and enhancements than cuts. This book is the product of the great response we got to the *First Look* book and the answer to the frequently asked question, "When are you guys going to do an update?" I'd say that this is quite a bit more than an update, however. We've included lots of new and revised material; there are too many changes to enumerate. There is even a section on best practices because at this point in time, the early adopters who shipped revised versions of their software that works with SQL Server 2005 have already had a few years to practice.

We did, however, wait for the "golden bits" to appear before embarking on the last of the series of revisions. This turned out to be a good move, as the implementation details of a few of the features changed slightly up until the last candidate release. This is a Sisyphus-like strategy for the most part, however, as the software keeps improving. As I write this, Service Pack 1 has been announced and may indeed change things slightly. Work has begun on the next release of SQL Server, code-named Katamai, and the next version of the .NET Framework is currently available in beta. Software products are never static. Dan and I will be including the code samples from the book and updates on our Web sites:

- http://www.SQLskills.com (Books section)
- http://www.pluralsight.com

We'll also be writing about SQL Server 2005 features and enhancements in our blogs.

The ANSI SQL 2003 specification "shipped," too, and included a slightly different version of Part 14: XML Related Specifications (SQL/XML). The W3C XQuery committee is closing in on becoming a recommendation. As an additional point of note, since the *First Look* book was published, both of Microsoft's biggest competitors in the database space have released .NET Framework procedure inclusion (although integration is not as tight) and have announced or released XQuery support.

By now, you probably have heard about the .NET Framework–based procedures, the inclusion of the XML data type and XQuery language, the enhancements to T-SQL to support robust error handling and queries against hierarchical data and open-schema based designs, and versioning-based transaction isolation. These features, however, combined with inclusion of an asynchronous messaging system, SQL Server Service Broker, permit SQL Server to move toward a Service Oriented Database Architecture. Event Notifications, Query Notifications, and database mail are the first manifestations of this type of architecture; it moves SQL Server toward being more of a system that responds asynchronously to external events, rather than being strictly connection-and-statement–based. Service Broker, combined with CLR procedural code and XML data support, enables database programmers to build their own service-based applications. The inclusion of support for Web Services as an alternate client stack is another manifestation of this architecture. This is such a compelling programming model that Microsoft plans to include similar functionality as part of the next series of .NET Framework enhancements. When this framework functionality is integrated with Service Broker's robust transport and built-in transactional and database support, it should make for a powerful combination. This architecture is a quantum change because it enables building scalable, robust, distributed database applications by designing distribution of processing in from the ground up.

It's still my conclusion that there's quite a bit in SQL Server 2005 for just about every developer, DBA, application designer, business analyst, and data miner. I'm still reading in some places (though not as many as in 2002) that the new features just aren't that interesting; they're more like a recitation of glitzy acronyms than substance. So I'll end this with the same mid-1981 personal history lesson.

I'm working for an insurance company in Seattle, and we're planning to convert our indexed file data, which we'd just converted from ISAM (indexed sequential access method) to VSAM (virtual storage access method), to a better, more robust database engine. The one we had in mind was IMS (IBM's Information Management System product). The salesperson, however, wants us to look at some newfangled database called SQL/DS (which eventually became DB2). After designing some tables and playing around with some queries, we asked some tough questions like "Why does it matter that a database engine is built on a mathematical theory?" and "Why would you want to learn a foreign query language called SQL rather than using nice, fast assembly language or COBOL programs?" and "Why did you just decompose our 2 nice, understandable records into 30 little tables just to join them back together again?" and "Why does it go so slow?" It was the beginning of the relational era. Relational engines weren't all that optimized yet, and smart programmers with custom navigation-based code could beat the engine every time.

In 1981, we sent the product back, and I didn't learn SQL until 1987. By then, I was a bit behind on the learning curve, but relational engines were a heck of a lot faster, and programmers wrote a little SQL and much less procedural and navigational code. And they got much more work done. So I smile when I see folks shake their heads about the XML data models or the XQuery Formal Semantics. I saw the same raised eyebrows when mixing service-oriented concepts and data first came on the scene. Maybe the head-shakers are right, but I'm not waiting until 2010 to learn XQuery or how to integrate messaging and databases. It doesn't matter whether you choose to wait, however, or use relational exclusively. SQL Server 2005 and .NET Framework 2.0 have the enabling engines for all these data storage, messaging, and query technologies. And the future portends even more work in these areas.

Portland, Oregon
March 2006

Dan Sullivan

This journey started well over two years ago, when Bob asked me whether I would be interested in joining him in creating a course and book about the "new" version of SQL Server that Microsoft was working on. He said that this would be the biggest release of SQL Server to date and that it would make both XML and the Common Language Runtime first-class citizens of Microsoft's database platform. That sounded good to me, so here I am writing a preface for a book about the shipping version of SQL Server 2005.

One of the first things I realized when I started digging into it was that XML and the CLR integration are just the tip of the iceberg. Just the enhancements to T-SQL are worth upgrading a server. The enhancements in ADO.NET, such as SqlDependency, which keeps an application and a database in sync, are in tune with the needs of applications, and having the same programming model on the client and server made life much simpler, too.

Direct support of XML as a first-class data type in the database gives you the choice of shredding XML data into tables, storing it natively, or even doing some of each based on the needs of the application, not the limitations of the platform.

Likewise, the direct integration of the CLR into the SQL Server runtime gives you a choice of how to implement an operation based on the needs of the application, not the limitations of the platform.

To carry XML and CLR further as first-class citizens, SQL Server 2005 hosts Web Services. Again, this lets you choose how an application connects to SQL Server 2005 based on applications' needs. Applications that connect to a Web Service don't need ADO.NET, ADO, OLE DB, or any other library to make the connections.

SQL Server 2005 opens your choices and widens its applicability to business problems.

But my favorite comes last: Service Broker, the framework for implementing business transactions. The first time I looked at Service Broker, I did a flashback to projects I had worked on in the past and was bowled over by it. It is right on target. All those busywork details I had to code just to move a few things around to match a business process or control resources are now done for me by Service Broker. Service Broker truly is the best thing since sliced bread.

Taken as whole or in pieces, SQL Server 2005 is a huge step forward. Working on the book and explaining to developers as it was changing underneath my feet was a challenge, but well worth it. I couldn't have met that challenge, of course, without the patience, understanding, and love of my wife, Alberta.

Bolton, Massachusetts
March 2006

Acknowledgments

WE'D LIKE TO convey a special thanks to our astute reviewers. Besides "keeping us honest," they made some comments that mentioned using the new features in ways we hadn't considered before. Without their input, this book wouldn't be nearly as good.

Tom Moreau

Greg Low

Roger Wolter

Pablo Castro

John Huschka

Jens Süßmeyer

Laura Blood

Umachandar Jayachandran

Matt Milner

Michiel Worries

Martin Heller

Keith Brown

Laurentiu Cristofor

Raul Garcia

Rushi Desai

Chris Lee

Jeff Currier

About the Authors

Bob Beauchemin is a database-centric application practitioner and architect, instructor, course author, writer, and Director of Developer Skills for SQL-skills. He's been an application developer and DBA with relational databases including Microsoft SQL Server, Oracle, Sybase, and DB2, as well as nonrelational databases including IMS/DB and IDMS. Over the past two years, he's been teaching his SQL Server 2005 course to 500 students worldwide through the Ascend program. Bob is lead author of *A First Look at SQL Server 2005 for Developers* and author of *Essential ADO.NET* (both from Addison-Wesley), and has written articles on SQL Server and other databases, database security, ADO.NET, and OLE DB.

Dan Sullivan runs his own consulting company. His work in the computer industry has stretched from hardware development, such the design of audio processing systems and Digital Equipment's PDP-11 computers, to software development for manufacturing automation and image processing products driven by databases. Dan has worked with many operating systems, including the first versions of DOS, Windows, and NT. He has worked with SQL Server since it was first distributed by Microsoft and ran on OS2. Dan has been a speaker at .NET Framework user groups and WinDev, has developed several programming courses, and currently does training for Pluralsight. Dan is the coauthor of *A First Look at SQL Server 2005 for Developers* (Addison-Wesley), and his articles have appeared in *MSDN Magazine* and *SQL Server Magazine*. His current interests include the .NET Framework, SQL Server, XML, and the new Microsoft technologies for building distributed systems.

▄ 1 ▪

Introduction

S QL SERVER 2005 contains features that constitute the biggest change
since the internal server rewrite of SQL Server 7. This is true from both
programmability and data model viewpoints. This chapter describes SQL
Server 2005 in terms of .NET Framework programmability, SQL:1999 compliance, user-defined types (UDTs), and XML integration to present a picture of holistic data storage, manipulation, and access.

The .NET Framework and the Microsoft Platform

The .NET Framework is Microsoft's latest environment for running program code. The concept of managed code, running under control of an execution engine, has quickly permeated all major operating systems, including
those from Microsoft. The .NET Framework is one of the core technologies
in Windows 2003 Server, Microsoft's latest collection of server platforms.
Handheld devices and computer-based mobile phones have quickly
acquired .NET Framework-based development environments. The .NET
Framework is an integral part of both Internet Information Server (IIS) and
Internet Explorer (IE). ASP.NET runs on the Windows 2000 version and up
of IIS 5.0. Internet Explorer 5.5, and can load and run .NET Framework
code referenced by `<object>` tags embedded in Web pages. Rich .NET
Framework–based Windows applications, based on the WinForms library
that comes with the .NET Framework, may be deployed directly from the

Internet and run on Windows-based desktops. So what is it about the .NET Framework that has caused it to catch on?

Managed code has made the .NET Framework so compelling. Development tools produce managed code using .NET Framework classes. Managed code is so named because it runs in an environment produced by `mscoree.dll`, the Microsoft common object runtime execution engine, which manages all facets of code execution. These include memory allocation and disposal, and class loading, which in traditional execution environments are major sources of programming errors. The .NET Framework also manages error recovery, and because it has complete information about the runtime environment, it need not always terminate an entire application in the face of an error such as an out-of-memory condition, but can instead terminate just a part of an application without affecting the rest of it.

.NET Framework code makes use of code access security that applies a security policy based on the principal running the code, the code itself, and the location from which the code was loaded. The policy determines the permissions the code has. In the .NET Framework, by default, code that is loaded from the machine on which it runs is given full access to the machine. Code loaded from anywhere else, even if run by an administrator, is run in a sandbox that can access almost nothing on the machine. Prior to the .NET Framework, code run by an administrator would generally be given access to the entire machine regardless of its source. The application of policies is controlled by a system administrator and can be very fine grained.

Multiple versions of the .NET Framework, based on different versions of user-written classes or different versions of the .NET base class libraries (BCL), can execute side by side on the same machine. This makes versioning and deployment of revised and fixed classes easier. The .NET Framework *kernel* or execution engine and the BCL can be written to work with different hardware. A common .NET Framework programming model is usable in x86-based 32-bit processors, like those that currently run versions of Windows $9x$, Windows NT, Windows 2000, and Windows XP, as well as mobile computers like the iPaq running on radically different processors. The development libraries are independent of chipset. Because .NET Framework classes can be Just-in-Time compiled (JIT compiled), optimization based on processor type can be deferred until runtime. This allows the .NET Framework to integrate more easily with the new versions of 64-bit processors.

.NET Framework tools compile code into an intermediate language (IL) that is the same regardless of the programming language used to author the program. Microsoft provides C#; Visual Basic .NET; Managed C++; JavaScript; and J#, a variant of the Java language that emits IL. Non-Microsoft languages such as COBOL.NET and Eiffel.NET are also first-class citizens. Code written in different languages can interoperate completely if written to the Common Language Specification (CLS). Even though language features might be radically different—as in Managed C++, where managed and unmanaged code can be mixed in the same program—the feature sets are similar enough that an organization can choose the language that makes the most sense without losing features. In addition, .NET Framework code can interoperate with existing COM (Component Object Model) code (via COM-callable wrappers and runtime-callable wrappers) and arbitrary Windows Dynamic Link Libraries (DLLs) through a mechanism known as Platform Invoke (PInvoke).

The .NET Framework's Effects on SQL Server

So the .NET Framework with managed code is so compelling because it improves developer productivity and the reliability and security of applications, provides interoperability among a wide variety of languages, and supports use of legacy Windows code not written using the .NET Framework. What does this mean with respect to SQL Server, Microsoft's flagship database management system (DBMS)? Originally, SQL Server shared ancestry with the Sybase relational database management system (RDBMS). SQL Server version 7 was split off from this common ancestry and rewritten using component-based programming. This makes adding new features at any level of functionality easier. Prior to version 7, SQL Server was a monolithic application. SQL Server version 7 factored code into layers, with communication between the relational and storage engines accessible through OLE DB. The SQL Server 7 component-based architecture is shown in Figure 1-1. In addition to easing accommodation of new features in future versions, such as SQL Server 2005, the new component-based

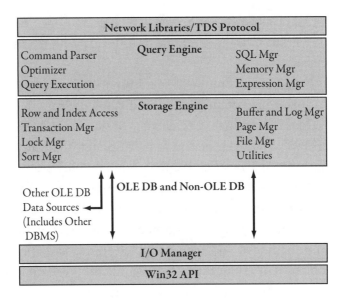

FIGURE 1-1: SQL Server architecture, version 7 and above

model offered a variety of form factors, from the SQL Server Enterprise Edition, that provided a data store for an entire enterprise to the Microsoft Data Engine (MSDE), which provided a data store for a single application. Separation of the relational engine from the storage engine in SQL Server 7 made it easier to accommodate other data sources, such as Exchange or WebDav, which are traditionally not thought of as databases. SQL Server's relational engine can load OLE DB rowsets from an Exchange or WebDav store just as though it were processing data managed by the storage engine.

In versions of SQL Server prior to 2005, there were two ways to write programs that ran in SQL Server: Transact-SQL (T-SQL) and extended stored procedures. T-SQL is Microsoft's proprietary implementation of persistent stored modules (SQL-PSM) as defined in SQL standards.

T-SQL code is highly integrated into SQL Server and uses data types that have the same representation in the storage engine as they do in T-SQL. Instances of these data types are passed between T-SQL and the storage engine without marshaling or conversion between representations. This makes T-SQL code as efficient in its use of data types as the compiled code that runs in the storage engine.

On the other hand, SQL Server interprets T-SQL code; it does not compile it prior to use. This is not as efficient an execution technique as is used by the compiled code in the storage engine but typically does not affect the performance of data access operations. It does affect, however, the performance of numeric and string-oriented operations. Prior to SQL Server version 7, T-SQL code was preparsed and precompiled into a tree format to alleviate some of this effect. Starting with SQL Server version 7, this is no longer done. An example of a simple T-SQL stored procedure is shown in Listing 1-1. Note that even though procedural code is interspersed with SQL statements, T-SQL variables passed between T-SQL and the storage engine are not converted.

LISTING 1-1: A simple stored procedure

```
CREATE PROCEDURE dbo.find_expensive (
   @category
   @price    MONEY,
   @verdict VARCHAR(20) OUTPUT
)
AS
IF (SELECT AVG(cost)
     FROM dbo.products WHERE cat = @category) > @price
   SET @verdict = 'Expensive'
ELSE
   SET @verdict = 'Good Buy'
```

Extended stored procedures are an alternative to interpreted T-SQL code and prior to SQL Server 2005 were the only alternative to T-SQL. Extended stored procedures written in a complied language, such as C++, do numeric and string operations more efficiently than T-SQL. They also have access to system resources such as files, the Internet, and timers that T-SQL does not. Extended stored procedures integrate with SQL Server through the Open Data Services API. Writing extended stored procedures requires a detailed understanding of the underlying operating system that is not required when writing T-SQL. Typically, more testing and debugging are needed to establish the reliability of an extended stored procedure than are needed for T-SQL stored procedures.

In addition, data access operations by an extended stored procedure are not as efficient as T-SQL. Data accessed using ODBC or OLE DB requires data type conversion that T-SQL does not. An extended stored procedure that does data access also requires a separate connection to the database even though it runs inside SQL Server itself. T-SQL directly accesses data in the storage engine and does not require a separate connection. Listing 1-2 shows a simple extended stored procedure written in C++.

LISTING 1-2: A simple extended stored procedure

```
ULONG __GetXpVersion()
{ return ODS_VERSION; }
SRVRETCODE xp_sayhello(SRV_PROC* pSrvProc)
{
    char szText[15] = "Hello World!";

    // error handling elided for clarity
    // describe the output column
    srv_describe(pSrvProc, 1, "Column 1",
                 SRV_NULLTERM, SRVVARCHAR,
                 strlen(szText), SRVVARCHAR, 0, NULL);

    // set column length and data
    srv_setcollen(pSrvProc, 1, strlen(szText));
    srv_setcoldata(pSrvProc, 1, szText);

    // send row
    srv_sendrow(pSrvProc);

    // send done message
    srv_senddone(pSrvProc,
                 (SRV_DONE_COUNT | SRV_DONE_MORE),
                 0, 1);
    return (XP_NOERROR);
}
```

SQL Server uses structured exception handling to wrap all calls to extended stored procedures. This prevents unhandled exceptions from damaging or shutting down SQL Server. There is, however, no way for SQL Server to prevent an extended stored procedure from misusing system resources. A rogue extended stored procedure could call the exit() function in the Windows runtime library and shut down SQL Server. Likewise, SQL Server cannot prevent a poorly coded extended stored procedure from writing over the memory SQL Server is using. This direct access to system resources is the reason that extended stored procedures are more efficient than T-SQL for non–data access operations but is also the reason that a stored procedure must undergo much more scrutiny before it is added to SQL Server.

Under SQL Server 2005, T-SQL code continues to operate mostly as before. In addition to providing complete compatibility with existing code, this enables the millions of current T-SQL programmers to continue to write high-performance data access code for the SQL Server relational engine. For these programmers, T-SQL is still their language of choice.

SQL Server 2005 adds the ability to write stored procedures, user-defined functions, and triggers in any .NET Framework–compatible language. This enables .NET Framework programmers to use their language of choice, such as C# or Visual Basic .NET, to write SQL Server procedural code.

The .NET Framework code that SQL Server runs is completely isolated from SQL Server itself. SQL Server uses a construct in the .NET Framework called an AppDomain. It completely isolates all resources that the .NET Framework code uses from the resources that SQL Server uses, even though SQL Server and the AppDomain are part of the same process. Unlike the technique used to isolate stored procedures, the AppDomain protects SQL Server from all misuse or malicious use of system resources.

.NET Framework code shares the advantage of compilation with extended stored procedures. .NET Framework code is Just-In-Time compiled into machine instructions at execution time. .NET Framework classes are objects that enable usage of object-oriented programming techniques. The execution engine controls storage allocation and memory management. This ensures that short of a bug in the engine itself, .NET Framework procedural code will never step on random memory buffers. In case of severe programmer error, the execution engine can always dispose of the offending thread or even an AppDomain while SQL Server continues to run without interruption. This is shown in Figure 1-2. Writing SQL Server procedural code is examined in detail in Chapters 3 and 4.

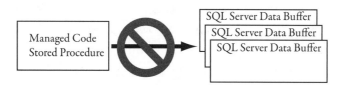

FIGURE 1-2: Preventing managed code from interfering with SQL Server processing or writing over buffers

SQL Server 2005 ships with an in-memory .NET Framework data provider to optimize data access from managed procedural code. When using this provider, programmers have a choice of using vanilla .NET Framework types or SQL types. Some vanilla .NET Framework types, like `System.Int32`, require no conversion or marshaling, but some, such as `System.Decimal`, are not exact matches. The .NET Framework classes in `System.Data.SqlTypes` correspond exactly to the corresponding SQL Server types. Using these types in .NET Framework procedures means no type conversion or marshaling is required, and that means faster execution. Enhancements to SQL Server 2005's ADO.NET provider, known as `System.Data.SqlClient`, also contains optimizations that permit .NET Framework procedural code to share an execution environment (including `Connection` and `Transaction`) with its caller. .NET Framework procedures can run in the security context of the user who cataloged the procedure or of the current user. Using the `SqlClient` data provider in .NET Framework procedures, triggers, and functions is discussed in Chapter 4.

The SQL:1999 Standard: Extending the Relational Model

Many of the interesting changes to the programmability and data type extensions in SQL Server 2005 are related to ongoing changes to the SQL standard, so it is instructive here to take a look at that standard. SQL:1999 is the latest version of ANSI standard SQL, although at this writing a newer version yet, known as SQL:2003, is in progress. Some of the features added to standard SQL in SQL:1999, such as triggers, have always been part of SQL Server. The more interesting features of SQL:1999 have to do with extending the type system to support extended scalar types, distinct types, and even complex types. In SQL Server 2005, you can add a new scalar type to the relational type system yourself without waiting for Microsoft to implement it in the engine. The most common use for SQL Server 2005 user-defined types will be to add new scalar types.

A distinct type extends simple data types (such as `integer` or `varchar`) with special semantics. A JPEG data type may be defined, for example. This type is stored as an IMAGE data type in SQL Server, but the IMAGE type is extended with user-defined functions such as `get_background_color` and `get_foreground_color`. Extending a simple type by adding *behaviors* was inspired by object-relational databases of the mid-1990s. Adding functions to the simple `IMAGE` type enables SQL queries that accomplish a task, such as "Select all the rows in the database where the `JPEG` column x has a background color of red." Without the user-defined functions to extend the type, the `IMAGE` would have to be decomposed into one or more relational tables for storage. As an alternative, the background color could be stored separately from the `IMAGE`, but this could introduce update anomalies if the `IMAGE` were updated but the background color was not. SQL:1999 codified the definition of the distinct type and defined some rules for its use. As an example, if the `JPEG` type and the `GIF` type are both distinct types that use an underlying storage type of `IMAGE`, `JPEG` types and `GIF` types cannot be compared (or otherwise operated on) without using the SQL `CAST` operator. `CAST` indicates that the programmer is aware that two distinct types are being compared. Using the `JPEG` type's `get_background_color` is likely to get incorrect results against a `GIF` column.

Complex types contain multiple data values, also called *attributes.* Including these data types in the SQL standard was inspired by the popularity of object-oriented databases in the early and mid-1990s. An example of a complex type is a *person* type that consists of a name, an address, and a phone number. Although these data types violate the first normal form of the relational data model and can be easily represented as a discrete table in a properly normalized database, these types have a few unique features. A diagram representing the data structures involved is shown in Figure 1-3.

The person type could be used in multiple tables while maintaining its "personness"—that is, the same attributes and functions are usable against the

OrderId	OrderDate	Customer						
		Name	Address					Phone
			Street	City	State	Postcode		

FIGURE 1-3: Complex types in otherwise-relational tables

person type even when the person column is used in three unrelated tables. In addition to allowing complex types, SQL:1999 defined types that could be references to complex types. A person type could contain a reference (similar to a pointer) to an address type in a different table, as shown in Listing 1-3.[1]

LISTING 1-3: Using SQL:1999 structured data types

```
CREATE TYPE PERSON (
    pers_first_name          VARCHAR(30),
    pers_last_name           VARCHAR(30),
    -- other fields omitted
    pers_address             REF(ADDRESS) SCOPE ADDR_TAB)
)

CREATE TYPE ADDRESS (
    addr_street              VARCHAR(20),
    addr_city                VARCHAR(30),
    addr_state_province      VARCHAR(10),
    addr_postal_code         VARCHAR(10)
)

CREATE TABLE ADDR_TAB (
    addr_oid                 BIGINT,
    addr_address             ADDRESS
)
```

In addition, complex type–specific methods could be defined, and the SQL language was extended to support using attributes of a complex type in queries. An example of a complex type and a SELECT statement that uses it would look like the following:

```
SELECT pers.address FROM ADDR_TAB
    WHERE ADDR.addr_city like 'Sea%'
```

SQL:1999 expanded the type system to add some less revolutionary types, such as the BOOLEAN data type (which can contain TRUE, FALSE, or NULL) and the LOCATOR and DATALINK data types, which point to other

---

1. Note that this code will not work in any version of SQL Server.

TABLE 1-1: New Data Types in SQL:1999

Data Type	Description
BOOLEAN	Bit switch
BLOB	Binary large object
CLOB	Character large object
Structured types	Distinct types and user-defined types
REF	Pointer to a persisted structured type
Array	Array
LOCATOR	Pointers to types inside the DBMS
DATALINK	Reference to an external data source

storage inside or outside the database. A complete list of the new types is shown in Table 1-1.

User-Defined Types and SQL Server

SQL Server has always supported its own concept of a user-defined data type. These data types are known as *alias types* and are defined by using the system stored procedure `sp_addtype`.[2] These data types share some functionality with SQL:1999 distinct types. They must be derived from a SQL Server built-in data type. You can add integrity constraints by using SQL Server RULES. You create a SQL Server RULE using CREATE RULE and associate a rule with a SQL Server user-defined type by using `sp_bindrule`. A single user-defined data type can be used in multiples tables, and a single SQL Server rule can be bound to more than one user-defined type. Creating two SQL Server data types, creating rules, and binding the rules to the types are shown in Listing 1-4.

---

2. In SQL Server 2005, alias types can also be defined with a new CREATE TYPE syntax.

LISTING 1-4: Creating types and binding them to rules

```
-- define two user-defined types
EXEC sp_addtype iq, 'FLOAT', 'NULL'
EXEC sp_addtype shoesize, 'FLOAT', 'NULL'

-- specify constraints
CREATE RULE iq_range AS @range between 1 and 200
CREATE RULE shoesize_range AS @range between 1 and 20

-- bind constraint to type
EXEC sp_bindrule 'iq_range', 'iq'
EXEC sp_bindrule 'shoesize_range', 'shoesize'
```

SQL Server user-defined types have some things in common with SQL distinct types. Like distinct types, they extend the SQL types by adding user-defined behaviors, in that a rule can be considered a behavior. Unlike SQL distinct types, they may not have associated user-defined functions that are scoped to the type. Although we defined the `shoesize` type and limited its values to floating-point numbers from 1 to 20, for example, we cannot associate a function named `derive_suit_size_from_shoesize` with the type. This would be possible if `shoesize` were a SQL standard derived type. In addition, SQL Server user-defined types are comparable based on where the underlying built-in type is comparable, without using the SQL CAST operator. The SQL specification mandates that a user-defined type must be cast to a built-in or user-defined type before it can be used in a comparison operation, but attempting to apply the CAST operator to a user-defined type in SQL Server causes an error. Listing 1-5 shows this difference in behavior.

LISTING 1-5: Comparing unlike user-defined types

```
-- use the type
CREATE TABLE dbo.people (
  personid      INTEGER,
  iq            iq,
  shoe          shoesize,
  spouse_shoe   shoesize
)

-- SQL Server syntax
SELECT * FROM dbo.people WHERE iq < shoe

-- SQL:1999  syntax
-- invalid in SQL Server
-- SELECT * FROM dbo.people
    WHERE CAST(iq AS shoesize) < shoe
```

SQL Server 2005 goes beyond previous versions in support of SQL:1999 distinct and complex user-defined types. Extended data types must be defined as .NET Framework classes and cannot be defined in T-SQL, although they are accessible in T-SQL stored procedures, user-defined functions, and other procedural code. These classes (types) may have member functions that are accessible in T-SQL à la SQL distinct types, and in addition, they may have mutator functions that are usable in T-SQL UPDATE statements.

In addition to enabling users to define distinct types based on a single built-in data type, SQL Server 2005 allows user-defined types to have multiple storage items (attributes). Such a user-defined data type is considered a complex type in SQL:1999. Once defined to the SQL Server catalog, the new type may be used as a column in a table. Variables of the type may be used in stored procedures, and the type's attributes and methods may be used in computed types and user-defined functions. Although we'll see how to define user-defined distinct and complex types in Chapter 5, Listing 1-6 shows an example of defining a user-defined complex type, SecondsDelay, and using it as a column in a table.

LISTING 1-6: Defining a user-defined type and using it in a table

```
CREATE TYPE SecondsDelay
AS EXTERNAL NAME SomeTypes.SecondsDelay
GO

CREATE TABLE Transforms(
    transform_id      BIGINT,
    transform_input,  SecondsDelay,
    transform_result SecondsDelay)
GO
```

After even a fundamental description, we should immediately point out that SQL Server complex types extend relational data types. The most common usage will not be to define "object" data types that might be defined in an object-oriented database, but to define new scalar types that extend the relational type system, such as the SecondsDelay type shown in Listing 1-6. In SQL Server 2005, the server is unaware of the inheritance relationships among types (although inheritance may be used in the implementation) or polymorphic methods, however, as in traditional object-oriented systems.

That is, although we can define a complex user-defined type called `Sec-ondsDelay` that contains multiple data fields (whole seconds, whole milliseconds) and instance methods, and define a complex type called `MinutesDelay` that inherits from `SecondsDelay` and adds a whole minutes field to it, we cannot invoke methods of the `SecondsDelay` type when using an `MinutesDelay` type or cast `MinutesDelay` to `SecondsDelay`.

In addition to supporting user-defined types, SQL Server 2005 supports user-defined aggregate functions. These types extend the concept of user-defined functions that return a single value and can be written in any .NET Framework language, but not T-SQL. The SQL specification defines five aggregates that databases must support (`MAX`, `MIN`, `AVG`, `SUM`, and `COUNT`). SQL Server implements a superset of the specification, including such aggregates as standard deviation and variance. By using SQL Server 2005 support for .NET Framework languages, users need not wait for the database engine to implement their particular domain-specific aggregate. User-defined aggregates can even be defined over user-defined types, as in the case of an aggregate that would perform aggregates over the `SecondsDelay` data type described earlier.

Support of user-defined types and aggregates moves SQL Server closer to SQL:1999 compliance, and it extends SQL:1999 in that SQL:1999 does not mention user-defined aggregates in the specification.

XML: Data and Document Storage

XML is a platform-independent data representation format based originally on Standard Generalized Markup Language (SGML). Since its popularization, it is becoming used as a data storage format. It has its own type system, based on the XML schema language (XSD). Both XML and XSD are W3C standards at the Recommendation level.[3] An XML schema defines the

---

3. The W3C defines seven levels of specification. These are (in order of importance) Recommendation, Proposed Recommendation, Candidate Recommendation, Working Draft in Last Call, Working Draft in Development, Requirements, and Note. This means that a W3C Recommendation is an agreed-upon standard.

format of an XML document as a SQL Server schema defines the layout of a SQL Server database.

The XML type system is quite rigorous, enabling definition in XML schema definition language of almost all the constructs available in a relational database. Because it was originally designed as a system that could represent documents with markup as well as what is traditionally thought of as "data," the XML type system is somewhat bifurcated into attributes and elements. Attributes are represented in the XML serialization format as HTML attributes are, using the `name='value'` syntax. Attributes can hold only simple data types, like traditional relational attributes. Elements can represent simple or complex types. An element can have multiple levels of nested subelements, as in the following example:

```
<table>
<row>
   <id>1</id>
   <name>Tom</name>
</row>
<row>
   <id>2</id>
   <name>Maureen</name>
</row>
</table>
```

This means that an element can be used to represent a table in a relational database. Each tuple (row) would be represented as a child element, with relational attributes (columns) represented as either attributes or subelements. The two ways of representing relational column data in XML are known as *element-centric mapping* (where each column is a nested subelement) and *attribute-centric mapping* (where each column is an attribute on an element tuple). These are illustrated in Listing 1-7.

LISTING 1-7: Element-centric mapping and attribute-centric mapping

```
<!-- element-centric mapping -->
<!-- all data values are element content -->

<table>
<row>
   <id>1</id>
   <name>Tom</name>
</row>
```

```
<row>
    <id>2</id>
    <name>Maureen</name>
</row>
</table>

<!-- same document in attribute-centric mapping-->
<!-- id and name are represented as attributes -->
<!-- and cannot themselves be complex types -->
<table>
    <row id="1" name="Tom" />
    <row id="2" name="Maureen" />
</table>
```

Because subelements can be nested in XML documents, a document more closely corresponds to a hierarchical form of data than to a relational form. This is reinforced by the fact that by definition, an XML document must have a single root element. Sets of elements that do not have a single root element are called *document fragments.* Although document fragments are not well-formed XML documents, multiple fragments can be composed together and wrapped with a root element, producing a well-formed document.

In addition to being able to represent relational and hierarchical data, XML schema definition language (XSD) can represent complex type relationships. XSD supports the notion of type derivation, including derivation by both restriction and extension. This means that XML can directly represent types in an object hierarchy.

A single XML schema document (which itself is defined in an XML form specified by the XML schema definition language) represents data types that scope a single XML namespace, although you can use XML namespaces in documents without having the corresponding XML schema. An XML namespace is a convenient grouping of types, similar to a schema in SQL Server. This is illustrated in Listing 1-8.

LISTING 1-8: An XML namespace defining a set of types

```
<schema targetNamespace="http://www.MyCompany.com/order.xsd"
    xmlns:po="http://www.MyCompany.com/order.xsd"
    xmlns="http://www.w3.org/2001/XMLSchema"
    elementFormDefault="qualified">

  <!-- define a new type -->
  <complexType name="PurchaseOrderType">
```

```
    <sequence>
      <element name="PONum" type="decimal"/>
      <element name="Company" type="string"/>
      <element name="Item" maxOccurs="1000">
        <!-- a nested anonymous type -->
        <complexType>
          <sequence>
            <element name="Part" type="string"/>
            <element name="Price" type="float"/>
          </sequence>
        </complexType>
      </element>
    </sequence>
  </complexType>

  <!-- global element definition using type above -->
  <element name="PurchaseOrder" type="po:PurchaseOrderType"/>
</schema>
```

An XML schema defines the namespace that its types belong to by specifying the `targetNamespace` attribute on the schema element. An XML document that uses types from a namespace can indicate this by using a default namespace or explicitly using a namespace prefix on each element or attribute of a particular type. Namespace prefixes are arbitrary; the `xmlns` attribute established the correspondence between namespace prefix and namespace. This is illustrated in Listing 1-9. This is analogous to using SQL Server two-part or three-part names in SQL statements.

LISTING 1-9: Referring to a type via namespace and namespace prefixes

```
<pre:PurchaseOrder
  xmlns:pre="http://www.MyCompany.com/order.xsd"
  xmlns:xsi="http://www.w3.org/2001/XMLSchema-instance"
  xsi:schemaLocation="http://www.MyCompany.com/order.xsd
              http://www.MyCompany.com/schemas/order.xsd">
  <pre:PONum>1001</pre:PONum>
  <pre:Company>SQL Traders</pre:Company>
  <pre:Item>
    <pre:Part>Dons Boxers</pre:Part>
    <pre:Price>11.95</pre:Price>
  </pre:Item>
  <pre:Item>
    <pre:Part>Essential ADO.NET</pre:Part>
    <pre:Price>49.95</pre:Price>
  </pre:Item>
</ pre:PurchaseOrder>
```

Only when an XML document contains types defined by XML schemas is it possible to determine the exact data types of elements or attributes. XML elements and attributes are data type `"string"` by definition, although the encoding used in the document can be defined in the XML document element. A predecessor of XML schemas, known as Document Type Definition (DTD), was primarily concerned with defining document structure and allowed only limited information about data types. XSD is a superset of the aforementioned type systems, including all the DTD structure types. Using an XSD schema or schemas to determine whether a document is "correct" is known as *schema validation*. Schema validation can be thought of as applying type constraints and declarative integrity constraints to ensure that an XML document is correct. A nonvalidated XML schema still must conform to XML "well-formedness" rules, and a single XML document adheres to a set of rules known as the XML Infoset, consisting of structure and some content information. Validating an XML document against one or more XML schemas produces what is called a Post Schema Validation Infoset (PSVI). The PSVI information makes it possible to determine a strong, well-defined type for each XML element and attribute.

SQL Server 2005 introduces an XML data type. This data type can be used in table definitions to type a column, as a variable type in T-SQL procedural code, and as procedure parameters. A definition of a simple table containing an XML type would look like a "normal" CREATE TABLE statement:

```
CREATE TABLE dbo.xml_tab(
  id       INTEGER PRIMARY KEY,
  xml_col  XML)
```

In addition, columns, variables, and parameters of the XML data type can be constrained by an XML schema. XML schemas are defined in the SQL Server catalog.

XML, like relational databases, has its own query language optimized for the data format. Because XML data is hierarchical, it's reminiscent of a hierarchical file system. The archetypical query language for XML documents is known as XPath. Queries in XPath reflect the hierarchical nature of XML, because nodesets are selected by using syntax similar to that used to specify files in the UNIX file system. As an example, when a typical XML document is queried using a hierarchical XPath query, the result is a nodeset containing all the nodes at that level of hierarchy. Listing 1-10 shows an example of an XPath query that, when run against the purchase-order document in Listing 1-9, produces a nodeset result containing all the item elements. Think of an XPath query as analogous to a SQL query.

LISTING 1-10: Simple XPath query

```
<!-- this query -->
//pre:Item

<!-- produces this nodeset -->
<!-- two Item nodes -->
  <pre:Item>
    <pre:Part>Dons Boxers</pre:Part>
    <pre:Price>11.95</pre:Price>
  </pre:Item>
  <pre:Item>
    <pre:Part>Essential ADO.NET</pre:Part>
    <pre:Price>49.95</pre:Price>
  </pre:Item>
```

Like a SQL query, an XPath query simply produces a resultset consisting of possibly multiple instances of items; unlike in SQL, these results are not always rectangular. XPath results can consist of nodesets of any shape or even scalar values. In SQL, database vendors can implement a variation of SQL-PSM that composes possibly multiple SQL queries and some procedural code to produce a more complex result. SQL Server's variation of SQL-PSM is known as T-SQL. XML processing libraries implement an analogous concept by using an XML-based nonprocedural language called XSLT (Extensible Stylesheet Language Transformations). Originally meant to produce nice-looking HTML pages from XML input, XSLT has evolved into an almost full-fledged programming language. Vendors have even added proprietary extensions to XSLT to allow it to execute code routines in procedural programming languages like Visual Basic and C#.

Because XPath and XSLT were not originally developed to process large amounts of data, a new programming language for XML, known as XQuery, has been developed under the auspices of the W3C. XQuery implements many of the best features of XPath and XSLT, is developed from the ground up to handle large documents, and is also designed specifically to be optimizable. In addition, it adds some of the syntax features of SQL. XQuery's data can be strongly typed; this also assists in query optimization. XQuery includes a query language, the equivalent of SQL Server SELECT, but does not define a standard implementation of the equivalent of SQL Server's INSERT, UPDATE, and DELETE statements.

SQL Server 2000 allows users to define mapping schemas (normal XML schemas with extra annotations that mapped XML items and concepts to SQL items and concepts) that represented all or a portion of the database as a virtual XML document, and to issue XPath queries against the resulting data structure. In addition, SQL Server 2000 extended T-SQL to enable relational resultsets to be returned as XML. This consists of support for a FOR XML clause; three different subcategories of FOR XML are supported. The SQL Server 2000 support allows XML document composition from relational data and XML document decomposition into multiple relational tables; this will be discussed further in Chapter 8.

SQL Server 2005 extends this support by adding direct support for XQuery. The XQuery engine runs directly inside SQL Server, as opposed to XPath support in SQL Server 2000. XPath support in SQL Server 2000 is accomplished by a portion of the SQL Server OLE DB provider (SQLOLEDB) that took a mapping schema and an XPath query, produced a SELECT ... FOR XML query, and sent that query to SQL Server. Native support for XQuery, combined with XQuery's design for optimization, and support for multiple documents (a series of XML columns) should improve on the already-good support for querying XML data.

Web Services: XML As a Marshaling Format

Marshaling data to unlike platforms has always been a problem. In the past, vendors could not even agree on a marshaling format, let alone a common type system. Microsoft used COM (component object model) for its distributed object model and marshaling format; it did not support CORBA (common object request broker architecture). Processor differences such as endianness (byte ordering), floating-point representation, and character set were considered in both these models. Marshaling between systems required a "reader–make right" approach—that is, the receiver of a message had to determine the format and convert it to something understandable to his processor. In addition, the distributed programming models were plagued by the requirement to have a specific naming model or security system. As an example, porting COM to the Solaris platform required installing the equivalent of a Windows Registry and an NTLM security service. But the biggest problems were network protocol and access to specific ports on network servers. COM not only used a proprietary protocol and network ports when run over TCP/IP, but also required opening port 135 for the naming service to operate correctly—something that few systems administrators would permit for security reasons. By contrast, most systems administrators gladly opened port 80 and allowed the HTTP protocol, even setting up special proxy servers rather than deny internal users access to the World Wide Web. Systems such as DCOM over HTTP and Java RMI over HTTP were the first steps away from a proprietary distributed programming system.

Vendors such as Microsoft, IBM, Oracle, and Sun are moving toward supporting distributed computing over HTTP using a framing protocol known as SOAP and using XML as a marshaling format. SOAP itself uses XML to frame XML-based payloads; elements and attributes used in SOAP are defined in two XSD schemas. SOAP also defines a portable way of representing parameters to remote procedure calls (RPCs), but since the completion and adaptation of XML schemas, a schema-centric format has been used. Using XML as a marshaling format, framed by SOAP, possibly over HTTP, is known as Web Services.

The popularity of XML and Web Services, like the popularity of SQL, is fairly easy to explain. Managers of computer systems have learned over time to shy away from proprietary solutions, mostly because companies often change hardware and operating system (and other) software over time. In addition, a company may have to communicate with other companies that use an unlike architecture. Therefore, protocols like HTTP; formats like XML and CSV (comma-separated value) files; and languages like SQL, XPath, XSLT, and XQuery tend to be used for a single reason: They are available on every hardware and software platform.

Consider as an example the RDS (remote data services) architecture used by Microsoft to marshal resultsets (known as `recordsets`) over HTTP in a compact binary format, as opposed to XML, a rather verbose text-based format. Because Microsoft invented the RDS marshaling format (known as Advanced Data Tablegrams, or ADTG), other vendors (such as Netscape) refused to support it. This is known as NIH (not invented here) syndrome. On the other hand, visit any large software or hardware manufacturer on the planet, and ask, "Who invented XML?" The answer is always the same: "We did." Because XML (or SQL, to expand the analogy) cannot possibly be perceived as "a Microsoft thing" or "an Oracle thing," support is almost universal.

SQL Server 2005 supports creating Web Services and storing data to be used in Web Services at a few different levels. The XML data type and XQuery support mentioned previously are a good start. Data can be stored in XML format inside SQL Server and used directly with XQuery to produce or consume Web Services. With the addition of direct support in SQL Server for HTTP, we could think of SQL Server 2005 as a "Web Services server." This reduces the three-tier architecture usually required to support Web Services (database, middle tier, and client) to a two-tier architecture, with stored procedures or XQuery/XSLT programs being used as a middle tier.

Client Access . . . And Then There Are Clients

Database programmers, especially those who specialize in procedural dialects of SQL, tend to forget that without client access libraries, a database is just a place to keep data. Although the SQL language itself was supposed to ensure that ordinary clients could access the data, performance issues and the complexity of SQL queries (and XPath and XQuery queries, for that matter) ensure that very few (if any) users actually go right to SQL Server Management Studio or Query Analyzer for the data they need, and no enterprise applications that we know of use SQL Server Management Studio as a front end to the database. Applications, both rich Windows applications and Web applications, are written using high-level programming languages like C++, Visual Basic, and the .NET Framework family of languages.

Client-Side Database APIs and SQL Server 2005

With all the new features in SQL Server 2005, client libraries such as OLE DB have quite a lot of work to do just to keep up. Although the designers of OLE DB and ADO designed support for user-defined types into the model, the intricacies of supporting them weren't made clear until support for these types was added to popular mainstream databases like SQL Server 2005. OLE DB and ADO are very `Rowset`/`Recordset`-centric and have limited support for user-defined types, invoking methods on database types and extending the type system. The next version of these libraries adds support for fetching complex types in a couple of different ways: as a data type `Object` or as a nested resultset (`Rowset` or `Recordset`). Most of the support in OLE DB and ADO leverages existing objects and methods, and extends them to support the new types. Support for the SQL:1999 information schema rowsets is another new feature in data access.

The client-side .NET Framework data provider for SQL Server, known as `SqlClient`, has an easier time of it. Because user-defined types are .NET Framework types, code to process these types might be downloaded to a client from a SQL Server or stored on a network share. It's possible to coerce a column in a `DataReader` from type `Object` to type `Person` and use it directly in a .NET Framework program. Techniques such as network-based code make this work. Handling complex data in situ or storing complex types in a .NET Framework `DataSet` presents a different set of problems. Bob Beauchemin's first book, *Essential ADO.NET* (Addison-Wesley, 2002), describes many of these problems and theoretical solutions to them based on the existing .NET Framework libraries. Now that SQL Server supports columns that are classes or columns that are XML, this becomes an interesting area.

One limitation of SQL Server clients was that only a single `Rowset` or `Recordset` could be active at a time in the default cursorless mode of SQL Server data access. Different APIs solved this problem in different ways, and we'll talk about the repercussions of this in Chapter 11. SQL Server 2005 breaks through the one-active-rowset barrier by allowing the user APIs to multiplex active results on a single connection. This empowering feature is known as MARS (multiple active resultsets).

Client-Side XML-Based APIs and SQL Server 2005 Integration

XML is ubiquitous in the SQL Server 2005–era client APIs. User-defined types use .NET Framework XML Serialization to be able to be marshaled or persisted as XML directly. The `FOR XML` syntax has been extended to allow a user to fetch data in an XML type. In addition, SQL Server Analysis Services can directly consume queries in XML format and produce XML results. This is called XML for Analysis and has been around for a while; in SQL Server 2005, it becomes a first-class API directly supported and on a par with OLE DB for Analysis. If you've gotten used to OLE DB for Analysis (or its automation equivalent, ADOMD), don't fret; XML for Analysis uses an OLE DB–style syntax for both queries and properties.

The XML data type and XQuery engine inside SQL Server 2005 are complemented by a rich middle-tier or client-side model for XML. This model exposes XML data outside the server using a variety of data models. These models include the XML Document Object Model (DOM) and abstract `XmlNavigator` model, in addition to streaming models known as `XmlReader` and `XmlWriter`. The standard XML query and transformation models, XPath and XSLT, have been part of the .NET Framework platform since its inception.

Extending SQL Server into the Platform: Service Broker and Notification Services

Finally, SQL Server 2005 adds two more pieces of data access and application programming functionality that bear mention. SQL Server Service Broker allows you to use T-SQL to send asynchronous messages. These messages can be exchanged only with SQL Server 2005, but the messages can be sent to the same database, between databases in the same instance, or to a different instance on the same machine or different machines. The asynchronous messages work similarly to a message queuing system (they even use queues), but because SQL Server is controlling both the database data and the messages, messages can participate in a local database transaction. The T-SQL language is being extended to support the handling of queued messages that can be retrieved asynchronously.

SQL Server Service Broker uses dialogs to achieve coordinated messaging with multimessage correlation semantics. A *dialog* is a bidirectional series of messages between two endpoints, in which each message contains a conversation ID to enable the other side to correlate messages, as shown in Figure 1-4.

One of the main advantages of a dialog is that it maintains message order across transactions, threads, applications, and database restarts—something no other messaging system does. A dialog also allows guaranteed delivery

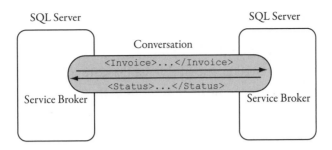

FIGURE 1-4: Messages and dialogs

of messages to a number of different subscribers. Multiple dialogs can be grouped into a single "application" known as a Conversation Group. A Conversation Group can maintain its state and share state among multiple dialogs. This goes beyond the concept of simple correlation ID message queuing systems, and it's handled automatically by Service Broker rather than manually by the application programmer.

Using asynchronous messaging inside the database enables building scalable systems, because work that had to be handled serially in the past can now be multiplexed in the same transaction. In addition, Service Broker guarantees that the messages will arrive in order, even across transactions, and guarantees once-only delivery.

SQL Server Notification Services is an easy-to-use but powerful framework around which you can build scalable "notification applications" that can notify millions of users about millions of interesting events, using standard notification protocols like SMS (Simple Message Service) and programs like MSN Messenger. The unique pieces, such as an application, are defined using XML and integrated with the framework (which runs as a series of stored procedures over a mostly system-defined schema).

We'll discuss Service Broker in Chapter 11 and Notification Services in Chapter 16. In addition, SQL Server 2005 adds a set of reporting tools to extend further the data-related platform. The Reporting Services feature is outside the scope of this book, but it does, among other things, allow users to get parameterized reports and to make a restricted set of ad hoc queries without the need to develop an application. Reporting Services continues the .NET Framework theme in SQL Server by allowing the use of .NET Framework classes to assist in building and displaying reports.

Where Are We?

In this chapter, we've had a whirlwind tour of the plethora of new technologies in SQL Server 2005; the problems they are intended to solve; and, in some cases, the entirely new data models they represent. SQL Server 2005 supports .NET Framework programming, user-defined data types and aggregates, and an XML data type. The support for these alternative data types extends from the server out to the client.

In the rest of the book, we're going to explore the implementation and best practices when using these new data models, and see that SQL Server 2005 and improvements to the client libraries truly represent the integration of relational data, object-oriented data and concepts, and XML data.

■ 2 ■
Hosting the Runtime: SQL Server As a Runtime Host

T HIS CHAPTER DISCUSSES what it means to be a .NET Framework runtime host. Topics include how SQL Server differs from other runtime hosts such as Internet Information Server (IIS) and Internet Explorer (IE) with respect to loading and running code. Finally, we'll show how you would catalog and maintain user assemblies stored in SQL Server.

Why Care How Hosting Works?

If you are an SQL Server developer or database administrator, you might be inclined to use the new Common Language Runtime (CLR) hosting feature to write stored procedures in C# or Visual Basic .NET (or establish a company policy forbidding its use) without knowing how it works. But you should care. SQL Server is an enterprise application, perhaps one of the most important in your organization. When the CLR was added to SQL Server, there were three goals in the implementation, considered in this order:

1. Security
2. Reliability
3. Performance

The reasons for this emphasis are apparent. Without a secure system, you have a system that can reliably run code, including code introduced by hackers, very quickly. It's not what you'd want for an enterprise application (or any application). Reliability comes next. Critical applications, like a database management system (DBMS), are expected to be available 99.999 percent of the time. You don't want to wait in a long line at the airport or the bank while the database restarts itself. Reliability, therefore, is considered over performance when the two clash; a decision might be whether to allow stack overflows potentially to bring down the main application or to slow processing to make sure they don't. Applications that perform transactional processing using SQL Server must ensure data integrity and its transactional correctness, which is another facet of reliability.

Performance is extremely important in an enterprise application as well. DBMSes can be judged on benchmarks, such as the TPC-C (Transaction Processing Performance Council benchmark C) benchmark, as well as programmer-friendly features. So although having stored procedures and user-defined types written in high-level languages is a nice feature, it had to be implemented in such a way as to maximize performance.

SQL Server introduced hosting APIs as one of the features in a series of vast internal changes. The changes are meant to encapsulate operating system services and are known collectively as the SQL Server Operating System (SQLOS). Hosting the .NET Framework runtime is only one of the reasons for the SQLOS and perhaps not even the main reason. SQLOS is a user-mode operating system that abstracts different Windows operating system–level services. Among the features that are enabled by SQLOS are better support for extended hardware architectures such as NUMA (Non-Uniform Memory Access), better support for operating system features such as the ability for SQL Server to recognize dynamically "hot-added" memory and processors, increased server reliability and scalability, a dedicated administrator connection, and a set of hosting APIs for hosted components. The .NET Framework runtime is one of the hosted components and is a consumer of many of the OS-level services that SQLOS provides, as shown in Figure 2-1.

Because SQL Server 2005 introduces fundamental changes, we'll first consider how SQLOS works as a .NET Framework runtime host; how it compares with other .NET Framework runtime hosts; and what special features of the runtime are used to ensure security, reliability, and performance.

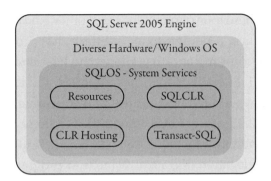

FIGURE 2-1: SQLOS services

You may already know that the latest version of the .NET Framework runtime, version 2.0, is required to use the .NET Framework in-process with SQL Server 2005. In this chapter, we'll explain why.

What Is a .NET Framework Runtime Host?

A *runtime host* is defined as any process that loads the .NET Framework runtime and runs code in a managed environment. The most common scenario is that a runtime host is simply a bootstrap entry point that executes from the Windows shell, loads the runtime into memory, and then loads one or more managed assemblies. An *assembly* is the unit of deployment in the .NET Framework roughly analogous to an executable program or DLL in prior versions of Windows.

A runtime host begins loading the runtime by calling `CorBindToRuntimeEx`, an export from `mscoree.dll` that is a shim DLL whose only job is to load the runtime. Only a single copy of the .NET Framework CLR engine can ever be loaded into a process during the process's lifetime. It is not possible to run multiple versions of the CLR within the same host. Four of `CorBindToRuntimeEx`'s parameters allow some customizing of runtime loading and behavior, namely the following:

- Server or workstation behavior
- Version of the CLR (for example, version 1.0.3705.0)
- Garbage-collection behavior
- Whether to share JIT compiled code across AppDomains (an AppDomain is a subdivision of the CLR runtime space)

In addition to these four parameters, three other parameters of CorBind-ToRuntimeEx request a pointer to an interface that provides methods to start and stop the runtime and that allows the host and runtime to communicate. In .NET Framework 1.1, hosts request the `ICorRuntimeHost` interface that allows limited host control of the runtime's behavior, but in .NET Framework 2.0, hosts can also request the `ICLRRuntimeHost` interface. This interface provides two methods, `GetCLRControl` and `SetHostControl`, that allow deep delegation of control to the host program—SQL Server, in this case. A series that a manager interface sets allow hosts to control

- Assembly loading
- Host protection
- Failure policy
- Memory
- Threading
- Thread pool management
- Synchronization
- I/O completion
- Garbage collection
- Debugging
- CLR events

SQL Server, in its role as a runtime host, uses almost every one of these control mechanisms to provide security, reliability, and performance when hosting the .NET Framework. The CLR requests interfaces to talk to SQL Server by using `IHostControl::GetHostManager`, and SQL Server (through SQLOS) uses `ICLRControl::GetCLRManager` to talk back. The exact details of every interface and method are beyond the scope of this book. Refer to *Customizing the Microsoft .NET Framework Common Language Runtime*, by Steven Pratschner (Microsoft Press, 2005), for a complete description. This excellent treatise on hosting was published before SQL Server 2005 and .NET Framework 2.0 shipped, so a few SQL Server–related details have changed since its publication.

Two examples of specialized runtime hosts are the ASP.NET worker process and IE. The ASP.NET worker process differs from the norm in code location and in how the executable code, threads, and AppDomains are organized. (We'll discuss AppDomains in the next section.) The ASP.NET worker process divides code into separate applications. *Application* is a term that is borrowed from IIS to denote code running in a virtual directory. Code is located in virtual directories, which are mapped to physical directories in the IIS metabase, a proprietary file maintained by IIS to store this and other configuration information. IE is another runtime host with behaviors that differ from the ASP.NET worker process or SQL Server 2005. IE loads code when it encounters a specific type of `<object>` tag in a Web page. The location of the code is obtained from an HTML attribute of the tag. SQL Server 2005 is an example of a specialized runtime host that goes far beyond ASP.NET or IE in specialization and control of CLR semantics.

SQL Server As a Runtime Host

SQL Server's special requirements of utmost security, reliability, and performance have necessitated an overhaul of how the managed hosting APIs work, as well as of how the CLR works internally. SQL Server is a specialized host like ASP.NET and IE rather than a simple bootstrap mechanism. The runtime is lazy loaded; if you never catalog a user assembly, or use a managed stored procedure or user-defined type, the runtime is never loaded. This is useful because loading the runtime takes a one-time memory allocation of approximately 10MB to 15MB in addition to SQL Server's buffers and unmanaged executable code. How SQL Server manages its resources and locates the code to load is unique as well. Figure 2-2 shows how SQL Server 2005 hosts the CLR.

SQL Server Resource Management

As mentioned previously, SQL Server 2005 handles resource management using a user-mode operating system known as SQLOS. SQL Server 2005's SQLOS provides management functionality such as:

- Nonpreemptive scheduling
- Memory management
- Resource monitoring

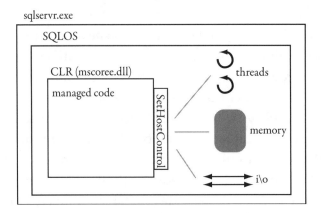

FIGURE 2-2: Hosting the CLR

- Exception handling
- Network and disk I/O
- Synchronization
- Hosting subsystems

Having all the features abstracted allows SQL Server to exploit different hardware configurations and different Windows operating system versions better. Note that there is almost a direct correlation between resources that the CLR allows the host to manage and those that SQLOS manages. SQLOS provides these features to manage all OS-level functions—not just those of the CLR—in an integrated and consistent manner. If SQL Server is running short on memory, for example, all subsystems are notified so that they can release memory to alleviate the shortage. The buffer pool may release some of its data buffers; the CLR might respond by performing eager garbage collection.

In .NET Framework runtime hosts, resources like memory and threads are usually managed by the CLR itself in conjunction with the underlying operating system. In SQLCLR (this is a term that is used for the functionality of the CLR running inside SQL Server), SQL Server controls these chores. SQL Server does this by informing, negotiating with, and layering over the CLR if needed by using the CLR hosting interfaces described previously, in conjunction with the SQLOS hosting interfaces. SQL Server uses its own memory allocation scheme, for example, managing real memory and mapping it to virtual memory as needed. The SQL Server buffer pool optimizes throughput by balancing memory usage among data and index buffers, plan caches, and other internal data structures. SQL Server can do a better job if it manages all the memory in its process. As an example, prior to SQL Server 2000, it was possible to specify that the TEMPDB database should be allocated in memory. In SQL Server 2000, that option was removed, because SQL Server can manage this better than the programmer or database administrator (DBA).

Clients of SQLOS in SQL Server 2005 (like the CLR) allocate memory using a SQLOS structure called a *memory clerk*. You can see all the memory clerks in a SQL Server instance by using the dynamic management view sys.dm_os_memory_clerks. Dynamic management views are new in SQL Server 2005 and allow administrators to look at much more of the inner workings of SQL Server than was possible in previous versions. These dynamic management views show real-time information. The dynamic views whose names begin with sys.dm_os display SQLOS internals, and those whose names begin with sys.dm_clr display information about SQLCLR internals.

SQL Server also uses its own thread scheduler, putting threads "to sleep" until it wants them to run. The DBA can configure SQL to use fibers rather than threads by adjusting the *lightweight pooling* configuration option, though this option is rarely used. In the Windows operating system, a thread represents an independent execution mechanism. A *fiber* is a lightweight thread that requires fewer resources; one Windows thread can be mapped to many fibers.[1] In SQLOS, schedulers manage *tasks*, which can be threads or fibers, depending on which mode SQL Server is using. Within the Windows operating system, the CLR usually maintains its own thread pools and allows programmers to create new threads; within SQL Server 2005, however, SQLCLR delegates the responsibility of managing pooling and scheduling to SQLOS. The key difference is the way threads are scheduled. SQL Server uses cooperative thread scheduling; the CLR natively

---

1. Fiber mode (lightweight pooling=1) is rarely used because not all components of SQL Server are supported in fiber mode.

uses preemptive thread scheduling. When a thread is cooperatively scheduled, it voluntarily yields control back to the operating system when it has completed its task. When a thread is preemptively scheduled, the operating system interrupts the thread when it has executed for a given time slice. SQL Server uses cooperative thread scheduling to minimize thread context switches. The CLR hosting APIs also define units of execution and scheduling in terms of tasks. The SQL scheduler manages blocking points, and hooks `PInvoke` and COM interop calls out of the runtime (which still use preemptive scheduling) to control switching the scheduling mode. The CLR hosting interfaces provide the hooks.

SQLOS also manages thread synchronization and locking for SQLCLR, using a combination of locks and latches. The physical implementation in SQLOS, such as a spinlock, is used to provide the implementation that SQLCLR uses when you request a monitor, semaphore, reader-writer lock, or critical section. The CLR delegates that responsibility to SQLOS, as opposed to using the Win32 API primitives, by using the host manager interfaces. It does the same type of delegation for I/O completion ports and other services usually provided directly by the underlying operating system.

Exceptional Condition Handling

In .NET Framework 1.1, certain exceptional conditions, such as an out-of-memory condition or a stack overflow, could bring down a running process. This cannot be allowed to happen in SQL Server. Although transactional semantics might be preserved, reliability and performance would suffer dramatically. In addition, unconditionally stopping a thread (using `Thread.Abort` or other API calls) can conceivably leave some system resources in an indeterminate state. Although using garbage collection reduces the severity of memory leaks, leaving system resources in an indeterminate state can still cause memory leaks. A subset of the .NET Framework base class libraries (BCL) has gone through more extensive testing and instrumentation, and in some cases, the libraries have been rewritten for .NET Framework 2.0 to guarantee that they do not leak unmanaged operating system handles or other unmanaged resources under exceptional conditions. The way this was accomplished in .NET Framework 2.0 was to use some new APIs (`Thread.BeginCriticalRegion` and `EndCriticalRegion`) to mark the beginning and ending of sections of code that could not be protected against leaks. If a thread must be terminated in a critical region, it might leak, and SQLOS will take appropriate action, such as unloading the AppDomain. And as we just discussed, SQL Server itself manages the memory.

Different runtime hosts deal with these hard-to-handle conditions in different ways. In the ASP.NET worker process, for example, recycling both the AppDomain and the process itself is considered acceptable, because disconnected, short-running Web requests would hardly notice. With SQL Server, rolling back all the in-flight transactions might take a few minutes (or a few hours). Process recycling would ruin long-running batch jobs in progress. Therefore, changes to the CLR exceptional condition handling needed to be made through the hosting APIs' exception escalation policy manager.

Out-of-memory conditions are particularly difficult to handle correctly, even when you leave a safety buffer of memory to respond to them. SQL Server attempts to use all memory available to it to maximize throughput. SQL Server 2005 works through the hosting interfaces to maintain a very small safety net and to handle out-of-memory conditions by providing memory for the CLR just-in-time. The .NET Framework 2.0 runtime and hosting APIs permit handling these conditions more robustly—that is, they guarantee availability and reliability after out-of-memory conditions without requiring a large safety net, letting SQL Server tune memory usage to the amount of physical memory. The CLR notifies SQL Server about the repercussions of failing each memory request. SQLOS monitors and responds to operating system memory pressure by using the `QueryMemoryResourceNotification` API, and it monitors and responds to CLR memory pressure by using the CLR host manager event infrastructure. Low-memory conditions may be handled by permitting the garbage collector to run more frequently, unloading AppDomains that are no longer being used, waiting for other procedural code to finish before invoking additional procedures, or even aborting running threads if needed.

There is also a failure escalation policy implemented via the hosting interfaces that allows SQL Server to determine how to deal with exceptions. SQL Server can decide to abort the thread that causes an exception and, if necessary, unload the AppDomain (we'll discuss AppDomains shortly). On resource failures, the CLR will unwind the entire managed stack of the session that takes the resource failure. If that session has any locks, the entire AppDomain in which the session is running is unloaded. The entire App-Domain must be unloaded, because having locks indicates that there is some shared state to synchronize and, thus, that shared state is not likely to be consistent if just the session was aborted. In certain cases, this might mean that finally blocks in CLR code may not run. In addition, *finalizers*—hooks that programmers can use to do necessary but not time-critical resource cleanup—might not get run. Except in UNSAFE mode (discussed later in the chapter), finalizers are not permitted in CLR user libraries that run in SQL Server.

Stack overflow conditions cannot be entirely prevented and are usually handled by implementing exceptional condition handling in the program. If the program does not handle these conditions, the CLR will catch these exceptions, unwind the stack, and abort the thread if needed. In exceptional circumstances, such as when memory allocation during a stack overflow causes an out-of-memory condition, recycling the AppDomain may be necessary.

In addition to exceptions that the programmer does not catch, there is the possibility that the database administrator can issue the Transact-SQL (T-SQL) KILL command. This command terminates a running SQL Server session or SPID (system process identifier). SQLCLR has an exception escalation policy, implemented through the hosting APIs that were mentioned at the beginning of the chapter and enforced by SQLOS. This is shown in Figure 2-3. To reiterate:

1. An unhandled exception or SQL KILL statement can cause a thread abort. The CLR has a certain amount of time to respond, configured through the hosting APIs.

2. If the CLR does not respond, this is escalated to a rude thread abort. In a rude thread abort, finally blocks may not run.

3. If the CLR does not respond to rude thread abort, this is escalated to AppDomain unload.

4. Finally, SQLOS will escalate to rude AppDomain unload.

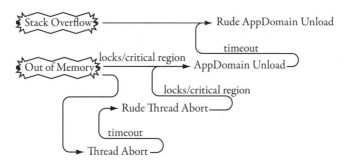

FIGURE 2-3: SQL Server 2005 unhandled exception escalation policy

In all the cases just mentioned, SQL Server will maintain transactional semantics. If the session is running SQLCLR code, how do the .NET Framework base class libraries guarantee that they clean up all unmanaged resources after a thread abort or an AppDomain unload?

In .NET Framework 2.0, a new set of classes was introduced to allow the CLR libraries to wrap operating system handles in a more robust manner. These classes all derive from the `SafeHandle` class. In implementations of `SafeHandle`, classes provide finalizers that are guaranteed to be run during rude thread abort or during AppDomain unload. This is because the `SafeHandle` class itself is derived from the `CriticalFinalizerObject` class. In this way, the base class libraries can provide guarantees to SQL Server that they will not leak handles over time.

Code Loading

SQL Server does not allow users to run arbitrary programs, because doing so might threaten the reliability of the server environment. Therefore, SQLCLR assemblies are loaded differently within SQLOS than CLR assemblies are loaded within Windows. The user or DBA must preload the code into the database and define which portions are invocable from T-SQL. Preloading and defining code uses ordinary SQL Server Data Definition Language (DDL) statements. Loading code as a stream of bytes from the database rather than from the file system makes SQL Server's class loader unique. Later in this chapter, we'll look at the exact DDL that is used to "create" an assembly in SQL Server (that is, load or refresh the bytes of code in the database) and manage the behavior of the assemblies.

The special subset of base class libraries that makes up the .NET Framework and has been approved for loading in SQL Server 2005 is treated differently from ordinary user .NET Framework assemblies in that the libraries are loaded from the global assembly cache (GAC) and are not defined to SQL Server or stored in SQL Server. Base class libraries that are not approved for loading must be treated as ordinary user assemblies—that is, stored in the database and loaded from the database. Most of the base class libraries are not on the approved list. Some portions of the base class libraries may have no usefulness in a SQL Server environment (for example, System.Windows.Forms); some may be dangerous to the health of the service process when used incorrectly (System.Threading) or may be a security risk (portions of System.Security). The architects of SQL Server 2005 have reviewed the class libraries that make up the .NET Framework, and only those deemed relevant are enabled for loading. This is accomplished by providing the CLR a list of libraries that are OK to load. Providing a list of libraries that are OK to load from the GAC, as well as overriding the .NET Framework's ordinary class loading mechanism, is accomplished through the CLR host management APIs described at the beginning of this chapter. The current list of libraries enabled for loading from the GAC is

- CustomMarshallers.dll
- Microsoft.VisualBasic.dll
- Microsoft.VisualC.dll
- mscorlib.dll
- System.dll
- System.Configuration.dll
- System.Data.dll
- System.Data.OracleClient.dll
- System.Data.SqlXml.dll
- System.Security.dll

- `System.Transactions.dll`
- `System.Web.Services.dll`
- `System.Xml.dll`

SQL Server will take responsibility for validating all user libraries and FX libraries that are not on the approved list, to determine that they are suitable for use within SQL Server. It will examine them, for example, to determine that they don't contain updatable static variables unless specially allowed because the assembly is registered as `PERMISSION_SET = UNSAFE`. SQL Server does not allow sharing state between user libraries and registers through the new CLR hosting APIs for notification of all interassembly calls. In addition, user libraries are divided into three categories for security purposes; two of these categories have similar reliability guarantees. Assemblies must be assigned to a category and use only the appropriate libraries for that category. We'll discuss this further after we've looked at the syntax involved in assembly definition.

Because code in SQL Server must be reliable, SQL Server will load only the latest version of the Framework class libraries it supports. This is analogous to shipping a particular tested version of ADO with SQL Server. Multiple versions of your code cannot run side by side in SQL Server 2005, although this is permitted by other .NET Framework runtime hosts.

Security

You may have noticed that we started this chapter by asserting that security is the most important consideration in an enterprise application, but in this discussion, we have saved it for last. This is because an entire chapter of this book is devoted to the subject of .NET Framework code access security (CAS), assembly security, user security, and other security enhancements in SQL Server 2005 (see Chapter 6). We'll talk about XML namespace security in Chapter 9, which discusses the `XML` data type.

At this point, suffice it to say that there are three categories of access security for managed code. These are `SAFE`, `EXTERNAL_ACCESS`, and `UNSAFE`, which we mentioned previously with respect to class loading. They allow the DBA to grant certain privileges to an assembly after (s)he has weighed the risks and benefits of doing so. SAFE and EXTERNAL_ACCESS assemblies have similar reliability guarantees; they are different only with respect to security. These categories equate to SQL Server–specific permission sets using CAS concepts. For ensuring the integrity of user-permissions defined in the database, we depend on the principal execution context of the stored procedure or user-defined function in combination with database roles. See Chapter 6 for the specifics of security enhancements.

Loading the Runtime: Processes and AppDomains

We've spoken of AppDomains quite a bit in previous paragraphs. It's time to describe exactly what they are and how SQL Server uses them. In the .NET Framework, processes can be subdivided into pieces known as application domains, or AppDomains. Loading the runtime creates a default AppDomain; user or system code can create other AppDomains. AppDomains are like lightweight processes themselves with respect to code isolation and marshaling. This means that object instances in one AppDomain are not directly available to other AppDomains by means of memory references; the parameters must be marshaled up and shipped across. In the .NET Framework, the default is not to marshal at all. If marshaling is allowed by specifying the Serializable attribute, the default is marshal-by-value; a copy of the instance data is made and shipped to the caller. Another choice is marshal-by-reference, in which the caller gets a locator or "logical pointer" to the data in the callee's AppDomain, and subsequent use of that instance involves a cross-AppDomain trip. This isolates one AppDomain's state from others and is shown graphically in Figure 2-4.

Each process that loads the .NET Framework creates a default App-Domain.[2] From this AppDomain, you can create additional AppDomains programmatically, as shown in Listing 2-1.

---

2. Technically, this describes the Windows .NET host AppDomain allocation.

LISTING 2-1: Creating AppDomains programmatically

```
public static int Main(string[] argv) {

 // create domain
 AppDomain child = AppDomain.CreateDomain("dom2");

 // execute yourapp.exe
 int r = child.ExecuteAssembly("yourapp.exe",null,argv);

 // unload domain
 AppDomain.Unload(child);

 return r;
}
```

Although there may be many AppDomains in a process, AppDomains cannot share class instances without marshaling.

SQL Server does not use the default AppDomain for database processing, although it is used to load the runtime. Exactly how AppDomains are allocated in SQL Server 2005 is not controllable by the user or DBA; AppDomains are scoped to the database, and a separate AppDomain is created for each assembly owner in a database. In the current implementation, there are two reasons that new AppDomains are created: to run DDL that creates assemblies and other database objects, and to run .NET Framework code. The DDL-AppDomains are transient and are destroyed as soon as the DDL completes. The AppDomains that run code are created when new .NET Framework code or updated .NET Framework code runs for the first time. The system dynamic management view sys.dm_clr_appdomains shows

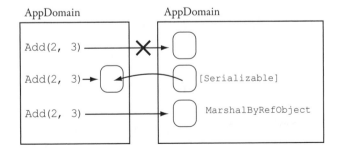

FIGURE 2-4: .NET Framework marshaling choices. The default is to not allow marshaling.

the code running AppDomains in the SQL Server process. Creation and destruction of AppDomains that run code produce messages in the SQL Server log. AppDomains are allocated based on the owner of the assembly. This isolates each assembly owner's code. This effectively prevents using code that is not type-safe to circumvent SQL Server permissions without the overhead of intercepting each call. The relationship among the SQL Server process, databases, and AppDomains is shown in Figure 2-5.

The runtime-hosting APIs also support the concept of domain-neutral code. Domain-neutral code means that one copy of the JIT compiled code is shared across multiple AppDomains. Although this reduces the working set of the process because only one copy of the code and supported structures exists in memory, it is a bit slower to access static variables, because each App-Domain must have its own copy of static variables, and this requires the runtime to add a level of indirection. There are four domain-neutral code settings:

1. No assemblies are domain neutral.
2. All assemblies are domain neutral.
3. Only strongly named assemblies are domain neutral.
4. The host can specify a list of assemblies that are domain neutral.

SQL Server 2005 uses the fourth option; it will share only a set of Framework assemblies. Strongly named assemblies cannot be shared, because these shared assemblies could never be unloaded.

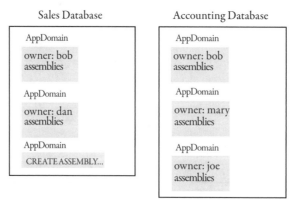

FIGURE 2-5: AppDomains in SQL Server databases

AppDomains do not have a concept of thread affinity—that is, all App-Domains share the common CLR thread pool. This means that although object instances must be marshaled across AppDomains, the marshaling is more lightweight than COM marshaling because not every marshal requires a thread switch. This also means it is possible to delegate the management of all threads to SQL Server while retaining the existing marshaling behavior with respect to threads.

Safe Code: How the Runtime Makes It Safer to Run "Foreign" Code

If you've used SQL Server for a while, you might be thinking at this point, "We've always been able to run code other than T-SQL inside the SQL Server process. OLE DB providers can be defined to load into memory. Extended stored procedures are written in C++ and other languages. What makes this scenario different?" The difference is that managed code is safe code. Except in the special UNSAFE mode, code is verified by the runtime to ensure that it is type-safe and validated to ensure that it contains no code that accesses memory locations directly. This all but eliminates buffer over-runs, pointers that point to the wrong storage location, and so on.

The unmanaged extended stored procedure code does run under structured exception handling. You cannot bring down a SQL Server process by branching to location zero, for example. Because an extended stored procedure runs directly in memory shared with SQL Server, however, it is possible for the procedure to access or change memory that it does not own. This can cause memory corruption and violate security, which is potentially more insidious.

Because managed code runs in its own AppDomain and is prevented from accessing memory except through the runtime, it is an order of magnitude safer than the extended stored procedures of the past. Note that it is possible to run unsafe .NET Framework code inside SQL Server, but this code must be defined using the UNSAFE option in the CREATE ASSEMBLY DDL statement. It is worth noting that UNSAFE assemblies may be catalogued only by SQL Server administrators that are granted UNSAFE ASSEMBLY permission. .NET Framework code in the Managed C++ compiler without the /safe compile switch and C# code that uses the unsafe keyword must use the UNSAFE declaration in the DDL. In addition to analyzing your code when it is catalogued to SQL Server, SQL Server also performs safety checks at runtime.

The Host Protection Attribute was invented in .NET Framework 2.0 to allow the host to have a say in running certain classes and methods based on information the author of the class or method provides. The System.Security.Permissions.HostProtectionAttribute class is applied to assemblies, classes, constructors, delegates, or methods to indicate that the item contains functionality that could cause instability in the host when invoked by user code. HostProtectionAttribute has a series of properties that can be set to indicate different potentially dangerous functionality types. The current set of properties is as follows:

- ExternalProcessMgmt[3]
- ExternalThreading
- SelfAffectingProcessMgmt
- SelfAffectingThreading
- MayLeakOnAbort
- Resources (this is a bitswitch of all the other properties of type HostProtectionResource)
- SecurityInfrastructure
- SharedState
- Synchronization
- UI

Applying the HostProtectionAttribute to a class or method creates a LinkDemand—that is, a demand that the immediate caller have the permission required to execute the method. The LinkDemand is checked against the permission set of the assembly and/or the procedural code. Setting permission sets on assemblies is shown in the section on CREATE

---

3. ExternalProcessMgmt (external process management) means that this code could create or destroy other processes.

ASSEMBLY later in the chapter. A HostProtectionAttribute differs from a normal security LinkDemand in that it is applied at the discretion of the host—in this case, SQL Server. Some hosts, such as IE, can choose to ignore the attribute, while others, such as SQL Server, can choose to enforce it. If the host chooses to ignore the HostProtectionAttribute, the LinkDemand evaporates—that is, it's not executed at all.

All the Framework class libraries permitted to load in SQL Server have been decorated with HostProtectionAttributes. In conjunction with CAS (discussed in Chapter 6), HostProtectionAttributes produce a SQL Server–specific sandbox based on a permission set that ensures that the code running with any permission set other than UNSAFE cannot cause instability or lack of scalability in SQL Server.

In addition to the usage of HostProtectionAttribute, there is a set of attributes that is disallowed in all SQL Server user assemblies. These attributes are deemed dangerous because they affect thread management or security. A few additional attributes are disallowed in SAFE and EXTERNAL_ACCESS assemblies but allowed in UNSAFE assemblies. The dangerous attributes are listed below:

- System.ContextStaticAttribute
- System.MTAThreadAttribute
- System.Runtime.CompilerServices.MethodImplAttribute
- System.Runtime.CompilerServices.CompilationRelaxations Attribute
- System.Runtime.Remoting.Contexts.ContextAttribute
- System.Runtime.Remoting.Contexts.Synchronization Attribute
- System.Runtime.InteropServices.DllImportAttribute
- System.Security.Permissions.CodeAccessSecurity Attribute
- System.STAThreadAttribute
- System.ThreadStaticAttribute
- System.Security.SuppressUnmanagedCodeSecurityAttribute
- System.Security.UnverifiableCodeAttribute

Where the Code Lives: Storing .NET Framework Assemblies (CREATE ASSEMBLY)

A .NET Framework assembly is catalogued in a SQL Server database by using the CREATE ASSEMBLY statement. The following lines of code define an assembly to SQL Server and assign it the symbolic name SomeTypes:

```
CREATE ASSEMBLY SomeTypes
  FROM 'C:\types\SomeTypes.dll'
```

This not only loads the code from the file, but also assigns a symbolic name to it—in this case, SomeTypes. The code can be loaded from a network share or from a local file system directory, and it must be a library (DLL) rather than directly executable from the command line (EXE). No special processing of the code is needed beyond normal compilation; SomeTypes.dll is a normal .NET Framework assembly. SomeTypes.dll must contain an assembly manifest, and although a .NET Framework assembly can contain multiple physical files, SQL Server does not currently support multifile assemblies. The complete syntax for CREATE ASSEMBLY follows:

```
CREATE ASSEMBLY assembly_name
[ AUTHORIZATION owner_name ]
FROM { < client_assembly_specifier > | < assembly_bits > [,...n] }
[ WITH PERMISSION_SET = { SAFE | EXTERNAL_ACCESS | UNSAFE } ]

< client_assembly_specifier > :: =
   '\\machine_name\share_name\[path\]manifest_file_name'
< assembly_bits > :: =
   { varbinary_literal | varbinary_expression }
```

where:

- assembly_name—Is the name of the assembly; the name should be a valid SQL Server identifier.
- client_assembly_specifier—Specifies the local path or the network location (as UNC Path) of the assembly being loaded, including the filename of the assembly.
- manifest_file_name—Specifies the name of the file that contains the manifest of the assembly. SQL Server will also look for the

dependent assemblies of this assembly, if any, in the same location—that is, the directory specified by `client_assembly_specifier`.

- `PERMISSION_SET = { SAFE | EXTERNAL_ACCESS | UNSAFE }`—Changes the .NET Framework Code Access Permission Set property granted to the assembly. We'll have more to say about this later in the chapter and in Chapter 6.

- `assembly_bits`—Supplies the list of binary values that constitute the assembly and its dependent assemblies. If `assembly_bits` is specified, the first value in the list should correspond to the root-level assembly—that is, the name of the assembly as recorded in its manifest should match the `assembly_name`. The values corresponding to the dependent assemblies can be supplied in any order.

- `varbinary_literal`—Is a `varbinary(max)` literal of the form 0x . . .

- `varbinary_expression`—Is an expression of type `varbinary(max)`.

When you catalog an assembly using CREATE ASSEMBLY, the symbolic name you assign to the assembly need not agree with the name in the assembly manifest. This allows you to catalog assemblies with the same name that differ in culture specifier. Multiple versions of an assembly that differ by version number are not permitted in SQL Server 2005.

The current user's identity is used (via impersonation) to read the assembly file from the appropriate directory. Therefore, the user must have permission to access the directory where the assembly is located. If you are logged into SQL Server using an SQL login, the credentials of the SQL Server service account are used to attempt to access the file. Note that using CREATE ASSEMBLY copies the assembly's bits into the database and stores them physically in a system table (`sys.assembly_files`). There is no need for SQL Server to have access to the file system directory to load the bits the next time SQL Server is started; when the CREATE ASSEMBLY statement completes, SQL Server never again accesses the location from which it loaded the assembly. If the file or bits that CREATE ASSEMBLY points to do not contain an assembly manifest, or if the manifest indicates that this is a multifile assembly, CREATE ASSEMBLY will fail.

SQL Server will verify that the assembly code is type-safe (except if PERMISSION_SET = UNSAFE) and validate the code when it is catalogued.

This not only saves time, because this is usually done by the runtime during the Just-in-Time (JIT) compilation process (at first load), but also ensures that only verifiable code is catalogued into SQL Server. Unverifiable code will cause CREATE ASSEMBLY to fail. What happens during validation depends on the value of the PERMISSION_SET specified. The default PERMISSION_SET is SAFE. Permission sets control CAS permissions when the code executes but also enforce semantics with respect to what kind of calls can be made. CREATE ASSEMBLY uses reflection[4] to ensure that you are following the rules.

There are three distinct PERMISSION_SETs:

SAFE—This is the default permission set. An assembly catalogued with the SAFE permission set cannot compromise the security, reliability, or performance of SQL Server. SAFE code cannot access external system resources such as the Registry, network, file system, or environment variables; the only CLR permission that SAFE code has is execution permission. SAFE code cannot access unmanaged code through runtime-callable wrappers or use PInvoke to invoke a native Windows DLL. SAFE code can make data access calls using the current context but cannot access external data through the SqlClient or other data providers. SAFE code cannot create threads or otherwise do any thread or process management. Attempting to use forbidden methods within a SAFE assembly will result in a security exception. The following example shows the security exception produced when a method in a SAFE assembly tries to connect to the Web using System.Net.WebRequest:

```
Msg 6522, Level 16, State 1, Procedure GetFromWeb, Line 0
A .NET Framework error occurred during execution of user defined routine
or aggregate 'GetFromWeb':
  System.Security.SecurityException:
  Request for the permission of type
    System.Net.WebPermission,
    System, Version=2.0.0.0,
    Culture=neutral,
    PublicKeyToken=b77a5c561934e089 failed.
at System.Security.CodeAccessSecurityEngine.Check(Object demand,
StackCrawlMark& stackMark, Boolean isPermSet)
at System.Security.CodeAccessPermission.Demand()...
```

---

4. *Reflection* is the ability to use assembly metadata to retrieve information about .NET Framework classes, fields, properties, and methods contained in that assembly.

EXTERNAL_ACCESS—Specifying EXTERNAL_ACCESS gives code the ability to access external system resources. As with SAFE, an assembly catalogued with the EXTERNAL_ACCESS permission set cannot compromise the reliability or performance of SQL Server. Unlike SAFE assemblies, EXTERNAL_ACCESS assemblies can pose a threat to security because they access resources outside the database process. The Registry, network file system, external databases, and environment variables are available through the managed code APIs, but EXTERNAL_ACCESS code cannot use COM-callable wrappers or PInvoke, or create threads. An administrator must have EXTERNAL ACCESS ASSEMBLY permission to catalog an EXTERNAL_ACCESS assembly with CREATE ASSEMBLY.

UNSAFE—UNSAFE code is not restricted in any way, including using unmanaged code. Because using UNSAFE could compromise SQL Server, only users with UNSAFE ASSEMBLY permission can catalog UNSAFE code. Usage permissions are described in Chapter 6. Although it seems unwise even to permit UNSAFE code to execute, UNSAFE code is really no more unsafe than an extended stored procedure.

In addition to CAS permission sets, which will be discussed in Chapter 6, there is a series of .NET Framework code requirements and coding constructs that can be used based on the PERMISSION_SET applied to the code. Table 2-1 shows a list of .NET Framework constructs and their permitted usage in the three permission sets.

Assembly Dependencies: When Your Assemblies Use Other Assemblies

Assemblies have a database-level scope. Because each database has its own set of AppDomains, as mentioned previously, and assemblies may not be shared among AppDomains, each assembly owner by a distinct owner must be loaded in a distinct AppDomain. However, you might want to share an assembly within a single database if the assemblies are owned by the same owner. Examples would be statistical packages or spatial data types that are referenced by many user-defined assemblies in multiple databases. System utilities, such as collection classes, and user-defined class libraries can be used in this manner.

TABLE 2-1: Code Requirements and Constructs, and SQL Server Permission Sets

Feature or Construct	SAFE	EXTERNAL_ACCESS	UNSAFE
Shared state	N	N	Y
Synchronization	N	N	Y
`Thread.Create`	N	N	Y
Class constructors	Y	Y	Y
Register for static events	N	N	Y
Finalizers	N	N	Y
`Debug.Break`	N	N	N
`ThreadException.EventHandler`	N	N	N
`AppDomain.DomainUnloadEvent`	N	N	N
PInvoke	N	N	Y
`IJW (Note: /clr:pure and / clr are supported)`	N	N	N
PE verification	Y	Y	Y
Metadata verification	Y	Y	Y
IL verification	Y	Y	Y
Non-read-only static fields/properties	N	N	Y
Code must be type safe	Y	Y	N
`HPA—ExternalProcessMgmt`	N	N	Y
`HPA—ExternalThreading`	N	N	Y
`HPA—Synchronization`	N	N	Y
`HPA—SharedState`	N	N	Y
`HPA—SelfAffectedProcessMgmt`	N	N	Y
`HPA—SelfAffectedThreading`	N	N	Y

To ensure that a library that's being referenced by multiple assemblies is not dropped when a single library that references it is dropped, SQL Server will reflect on the assembly when CREATE ASSEMBLY is executed, to determine the dependencies. It automatically catalogs these dependencies in the SQL metadata tables. As an example, let's assume that both the Payroll department and the HR department reference a common set of formulas to calculate an employee's years of service. This library is called EmployeeRoutines.

When Payroll routines and HR routines are declared (in assemblies of analogous names), they each reference EmployeeRoutines as follows:

```
-- SQL Server reflection determines
-- that PayrollRoutines references EmployeeRoutines
-- EmployeeRoutines is cataloged too
CREATE ASSEMBLY PayrollRoutines FROM
      'C:\types\PayrollRoutines.DLL'
GO

-- SQL Server reflection determines
-- that HRRoutines references EmployeeRoutines
-- this sets up another reference to EmployeeRoutines
CREATE ASSEMBLY HRRoutines FROM
      'C:\types\HRRoutines.DLL'
GO
```

With the previous declarations, neither the Payroll programmers nor the HR programmers can change or drop the EmployeeRoutines without the consent of the other. We'll look at how you'd set up the permissions for this in Chapter 6, the security chapter.

Assemblies and SQL Schemas: Who Owns Assemblies (Information Schema)

Assemblies, like other SQL Server database objects, are the property of the user who catalogs them using CREATE ASSEMBLY: the owner. This has security repercussions for the users who wish to use the procedures, triggers, and types within an assembly. Though we'll go over all the security details in Chapter 6, we'd like to discuss execution context here. In addition, we'll see exactly where in the system tables information about assemblies is stored.

System Metadata Tables and INFORMATION_SCHEMA

Information about assemblies, assembly code, and code dependencies is stored in the system metadata tables, which in general store information about SQL Server database objects, such as tables and indexes. Some metadata tables store information for the entire database instance and exist only in the MASTER database; some are replicated in every database, user databases as well as MASTER. The names of the tables and the information they contain are proprietary. System metadata tables are better performing, however, because they reflect the internal data structures of SQL Server. In the big rewrite that took place in SQL Server 7, the system metadata tables remained intact. In SQL Server 2005, the metadata tables have been overhauled, revising the layout of the metadata information and adding metadata for new database objects. In addition, programmers and DBAs can no longer write to a system metadata table. It is really a read-only view.

The SQL INFORMATION_SCHEMA, on the other hand, is a series of metadata views defined by the ANSI SQL specification as a standard way to expose metadata. The views evolve with the ANSI SQL specification; SQL:1999 standard INFORMATION_SCHEMA views are a superset of the SQL-92 views. SQL Server 2000 supports the INFORMATION_SCHEMA views at the SQL-92 standard level; there are few changes to this support in SQL Server 2005. Listing 2-2 shows code that can be used to retrieve the list of tables in a specific database. The sample uses the system metadata tables, followed by analogous code using the INFORMATION_SCHEMA views. Note that neither query (in SQL Server, the SQL:1999 spec seems to indicate otherwise) includes the system tables in the list of tables.

LISTING 2-2: Getting metadata from SQL Server

```
-- this uses the old system metadata tables, supported for compatibility
SELECT * FROM sysobjects
    WHERE type = 'U'

-- this uses the INFORMATION_SCHEMA
SELECT * FROM INFORMATION_SCHEMA.TABLES
    WHERE TABLE_TYPE = 'BASE TABLE'
```

SQL Server 2005 includes a reorganization of the system metadata tables. This includes renaming the tables to use an arbitrary schema (named SYS) as well as table renames and reorganization of some of the information. The goal, once again, is speed and naming consistency. The equivalent query to the previous two using the new system metadata tables would be as follows:

```
SELECT * FROM sys.tables
```

Note that the information returned by all three queries differs in the number of columns returned, the column names used, and the information in the rowset. Although a complete description of all the new metadata tables is beyond the scope of this book, we'll discuss the metadata information that is stored when CREATE ASSEMBLY is executed and explain assembly properties.

Assembly Metadata

Information about assemblies and the assembly code itself is stored in three metadata tables. These tables exist in each database, because assemblies are scoped to the database.

sys.assemblies stores information about the assembly itself as well as schema_id, assembly_id, and the .NET Framework version number. The complete list of columns in sys.assemblies is shown in Table 2-2.

The assembly dependencies are stored in sys.assembly_references, one row per assembly-reference pair. Table 2-3 shows the columns in sys.assembly_references. Note that this table does not contain information about which base class libraries an assembly references.

Finally, the assembly code itself is catalogued in sys.assembly_files. In all cases, this table contains the actual code rather than the name of the file where the code resided when it was catalogued. The original file location is not even kept as metadata. In addition, if you have added a debugger file, using a DDL statement such as ALTER ASSEMBLY ADD FILE, the debug information will appear as an additional entry in the sys.assembly_files table. Table 2-4 shows the contents of the sys.assembly_files table.

We'll further discuss declaring routines and types in the CREATE ASSEMBLY DDL statement in Chapters 3 and 4. Notice that you can define an assembly that is "invisible" with respect to defining routines and types to the runtime. Lack of visibility is the default when SQL Server loads

TABLE 2-2: Contents of sys.assemblies

Column Name	Data Type	Description
name	sysname	Name of assembly, unique within schema.
principal_id	int	ID of the principal that owns this schema.
assembly_id	int	Assembly identification number, unique within a database.
clr_name	nvarchar (4000)	Canonical string that encodes the simple name, version number, culture, and public key of the assembly. It uniquely identifies the assembly on the CLR side.
permission_set	tinyint	Permission set/security level for assembly, one of: 1 = Safe access only. 2 = External access allowed. 3 = Unsafe access allowed.
permission_set_desc	nvarchar(60)	Description of permission set/security level for assembly, one of: SAFE_ACCESS. EXTERNAL_ACCESS. UNSAFE_ACCESS.
is_visible	bit	1 if the assembly is visible to register T-SQL entry points (functions/procs/triggers/types/aggregates); 0 if it is intended only for managed callers (that is, provides internal implementation for other assemblies in the database).
create_date	datetime	Date assembly was created or registered.
modify_date	datetime	Date assembly was modified.

TABLE 2-3: Contents of sys.assembly_references

Column Name	Data Type	Description
assembly_id	int	ID of assembly to which this reference belongs
referenced_assembly_id	int	ID of assembly being referenced

TABLE 2-4: Contents of sys.assembly_files

Column Name	Data Type	Description
assembly_id	int	ID of assembly to which this file belongs
name	nvarchar(260)	Name of assembly file
file_id	int	ID of file, unique within an assembly
content	varbinary(max)	Bytes of assembly or debug symbols

dependent assemblies of an assembly defined using CREATE ASSEMBLY. You might do this, for example, to define a set of utility routines to be invoked internally only. If you specify VISIBILITY=ON (the default), this means that methods and types in this assembly can be declared as SQL Server stored procedures, user-defined functions, triggers, and types through DDL.

Maintaining User Assemblies (ALTER ASSEMBLY, DROP ASSEMBLY)

Although we stated earlier in this chapter that SQL Server loads only a single version of the .NET Framework runtime and base class libraries on the approved list, assemblies may be updated, their code reloaded, and properties (including the set of dependent assemblies) altered via DDL. Assemblies may also be dropped via DDL, subject to whether they are currently used by other system objects. An example of dropping the SomeTypes assembly defined earlier follows:

```
DROP ASSEMBLY SomeTypes
```

The complete syntax for dropping a defined assembly follows:

```
DROP ASSEMBLY assembly_name
  [WITH NO DEPENDENTS]
```

Note that the DROP ASSEMBLY statement will fail if any existing database objects reference the assembly. We'll get back to dependent assemblies in a moment.

You may change the properties of an assembly or even modify the assembly code in place using the ALTER ASSEMBLY statement. Let's assume that we have decided that the SomeTypes assembly mentioned earlier needs to be present in SQL Server, but it need not be visible (for example, it is accessed only by other assemblies and not from the outside). To prevent routines in this assembly from inadvertently being declared publicly via DDL, we can alter its visibility like this:

```
ALTER ASSEMBLY SomeTypes
  WITH VISIBILITY=OFF
```

To reload the SomeTypes assembly, as long as it is not currently being referenced, we can use the following syntax:

```
ALTER ASSEMBLY SomeTypes
  FROM 'C:\types\SomeTypes.dll'
```

The complete syntax for ALTER ASSEMBLY follows. We'll discuss uses of some of the more esoteric options in Chapter 5 and the security options in Chapter 6.

```
ALTER ASSEMBLY assembly_name
  [ FROM { < client_assembly_specifier > | < assembly_bits > [ ,...n ] ]
  [ WITH < assembly_option > [ ,...n ] ]
  [ DROP FILE { file_name [ ,...n ] | ALL } ]
  [ ADD FILE FROM { client_file_specifier
    [ AS file_name ] | file_bits AS file_name } [,...n ]

< client_assembly_specifier > :: =
    '\\computer_name\share-name\[path\]manifest_file_name'

< assembly_bits > :: =
    { varbinary_literal | varbinary_expression }

< assembly_option > :: =
    PERMISSION_SET { SAFE | EXTERNAL_ACCESS | UNSAFE }
    | VISIBILITY { ON | OFF }
    | UNCHECKED DATA
```

In order to change the permission set with ALTER ASSEMBLY, you must have analogous permissions as with CREATE ASSEMBLY—that is, you need EXTERNAL ACCESS ASSEMBLY permission to alter an assembly to the EXTERNAL_ACCESS safety level, and you must have UNSAFE ASSEMBLY permission to alter an assembly to UNSAFE. You also must have analogous file access permissions as with CREATE ASSEMBLY if you are going to load any new code from a file.

You can use ALTER ASSEMBLY not only to change individual metadata properties, but to update or reload the code as well. Reloading the code (by using the FROM clause) not only reloads, but revalidates code as well. Of course, this code must be built against the same version of the runtime and the same base class libraries as the original.

If there are references to the assembly, none of the method signatures of the methods defined as stored procedures, triggers, and user-defined functions is allowed to change. If your new version contains user-defined types, ALTER ASSEMBLY not only checks all the methods' signatures, but also, if the serialization format is Native, all the data members must be the same so that the user-defined type instances that have been persisted (as column values in tables) will still be usable. Other types of persisted data will be checked, too, if your assembly contains the following:

- Persisted computed columns that reference assembly methods
- Indexes on computed columns that reference assembly methods
- Computed columns with expressions that reference assembly user-defined functions
- Columns with check constraints that reference assembly user-defined functions (UDFs)

You can bypass checking persisted data by specifying the UNCHECKED DATA option; you must be db_owner or db_ddlowner or must have equivalent permissions to use this option. The metadata will indicate that the data is unchecked until you use the command DBCC CHECKTABLE to check the data in each table manually. You must be sure that the formulas (content) of UDFs have not changed before you use the UNCHECKED DATA option, or else corrupted data could result.

When you use ALTER ASSEMBLY, there may be user sessions using the old version of the assembly. In order not to disrupt those sessions, SQL Server will create a new AppDomain to load your new code. Existing sessions continue to use the old code in the original AppDomain until logoff; new sessions will be routed to the new AppDomain. When all the existing sessions finish, the old AppDomain is shut down. This is the only (transient) case where two different versions of your code can be running at the same time but is not the same as side-by-side execution.

One common requirement for programmers will be to add debugging information to use during development. A .NET Framework assembly can be debugged inside SQL Server with any of the usual .NET Framework debuggers—for example, Visual Studio 2005. You may have noticed that one of the metadata tables (`sys.assembly_files`) contains an additional entry if you have added the .NET Framework debugging symbols for the assembly. This file usually has a `.pdb` extension when it is produced by the compiler. To add a debug symbols file for the assembly that we defined earlier, we can execute the following statement:

```
ALTER ASSEMBLY SomeTypes
ADD FILE FROM 'C:\types\SomeTypes.pdb'
GO
```

The Database Project in Visual Studio 2005 will perform this step automatically when you use the Deploy menu entry.

Specification Compliance

The ANSI SQL specification attempts to standardize all issues related to relational databases, not just the SQL language. Although some databases allow external code to run inside the database (SQL Server permits this through extended stored procedures), this was not part of the SQL specification until recently. Two specifications that appeared at the end of the SQL:1999 standardization process relate to the concepts we're going to be covering in the SQL Server–.NET Framework integration portion of this book. The specifications related to the concept of managed code running inside the database and the interoperation of managed types and unmanaged types are called SQL/J part 1 and SQL/J part 2. There are two interesting features of these specs:

- They were added as addenda to SQL:1999 after the specification was submitted. SQL/J part 1 became SQL:1999 part 12, and SQL/J part 2 became SQL:1999 part 13. This specification was consolidated as part 13 of SQL:2003 and is there known as SQL-Part 13: Java Routines and Types (SQL/JRT).

- Although the specs are part of the ANSI SQL specification, the only managed language they address is Java, which is itself not a standard. Java was withdrawn from the ECMA (European Computer Manufacturers Association) standardization process. On the other hand, the .NET Framework CLR is an ECMA standard.[5]

Nevertheless, it is interesting at least to draw parallels.

The closest equivalents to SQL Server 2005's CREATE ASSEMBLY/ALTER ASSEMBLY/DROP ASSEMBLY statements are SQL/J's SQLJ.INSTALL_JAR, SQLJ.REMOVE_JAR, and SQLJ.REPLACE_JAR procedures. These procedures are not implemented by all the implementers of the standard. Because the SQL/J standard does not state that the actual code needs to be stored in the database, you can also change the defined path where the jar file[6] resides with SQLJ.ALTER_JAR_PATH. Because SQL Server assemblies are stored inside the database, an equivalent function is unnecessary.

Some of the ancillary concepts are analogous with respect to deploying the items that an assembly or jar file contains. The specification includes a bit to indicate whether a deployment descriptor included in the jar file should be read; an analogous concept would be the list of publicly declared methods and types in the CREATE ASSEMBLY or ALTER ASSEMBLY statement. Visibility of classes and methods is defined by using the public or private keywords, as it is in SQL Server 2005, but no notion of visibility at the jar level exists in the SQL specification to correspond to the SQL Server 2005 notion of assembly visibility. References are defined in the ANSI specification only with respect to pathnames; there is no concept of keeping references in the schema. The ANSI specification contains no notion of CAS level and execution context. Database permissions for managed code within an assembly are part of SQL Server 2005 and, to an extent, the code within a SQL/JRT file as well. We'll discuss this in Chapter 6, which covers security.

---

5. Information about the .NET Framework–related ECMA standards can be found at http://msdn.microsoft.com/netframework/ecma.

6. A jar file is a container for Java class files.

Conclusions

If your assembly is SAFE or EXTERNAL_ACCESS, nothing you can do will affect SQL security, reliability, or performance. You'll have to work hard to make your app itself unreliable and nonscalable at these safety levels. SAFE or EXTERNAL_ACCESS levels enforce the general principles of no-shared-state and no multithreaded programming. Writing secure, reliable, and performant code that doesn't follow these tenets is harder, and such assemblies must be catalogued as UNSAFE.

Where Are We?

We've seen that SQL Server 2005 is a full-fledged runtime host and can run your managed code. SQL Server's choices as a runtime host are geared to security and reliability, with an eye to performance.

We've seen how to define an assembly (managed DLL) to SQL Server for storage inside the server and how to specify the execution context (identity) and degree of safety with which the code runs. The CLR's class libraries are even categorized by degree of safety; this should ameliorate some of the DBA's concerns.

In the next chapter, we'll look at some of the specific code you'd write as managed—stored procedures, user-defined functions, and triggers—and see how this code is defined to SQL Server so that it's indistinguishable from T-SQL procedures to the caller.

■ 3 ■

Procedures and Functions in .NET CLR Languages

S QL SERVER 2005 ADDS Common Language Runtime (CLR) languages as an alternative way to extend the functionality of SQL Server.

Any language capable of creating a DLL or a COM component can be used to extend the functionality of SQL Server. But extended stored procedures and COM components lack the security, reliability, and, in many cases, performance that Transact-SQL (T-SQL) provides. With SQL Server 2005, any .NET CLR language can be used to add stored procedures, user-defined functions, and triggers to extend the functionality of SQL Server with the same level of security, reliability, and performance that T-SQL provides.

Extending SQL Server

SQL Server's query functionality can be extended by using T-SQL. It can encapsulate common tasks and make it easier to maintain and perform them. It in effect allows you to write SQL batches that perform common tasks and store those batches directly in SQL Server for later reuse.

Much of the functionality associated with SQL Server does not come from the SQL programming language; it comes from extensions that Microsoft has added to SQL Server using T-SQL, its proprietary language for writing imperative code.

There is, for example, a Microsoft-written stored procedure to add a new user to a database called `sp_adduser`. This stored procedure is deprecated in SQL Server 2005 but is still supported so that existing scripts from previous versions of SQL Server can be used on SQL Server 2005. It has been replaced by the CREATE USER expression. Both of these work. This stored procedure inserts the parameters you pass in—login name and username—into appropriate database tables. If you use `sp_adduser` to add a user to the database you do not need to know the details of what happens inside the database. In fact, Microsoft could completely change how SQL Server maintains users in a database, and it would not affect the way you add users to a database.

Prior to SQL Server 2005, the only ways to extend SQL Server were to use T-SQL, or write an extended stored procedure or a COM component. T-SQL required you to know the T-SQL language. For many, this meant learning an alternative programming language that they used much less than their primary language. For a Visual Basic 2005 programmer, this might have meant stumbling through something like "Dim id. Whoops, no; Declare id. Whoops, no; Declare @id int." Similar relearn-by-syntax-error journeys await programmers from other languages whenever they attempt to write a T-SQL–based stored procedure.

Extended stored procedures require a rather tedious DLL to be created. C++ programmers, however, can use a wizard in Visual Studio to create this DLL and just fill in the functionality they choose. Likewise, Visual Basic 6 programmers can create a COM component and use it in SQL Server through the `sp_OACreate` stored procedure. This allows C++ or Visual Basic 6 programmers to use a familiar programming environment to extend SQL Server. Extended stored procedures and COM components have capabilities that T-SQL does not, because they can access system services that are outside SQL Server. The extension to SQL Server that allows it to send e-mail, for example, is an extended stored procedure. It could not have been written in T-SQL.

Extended stored procedures have their own issues. Although it is possible to write extended stored procedures that are secure and reliable, the languages used to create them make this very difficult to do. In general, an extended stored procedure or a COM component must stand a much higher level of scrutiny than a T-SQL–based stored procedure and in some cases cannot match the performance of T-SQL.

SQL Server 2005 changes all this. Any CLR language can extend SQL Server. The CLR is part of the .NET Framework. Extensions running in the CLR can be as safe and reliable as T-SQL and as flexible as an extended stored procedure or a COM component. This means that non–T-SQL developers can use a familiar development environment to extend the functionality of SQL Server.

In addition, there are some tasks for which the CLR is just better suited. Typically, the CLR is a better choice for operations that involve numeric computations or string manipulation.

If you hear anyone say, "Now that SQL Server 2005 uses the CLR, every Visual Basic and C# programmer is a database programmer!", run away quickly. The CLR is not better suited for doing set operations; SQL is the clear winner here. However, the CLR can execute SQL expressions, just as T-SQL can, and with about the same efficiency. Being able to write code in a CLR language will not be a substitute for knowing how to write `SELECT DISTINCT A.au_fname, A.au_lname FROM authors A JOIN titleauthors T ON A.au_id = T.au_id` when you need to find all the authors who have publications.

Chapter 2 focuses on how SQL Server 2005 hosts the CLR and, as part of that, how assemblies are loaded into SQL Server 2005. This chapter focuses on the mechanics of using the methods in those assemblies as stored procedures, functions, and triggers for operations that do not access SQL Server. Chapter 4 explains how these methods can access SQL Server directly, in a performant way.

CLR Extension Basics

A public static method of a public class from a CLR-based language can, with some restrictions, be used as a stored procedure, user-defined function, or trigger in SQL Server. Later, we will cover the specific restrictions, but in general, they limit the method parameters to those that make sense when used inside SQL Server and map directly to a SQL Server type.

To illustrate the use of CLR methods in SQL Server, we will look at a database for a company that makes pulley/belt drives. A pulley/belt drive is a kind of transmission; it has two round pulleys with a belt wrapped around them. Lots of kinds of equipment, from lawnmowers to drill presses, use the pulley/belt transmissions. Figure 3-1 shows an example of a pulley/belt drive.

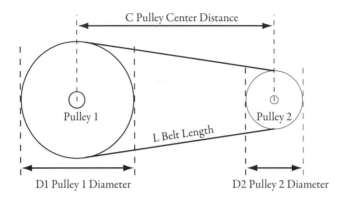

FIGURE 3-1: Pulley system

A belt, whose length is L, wraps around pulley 1 and pulley 2. D1 is the diameter of pulley 1, and D2 is the diameter of pulley 2. C is the distance from the center of pulley 1 to pulley 2.

Our pulley/belt company uses a database to keep track of the kinds of pulleys and belts it stocks. The database has a pulley table that lists each pulley by part number and diameter in inches. It has a belt table that lists each belt by part number and length in inches. Any combination of two pulleys and a belt can be used to make a transmission, provided that the pulleys can be placed far enough apart to not touch each other and still allow the belt to go around them.

This company wants a view that will show it all the possible transmissions that the company can make from the parts that it stocks. The transmission view should show the part numbers for the pulleys and belt, and it must also show the distance between the centers of the pulleys. This view will have to eliminate any combinations of pulleys and belt that would overlap the pulleys, of course.

The distance between the pulleys requires a geometric calculation. Figure 3-2 shows a function that calculates the approximate distance (3) between the two pulleys of a pulley/belt transmission, given the pulley sizes and belt length. The PulleyDistance method (1) in the C# Pulley class satisfies the requirements of a CLR method to be used in SQL Server 2005. The calculation of the distance (3) is based on a formula from the *McGraw-Hill Machining and Metalworking Handbook,* by Ronald

```
public class Pulley {
①  public static double PulleyDistance(
      double Pulley1Diameter, double Pulley2Diameter,
      double BeltLength) {
   ②  double distance = 0, a = 2.0;
      double b = BeltLength - 1.57 *
         (Pulley1Diameter + Pulley2Diameter);
      double c = Math.Pow(Pulley1Diameter
③         - Pulley2Diameter, 2.0);
      double b1 = Math.Pow(b, 2.0) - (4 * a * c);
      if (b1 > 0) {
         distance = (b + Math.Sqrt(b1)) / (2 * a);
         if (distance <
            ((Pulley1Diameter + Pulley2Diameter) / 2)){
      ④  distance = 0;
         } }
   ⑤  return Math.Round(distance, 1);
   }
};
```

FIGURE 3-2: Pulley distance calculation

Walsh (McGraw-Hill, 1994). By convention, the distance (4) is zero if the BeltLength would make the pulleys overlap. The calculation is returned (5) rounded to one decimal place.

A CLR method has to be loaded into SQL Server 2005 before it can be used, as shown in Figure 3-3. The assembly that contains the method must

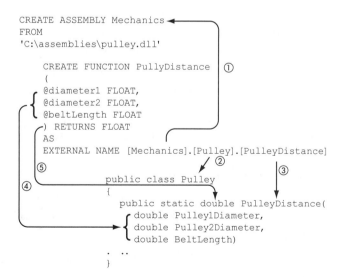

FIGURE 3-3: Create function

be catalogued as shown in Chapter 2. When the assembly has been cata-logued, the PulleyDistance function must be created in a way similar to the way a T-SQL function would be, using a CREATE FUNCTION expression.

Instead of the function body that a T-SQL user-defined function would have, there is an EXTERNAL NAME clause. The EXTERNAL NAME is broken into three parts separated by periods. The first part (1) is the name used to cat-alog the assembly. The second part (2) is the name of the class that holds the CLR method that implements the function. The third part (3) is the name of the CLR method that implements the function.

Note that the name of the T-SQL function does not have to be the same as the name of the CLR method that implements it. The name of the assembly (1), as shown in Figure 3-3, is not case sensitive, but the names of the class (2) and method (3) are case sensitive. For case-insensitive lan-guages such as Visual Basic, the case used in the external name for the class and method must be the same as in the Visual Basic source code that contains them.

Note that each of the parts of the EXTERNAL NAME is enclosed in square brackets. These part names must be treated as any name on SQL Server would be. In this example, they are not necessary, but some CLR languages support namespaces. In those cases, the class name might itself include periods, and the square brackets prevent SQL Server from interpreting them as a part separator in the EXTERNAL NAME.

There must be the same number of parameters in the CREATE FUNCTION expression as there are in the CLR method. The names of the parameters do not have to be the same as those in the CLR method (4), but the T-SQL data types must be exactly compatible with the ones used in the CLR method—that is, there is no conversion between compatible types. Like-wise, the return value (5) of the CLR method must match the RETURNS type of the function.

Listing 3-1 shows the complete listing for the C# file, pulley.cs, that implements the PulleyDistanceFunction. It must be built as a CLR library. Figure 3-4 shows csc, the command-line C# compiler, being used to compile pulley.cs into a CLR library assembly. Listing 3-2 shows the assembly being catalogued into a database, the PulleyDistance function being catalogued, and then the PulleyDistance function being executed.

LISTING 3-1: Pulley code

```
-- pulley.cs
using System;

public class Pulley
{
  public static double PulleyDistance(
    double Pulley1Diameter,
    double Pulley2Diameter,
    double BeltLength)
  {
    double length = 0, a = 2.0;
    double b = BeltLength - 1.57 *
      (Pulley1Diameter + Pulley2Diameter);
    double c = System.Math.Pow(Pulley1Diameter - Pulley2Diameter, 2.0);
    // if this is not positive no chance the pulleys will fit
    double b1 = (b * b) - (4 * a * c);
    if (b1 > 0)
    {
      length = (b + Math.Sqrt(b1)) / (2 * a);
      // check that pulleys fit
      if (length < ((Pulley1Diameter + Pulley2Diameter) / 2))
        {
          // return 0 if pulleys don't fit
          length = 0;
        }
    }
    // one decimal point is enough
    return System.Math.Round(length, 1);
  }
};
```

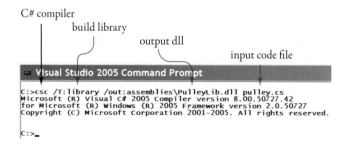

FIGURE 3-4: Building assembly

LISTING 3-2: Cataloguing PulleyDistance function

```
CREATE ASSEMBLY Mechanics
FROM 'C:\Assemblies\PulleyLib.dll'
GO

CREATE FUNCTION PulleyDistance
(@diameter1 FLOAT,
@diameter2 FLOAT,
@beltLength FLOAT
) RETURNS FLOAT
AS EXTERNAL NAME
[Mechanics].[Pulley].[PulleyDistance]
GO

SELECT dbo.PulleyDistance(3,2,100)
```

Using a user-defined function that is based on a CLR method is no different from using a user-defined function that is based on T-SQL; in fact, you really can't tell the difference in usage. Figure 3-5 shows a SELECT statement (1) that uses the PulleyDistance function. The results (2) show that for a 3-inch pulley, a 2-inch pulley, and a 100-inch belt, the distance between the centers of the pulleys would be 46.1 inches.

In usage, there is no difference between T-SQL– and CLR-based user-defined functions and stored procedures. The INFORMATION_SCHEMA. ROUTINES view, however, does distinguish between them. Figure 3-6 shows a query (1) that returns the names of routines and how they are implemented. The results show that PulleyDistance (2) is implemented externally (that is, not in T-SQL) and that the routine SalesByMedian-ByState (3) is implemented with T-SQL.

The PulleyDistance function could have been implemented using T-SQL as shown in Figure 3-7. One of the reasons for choosing to use a CLR language in SQL Server 2005 is that in some cases, the CLR-based version will provide better performance. The strong point of T-SQL is set arithmetic, not

FIGURE 3-5: Using a CLR function

```
① SELECT ROUTINE _ NAME, ROUTINE _ BODY
   from INFORMATION _ SCHEMA.ROUTINES
```

	ROUTINE_NAME	ROUTINE_BODY
② 96	PullyDistance	EXTERNAL
③ 97	SalesMedianByState	SQL

FIGURE 3-6: INFORMATION_SCHEMA.ROUTINES

numeric arithmetic. Some people have ported complex financial calculations from T-SQL to a CLR language and found noticeable improvements in performance.

Figure 3-8 shows a simple loop (1) that determines approximately how long it takes the PulleyDistance function to do 1 million calculations. Running this loop takes about 18 seconds (2) on our test system. If the Pulley-Distance function (3) is replaced with the PulleyDistanceTSQL function, the time to run the loop increases to 30 seconds (4).

Note that comparisons like this are always a bit suspect; some applications spend very little time doing numeric arithmetic, and sometimes, there

```
CREATE FUNCTION PulleyDistanceTSQL
(@Diameter1 FLOAT, @Diameter2 FLOAT, @BeltLength FLOAT)
RETURNS FLOAT AS
BEGIN
DECLARE @distance FLOAT
SET @distance = 0
DECLARE @a FLOAT
SET @a = 2.0
DECLARE @b FLOAT
SET @b = @BeltLength -
   1.57 * (@Diameter1 + @Diameter2)
DECLARE @c FLOAT
SET @c = (@diameter1 - @diameter2)
   *(@diameter1 - @diameter2)
DECLARE @b1 FLOAT
SET @b1 = (@b * @b) - (4 * @a * @c)
IF @b1 > 0
BEGIN
   SET @distance = (@b + SQRT(@b1)) / (2 * @a)
   IF @distance < ((@diameter1 + @diameter2) / 2)
      SET @distance = 0
   END
return ROUND(@distance, 1)
END
```

FIGURE 3-7: T-SQL PulleyDistance

```
① DECLARE @pass INT
  DECLARE @start DATETIME
  SET @start = GETDATE()
  DECLARE @result FLOAT
  SET @pass = 1000000
  redo:                           ③
  SET @result =  dbo.PulleyDistance(
  @pass % 5, @pass % 4, @pass % 100)
  SET @pass = @pass - 1
  IF @pass <> 0 GOTO redo
  print DATEDIFF(second, @start, GETDATE())
```

```
    PulleyDistance        PulleyDistanceTSQL
  ②  ▣ Results           ④  ▣ Results
        18                      30
```

FIGURE 3-8: PulleyDistance comparison

are much better solutions that require very little calculation. The example does illustrate, however, that in general, CLR languages have the edge for numeric calculations.

There is another area in which CLR methods are useful: string operations. No good database accepts a string at face value; it should validate that a string is properly formatted before using it.

A United States Social Security number (SSN) is three integer numbers separated by dashes. An example of an SSN is 123-45-6789. T-SQL can be used to validate a string that is supposed to be an SSN, and Figure 3-9 shows a user-defined function, ValidateSSNTSQL (1), that does this. It checks (2) to make sure only numerics are used. If so, it returns 1; otherwise (3), it returns 0.

```
①CREATE FUNCTION ValidateSSNTSQL(@ssn CHAR(11))
  RETURNS BIT
  BEGIN
  RETURN CASE
  ② WHEN @ssn LIKE
        '[0-9][0-9][0-9]-[0-9][0-9]-[0-9][0-9][0-9][0-9]'
     THEN 1
  ③ ELSE 0
  END
  END
```

FIGURE 3-9: T-SQL SSN validation

```
  print dbo.ValidateSSNTSQL('asdf')
① print dbo.ValidateSSNTSQL('123-45-6789')
  print dbo.ValidateSSNTSQL('123-45.6789')
  print dbo.ValidateSSNTSQL('123-45-6a89')
```

```
  Results
     0
②  1
     0
     0
```

FIGURE 3-10: Using the ValidateSSNTSQL
function

Figure 3-10 shows that using the ValidateSSNTSQL with a valid SSN (1)
produces a one (2) as output but otherwise produces a zero. There may well
be better implementations of the ValidateSNNTSQL functions, but in general, they will all involve some kind of chopping up of the input string and
testing the pieces.

The CLR has capability similar to LIKE called a regular expression.
Figure 3-11 shows a C# function that checks a string to see whether it is a
properly formatted SSN. This function uses a regular expression (1), rather
than imperative code, to define the format of an SSN. The ValidateSSN
function uses the Match (2) method to check that the string passed in as a
parameter is properly formatted.

Figure 3-12 shows that the ValidateSSN function (2) produces the
same results (3) that the ValidateSSNTSQL function did. As with any
CLR-based user-defined function, it has to be added (1) to the database
before it can be used.

```
public class ValidationFunctions
{
    static readonly Regex SSNRegex;
    static ValidationFunctions()
    {
    ①  SSNRegex = new Regex(@"\d{3}-\d{2}-\d{4}");
    }
    public static int ValidateSSN(string ssn)
    {
    ②  return SSNRegex.Match(ssn).Success ? 1 : 0;
    }
};
```

FIGURE 3-11: CLR-based validation

```
① CREATE FUNCTION ValidateSSN(@ssn NCHAR(11))
  RETURNS int
  AS EXTERNAL NAME
  ValidationAsm.ValidationFunctions.ValidateSSN

② print dbo.ValidateSSN('asdf')
  print dbo.ValidateSSN('123-45-6789')
  print dbo.ValidateSSN('123-45.6789')
  print dbo.ValidateSSN('123-45-6a89')
```

④
```
Results
0
1
0
0
```

FIGURE 3-12: Using ValidateSNN

One of the things you can notice about the ValidateSSN function shown in Figure 3-11 is that it does not use a sequence of code to validate the SSN; it uses a regular expression to define its format. To make use of this technique, of course, you will have to learn about regular expressions, but if you have to work with strings, regular expressions are your friend. Regular expressions are documented in the MSDN documentation that comes with .NET Framework. The book *Mastering Regular Expressions*, by Jeffrey E.F. Friedl (O'Reilly), is a good place to start learning about them. http://www.regexlib.com is a Web site that maintains an online library of regular expressions.

Let's expand the ValidateSSN function a bit just to show how useful regular expressions are. It turns out that there are some restrictions on what numbers can be used in a SSN. 078-05-1120, for example, is not

```
public partial class UserDefinedFunctions
{                            ①
    static readonly Regex ssnRegex
    = new Regex(             ②
@"^(?!078-05-1120)(?!000)\d\d\d-(?!00)\d\d-(?!0000)\d\d\d\d$"
    ,RegexOptions.Compiled | RegexOptions.Singleline
    );

    public static bool CheckSSN(string ssn)
    {
        if(ssn == null) return false;
        Match m = ssnRegex.Match(ssn);
        return m.Success;③
    }
};
```

FIGURE 3-13: Improved SSN validation

a valid SSN because of a newspaper advertisement in 1938! Check out http://en.wikipedia.org/wiki/Social_security_number to find out the details. Also, none of the three numbers may be made up of all zero digits. 0000-45-9789, for example, is not a valid SSN. Last, the regular expression used in the `ValidateSSN` CLR method was not correct, as it allows extra characters to slip in. Let's make an improved version of ValidateSNN, called ValidateSSNFull, that checks for all these things. We will use and enhance this new version to illustrate the rest of the features of using the CLR to enhance SQL Server 2005.

Figure 3-13 shows the improved `ValidateSSNFull` implementation. It uses an improved regular expression (2). A full description of regular expressions is beyond the scope of this book, but make use of the references previously mentioned. In this case, in the regular expression the ^ and $ characters bound the length of the string to ensure that it is the exact size it should be. The `(!!078-05-1120)` part of the expression is testing to make sure that is not the invalid SSN from 1938. Likewise, similar parts of the expression test all zero numbers. The regular expression is matched (3) against the input string, and true is returned if the match was successful.

The regular expression itself is stored in a variable named `ssnRegex` (1). The variable is static because a regular expression must be compiled before it is used. When it is put in a static variable, this happens only once, even though it is used over and over.

Chapters 2 and 6 both make the point that it is important that assemblies be loaded `WITH PERMISSION_SET = SAFE` if possible. The ssnRegex variable is marked as being read-only to allow this. Any assembly that contains a mutable static variable must be loaded `WITH PERMISSION_SET = UNSAFE`.

Now the input parameter is tested to see whether it is null (2), and if it is, `ValidateSSNFull` returns false. This is probably not a good choice, but we will talk later in this chapter about more SQL types that can always be NULL and CLR types that sometimes cannot be, and how to make the two type systems work together.

We can easily expand the T-SQL implementation of the SSN checker to do these extra checks just by adding a few more WHEN clauses to the code shown in Figure 3-9. In the end, regular expressions and T-SQL have about the same capabilities for checking the validity of a string. Why go to the trouble of using the CLR to do this?

You will find that the CLR/regular expression implementation is faster than the T-SQL implementation, but not by a lot. The real value of regular expressions is that they are declarative expressions that can be used outside T-SQL. Regular expressions are widely supported. A middle-tier or client application can use the same regular expression this function did and get the same results. In fact, if you are going to use regular expressions like this in SQL Server 2005, you should consider making them available to clients from the database itself, rather than a specification. Listing 3-3 is an example of a method that could be added to the implementation shown in Figure 3-13 and catalogued as a function in SQL Server 2005. Clients use this to keep in sync with the regular expression being used to check SSNs.

LISTING 3-3: Regular expression for checking SSN

```
public static string SSNRegex()
{
return ssnRegex.ToString();
}
```

In fact, if the language is one supported by the CLR, it can use the same assembly that was catalogued in SQL Server 2005! There's no more misinterpreting a specification of a string format; the server and the client can use the same code, via a regular expression, to do validation.

There are more things we should test for, but what we have done in `ValidateSSNFull` is enough to show that regular expressions in the CLR are very useful additions to SQL Server 2005.

CLR Extension Details

So far, we have covered the basics of using the CLR to extend the functionality of SQL Server 2005; we have looked at exposing a public static method of a public class as a function that can be accessed by T-SQL. Now we are going to dig into the details.

The assembly and methods in the previous example functions do not contain enough information for SQL Server 2005 to manage them in the same way that it manages T-SQL functions. Figure 3-14, for example, shows a trivial T-SQL function that returns whatever string is passed into it. If we

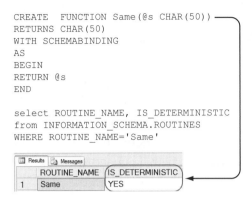

```
CREATE   FUNCTION Same(@s CHAR(50))
RETURNS CHAR(50)
WITH SCHEMABINDING
AS
BEGIN
RETURN @s
END

select ROUTINE_NAME, IS_DETERMINISTIC
from INFORMATION_SCHEMA.ROUTINES
WHERE ROUTINE_NAME='Same'
```

	ROUTINE_NAME	IS_DETERMINISTIC
1	Same	YES

FIGURE 3-14: Deterministic function

look this function up in the INFORMATION_SCHEMA, we can see that it has a property that says it is deterministic. In SQL Server, a *deterministic function* is one that for a given input always returns the same result, as this trivial function does. There are some cases when a function is required to be deterministic—when it is used to calculate the value of a persisted computed column of a table, for example.

Nothing in the function definition in Figure 3-14 says it is deterministic, so how does SQL Server determine this? SQL Server does this by analyzing the code and sees that it is not calling any functions that are not deterministic; neither does its return value depend on the state of the database.

SQL Server does not analyze the code in CLR methods; instead, it depends on metadata added to the assembly to provide the information it would get by analyzing a T-SQL function. It does this by using a feature of the CLR called an attribute. See the MSDN documentation for .NET Framework for a discussion of "Attribute class" for more information.

In simple terms, SQL Server makes use of attributes to attach name–value pairs to the CLR method that implements a user-defined function. SQL Server reads these name–value pairs when the function is catalogued. Attributes in the CLR are similar in concept and usage to extended properties in SQL Server, which allows arbitrary name–value pairs to be added to database objects.

Several attributes can be applied to CLR methods that implement stored procedures, functions, or triggers: SqlProcedure, SqlFunction, and SqlTrigger, respectively. All these attributes are in the Microsoft.

SqlServer.Server namespace. SQL Server uses only one of these attributes, the SqlFunction attribute; later in this chapter, we will discuss the uses of the others.

Figure 3-15 shows a C# implementation of the trivial T-SQL function shown in Figure 3-3. It uses the SqlFunction attribute to add metadata to the Same CLR function that indicates that it is deterministic. If, after we catalog it in SQL Server 2005, we look up this function in the INFORMATION_ SCHEMA, we see that SQL Server has used the SqlFunction attribute to determine that this function is deterministic.

SQL Server uses five properties in the SqlFunction attribute: DataAccess, SystemDataAccess, IsDeterministic, IsPrecise, and FillRowMethod-Name. Later, we will discuss the details of these properties. Note that System DataAccess and DataAccess will be more fully discussed in Chapter 4.

Listing 3-1, Figure 3-4, and Listing 3-2 show how to create and catalog a function. Visual Studio 2005 is tightly integrated with SQL Server and can deploy functions, stored procedures, and triggers directly into SQL Server 2005—that is, you need not use a command-line compile, as shown in Figure 3-4, or an install script, as shown in Listing 3-2. In Visual Studio 2005, you can just press F5, as you would to debug a C# or Visual Basic program; it will compile, deploy into SQL Server 2005, and start debugging the code, even stepping into SQL Server.

Visual Studio needs additional information to do this. It gets this information from the SqlFunction, SqlProcedure, and SqlTrigger attributes,

```
[Microsoft.SqlServer.Server.SqlFunction(
   IsDeterministic=true)]
public static string SameCLR(string s)
{
    return s;
}

select ROUTINE_NAME, IS_DETERMINISTIC
from INFORMATION_SCHEMA.ROUTINES
WHERE ROUTINE_NAME='Same'
```

	ROUTINE_NAME	IS_DETERMINISTIC
1	SameCLR	YES

FIGURE 3-15: SqlFunction usage

and from some other attributes we will discuss in Chapter 5. See Appendix C for an overview of using Visual Studio 2005 with SQL Server.

System.Data.SqlTypes

There are limitations in what types of parameters can be used in CLR methods that extend SQL Server 2005; in general, they fall under the advice that they must make "sense" to SQL Server 2005. There are also some limitations on the design of the class that implements the methods used through T-SQL. We are going to discuss these issues and some new classes that have been added to the CLR, from the System.Data.SqlTypes namespace, that better match the types in SQL Server 2005 than other CLR types do.

The CheckSSN CLR function from Figure 3-13 in the preceding section, though useful, does not have all the capabilities of a native T-SQL function. Figure 3-16 shows what happens when a NULL is passed into CheckSSN (1). As expected, it returns a zero (2). But does this really make sense? In a database, NULL is supposed to represent a missing or inapplicable value. If the value is missing or inapplicable, you can't determine whether it is valid or not.

A Few Words About Null Values

Most languages provide some way to represent something that they call null. It is meant to be something you can use when a value is needed, but you don't have one. For clarity, we will generically call the thing these languages are trying to represent a *null value*, because the term null is highly overloaded in meaning and usage. So SET @a = NULL in a T-SQL script and a = null; in a C# program are both setting variables to a null value.

This can lead to confusion, because a null value in set theory has a very specific behavior that is supported by relational databases like SQL Server 2005, but typically is not supported in programming languages like C# or

FIGURE 3-16: Questionable result produced by NULL

Visual Basic. In a database, for example, a comparison to a null value typically is false, even if both values are null values. In C#, the comparison of one null value to another typically is true. In fact, C# has several ways to represent a null value.

The data types in the System.Data.SqlTypes namespace are meant to help bridge the differences in how SQL Server 2005 treats null values and how CLR languages typically treat null values. Let's take a look at why we need the System.Data.SqlTypes.

SQL Server 2005 offers reasonably seamless integration of T-SQL and CLR languages except in one area: the use of null values. How a null value is treated depends on the context in which it is used. Figure 3-17 shows one of the differences in the way that T-SQL and C# treat null values. At first glance, they appear to be the same program. Both create two strings, one of which is a null value, and then concatenate them. The result of the concatenation in T-SQL (1) is a null value. The C# program, however, treats the null value as though it were a zero-length string and produces (2) an actual value as a result.

The C# program shown in Figure 3-17 could have been written in Visual Basic and produced the same results. That does not mean, however, that C# and Visual Basic treat null values in the same way. Figure 3-18 shows Visual Basic and C# programs similar to the ones in Figure 3-17. The difference in the programs in Figure 3-18 is that neither the Visual Basic (1) nor the C# (2)

```
DECLARE @s1 VARCHAR(MAX)
SET @s1 = 'asdf'
DECLARE @s2 VARCHAR(MAX)
SET @s2 = NULL
DECLARE @s3 VARCHAR(MAX)
SET @s3 = @s1 + @s2
SELECT @s3 AS [string + NULL]
```

	Results	Messages
	string + NULL	
① | 1 | NULL |

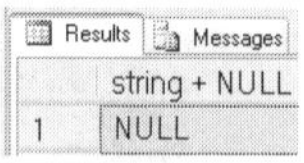

```
static void Main(string[] args)
{
    string s1 = "asdf";
    string s2 = null;
    string s3 = s1 + s2;
    Console.WriteLine(s3);
}
```

② Visual Studio 2005 Command Prompt
```
C:>UsingNullString.exe
asdf

C:>
```

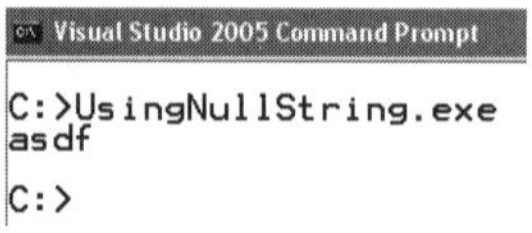

FIGURE 3-17: Null values in T-SQL and C#

```
Module Module1
Sub Main()
   Dim s1 As String
① Dim s2 As String
   s1 = "asdf"
   Dim s3 As String
   s3 = s1 + s2
   Console.WriteLine(s3)
End Sub
End Module
```

```
class Program
{
    static void Main(string[] args)
    {
        string s1 = "asdf";
②   string s2;
        string s3 = s1 + s2;        ③
        Console.WriteLine│Use of unassigned local variable 's2'│
    }
}
```

FIGURE 3-18: Visual Basic and C#
treatment of unassigned variable

program specifically assigns the second string a null value. In the case of
the Visual Basic program, it will treat the second string as a null value; the
C# program will not even compile, because it specifically does not allow the
use of unassigned variables.

The takeaway from Figure 3-17 and Figure 3-18 is that there is very little commonality in the treatment of null values among T-SQL and the CLR
languages. If you are proficient in using T-SQL and now want to integrate
the use of a CLR language into your applications, it is important that you
take the time to understand the specifics of how the CLR language of your
choice treats null values. Likewise, if you are proficient in the use of CLR
language and now want to integrate that language into SQL Server 2005, it
is important that you take the time to understand how SQL Server treats
null values.

It is beyond the scope of this book to cover the treatment of null values
in T-SQL or the CLR languages. This book will follow a convention when
referencing null values, however. The term *null value* will be used to refer to
the generic concept of a null value, regardless of its source. The term *NULL*
will be used to mean a null value from SQL Server. The term *null*, when not
followed by *value*, will be used to mean a null value from C#, and the term
nothing will be used to refer to a null value from Visual Basic.

Using SqlTypes

The scalar data types in SQL Server 2005 sometimes differ from those in the CLR in how they are physically represented in SQL Server and in how null values are represented and used. A new set of data types in the System.Data. SqlTypes namespace is used to mimic the physical representation and the representation on operation of null in SQL Server data types.

System.Data.SqlTypes provides type definitions for data types typically found in databases that map to CLR types and, through additional properties, supports the concept of a NULL the way SQL Server 2005 does.

One of the things added to the CLR, which at first might seem useful for mimicking the data types in SQL Server 2005, is support for templates that are documented in MSDN under "Templates." In short, a template is a way to add methods to an existing type without deriving from it, and this feature is used to make new types that act like value types but can be null. You can declare a variable as being of type `System.Nullable<int>`, for example, and it will be a value type but can be set to null. In C#, the synonym `int?` can be used for `System.Nullable<int>`.

The reason for discussing the new CLR nullable types is that even though in many ways they behave the way the types in `System.Data.SqlTypes` do, they may not be used for parameters or return values for functions and stored procedures, because they do not map to any SQL Server 2005 types. You must use the types from `System.Data.SqlTypes` for nullable value types when they are needed.

Figure 3-19 shows the SSN validation function from Figure 3-13 reworked to be more T-SQL–like. It uses the `SqlBoolean` type (1) from

```
static readonly Regex SSNRegex = new Regex(
@"^(?!078-05-1120)(?!000)\d\d\d-(?!00)\d\d-(?!0000)\d\d\d\d$"
    ,RegexOptions.Compiled | RegexOptions.Singleline
    );
public static SqlBoolean①
  ValidateSSNFullNull(SqlString ssn)
{
  if (ssn.IsNull)
  {
    return SqlBoolean.Null;②
  }
  Match match = SSNRegex.Match(ssn.Value);
  return match.Success;③
}
```

FIGURE 3-19: T-SQL–like SSN validation

System.Data.SqlTypes namespace for the return value and the SqlString type, also from System.Data.SqlTypes namespace, for the input parameter, ssn. It tests the ssn to see whether it is null and returns a null (2) if it is. If ssn is not null, it tests it against a regular expression—the same one used in Figure 3-13—and returns true if the match was successful.

The T-SQL ValidateSSNTSQL function in Figure 3-9 could have also tested for NULL and returned a NULL. T-SQL functions can also be created with the RETURNS NULL ON NULL INPUT function option so that you don't have to test inputs for NULL. You could use the same function option on ValidateSSNFullNull when you catalog it in SQL Server 2005, but you still should test for a null input; this is CLR code, and it might be called from code other than T-SQL.

All the data types from the System.Data.SqlTypes namespace have three properties: Null, IsNull, and Value. The IsNull property corresponds to the IS NULL clause in T-SQL, and the Null property corresponds to the NULL keyword in T-SQL. The IsNull and Null properties allow a CLR-based method to treat null values in the same way that they are treated in T-SQL, as shown in Figure 3-19.

Every data type in System.Data.SqlTypes has an underlying CLR data type. The underlying data type is accessed through the Value property. Note that if IsNull for an instance of a System.Data.SqlTypes type returns true, accessing its Value property will produce an exception, as accessing any null value in the CLR would.

The value returned by the Null property of a System.Data.SqlTypes type is itself typed—that is, it is unlike the NULL in SQL Server 2005 or the nulls and nothings found in C# and Visual Basic, respectively. Both SqlBoolean b2 = SqlInt32.Null; and SqlBoolean b3 = null; will produce a compile-time error. You must return SqlBoolean.Null to represent null if the return type is SqlBoolean. There is no generic null as there is in the T-SQL and CLR languages.

Note that System.Data.SqlTypes are usually larger (take up more memory) than their underlying CLR types.

By convention, the suffix of the name of a System.Data.SqlType type is that of the underlying CLR type. Note that many languages, including C# and Visual Basic 2005, alias the CLR type name. The underlying data type for SqlInt32, for example, is System.Int32 in the CLR type system and int in C#. The columns, from left to right, in Table 3-1 show the mapping between a type from `System.Data.SqlTypes`, the native types it represents on SQL Server, the underlying type in the CLR, the alias used for the type in C#, and the type used for an ADO.NET SqlParameter.

TABLE 3-1: SqlTypes Mappings to Other Types

SqlTypes	SQL Server	Underlying CLR Type	C# Alias	ADO.NET
SqlBinary	BINARY VARBINARY	Byte[]	byte[]	Binary VarBinary TimeStamp Image
SqlInt64	BIGINT	Int64	Long	BigInt
SqlInt32	INT	Int32	Int	Int
SqlInt16	SMALLINT	Int16	Short	SmallInt
SqlByte	TINYINT	Byte	Byte	Byte
SqlChars	NVARCHAR(MAX)	String	String	NVarChar
SqlString	NVARCHAR	String	String	Char VarChar
	NCHAR			NChar
SqlDateTime	DATETIME	DateTime	DateTime	DateTime
	SMALLDATETIME			SmallDateTime
SqlDecimal	DECIMAL	Decimal	Decimal	Decimal
	NUMERIC			Numeric
SqlDouble	FLOAT	Double	Double	Float
SqlSingle	REAL	Single	Float	Real
SqlMoney	MONEY	Decimal	Decimal	Money
	SMALLMONEY			SmallMoney
SqlGuid	UNIQUEIDENTIFIER	Guid	Guid	UniqueId
SqlBoolean	BIT	Boolean	Bool	Boolean

```
    DECLARE @i INT
    DECLARE @s VARCHAR(10)
①  SET @s = 3
②  SET @i = '1' + @s
    SELECT @i
③  SET @i = 1 + '2'
    SELECT @i
```

FIGURE 3-20: Using types in T-SQL

When you are working in T-SQL, quite often, you can ignore the type of a variable. Figure 3-20 is an example of this. It shows that string type can be set (1) with an integer value. Likewise, a string value can be added (2) to an integer variable, and an integer can even be added (3) to a string. This is called *implicit conversion.*

Sometimes, the implicit conversion that is done by T-SQL isn't what you really want. Figure 3-21 shows an example where T-SQL has concatenated (1) two strings. If what you really want to do is do an arithmetic addition, you must CAST one of the strings (2) to an INT. This is called *explicit conversion,* in which you specify explicitly how you want the conversion done.

Most CLR languages have implicit and explicit conversion capabilities similar to those in T-SQL. Table 3-2 shows the conversion capabilities between SqlTypes and their associated CLR types. Not all the implicit conversions are shown; there is an implicit conversion from the underlying CLR type, as shown in Table 3-1, to its associated SqlTypes type except for SQLBinary, SqlBytes, and SqlChars.

In Table 3-2, an I indicates an implicit conversion to the type that is to the left of the I from the type that is listed above the I. An E indicates an explicit conversion to the type listed to the left of the E from the type listed above the E.

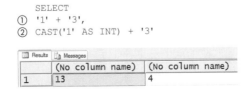

FIGURE 3-21: Casting types

TABLE 3-2: SqlTypes Conversions

To From	SqlBinary	SqlByte	SqlBytes	SqlBoolean	SqlChars	SqlDateTime	SqlDecimal	SqlDouble	SqlGuid	SqlInt16	SqlInt32	SqlInt64	SqlMoney	SqlSingle	SqlString
SqlBinary	E								E						E
SqlByte	E	E					E	E		E	E	E	E	E	E
SqlBytes	E		E												
SqlBoolean	E	E		E			E	E		E	E	E	E	E	E
SqlChars	E				E										E
SqlDateTime						E									E
SqlDecimal				E			E	E		E	E	E	E	E	E
SqlDouble				E			E	E		I	I	I	I	I	E
SqlGuid	E								E						E
SqlInt16		I		E			E	I		E	E	E	E	E	E
SqlInt32		I		E			E	I		I	E	E	E	E	E
SqlInt64		I		E			E	I		I	I	E	E	E	E
SqlMoney		I		E			EI	E		I	I	I	E	E	E
SqlSingle		I		E			I	I		I	I	I	I	E	E
SqlString	E	E		E	E	E	E	E	E	E	E	E	E	E	E

An implicit conversion, as the name implies, is done automatically by the CLR languages that support it. Each CLR language that supports explicit conversions has its own syntax for doing so, however. Figure 3-22 shows an example of conversions done using C#. It shows an implicit conversion (1) from an `int` to a `SqlInt32`. There is also an explicit conversion (2) from a `SqlInt32` to an `int`. There is no implicit conversion (3) from `SqlInt32` to `int`, and attempting to do this will produce a compile time-error. Many of the `SqlTypes` can be explicitly converted (4) to a `SqlString`.

Data types in the CLR support implicit and explicit conversions by implementing the well-known methods `op_Implicit` and `op_Explicit`, respectively. `SqlInt32`, for example, implements the methods `op_Implicit (Int32)`, `op_Implicit (SqlByte)`, and `op_Implicit (SqlInt16)`, as shown in MSDN documentation under "`SqlInt32.op_Implicit`." This is why the columns headed by `SqlByte`, `SqlInt16`, and `SqlInt32` of Table 3-2 have an I in the row with `SqlInt32` on its left.

A `SqlString` can be explicitly converted to most `SqlTypes`, but this capability should be used with care. Figure 3-23 shows an attempt to do an explicit conversion (1) of a `SqlString` that is not a number to a `SqlInt32`; this will result in a runtime exception. Every `System.Data.SqlTypes` type has a static `Parse` method that can also be used to convert (2) a `System.String` into that data type. Both of these techniques for converting text into a `System.Data.SqlTypes` type will produce a runtime exception if the string is not properly formatted.

Many of the CLR numeric types implement a static method called `TryParse` that allows text to be tested for correct format without producing

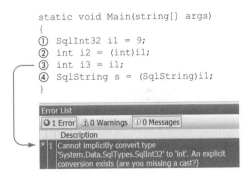

```
static void Main(string[] args)
{
①   SqlInt32 i1 = 9;
②   int i2 = (int)i1;
③   int i3 = i1;
④   SqlString s = (SqlString)i1;
}
```

Error List
● 1 Error ⚠ 0 Warnings ⓘ 0 Messages
      Description
✱ 1 Cannot implicitly convert type
     'System.Data.SqlTypes.SqlInt32' to 'int'. An explicit
     conversion exists (are you missing a cast?)

FIGURE 3-22: CLR conversions

```
static void Main(string[] args)
{
    SqlString s = "A123";
①  SqlInt32 i1 = (SqlInt32)s;
②  SqlInt32 i2 = SqlInt32.Parse(s.Value);
    SqlInt32 i3;
    Int32 i;
③  if (Int32.TryParse(s.Value, out i))
    {
        i3 = i;
    }
}
```

⚠ FormatException was unhandled
Input string was not in a correct format.

FIGURE 3-23: Converting SqlString

a runtime exception if the format is incorrect. None of the SqlTypes types implements a method like this. Figure 3-23 also shows a way to use (3) the TryParse method from the underlying CLR type for the SqlTypes type to test text before converting it to a System.Data.SqlTypes type.

There are some cases where the types in the System.Data.SqlTypes namespace behave a bit differently from their underlying CLR data types. SqlDouble and SqlSingle cannot represent NaN (not a number), meaning an underlying byte representation that does not represent any number, or infinity. CLR floating-point types can represent both of these. An attempt to set a SqlDouble or SqlSingle to either of these will result in a runtime error.

Figure 3-24 shows a SqlDouble that uses implicit conversion to be assigned (1) a value of a System.Double—that is, a C# double. A System.

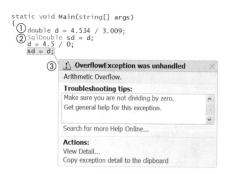

FIGURE 3-24: SqlTypes overflow

Double, or double in C#, can represent infinity (2) and NaN floating-point values, but SqlDouble and SqlSingle cannot. An attempt to set a SqlDouble or SqlSingle to System.Double that represents an infinite value (2) or NaN will result in a runtime exception (3).

The underlying CLR data type for SqlDecimal does not have the same numeric range as its corresponding T-SQL data types, DECIMAL and NUMERIC. Figure 3-25 shows a T-SQL DECIMAL variable being set (1) to a large value. An attempt to initialize a SqlDecimal variable (2) with the same value results in a compile-time error (3) because the number is outside the range of the underlying Decimal data type. Likewise, if the large value were in a variable, it would cause a runtime exception.

Most CLR languages include special operator symbols for doing common operations:+ for addition, – for subtraction, and so on. When a CLR language—C#, for example—sees a + sign between two values, it must find and use a method that will add those two values. There is no + method in the CLR, and in any case, it is possible that the data types on either side of the + sign are implemented in different CLR languages.

The CLR uses well-known names for methods that implement common operations. All these names start with the prefix op_. The method for a method used to do addition is op_addition. These are documented in the MSDN documentation; look up "op_Addition" in the index to see all of them.

It is a great convenience to be able to use simple operators on System.Data.SqlTypes data types, and a number of them are implemented for these types. Figure 3-26 shows the signature for the op_addition (1) static method that implements addition for the SqlInt32 type. The C# language uses this method to implement the + operator (2).

The result of using one of these operators is defined by the data type itself, and not all the System.Data.SqlTypes data types implement all of

```
DECLARE @d DECIMAL(38)
SET @d = ① 79228162514264337593543950336
SELECT @d

SqlDecimal sqlDecimal =
    new SqlDecimal( ② 79228162514264337593543950336M);

③ Error      1 Floating-point constant is outside the
range of type 'decimal'
```

Figure 3-25: SqlDecimal limits

```
① public static op_addition(SqlInt32 x, SqlInt32 y);
    SqlInt32 i1= 10;
    SqlInt32 i2 = 9;
② SqlInt32 sum = i1 + i2;
```

FIGURE 3-26: SqlTypes addition

the operators. The `op_addition` operator for `SqlInt32`, for example, does an arithmetic sum, but the same operator for `SqlString` does a concatenation. Table 3-3 shows the operator methods implemented by the data types in the `System.Data.SqlTypes` namespace. An X symbol in the table indicates that the method listed above it is implemented by the System.Data. SqlTypes type to the left of it. You will have to look into the MSDN documentation to see the specifics of what the particular operator does, but in most cases, you will find that the operator does what you would intuit.

There are an `op_Equality` and an `op_Inequality` for comparing `SqlBooleans`. Even though the underlying data type is `System.Boolean`, the results of using these comparisons are not the same as those for `System.Boolean`.

Figure 3-27 contains some C# code that shows usages of `SqlBoolean`. An attempt to assign the result (1) of comparing two `SqlBooleans` to a `bool` will produce a compile-time error, because the result is a `SqlBoolean` and there is no implicit conversion from `SqlBoolean` to `System.Boolean`.

The underlying type of the result of comparing two `SqlBooleans` is a `System.Boolean`, so its `Value` (2) property can be assigned to a `System. Boolean`. Last, because the result is a `SqlBoolean`, it can be explicitly cast (3) to a `System.Boolean`.

CLR types and SqlTypes types handle null differently. Figure 3-28 shows a C# program that shows those differences. It starts by comparing two instances of the `int?` C# type. This is `System.Nullable<System.Int32>` nullable type that in some way is similar to the `SqlTypes` types in that it can be `null`, though any CLR type that can be set to null will exhibit the behavior shown. Note that when the two instances of `int?` are compared (1) for equality, the result is true, and the code prints this out.

When the two instances of `SqlInt32` are compared for equality, however, the result is false, and nothing prints out. Likewise, when the two

TABLE 3-3: CLR Operations Supported by SqlTypes

	op_Addition	op_BitwiseAnd	op_BitWiseOr	oop_Division	op_Equality	op_ExclusiveOr	op_False	op_GreaterThan	op_GreaterThanOrEqual	op_Inequality	op_LessThan	op_LessThanOrEqual	op_LogicalNot	op_OnesComplement	op_Modulus	op_Multiply	op_True	op_Subtration	op_True	op_UnaryNegation
SqlBinary	X				X			X	X		X	X								
SqlByte	X	X	X	X	X	X		X	X	X	X	X			X	X	X		X	
SqlBytes																				
SqlBoolean		X	X		X	X	X	X	X	X	X	X	X	X			X			
SqlChars																				
SqlDateTime	X				X			X	X	X	X	X						X		
SqlDecimal	X			X	X			X	X	X	X	X				X		X		X
SqlDouble	X			X	X			X	X	X	X	X				X		X		X
SqlGuid					X			X	X	X	X	X								
SqlInt16	X	X	X	X	X	X		X	X	X	X	X			X	X	X		X	X
SqlInt32	X	X	X	X	X	X		X	X	X	X	X			X	X	X		X	X
SqlInt64	X	X	X	X	X	X		X	X	X	X	X			X	X	X		X	X
SqlMoney	X	X	X	X	X	X		X	X	X	X	X			X	X	X		X	X
SqlSingle	X	X	X	X	X	X		X	X	X	X	X			X	X	X		X	X
SqlString	X	X	X	X	X	X		X	X	X	X	X			X	X	X		X	X
SqlBinary	X	X	X	X	X	X		X	X	X	X	X			X	X	X		X	X

instances of `SqlInt32` are compared for inequality, the result is also false. This mimics the SQL Server 2005 behavior that a comparison involving a NULL is always false. Note that this behavior in SQL Server 2005 can be configured to act as the CLR does with NULL.

```
static void Main(string[] args)
{
    SqlBoolean b1 = SqlBoolean.True;
    SqlBoolean b2 = SqlBoolean.False;
①   bool compare1 = b1 == b2;
②   bool compare2 = (b1 == b2).Value;
③   bool compare3 = (bool)(b1 == b2);
}
```

Description
⊘ 1 Cannot implicitly convert type
'System.Data.SqlTypes.SqlBoolean' to 'bool'. An explicit
conversion exists (are you missing a cast?)

FIGURE 3-27: Using SqlBoolean

T-SQL supports a data type called SQL_VARIANT that is typically used to support the data types used in the Microsoft Component Object Model (COM). There is no System.Data.SqlTypes data type that is the equivalent of SQL_VARIANT. In CLR methods, a T-SQL SQL_VARIANT is represented by a System.Object data type. A SQL_VARIANT variable can be used to hold most types of data.

Figure 3-29 shows a function named ObjectType written in C# that has a single input parameter and returns the name (1) of the type of object passed in as a SqlString. This function is invoked using T-SQL. In the first case (2), a numeric 1 is passed into the ObjectType, and it returns the string "System.Data.SqlTypes.SqlInt32"—that is, the type of the numeric 1 passed in.

In the second case (3), an uninitialized T-SQL INT variable is passed in. ObjectType for this case returns "System.DBNull", a data type in the CLR

```
static void Main(string[] args)
{
    int? a = null;
    int? b = null;
① if (a == b) Console.WriteLine("int? ==");
    if (a != b) Console.WriteLine("int? !=");

    SqlInt32 c = SqlInt32.Null;
    SqlInt32 d = SqlInt32.Null;
② if (c == d) Console.WriteLine("SqlInt32 ==");
    if (c != d) Console.WriteLine("SqlInt32 !=");
}
```

■ C:\WINDOWS\system32\cmd.exe
```
int? equal
Press any key to continue . . .
```

FIGURE 3-28: Comparing nulls

```
public static SqlString ObjectType(object obj)
{
①  return new SqlString(obj.GetType().ToString());
}

DECLARE @f FLOAT
SET @f = 7
DECLARE @i INT
DECLARE @v SQL _ VARIANT
SET @v = 'abc'
SELECT                        ②
dbo.ObjectType(1) AS Col1,
                              ③
dbo.ObjectType(@i) AS Col2
                              ④
dbo.ObjectType(@v) AS Col3
```

Col1
System.Data.SqlTypes.SqlInt32

Col2
System.DBNull

Col3
System.Data.SqlTypes.SqlString

FIGURE 3-29: Using system.object

meant to be used to represent a database NULL. Last (4), a SQL_VARIANT
variable is initialized as a string and passed in. Note here that ObjectType
cannot tell that a SQL_VARIANT was passed in; it returns "System.Data.
SqlTypes.SqlString"—that is, the type of the value that was used to initialize the SQL_VARIANT.

In general, working with System.Object as an input parameter
requires testing it to determine what type was passed in. Figure 3-30

```
public static SqlString ProcessObject(object obj)
{
    if (obj is SqlInt32)
    {
①  return (((SqlInt32)obj).Value + 1).ToString();
    }
    if (obj is SqlBoolean)
    {
        return (!((SqlBoolean)obj)).ToString();
    }
    if (obj is SqlString)
    {
        return ((SqlString)obj).Value.ToUpper();
    }
②  return SqlString.Null;
}

DECLARE @b bit
SET @b = 1                            ③
select dbo.ProcessObject(1) AS Col1,

dbo.ProcessObject(@b) AS Col2,

dbo.ProcessObject('abc') AS Col3
```

Col1
2

Col2
False

Col3
ABC

FIGURE 3-30: Processing system.object

shows an example of a function implemented in C# that processes an input parameter of type System.Object and returns a SqlString. The kind of processing it does depends on the type of object passed into it. You can think of this as an overloaded function; it does something different when a SqlInt32 is passed in than it does when a SqlBoolean is passed in.

When a SqlInt32 is passed in, its value is incremented (1) by one, and the result is returned as a string. If the input parameter type is a SqlBoolean, the value is complemented and returned as a string, and so on. If the input parameter is a type it does not support, it returns a null (2).

When this function is invoked from T-SQL, as is also shown in Figure 3-30, when a numeric 1 is passed in (3), a 2 is returned. Likewise, when BIT initialized to 1 is passed in, a False is returned.

The SqlString data type needs some special consideration. The CLR supports only Unicode strings. This means that when a CLR method is catalogued into SQL Server 2005, the NCHAR or NVARCHAR data type must be used for string parameters and return values; CHAR and VARCHAR may not be used. NVARCHAR(MAX) most closely matches the CLR System.String data type, string in C#.

Note that if a limited-size NVARCHAR is used—for example, NVARCHAR(10) is used for a return value or output parameter—the CLR will produce an exception if the method involved attempts to return a string of more than the size limit specified by the NVARCHAR. In the case of return values or output parameters specified with NCHAR, the results will be truncated, and no exception will be thrown.

Also note that when Visual Studio 2005 deploys a function or stored procedure, it uses NVARCHAR(4000) for strings.

To summarize what we have covered on SqlTypes, we can say that a SqlTypes type is a type that can represent a null value in a way similar to the way a null value is represented in a database but otherwise behaves much like its underlying CLR type. A SqlTypes type is used when it is desirable to copy the behavior of a SQL Server type. A SqlTypes type has a Value property, which has its value in terms of its underlying CLR type. A SqlTypes type can be converted to some other SqlTypes type and to a CLR type, and some CLR types can be converted to a SqlTypes type.

Parameters and Return Value

Best practice is to use the types from the `System.Data.SqlTypes` namespace for parameters and the return value of CLR methods that will be used to implement T-SQL stored procedures and functions. In addition to these types, any of the underling CLR types, shown in the Underlying CLR Type column of Table 3-1, can be used along with `System.Object` from the CLR type system and any user-defined type. User-defined types are discussed in Chapter 5.

There are further restrictions on parameters and return values that are specific to user-defined functions and stored procedures, which will be discussed in the "User-Defined Functions" and "Stored Procedures" sections later in this chapter.

User-Defined Functions

SQL Server 2005 supports both scalar and table-valued user-defined functions implemented in the CLR. User-defined functions in T-SQL have some properties that are used by SQL Server 2005 to assess their use in various tasks. Two of the important properties are `IsDeterministic` and `IsPrecise`.

`IsDeterministic` means that for a given input, the results are always the same. A function that adds two numbers and returns their sum, for example, is deterministic; 1 + 2 always equals 3. Functions that do not use the `REAL` or `FLOAT` data types for parameters or return type or for internal calculations are considered to be `IsPrecise`. It is beyond the scope of this book to discuss why these data types are not precise, but it has to do with how floating-point calculations are implemented in hardware.

SQL Server 2005 can analyze a T-SQL–based user-defined function to find out whether it is deterministic or precise, or both. Figure 3-31 shows a T-SQL function named `Same` (1) that returns whatever string is passed into it. This function is deterministic, because for a given input, the return value is always the same.

The second T-SQL function in Figure 3-31 is named `AddUser` (2), and it returns the string passed into it with the current user's name appended to it. This function is not deterministic, because what it returns depends on who the current user is.

```
     CREATE FUNCTION Same(@s CHAR(50)) RETURNS CHAR(50)
     WITH SCHEMABINDING AS BEGIN
①   RETURN @s
     END

     CREATE FUNCTION AddUser(@s CHAR(50)) RETURNS CHAR(50)
     WITH SCHEMABINDING AS BEGIN
②   RETURN @s + USER
     END

③   Select routine _ name, is _ deterministic
     from INFORMATION _ SCHEMA.ROUTINES
     where routine _ name = 'Same'
     OR routine _ name = 'AddUser'
```

④

	routine_name	is_deterministic
1	Same	YES
2	AddUser	NO

FIGURE 3-31: T-SQL function calculation properties

The ANSI INFORMATION_SCHEMA.ROUTINES view is implemented by SQL Server 2005, and it can be used to see how SQL Server 2005 categorizes (3) these functions with respect to IsDeterministic. The Same function is in fact deterministic (4), and the AddUser routine is not. SQL Server 2005 has analyzed the code for each of these functions and has determined that the Same function consistently returns the same thing, but the AddUser function uses the USER keyword, which may return a different result every time it is called.

SQL Server 2005 does not analyze the details of the code from a user-defined function implemented in a CLR language. Instead, it depends on information passed in the Microsoft.SqlServer.Server.SqlFunction attribute optionally used to decorate the method definition. Figure 3-32 shows some CLR-implemented functions that are similar to the ones in Figure 3-31. The first CLR function, SameCLR, in Figure 3-32 uses the SqlFunction attributes (1) to identify itself as being an IsDeterministic function. The second CLR function, AddUserCLR, uses the SqlFunction attribute (2) to identify itself as not being an IsDeterministic function. As shown in Figure 3-31, the INFORMATION_SCHEMA.ROUTINE view (3) is used to see how SQL Server 2005 classifies these functions. The output (4) reflects the information in the corresponding SqlFunction attribute.

There is a slight difference in the way T-SQL and CLR functions treat IsDeterministic and IsPrecise. A T-SQL function will always be classified as not being IsDeterministic and not being IsPrecise if the function was created without the WITH SCHEMABINDING function option,

① ```
[SqlFunction(IsDeterministic = true)]
public static SqlString SameCLR(SqlString s)
{
    return s;
}
```

② ```
[SqlFunction(IsDeterministic = false)]
public static SqlString AddUserCLR(SqlString s)
{
    return s + System.Environment.UserName;
}
```

③ ```
Select routine_name, is_deterministic
from INFORMATION_SCHEMA.ROUTINES
where routine_name = 'SameCLR'
OR routine_name = 'AddUserCLR'
```

④

| | routine_name | is_deterministic |
|---|---|---|
| 1 | AddUserCLR | NO |
| 2 | SameCLR | YES |

FIGURE 3-32: CLR function calculation properties

regardless of the content of the function body. The CREATE FUNCTION statement for a CLR function is not allowed to use the WITH SCHEMABINDING function option, so it will always be classified according to the IsDeterministic and IsPrecise properties of the SqlFunction attribute.

It is important to specify correctly the IsDeterministic and IsPrecise properties of the SqlFunction attribute. An incorrect specification of one of these properties—saying that a function IsPrecise when in fact it does do floating-point operations, for example—may result in subtle, very hard-to-find errors in data.

The SqlFunction attribute has a number of properties that are summarized in Table 3-4; some are used by SQL Server 2005, and some are used by Visual Studio 2005 when it deploys the function into an instance of SQL Server 2005. Appendix C discusses using Visual Studio 2005 projects that can deploy a CLR extension directly into SQL Server 2005.

The DataAccess and SystemDataAccess properties of the SqlFunction attribute have two possible enumerated values; None and Read. DataAccess = None means that the function will not access any user objects in SQL Server. Likewise, SystemDataAccess = None means that the function will not access any system objects in SQL Server. When the Read enumeration is used for either of these properties, it means that the corresponding objects
```

TABLE 3-4: SqlFunction Properties

SqlFunction Property	Use	Default
DataAccess	Accesses user objects	None
IsDeterministic	Specifies IsDeterministic property	False
IsPrecise	Specifies IsPrecise property —that is, whether the function uses floating-point arithmetic	False
FillRowMethodName	Table-valued function column decoder	Null
Name	Name for deployment (Visual Studio only)	Null
TableDefinition	Table definition for table-valued function (Visual Studio only)	Null
SystemDataAccess	Accesses system objects	None

may be accessed. Note that specifying None will prevent access to the corresponding objects. Chapter 4 discusses the details of accessing SQL Server from within a CLR-based user-defined function. Note that in no case can a CLR user-defined function change the state of a database—do an INSERT, for example—just as is the case for a T-SQL user-defined function.

The Name property is used by Visual Studio 2005 when it deploys the method. The value Name property will be used to refer to the function in T-SQL if it is not null.

The TableDefinition and FillRowMethodName are used by table-valued user-defined functions and will be discussed later in this chapter.

There are two kinds of user-defined functions: scalar and table valued. A scalar user-defined function returns a scalar. So far in this chapter, all the examples discussed have been scalar functions, such as the Validate-FullNull function in Figure 3-19.

The general form of all CLR based user-defined function requires that the CLR method be a top-level static public method of a public class. Method names may not be overloaded. The SqlFunction attribute is optional for scalar user-defined functions that are neither deterministic nor

```
① public class Math
   {
② [SqlFunction(IsPrecise=true,
   IsDeterministic=true)
③ static public SqlInt32 AddInt32
      (SqlInt32 a, SqlInt32 b)
   {
      return a + b;
   }
④ static public SqlSingle AddSingle
      (SqlSingle a, SqlSingle b)
   {
      return a + b +
         System.Environment.UserName.Length;
   }
}
```

FIGURE 3-33: SqlFunction usage

precise and that do not access database objects. Note that the SqlFunction attribute is required if the function is to be deployed by Visual Studio 2005.

Figure 3-33 shows some CLR methods in a C# class that can be used as scalar user-defined functions. The class Math (1) is public. It contains two public methods: AddInt32 (3) and AddSingle (4). The AddInt32 is decorated with a SqlFunction attribute (2) that marks it as being both IsPrecise and IsDeterministic. If this attribute were not used, SQL Server 2005 would assume that this function was neither IsPrecise or IsDeterministic, which would limit its use in indexes, for example.

The AddSingle function in Figure 3-33 in fact is neither IsDeterministic nor IsPrecise and does not access database objects, so it does not require a SqlFunction attribute to be loaded properly into SQL Server 2005. Best practice, however, is always to use the SqlFunction attribute for clarity.

The CLR supports the nesting of class definitions, as shown in Figure 3-34. The class Math (1) contains the definition of the class Numeric (2). Both of these classes are public. The class Numeric contains a static public method named AddInts (3). Attempting to load the AddInts method as a T-SQL function will produce an error (4).

SQL Server 2005 does not support method overloading, even when only one of the methods will be used as a T-SQL function. Figure 3-35 shows some C# methods from a class, which is grammatically correct. It has two overloaded methods. Both methods have the same name, Add. One has SqlInt32 parameters (1), and the other has SqlInt16 parameters (2).

```
①  public class Math
    {
    ②  public class Numeric
        {
            [SqlFunction(IsPrecise = true,
                IsDeterministic = true)]
        ③  static public SqlSingle AddInts(
                SqlSingle a, SqlSingle b)
            {
                return a + b;
            }
        }
    }
```

④ Error List

❸ 1 Error	⚠ 0 Warnings	ⓘ 0 Messages

Description

❸ 1 The method "AddInts" in class "Math+Numeric" cannot be mapped to a SQL Server object because it is inside a nested class.

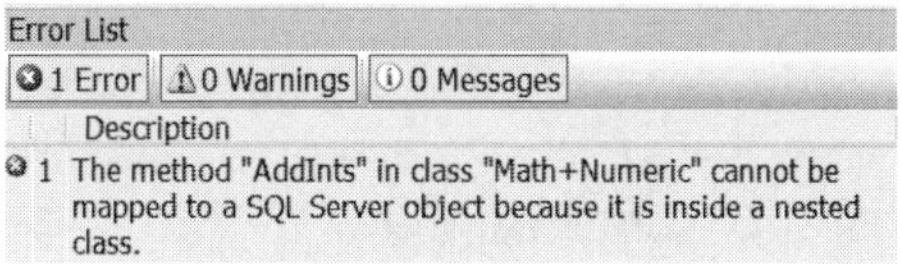

FIGURE 3-34: Nested class

Attempting to load either one of these methods will produce an overloaded error (3), even if the other method is not loaded as a T-SQL function.

The data types of the parameters and return value of scalar user-defined functions can be any of those mentioned in the "Parameters and Return Value" section earlier in this chapter. All the parameters must be input only, as is the case for T-SQL–based user-defined functions. This is the default for parameters in C# and Visual Basic .NET. This means that in C#, parameters

```
    [SqlFunction(IsPrecise = true,
        IsDeterministic = true)]
    static public SqlInt32
①      Add(SqlInt32 a, SqlInt32 b)
    {
        return a + b;
    }
    static public SqlInt32
②      Add(SqlInt16 a, SqlInt16 b)
    {
        return a + b;
    }
```

③ Error List

❸ 1 Error	⚠ 0 Warnings	ⓘ 0 Messages

Description

❸ 1 More than one method, property or field was found with name 'Add' in class 'Math' in assembly 'FunctionLimits'. Overloaded methods, properties or fields are not supported.

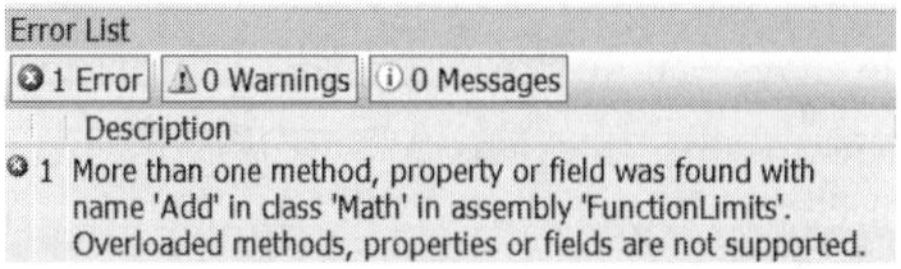

FIGURE 3-35: Method overload

```
[SqlFunction(IsPrecise = true,
   IsDeterministic = true)]
 static public SqlInt32 AddInt16(
① ref SqlInt32 a, SqlInt32 b)
 {
② a = a + 1;
   return a + b;
 }


CREATE FUNCTION [AddInt16]
(                             ── illegal
③ @a int OUTPUT,
   @b int
)
RETURNS [int]
AS EXTERNAL NAME [Math].[AddInt16]
```

FIGURE 3-36: Function output error

must be marked as IN or not at all, and they may not be marked as OUT or REF. In Visual Basic, parameters may not by marked as BY REF.

Figure 3-36 shows a C# method that uses a ref parameter (1) named a. It uses the ref parameter to return (2) an extra value to the caller. This feature cannot be used in T-SQL, because it would require that corresponding parameter in the T-SQL function definition use the OUTPUT (3) keyword, which is not allowed for parameters of user-defined functions in T-SQL.

Table-Valued Functions

A table-valued function is implemented in the CLR by a method that returns an IEnumerable interface along with some other helper constructs. A table-valued function in T-SQL returns rows to SQL Server 2005. In the CLR, the IEnumerable interface is used to obtain an IEnumerator interface. The main things of interest to SQL Server 2005 in the IEnumerator interface are the MoveNext method and the Current property. MoveNext returns true and moves on to the next object, if there is one; otherwise, it returns false. Current returns the "current" object. Enumerators always start pointed before the first object, so you have to call MoveNext first.

When SQL Server 2005 executes a table-valued function that is implemented by the CLR, it calls MoveNext and then uses Current to get the current object until MoveNext returns false. There is a problem, though: SQL Server 2005 needs the set of columns for the row, not an object.

The implementation of the table-valued function must also provide SQL Server 2005 a helper method that it can use to convert the object returned by Current to the column values SQL Server 2005 needs. This helper method is called the FillRowMethod, and its name is passed to SQL Server 2005 in the FillRowMethodName property of the SqlFunction attribute, much as the IsDeterministic property is used to inform SQL Server 2005 as to whether the function is deterministic.

Implement IEnumerable isn't hard but is very tedious, as a lot of bookkeeping boilerplate is involved in making it work. C# will implement all the boilerplate for you, as you will see later in this chapter.

Methods that return the IEnumerable interface are used by some CLR language constructs to loop though an enumeration of values—for example, foreach in C# or For Each in Visual Basic. SQL Server 2005 uses a construct like this to treat the method as though it were a read-only, forward-only cursor.

Figure 3-37 shows a C# example of an enumerator method, EnumNumbers1to4 (1), and its typical use. The body of the method is a loop that counts from one to four. Inside the loop is a yield return instruction that runs each time the loop is run and returns the value produced by the loop.

```
class SimpleEnum {
①  static public IEnumerable EnumNumbers1to4()
    {
        for (int index = 1; index < 5; index++)
        {
②          yield return index;
        }
    }
}
class Program {
    static void Main(string[] args)
    {
③      foreach(int i in SimpleEnum.EnumNumbers1to4())
        {
            Console.WriteLine(i);
        }
    }
}
```

④ **Visual Studio**
```
C>SimpleEnum.exe
1 2 3 4
C>
```

FIGURE 3-37: Simple enumeration

`yield return` greatly simplifies the implementation of IEnumerable. Putting a `yield` in front of a `return` causes the current state of the method involved to be saved—in particular, all the local variables—and the location of the `yield`, but the method still returns. The next time the method is called, it will continue at the line immediately after the `yield`, with all its local variables in the same state they were in on the previous call.

This `yield` can be used in a C# `foreach` statement, as is shown in the main program (3) in Figure 3-37. The body of the `foreach` is run once for each `yield return` that is executed in the `EnumNumbers1to4` method. The results of running the program (4) are the numbers from one to four printed in the screen.

It is not obvious what function is being called to make `yield` save the local state, because under the covers, C# has written a lot of boilerplate code to implement `IEnumerable`. In effect, what is happening is that every time the `foreach` loop (3) in `Main` cycles, the `yield` (2) in `EnumNumbers1to4` is being called.

Let's look at a table-valued function that can be used to create a set of logarithmic range values. The goal is to break an overall range of values into a set of log ranges such that the first log range covers twice the range of the second, and so on. Later, we will use this table in a query to categorize values according to the log range they fall into.

Figure 3-38 illustrates an overall range of ten broken into five log ranges. Log range 1 covers a range of 5.161. Log range 2 covers $7.742 - 5.161 = 2.581$, or about half of what log range 1 covers—likewise for the remaining log ranges.

We will create a table-valued function named `LogRange` that, given a minimum value, a maximum value, and a number of log ranges, will produce a table that includes the minimum and maximum value for each log range. The table in Figure 3-39 shows what we want to produce for a minimum value

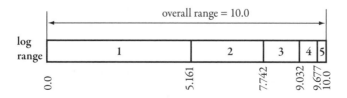

FIGURE 3-38: Log ranges

MinValue	MaxValue	RangeNumber
-1.79769313486232E+308	5.16129032258065	1
5.16129032258065	7.74193548387097	2
7.74193548387097	9.03225806451613	3
9.03225806451613	9.67741935483871	4
9.67741935483871	1.79769313486232E+308	5

FIGURE 3-39: Log-Range table

of zero, a maximum value of ten, and five log ranges. Note that the minimum value for RangeNumber 1 is the smallest number, and likewise, the MaxValue for RangeNumber 5 is the largest number. Also, the MaxValue is repeated as the MinValue for the next row, except for the last row.

Given a table like the one in Figure 3-39, we can easily categorize values logarithmically from one through ten. Figure 3-42 shows the implementation of the LogRange function that will produce the table shown in Figure 3-39.

It takes a bit of more work to make a table-valued function than to make a scalar one, because the yield return will return only a single object. Figure 3-40 shows a C# struct named Range (1) that can be used to hold the three columns of the table-valued function. Each one of the columns is represented by a field (2) in the Range struct. There must be one field for each column in the table. The constructor (3) for the Range class initializes these fields.

SQL Server 2005 will get an instance of the Range struct for each row in the table. It is going to need a FillRowMethod to extract the column values from an instance of the Range struct. The FillRowMethod takes as input an object and returns an output parameter for each column in the table. Figure 3-41 shows the GetRow method (1) that satisfies this requirement.

```
①  struct Range
    {
②  public readonly double minValue;
    public readonly double maxValue;
    public readonly int rangeNumber;
③  public Range(double minValue,
        double maxValue, int rangeNumber)
    {
        this.minValue = minValue;
        this.maxValue = maxValue;
        this.rangeNumber = rangeNumber;
    }
    }
```

FIGURE 3-40: Range class

```
    public class RangeFunctions
    {
①   static public void GetRow(Object obj,
②       out SqlDouble minValue,
        out SqlDouble maxValue,
        out SqlInt32 rangeNumber)
    {
③   Range r = (Range)obj;
        minValue = r.minValue;
        maxValue=r.maxValue;
        rangeNumber = r.rangeNumber;
    }
}
```

FIGURE 3-41: GetRow method

SQL Server 2005 will call the GetRow method once for each row and pass into it the object it received from the enumerator. The output parameters (2) return the column values.

The object that is passed in is always an instance of a Range struct (3), and as you will see, the implementation guarantees this. Note that this method must be a member of the same class that implements the method for the table-valued function—in this example, the RangeFunctions class.

Now we have the basic pieces we need to implement the LogRange table-valued function; a method that implements the IEnumerable interface. Each time MoveNext is called, Current returns an instance of the Range struct. The GetRow method extracts the column values from the Range struct.

Figure 3-42 shows the implementation of LogRange. The SqlFunction attribute that decorates it contains two pieces of information. The Fill-RowMethodName property (1) of the SqlFunction attribute contains the name of the FillRowMethod method SQL Server 2005 must use to extract the column information from an instance of the Range struct. The TableDefinition property (2) contains the name and data type for each column in the table produced by the table-valued function. The format of this information is the same as it would be in a T-SQL table-valued function. When the LogRange function is catalogued, SQL Server 2005 will get the name of the FillRowMethod from the SqlFunction attribute. SQL Server, however, does not use the TableDefinition property; that is used only by Visual Studio 2005 when it deploys the function.

The beginning of the body of the LogRange method contains some arithmetic needed to calculate the log ranges. The first row of the table is

```
public class RangeFunctions
{
[Microsoft.SqlServer.Server.SqlFunction
① (FillRowMethodName="GetRow",
② TableDefinition =
  "MinValue FLOAT, MaxValue FLOAT, RangeNumber INT"
  )]
public static IEnumerable LogRange(
  SqlDouble minValue,
  SqlDouble maxValue,
  SqlInt32 count)
  {
    double factor = (Math.Pow(2.0, count.Value) - 1)
      /Math.Pow(2.0, count.Value - 1.0);
    double lastTop = double.MinValue;
    double thisTop = minValue.Value + range/2;
③ yield return new Range(lastTop, thisTop, 1);
    lastTop = thisTop;
    range /= 2;
    for (int index = 1; index < (count-1); index++)
    {
      thisTop = lastTop + range / 2.0;
      yield return
④ new Range(lastTop,thisTop, index + 1);
      lastTop = thisTop;
      range /= 2.0;
    }
⑤ yield return new
      Range(lastTop, double.MaxValue, count.Value);
  }
}
```

FIGURE 3-42: CLR table-valued function

output (3) by doing a `yield return` of a `Range` struct that contains the smallest number, the maximum value of the first log range, and the number of the log range.

The `for` loop in Figure 3-42 uses a `yield return` (4) to output all the subsequent rows except the last. Finally, the last row is output (5) with the minimum value for the last log range and the largest number for its maximum value.

Listing 3-4 shows the T-SQL script to catalog the `LogRange` function. As with any CLR function, the types used as parameters in the T-SQL script must match those in the CLR implementation. Also, a table-valued function must use `RETURNS TABLE`, and in the case of a CLR table-valued function, it must specify the names and types of the columns of the table. If Visual Studio 2005 were deploying this function, it would get the specification of the table columns from the `TableDefinition` property of the `SqlFunction` attribute.

LISTING 3-4: Cataloguing table-valued functions

```
CREATE ASSEMBLY [RangeTable]
FROM 'C:\assemblies\Range.dll'
GO

CREATE FUNCTION [LogRange]
(
   @minValue float,
   @maxValue float,
   @count int
)
RETURNS TABLE(
MinValue FLOAT, MaxValue FLOAT, RangeNumber INT
) AS
EXTERNAL NAME [RangeTable].[RangeFunctions].[LogRange]
```

Figure 3-43 shows the use of the LogRange function (1) and the table it produces. The first row of the table is produced by the first yield return (3) in the LogRange method. The middle rows are produced by the yield return (4) inside the for loop of the LogRange method. Finally, the last row is produced by the last yield return (5) of the LogRange method.

When it has been catalogued, the LogRange function is just like any other table-valued function in SQL Server 2005. It can be joined to other tables in a SELECT expression, for example.

Figure 3-44 shows a summary of what is needed to make a table-valued function: a class, Range in this case (1), to encapsulate the column values that will be returned to SQL Server 2005; a FillRowMethod (4), in this case the GetRow method, that can extract the column values from instances of the Range class; a function that returns an IEnumerable interface (3),

FIGURE 3-43: Using LogRange

```
①  struct Range
    {
       ...
    }
    public class RangeFunctions
    {
    ②  [Microsoft.SqlServer.Server.SqlFunction
           (FillRowMethodName="GetRow",
           TableDefinition = "MinValue ..."
           )]
    ③  public static IEnumerable LogRange(
           SqlDouble minValue,
           SqlDouble maxValue,
           SqlInt32 count)
       {
          ...
       }
    ④  static public void GetRow(Object obj,
           out SqlDouble minValue,
           out SqlDouble maxValue,
           out SqlInt32 rangeNumber)
       {
          ...
       }
    };
```

FIGURE 3-44: Summary of a table-valued function

LogRange in this case; and a SqlFunction attribute (2) that decorates the
LogRange method and specifies the name of the FillRowMethod. The
TableDefinition property of the SqlFunction documents the table definition and will be used by Visual Studio 2005 if it is used to deploy this
function.

Stored Procedures

A T-SQL stored procedure is similar to a T-SQL user-defined function in
that it has input parameters and a return value. There is more flexibility
in what can be done with the input parameters and less in what can be
done with the return value. In addition, a stored procedure is permitted
to make changes to a database. Chapter 4 covers the techniques for actually doing this; this chapter concentrates on the mechanics of CLR-based
stored procedures.

Parameters for a stored procedure have directionality. By default, a
parameter is an input parameter. If it includes the OUTPUT phrase, it is an
input/output parameter similar to ref in C# or By Ref in Visual Basic.

A stored procedure returns a status value. The return value is meant to indicate the status of the results of the stored procedure, with zero indicating that it operated properly. It is not meant to be used to return the results of a stored procedure.

Figure 3-45 shows a C# method, Div (1), that can be used as a stored procedure. Its purpose is to calculate both the quotient and remainder of the parameters passed into it. The first parameter, dividend (2), is an input parameter. The second parameter, divisor_quotient (3), is an input/output parameter; it both passes in the divisor and returns the quotient. The last parameter, remainder, is an output parameter. If either the dividend or divisor_quotient is null (5), the stored procedure returns one, indicating that it was not successful. Note that because remainder is an out parameter, it must be set to a value before returning. If it is successful (6), Div returns a zero.

Typically, a stored procedure will return resultsets, make changes to the state of the database, or both. Chapter 4 discusses how to do this using the CLR. The example shown here returns two values, which cannot be done in a scalar-valued stored procedure unless it returns a user-defined type. Chapter 5 discusses user-defined types.

Figure 3-46 shows the Div stored procedure being catalogued. The syntax is the same as for creating a T-SQL stored procedure (1) except that the AS clause contains an EXTERNAL NAME instead of a body. The second parameter (2)

```
   public class Math {
①  public static SqlInt32 Div(
②     SqlInt32 dividend,
③     ref SqlInt32 divisor_quotient,
④     out SqlInt32 remainder)
      {
         if (dividend.IsNull || divisor_quotient.IsNull)
         {
            remainder = SqlInt32.Null;
⑤        return 1;
         }
         remainder = dividend.Value
            % divisor_quotient.Value;
         divisor_quotient =
            dividend.Value / divisor_quotient.Value;
⑥     return 0;
      }
   }
```

FIGURE 3-45: CLR stored procedure

```
CREATE ASSEMBLY Numeric
FROM 'C:\assemblies\math.dll'

① CREATE PROCEDURE [Div]
     @dividend int,
   ② @divisor _ quotient int OUTPUT,
   ③ @remainder int OUTPUT
AS
EXTERNAL NAME [Numeric].Math.Div
```

FIGURE 3-46: Loading stored procedure

and the third parameter (3) both include the OUTPUT phrase to correspond to the ref and out keywords used in the CLR implementation.

The CLR supports parameters that are input only, output only, and input/output. T-SQL supports only parameters in stored procedures that are input only or input/output. T-SQL does not support output-only parameters, even though the keyword OUTPUT implies that it does. T-SQL parameters marked as OUTPUT are always input/output parameters.

As with CLR-based functions, in usage, CLR-based stored procedures are no different from T-SQL–based stored procedures. Figure 3-47 shows the Div (1) stored procedure being executed. The results (2) show that a quotient of 11 divided by 3 is 3, and the remainder is 2.

There is an attribute that may be added to a CLR method that implements the stored procedure: the SqlStoredProcedure attribute. It has a single property, Name. This attribute is used by Visual Studio 2005 to deploy the stored procedure. SQL Server 2005 doesn't use the information provided by the SqlStoredProcedure attribute.

```
DECLARE @i INT
DECLARE @b INT
SET @b = 3
① EXEC Div 11, @b OUTPUT, @i OUTPUT
SELECT @b, @i
```

②
	Results	Messages	
		(No column name)	(No col
	1	3	2

FIGURE 3-47: Using stored procedure

```
  .    public class Triggers
       {
   ① public static OnMyUpdate()
       {
         ② ... code that checks/modifies database
       }
   }
```

FIGURE 3-48: CLR trigger

Triggers

A trigger in SQL Server 2005 may be implemented by a CLR method. Methods that implement a trigger return a void and take no parameters. Figure 3-48 shows a C# CLR method (1) that can be used as a trigger. As with functions and stored procedures, it must be a static public method in a public class. Its body accesses and possibly modifies the database (2). Chapter 4 discusses how to access a database in a trigger and shows examples of their use.

A CLR-based trigger must be added to SQL Server. Figure 3-49 shows the syntax to create a trigger, which is the same as that for a T-SQL trigger except that the AS phrase is followed by an EXTERNAL NAME clause (2).

The SqlTrigger attribute may optionally be added to a CLR method that implements a trigger. SQL Server 2005 does not use the information in this attribute. This attribute has three properties that SQL Server 2005 uses to deploy the trigger. The Name property is used to name the trigger. If it is absent, the name of the CLR method is used as the name of the trigger. The Target property is used to name the table to which the trigger is being added. The Target property is the equivalent of the ON clause in the T-SQL CREATE TRIGGER statement. The Event property specifies the type of trigger—for example, "FOR UPDATE." The Name property is optional, but both the Target and Event properties are required for Visual Studio 2005 to be able to deploy the trigger.

```
   ① CREATE TRIGGER reminder
     ON Sales
     AFTER INSERT, UPDATE
     AS
   ② EXTERNAL NAME Rules.Triggers.OnMyUpdate
```

FIGURE 3-49: Loading trigger

Where Are We?

This chapter shows that CLR functions can be used to implement T-SQL stored procedures, functions, and triggers. CLR languages typically are better suited to doing numeric computations and also offer a familiar programming environment for problem space experts who typically don't write T-SQL applications. The `System.Data.SqlTypes` namespace provides data types that can be used in the CLR but that operate like the corresponding data types in SQL Server.

■ 4 ■
In-Process Data Access

W HETHER YOU ACCESS data from the client, middle tier, or server, when you're using SQL Server and the .NET Framework, you use the `SqlClient` data provider. Your data access code is similar regardless of its location, but the .NET Framework 2.0 version of `SqlClient` contains code to encapsulate differences when you're programming inside SQL Server and optimize the in-server programming environment.

Programming with SqlClient

Accessing data from outside SQL Server entails connecting to SQL Server through a network library and a client library. When you use the .NET Framework with SQL Server, you use System.Data.dll as the client library and the ADO.NET programming model. ADO.NET is a provider-based model, similar in concept to ODBC, OLE DB, and JDBC. The model uses a common API (or a set of classes) to encapsulate data access; each database product has its own provider. ADO.NET providers are known as *data providers,* and the data provider for SQL Server is `SqlClient`. The latest release of `SqlClient`, installed with .NET Framework 2.0, includes new client-side functionality to take advantage of new features in SQL Server 2005. In addition, `SqlClient` contains extensions to allow ADO.NET code to be used inside the database itself. Though T-SQL is usually preferred when a stored procedure, user-defined function, or trigger accesses database data, you can also use ADO.NET when writing procedural code in the

.NET Framework. The programming model when using SqlClient in .NET Framework stored procedures is similar to client-side code but in-database access is optimized because no network libraries are needed. Let's start by writing some simple client database code and then convert it to run on the server.

Simple data access code is very similar regardless of the programming model used. To summarize, using ADO.NET and SqlClient as an example:

1. Connect to the database by instantiating a SqlConnection class and calling its Open method.

2. Create an instance of a SqlCommand class. This instance contains a SQL statement or procedure name as its CommandText property. The SqlCommand is associated with the SqlConnection.

3. Execute the SqlCommand, and return either a set of columns and rows called SqlDataReader or possibly only a count of rows affected by the statement.

4. Use the SqlDataReader to read the results, and close it when finished.

5. Dispose of the SqlCommand and SqlConnection to free the associated memory, network, and server resources.

The ADO.NET code to accomplish inserting a row into a SQL Server table would look like Listing 4-1.

LISTING 4-1: Inserting a row using SqlClient from the client

```
// Code to insert data from client
//   See chapter 14 for an implementation of
//   the GetConnectionStringFromConfigFile method.
string connStr = GetConnectionStringFromConfigFile();
SqlConnection conn = new SqlConnection(connStr);
conn.Open();
SqlCommand cmd = conn.CreateCommand();
cmd.CommandText = "insert into test values ('testdata')";
int rows_affected = cmd.ExecuteNonQuery();
cmd.Dispose();
conn.Dispose();
```

The previous ADO.NET code ignored the fact that an exception might cause the execution of cmd.Dispose or conn.Dispose to be skipped. The preferred and simple way to prevent this from happening is to use the using syntax in C#. One or more object instance declarations are followed by a block of code. The `Dispose` method is called automatically at the end of the code block. We'll be using the `using` construct a lot in the code in this book. Rewritten using this syntax, the code above would look like Listing 4-2.

LISTING 4-2: Inserting a row using SqlClient from the client, C# using construct

```
//code to insert data from client
string connStr = GetConnectionStringFromConfigFile();
using (SqlConnection conn = new SqlConnection(connStr))
using (SqlCommand cmd =
  new SqlCommand("insert into test values ('testdata')", conn))
{
  conn.Open();
  int rows_affected = cmd.ExecuteNonQuery();
}  // Dispose called on cmd and conn here
```

Other classes in a typical ADO.NET data provider include a transaction class (`SqlTransaction`) to tie Connections and Commands to a database transaction, a parameter collection (`SqlParameterCollection`) of parameters (`SqlParameter`) to use with parameterized SQL queries or stored procedures, and specialized Exception and Error classes (`SqlException`, `SqlErrorCollection`, `SqlError`) to represent processing errors. `SqlClient` includes all the typical classes; Figure 4-1 shows the object model.

The same basic model is used inside the server to access data in .NET Framework stored procedures. It's familiar to ADO.NET programmers, and using it inside the server makes it easy for programmers to use their

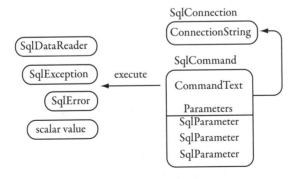

FIGURE 4-1: The SqlClient provider object model
(major classes only)

existing skills to write procedures. The big difference is that when you're writing a .NET Framework procedure, you're already inside the database. No explicit connection is needed. Although there is no network connection to the database, there is a SqlConnection instance. The difference is in the connection string. Outside the database, the connection string should be read from a configuration file and contains items like the SQL Server instance to connect to (server keyword), the SQL Server login (either User ID and Password keywords or Integrated Security=true), and the initial database (database keyword). The connection string that indicates to SqlClient that we're already inside the database and the provider should just use the existing database context contains only the keyword "context connection=true". When you specify "context connection=true", no other connection string keyword can be used. Listing 4-3 is the same code as above but executing inside a .NET Framework stored procedure.

LISTING 4-3: Inserting a row using SqlClient in a SQLCLR stored procedure

```
//code to insert data in a stored procedure
public static void InsertRowOfTestData()
{
  string connStr = "context connection=true";
  using (SqlConnection conn = new SqlConnection(connStr))
  using (SqlCommand cmd =
    new SqlCommand("insert into test values ('testdata')", conn))
  {
    conn.Open();
    int rows_affected = cmd.ExecuteNonQuery();
  }
}
```

Note that this code is provided as a stored procedure only to explain how to access data on the server. Not only is the code faster as a Transact-SQL (T-SQL) stored procedure but also SQL Server will check the SQL statements for syntactic correctness at CREATE PROCEDURE time. This is not the case with the .NET Framework stored procedure above. When you execute SQL statements by using SqlCommand, it's the equivalent of using sp_executesql (a system-supplied store procedure for dynamic string execution of commands) inside a T-SQL stored procedure. There is the same potential for SQL injection as with sp_executesql, so don't execute commands whose CommandText property is calculated by using input parameters passed in by the procedure user.

This code is so similar to the previous client-side code that if we knew whether the code was executing in a stored procedure on the server or on the client, we could use the same code, changing only the connection string. But a few constructs exist only if you are writing server-side code. Enter the `SqlContext` class.

Context: The SqlContext Class

The `SqlContext` class is one of the new classes that are available only if you're running inside the server. When a procedure or function is executed, it is executed as part of the user's connection. Whether that user connection comes from ODBC, ADO.NET, or T-SQL doesn't really matter. You are in a connection that has specific properties, environment variables, and so on, and you are executing within that connection; you are in the context of the user's connection.

A command is executed within the context of the connection, but it also has an execution context, which consists of data related to the command. The same goes for triggers, which are executed within a trigger context.

Prior to SQL Server 2005, the closest we came to being able to write code in another language that executed within the process space of SQL Server was writing extended stored procedures. An *extended stored procedure* is a C or C++ DLL that has been catalogued in SQL Server and therefore can be executed in the same manner as a "normal" SQL Server stored procedure. The extended stored procedure is executed in process with SQL Server and on the same Windows thread[1] as the user's connection.

Note, however, that if you need to do any kind of database access—even within the database to which the user is connected—from the extended stored procedure, you still need to connect to the database explicitly through ODBC, OLE DB, or even DBLib exactly as you would do from a client, as Figure 4-2 illustrates. Furthermore, when you have created the connection from the procedure, you may want to share a common transaction lock space with the client. Because you now have a separate connection, you need to

---

1. Strictly speaking, thread or fiber, depending on the setting in the server. See Chapter 2 for information about fiber mode.

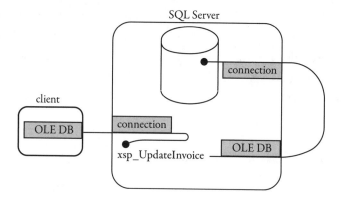

FIGURE 4-2: Connections from extended stored procedures

ensure explicitly that you share the transaction lock space by using the srv_getbindtoken call and the stored procedure sp_bindsession.

In SQL Server 2005, when you use the .NET Framework to write procedures, functions, and triggers, the SqlContext is available. The original program can now be rewritten in Listing 4-4 so that the same code works either on the client/middle tier or in the server if it's called as part of a stored procedure using the SqlContext static IsAvailable property.

LISTING 4-4: Using IsAvailable to determine whether the code is running on the server

```
// other using statements elided for clarity
using System.Data.SqlClient;
using Microsoft.SqlServer.Server; // for SqlContext

public static void InsertRowOfTestData2()
{
  string connStr;
  if (SqlContext.IsAvailable)
    connStr = "context connection=true";
  else
    connStr = GetConnectionStringFromConfigFile();
  // the rest of the code is identical
  using (SqlConnection conn = new SqlConnection(connStr))
  using (SqlCommand cmd =
    new SqlCommand("insert into test values ('testdata')", conn))
  {
    conn.Open();
    // The value of i is the number of rows affected
    int i = cmd.ExecuteNonQuery();
  }
}
```

You can see the `SqlContext` as a helper class; static read-only properties that allow you to access the class encapsulate functionality that exists only on the server. These properties are shown in Table 4-1.

Using `SqlContext` is the only way to get an instance of the classes in Table 4-1; you cannot create them by using a constructor (`New` in Visual Basic .NET). You can create the other classes that are part of the `SqlClient` provider in the same way that you normally would create them if used from an ADO.NET client. Some of the classes and methods in `SqlClient` act a little differently if you use them on the server, however.

SQLCLR stored procedures can do data access by default, but this is not the case with a SQLCLR user-defined function. As was discussed in the previous chapter, unless `DataAccessKind` or `SystemDataAccessKind` is set to `DataAccessKind.Read`/`SystemDataAccessKind.Read`, any attempt to do data access using the `SqlClient` provider will fail. Even if `DataAccessKind` is set to `DataAccessKind.None` (the default), however, `SqlContext.IsAvailable` returns true. `SqlContext.IsAvailable` is an indication of whether you're running in the server, rather than whether data access is permitted.

By now, you may be wondering: If some of the managed classes are calling into SQL Server, does that mean that the internals of SQL Server are managed as well, and if not, are interoperability calls between managed and native code space happening? The answers are no and yes. No, the internals of SQL Server are not managed; Microsoft did not rewrite the whole of SQL Server in managed code. And yes, interoperability calls happen. The managed classes are making Platform Invoke (PInvoke) calls against the executable of SQL Server, `sqlservr.exe`, as shown in Figure 4-3, which exposes a couple dozen methods for the CLR to call into.

TABLE 4-1: SqlContext Static Properties

Property	Return Value
IsAvailable	Boolean
WindowsIdentity	System.Security.Principal.WindowsIdentity
Pipe	Microsoft.SqlServer.Server.SqlPipe
TriggerContext	Microsoft.SqlServer.Server.SqlTriggerContext

sqlservr.exe

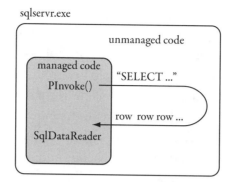

FIGURE 4-3: Interop between .NET framework and SQL Server code in process

When you read this about interop, you may become concerned about performance. Theoretically, a performance hit is possible, but because SQL Server hosts the CLR (as discussed in Chapter 2), and the SqlClient provider runs in process with SQL Server, the hit is minimal. In the last sentence, notice that we said *theoretically*. Remember that when you execute CLR code, you will run machine-compiled code, which is not the case when you run T-SQL. Therefore, for *some* code executing in the CLR, the result may be a performance improvement compared with pure T-SQL code.

Now that we have discussed the SqlContext class, let's see how we go about using it.

Connections

As already mentioned, when you are at server side and a client executes, you are part of that client's connection context, which in SQL Server 2005 is exposed by using a special connection string. The SqlConnection object exposes the public methods, properties, and events listed in Table 4-2. (Note that the table doesn't show members inherited from System.Object.)

You can create only one SqlConnection at a time with the special "context connection=true" string. Attempting to create a second SqlConnection instance will fail, but you can create an "internal" SqlConnection and another external SqlConnection back to the same instance using an ordinary connection string. Opening this additional SqlConnection

TABLE 4-2: Public Members of SqlConnection

Name	Return Value/Type	Member Type
Constructor		Constructor
Constructor(String)		Constructor
BeginTransaction()	SqlTransaction	Method
BeginTransaction (IsolationLevel)	SqlTransaction	Method
BeginTransaction (IsolationLevel, String)	SqlTransaction	Method
BeginTransaction(String)	SqlTransaction	Method
ChangeDatabase(String)	void	Method
ChangePassword (String, String)	void	Static Method
ClearAllPools	void	Static Method
Close()	void	Method
CreateCommand()	SqlCommand	Method
EnlistDistributedTransaction (ITransaction)	void	Method
EnlistTransaction (Transaction)	void	Method
GetSchema()	DataTable	Method
GetSchema(String)	DataTable	Method
GetSchema(String, String[])	DataTable	Method
Open()	void	Method
ResetStatistics	void	Method
RetrieveStatistics	Hashtable	Method
ConnectionString	String	Property

(Continued)

TABLE 4-2: Public Members of SqlConnection (*Continued*)

Name	Return Value/Type	Member Type
ConnectionTimeout	Int32	Property
Database	String	Property
DataSource	String	Property
FireInfoMessageOnUserErrors	Boolean	Property
PacketSize	Int32	Property
ServerVersion	String	Property
State	String	Property
StatisticsEnabled	Boolean	Property
WorkStationId	String	Property
InfoMessage	SqlInfoMessage EventHandler	Event

will start a distributed transaction, however,[2] because you have multiple SPIDs (SQL Server sessions) possibly attempting to update the same data. There is no way to knit the two sessions together through the ADO.NET API into a single local transaction, however, as you can in an extended stored procedure with sp_bindtoken. You can call the SqlConnection's Close() method and reopen it, if you like, although it's unlikely that you ever actually need to do this. Keeping the SqlConnection open doesn't use any additional resources after you originally refer to it in code.

Although the same System.Data.SqlClient.SqlConnection class is used for both client and server code, some of the features and methods will not work inside the server:

- ChangePassword method
- GetSchema method

2. Technically, you can avoid a distributed transaction by using "enlist=false" in the connection string of the new SqlConnection. In this case, the second session does not take part in the context connection's transaction.

- Connection pooling and associated parameters and methods
- Transparent failover when database mirroring is used
- Client statistics
- `PacketSize, WorkstationID`, and other client information

Commands: Making Things Happen

The `SqlClient` provider implements the `SqlCommand` class to execute action statements and submit queries to the database. When you have created your connection, you can get the command object from the `Create-Command` method on your connection, as the code in Listing 4-5 shows.

LISTING 4-5: Create a command from the connection object

```
//get a command through CreateCommand
SqlConnection conn = new SqlConnection("context connection=true");
SqlCommand cmd = conn.CreateCommand();
```

Another way of getting to the command is to use one of the `SqlCommand`'s constructors, which Listing 4-6 shows.

LISTING 4-6: Using SqlCommand's constructor

```
//use constructor that takes a CommandText and Connection
string cmdStatement = "select * from authors";
SqlConnection conn = new SqlConnection("context connection=true");
SqlCommand cmd = new SqlCommand(cmdStatement, conn);
```

We have seen how a `SqlCommand` is created; now let's look at what we can do with the command. Table 4-3 lists the public methods, properties, and events. (The table doesn't show public members inherited from `System.Object` or the extra asynchronous versions of the execute-related methods.)

For those of you who are used to the `SqlClient` provider, most of the members are recognizable, but as with the connection object when used inside SQL Server, there are some differences:

- The new asynchronous execution methods are not available when running on the server.
- You can have multiple `SqlCommands` associated with the special context connection, but cannot have multiple active `SqlDataReaders` at

TABLE 4-3: Public Members of SqlCommand

Name	Return Value/Type	Member Type
Constructor()		Constructor
Constructor(String)		Constructor
Constructor(String, SqlConnection)		Constructor
Constructor(String, SqlConnection, SqlTransaction)		Constructor
Cancel()	void	Method
CreateParameter()	SqlParameter	Method
Dispose()	void	Method
ExecuteNonQuery()	int	Method
ExecuteReader()	SqlDataReader	Method
ExecuteReader (CommandBehavior)	SqlDataReader	Method
ExecuteScalar()	Object	Method
ExecuteXmlReader()	XmlReader	Method
Prepare()	void	Method
ResetCommandTimeout	void	Method
CommandText	String	Property
CommandTimeout	int	Property
CommandType	CommandType	Property
Connection	SqlConnection	Property
Notification	SqlNotificationRequest	Property
NotificationAutoEnlist	Boolean	Property
Parameters	SqlParameterCollection	Property

(Continued)

TABLE 4-3: Public Members of SqlCommand (*Continued*)

Name	Return Value/Type	Member Type
Transaction	SqlTransaction	Property
UpdatedRowSource	UpdateRowSource	Property
StatementCompleted	StatementCompleted EventHandler	Event

the same time on this connection. This functionality, known as *multiple active resultsets* (MARS), is available only when using the data provider from a client.

- You cannot cancel a `SqlCommand` inside a stored procedure using the `SqlCommand`'s `Cancel` method.
- `SqlNotificationRequest` and `SqlDependency` do not work with commands issued inside SQL Server.

When you execute parameterized queries or stored procedures, you specify the parameter values through the `Parameters` property of the `Sql-Command` class. This property can contain a `SqlParameterCollection` that is a collection of `SqlParameter` instances. The `SqlParameter` instance contains a description of the parameter and also the parameter value. Properties of the `SqlParameter` class include parameter name, data type (including precision and scale for decimal parameters), parameter length, and parameter direction. The `SqlClient` provider uses named parameters rather than positional parameters. Use of named parameters means the following:

- The parameter name is significant; the correct name must be specified.
- The parameter name is used as a parameter marker in parameterized SELECT statements, rather than the ODBC/OLE DB question-mark parameter marker.
- The order of the parameters in the collection is not significant.
- Stored procedure parameters with default values may be omitted from the collection; if they are omitted, the default value will be used.
- Parameter direction must be specified as a value of the `ParameterDirection` enumeration.

This enumeration contains the values Input, Output, InputOutput, and ReturnCode. Although Chapter 3 mentioned that in T-SQL, all parameters defined as OUTPUT can also be used for input, the SqlClient provider (and ADO.NET is general) is more precise. Attempting to use the wrong parameter direction will cause an error, and if you specify ParameterDirection.Output, input values will be ignored. If you need to pass in a value to a T-SQL procedure that declares it as OUTPUT, you must use ParameterDirection.InputOutput. Listing 4-7 shows an example of executing a parameterized T-SQL statement.

LISTING 4-7: Using a parameterized SQL statement

```
SqlConnection conn = new SqlConnection("context connection=true");
conn.Open();
SqlCommand cmd = conn.CreateCommand();

// set the command text
// use names as parameter markers
cmd.CommandText =
  "insert into jobs values(@job_desc, @min_lvl, @max_lvl)";

// names must agree with markers
// length of the VarChar parameter is deduced from the input value
cmd.Parameters.Add("@job_desc", SqlDbType.VarChar);
cmd.Parameters.Add("@min_lvl", SqlDbType.TinyInt);
cmd.Parameters.Add("@max_lvl", SqlDbType.TinyInt);

// set values
cmd.Parameters[0].Value = "A new job description";
cmd.Parameters[1].Value = 10;
cmd.Parameters[2].Value = 20;

// execute the command
// should return 1 row affected
int rows_affected = cmd.ExecuteNonQuery();
```

Obtaining Results

Execution of SQL commands can return the following:

- A numeric return code
- A count of rows affected by the command
- A single scalar value

- One or more multirow results using SQL Server's default (cursorless) behavior
- A stream of XML

Some commands, such as a command that executes a stored procedure, can return more than one of these items—for example, a return code, a count of rows affected, and many multirow results. You tell the provider which of these output items you want by using the appropriate method of `SqlCommand`, as shown in Table 4-4.

When you return data from a `SELECT` statement, it is a good idea to use the lowest-overhead choice. Because of the amount of internal processing and the number of object allocations needed, `ExecuteScalar` may be faster than `ExecuteReader`. You need to consider the shape of the data that is returned, of course. Using `ExecuteReader` to return a forward-only, read-only cursorless set of results is always preferred over using a server cursor. Listing 4-8 shows an example of when to use each results-returning method.

LISTING 4-8: Returning rows with SqlClient

```
SqlConnection conn = new SqlConnection("context connection=true");
conn.Open();
SqlCommand cmd = conn.CreateCommand();

// 1. this is a user-defined function
// returning a single value (authorname) as VARCHAR
cmd.CommandText = "GetFullAuthorNameById";
// required from procedure or UDF
cmd.CommandType = CommandType.StoredProcedure;
cmd.Parameters.AddWithValue("@id", "172-32-1176");

String fullname = (String)cmd.ExecuteScalar();
// use fullname
cmd.Parameters.Clear();

// 2. returns one row
cmd.CommandText = "GetAuthorInfoById";
// required from procedure or UDF
cmd.CommandType = CommandType.StoredProcedure;
cmd.Parameters.AddWithValue("@id", "172-32-1176");

SqlDataReader rdr1 = cmd.ExecuteReader();
// use fields in SqlDataReader
```

```
rdr1.Close();
cmd.Parameters.Clear();

// 3. returns multiple rows
cmd.CommandText = "select * from authors";
cmd.CommandType = CommandType.Text;

SqlDataReader rdr2 = cmd.ExecuteReader();
while (rdr2.Read())
  // process rows in SqlDataReader
  { }
rdr2.Close();
```

SqlDataReader encapsulates multiple rows that can be read in a forward-only manner. You move to the next row in the set by using the SqlDataReader's Read() method, as shown in Listing 4-8. After you call ExecuteReader, the resultant SqlDataReader is positioned before the first row in the set, and an initial Read positions it at the first row. The Read method returns false when there are no more rows in the set. If more than one rowset is available, you move to the next rowset by calling SqlDataReader's NextResult method. While you are positioned on a row, the IDataRecord interface can be used to read data. You can use loosely typed ordinals or names to read the data in single columns. Using ordinals or names is a syntactic shortcut to using IDataRecord.GetValue(n). This returns the value as a .NET Framework System.Object, which must be cast to the correct type.

TABLE 4-4: How to Obtain Different Result Types

Result Desired	Mechanism to Obtain It
Return code	Parameter with ParameterDirection of ReturnCode
Count of rows affected	Returned value from SqlCommand.ExecuteNonQuery or Use SqlCommand.ExecuteReader and SqlDataReader.RecordsAffected
Scalar value	Use SqlCommand.ExecuteScalar
Cursorless mode results	Use SqlCommand.ExecuteReader
XML stream	Use SqlCommand.ExecuteXmlReader

If you know the data type of the value, you can use more strongly typed column accessors. Both SQL Server providers have two kinds of strongly typed accessors. `IDataReader.GetDecimal(n)` is an example; this returns the value of the first column of the current row as a .NET Framework `System.Decimal` data type. If you want full SQL Server type fidelity, it is better to use `SqlDataReader`'s SQL Server–specific accessors, such as `IDataReader.GetSqlDecimal(n)`; these return instances of structures from the `System.Data.SqlTypes` namespace. These types are isomorphic with SQL Server data types; examples of their use and reasons why they are preferable to the .NET Framework base data types when used inside the server are covered in Chapter 3. Listing 4-9 shows an example of using each type.

LISTING 4-9: Getting column values from a SqlDataReader

```
SqlConnection conn = new SqlConnection("context connection=true");
conn.Open();
SqlCommand cmd = conn.CreateCommand();
cmd.CommandText = "select * from authors";
cmd.CommandType = CommandType.Text;

SqlDataReader rdr = cmd.ExecuteReader();
while (rdr.Read() == true)
{
  string s;
  // 1. Use ordinals or names
  //    explicit casting, if you know the right type
  s = (string)rdr[0];
  s = (string)rdr["au_id"];

  // 2. Use GetValue (must cast)
  s = (string)rdr.GetValue(0);

  // 3. Strong typed accessors
  s = rdr.GetString(0);

  // 4. Accessors for SqlTypes
  SqlString s2 = rdr.GetSqlString(0);
}
```

Although you can process results obtained inside .NET Framework procedural code, you can also pass these items back to the client. This is accomplished through the `SqlPipe` class, which is described later in the chapter. Note that each of the classes returns rows, which must be processed sequentially; these results cannot be updated in place.

Transactions

Multiple SQL operations within a stored procedure or user-defined function can be executed individually or composed within a single transaction. Composing multistatement procedural code inside a transaction ensures that a set of operations has ACID properties. *ACID* is an acronym for the following:

- *Atomicity*—All the operations in a transaction will succeed, or none of them will.
- *Consistency*—The transaction transforms the database from one consistent state to another.
- *Isolation*—Each transaction has its own view of the database state.
- *Durability*—These behaviors are guaranteed even if the database or host operating system fails—for example, because of a power failure.

You can use transactions in two general ways within the `SqlClient` managed provider: by starting a transaction by using the `SqlConnection`'s `BeginTransaction` method or by using declarative transactions using `System.Transaction.TransactionScope`. The `TransactionScope` is part of a new library in .NET Framework 2.0: the `System.Transactions` library. Listing 4-10 shows a simple example of each method.

LISTING 4-10: SqlClient can use two different coding styles for transactions

```
// Example 1: start transaction using the API
SqlConnection conn = new SqlConnection("context connection=true");
conn.Open();
SqlTransaction tx = conn.BeginTransaction();
// do some work
tx.Commit();
conn.Dispose();
```

```
// Example 2: start transaction using Transaction Scope
using System.Data.SqlClient;
using System.Transactions;

using (TransactionScope ts = new TransactionScope())
{
  SqlConnection conn = new SqlConnection("context connection=true");
  // connection auto-enlisted in transaction on Open()
```

```
conn.Open();
// transactional commands here
conn.Close();
ts.Complete();
} // transaction commits when TransactionScope.Dispose called implicitly
```

If you've done any ADO.NET coding before, you've probably run into the `BeginTransaction` method. This method encapsulates issuing a BEGIN TRANSACTION statement in T-SQL. The `TransactionScope` requires a bit more explanation.

The `System.Transactions` library is meant to provide a representation of the concept of a transaction in the managed world. It is also a lightweight way to access MSDTC, the distributed transaction coordinator. It can be used as a replacement for the automatic transaction functionality in COM+ exposed by the `System.EnterpriseServices` library, but it does not require the components that use it to be registered in the COM+ catalog. `System.EnterpriseServices` cannot be used in .NET Framework procedural code that runs in SQL Server. To use automatic transactions with `System.Transactions`, simply instantiate a `TransactionScope` object with a `using` statement, and any connections that are opened inside the `using` block will be enlisted in the transaction automatically. The transaction will be committed or rolled back when you exit the `using` block and the `TransactionScope`'s `Dispose` method is called. Notice that the default behavior when `Dispose` is called is to roll back the transaction. To commit the transaction, you need to call the `TransactionScope`'s `Complete` method.

In SQL Server 2005, using the `TransactionScope` starts a local, not a distributed, transaction. This is the behavior whether `TransactionScope` is used with client-side code or SQLCLR procedures unless there is already a transaction started when the SQLCLR procedure is invoked. This phenomenon is illustrated below:

```
-- Calling a SQLCLR procedure that uses TransactionScope

EXECUTE MySQLCLRProcThatUsesTransactionScope -- local transaction
GO

BEGIN TRANSACTION
-- other T-SQL statements
EXECUTE MySQLCLRProcThatUsesTransactionScope -- distributed transaction
COMMIT
GO
```

The transaction actually begins when Open is called on the SqlConnection, not when the TransactionScope instance is created. If more than one SqlConnection is opened inside a TransactionScope, both connections are enlisted in a distributed transaction when the second connection is opened. The transaction on the first connection actually changes from a local transaction to a distributed transaction. Recall that you can have only a single instance of the context connection, so opening a second connection really means opening a connection using SqlClient and a network library. Most often, you'll be doing this specifically to start a distributed transaction with another database. Because of the network traffic involved and the nature of the two-phase commit protocol used by distributed transactions, a distributed transaction will be much higher overhead than a local transaction.

BeginTransaction and TransactionScope work identically in the simple case. But some database programmers like to make each procedure usable and transactional when used stand-alone or when called when a transaction already exists. To accomplish this, you would put transaction code in each procedure. When one procedure with transaction code calls another procedure with transaction code, this is called *composing transactions.* SQL Server supports nesting of transactions and named savepoints, but not autonomous (true nested) transactions. So using a T-SQL procedure X as an example,

```
CREATE PROCEDURE X
AS
BEGIN TRAN
-- work here
COMMIT
```

calling it stand-alone (EXECUTE X) means that the work is in a transaction. Calling it from procedure Y

```
CREATE PROCEDURE Y
AS
BEGIN TRANSACTION
-- other work here
EXECUTE X
COMMIT
```

doesn't start an autonomous transaction (a second transaction with a different scope); the BEGIN TRANSACTION in X merely increases a T-SQL variable

@@TRANCOUNT by one. Two error messages are produced when you roll back in procedure X while it's being called by procedure Y:

```
Msg 266, Level 16, State 2, Procedure Y, Line 0
Transaction count after EXECUTE indicates that a COMMIT or ROLLBACK
TRANSACTION statement is missing. Previous count = 1, current count = 0.
Msg 3902, Level 16, State 1, Procedure X, Line 5
The COMMIT TRANSACTION request has no corresponding BEGIN TRANSACTION.
```

I'd like to emulate this behavior in SQLCLR—that is, have a procedure that acts like X and that can be used stand-alone or composed. I can do something akin to T-SQL (and get the interesting rollback behavior with a slightly different error number) using the BeginTransaction method on the context SqlConnection. Using a TransactionScope has a different behavior, however. If I have a SQLCLR proc that looks like this (condensed version),

```
public static void X {
   using (TransactionScope ts = new TransactionScope())
   using (
     SqlConnection conn = new SqlConnection("Context connection=true"))
   {
   conn.Open();
   ts.Complete();
   }
}
```

and if SQLCLR X is used stand-alone, all is well, and the TransactionScope code gets a local transaction. If SQLCLR X is called from procedure Y (above), SqlConnection's Open starts a distributed transaction. Apparently, it *has* to be this way, at least for now, because of how TransactionScope works. Local transactions don't expose the events that TransactionScope needs to compose transactions.

If you *want* a distributed transaction composed with your outer transaction (your SqlConnection is calling to another instance, for example), use TransactionScope; if you *don't* want one, use SqlConnection's BeginTransaction. It won't act any different from T-SQL (except you do get a different error number) if you roll back inside an "inner" transaction. But you get a nesting local transaction with BeginTransaction.

Listing 4-11 shows an example of using a distributed transaction with TransactionScope.

LISTING 4-11: A distributed transaction using TransactionScope

```
public static void DoDistributed() {
  string ConnStr =
    "server=server2;integrated security=sspi;database=pubs";
  using (TransactionScope ts = new TransactionScope())
  using (SqlConnection conn1 =
        new SqlConnection("Context connection=true"))
  using (SqlConnection conn2 =
        new SqlConnection(ConnStr))
  {
  conn1.Open();
  conn2.Open();
  // do work on connection 1
  // do work on connection 2
  // ask to commit the distributed transaction
  ts.Complete();
  }
}
```

TransactionScope Exotica

You can use options of the `TransactionScope` class to compose multiple transactions in interesting ways. You can start multiple transactions, for example (but not on the context connection), by using a different `TransactionScopeOption`. Listing 4-12 will begin a local transaction using the context connection and then begin an autonomous transaction using a connection to the same server.

LISTING 4-12: Producing the equivalent of an autonomous transaction

```
public static void DoPseudoAutonomous() {
  string ConnStr =
    "server=sameserver;integrated security=sspi;database=samedb";
  using (TransactionScope ts1 = new TransactionScope())
  using (SqlConnection conn1 =
        new SqlConnection("context connection=true"))
  {
  conn1.Open();
  // do work on connection 1, then
  {
      using (TransactionScope ts2 =
            new TransactionScope(TransactionScopeOption.RequiresNew))
      using (SqlConnection conn2 = new SqlConnection(ConnStr))
      {
```

```
        conn2.Open();
        // do work on connection 2
        ts2.Complete();
    }
  // ask to commit transaction1
  ts1.Complete();
  }
}
```

This code works because it uses a second connection to the same server to start a second transaction. This second connection is separate from the first one, not an autonomous transaction on the same connection. The result is the same as you would get from an autonomous transaction; you just need two connections (the context connection and a second connection) to accomplish it.

Attempting to use any `TransactionScopeOption` other than the default `TransactionRequired` fails if there already is an existing transaction (as we saw before, when `BEGIN TRANSACTION` was called in T-SQL before `EXECUTE` on the SQLCLR procedure) and you attempt to use context connection, as shown in Listing 4-13. You'll get a message saying "no autonomous transaction".

LISTING 4-13: Attempting to use autonomous transactions on a single connection fails

```
-- Calling a SQLCLR procedure that uses TransactionScope
-- with an option other than TransactionRequired

EXECUTE DoPseudoAutonomous -- works
GO

BEGIN TRANSACTION
-- other T-SQL statements
EXECUTE DoPseudoAutonomous -- fails, "no autonomous transaction"
COMMIT
GO
```

This is because SQL Server doesn't support autonomous transactions on a single connection.

Best Practices

With all these options and different behaviors, what's the best and easier thing to do to ensure that your local transactions always work correctly in SQLCLR procedures? At this point, because SQL Server 2005 doesn't support autonomous transactions on the same connection, SqlConnection's BeginTransaction method is the best choice for local transactions. In addition, you need to use the Transaction.Current static properties in System.Transactions.dll to determine whether a transaction already exists—that is, whether the caller has already started a transaction. Listing 4-14 shows a strategy that works well whether or not you compose transactions.

LISTING 4-14: A generalized strategy for nesting transactions

```
// Works whether caller has transaction or not
public static int ComposeTx()
{
  int returnCode = 0;
  // determine if we have transaction
  bool noCallerTx = (Transaction.Current == null);
  SqlTransaction tx = null;

  SqlConnection conn = new SqlConnection("context connection=true");
  conn.Open();

  if (noCallerTx)
    tx = conn.BeginTransaction();

  try {
    // do the procedure's work here
    SqlCommand workcmd = new SqlCommand(
      "INSERT jobs VALUES('New job', 10, 10)", conn);
    if (tx != null)
      workcmd.Transaction = tx;
    int rowsAffected = workcmd.ExecuteNonQuery();

    if (noCallerTx)
      tx.Commit();
  }

  catch (Exception ex) {
    if (noCallerTx) {
      tx.Rollback();
      // raise error - covered later in chapter
    }
    else {
      // signal an error to the caller with return code
      returnCode = 50010;
    }
  }
  conn.Dispose();
  return returnCode;
}
```

For distributed transactions as well as the pseudoautonomous transactions described earlier, you must use `TransactionScope` or a separate second connection back to the server using `SqlClient`. If you don't mind the behavior that nesting transactions with `TransactionScope` force a distributed transaction and the extra overhead caused by MSDTC, you can use `TransactionScope` all the time. Finally, if you know your procedure won't be called with an existing transaction, you can use either `BeginTransaction` or `TransactionScope`. Refraining from nesting transactions inside nested procedures may be a good strategy until this gets sorted out.

Pipe

In the section on results earlier in this chapter, we mentioned that you have a choice of processing results in your procedural code as part of its logic or returning the results to the caller. Consuming `SqlDataReaders` or the stream of XML in procedural code makes them unavailable to the caller; you cannot process a cursorless mode result more than once. The code for in-process consumption of a `SqlDataReader` is identical to `SqlClient`; you call `Read()` until no more rows remain. To pass a resultset back to the client, you need to use a special class, `SqlPipe`.

The `SqlPipe` class represents a channel back to the client; this is a TDS (Tabular Data Stream) output stream if the TDS protocol is used for client communication. You obtain a `SqlPipe` by using the static `SqlContext.Pipe` property. Rowsets, single rows, and messages can be written to the pipe. Although you can get a `SqlDataReader` and return it to the client through the `SqlPipe`, this is less efficient than just using a new special method for the `SqlPipe` class: `ExecuteAndSend`. This method executes a `SqlCommand` and points it directly to the `SqlPipe`. Listing 4-15 shows an example.

LISTING 4-15: Using SqlPipe to return rows to the client

```
public static void getAuthorsByState(SqlString state)
{
  SqlConnection conn = new SqlConnection("context connection=true");
  conn.Open();
  SqlCommand cmd = conn.CreateCommand();
  cmd.CommandText = "select * from authors where state = @state";
  cmd.Parameters.Add("@state", SqlDbType.VarChar);
```

```
    cmd.Parameters[0].Value = state;
    SqlPipe pipe = SqlContext.Pipe;
    pipe.ExecuteAndSend(cmd);
}
```

In addition to returning an entire set of results through the pipe, SqlPipe's Send method lets you send an instance of the SqlDataRecord class. You can also batch the send operations however you like. An interesting feature of using SqlPipe is that the result is streamed to the caller immediately, as fast as you are able to send it, taking into consideration that the client stack may do row buffering. This may improve performance at the client because you can process rows as fast as they are sent out the pipe. Note that you can combine executing a command and sending the results back through SqlPipe in a single operation with the ExecuteAndSend convenience method, using a SqlCommand as a method input parameter.

SqlPipe also contains methods for sending scalar values as messages and affects how errors are exposed. We'll talk about error handling practices next. The entire set of methods exposed by SqlPipe is shown in Table 4-5.

There is also a boolean property on the SqlPipe class, IsSendingResults, that enables you to find out whether the SqlPipe is busy. Because multiple active resultsets are not supported when you're inside SQL Server,

TABLE 4-5: Methods of the SqlPipe Class

Method	What It Does
ExecuteAndSend(SqlCommand)	Executes command, returns results through SqlPipe
Send(String)	Sends a message as a string
Send(SqlDataReader)	Sends results through SqlDataReader
Send(SqlDataRecord)	Sends results through SqlDataRecord
SendResultsStart (SqlDataRecord)	Starts sending results
SendResultsRow (SqlDataRecord)	Sends a single row after calling SendResultsStart
SendResultsEnd()	Indicates finished sending rows

attempting to execute another method that uses the pipe while it's busy will procedure an error. The only exception to this rule is that SendResultsStart, SendResultsRow, and SendResultsEnd are used together to send results one row at a time.

SqlPipe is available for use only inside a SQLCLR stored procedure. Attempting to get the SqlContext.Pipe value inside a user-defined function returns a null instance. This is because sending rowsets is not permitted in a user-defined function. Within a stored procedure, however, you can not only send rowsets through the SqlPipe by executing a command that returns a rowset, but also synthesize your own. Synthesizing rowsets involves the use of two server-specific classes we haven't seen before: SqlDataRecord and SqlMetaData.

Creating and Sending New Rowsets

You've already seen that you can execute commands that return rowsets and send these to the client. You might want to execute a command that returns a rowset and then augment or change the rowset before sending it on. Or you might get data that is not in the database, such as an RSS feed or other Web Service, and choose to expose that data as a set of columns and rows. This is similar to the functionality that you can expose using table-valued functions, but without the capability to perform SQL using a where clause on the result. Your rowset will appear as one of the outputs of the stored procedure just as though it came from SQL Server's data.

You'd accomplish creating and sending a rowset by using the following steps:

1. Create an array of SqlMetaData instances that describes the data in each column.
2. Create an instance of SqlDataRecord. You must associate the array of SqlMetaData instances with the SqlDataRecord.
3. Populate the values in the SqlDataRecord using either weakly or strongly typed setter methods.
4. Call SqlPipe's SendResultsStart method to send the first row. This sends the metadata back to the client.
5. Populate the values in the SqlDataRecord using either weakly or strongly typed setter methods.

6. Use `SqlPipe`'s `SendResultsRow` method to send the data.

7. Use `SqlPipe`'s `SendResultsEnd` method to indicate that the rowset is complete.

First, we'll talk about using the `SqlMetaData` class. `SqlMetaData` is a class that is used to describe completely a single column of data. It can be used with `SqlDataRecord` instances. `SqlMetaData` instances encapsulate the information in the extended metadata from new format-extended TDS *describe packets* used by SQL Server 2005, as well as work with earlier versions of TDS. Listing 4-16 lists the properties exposed by the `SqlMetaData` class.

LISTING 4-16: Fields of the SqlMetaData class

```
class SqlMetaData {

    //data type info
    public SqlDbType SqlDbType;    // SqlDbType enum value
    public DbType DbType;          // DbType enum value
    public Type Type;              // .NET Framework data type
    public string TypeName;        // .NET Framework type name
    public string UdtTypeName;     // SQL Server 3-part type name

    //metadata info
    public bool IsPartialLength;
    public long LocaleId;
    public long Max;
    public long MaxLength;
    public byte Precision;
    public byte Scale;
    public string Name;            // column name
    public SqlCompareOptions CompareOptions;

    // XML schema info for XML data type
    public string XmlSchemaCollectionDatabase;
    public string XmlSchemaCollectionName;
    public string XmlSchemaCollectionOwningSchema;
};
```

Let's use `SqlDataRecord`, `SqlMetaData`, and `SqlPipe` to create and send rows from a simple synthesized rowset. The code for this is shown in Listing 4-17. The `Thread.Sleep()` calls are inserted so that you can observe pipelining in action with this type of rowset. Rows are sent as soon as the SQL engine has spare cycles to send them.

LISTING 4-17: Synthesizing a rowset using SqlDataRecord and SqlMetaData

```
// other using statements elided for clarity
using System.Threading;
using Microsoft.SqlServer.Server;
public static void Pipeline()
{
  SqlPipe p = SqlContext.Pipe;

  // a single column in each row
  SqlMetaData[] m = new SqlMetaData[1]
     {new SqlMetaData("colname", SqlDbType.NVarChar, 5) };
  SqlDataRecord rec = new SqlDataRecord(m);
  rec.SetSqlString(0, "Hello");

  p.SendResultsStart(rec);
  for (int i=0;i<10000;i++)
     p.SendResultsRow(rec);

  Thread.Sleep(10000);
  for (int i = 0; i < 10000; i++)
     p.SendResultsRow(rec);

  Thread.Sleep(10000);
  for (int i = 0; i < 10000; i++)
     p.SendResultsRow(rec);

  Thread.Sleep(10000);
  p.SendResultsEnd();
}
```

Using the WindowsIdentity

Procedural code executes SQL in the context of the caller by default. In SQL Server 2005, you can also specify alternative execution contexts by using the new WITH EXECUTE AS clause. (We'll talk more about this clause in Chapter 6.) When you're using an assembly created with the EXTERNAL_ACCESS or UNSAFE permission sets, however, you're allowing to access resources outside SQL Server. These resources can include other database instances, the file system, and external Web Services. Some of these resources may require authentication using a Windows security principal. If you're running the stored procedure as a SQL Server user associated with a Windows login, you can choose to impersonate the logged-in user. If you don't choose to impersonate the logged-in user (or if you're running the procedure while logged in as a SQL login), all external access takes place under the identity of the Windows principal running the SQL Server process. Under the *principal of least privilege*, this most likely should be a user with only the privileges required to run SQL Server. This principal probably won't have access to the external resources that you want.

You can get the Windows identity of the user running the procedure by using the `SqlContext.WindowsIdentity` property, as shown in Listing 4-18.

LISTING 4-18: Using impersonation in a SQLCLR stored procedure

```
// other using statements elided for clarity
using System.Security.Principal;
using Microsoft.SqlServer.Server
public static void GetFile(string filename)
{
  string s;
  using (WindowsIdentity id = SqlContext.WindowsIdentity)
  {
    WindowsImpersonationContext c = id.Impersonate();
    StreamReader sr = new StreamReader(filename);
    s = sr.ReadLine();
    sr.Close();
    c.Undo();
  }
    SqlContext.Pipe.Send(s);
}
```

When you have the `WindowsIdentity instance`, you can call its `Impersonate` method. Be sure to save the `WindowsImpersonationContext` that is returned, because you'll have to call its `Undo` method to undo the impersonation. Note that you can do data access only before calling `Impersonate` or after calling `Undo`. Attempting to use an impersonated context for data access will fail. Also, bear in mind that if you're executing the stored procedure as a SQL login rather than a Windows login, the `WindowsIdentity` instance will be null.

Calling a Web Service from SQLCLR

You most likely would be using impersonation from within a procedure in an assembly that is catalogued as PERMISSION_SET = EXTERNAL_ACCESS or UNSAFE. This is because when accessing external Windows resources, you'll need to impersonate the login that executed the procedure. One such case is calling a Web Service.

If you call a Web Service from a .NET Framework function or procedure by using the low-level APIs in `System.Web`, no special considerations other than impersonation apply. If you are using the Web Service client proxy classes generated by the .NET Framework `WSDL.exe` utility (or Add Web Reference from within Visual Studio 2005), however, you need to perform a few extra steps. The Web Service proxy classes generated will attempt to use dynamic assembly generation at procedure runtime to build and load the `XmlSerializer` classes that it uses to communicate with the Web Service. This is not allowed in SQLCLR, regardless of the `PERMISSION_SET` of the assembly. The way around this limitation is to build your `XmlSerializer` classes in advance, using a command-line utility, SGEN.exe. Here's how you would accomplish this.

I'd like to call a Web Service named `StockService` and have a URL, `http://stockbroker/StockService?WSDL`, where I can obtain Web Service Description Language—metadata that is needed to build the client proxy. To build the proxy, issue the following command:

```
WSDL.exe http://stockbroker/StockService?WSDL
```

Additional parameters available for the WSDL.exe utility are outside the scope of this discussion. Now that you have the proxy class (in the default case, it will be named `StockService.cs`), you compile it into an assembly and reference it in your program. This class consists of an object that represents your Web Service call, so calling out to the Web Service is no more complex than calling a method on an object. In your SQLCLR procedure, the code to call the Web Service looks like Listing 4-19.

LISTING 4-19: Calling a Web Service from a SQLCLR user-defined function

```
[Microsoft.SqlServer.Server.SqlFunction]
[return: SqlFacet(Precision = 9, Scale = 2)]
public static decimal GetStockWS(string symbol)
{
Decimal price;
using (WindowsIdentity id = SqlContext.WindowsIdentity)
  {
    WindowsImpersonationContext c = id.Impersonate();
    StockService s = new StockService();
```

```
    // use the current credentials
    s.Credentials =
      System.Net.CredentialCache.DefaultNetworkCredentials;
    price = s.GetStockPrice(symbol);
    c.Undo();
  }
return price;
}
```

For this code to work, you must pregenerate the required serializer for the proxy with the SGEN.exe utility, like this:

```
SGEN.exe StockService.dll
```

The utility produces an assembly named `StockService.XmlSerializers.dll`. You must catalog this assembly to SQL Server so that your Web Service client stored procedure (`GetStockWS` above) can use it. But there's another SQLCLR reliability–related issue to address before you do this. Our overall build steps for the proxy so far look as shown in Figure 4-4.

Use the WSDL (1) utility to build a proxy from the URL for the Web Service. It will build a C# file whose name is based on the name of the service—in this case, StockService.cs. StockService.cs will include both a synchronous and asynchronous implementation of the proxy. You must remove the asynchronous one by removing it. You need keep only the constructor and

```
   rem from the Command line
   rem(ensure these .NET utilities are in your path)
   cd \temp
   rem produce StockService.cs, need to edit this file
 ① C:temp>WSDL.exe http://stockbroker/StockService?WSDL
   rem produce StockService.dll
 ② C:temp>CSC /target:library StockService.cs
   rem produce StockService.XmlSerializers.dll
 ③ C:\temp>SGEN StockService.dll

   -- From SQL Server Management Studio
 ④ CREATE ASSEMBLY stockproxy
   FROM 'c:\temp\StockService.dll'
   GO
 ⑤ CREATE ASSEMBLY stockser
   FROM 'c:\temp\StockService.XmlSerializers.dll'
   GO
   -- now, reference both of these
   -- assemblies in your SQLCLR project
```

FIGURE 4-4: Building a Web Service proxy and cataloguing it to SQL Server

```
public partial class Service … {
    private System.Threading.SendOrPostCallback
        GetStockPriceOperationCompleted;

  public Service() {…
② public float GetStockPrice(string Symbol) {

    …
    }
    public System.IAsyncResult BeginGetStockPrice(…
    public float EndGetStockPrice(…
    public void GetStockPriceAsync(…
    public void GetStockPriceAsync(…
③ private void OnGetStockPriceOperationCompleted(…
    public new void CancelAsync(…
    public delegate void
        GetStockPriceCompletedEventHandler(…
    public partial class GetStockPriceCompletedEventArgs…
}
```

FIGURE 4-5: Commenting out the asynchronous methods
in a WSDL.exe–generated proxy

the methods (2) and remove everything else (3). Build a library out of StockService.cs using the C# compiler (4). You must also build an assembly that contains the XML serialization code using the SGEN utility (5). This utility produces a DLL (6) that contains the XML serialization implementation.

The only problem with this is that when WSDL.exe produces an "automatic" proxy class, two types of invocation methods are produced: a method to execute the Web Service synchronously (GetStockPrice, in this case) and a pair of methods to execute the Web Service asynchronously (BeginGetStockPrice and EndGetStockPrice). The asynchronous methods must be edited out before compiling StockService.cs, or the resulting assembly will need to be catalogued with PERMISSION_SET = UNSAFE.[3] If your DBA doesn't mind PERMISSION_SET = UNSAFE, this is fine, but you won't be using the methods, so let's go in and remove them. In the generated code StockService.cs, remove or comment out the following (a subset of the four changes you have to make is shown in Figure 4-5):

1. The BeginGetStockPrice and EndGetStockPrice methods

2. The GetStockPriceCompletedEventHandler variable

---

3. In addition to commenting these methods out by hand, you can use a WSDL.exe configuration file to generate the class without these methods. Using a Visual Studio 2005 SQL Server Project and Add Web Reference also do not generate these methods.

3. The GetStockPriceCompletedEventHandler method

4. The GetStockPriceCompletedEventHandlerEventArgs method

Now our proxy class assembly, StockService.dll, will be able to use PERMISSION_SET = SAFE. We'll return to the subject of XmlSerializers in Chapter 5 and see how they are used by user-defined types.

Exception Handling

One of the reasons .NET Framework procedures are appealing is that the .NET Framework has real structured exception handling. SQL Server 2005 includes improvements in error handling (see BEGIN/END TRY, BEGIN/END CATCH in Chapter 8), but this isn't true of structured exception handling. With .NET Framework procedures, you can accomplish something that wasn't available in previous versions of SQL Server. You can choose to consume the exception and not return the error to the caller, as shown in Listing 4-20.

LISTING 4-20: Result of consuming an exception in a SQLCLR procedure

```
public static void EatException()
{
  try
  {
    // cause a divide-by-zero exception
    int i = 42;
    int j = 0;
    j = i / j;
  }
  catch (Exception e)
  {
    SqlContext.Pipe.Send("Ate the exception");
    SqlContext.Pipe.Send(e.Message);
  }
}


-- Run this T-SQL code to test it
-- The transaction commits and the row is inserted
-- prints:
--    (1 row(s) affected)
--    Ate the exception
--    Attempt to divide by zero
BEGIN TRANSACTION
INSERT INTO jobs VALUES('before exception', 10, 10)
EXECUTE EatException
COMMIT
```

You can even catch an error in .NET Framework code and rethrow it as a user-defined exception. There is a catch (pun intended), however. Any unhandled exceptions that make their way out of your CLR procedure result in the same error at the client, whether the client is SQL Server Management Studio or a user application. If you are called from a .NET Framework `try/catch` block inside another .NET Framework stored procedure, however, that procedure can catch your exception without causing an underlying T-SQL exception. Listing 4-21 illustrates this.

LISTING 4-21: Catching an exception and rethrowing it using SQLCLR

```
public static void ExceptionThrower()
{
  try
  {
    int i = 42;
    int j = 0;
    j = i / j;
  }
  catch (Exception e)
  {
    SqlContext.Pipe.Send("In exception thrower");
    SqlContext.Pipe.Send(e.Message);
    throw (e);
  }
}

public static void ExceptionCatcher()
{
  using (SqlConnection conn =
    new SqlConnection("context connection=true"))
  using (SqlCommand cmd = new SqlCommand("ExceptionThrower", conn))
  {
    try
    {
      cmd.CommandType = CommandType.StoredProcedure;
      conn.Open();
      cmd.ExecuteNonQuery();
      SqlContext.Pipe.Send("Shouldn't get here");
    }
    catch (SqlException e)
    {
      SqlContext.Pipe.Send("In exception catcher");
      SqlContext.Pipe.Send(e.Number + ": " + e.Message);
    }
  }
}
```

The results of using the ExceptionThrower procedure, both stand-alone and from the ExceptionCatcher, are shown in Listing 4-22.

LISTING 4-22: Results of catching and rethrowing an exception

```
-- exception thrower standalone
BEGIN TRANSACTION
INSERT INTO jobs VALUES('thrower', 10, 10)
EXECUTE ExceptionThrower
COMMIT


-- results in the messages window
(1 row(s) affected)
In exception thrower
Attempted to divide by zero.
Msg 6522, Level 16, State 1, Procedure ExceptionThrower, Line 0
A .NET Framework error occurred during execution of user defined routine
or aggregate 'ExceptionThrower':
System.DivideByZeroException: Attempted to divide by zero.
System.DivideByZeroException:
   at StoredProcedures.ExceptionThrower()

-- exception catcher calls exception thrower
BEGIN TRANSACTION
INSERT INTO jobs VALUES('catcher', 10, 10)
EXECUTE ExceptionCatcher
COMMIT


(1 row(s) affected)
In exception catcher
6522: A .NET Framework error occurred during execution of user defined
routine or aggregate 'ExceptionThrower':
System.DivideByZeroException: Attempted to divide by zero.
System.DivideByZeroException: at StoredProcedures.ExceptionThrower().
In exception thrower
Attempted to divide by zero.
```

Note that in each case, the transaction will commit. The only thing that would cause the transaction to roll back would be if the call to the stand-alone ExceptionThrower were called from a T-SQL TRY/CATCH block. In the case of ExceptionCatcher, it catches and discards the exception raised by the ExceptionThrower (the error message comes from Exception-Catcher's write of e.Message to the SqlPipe). The only unusual thing is that we don't see the messages sent by the ExceptionThrower.

A disappointing thing about errors from SQLCLR procedures is that they are always wrapped in a general error with error number 6522. This makes it more difficult to get the actual error from a client. ADO.NET or OLE DB clients can return a stack of errors, but the actual error does not appear in the error stack. Note that SQL Server Management Studio is an ADO.NET application, so when we execute the code in SSMS, we get both errors. The 6522 contains the complete text and error number of the inner (actual) error.

From ODBC and (especially) from T-SQL callers, the picture is not as rosy, however. If you've not updated your error handling to use TRY/CATCH, you're looking just at the value of @@ERROR. That value is always 6522, which makes determining what happened rather difficult. In this case, your only alternative is to expose your own error via the SqlPipe, as we'll show you soon. An inelegant workaround is always to use SqlPipe's ExecuteAndSend method inside of a .NET Framework try block that is followed by a dummy (do-nothing) catch block. In this case, provided that you are also using T-SQL's new TRY/CATCH functionality, the outer (6522) error is stripped off, and the actual error information is available through the ERROR_NUMBER, ERROR_MESSAGE, and other new T-SQL functions we'll be looking at soon. Be very careful to keep the 6522 wrapper error in mind as you plan for overall error handling strategy.

To return a custom error, the tried-and-true method is best. In fact, it is the only strategy that works regardless of the client stack you're using and whether or not you're being called by T-SQL:

1. Define your error to the SQL Server error catalog with sp_addmessage.

2. Use the T-SQL RAISERROR command in SqlCommand.Text.

3. Use SqlPipe's ExecuteAndSend method to return the error. Wrap the call to in a .NET Framework try/catch block with an empty catch clause.

Listing 4-23 shows this method.

LISTING 4-23: Returning a user error from a SQLCLR procedure

```
public static SqlInt32 getAuthorWithErrors(
  SqlString au_id, out SqlString au_info)
{
  // -- In SQL Server Management Studio add custom message to be used
  // -- when an author cannot be found
```

```
// sp_addmessage 50005, 16,
//   'author with ssn: %s, not found in the database'
// go

// build a command
SqlConnection conn = new SqlConnection("context connection=true");
conn.Open();
SqlCommand cmd = conn.CreateCommand();
// build command text
cmd.CommandText =
    "select address, city, state, zip" +
    " from authors where au_id = @au_id";

// make a parameter to hold the author id
cmd.Parameters.Add("@au_id", SqlDbType.VarChar);
// put in the value of the author id
cmd.Parameters[0].Value = au_id;

SqlDataReader rec = cmd.ExecuteReader();
// make SqlString to hold result
// note that if you do not give this
// string a value it will be null
au_info = new SqlString();

// check to see if lookup was successful
if (rec.Read() == false)
{
  rec.Close();
  // lookup was not successful, raise an error
  cmd.CommandText = "Raiserror (50005, 16, 1, '" +
    au_id.ToString() +"') with seterror";
  // use the try-catch with empty catch clause
  try   { SqlContext.Pipe.ExecuteAndSend(cmd); }
  catch { }
  // this return statement will never be executed
  return 0;
}
else
{
  // lookup was successful, set au_info to information string
  au_info = String.Format("{0} {1} {2} {3}",
    rec["address"], rec["city"], rec["state"], rec["zip"]);
  rec.Close();
}
// nothing to return, either success returned author info in au_info
// or error was raised
return 0;
}
```

This procedure will return the correct custom error (and not return error 6522) when invoked from T-SQL, whether T-SQL's `@@ERROR` or the new T-SQL `TRY/CATCH` construct is used to return error information.

SqlTriggerContext

SQL triggers have an execution context (represented by `SqlContext`) just as stored procedures and UDFs do. The environment settings, temporary tables in scope, and so on are available to a trigger. But triggers have additional context information; in T-SQL, this information consists of logical tables for DML (data manipulation language) statements, as well as information about which columns were updated, in the case of an update statement. In CLR triggers, this information is made available through the `SqlTriggerContext` class. You obtain the `SqlTriggerContext` through the `SqlContext`, as shown in the following example. `SqlTriggerContext` has a property to tell you whether the triggering action was an `INSERT`, `UPDATE`, `DELETE`, or one of the new DDL or event triggers. This is handy if your trigger handles more than one action. The `IsUpdatedColumn(n)` returns information about whether the *n*th column in the table or view has been changed by the `INSERT` or `UPDATE` statement that caused the trigger to fire. Finally, because SQL Server 2005 adds DDL and Event triggers to the mix, a property that exposes the `EventData` XML structure provides detailed information.

The `INSERTED` and `DELETED` logical tables work the same way that they do in T-SQL triggers; they are visible from any `SqlCommand` that you create inside your trigger. This is shown in Listing 4-24. Because individual SQL statements (including triggers) are transactional, triggers in T-SQL use the `ROLLBACK` statement if the logic in the trigger determines that a business rule has been violated, for example. Although inside a trigger, the context transaction is visible, rolling it back produces an error just as in other CLR procedural code. The way to roll back the statement inside a trigger is to use the `System.Transactions.Transaction.Current` property. Listing 4-24 shows an example of this. Note that this example is meant only to show the coding techniques involved; using T-SQL actually would be a better choice for triggers like this.

LISTING 4-24: A SQLCLR trigger that rolls back the transaction in progress

```csharp
// other using statements elided for clarity
using System.Data.SqlClient;
using System.Transactions;

public static void AddToObsolete()
{
  // get the trigger context so you can tell what is
  // going on
  SqlTriggerContext tc = SqlContext.TriggerContext;

  // this trigger is for deletes
  if (tc.TriggerAction == TriggerAction.Delete)
  {
    // Make a command
    SqlConnection conn = new SqlConnection("context connection=true");
    conn.Open();
    SqlCommand cmd = conn.CreateCommand();
    // make a command that inserts the deleted row into
    // the obsoletejobs table
    cmd.CommandText = "insert into obsoletejobs select * from deleted";

    // move the rows
    int rowsAffected = (int)cmd.ExecuteNonQuery();

    if (rowsAffected == 0)
    {
      // something bad happened, roll back
      Transaction.Current.Rollback();
    }
  }
}
```

SqlClient Classes That You Can't Use on the Server

Although the same provider is used on the client and server, some of the classes that contain ancillary functionality will not be available on the server. Most often, they are not available because they don't make sense inside the database or couldn't be hooked up to the internal context. We've mentioned most of the "prohibited on the server" constructs in the `SqlConnection` and `SqlCommand` sections. Another class that won't work in the server is `SqlBulkCopy`, which you'll see (from the client side) in Chapter 14.

In addition, you must use the `SqlClient`–specific classes inside .NET Framework procedural code. Chapter 14 discusses the fact that .NET Framework data providers are now base class–based. Using the base classes such as `DbConnection`, `DbCommand`, and so on inside the server is not supported. Finally, Chapter 14 discusses the tracing facility in ADO.NET 2.0. This built-in tracing facility is not available inside server code.

Where Are We?

This chapter looked at using the `SqlClient` managed provider inside .NET Framework procedural code in depth. In Chapter 3, however, we stated that T-SQL is almost always best for data-centric code. When, then, is the best time to use the provider in process? These cases include when it's appropriate to mix .NET Framework–specific logic with data access code. Another case might be where structured exception handling is desired. In addition, because the programming model is similar enough (though not identical) to using `SqlClient` on the client, middle tier, and server, some existing .NET Framework code might be moved into the server for locality-of-reference benefits.

◼ 5 ◼
User-Defined Types and Aggregates

S QL SERVER PROVIDES types for scalars like FLOAT and CHAR. These can be represented by a single value, such as a number or a string. Some scalars, such as a date, require more than one value to be represented. A date has a month, day, and year value in its representation. SQL Server provides the DATETIME scalar type for dates. There are other scalars that require more than one value to represent them for which SQL Server does not provide a scalar type. Dimensions in a mechanical drawing, for example, have quantity value and unit value, like "12 in." SQL Server 2005 allows a Common Language Runtime, CLR, language to be used to add scalar types and aggregates to SQL Server that can be used in the same way that any built-in scalar type or aggregate is.

Why Do We Need User-Defined Types?

User-defined types in SQL Server 2005 are used to extend its scalar type system. A column in a table is meant to hold a scalar. If you were given a sample set of data that looked like 12 4 9, 13 5 2, 9 14 11, you would say, "Those are triples of numbers, so each must be a vector, and I will need three columns to represent each one." You would know from experience and the first normal form that trying to squeeze each triple into a single column would be a false economy.

But not all triples are vectors. Consider this set of data: 10 13 1966, 6 15 1915, 7 3 1996. Writing this set as follows might make it clearer that these are dates: 10/13/1966, 6/15/1915, 7/3/1996. Again, from experience, you would know that storing a date in three columns would make it difficult to work with. The triple, in this case, would use a single column. The reason you would want to use a single column is that storing a date in three columns makes no more sense or utility than storing the number 123 in three single-digit columns. The reason you can do this is that the SQL-92 specification realized how important it was to have a scalar type for a date, so it included a number of types for it, including DATETIME, which SQL Server implements.

There are other multifield values that are scalars. Angles, such as latitude and longitude, are written as having four fields: degrees, minutes, seconds, and direction. Geographic Information Systems (GIS) often have values that look like 34°6′12″N, 61° 35′ 19″W. Unfortunately, the SQL Server scalar type system is missing the Latitude and Longitude data types. User-defined types allow you to make your own Latitude and Longitude types and use them in the same convenient way you use the DATETIME type.

Scalars often have type-specific functions associated with them. Numerous functions, for example, such as ASIN and CEILING, are associated with numerical scalars. A user-defined type may also implement functions specifically associated with it. In some cases, it may be useful to implement a user-defined type that is based on a built-in scalar type so that you may encapsulate some functionality with it.

Overview of User-Defined Types

A user-defined type is implemented by a public CLR class that meets a set of requirements discussed later in this chapter. There is no way to implement a user-defined type using Transact-SQL (T-SQL). This class must implement the three key features of a user-defined type: a string representation, a binary representation, and a null representation. The string representation is the form of the user-defined type that a user will see. One string representation of a Date, for example, is "2/5/1988". The binary representation is the form of the user-defined type that SQL Server will use to persist its value on disk. Last, a scalar in SQL Server must be able to have a null value, so the user-defined type must implement this too. See "A Few Words About Null Values" in Chapter 3 for a discussion of null values and their syntax and usage in various languages.

The class that implements the user-defined type must be in an assembly that has been catalogued, as described in Chapter 2, into any database that uses it. The CREATE TYPE command, shown in Figure 5-20 later in this chapter, is used to add the user-defined type in the class to the scalar type system for a database, much as CREATE PROCEDURE, FUNCTION, and TRIGGER are used to add procedures, functions, and triggers based on CLR methods to a database.

User-defined types are similar to the DATETIME type in that they are inserted into a column as a string but stored as a stream of bytes—that is, they are entered using their string representation but stored using their binary representation. Figure 5-1 shows a table, Dates, that has a single column (1) of type DATETIME. A single row is inserted (2) into it. A SELECT statement (3) selects the date in two forms: as a string and as a binary number. The result (4) of the select shows the date as a 16-byte binary number.

This gives us the best of both worlds. We can write and read dates in a familiar notation and conveniently write predicates like (WHERE '1/1/1997' < InstallDate). User-defined types can also support this convenient comparison feature if their binary representation is appropriately designed, though they are not required to.

```
    CREATE TABLE Dates
    (
①    Date DATETIME
    )
②  INSERT INTO Dates VALUES ('10/2/1901')
③  SELECT Date,
        CONVERT(VARBINARY(8), Date) AS Binary
        FROM Dates
```

④

	String	Binary
1	1901-10-02 00:00:00.000	0x0000027F00000000

FIGURE 5-1: Date as binary number

SQL Server 2005 provides a number of aggregate functions, such as MAX and AVG, for many of its scalar types. Likewise, in SQL Server 2005, you can create user-defined aggregates for the user-defined types that you create and for the built-in SQL Server 2005 scalar types. You can also create used-defined aggregates for SQL Server 2005 built-in scalar types.

To illustrate a user-defined type, we will implement one that supports a simple linear dimension that might be used in a mechanical drawing. It is called LDim. An instance of this type will contain a numeric value and units. The units can be any of "in," "ft," or "yd." A typical LDim we might write would look like "1.34 ft" or "7.9 yd". We want to be able to treat LDim as we would any other scalar variable, so we will also implement an aggregate function, SumLDim, for it.

Figure 5-2 shows that a user-defined type, LDim, can be used in the same way as any other scalar. It is used as the data type for the Length and Width columns (1) in a table named Tiles. The string representation (2) of an LDim can be inserted into the Tiles table and can be used as part of a predicate (3) in a query. The results of the query show that tiles 1 and 3 have a Length greater than 18 in. Note that the comparison was done on the actual dimension, not its string representation; tile 1 has a Length of 2 yd, which is, of course, greater than 18 in.

```
     CREATE TABLE Tiles (
     Id INT PRIMARY KEY,
(1)  Length LDim,
     Width LDim
     )
                                           (2)
     INSERT INTO Tiles VALUES (1, '2 yd', '2 in')
     INSERT INTO Tiles VALUES (2, '7 in', '1 in')
     INSERT INTO Tiles VALUES (3, '2 ft', '3 in')
     INSERT INTO Tiles VALUES (4, NULL, NULL)
                                        (3)
     SELECT Id FROM Tiles WHERE Length > '18 in'
```

(4)

	Id
1	1
2	3

FIGURE 5-2: Using a user-defined type

Creating a User-Defined Type

Now we will look at how to create the LDim user-defined type used in the previous example in this chapter. It has two parts: value and units. The value is a numeric, and the units can be one of "in" for inches, "ft" for feet, and "yd" for yard. We are going to add a couple of real-world constraints to it, though.

It is often tempting to say, "There is something we have to measure, so let's just use a double to represent it; that way, we can be sure it will have enough range and accuracy." It is important to determine the range and accuracy of any value you want to store before you select the data type you will use to represent it. In the case of LDim, we want to be able to measure a distance of up to about ten miles with an accuracy of a thousandth of an inch. We also want accurate arithmetic calculation, so we will not want to use either float or double. Any calculation can become inaccurate if it goes though enough operations, of course, but with floats or doubles, the operations that produce inaccurate results can be deceptively simple.

Figure 5-3 shows a comparison of simple arithmetic results using the C# double and decimal data type. Two double types (1) are added, and their nominal sum is subtracted. The result (2) is sent to standard out. The same operation is repeated (3) using the decimal data type, and its result (4) is

```
static void Main(string[] args)
{
① double doubleValue1 = 5.1;
   double doubleValue2 = 0.8;
   double doubleResult =
      doubleValue1 + doubleValue2 - 5.9;
② Console.WriteLine("doubleResult {0}",
      doubleResult);
③ decimal decimalValue1 = 5.1M;
   decimal decimalValue2 =   0.8M;
   decimal decimalResult =
      decimalValue1 + decimalValue2 - 5.9M;
④ Console.WriteLine("decimal result: {0}",
      decimalResult);
}
```

⑤ **C:\WINDOWS\system32\cmd.exe**
```
doubleResult -8.88178419700125E-16
decimal result: 0.0
Press any key to continue . . .
```

FIGURE 5-3: Comparison of numeric results

sent to standard out. Running this program (5) shows that the simple addition operation using double has introduced a small error, but the one using decimal has not.

Does this mean you should always use decimal for arithmetic operations? Definitely not. A CLR decimal data type is larger and operations on it in general are slower than for doubles. It's a matter of deciding what is appropriate for the calculations that will be done with the data.

Note that we have also put limits on both the accuracy—one thousandth of an inch—and range—ten miles—for LDim, because those are the requirements we have. Later, the fact that we have limited LDim to a given range and accuracy will be very useful to us.

The basis of a user-defined type is a public class. In general, any public class, with some limitations, can be the basis of a user-defined type. In practice, the class should represent a scalar value. We will cover the specific limitations and what it means to be a scalar as we go through this chapter.

Figure 5-4 shows a C# struct, which is a class that can be used as the basis of a user-defined type. Note that C# uses the keyword struct to define a *value type*, which is a class that derives from System.ValueType. See the MSDN documentation for a discussion of the tradeoffs between value types and reference types—that is, classes that do not derive from System.ValueType.

There are no strict rules for choosing a value or reference type as the basis for a user-defined type. Value types do not allocate any memory from the heap, so in general, they do not require any resources to be cleaned up. On the other hand, value types must be copied when passed as a parameter or returned as a value, where reference types are not copied. Unfortunately, you cannot start with a value type as the basis for the user-defined

```
namespace Dimensions
{
① public struct LDim
    {
    ② private decimal value;
    ③ private string units;
    }
}
```

FIGURE 5-4: Basis for LDim

type and later change it to a reference type, as that change would quite likely break the code using the user-defined type.

The struct, named LDim, is public (1) and contains two fields. One is value (2), which will hold the numeric part of the dimension. The other is units (3), which will hold the name of the units for the dimension.

Three things must be supported by a user-defined type: a null value representation, a string representation, and a binary representation. The null value representation is supported by implementing the INullable interface and the well-known (a defined requirement rather than inherited from a base class) static property named Null. The string representation is supported by overriding System.Object.ToString method and implementing the well-known method Parse. The binary representation can be implemented by SQL Server 2005 to the CLR or by implementing the IBinarySerialize interface. The size of the binary representation is limited to 8,000 bytes regardless of the implementation. Note that all classes in the CLR ultimately derive from System.Object and can override the ToString method.

Figure 5-5 shows a skeleton of the class we will use to implement LDim. The SqlUserDefinedType attribute (1) decorates the class; this is a requirement of any class that implements a user-defined type. The NULL implementation (2) is the static property Null and the instance property IsNull. The string implementation (3) is the methods ToString and Parse. The binary implementation (4) is the Read and Write methods.

```
namespace Dimensions
{
①  [SqlUserDefinedType(…)]
    public struct LDim : INullable, IBinarySerialize
    {
       private decimal value;
       private string units;
       static public Null {…}
②      public Boolean IsNull() {…}
       public override String ToString() {…}
③      public LDim Parse() {…}
       public void Read(BinaryReader rdr) {…}
④      public void Write(BinaryWriter wtr) {…}
    }
}
```

FIGURE 5-5: Skeleton of LDim implementation

One thing to note about this skeleton is that except for the INullable interface, no base class or interface defines what you must implement—just a number of well-known methods and properties.

Null Value Implementation

Figure 5-6 shows a T-SQL batch that uses NULL in conjunction with a user-defined type, a variable named @ldim of type LDim. SQL Server 2005 uses the static Null property shown in the skeleton in Figure 5-5 to make an instance of LDIM that is a null value, and it assigns (1) to @ldim. SQL Server 2005 uses the IsNull instance property shown in Figure 5-5 to test @ldim (2) to see if it is a null value.

For the example shown in Figure 5-6 to work, the LDim class will need some way to keep track of whether or not an instance is a null value. There are two ways it can do this: One is to have a Boolean field that indicates whether the instance is a null value, and the other is to store values in the value and units fields that are not possible when an instance of LDim is not a null value. LDim uses the latter technique and sets the units field to null to indicate that the instance is a null value.

Figure 5-7 shows how LDim implements the null value representation. The indicator that an instance is a null value is that the units field is null. The IsNull instance property just returns (1) the results of testing the units field to see if it is null.

The static Null property returns a newly created instance of LDim (2). The CLR guarantees that contents of the units field will be null and that the value field will be initialized with zeros.

String Implementation

Figure 5-8 shows a T-SQL batch that uses the string representation of a user-defined type in conjunction with a variable named @ldim of type LDIM. SQL Server 2005 uses the Parse method from the skeleton shown in Figure 5-5 to convert the '1 ft' string to an instance of an LDIM and assign

```
          DECLARE @ldim LDIM
      ① SET @ldim = NULL
      ② IF @ldim IS NULL
             PRINT '@ldim is null'
```

FIGURE 5-6: Using NULL

```
public bool IsNull
{
  get
  {
①    return units == null;
  }
}
public static LDim Null
{
  get
  {
②    return new LDim();
  }
}
}
```

FIGURE 5-7: Implementation
of null

it (1) to @ldim. It uses the ToString() method shown in Figure 5-5 to cast (2) @ldim to a VARCHAR.

The implementation of ToString is less involved than that of Parse, so we will look at that first; it's shown in Figure 5-9. The implementation overrides (1) the ToString method from System.Object, which all classes in the CLR ultimately derive from. See the MSDN documentation for a complete description of the class hierarchy in the CLR.

The ToString implementation first tests (2) to see if the instance of LDIM is a null value. Note that it uses the IsNull property that is part of the null representation implementation. If the instance is not a null value, it returns (3) a string, which is the string representation of the value field concatenated with a space and the units field.

The implementation of the Parse method is a bit more involved, because it has to extract the value and units from a string in a reliable manner. Parse takes a SqlString as an input parameter and returns an instance of an LDim. As with any string passed into a SQL Server stored procedure or function, it is very important that its format be verified before it is used. For example, what would happen if the string "10 light years" was passed in? If its format was not validated, the units field of the LDim struct could be set to

```
DECLARE @ldim LDIM
① SET @ldim = '1 ft'
② PRINT CAST(@ldim AS VARCHAR(50))
```

FIGURE 5-8: Using string

```
      ①
   public override string ToString()
   {
②  if (IsNull)
   {
      return null;
   }
③  return String.Format("{0} {1}", value, units);
   }
```

FIGURE 5-9: Implementation of ToString

an invalid value. In addition, the Parse implementation will have to parse the numeric part of the string and if it is not properly formatted this will throw an exception which the Parse implementation will not be able to control.

An instance of the Regex class, named vu, is initialized with a string, as shown in Figure 5-10. The string that initializes vu is a regular expression that can be used to both validate and parse the input to the Parse method. For convenience, the string that is used to initialize the vu is the concatenation of two strings. The parts of the initialization string enclosed in parentheses are called groups; later, we will see that they can be used to extract the parts of a string that matches regular expression. The first group (1) matches a floating-point number—a sequence of digits with at most a single decimal point. The second group (2) matches the possible units strings that may be used in a LDim.

Figure 5-11 shows the implementation of Parse (1). If the SqlString is null, it returns a LDim (2) that is a null value. Note that the static Null property that is part of the null representation implementation is used to make a null instance of LDim.

The input string is validated (3) by using a regular expression in vu discussed previously. It is beyond the scope of this book to explain the details of regular expressions, but they are the preferred way to validate and parse strings in the CLR. See Chapter 3 for some references to learn about regular expressions.

```
   string fp = @"-?([0-9]+(\.[0-9]*)?|\.[0-9]+)";
   Regex vu = new Regex(
         @"(?<v>" + fp + @")" (?<u>in|ft|yd)");
                    ①              ②
```

FIGURE 5-10: Regular expression for validation

In Figure 5-11, the `IsMatch` method of a `Regex` class tests (3) an input string against the regular expression and returns false if the input string does not match. If it does not match, `Parse` throws an exception. The "Bad format" string thrown in the exception should be more descriptive, but for simplicity of the example, it is not.

The `Match` method of the `Regex` class is used to extract (4) the parts of the strings that match groups in a regular expression. It produces a `Match` object. The `Result` method of a `Match` object can be used to extract the groups by name.

A new instance of an `LDim` is created and will be returned at the end of the method, as shown in Figure 5-11. The string for the units is in the "${u}" group (5), is extracted using the `Result` method of `Match` object, and is then assigned to the units field of the new `LDim`. Likewise, the string for the value is the "${v}" group (6), is extracted using the `Result` method again, and is then converted to a decimal using the static `Parse` method of the decimal class. Note that these strings can be processed further without checking because the overall format was validated by the `IsMatch` method (3).

The last thing `Parse` has to do is check to be sure that the value of the `LDim` meets our range and accuracy requirements. If it does not (7), the `Parse` method throws an exception to indicate this. SQL Server 2005 will

```
① public static LDim Parse(SqlString s)
   {
       if (s.IsNull)
②      return Null;
       string fp = @"-?([0-9]+(\.[0-9]*)?|\.[0-9]+)";
       Regex vu = new Regex(
          @"(?<v>" + fp + @") (?<u>in|ft|yd)");
③    if (!vu.IsMatch(s.Value))
       {
           throw new Exception("Bad format", null);
       }
④    Match m = vu.Match(s.Value);
       LDim d = new LDim();
⑤    d.units = m.Result("${u}");
⑥    d.value = decimal.Parse(m.Result("${v}"));
⑦    if (!CheckRangeAndAccurcy(d))
       {
           throw new Exception(
           "Out of range or accuracy", null);
       }
       return d;
   }
```

FIGURE 5-11: Implementation of parse

send this to the client as a RAISERROR with an error number of 6522. Part of the error message will include the string "Out of range or accuracy" that was part of the exception. Likewise, the exception thrown when the Parse method finds the string not properly formatted results in a 6522 error, but in this case, the error message will have "Bad format" embedded in it.

Figure 5-12 shows the CheckRangeAndAccurcy method that is used to check an LDim to see if it meets our requirement of being no more accurate than one-thousandth of an inch with a range of ten miles.

```
static bool CheckRangeAndAccurcy(LDim d)
{
  decimal value = d.value;
  // check overall range
  if (d.units == "in")
  {
    if ((value > (52800M * 12M)) ||
      (value < -(52800M * 12M)))
    {
      return false;
    }
  }
  if (d.units == "ft")
  {
    if ((value > 52800M) ||
      (value < -52800M))
    {
      return false;
    }
  }
  if (d.units == "yd")
  {
    if ((value > (52800M / 3M)) ||
      (value < -(52800M) / 3M))
    {
      return false;
    }
  }
  // check accuracy to 0.001 inches
  if (d.units == "ft")
  {
    value *= 12M;
  }
  if (d.units == "yd")
  {
    value *= 36M;
  }
  decimal norm = value * 1000M;
  norm = decimal.Round(norm);
  if ((norm - (value * 1000M)) != 0M)
  {
    return false;
  }
  return true;
}
```

FIGURE 5-12: Checking range and accuracy

Binary Implementation

One of the requirements of a user-defined type is that the class that implements it must be decorated with a `SqlUserDefinedType` attribute, as shown in the skeleton in Figure 5-5 earlier in this chapter. The `SqlUserDefined-Type` attribute is used to specify how the binary representation will be implemented. There are two choices for implementing the binary representation: SQL Server 2005 can do the implementation, or the class itself can do the implementation.

The Format property of the `SqlUserDefinedType` attribute indicates how the binary representation will be implemented. `SqlUserDefinedType.Format=UserDefined` indicates that the class will implement `IBinary Serialize` to implement the binary representation.

`SqlUserDefinedType.Format=Format.Native` indicates that SQL Server will implement the binary representation. SQL Server can implement the binary representation only if all the fields in the class, even private ones, come from a restricted set of data types. The acceptable data types are listed in Figure 5-13. There is no default value for `SqlUserDefinedType.Format`; it must be specified. We will look at using `Format.Native` later in this chapter, in the section on user-defined aggregates. User-defined aggregates have the same serialization issues as user-defined types.

`LDim` has member fields of type string and decimal, neither of which is listed in Figure 5-13, so `LDim` must use `SqlUserDefinedType.Format=Format. UserDefined`. When `Format.UserDefined` is used, SQL Server 2005 requires other pieces of information.

SQL Server will store the binary representation of `LDim` in a stream, and it needs to know how much space to allocate in that stream for it. The `MaxByteSize` property (2), shown in Figure 5-14, is the maximum number of bytes that the binary representation might require. As noted earlier, `MaxByteSize` may not be greater than 8,000. If `SqlFormatUserDefined-Type.Format=Format.UserDefined`, `MaxByteSize` must be specified; otherwise, it may not be specified.

Just as there is a tradeoff between fixed and variable sized strings in T-SQL, there is one for `SqlUserDefinedType.Format=Format.UserDefined`. If the length of the stream required to store the binary representation is fixed, SQL Server 2005 can store it more efficiently if it knows this. The `SqlUserDe-finedType.IsFixedLength=true` (3) indicates that this is the case for `LDim`. The default value for `SqlUserDefinedType.IsFixedLength` is false.

System.Boolean

System.Byte

System.SByte

System.Int16

System.Int32

System.Int64

System.UInt16

System.UInt32

System.UInt64

System.Single

System.Double

System.Data.SqlTypes.SqlBoolean

System.Data.SqlTypes.SqlByte

System.Data.SqlTypes.Int16

System.Data.SqlTypes.SqlInt32

System.Data.SqlTypes.DateTime

System.Data.SqlTypes.SqlMoney

System.Data.SqlTypes.SqlDouble

System.Data.SqlTypes.SqlSingle

System.Data.SqlTypes.SqlInt64

FIGURE 5-13: Format=Native data types

When `SqlUserDefinedType.Format=Format.UserDefined` is used, the `SqlUserDefinedType.IsByteOrdered` property indicates whether an instance of the type can be sorted; true indicates it can be sorted, and false indicates that it cannot be sorted. Sorting is not automatically provided for user-defined types; the implementation has to take this into account, which we will see shortly. `LDim` will be sortable (4). The default value for `SqlUserDefinedType.IsByteOrdered` is `false`, and it must be `false` when `SqlUserDefinedType.Format=Format.Native`.

Figure 5-14 shows the `SqlUserDefined` attribute used to decorate the `LDim` class.

```
① [SqlUserDefinedType(Format.UserDefined,
②   MaxByteSize = 5,
③   IsFixedLength = true,
④   IsByteOrdered = true
   )]
```

FIGURE 5-14: SqlUserDefinedType for LDim

SQL Server 2005 sorts user-defined types with `SqlUserDefinedType`. `Format=Format.UserDefined` by the byte, from high-order byte to low-order byte. Figure 5-15 shows a table, named `BOrder`, that contains a single column (1) of type `VARBINARY`. `BOrder` is filled (2) with four rows. The rows are selected (3) and sorted. The results (4) show that the byte, starting with the high-order byte, of the binary data is sorted, then the next, and so on. Binary data is byte ordered, and user-defined types are sorted as binary data based on their binary representation, if `SqlUserDefinedType`. `IsByteOrdered=true`.

IBinarySerialize.Read/Write

The `IBinarySerialize` interface has two methods in it: `Write` and `Read`. The `Write` method has a single parameter: a `BinaryWriter` that is used to write the binary representation. A trivial implementation of the `Write` method (1) is shown in Figure 5-16. It uses the built-in serialization

```
CREATE TABLE BOrder
(
① data VARBINARY(10)
)

② INSERT INTO BOrder values (0xFFA012)
   INSERT INTO BOrder values (0x0ABC)
   INSERT INTO BOrder values (0x19A0)
   INSERT INTO BOrder values (0x0A11BC)

③ SELECT * FROM BOrder ORDER BY data
```

④

	data
1	0x0A11BC
2	0x0ABC
3	0x19A0
4	0xFFA012

FIGURE 5-15: Sort by byte

```
① public void Write(System.IO.BinaryWriter w)
  {
     // serialize intance into w
② w.Write(value);
③ w.Write(units);
  }
```

FIGURE 5-16: Trivial implementation of write

capability of the CLR to write the `value` (2) and `units` (3) into the stream passed into the Write method.

The trivial Write implementation shown in Figure 5-16 is not suitable for LDim, because one of the requirements of LDim is that it be sortable. The implementation of the binary representation must ensure that it is byte ordered. The binary representation of CLR numeric types are not byte ordered. Figure 5-17 shows a numeric sort of decimal numbers minus one, zero, and one compared with a byte-order sort of the same numbers. To the right of each number is its binary representation when serialized by the CLR. Note that the high-order byte of the number zero is zero, so it will come before the number minus one and one because the value of their high-order byte is one.

One way to force the binary representation is to encode the value of the user-defined type so that it is byte ordered. In general, making a byte-ordered encoding is a bit of work. LDim encodes the value and units into 5 bytes. It makes use of the fact that unsigned integers are, in fact, byte ordered.

Figure 5-18 shows the implementation of `Write` and `Read` for `IBinary-Serialize`. Some helper methods that we will look at later in this chapter

numeric sort

```
-1 0100000000000000000000000000000080
 0 0000000000000000000000000000000000
 1 0100000000000000000000000000000000
```

byte order sort

```
 0 0000000000000000000000000000000000
 1 0100000000000000000000000000000000
-1 0100000000000000000000000000000080
```

decimal binary representation

FIGURE 5-17: Comparison of numeric and byte-ordered sort

```
public void Write(System.IO.BinaryWriter w)
{
① byte[] bytes = ToBytes();
   foreach (byte b in bytes)
   {
② w.Write(b);
   }
}

public void Read(System.IO.BinaryReader r)
{
③ byte[] bytes = r.ReadBytes(5);
④ FromBytes(bytes);
}
```

FIGURE 5-18: Implementation of write and read

are involved. The Write method uses the ToBytes helper method to convert the value of LDim to an array (1) of 5 bytes. It writes (2) those bytes into the stream provided by SQL Server 2005.

The Read method works in a complementary fashion. It reads 5 bytes (3) from the stream provided by SQL Server 2005 and then uses the FromBytes helper method to convert the array to an LDim.

All implementations of IBinarySerialize work this way; they convert the value they represent to or from a stream of bytes. The real effort, of course, is in those helper methods.

The basic algorithm to convert an LDim to a stream of bytes is to normalize the LDim to inches and break it into four parts. The top of Figure 5-19 shows how the normalized LDim is broken into its constituent parts, which are a sign, a normalized whole number of inches, the number of thousandths, and the units. The bottom shows how the parts are mapped into

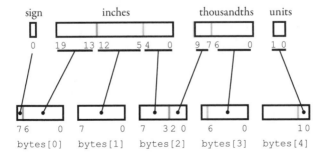

FIGURE 5-19: Encoding of LDim

5 bytes, which in turn are written and read by the `Write` and `Read` functions shown in Figure 5-18.

The actual mapping is done by several helper methods that are in the source for the `LDim` class shown in Listing 5-1 later in this chapter. The `MoveBitsFromIntToByte` method masks bits from and maps them into a byte. `MoveBitsFromIntToByte` (i, 3, 5, ref b, 1), for example, will copy bits 3 though 7 from `int` i into bits 1 through 4 in `byte` b. The `MoveBits-FromByteToInt` complements this method by moving bits from a `byte` into an `int`. The `FromBytes` and `ToBytes` methods are used by the `MoveBits-FromIntToByte` and `MoveBitsFromByteToInt` to encode `LDim` into/from bytes, as shown in Figure 5-19.

Creating User-Defined Types

The `CREATE TYPE` statement in T-SQL is used to create a user-defined type that is implemented by the CLR. Figure 5-20 shows a user-defined type being loaded prior to use. Before the user-defined type can be loaded, the assembly that contains it must be catalogued (1), as with any type of CLR extension to SQL Server 2005 and as discussed in Chapter 2. The `CREATE TYPE` statement names the type (3) and, in a way similar to CLR-based functions and stored procedures, identifies the class that implements the user-defined type with a two-part (2) `EXTERNAL NAME`. The parts are separated by a period. The `CREATE TYPE` statement in Figure 5-20 adds a new type to SQL Server 2005: `LDim`, which is implemented by the class `Dimensions.LDim` in the assembly named `Geo`.

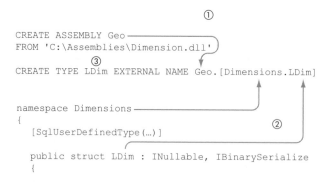

FIGURE 5-20: Creating a user-defined type

Figure 5-21 shows LDim being used in a T-SQL batch. A variable of type LDim is set to '1 ft'. It is selected both in its raw form (1) and cast (2) to an VARCHAR. The results (3) show that the raw representation is a binary number, not the string representation of an LDim. It might seem strange that selecting an LDim does not automatically produce its string representation, but the code required to do this is part of the class that implements LDim. SQL Server 2005 streams the binary representation of a user-defined type to the client, not the string representation.

The results shown in Figure 5-21 were produced by SQL Server Management Studio, but any client application would have the same results. As Chapter 13 shows, a client application could use the LDim class to convert the binary representation to the string representation. Both SQL Server Management Studio and SQLCMD, however, prevent the use of the class that implements a user-defined type to minimize the security surface area of those products.

SQL Server Management Studio and SQLCMD must convert a user-defined type to a string representation on the server if they want the string representation. Both disallow the use of the assemblies that implement user-defined types to minimize their surface area for security purposes. The examples in the rest of this chapter use the CAST function to do this. Later, we will see that T-SQL can access the public methods of a user-defined type, so the ToString method could also be used to convert a user-defined type to a string on the server.

Figure 5-22 shows LDim in use. The Tiles table shown in Figure 5-2 earlier in this chapter has been loaded with different data (1). The rows are selected from the Tiles table ordered by Length (2). The results (3) show that NULL is sorted first. The figure also shows that negative dimensions are

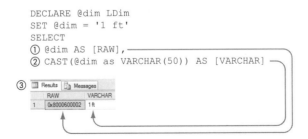

Figure 5-21: Casting LDim to VARCHAR

```
① INSERT INTO Tiles VALUES(1, '12.001 in', '0 in')
  INSERT INTO Tiles VALUES(2, '2 ft', '-1 in')
  INSERT INTO Tiles VALUES(3, NULL, '-1 in')
  INSERT INTO Tiles VALUES(4, '-200 yd', '-1 in')
  INSERT INTO Tiles VALUES(5, '-600.001 ft', '-1 in')
② SELECT CAST(Length AS VARCHAR(20)),
  CAST(Width AS VARCHAR(20)),
  ID FROM Tiles
  ORDER BY Length
```

③

	Len	Width	ID
1	NULL	-10 in	3
2	-600.001 ft	-1 in	5
3	-600 ft	-1 in	6
4	-200 yd	-1 in	4
5	-200 ft	-1 ft	7
6	0 ft	-1 in	13
7	1 ft	-21 in	9
8	12.001 in	0 in	1
9	1.001 ft	-31 in	11
10	1.1 ft	-1 yd	10
11	2 ft	-19 in	2
12	20 ft	-1 in	8
13	52800 ft	-1 in	12

FIGURE 5-22: Selecting and sorting user-defined types

sorted before zero, which in turn is sorted before the positive dimensions. Also note that 12.001 in is sorted before 1.001 ft, as it should be.

User-defined types like LDim can be used in comparison predicates. too. Figure 5-23 shows a SELECT statement (1) that selects tiles whose length is greater than 1.02 ft and less than 3 yd. The results (2) show that only two of the tiles in this table meet the criteria expressed in the predicate.

Typically, it is a fair amount of work to get a byte-ordered representation of a user-defined type. It is worth the effort, though, because when completed, that value can easily be treated the same way as any other scalar in SQL Server 2005.

SQL Server 2005 will not use the IComparable interface if a user-defined type implements it. Implementing it, however, is good practice so that client code that uses the user-defined type has access to it. IComparable is the

```
① SELECT CAST(Length AS VARCHAR(20)) AS Length,
  ID FROM Tiles
  WHERE Length > '1.02 ft'
  AND Length < '3 yd'
```

②

	Length	ID
1	2 ft	2
2	1.1 ft	10

FIGURE 5-23: UDT and comparison

CLR interface that by convention implements comparison. The `System.Array.Sort` method in the CLR uses it, for example. See "IComparable" in the MSDN documentation for a discussion of it.

Public Properties, Fields, and Methods

A user-defined type is a class. It is common to encapsulate into a class methods that can be used on instances of that class. SQL Server 2005 supports this programming technique for user-defined types. Every public field, method, and read–write property in the class that implements a user-defined type can be accessed with T-SQL as long as it involves data types that T-SQL understands. In some cases, a dotted syntax is used; in others, a double-colon syntax is used.

Any public-instance property or field in the class that implements a user-defined type can be accessed by T-SQL through a dotted syntax. Figure 5-24 shows the `Inches` property that is part of the class that implements `LDim`. The `Inches` property is public and of type `SqlDecimal` (1). The `SqlFacet` attribute is used to specify the precision and scale of the returned value. The `get` (2) method of the property converts the value to inches, if needed, and returns it. The `set` method of the property will not set a null instance of an `LDim` to a value; because nulls are immutable, they may not be changed into a concrete value.

```
① [SqlFacet(Precision = 9, Scale = 3)]
  public SqlDecimal Inches   {
② get {
      SqlDecimal d;
      if (IsNull) return SqlDecimal.Null;
      if (units == "in") {
        return this.value;
      }
      if (units == "ft") {
        d = this.value * 12.0M;
        return this.value * 12.0M;
      }
      return 36.0M * this.value;
    }
③ set {
      if (units != null) {
        this.value = value.Value;
        units = "in";
      }
    }
  }
```

FIGURE 5-24: Inches property

The SqlFacet attribute is used by SQL Server 2005 to determine characteristics of values returned from methods, parameters, properties, and fields. The SqlFacet attribute can be used to specify the maximum length of a returned SqlString. Figure 5-25 shows the usage of SqlFacet in a C# method and the equivalent type usage in a T-SQL function. See "SqlFacetAttribute" in the MSDN documentation for a more detailed discussion.

Figure 5-26 shows the Inches property being used in a SELECT (1) expression. A SELECT uses the get method of a property. The Length column from the Tiles tables, used in the previous example, has a period and the name of the property, Length, appended to it. This produces (2) a column with the dimension converted to inches.

A property of a user-defined type can also be used to update or set it. Figure 5-27 shows an UPDATE expression being used to set (1) the Length column of the Tiles table to 10 inches. The SELECT statement that follows (2) shows (3) that the column was set to 10 inches.

A common object-oriented technique is to encapsulate the methods used to manipulate an object with the class for the object; these are sometimes called instance methods because you call them on an instance of the class. SQL Server 2005 supports this in user-defined types by allowing any public method or property to be accessed by appending a period and its name to a column or variable that is of that user-defined type.

Figure 5-28 shows the LDim class in skeleton form (Listing 5-1 later in this chapter shows the complete source code for LDim), the public members of the LDim class being accessed from T-SQL, and the results of the T-SQL usage. Note that a C# struct is a class in the CLR.

```
[return:SqlFacet(MaxSize=30)]
public SqlString GetDescription(
  [SqlFacet(MaxSize=-1)]
  SqlString intro,
  [SqlFacet(Scale=8, Precision=4)]
  SqlDecimal weight)
{
...

CREATE FUNCTION GetDescription(@intro NVARCHAR(MAX),
  @weight DECIMAL(8, 4))
  RETURNS NVARCHAR(30)
AS
...
```

FIGURE 5-25: Using SqlFacet

```
  SELECT CAST(Length as VARCHAR(50)) as [LEN],
① Length.Inches AS Inches
  FROM Tiles
```

②
7	-200 ft	-2400.000
8	20 ft	240.000
9	1 ft	12.000
10	1.1 ft	13.200

FIGURE 5-26: Selecting the inches property

Inches (1) is a public-instance property—that is, a property that can be accessed though an instance of the LDim class. The Inches property represents the value of the LDim instance in inches. In the CLR, a property may have a get and a set method. The set method modifies the value of the property and is accessed in T-SQL by appending a period and the name of the property to a T-SQL variable or column and using it in a statement that modifies a value—in this example, SET @dim.Inches='1 ft'.

The get method of a property is accessed with the same syntax as the set method but is used in a statement that returns a value—in this example, SELECT @dim.Inches. Note that a public field in a class is accessed the same way as a public property.

A static field in the CLR is a field that is marked as static and that may be accessed without using an instance of the class. Setback (2) is a public, static field in LDim. Note that Setback is also marked as read-only, as it is meant to be a source of a constant. There is no requirement for a static field to be marked as read-only, but if it is not marked read-only, the assembly that contains it must be catalogued with PERMISSION_SET=UNSAFE, which in practice greatly limits its utility.

T-SQL can access a static field by prefacing it with the name of the user-defined type and two colons. When used in a statement that returns a

```
  UPDATE Tiles
① SET Length.Inches = 10 WHERE ID = 7

② SELECT CAST(Length as VARCHAR(50)) AS Length
  from Tiles WHERE ID = 7
```

③
	Length
1	10 in

FIGURE 5-27: Updating the property

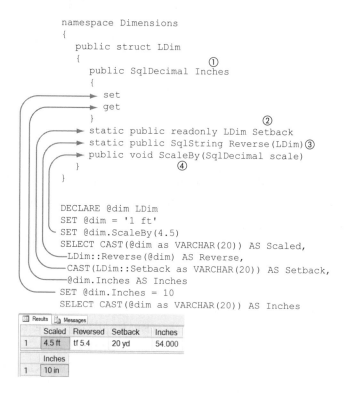

FIGURE 5-28: Using methods, fields, and properties

value—in this example, SELECT LDim::Setback—the value of the static field is returned. It is possible to modify a static field in T-SQL if it is not marked as read-only in the CLR, but again, this practice is not recommended.

Reverse (3) is a static-instance method in the LDim class that returns the reversed string representation of the instance of LDim passed into it. T-SQL can access a static method in a class by prefacing the method name with the name of the user-defined type and two colons—LDim::Reverse, in this example.

T-SQL can access a public-instance method of a class (a method that is not marked as static) by appending a period and the name of the method to a variable or column. ScaleBy (4) is a public-instance method—in this example, the LDim class that modifies the value of the instance by scaling it by the parameter passed into it. In this example, T-SQL accesses it as SET @dim.ScaleBy(4.5).

Figure 5-28 and the explanation accompanying it show the usage of member of a class that defines a user-defined type but do not show the metadata

SQL Server 2005 needs to manage the usage of these members. The `ScaleBy` instance method, for example, changes the value of a variable or column and so may not be used in a `SELECT` statement. A method that changes the value of an instance of a user-defined type is said to be a *mutator.*

`ToString` is an example of one of the public-instance methods in `LDim`. One of the public properties in `LDim` is `IsNull`. Note that a property in the CLR is just shorthand for creating a related pair of `set` and `get` methods, so it also is an instance method. Both of these can be accessed by T-SQL.

T-SQL can access any public method of a user-defined type if its return value and parameters can be mapped to T-SQL types. There are in essence two kinds of methods: those that can change the value of the instance of the user-defined type they are associated with and those that can't. A method that can change the value of an instance of a user-defined type is said to be a mutator. The `SqlMethod` attribute is used to specify this.

Methods that are mutators must set the `IsMutator` property of the `SqlMethod` attribute to `true` and return a void. Those that can't change the value set the `IsMutator` property of the `SqlMethod` to false and return a scalar value.

The `SqlMethod` attribute derives from the `SqlFunction` attribute and in usage is much like a `SqlFunction`. All the parameters for a `SqlMethod` must be input parameters; no out or ref parameters are allowed. `Sql-Method` adds three properties to `SqlFunction`: `IsMutator`, `OnNullCall`, and `InvokeIfReceiverIsNull`. A SqlMethod may not use the `Table Definition` or `FillRowMethodName` properties, because a `SqlMethod` may not return a table—only a scalar or user-defined type.

Figure 5-29 shows an instance method, `ScaleBy`, that is part of the `LDim` user-defined type. Its purpose is to scale the `LDim` it is associated with by the scale factor passed in to it. The `SqlMethod` attribute has the `IsMutator` property (1) set to `true`. The `IsMutator` property indicates to SQL Server 2005 that this method may change the value of the `LDim` and will limit its use to those places where side effects are allowed—that is, not in a `SELECT` statement. It is important to set the value of `IsMutator` properly to reflect what the method actually does, because if it is incorrectly set, it may lead to hard-to-diagnose bugs or corrupted data in a database.

The `OnNullCall` property indicates how SQL Server 2005 should treat calls to this method if one of the input parameters is a null value.

```
             ①                        ②
[SqlMethod(IsMutator=true, OnNullCall=true)]
public void ScaleBy(SqlDecimal scale)
{
③if (!IsNull && !scale.IsNull)
  {
    Decimal oldValue = this.value;
    this.value *= scale.Value;
  ④if (!CheckRangeAndAccurcy(this))
    {
      this.value = oldValue;
    }
  }
}
```

FIGURE 5-29: User-defined-type mutator method

If OnNullCall = false, SQL Server 2005 will shortcut things by not calling this method if it is invoked with any null parameters and directly return a NULL. If OnNullCall = true, SQL Server 2005 will call this method even if some of the parameters are null values.

In the case of the ScaleBy method in Figure 5-29, OnNullCall = true (2). The ScaleBy method must check (3) to make sure that both its instance and input parameters are not null values and make no changes to the LDim if either is a null value. When it does make a change, it checks that change (4) to see whether the new value is in an acceptable range and accuracy. If not, the method reverts to the original value.

Figure 5-30 shows the use of the ScaleBy method. An LDim variable, @d1, is set (1) to 1.1 ft. Next, it is changed (2) by use of the ScaleBy instance method. The results (3) show the ScaleBy method multiplied @d1 to 2.2 ft, as expected.

A user-defined type method that uses IsMutator=false may return a value and be used in a SELECT or similar statement. Figure 5-31 shows the GetScaled method. It returns a new LDim that is a scaled version of the LDim on which it was called. OnNullCall = false (1) for this method,

```
DECLARE @d1 LDIM
① SET @d1 = '1.1 ft'
② SET @d1.ScaleBy(2.0)
   SELECT CAST(@d1 as VARCHAR(50))

③   Amount
   1  2.2ft
```

FIGURE 5-30: Using ScaleBy

```
① [SqlMethod(IsMutator = false, OnNullCall = false)]
  public LDim GetScaled(SqlDecimal scale)
  {
   LDim ldim = new LDim();
② if (!IsNull)
   {
    ldim.value = this.value;
    ldim.units = this.units;
    ldim.value *= scale.Value;
③ if (!CheckRangeAndAccurcy(ldim))
    {
     ldim = this;
    }
   }
   return ldim;
  }
```

FIGURE 5-31: User-defined-type nonmutator method

which means that if the scale input parameter is a null value, SQL Server 2005 will not call this method but directly return a NULL. Unlike the ScaleBy method, this method will not be called by T-SQL if the scale parameter is a null value, but it does check it for null value for those cases where it is used outside T-SQL. Like ScaleBy, this method also checks to make sure that the new LDim is in the proper range and accuracy. If not, the method returns a copy of the original value.

Note that SQL Server Management Studio (SSMS) treats null instances of a user-defined type as an error, which is different from the way it treats a built-in scalar type that is a null value, as shown in Figure 5-32.

Figure 5-33 shows the use of the GetScaled method. An LDim variable, @dim, is set to 1 ft. Then a SELECT statement uses the return value of the

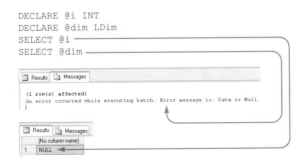

FIGURE 5-32: NULL user-defined type

```
    DECLARE @dim LDIM
①  SET @dim = '1 ft'
②  SELECT CAST(@dim.GetScaled(2) AS VARCHAR(MAX))

③  │ (No column name) │
   │ 1 │ 2 ft │
```

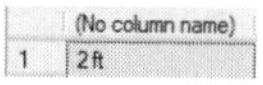

FIGURE 5-33: Using GetScaled

GetScaled method (2). The result (3) shows that the value of the returned LDim is twice that of the original.

There is a difference between user-defined-type instance methods and those in object-oriented languages. An instance method may be invoked on a user-defined type if the method is marked IsMutator = false. Figure 5-34 shows an LDIM variable, @dim, being set to NULL (1). Next, the GetScaled method is called (2) on it. It succeeds and returns (3) a NULL instance of an LDIM.

Invoking an instance method of a user-defined type that is a null value and that is marked IsMutator = true will produce a runtime error.

The InvokeIfReceiverIsNull property of the SqlMethod attribute determines what SQL Server 2005 will do if an instance method is called on a null value. By default, InvokeIfReceiverIsNull is false, and SQL Server 2005 will not call the method but instead will directly return NULL. This is the case for the example in Figure 5-34.

If InvokeIfReceiverIsNull=true, the method will be called even if the instance is a null value. This means that SQL Server 2005 will make an instance of the user-defined type using the static Null property of the class that implements the user-defined type, call the method on that instance, and then not use that instance again.

```
    DECLARE @i INT
    DECLARE @dim LDim
    IF @i IS NULL print '@i is null'
①  IF @dim IS NULL print 'IS NULL @dim is null'
②  IF @dim.IsNull=1  print 'IsNull @dim is null'
    SELECT @dim.IsNull

    ▣ Results │ Messages
    │ (No column name) │
    │ 1 │ NULL ◄
    
    ▣ Results │ Messages
    @i is null
    IS NULL @dim is null
    ◄
    (1 row(s) affected)
```

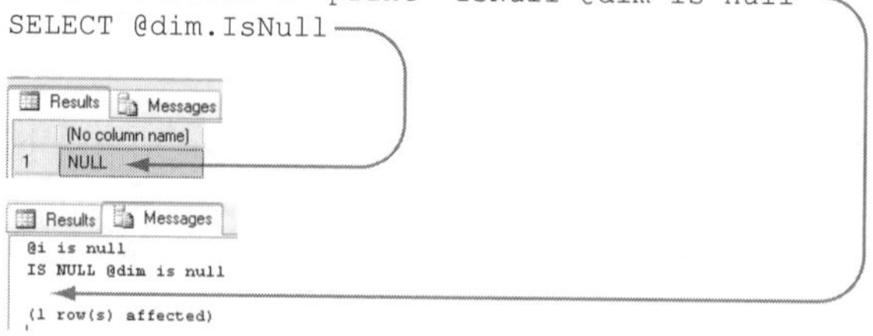

FIGURE 5-34: Using method on null instance

The best practice for testing a variable or column to see if it is null is to use the IS NULL clause. This works for user-defined types in the same way as it does for built-in scalars, as shown (1) in Figure 5-35.

Every user-defined type, however, implements the IsNull property that will return a true if the user-defined type is null. This may produce unexpected results when invoked from T-SQL. The IsNull property of a user-defined property will return NULL, not one, if the get method of the IsNull property is not attributed with [SqlUserDefinedType(InvokeIf ReceiverIsNull=true)]. The result, shown in Figure 5-35, is that a null value may appear not to be a null value (2) when in fact it is.

There is no way to prevent a T-SQL user from invoking the IsNull property of a user-defined type, which in turn will lead to unexpected results. Because of this, it is a best practice to include InvokeIfReceiverIs-Null=true on the get method of the IsNull property of a user-defined type, as shown in Figure 5-36, to force SQL Server 2005 to call the IsNull property in all cases and get the appropriate zero or one value.

Helper Functions

Chapter 3 discusses using the static methods of a CLR class to make functions that T-SQL can use. These functions can return or use as parameters user-defined types. Table 3-3 in Chapter 3 lists the standard operators used in the CLR—for example, op_Addition. In general, it is a good idea to implement those operators that make sense for a user-defined type.

Figure 5-37 shows a static method that implements the + operator (2) for the LDim class. The + operator in C# is mapped to the op_Addition method. This method is decorated with the SqlFunction attribute. The Name property of the SqlFunction attribute is set to "LDimAdd" (1). SQL Server 2005 does not use this property, but Visual Studio 2005 does when it deploys this function. Even if Visual Studio 2005 is not going to be used to deploy this function, this is a good place to note what it should be named in SQL Server 2005.

```
     DECLARE @dim LDIM
 ①  SET @dim = NULL
 ②  SELECT CAST(@dim.GetScaled(2) AS VARCHAR(MAX))

 ③    (No column name)
     1   NULL
```

FIGURE 5-35: Comparing iS NULL to IsNull

```
public bool IsNull
{
    [SqlMethod(InvokeIfReceiverIsNull=true)]
    get
    {
        return units == null;
    }
}
```

FIGURE 5-36: Ensuring that IsNull works as
expected

There is no requirement that a function that uses a particular user-
defined type as a parameter or return value be implemented in the same
class as the user-defined type itself, but sometimes, as in this case, it is convenient to use this implementation.

The method in Figure 5-37 returns a null instance of LDim if (3) either of
the input parameters is null. If both of the input parameters have the same
units (4), those units are used for the return value. If the units are different,
inches (5) are used for the units of the return value.

Figure 5-38 shows the LDimAdd (1) function being used by T-SQL. Note
that T-SQL never uses any of the arithmetic operators for a user-defined
type; it can use the function only by name. The results show (3) that the
units were preserved and that the dimensions were added.

```
① [SqlFunction(Name = "LDimAdd")]
   static public LDim
② operator +(LDim d1, LDim d2)
   {
③ if (d1.IsNull || d2.IsNull)
      {
          return Null;
      }
④ if (d1.units == d2.units)
      {
          LDim dim = new LDim();
          dim.units = d1.units;
          dim.value = d1.value + d2.value;
          return dim;
      }
⑤ LDim dim1 = new LDim();
   dim1.units = "in";
   dim1.value =
      d1.Inches.Value + d2.Inches.Value;
   return dim1;
   }
```

FIGURE 5-37: Implementing add

```
      DECLARE @d1 LDim
      DECLARE @d2 LDim
      DECLARE @dsum LDim
      SET @d1 = '1 ft'
      SET @d2 = '2 ft'
   ①SET @dsum = dbo.LDimAdd(@d1, @d2)
      SELECT CAST(@dsum as VARCHAR(50))
```

(No column name)
② 1   3 ft

FIGURE 5-38: Using add

Why go to the trouble of implementing "operator +" and renaming it for SQL Server 2005 instead of just naming it LDimSum in the first place? There are a couple of reasons for this. In C# and most CLR languages, the actual name of "operator +" is always op_Addition for all data types. T-SQL cannot deal with method overloading, so it would be possible to implement "operator +" for only a single user-defined data type.

Figure 5-39 shows an example of a C# console application (1) that uses the LDim user-defined data type. Another reason to implement the "+" (2) is that it allows client-side applications that use user-defined types to use standard operator symbols to manipulate them.

So the real reason to implement "operator +", and all the other arithmetic operators in the CLR, is to make it easier to use the user-defined type in CLR languages. One of the strengths of a user-defined type is that it can be used in both T-SQL and CLR languages. Chapter 13 shows how to return an instance of a user-defined type to a client program.

User-Defined-Type Validation

It is possible to insert a value into any an instance of any SQL Server 2005 scalar data type just by inserting its binary representation. Figure 5-40

```
① static void Main(string[] args)
   {
       LDim d1 = LDim.Parse("1 ft");
       LDim d2 = LDim.Parse("3 ft");
   ② LDim d3 = d1 + d2;
       Console.WriteLine(d3);
   }
```

FIGURE 5-39: Client program using
LDimAdd

```
      DECLARE @d1 LDim
  ①  SET @d1 = CAST(0xCD59000002 as LDIM)
  ②  SELECT CAST(@d1 as VARCHAR(50))
```

③

(No column name)
1 52802.6666666666666666666667 ft

FIGURE 5-40: Invalid LDim

shows an LDim variable, @d1, being set (1) with a 5-byte binary number. Doing a SELECT (2) on @d1 and casting to a string shows (3) that its value is 52802.6666666666666666666667 ft.

This value is invalid according to the limits on both range and accuracy we specified for LDim at the beginning of this chapter. In fact, Figure 5-41 shows that if we try to SET an LDim variable (1) with the value 52802.666-6666666666666666667 ft, it produces an "Out of range or accuracy" error (2) from the code that LDim uses to check range and accuracy.

Invalid direct binary input of data can be prevented by adding a validation method to the LDim implementation. We almost have one already: the static bool CheckRangeAndAccurcy(LDim d) in LDim that the Parse and other methods use to validate input, except that it does not have the correct signature. A validation method must be an instance method, return a Boolean, and take no parameters. A return value of false indicates that the LDim is not valid.

The CheckDirectInput method is shown in Figure 5-42. The ValidationMethodName property (1) of the SqlUserDefinedType attribute is used to indicate the method (2) that SQL Server 2005 should use to validate any binary input directly inserted into an LDim. SQL Server 2005 uses this method whenever it casts a value to a user-defined type, for example.

```
      DECLARE @d1 LDim
  ①  SET @d1 = '52802.6666666666666666666667 ft'

      Msg 6522, Level 16, State 2, Line 2
      A .NET Framework error occurred during execution
      of user defined routine or aggregate 'LDim':
  ②  System.Exception: Out of range or accuracy
      System.Exception:
      at Dimensions.LDim.Parse(SqlString s)
```

FIGURE 5-41: Range error

```
  [SqlUserDefinedType(Format.UserDefined,
  MaxByteSize = 5,
  IsFixedLength = true,
  IsByteOrdered = true,
① ValidationMethodName="CheckDirectInput"
  )]
  public struct LDim : INullable, IBinarySerialize


② bool CheckDirectInput()
  {
      return CheckRangeAndAccurcy(this);
  }
③ static bool CheckRangeAndAccurcy(LDim d)
  {
```

FIGURE 5-42: Validation method

The `CheckDirectInput` method delegates the actual checking to the `CheckRangeAndAccurcy` method (3) that `LDim` already uses to check input from the `Parse` method.

Figure 5-43 shows that if an out-of-range or -accuracy binary number is inserted into an `LDim` (1), it will produce an error that shows that the validate method (2) `LDim` class has failed.

Maintaining User-Defined-Type Definitions

There are two ways to replace a user-defined type. One is to use DROP TYPE followed by CREATE TYPE. The other is to use the ALTER ASSEMBLY command to replace the assembly that contains the implementation of the user-defined type.

Changing a user-defined type is a fundamental change to a database. Think about how you would feel if Microsoft said it was going to change how

```
  DECLARE @d1 LDim
① SET @d1 = CAST(0xCD59000002 as LDIM)

  Msg 6522, Level 16, State 2, Line 2
  A .NET Framework error occurred during execution of
  user defined routine or aggregate 'LDim':
  System.Data.SqlServer.Internal.UdtValidationException:
② The Validate Method of the UDT has return False
  System.Data.SqlServer.Internal.UdtValidationException:
      at LDim::.DeserializeValidate(IntPtr , LDim& )
```

FIGURE 5-43: Validation error

the SQL DECIMAL data type works, even if Microsoft said it would just "improve the accuracy of decimal." The fact that calculations you had done in the past might produce different, albeit more accurate, results could easily have an overwhelming impact on your database, because things that compared as equal in the past might not do so after the change. You must keep this level of impact in mind whenever you make a change to a user-defined type.

The safest way to change a user-defined type is to export tables that refer to the type to a text file using SQL Server Integration Services (SSIS), drop and re-create the type and everything that references it, and then reload the tables. You will not miss anything that refers to the user-defined type, because you cannot drop a type if any table, stored procedure, and so on references it. All UDTs, by definition, support conversion to and from a string, so SSIS will work with any UDT.

This is safest because it guarantees that any changes to the semantics of the type and how it is represented will be propagated to the entire database. Note that it may not be possible to reimport some of the data, because the new type definition may not allow it. What if one of the changes to the user-defined type was to the validation method, for example? It will, however, guarantee the integrity of the database, which is paramount in any change.

In many cases, you will not be changing something as fundamental as the semantics of the type or how it is represented. In these cases, you can use the ALTER ASSEMBLY command, described in Chapter 2. The ALTER ASSEMBLY expression can replace an existing assembly with user-defined types in it without dropping objects such as tables and stored procedures that reference those types.

ALTER ASSEMBLY is meant to be used to make bug changes or improve implementations, not semantic or operational changes. You cannot use ALTER ASSEMBLY, for example, to replace an assembly with one whose assembly name is different in anything other than the revision of the assembly. Note that the revision is the fourth of the dotted list of numbers that specifies an assembly version. In the assembly version "1.2.3.4," "4" is the revision of the assembly.

It is your responsibility, however, when changing an assembly this way to ensure that the meaning, sorting, and so on of any data persisted by user-defined types is not changed by replacing the assembly. The ALTER ASSEMBLY expression can check for some of these issues, but not all. Keep this in mind when deciding between drop and re-create, and ALTER ASSEMBLY. Maintaining integrity of data should always be the most important factor when you are making this decision.

User-Defined Types and XML

XML has been tightly integrated into the CLR since its first release. Part of the support of XML is provided in the System.Xml.Serialization namespace, which provides support for the serialization of an instance of a CLR class to and from XML. Because a user-defined type is a CLR class, instances of it can be serialized to and from XML.

SQL Server 2005 also provides support for XML. The xml data type is supported, and so is the FOR XML phrase, which can be added to a SELECT expression. User-defined types, however, cannot be implicitly converted to or from XML; conversions must be explicit. Figure 5-44 shows an instance of the LDim user-defined type being cast to and from XML. It sets @d, an instance of an LDim, to 2 ft, and then casts it to XML and sets it into @x, an xml variable. Then it casts @x back to an LDim and shows the result.

A user-defined type must be cast to xml if it is part of a SELECT expression that uses a FOR XML clause, as shown in Figure 5-45. A table, Lengths (1), has a column that is a user-defined type. A SELECT expression (2) selects that column, Value, using a FOR XML clause. As part of the SELECT expression, the Value column is cast to xml. The result (3) shows the xml serialized form of the user-defined type. If the Value column were selected directly, this SELECT statement would have produced an error when it was run.

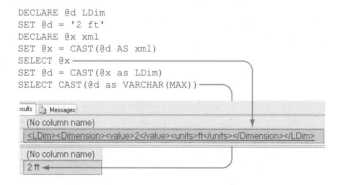

FIGURE 5-44: Casting a user-defined type to and from XML

```
①CREATE TABLE Lengths
  (
  ID int IDENTITY PRIMARY KEY,
  Value LDim
  )

②SELECT ID, CAST(Value as XML) as Value
    FROM Lengths FOR XML AUTO

③<Lengths ID="1">
    <Value>
      <LDim>
        <Dimension>
          <value>1</value>
          <units>ft</units>
        </Dimension>
      </LDim>
    </Value>
  </Lengths>
  <Lengths ID="2">
    <Value>
      <LDim>
        <Dimension>
          <value>1.54</value>
          <units>ft</units>
        </Dimension>
      </LDim>
    </Value>
  </Lengths>
  <Lengths ID="3">
    ...
```

FIGURE 5-45: Using FOR XML

By default, the CLR will build an assembly dynamically at runtime to serialize a CLR class to or from XML; SQL Server 2005 does not support this feature of the CLR, however. User-defined types must include the code that supports xml serialization with using this feature. The SGen utility is used to generate an assembly and optionally the source code that supports xml serialization from the assembly that implements a user-defined type.

Figure 5-46 shows SGen being used to create an assembly and C# source code that supports the xml serialization of LDim from Dimension.dll, the assembly that implements LDim. SGen is run (1) from the command line with the /K and /O switches. The /K switch keeps the source code for the assembly SGen creates. The /O switch is used to specify the directory the SGen should write its results to—in this example, the xml directory. The output of SGen is also shown, including the assembly it has created (2) and the source code for that assembly (3). Note also that the switches used to run the C# compiler are in the file with the .cmdline

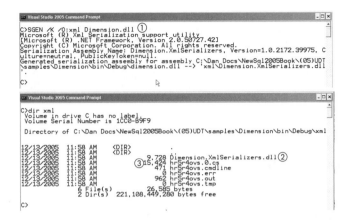

C>SGEN /K /O:xml Dimension.dll ①
Microsoft (R) Xml Serialization support utility
[Microsoft (R) .NET Framework, Version 2.0.50727.42]
Copyright (C) Microsoft Corporation. All rights reserved.
Serialization Assembly Name: Dimension.XmlSerializers, Version=1.0.2172.39975, C
ulture=neutral, PublicKeyToken=null.
Generated serialization assembly for assembly C:\Dan Docs\NewSql2005Book\(05)UDT
\samples\Dimension\bin\Debug\dimension.dll --> 'xml\Dimension.XmlSerializers.dll
'.

C>

C>dir xml
 Volume in drive C has no label.
 Volume Serial Number is 1CC0-B9F9

 Directory of C:\Dan Docs\NewSql2005Book\(05)UDT\samples\Dimension\bin\Debug\xml

12/13/2005 11:58 AM   <DIR>   .
12/13/2005 11:58 AM   <DIR>   ..
12/13/2005 11:58 AM   9,728 Dimension.XmlSerializers.dll ②
12/13/2005 11:58 AM   ③   15,424 hr5r4ovs.0.cs
12/13/2005 11:58 AM   471 hr5r4ovs.cmdline
12/13/2005 11:58 AM   0 hr5r4ovs.err
12/13/2005 11:58 AM   962 hr5r4ovs.out
12/13/2005 11:58 AM   0 hr5r4ovs.tmp
               6 File(s)   26,585 bytes
               2 Dir(s) 221,108,449,280 bytes free

C>

FIGURE 5-46: Using SGen

extension and that the output of running the C# compiler is in the file with
the .out extension.

A full discussion of what is produced by SGen is beyond the scope of this
book. One of the things in the assembly produced by SGen—Dimension.
XmlSerializers.dll in Figure 5-46—is a class named XmlSerializer-
Contract. This class in effect provides a method that SQL Server 2005 can
use to look up the classes needed to support the xml serialization of the
LDim class.

The last thing to do to tie everything together is to let SQL Server 2005
know which assembly contains the xml serialization support for a user-
defined type. This is done by decorating the class that implements the user-
defined type with a XmlSerializerAssembly attribute. The xml serialization
support can be provided from the assembly generated by SGen, Dimension.
XmlSerializers.dll (2) in Figure 5-46, or it can be provided by compiling the source code generated by SGen, hr5r4ovs.0.cs (3), into the assembly that contains the user-defined type.

To use the assembly created by SGen, the assembly must be catalogued
into the same database as the user-defined type is. The logical name of the
assembly doesn't matter. In addition, the XmlSerializerAssembly attribute
must be initialized with the full name of the assembly.

Figure 5-47 shows LDim (1), the class that implements the user-defined
type, decorated with an XmlSerializerAssembly attribute. The Assem-
blyName property of the XmlSerializerAssemblyAttribute is set to the

```
  [XmlSerializerAssemblyAttribute(AssemblyName =
     "dimension.xmlserializers, version=0.0.0.0,
     culture=neutral, publickeytoken=null,
     processorarchitecture=msil")]
① public struct LDim …

② CREATE ASSEMBLY [DimensionXmlSupport]
   FROM
   'C:\Dimension\xml\Dimension.XmlSerializers.dll'
```

FIGURE 5-47: Using an assembly created by SGen

full name of the assembly that was created by SGen. Note that the full assembly name is broken into multiple lines for the convenience of the diagram. In actual usage, it must be a single line.

The assembly created by SGen is catalogued using a CREATE ASSEMBLY (2) statement. When SQL Server 2005 needs to convert an LDim to or from xml, as shown in Figure 5-44 earlier in this chapter, it will use the Dimension.XmlSerializers assembly to get the code it needs to do this conversion.

An alternative way to use the xml support generated by the SGen utility is to compile the source code it creates into the assembly that implements the user-defined type. An advantage to this technique is that there is no need for an extra step to catalog the assembly generated by SGen. When the user-defined type is catalogued, its xml serialization support will be catalogued along with it. When the code generated by SGen is compiled with the assembly that implements the user-defined type, the XmlSerializerAssemblyAttribute is used without any assembly name, as shown in Figure 5-48.

The format of the XML produced by casting a user-defined type to xml is determined by the class that implements the user-defined type. By default, the values of all public properties and fields will output as content of elements named for the corresponding property or field. Note that the default

```
  [XmlSerializerAssemblyAttribute]
  public struct LDim …
  {
```

FIGURE 5-48: Built-in XML serialization

format requires that all information included in the xml be in public fields and properties and that all other information be in nonpublic fields and properties.

In general, the requirement that information must be in a public field or property to be serialized into xml can be difficult to meet, so there are two ways to control the format of the output. One is to use attributes from the `System.Xml.Serialization` namespace. The `XmlIgnore` attribute, for example, can be used to prevent a field or property from being serialized to xml, as shown in Figure 5-49.

Several of these attributes can be used to control xml serialization; search for "Introducing XML Serialization" in the MSDN documentation for a discussion of them. Note that there are attributes that can be used force a nonpublic member to be serialized.

The second way to control the serialization of a user-defined type into xml is to control it directly by implementing the `IXmlSerializable` interface. This interface has three methods: one named `WriteXml`, to serialize the user-defined type into xml; one named `ReadXml`, to serialize it from xml; and one named `GetSchema`, to provide the xml schema for the serialization format. The `ReadXml` and `WriteXml` methods completely override the default xml serialization and any attributes from the `System.Xml.Serialization` namespace.

A discussion of xml serialization and Xml Schema is beyond the scope of this book, but we will look briefly at the implementation of `IXmlSerializable`. Figure 5-50 shows the `WriteXml` method for the `LDim` user-defined type. An `XmlWriter` is passed into the method. The serialized form of the `LDim` is written into this stream. Note that the first write into an `XmlWriter` must be done with `XmlWriter.StartDocument()` and that the last write must be done with `XmlWriter.EndDocument()`; neither is done

```
public struct LDim …
{

    [SqlFacet(Precision = 9, Scale = 3)]
    [XmlIgnore]
    public SqlDecimal Inches
    {
…
```

FIGURE 5-49: XmlIgnore attribute

```
void IXmlSerializable.WriteXml(
① System.Xml.XmlWriter writer)
{
  if (!IsNull)
  {
  ② writer.WriteStartElement("Dimension");
    writer.WriteElementString("value",
      value.ToString());
    writer.WriteElementString("units", units);
    writer.WriteEndElement();
  }
  else
  {
  ③ writer.WriteStartElement("Dimension");
    writer.WriteAttributeString("nil",
      "http://www.w3.org/2001/XMLSchema-instance",
      "true");
    writer.WriteEndElement();
  }
}
```

FIGURE 5-50: WriteXml

in this method. SQL Server 2005 has already called this method and inserted the open tag for an "LDim" element—an element whose name is the same as that of the class that implements the user-defined type. Likewise, when the WriteXml method returns, SQL Server 2005 will insert the closing tag for the "LDim" element and call the XmlWriter.EndDocument() method.

The format for a non-null (2) LDim is just a value and units element. The format for a null LDim uses the convention as an element that includes the xsi:nil attribute. The WriteXml method shown in Figure 5-50 produced the xml output shown in Figure 5-44 and Figure 5-45.

The IXmlSerializable.ReadXml method is used to serialize xml into an LDim. Figure 5-51 shows the implementation of ReadXml for the LDim user-defined type. An XmlReader is passed in to (1) this method. The method must extract the information it needs to initialize the user-defined type. An XPath-Navigator is used to do this. XPathNavigator is the CLR class that typically is used to extract information from xml and is discussed in the MSDN documentation. If the xml passed into ReadXml is for a null instance of an LDim, the value and units fields (2) are appropriately initialized. If the xml is for a non-null instance of LDim, the value and units elements are extracted, and their string representation is parsed (3) using the Parse function. This is done both to convert the strings found in the xml to an LDim and to ensure that the range and precision meet the requirements we have set for LDim dimensions.

```
void IXmlSerializable.ReadXml(
①System.Xml.XmlReader reader)
{
  XPathDocument xdoc = new XPathDocument(reader);
  XPathNavigator nav = xdoc.CreateNavigator();
  XmlNamespaceManager nm =
    new XmlNamespaceManager(nav.NameTable);
    nm.AddNamespace("xsi",
      "http://www.w3.org/2001/XMLSchema-instance");
    if ((bool)(nav.Evaluate(
      "boolean(//@xsi:nil = 'true')",
      nm)))
    {
    ②value = 0;
      units = null;
    }
    else
    {
    ③LDim dim = Parse((string)(nav.Evaluate(
        "concat(//value, ' ', //units)")));
      units = dim.units;
      value = dim.value;
  }
}
```

FIGURE 5-51: ReadXml

The `IXmlSerializable.GetSchema` method returns a schema that defines the format used by the `ReadXml` and `WriteXml` methods. SQL Server 2005 does not use this method during the serialization of user-defined types, and it is permissible for it to return null. The `GetSchema` method, however, is used by SQL Server 2005 when it generates a WSDL file for a Web Service that uses a user-defined type as an argument. Chapter 12 discusses Web Services and WSDL files. Best practice would be for GetSchema to return an appropriate XML Schema. A discussion of XML Schema is beyond the scope of this book, but many resources do discuss it. The primer on the www.w3.org site is a good place to start; it is at http://www.w3.org/TR/2004/REC-xmlschema-0-20041028/.

Should Objects Be Represented by User-Defined Types?

If the object represents a scalar and requires more than one field to be described, or if you want to encapsulate some methods with it, a user-defined type should be used to represent it; otherwise, it should not. By definition, a column in a row of a relational table holds a scalar, so it can hold any object that is a scalar. This definition is crucial to features we associate with a relational database—such as the ability to have efficient declarative referential integrity via foreign keys and to order rows when they are used rather than when they are inserted.

A *scalar* is a value that can be represented in a single dimension. A value that requires more than one dimension to be represented is not a scalar. Note that the number of fields required to represent a value does not determine whether it is a scalar; the date example at the beginning of this chapter had three fields but was still a scalar.

Is a geometric point a scalar? No, because its representation requires two dimensions, not just two numbers. But why is a date that has three numbers a scalar, whereas a point that has only two numbers associated with it is not a scalar? You can ask of any dates something like "Is date d2 between date d1 and date d3?" and get a consistent answer. But there is no way in general to answer consistently the question "Is point p2 between point p1 and point p3?" The reason you can't get a consistent answer to this question for points is that each answer to a "between" question makes a commitment to the next. Consider the following questions and answers:

"Is date d2 between date d1 and date d3?" "Yes."
"Is date d4 between date d1 and date d2?" "Yes."

If someone then asks, "Is date d4 between date d1 and date d3?", the answer must be "Yes." This is because dates have an order; they in effect map onto the real number line. In fact, internally, SQL Server can use integer numbers to represent dates because of this. Figure 5-52 pictorially illustrates this.

This is not true for points, because they are not scalars. One of the problems with asking a "between" question of points is that our conventional

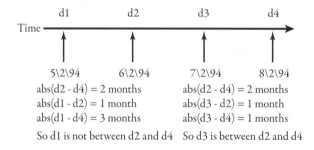

FIGURE 5-52: Answering the "between" question for dates

notion of "between" would require all three of the points involved to be on the same line. If we use this kind of definition of "between" for points, there are many points for which we cannot answer the "between" question, because it makes no sense.

But if we can just come up with an alternate definition of "between" that works consistently, we can still consider points to be scalars. Let's try to make up something that is similar to the way "between" works for dates. For dates, we can say that d2 is between d1 and d3 if both `abs(d2-d1) <` `abs(d1-d3)` and `abs(d2-d3) < abs(d1-d3)` are true. The `abs()` function means absolute value, which we can think of as a distance or a number with any associated minus sign removed.

The date d3 is between the dates d2 and d4 because both the distance between d3 and d2 and the distance between d3 and d4 are less than the distance between d2 and d4. Likewise, d1 is not between d2 and d4, because the distance between d1 and d4 is greater than the distance between d2 and d4.

We can try to apply a similar rule for points. Figure 5-53 shows four points and their relationships to one another in terms of distance.

Because the distance between p1 and p2 and between p2 and p3 is less than the distance between p1 and p3, p2 is between p1 and p3, by our definition of "between." Also, the distance between p4 and p1 and between p4 and p2 is less than the distance between p1 and p2, so p4 is between p1 and p2, by our definition of "between." If our "between" definition is consistent, P4 is then between p1 and p3. But it is obvious that the distance between p4 and p3 is greater than the distance between p1 and p3, so p4

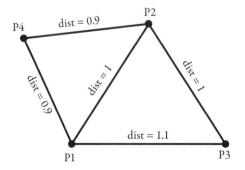

FIGURE 5-53: Answering the "between" question for points

could not be considered to be between p1 and p3, even though it is between p1 and p2. So it is not behaving like a scalar.

If you could find a set of rules for answering the "between" question consistently for points, you could consider a point to be a scalar. No such set of rules exists, however, so a point is not a scalar, even though it has fewer fields than a date does.

User-defined types should be used only for objects that represent scalars, even though it is physically possible to use user-defined types to represent any object whose state is less than 8,000 bytes, just by implementing IBinarySerialize.

Just because an application uses objects to represent things that are not scalars does not mean that the database has to. Chapter 8 covers the XML data type. SQL Server 2005 also still supports SQLXML. These technologies, and simple object-relational mappings, are much more efficient for persisting objects in a relational database than user-defined types are.

Listing 5-1 puts together the things we have been discussing to implement the LDim user-defined type in one place. Note that it includes a lot of arithmetic calculations that have very few comments. The purpose of this example is to show the structure of a user-defined type and the things that must be done so that it can be sorted and validated, not to cover the specifics of how this is done.

LISTING 5-1: LDim source code

```
using System;
using System.Data.SqlClient;
using System.Data.SqlTypes;
using System.Text.RegularExpressions;
using System.IO;
using Microsoft.SqlServer.Server;
using System.Xml.Serialization;
using System.Xml.Schema;
using System.Xml;
using System.Xml.XPath;

namespace Dimensions
{
  [SqlUserDefinedType(Format.UserDefined,
  MaxByteSize = 5,
  IsFixedLength = true,
  IsByteOrdered = true,
  ValidationMethodName = "CheckDirectInput"
  )]
```

```csharp
[XmlSerializerAssemblyAttribute]
// source code modules produced by SGen /K
// also compile in this assembly

public struct LDim : INullable,
 IBinarySerialize, IXmlSerializable
{


 private decimal value;
 private string units;
 public override string ToString()
 {
  if (IsNull)
  {
   return null;
  }

  // Put your code here
  return String.Format("{0} {1}", value, units);
 }
 public bool IsNull
 {
  [SqlMethod(InvokeIfReceiverIsNull = true)]
  get
  {
   return units == null;
  }
 }
 public static LDim Null
 {
  get
  {
   return new LDim();
  }
 }
 [SqlFacet(Precision = 9, Scale = 3)]
 // Prevents this property from being
 // xml serialized if default serialization used
 [XmlIgnore]
 public SqlDecimal Inches
 {
  get
  {
   SqlDecimal d;
   if (IsNull) return SqlDecimal.Null;
   if (units == "in")
   {
    return this.value;
   }
```

```
  if (units == "ft")
  {
   d = this.value * 12.0M;
   return this.value * 12.0M;
  }
  return 36.0M * this.value;
 }
 set
 {
  if (units != null)
  {
   this.value = value.Value;
   units = "in";
  }
 }
}
[SqlFunction(Name = "LDimAdd")]
static public LDim operator +(LDim d1, LDim d2)
{
 if (d1.IsNull || d2.IsNull)
 {
  return Null;
 }
 if (d1.units == d2.units)
 {
  LDim dim = new LDim();
  dim.units = d1.units;
  dim.value = d1.value + d2.value;
  return dim;
 }
 LDim dim1 = new LDim();
 dim1.units = "in";
 dim1.value = d1.Inches.Value + d2.Inches.Value;
 return dim1;
}
bool CheckDirectInput()
{
 return CheckRangeAndAccurcy(this);
}
static bool CheckRangeAndAccurcy(LDim d)
{
 decimal value = d.value;
 // check overall range
 if (d.units == "in")
 {
  if ((value > (52800M * 12M)) ||
  (value < -(52800M * 12M)))
  {
   return false;
  }
 }
```

```
 if (d.units == "ft")
 {
  if ((value > 52800M) ||
  (value < -52800M))
  {
   return false;
  }
 }
 if (d.units == "yd")
 {
  if ((value > (52800M / 3M)) ||
  (value < -(52800M) / 3M))
  {
   return false;
  }
 }
 // check accuracy to 0.001 inches
 if (d.units == "ft")
 {
  value *= 12M;
 }
 if (d.units == "yd")
 {
  value *= 36M;
 }
 decimal norm = value * 1000M;
 norm = decimal.Round(norm);
 if ((norm - (value * 1000M)) != 0M)
 {
  return false;
 }
 return true;
}

static void MoveBitsFromIntToByte(
 // source int
    uint i1,
 // start at this bit
    int start1,
 // take this many bits
    int width,
 // insert into this byte
    ref byte b2,
 // starting here
    int start2)
{
 uint mask = 0xFFFFFFFF;
 mask = 1U << start1 + 1;
 mask -= 1;
 uint mask2 = 1U << (start1 - (width - 1));
 mask2 -= 1;
```

```
    mask2 ^= 0xFFFFFFFF;
    mask &= mask2;
    i1 &= mask;
    int shift = start2 - start1;
    if (shift < 0)
    {
     i1 >>= -shift;
    }
    if (shift > 0)
    {
     i1 <<= shift;
    }
    mask = 1U << start2 + 1;
    mask -= 1U;
    mask2 = 1U << (start2 - (width - 1));
    mask2 -= 1;
    mask2 ^= 0xFFFFFFFF;
    mask &= mask2;
    b2 |= (byte)(i1 & mask);

}
static void MoveBitsFromByteToInt(
 // source byte
    byte b1,
 // start at this bit
    int start1,
 // take this many bits
    int width,
 // insert bits into this int
    ref uint i2,
 // starting at this bit
    int start2)
{
 uint bvalue = b1;
 uint mask = 1U << (1 + start1);
 mask -= 1U;
 uint mask2 = 1U << (start1 - (width - 1));
 mask2 -= 1;
 mask ^= mask2;
 bvalue &= mask;
 mask = 1U << (1 + start2);
 mask -= 1U;
 mask2 = 1U << (1 + start2 - width);
 mask2 -= 1;
 mask ^= mask2;
 mask ^= 0xFFFFFFFF;
 i2 &= mask;
 int shift = start2 - start1;
 if (shift < 0)
```

```
  {
   bvalue >>= -shift;
  }
  if (shift > 0)
  {
   bvalue <<= shift;
  }
  i2 |= bvalue;
}
public static LDim Parse(SqlString s)
{
 if (s.IsNull)
  return Null;
 // regular expression to test, extract
 string fp = @"-?([0-9]+(\.[0-9]*)?|\.[0-9]+)";
 Regex vu = new Regex(@"(?<v>" + fp + @") (?<u>in|ft|yd)");

 if (!vu.IsMatch(s.Value))
 {
  throw new Exception("Bad format", null);
 }

 Match m = vu.Match(s.Value);
 LDim d = new LDim();

 d.units = m.Result("${u}");
 d.value = decimal.Parse(m.Result("${v}"));
 if (!CheckRangeAndAccurcy(d))
 {
  throw new Exception("Out of range or accuracy", null);
 }
 return d;
}
[SqlMethod(IsMutator = true, OnNullCall = true)]
public void ScaleBy(
  [SqlFacet(Precision = 10, Scale = 15)]
        SqlDecimal scale)
{
 if (!IsNull && !scale.IsNull)
 {
  Decimal oldValue = this.value;
  this.value *= scale.Value;
  if (!CheckRangeAndAccurcy(this))
  {
   this.value = oldValue;
  }
 }
}
[SqlMethod(IsMutator = false, OnNullCall = false)]
```

```
public LDim GetScaled(SqlDecimal scale)
{
 LDim ldim = new LDim();
 if (!IsNull)
 {
  ldim.value = this.value;
  ldim.units = this.units;
  ldim.value *= scale.Value;
  if (!CheckRangeAndAccurcy(ldim))
  {
   ldim = this;
  }
 }
 return ldim;
}
[SqlMethod(IsMutator = true, OnNullCall = false)]
public void ToIn()
{
 if (units == "ft")
 {
  value *= 12M;
 }

 if (units == "yd")
 {
  value *= 36M;
 }

 units = "in";
}
public void Write(System.IO.BinaryWriter w)
{
 byte[] bytes = ToBytes();
 foreach (byte b in bytes)
 {
  w.Write(b);
 };
}

public byte[] ToBytes()
{
 byte[] bytes = new byte[5];
 if (IsNull)
 {
  bytes[0] = bytes[1] = bytes[2] = bytes[3] = bytes[4] = 0;
 }
 else
 {
  // store as inches and thousandths of an inch
  int thousandths;
```

```
uint sign = 1;
Decimal floor = 0M;
Decimal d = this.Inches.Value;
int inches;
if (d < 0M)
{
 floor = Decimal.Floor(-d);
 thousandths = (int)((-d - floor) * 1000M);
 sign = 0;
}
else
{
 floor = Decimal.Floor(d);
 thousandths = (int)((d - floor) * 1000M);
}
inches = (int)floor;

if (sign == 0)
{
 // this is negative dim
 inches = 10 * 5280 * 12 - inches;
 thousandths = 1000 - thousandths;
}
// max number of inches is 633600 or 0x9AB00
// this fits in about 2.5 bytes or 20 bits
// thousandths (0-999) fits about 1.5 bytes or 10 bits
// sign takes 1 bit
// units takes 2 bits
// store as inches. note as calculated inches is never negative
// total bits needed is 20 + 10 + 1 + 2 or 33
// storage then will be 5 bytes
byte b = 0;
MoveBitsFromIntToByte(sign, 0, 1, ref b, 7);
// move bit 19 to position 6
MoveBitsFromIntToByte((uint)inches, 19, 7, ref b, 6);
//w.Write(b); //1
bytes[0] = b;
// move bit 11 to position 7
b = 0;
MoveBitsFromIntToByte((uint)inches, 12, 8, ref b, 7);
//w.Write(b); //2
bytes[1] = b;
// move bit 4 to position 7
b = 0;
MoveBitsFromIntToByte((uint)inches, 4, 5, ref b, 7);
// move bit 10 to position 2
MoveBitsFromIntToByte((uint)thousandths, 9, 3, ref b, 2);
//w.Write(b); //3
bytes[2] = b;
// move bit 7 to position 7
```

```
 b = 0;
 MoveBitsFromIntToByte((uint)thousandths, 6, 7, ref b, 6);
 //w.Write(b); //4
 bytes[3] = b;
 // no add units 1=in, 2=ft, 3=yd
 if (units == "in")
 {
  b = 1;
 }
 if (units == "ft")
 {
  b = 2;
 }
 if (units == "yd")
 {
  b = 3;
 }
 //w.Write(b); //5
 bytes[4] = b;
 }
 return bytes;
}
public void Read(System.IO.BinaryReader r)
{
 byte[] bytes = r.ReadBytes(5);
 FromBytes(bytes);
}
public void FromBytes(byte[] bytes)
{
 // if all bytes are zero this is null instance
 if (
 (bytes[0] == 0)
 && (bytes[1] == 0)
 && (bytes[2] == 0)
 && (bytes[3] == 0)
 && (bytes[4] == 0)
 )
 {
  units = null;
  value = 0M;
  return;
 }

 uint sign = 0;
 MoveBitsFromByteToInt(bytes[0], 7, 1, ref sign, 0);
 uint inches = 0;
 MoveBitsFromByteToInt(bytes[0], 6, 7, ref inches, 19);
 MoveBitsFromByteToInt(bytes[1], 7, 8, ref inches, 12);
 MoveBitsFromByteToInt(bytes[2], 7, 5, ref inches, 4);
 uint thousandths = 0;
```

```
   MoveBitsFromByteToInt(bytes[2], 2, 3, ref thousandths, 9);
   MoveBitsFromByteToInt(bytes[3], 6, 7, ref thousandths, 6);
   uint u = 0;
   MoveBitsFromByteToInt(bytes[4], 1, 2, ref u, 1);
   if (sign == 0)
   {
    inches = 10 * 5280 * 12 - inches;
    thousandths = 1000 - thousandths;
   }
   value = thousandths;
   value /= 1000M;
   value += inches;
   switch (u)
   {
    case 1: units = "in"; break;
    case 2:
     units = "ft";
     value /= 12;
     break;
    case 3:
     units = "yd";
     value /= 36;
     break;
   }

   if (sign == 0)
   {
    value = -value;
   }
  }

  #region IXmlSerializable Members
  System.Xml.Schema.XmlSchema IXmlSerializable.GetSchema()
  {
   System.IO.StringReader sr = new StringReader(@"
<xsd:schema xmlns:xsd='http://www.w3.org/2001/XMLSchema'>
<xsd:element name='LDim'>
<xsd:complexType>
<xsd:sequence>
<xsd:element name='Dimension'>
<xsd:element name='value' type='xsd:float'/>
<xsd:element name='units:'>
<xsd:simpleType>
<xsd:restriction>
<xsd:enumeration value='ft'/>
<xsd:enumeration value='in'/>
<xsd:enumeration value='yd'/>
</xsd:restriction>
</xsd:simpleType>
</xsd:element>
```

```
</xsd:element>
</xsd:sequence>
</xsd:complexType>
</xsd:element>
</xsd:schema>");
    XmlSchema schema = XmlSchema.Read(sr, null);
    return null;
  }


  void IXmlSerializable.ReadXml(System.Xml.XmlReader reader)
  {
   XPathDocument xdoc = new XPathDocument(reader);
   XPathNavigator nav = xdoc.CreateNavigator();
   XmlNamespaceManager nm = new XmlNamespaceManager(nav.NameTable);
   nm.AddNamespace("xsi", "http://www.w3.org/2001/XMLSchema-instance");
   if ((bool)(nav.Evaluate("boolean(//@xsi:nil = 'true')", nm)))
   {
    value = 0;
    units = null;
   }
   else
   {
    LDim dim = Parse((string)(nav.Evaluate(
    "concat(//value, ' ', //units)")));
    units = dim.units;
    value = dim.value;
   }
  }


  void IXmlSerializable.WriteXml(System.Xml.XmlWriter writer)
  {
   if (!IsNull)
   {
    writer.WriteStartElement("Dimension");
    writer.WriteElementString("value", value.ToString());
    writer.WriteElementString("units", units);
    writer.WriteEndElement();
   }
   else
   {
    writer.WriteStartElement("Dimension");
    writer.WriteAttributeString("nil",
        "http://www.w3.org/2001/XMLSchema-instance", "true");
    writer.WriteEndElement();
   }
  }
  #endregion
 }
}
```

User-Defined Aggregates

An aggregate function operates on a set and produces a scalar. The SUM function in SQL Server is an example of an aggregate. A SELECT statement is used to produce a set of rows, and the SUM function produces the arithmetic sum of some column in the rows produced by the SELECT statement. Figure 5-54 shows an example of a SQL batch using the SUM function.

The SELECT statement made a set of all the rows (1) from the Items table where the size=3; then the SUM function added each of the price columns from those rows to produce 15 (2).

This ability to do operations that produce a scalar result on sets of data is a key feature of a relational database. In fact, the SQL-92 specification requires that a database implement the COUNT, SUM, AVG, MAX, and MIN aggregate functions for compliance. SQL Server includes these aggregate functions and several others—for example, COUNT and COUNT_BIG, plus a number of statistical aggregates, such as STDEV and VAR, for standard deviation and variance.

You can create your own user-defined aggregates with SQL Server 2005. One reason you might want to do this is if you have created your own user-defined type and need to be able to aggregate it. None of the built-in aggregates in SQL Server will work with a user-defined type, so you may have to create your own in this case.

A second reason is performance. You do not need the SUM aggregate to calculate the sum of a column. Figure 5-55 shows a SQL batch that calculates the sum of prices that the example in Figure 5-54 does, but it does not use the SUM aggregate function.

```
CREATE TABLE Items
(
    size int, price float
)

① INSERT INTO Items VALUES (3, 12.0)
   INSERT INTO Items VALUES (5, 10.0)
   INSERT INTO Items VALUES (3, 1.0)
   INSERT INTO Items VALUES (3, 2.0)

   SELECT SUM(price) FROM ITEMS WHERE size = 3
```

② Results | Message
(No column name)
1	15

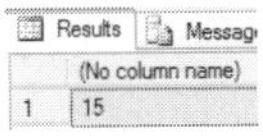

Figure 5-54: Using the SUM aggregate function

```
    DECLARE sumCursor CURSOR
①  FOR SELECT price FROM ITEMS WHERE size = 3
    OPEN sumCursor
    DECLARE @sum float
    SET @sum = 0
    DECLARE @price float
②  FETCH NEXT FROM sumCursor INTO @price
    WHILE @@FETCH_STATUS = 0
    BEGIN
    SET @sum = @sum + @price
③  FETCH NEXT FROM sumCursor INTO @price
    END
④  SELECT @sum
    CLOSE sumCursor
    DEALLOCATE sumCursor
```

FIGURE 5-55: Calculating a sum without an aggregate

The sum technique shown in Figure 5-55 uses a CURSOR (1) to iterate through the results of a query and add up the prices. The first row is read (2); then all the rest of the rows are read (3). At each step along the way, the @sum variable is incremented by the price that is read and then selected (4). It typically is orders of magnitude slower than using the built-in SUM aggregate and uses a lot more resources on the server because of the CURSOR. Prior to SQL Server 2005, if you needed an aggregate other than one of the built-in ones provided by SQL Server, you might have used this technique to create your own aggregation.

Note that it is possible to build fairly complicated aggregates out of the ones built into SQL Server 2005. Figure 5-56 shows, in effect, a product

```
    CREATE TABLE Measurements
    (
①      dist float
    )

②  INSERT INTO Measurements VALUES(2)
    INSERT INTO Measurements VALUES(.5)
    INSERT INTO Measurements VALUES(4)
    INSERT INTO Measurements VALUES(.25)

③  SELECT EXP(SUM(LOG(dist))) AS Product
        FROM Measurements
```

④
Results	
	Product
1	1

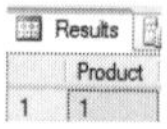

FIGURE 5-56: Product aggregate

aggregate; it calculates the product of all the numbers passed into it. A simple table (1) named Measurements has some floating-point distances in it. Some distances are inserted (2) into Measurements. The product aggregate is calculated (3) by summing the logarithms of the distances and raising ten to that sum that is produced (4). As a point of interest, this is how an old analog calculator known as a slide rule did multiplication, and using this technique to calculate the product of signed numbers has the same issues it did with a slide rule.

In many cases, combining existing T-SQL scalar and aggregate functions is a better choice than a user-defined aggregate when possible. The example shown in Figure 5-56 would not work, however, if the dist column of the Measurements table were of type DECIMAL, because the LOG and EXP functions require a float as input.

The example in Figure 5-56, of course, could be made to work by casting the dist to a float before computing the logarithm, but a float is not big enough to hold all possible decimal values; besides, we saw at the beginning of this chapter that floats can easily lead to inaccurate results.

Prior to SQL Server 2005, if you wanted to make an aggregate like the one shown in Figure 5-56 but maintain the accuracy of the DECIMAL type, you would have to use the CURSOR technique shown in Figure 5-55. In SQL Server 2005, you can write your own aggregate, and its performance will be on the order of the built-in aggregates instead of orders of magnitude slower, as the CURSOR-based technique would be.

In the end, if we are going to have a user-defined type, we should be able to aggregate it just as we can a built-in scalar type, and that is what we are looking at in the next section.

Implementing a User-Defined Aggregate

In this section, we look at creating a user-defined aggregate that is the equivalent of SUM for the LDim user-defined type. Note that even though you can create a new aggregate function, there is no way to extend an existing aggregate function to support additional data types—that is, there is no way to extend the SUM aggregate to support user-defined types such as LDim.

We will call this new aggregate SumLDim, and it will produce an LDim that represents the arithmetic sum of the LDims that it processes. Figure 5-57 shows a SQL batch that makes use of the SumLDim aggregate function.

```
CREATE Table Lengths
(
    ID int IDENTITY PRIMARY KEY,
    value LDim
)

INSERT INTO Lengths VALUES ('1 ft')
INSERT INTO Lengths VALUES ('1 ft')
INSERT INTO Lengths VALUES ('1 in')
INSERT INTO Lengths VALUES ('1 ft')
INSERT INTO Lengths VALUES ('1 ft')
INSERT INTO Lengths VALUES ('1 yd')


select CAST (dbo).SumLDim(value)
    as VARCHAR(MAX)) from Lengths AS TotalLength
```

Results	Messages
TotalLength	
1	85 in

FIGURE 5-57: Using a user-defined aggregate

Note that a user-defined aggregate function must be referenced with a two-part name.

A user-defined aggregate is implemented by a public class, decorated with the SqlUserDefinedAggregate attribute, that implements four well-known methods: Init, Aggregate, Merge, and Terminate. User-defined aggregates must be serialized, and the serialization can be done by either SQL Server 2005 itself or via IBinarySerialize, just as is done with user-defined functions.

Figure 5-58 shows a skeleton of the implementation of the SumLDim aggregate. This aggregate uses Format.Native (2) serialization, meaning that it is going to let SQL Server do the serialization. SQL Server is going

```
① [Serializable]
   [Microsoft.SqlServer.Server.SqlUserDefinedAggregate
② ( Format.Native,
③    IsInvariantToNulls=true,
④    IsInvariantToOrder=true
   )]
   public struct SumLDim
   {
       ...
   }
```

FIGURE 5-58: SumLDim implementation skeleton

to use the CLR to do the actual serialization, and because of this, the class that implements LDim must be marked with the Serializable attribute. The CLR will not serialize classes that are not marked with this attribute.

This implementation makes use of some optimizations. Many aggregates will ignore a null value—that is, they will not include it in the aggregate calculation. The IsInvariantToNulls property of the SqlUserDefinedAggregate is used to indicate this. If the aggregate is going to ignore null, the IsInvariant-ToNulls property should be set to true. When this is set to true, SQL Server 2005 may skip passing NULLs to the aggregate as an optimization. Note that the implementation of the aggregate must still be able to process null values, as IsInvariantToNulls is only a hint and is used only if the query processor finds it will be helpful.

In general, and specifically in the case of LDim, aggregates don't care about the order in which rows are processed. Some interesting aggregates could be implemented, however, if the order in which rows were processed could be controlled. In Figure 5-58, the IsInvariantToOrder property of the SqlUserDefinedAggregate attribute is used to indicate whether the aggregate expects the rows to be processed in some particular order. IsInvariantToOrder=true indicates that the aggregate does not care in what order the rows are processed; IsInvariantToOrder=false indicates that the aggregate requires rows to be processed in the order in which they are sorted.

SQL Server 2005 ignores the value of IsInvariantToOrder, but some future version of SQL Server may respect this setting. To respect this setting, SQL Server 2005 would have to either use or build an index when processing the aggregate function, which it never does. Best practice is to set this property to true so that if this aggregate is used with a version of SQL Server that supports IsInvariantToOrder, its performance will not be compromised by SQL Server's sorting rows before they are processed by the user-defined aggregate.

Two other properties of the SqlUserDefinedAggregate attribute should also be considered: IsInvariantToDuplicates and IsNullIfEmpty. Some aggregates can ignore duplicate values; the MIN and MAX aggregate functions are examples of these. A user-defined aggregate can, as an optimization hint, set IsInvariantToDuplicates=true if it is like MAX and MIN in that it need not have the same value passed in to it multiple times to make a correct calculation. The default value for IsInvariantToDuplicates is false, and this is the case for SumLDim, so it need not be specified.

The `IsNullIfEmpty` property is used to indicate that the aggregate function will return NULL if there are no rows to process. The SUM aggregate function returns a NULL if no rows are passed to it, for example. If `NullIfEmpty = true`, SQL Server 2005 may skip using the user-defined aggregate and directly return a NULL if there are no rows for the aggregate to process.

Both `IsInvariantToDuplicates` and `IsNullIfEmpty` are only hints; even if they are set to true, the user-defined aggregate must work property if they are ignored.

The underlying data type for an `LDim` is decimal; that was chosen to maintain the accuracy of arithmetic calculations as much as possible. The `SumLDim` should likewise use decimal for its calculations so that it can also preserve arithmetic accuracy as much as possible. One of the issues we ran into in the implementation of `LDim` was that the CLR decimal type must be serialized using `Format.UserDefined`.

A user-defined aggregate must store some kind of accumulator to build up the final result as rows are passed in to it. In the case of `SumLDim`, this accumulator will in effect be an `LDim`. In fact, the accumulator will accumulate inches and be a decimal.

It is possible to use `Format.Native` to serialize the internal representation of a decimal data type. Internally, a decimal data type is made up of four ints, which can be obtained by the `decimal.GetBits` method. Given the internal representation, a new decimal data type can be instantiated from these four ints. So by representing a decimal data type as four ints, we can serialize it using `Format.Native`.

Figure 5-59 shows how `SumLDim` stores a decimal type (1) as four ints. Two helper methods save and restore a decimal from these four ints. The `SaveSum` method (2) takes a decimal as an input parameter and then uses the `decimal.GetBits` method to extract the four ints that make it up. The `GetSum` method (3) returns a decimal by using the constructor for a decimal that takes as input an array of four ints.

The well-known method `Init` in the class that implements a user-defined type is used to initialize the accumulator for the aggregate. Init is guaranteed to be called once for an aggregate calculation, and it will be called before any of the other well-known methods are. Figure 5-60 shows the implementation of the `Init` method. It uses the `SaveSum` method (1) to save a zero. It might seem to be a better idea to have initialization for a class done in its constructor.

```
public struct SumLDim {
① int int0;
   int int1;
   int int2;
   int int3;
② void SaveSum(decimal d) {
      int[] ints = decimal.GetBits(d);
      int0 = ints[0];
      int1 = ints[1];
      int2 = ints[2];
      int3 = ints[3];
   }
③ decimal GetSum() {
      int[] ints = new int[4];
      ints[0] = int0;
      ints[1] = int1;
      ints[2] = int2;
      ints[3] = int3;
      return new decimal(ints);
   }
   ...
```

FIGURE 5-59: Representing decimal

Initialization for a user-defined aggregate, however, must be done in the `Init` method. SQL Server 2005 may, as an optimization, reuse an instance of the class that implements a user-defined aggregate rather than construct a new one.

The well-known method `Accumulate` is the method that does the actual aggregation. `SumLDim` aggregates `LDims` so that its input parameter type is `LDim`. Figure 5-61 shows the implementation of the `Accumulate` method. This method is called by SQL Server 2005 once for each row that is aggregated in a query. Note that it does check (1) the value passed in and does not process it if it is null, even though `IsInvariantToNulls` = `true`, because `IsInvariantToNulls` is only a hint. The input value is processed (2) by converting the `LDim` input value to inches, adding the current sum to it, and then saving the result in the four `ints` used to save the decimal value.

SQL Server 2005 may, in some cases, use more than one instance of a user-defined aggregate while doing an aggregate calculation. The well-known

```
public void Init()
{
① SaveSum(0M);
}
```

FIGURE 5-60: Imple-
mentation of init

```
public void Accumulate(LDim Value)
{
① if(!Value.IsNull)
  {
  ② SaveSum((Value.Inches.Value + GetSum()));
  }
}
```

FIGURE 5-61: Implementation of accumulate

method `Merge` is called by SQL Server when it needs to combine two instances of a user-defined aggregate. The `Merge` method may be called zero or more times. Figure 5-62 shows the implementation of `Merge`. It simply adds (1) the current sum in the instance with the sum from the other instance and saves the result into the four `int`s used to save the decimal value.

At the end of an aggregate calculation, SQL Server 2005 will call the well-known `Terminate` method to get the results of the aggregate calculation. The `Terminate` method will be called only once. Figure 5-63 shows the implementation of the `Terminate` method. It creates a new instance of an `LDim` (1) initialized to zero. Next, it uses the `Inches` property of `LDim` instance to set (2) it directly to the sum that was accumulated. Last, the new instance of `LDim` is returned (3).

Creating User-Defined Aggregate

A CREATE AGGREGATE statement is used to add an aggregate to SQL Server 2005, as shown in Figure 5-64. The assembly must already be loaded (1) into SQL Server. The syntax for CREATE AGGREGATE is similar to that for a function. The type of the input parameter (2) and return value (3) must be specified.

There is no requirement that a user-defined aggregate return the same type that it takes as an input. The `SumLDim`, for example, could have returned a float that by convention was the number of inches accumulated.

```
public void Merge(SumLDim Group)
{
① SaveSum(GetSum() + Group.GetSum());
}
```

FIGURE 5-62: Implementation of merge

```
public LDim Terminate()
{
① LDim ldim = LDim.Parse("0 ft");
② ldim.Inches=GetSum();
③ return ldim;
}
```

FIGURE 5-63: Implementation
of terminate

Format.Native vs. Format.UserDefined

You can also see in the SumLDim that implementing Format.Native is very simple, and the implementation of the user-defined type LDim would have been much easier if this technique had been used.

There were two reasons for using Format.UserDefined in the implementation of LDim. One was simply to provide an example of an implementation that used Format.UserDefined. The second reason was so that we could control the sorting order. Implementations that use Format.Native will be sorted according to the order of the fields in their class definition. Ordering in this case will be done numerically, not by byte order.

Unfortunately, that leaves us between a rock and a hard place with respect to controlling the sort order of the decimal type. If LDim used the four ints technique that SumLDim does, the order would not reflect the numeric order of decimal numbers.

In addition, the units would have to be taken into account. They could be represented as the numbers 0, 1, 2 and 3, but that would just compound the ordering problem.

To control the sort order of a Format.Native type closely, you can add a field that precedes all other fields in the class and have that field be maintained with a number that represents the order. You could add a float field

```
CREATE ASSEMBLY Geo①
FROM 'C:\Assemblies\Dimension.dll'
                            ②
CREATE AGGREGATE SumLDim(@dim LDIM)
RETURNS LDIM③
EXTERNAL NAME Geo.[SumLDim]
```

FIGURE 5-64: Loading a user-defined
aggregate

and cast the decimal into it, for example, but this would lead to range problems and accuracy.

In the end, if your implementation of a user-defined type is based on a type that cannot be serialized by Format.Native, you probably will find that techniques similar to those shown in the LDim implementation will be required to achieve both accuracy and a desired sort order. Listing 5-2 shows source code for the SumLDim aggregate.

LISTING 5-2: Source code for SumLDim

```
using System;
using System.Data;
using System.Data.SqlClient;
using System.Data.SqlTypes;
using Microsoft.SqlServer.Server;
using Dimensions;

[Serializable]
[Microsoft.SqlServer.Server.SqlUserDefinedAggregate(
 Format.Native,
 IsInvariantToNulls = true,
 IsInvariantToOrder = true

 )]
public struct SumLDim
{
 int int0;
 int int1;
 int int2;
 int int3;
 void SaveSum(decimal d)
 {

  int[] ints = decimal.GetBits(d);
  int0 = ints[0];
  int1 = ints[1];
  int2 = ints[2];
  int3 = ints[3];
 }
 decimal GetSum()
 {
  int[] ints = new int[4];
  ints[0] = int0;
  ints[1] = int1;
  ints[2] = int2;
  ints[3] = int3;
  return new decimal(ints);
 }
```

```
public void Init()
{
 SaveSum(0M);
}

public void Accumulate(LDim Value)
{
 if (!Value.IsNull)
 {
   SaveSum((Value.Inches.Value + GetSum()));
 }
}

public void Merge(SumLDim Group)
{
  SaveSum(GetSum() + Group.GetSum());
}

public LDim Terminate()
{
 LDim ldim = LDim.Parse("0 ft");
 ldim.Inches = GetSum();
 return ldim;
}

}
```

Where Are We?

User-defined types are extensions to the SQL Server built-in scalar types. They are used in the same way and for the same purpose. They allow us to use an application-specific format for the string representation of a value— for example, "1 ft"—in much the same way that we use a string representation of a date—such as "12/1/1998"—for a DATETIME built-in data type. They also allow us to encapsulate functionality for a type with the type itself.

A user-defined type is implemented by a CLR class that implements a number of well-known methods and is decorated with the SqlUserDe-finedType attribute. It can be accessed from within SQL Server when its assembly has been added to a database and CREATE TYPE has been used to create the user-defined type.

The user-defined type can be used in the definition of a column type for a table, a variable type, or a parameter type in a stored procedure or function. It is often useful to add user-defined-type-specific methods that can manipulate or extract information from an instance of that type. It is often useful also to add utility functions that can create initialized instances of a user-defined type.

User-defined types can also expose their properties and fields. This is useful when one of the fields of a user-defined type must be accessed or manipulated.

A user-defined aggregate is implemented using a CLR language. There is no way to create an aggregate function using T-SQL. Aggregate functions are often created for use with user-defined types. They may also be created for built-in types.

Both user-defined type and user-defined aggregate implementations must always be aware that they are manipulating data in SQL Server at a very low level and will often require extra code beyond the function they are implementing, to ensure that the data is not corrupted.

We've covered most of the new features of SQL Server 2005 that directly relate to .NET Framework, finishing with user-defined types and user-defined aggregates. Chapter 2 pointed out that no matter how flexible or powerful a database is, a database without security is less than useful. The next chapter talks about how security has been considered at every level when the new functionality was designed. In addition, we'll see how permissions work with the .NET Framework features.

▪ 6 ▪
Security

C HANGES IN SQL Server 2005 help make SQL Server more secure and security more approachable for the developer and the administrator. An entire new set of security requirements when hosting .NET Framework code inside SQL Server is addressed by using traditional user- and role-based security combined with .NET Framework hosting APIs and attribute-based security. Classic SQL security is improved by separating users from schemas and integrating password management with Windows Server 2003, and the attack surface of SQL Server is reduced by having many options turned off by default.

New Security Features in SQL Server 2005

SQL Server 2005 adds new security features, not only to make SQL Server more secure, but also to make security more understandable and easier to administer. Some of these features will permit programmers to develop database applications while running with the exact privileges that they need. This is known as *the principle of least privilege*. No longer does every programmer need to run as the SQL Server administrative login, sa.

- Security for .NET Framework executable code—Administration and execution of .NET Framework code is managed through a combination of SQL Server permissions, Windows permissions, and .NET Framework code access security. What user code can or cannot do inside and outside SQL Server is defined with three distinct levels.

- Password policies for SQL Server users—If you run SQL Server 2005 on a Windows 2003 Server, SQL users can go by the same policies as integrated security users.

- Separation of users and schemas—SQL Server 2005 schemas are first-class objects that can be owned by a user, role, group, or application roles. The capability to define synonyms makes this easier to administer.

- Granting permissions—No longer do users or logins have to be in special roles to have certain permissions; they are all grantable with the GRANT, DENY, and REVOKE verbs.

- New security on SQL Server metadata—New metadata views are not directly updatable, and users can list metadata only about objects to which they have permission.[1] There is also a new grantable VIEW DEFINITION permission.

- Execution context for procedural code—You can set the execution context for stored procedures and user-defined functions. You can also use the EXECUTE AS syntax to change the current user.

- Support of certificates and encryption keys—SQL Server 2005 can manage certificates and encryption keys for use with Service Broker, with Web Services Secure Sockets Layer (SSL), and for new data encryption functions.

- Code signing of procedural code—You can use a certificate or asymmetric key to sign procedural code.

We'll look at these features in detail in this chapter. Running non–Transact-SQL (T-SQL) code in a secure and reliable fashion inside SQL Server is a new concept, and we'll spend a lot of this chapter examining how SQL Server's new security features combine with the latest .NET Framework runtime version to make this possible. We include a review of how security currently works in SQL Server in general to establish a baseline of knowledge.

---

1. An exception to this rule is the sys.databases view. Public is granted VIEW DEFINITION on this view.

We will start by looking at a change in the general policy of how SQL Server is configured. Microsoft refers to this as the 3 Ds: Secure by Design, Secure by Default, and Secure by Deployment. Though having optional features turned off by default technically is not a feature as such, most will consider it an important step forward in securing SQL Server.

Optional Features Are Turned Off by Default

The SQL Server product has always been known for being feature rich. A multitude of new features is added with each release, sometimes too many for many DBAs to keep track of. Although it's a treat to see new features (that's what this book is about, after all), in previous releases they usually arrived with the product, installed and enabled by default. And enabled features that you don't know exist can hurt you by increasing the surface area exposed to attackers. These bad guys probe for any weakness in existing and new features, which in past releases included goodies such as command-line program invocation (xp_cmdshell), sending mail messages (xp_sendmail), and invocation of COM classes (sp_OACreate). Most of these features will run as the user that runs the SQL Server service process. Sometimes, for ease of installation, this is set to LocalSystem, a Windows superuser account. And if you are running in mixed security mode, and you've set your "sa" password to null (that is, no password), you're wide open, although it must be pointed out that neither running as LocalSystem, enabling mixed security, nor a blank password is the default, and a blank password is strongly discouraged throughout the product and all utilities.

Configuring Security Settings

SQL Server 2005 ships with a new configuration utility named SQL Server Surface Area Configuration Utility. This program lets the DBA configure the database on two levels: services/connections and features. When you bring up the utility, the startup screen gives you the capability of configuring SQL Server instances on a local or remote machine. The services for the database engine itself and any additional services are configurable. Note that in the SQL Server 2005 release, the SQL Browser service is a separate service, as is SQL Server Integration Services. In addition, this panel will allow you to configure remote connections to SQL Server instances. Some administrators were surprised to find that all remote database connections are OFF as a starting point in SQL Express and SQL Server Developer Edition. You can also configure connections on a per-protocol basis. The second screen allows you to turn SQL Server 2005 features on and off. In addition to new features, existing features have been turned off; if existing applications need them, you must turn them back on. The features that are off by default include

- Ad-hoc remote queries (OPENROWSET and OPENQUERY)
- Database mail and SQL mail
- Remote access to the dedicated administrator connection
- OLE automation (sp_OACreate and friends)
- xp_cmdshell
- CLR integration
- Web Assistant

Finally, no Service Broker or HTTP ENDPOINTs are created by default; you need to create them explicitly. Figure 6-1 shows the Security Configuration Manager screen for configuring features. It is shown being used to enable the CLR on an instance of SQL Server. Note that this is the equivalent of using the T-SQL batch shown in the inset in the figure.

In the SQL Server 2005 release, care has been taken to require that SQL Server passwords be stronger. You'll read later in this chapter about improvements when using SQL Server logins and passwords. With regard to feature enabling, two good examples of the new policy are ENDPOINTs used for HTTP (discussed in Chapter 12) and SQLCLR features (discussed in Chapters 2 through 5).

HTTP ENDPOINTs (endpoints that allow SQL Server to expose stored procedures as Web Services) are not enabled by default. Someone with an extended privilege must explicitly invoke CREATE ENDPOINT; there are no "default endpoints" set up on install. ENDPOINT definition prohibits using any security style but Windows integrated choices (Windows integrated security never sends passwords over the network, even in encrypted form) unless you are using the SSL. SSL, though not as robust as Windows

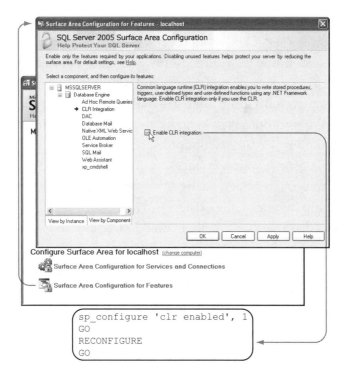

FIGURE 6-1: Surface area configuration for features

integrated (NTLM or Kerberos) authentication, does at least encrypt all network traffic for the connection. It's the same encryption you use to send credit-card numbers over the Internet when you purchase products on the Web. When an ENDPOINT is defined, it's not ON by default; you must create it as ENABLED or explicitly enable it with an ALTER ENDPOINT command. No Web Services or batch access (available separately) are enabled by default within an ENDPOINT, either.

Security and Metadata

One of the ways to gain information about a SQL Server database is to rummage through the system metadata views. In previous versions of SQL Server, you could retrieve metadata information on other users' database objects that you did not own or have access to. SQL Server 2005 remedies this situation.

One of the new permissions added to SQL Server 2005 is the VIEW DEF-INITION permission. Not only are the new system metadata views (which start with the identifier sys.) read-only, but also, you can use the VIEW DEFINITION privilege to permit or prohibit access to metadata. This privilege is exposed on individual database objects; it's also very useful at the schema level. If you do not have VIEW DEFINITION permission, system views and stored procedures will not list object information (for example, through sp_helptext) or metadata.

Error messages have been changed as well, so as not to provide information that would indicate the existence of objects you don't have access to. Attempting to drop a procedure that you don't "know about," for example, produces the following error message: "Cannot drop the procedure 'foo,' because it does not exist or you do not have permission." Although this feature does not stop "guessing attacks," it makes SQL Server metadata less subject to random browsing.

A Quick Review of SQL Server Security Concepts with Enhancements

SQL Server 2005 extends the SQL Server security system to handle .NET Framework assemblies and the calls that these assemblies might make. With a .NET Framework assembly, we are concerned with both internal calls (calls to other assemblies, or "ordinary" stored procedure and table access) and external calls (calls from a .NET Framework assembly to the world outside the SQL Server process) in SQL Server 2005. Because the new security is based on the original SQL Server security system, and because there have been many enhancements to SQL Server security in SQL Server 2005, it helps to start with a quick review of how SQL Server security works in general.

Authentication and Authorization: Principals and Permissions

Any security system is concerned with two main concepts: authentication and authorization. *Authentication* is the process of identifying a principal with strong evidence; *authorization* is determining what operations a principal can perform. In SQL Server, a login is a principal, and authentication is done by SQL Server when a user logs in to it. When a user—let's call him Bob—has identified himself to the SQL Server instance by logging in (that is, SQL Server is aware that the user session "5" is actually "bob"), he can do whatever operations, such as add records to tables or query tables, he has authorization to do. The operation can include access to SQL Server objects, as well as the ability to use functionality. One example of the latter is the `ALTER TRACE` permission that secures SQL Server tracing. These objects and functionality groups are known as *securables*. This is shown in Figure 6-2.

A SQL Server process is called an instance, as in "an instance of the service process `sqlservr.exe`." One or more SQL Server instances can run on one machine running Windows. Authentication is done per instance of SQL Server. Principals—that is, *logins*—that can log in to an instance were identified to SQL Server in previous releases by using system stored procedures and stored in a system view, `syslogins`. In SQL Server 2005, this information

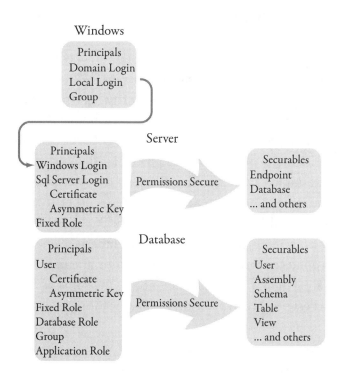

FIGURE 6-2: Principals, permissions, and securables in SQL Server 2005

is defined and maintained through the CREATE LOGIN DDL statement and exposed through sys.server_principals and sys.sql_logins.

SQL Server supports Windows users and groups as logins and SQL Server–specific logins, but it may be configured to support only Windows users as logins, which is recommended practice.[2] Windows user accounts may be local to the machine running SQL Server or accounts in the Active Directory for the enterprise to which SQL Server belongs. SQL Server no longer supports permitting only SQL Server logins.

In SQL Server 2000, the DBA defines Windows logins to SQL Server using the sp_grantlogin system stored procedure. SQL Server–defined users are assigned their login name, password, and (optionally) language and default database using the sp_addlogin system stored procedure. These system stored procedures still exist in SQL Server 2005 but should be considered deprecated; the equivalent functionality is exposed in the CREATE LOGIN DDL statement in SQL Server 2005, which should be used instead. In SQL Server 2005, you can also use the ALTER LOGIN DDL statement to DISABLE a LOGIN or to RENAME a LOGIN. You could rename the special "sa" login to a different name, like "Fred." In SQL Server 2005, there is also the ability to create logins that are associated with certificates and asymmetric keys. These logins cannot be used to log in to SQL Server from a client but are used for some advanced security features we'll be covering in the chapter, as well as with Service Broker endpoints.

Authenticated logins of a particular SQL Server instance can be mapped to principals called *users* in a particular database. Each login can have a default database; logging in will drop the user into this database. Logins may also be allowed to access databases other than their default database, as defined by the administrator. In SQL Server, the term *user* refers to a *login*'s identity in a particular database. Depending on how users are mapped to logins by the administrator, the user ID for a particular user in a particular database may not be the same as the login ID. It is, however, a best practice to make the user name the same as the login name.

---

2. It should be pointed out that even if the instance is configured to accept Windows authentication only, SQL-based logins (server principals) can exist in the server, with the difference that they will not be allowed to connect to the server (authenticate).

A login can have only a single user in a given database, as the following code illustrates:

```
CREATE LOGIN bob WITH PASSWORD='m8b#5pL'
GO

USE PUBS
GO

CREATE USER pubsbob FOR LOGIN bob

--the following will fail, login bob
-- may only have a single user in a database
CREATE USER otherPubsBob FOR LOGIN bob
```

Figure 6-3 shows the relationship between logins and users.

Figure 6-3 shows an instance of SQL Server with two logins: bob and niels. The login bob is mapped to the user bob in the pubs database. The login bob has a default database of pubs, so when bob logs in, by default, he will be referencing the pubs database as user bob. The login niels is mapped to the user nielsB on the database pubs, but the default database for this login is nwnd. The login niels will have to use a three-part name to reference pubs, and when he does, he will be referencing it as the user

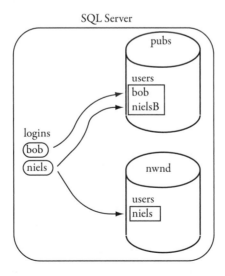

FIGURE 6-3: Defining database users for SQL Server logins

nielsB. The login niels is also mapped to the nwnd database as user niels, which is the default database for that login. When niels logs in, by default, he will connect to the nwnd database and do so as the user niels. Note that login niels has a different user name on pubs than on nwnd.

If a user has not been granted access to a database, and the "guest" user is enabled on that database, he accesses the database as a user called "guest." The guest user is off by default in new databases and must be enabled if needed. If a user has been granted access to a database but has no explicit user mapped to it, the token created for the user will have all the user's information except for a primary ID, so "public" will be used instead (the user_name() function returns the login name in this case). The most common example of this is when access to a database is granted via a Windows group membership.

In SQL Server 2005, you create a user with the CREATE USER DDL statement. The sp_adduser system stored procedure is retained for backward compatibility and acts a little differently from CREATE USER with respect to SCHEMAs, as you'll see soon. In SQL Server 2005, you can also create users who are associated with asymmetric keys and certificates, as you can with logins. In addition, you can create users who are not tied to logins by using the CREATE USER ... WITHOUT LOGIN statement. The reason for users without logins is to represent the identity associated with a partner's certificate when using Service Broker remotely. We'll talk more about Service Broker in Chapter 11.

A SQL Server user in a particular database can be permitted to perform DDL and DML operations; therefore, a database in SQL Server (rather than an instance) usually is the authorization domain. Users are granted permissions using the GRANT DDL statement, such as the following:

```
GRANT SELECT ON SOMESCHEMA.SOMETABLE TO SOMEUSER
```

In SQL Server 2005, permissions can also be granted on instance-level objects like ENDPOINTs and even commands like SHUTDOWN.

Permissions on a database table, view, or stored procedure, as well as other database object permissions, are granted to a user by the object's owner. A permission can be granted to each user, but this would be cumbersome and unwieldy as many users are added to the database. Therefore, SQL Server users can be grouped into *roles.* In addition to custom roles—which can be defined, for example, for users of a specific application—a few special, built-in roles exist. The only special role we'll mention here is db_owner, the database owner role. Multiple users can be assigned to the db_owner role for a particular database, and this role gives the user unlimited privilege inside that database. Note that the db_owner role is not the same as DBO, the special database owner principal. There can only be one DBO per database. There is also the special principal public that refers to anyone who has access to a particular database. Public appears along with the database roles in some graphic user interface tools, though technically, it's not a role. In addition to roles, SQL Server authorization is aware of *Windows groups*, if database users were derived from Windows-based logins, but Windows groups do not have any correspondence to database roles.

In addition to user-based security, SQL Server has the notion of application-based security. Some administrators might wish to permit or deny access based on the current application, rather than the user. For this purpose, SQL Server permits definition of *application roles.* Application roles are different from roles in that they contain no users. In fact, when a SQL Server user assumes an application role, because code in an application (for example, an inventory control application) issues a statement such as the following,

```
exec sp_setapprole @role='inventoryrole',
                    @password= 'AStrongPW!'
```

the user gives up all the permissions granted him as a user. The user can access only those database objects that the role has permission to access. A new feature in SQL Server 2005 allows unsetting an application role as well as setting it. To maintain security, when using this feature, you must use an option on sp_setapprole that returns a cookie. The cookie is required for sp_unsetapprole; this prohibits users from arbitrarily calling sp_unsetapprole. Listing 6-1 shows an example.

LISTING 6-1: Using sp_unsetapprole requires a cookie

```
sp_addapprole 'myapp', 'StrongPW1'
GO

DECLARE @theCookie varbinary(256)
EXEC sp_setapprole 'myapp', 'StrongPW1',
    @fCreateCookie = true, @cookie = @theCookie OUTPUT

-- Check user, should be myapp
```

```
SELECT USER_NAME()

-- now, unset it
EXEC sp_unsetapprole @theCookie
-- Check user, should be original user
SELECT USER_NAME()
GO
```

Application roles are not used as much as they could be because of issues with connection polling. The application role is not reset when a connection is returned to the pool automatically. If, however, the programmer remembers always to reset the identity using `sp_unsetapprole`, connection pooling should be able to coexist with application roles.

The following object-level permissions can be granted to a user, a role, an application role, or a Windows group:

- SELECT

- UPDATE

- DELETE

- INSERT

- EXECUTE

- REFERENCES

In SQL Server 2000, SELECT, INSERT, UPDATE, and DELETE are permissions that can be granted on SQL Server table and views. EXECUTE permission can be granted on a stored procedure or user-defined function. REFERENCES permission means that a user who is the owner of table A can define a foreign key to table B, which she does not own, if she has REFERENCES permission on table B. REFERENCES permission is also used to allow a user to define a VIEW or UDF using the SQL WITH SCHEMABINDING option if the view or UDF uses a table or view that is owned by a different owner. You can also use GRANT to grant a permission and give the user permission to grant access to others; this is called GRANT WITH GRANT OPTION. In SQL Server 2005, these permissions can also be granted at a higher scope—for example, at the SCHEMA scope.

SQL Server 2005 adds the following new object-level permissions:

- ALTER

- CONTROL

- SEND
- RECEIVE (Service Broker queues)
- TAKE OWNERSHIP
- VIEW DEFINITION

If a user is permitted to create objects like tables, views, or stored procedures, when the user issues the CREATE statement, in SQL Server 2000 she becomes the owner of the object. This changes in SQL Server 2005, as the object owner is the schema owner by default. Object owners have unlimited permissions on objects, including the permission to grant other users permissions. One special case is that if the user is a member of the special DBO principal, objects created by that user are considered owned by DBO. Because different users can define objects having the same name— that is, BOB.SOMETABLE and MARY.SOMETABLE—many SQL Server installations prefer to have all database objects defined and owned by DBO, although this can be done differently in SQL Server 2005 with the introduction of schemas (discussed later in this chapter). This simplifies determining permissions, which can become quite complicated, as we'll see later in this chapter.

As an aside, when anyone in the SQL Server system role sysadmin logs on to a SQL Server instance (this includes Windows system administrators by default), she automatically becomes DBO in every database by default. Programmers should always test their programs by running the program when logged on to Windows as nonadministrators to prevent surprises at deployment time. Obviously, security makes SQL DML statements act differently depending on the user who executes them. In addition, because changing databases inside a SQL Server instance using the USE SOMEOTHERDATABASE statement is an expensive operation, a best practice when using SQL Server from an application server (where like sessions will be pooled using connection pooling) is to define a special user for each distinct application in the application server and to give that user a default database that is appropriate for that application. When users must be distinctly identified inside SQL Server—for example, for auditing—this is not possible, of course, although each user should have a default database that corresponds to the database he will be working in most often.

Execution Context and Ownership Chaining

When you execute a stored procedure or user-defined function, or use a VIEW prior to SQL Server 2005, access to objects inside the stored procedure always occurs using the identity of the caller of the stored procedure. Many people don't recognize this at first glance, because permissions are checked only when the owner of the stored procedure is different from the owner of the object the stored procedure is accessing. This permits giving users access to database tables only through sanctioned stored procedures while denying them access to the underlying tables directly.

In the following example, let's say the same user, FRED, owns both the employee table and the update_salary stored procedure. FRED does not grant BOB permission to access the employee table but does grant BOB permission to execute the update_salary stored procedure. Now BOB can update the employee table, but only through the stored procedure:

```
--Logged in as FRED
CREATE TABLE FRED.employee (
  -- other fields elided for clarity
  emp_id   INT,
  name     VARCHAR(20),
  address VARCHAR(50),
  phone    VARCHAR(15),
  salary_grade INT,
  salary  MONEY
)
GO

-- procedure for update
CREATE PROCEDURE FRED.update_salary(
 @EMP_ID INT,
 @NEW_SALARY MONEY)
AS
UPDATE FRED.employee SET salary = @NEW_SALARY
  WHERE emp_id = @EMP_ID
GO

-- BOB can only execute the procedure
GRANT EXECUTE ON FRED.update_salary to BOB
GO
```

If the same user (FRED) owns both the stored procedure and the table, permissions are never checked when the stored procedure accesses the table using DML statements. Because BOB has EXECUTE permission on the stored procedure, the stored procedure works. This is shown in Figure 6-4.

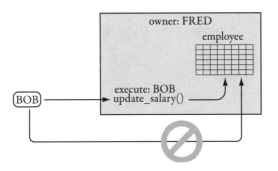

FIGURE 6-4: An ownership chain. **BOB** can access the table only through the stored procedure.

If, however, FRED alters the stored procedure also to access another table owned by a different user (say, ALICE) inside the stored procedure, the ability of BOB (not FRED) to access the salary_audit table is checked:

```
-- procedure for update
-- FRED owns the PROCEDURE
ALTER PROCEDURE FRED.update_salary(
 @EMP_ID INT,
 @NEW_SALARY MONEY)
AS
-- FRED owns the employee table
UPDATE FRED.employee SET salary = @NEW_SALARY
  WHERE emp_id = @EMP_ID

-- But ALICE owns the salary_audit table
INSERT INTO ALICE.salary_audit values(@EMP_ID, @NEW_SALARY)
GO
```

Figure 6-5 illustrates ownership chaining.
Notice two things about this diagram:

- Because BOB is invoking a stored procedure owned by FRED, BOB must have EXECUTE permission on the stored procedure. He need not have access to the underlying tables as long as FRED also owns the tables.
- Because FRED is the owner of the stored procedure but does not own the ALICE.salary_audit table, permission of the caller (BOB) on the ALICE.salary_audit is checked.

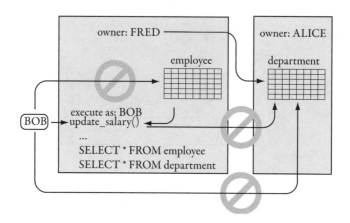

FIGURE 6-5: If **FRED**'s stored procedure accesses **ALICE**'s table, this breaks the ownership chain.

In general, SQL Server checks permissions only when an object accesses an object that is not owned by the same accessor. If the same user owns two objects, and one object accesses the other, permissions are not checked at all, at any level. This is known as an *ownership chain*. If, at any level, an object accesses another object that is not owned by the accessor, permissions are checked because the ownership chain has been broken.

Until SQL Server 2000 SP3, ownership chains were permitted across databases. After SP3, this is no longer the default, but you can enable cross-database ownership chains on a per-database basis as an option, using the following statement (this is not a recommended practice):

```
USE master
EXEC sp_dboption MyDatabase, 'db chaining', 'true'
GO
```

In addition, permissions are always checked when you are using dynamic SQL inside a stored procedure. A different implementation of the update_salary stored procedure is shown in the following code:

```
-- procedure for update
-- FRED owns the PROCEDURE
ALTER PROCEDURE FRED.update_salary(
  @in_emp_id INT,
  @in_new_salary MONEY)
AS
```

```
-- FRED owns the employee table
-- table is accessed through dynamic SQL
EXECUTE sp_executesql
N'UPDATE FRED.employee SET salary = @new_salary
  WHERE emp_id = @emp_id',
N'@new_salary MONEY, @emp_id INT',
@new_salary = @in_new_salary, @emp_id = @new_emp_id
GO
```

In SQL Server, access is always checked when dynamic SQL is invoked, regardless of the owner of the object that the dynamic SQL statement accesses. Because we're using dynamic SQL, when BOB executes the stored procedure, BOB's access to the employee table is checked. Because BOB does not have access to the table, the stored procedure fails.

In SQL Server 2005, the concept of ownership chaining remains tied to the object owner, but in most cases, the object owner will be the schema owner. SQL Server 2005 also introduces the notion of execution context other than "current user." Setting execution context can solve the dynamic SQL problem just described but must be managed carefully. We'll discuss it later in this chapter.

SQL Server Password Policies and Credentials

SQL Server 2005 tightens authentication for SQL Server logins when SQL Server runs under Windows Server 2003, and there are also some updates to authentication when SQL Server runs on other operating systems. As we mentioned at the beginning of this chapter, users can use Windows authentication or SQL Server authentication to log in to SQL Server. Windows authentication is very secure because a user's password is never sent across the network, and the domain or machine administrator can enforce password policy. The password policy can require that users change their passwords at the first login to the NT domain or machine. The policy can require users to use strong passwords—for example, at least eight characters, including at least one number, letter, and special character. The policy can also require users to change their passwords every so often. The policy can specify that a login will be locked out after a certain number of bad password attempts. When a database administrator uses only Windows logins, SQL Server inherits this level of enforceable security. Until SQL Server 2005, SQL Server logins had none of these necessary security characteristics. And weak passwords are acknowledged to be the weakest link in most security systems.

With the new SQL Server 2005 security features, SQL Server logins will have all the same security policy features available. Both SQL Server users and application roles will use the policy. With Windows Server 2003 or later, the policy will be implemented via an OS-level call, `NetValidatePassword-Policy`, so that the administrator can use the same policy for both Windows integrated and SQL Server logins. To give companies that convert to SQL Server 2005 time to analyze how the policy will affect existing applications, these policies can be turned off on a per-login basis. Obviously, this is not recommended. The `CHECK_EXPIRATION` policy is set to `OFF` by default, because organizations and software vendors will have to add password-changing capabilities to each application. As Windows provides users the ability to change their passwords at login time (or while logged on to Windows), SQL Server users will have the ability to change their passwords during login. Client APIs, such as OLE DB, ODBC, and ADO.NET, and the client tools, such as SQL Server Management Studio, have been enhanced to support this.

Password policy is set by using the Active Directory Users and Computers tool if you're using Active Directory or by using the Local Security Settings administrator tool if you're administering a nondomain computer. Table 6-1 shows the settings that are exposed using Local Security Settings.

Note that Account Lockout Duration (the amount of time accounts are locked out when you reach the Account Lockout Threshold) and Reset Lockout Counter After (the amount of time after which the invalid login attempts revert to zero, if you haven't exceeded them) are not applicable until you set Account Lockout Threshold to something other than zero.

There are two password options for SQL Server logins: `CHECK_EXPIRATION` and `CHECK_POLICY`. `CHECK_EXPIRATION` encompasses minimum and maximum password age, and `CHECK_POLICY` encompasses all the other policies. When you run afoul of either policy, the SQL Server login must be unlocked by the DBA, as shown in an example later in this chapter.

An administrator can add a new login through SQL Server Management Studio or by using the T-SQL statement `CREATE LOGIN`. The legacy stored procedure `sp_addlogin` will be supported for backward compatibility but will not expose the new features. As shown in the following example, you can create a new SQL Server login that requires the password to be changed on the user's first login attempt by using the `MUST_CHANGE` keyword.

TABLE 6-1: Security Policies for Windows and SQL Server 2005 Logins

Policy Category	Policy Name	Default (Local Server)
Password Policy	Enforce Password History	0 passwords remembered
	Maximum Password Age	42 days
	Minimum Password Age	0 days
	Minimum Password Length	0 characters
	Password Must Meet Complexity Requirements	Disabled
	Store Passwords Using Reversible Encryption	Disabled
Account Lockout Policy	Account Lockout Duration	Not applicable
	Account Lockout Threshold	0 invalid login attempts
	Reset Lockout Counter After	Not applicable

Attempting to access the SQL Server instance without changing the password will result in an error:

```
CREATE LOGIN FRED WITH PASSWORD = 'hy!at54Cq' MUST_CHANGE,
   DEFAULT_DATABASE = pubs,
   CHECK_EXPIRATION = ON,
   CHECK_POLICY = ON
GO
```

When FRED attempts to log into the database, he'll get a "Must change password on first login" error. The database administrator can manage password-policy problems with DDL. If login FRED has been locked out, for example, after three bad login attempts, the database administrator can unlock the login by using the following code:

```
ALTER LOGIN FRED WITH PASSWORD = 'fredsNewpassword#' UNLOCK
GO
```

In those rare cases where the database administrator wants to turn off the password expiration enforcement or security policy enforcement, ALTER LOGIN can accomplish this. Neither of the following statements will work when the MUST_CHANGE flag is set and the user has not yet changed his password:

```
ALTER LOGIN FRED WITH CHECK_EXPIRATION = OFF
GO

ALTER LOGIN FRED WITH CHECK_POLICY = OFF
GO
```

Encryption Keys and Built-In Encryption Functions

Industries and governments are beginning to demand the encryption of database data. In the United States, the health-care and credit-card industries are the first industries to be affected. Because of new laws, for example, doctors are not automatically permitted access to other doctors' patient records. Before SQL Server 2005, data encryption was supported only by third-party encryption products. In SQL Server 2005, data encryption is a built-in function. Data encryption is sometimes accomplished in other databases at a column level, by declaring a column to be encrypted through a DDL extension. This type of encryption will not be sufficient for the doctors example unless each doctor's patients are stored in a different table. SQL Server 2005 does not implement column-level encryption; it provides data encryption functions instead. It's up to the developer to call these functions, manually encrypt the data during an INSERT statement, and decrypt it during SELECT statements.

To encrypt and decrypt data, we need encryption keys. So the first questions to be answered are "Where will the encryption keys be stored?" and "How will the keys themselves be encrypted?" Before covering the encryption functions themselves, we need to answer these questions.

SQL Server 2005 stores and manages secrets by making them database objects and managing them through normal DDL statements, for the most part. Keys are tied to databases, and the encryption objects are arranged hierarchically. At the top of the chain is the service master key. This key is generated automatically when SQL Server 2005 is installed, and it's generated and stored using the DPAPI (data protection API, a Windows operating system feature). This key is stored in the master database. Key generation uses the principal that is running the SQL Server service as the starting point for the key. We'll get back to how you back up and restore the key, and to the repercussions this has when the SQL Server service principal is changed, in a moment. Each database can have a database master key. The database master key is not generated automatically for each new database; it is optional. It can be generated manually using the CREATE MASTER KEY DDL statement, as follows:

```
-- Generating the database master key
CREATE MASTER KEY ENCRYPTION BY PASSWORD = 'StrongPW#'
```

The database master key is a 128-byte DES3 key. When the database master key is generated, it is stored in two places. One copy is encrypted with the service master key and stored in the master database; one copy is encrypted with the supplied password and stored in the database itself. The database master key is required for functions such as encrypted conversations when using the Service Broker feature. We'll have more to say about this in the Service Broker chapter (Chapter 11).

The three key types that SQL Server can store are X.509 certificates, symmetric keys, and asymmetric keys. These secrets are defined at a database level; they are not part of a database schema. Symmetric keys and asymmetric keys are used to encrypt and decrypt data, and possibly other secrets. Certificates can be used for data and secret encryption but can also be used for other SQL Server 2005 functionality, such as SSL encryption on HTTP endpoints. SQL Server 2005 can generate its own certificates or use certificates generated from outside sources. When it uses certificates generated from outside sources, certificate authentication chains, expiration policies, and revocation lists are not used. You can generate a certificate (good for one year) with the following DDL statement:

```
-- Generating a certificate,
-- no password, so encrypted by database master key
CREATE CERTIFICATE mycert
 AUTHORIZATION certuser WITH SUBJECT = 'Cert for certuser'
```

Each type of secret can be protected by a variety of mechanisms. Table 6-2 shows the protection possibilities for each type of secret.

When you create symmetric and asymmetric keys using DDL statements, you specify the key, the owner, the encryption algorithm that the key uses, and the mechanism used to encrypt the key itself. A variety of encryption algorithms are supported.

Now that we have the basic information down, let's walk through a scenario for using encryption keys and show the entirety of the DDL involved.

A table contains a column with encrypted data. User1 and User2 should be able to see only their own encrypted data. Admin1 should be able to see data encrypted by both User1 and User2. Listing 6-2 illustrates creating the appropriate SYMMETRIC KEYs and the CERTIFICATEs to protect them. Each CERTIFICATE and SYMMETRIC KEY is owned by the corresponding user, as shown in Listing 6-2. Admin1 (the administrator) must have access to both keys and both certificates.

LISTING 6-2: Creating symmetric keys that are protected by certificates

```
-- Generate a certificate for user1 and user2
CREATE CERTIFICATE User1cert
    AUTHORIZATION User1 WITH SUBJECT = 'Cert for User1'
CREATE CERTIFICATE User2cert
    AUTHORIZATION User2 WITH SUBJECT = 'Cert for User2'
GO
-- symmetric keys to be used for encryption
-- they are faster than certificates
CREATE SYMMETRIC KEY Key1 AUTHORIZATION User1
   WITH ALGORITHM = TRIPLE_DES³ ENCRYPTION BY CERTIFICATE User1cert
CREATE SYMMETRIC KEY Key2 AUTHORIZATION User2
   WITH ALGORITHM = TRIPLE_DES ENCRYPTION BY CERTIFICATE User2cert
GO
```

The service master key, database master keys, and certificates must be backed up, restored, and maintained just like other database objects. Certificates, symmetric keys, and asymmetric keys can be backed up and

---

3. Not all encryption algorithms are available on all operating system versions. The AES algorithm may be a better choice here, but we're going with an algorithm that is available on every Windows OS that supports SQL Server 2005.

TABLE 6-2: Encryption Choices for SQL Server Security Secrets

Secret Type	Can Be Encrypted By	Multiple Encryptions Possible?
(Database) Master key	Password (1 or more), service master key (default, but it is optional and can be dropped)	Yes
Certificate (private key)	DB master key, password	No
Asymmetric key (private key)	DB master key, password	No
Symmetric key	Password, certificate, asymmetric key, symmetric key	Yes

restored with the database. Certificates can also be backed up to disk or restored from disk separately. Backing up and restoring only the public key or the public–private key pair is supported for certificates. The database master key is just another symmetric key, but there is special DDL to create and manipulate it. When you detach a database with a database master key and attach it to another instance, you need to open (via a password) the database master key and encrypt it using the service master key of the new instance. It is also possible to use a database master key without having the database master key encrypted by the service master key and stored in the master database. More on this later.

The service master key is special because:

- It is tied to the principal that runs the SQL Server service process.
- It is used to encrypt database master keys.
- It is used to encrypt other credentials at server scope, such as credentials.

You can back up and restore this key with DDL statements, like you can with database master keys and certificates. You cannot change the identity of the principal running the SQL Server service process, however, without explicitly decrypting and reencrypting the service master keys. Doing so could make all your keys unusable. The SQL Server Configuration Manager contains a special function to accomplish changing a SQL Server service principal. You must use this utility to protect the viability of your keys.

Encryption Functions

Now that we have the proper keys in place, let's discuss the functions used for data encryption. There are 15 T-SQL built-in functions defined for this purpose and a related helper function:

- `EncryptByAsymKey`
- `DecryptByAsymKey`
- `EncryptByCert`
- `DecryptByCert`
- `EncryptByPassPhrase`
- `DecryptByPassPhrase`
- `EncryptByKey`
- `DecryptByKey`
- `DecryptByKeyAutoCert`
- `DecryptByKeyAutoAsymKey`
- `SignByAsymKey`
- `SignByCert`
- `VerifySignedByAsymKey`
- `VerifySignedByCert`
- `HashBytes`

First, a word about keys and encryption/decryption functions. Symmetric keys use the same key for encryption and decryption. This presents a key-distribution problem, as the key must be distributed unchanged to both sides. Symmetric keys, however, are orders of magnitude faster for encryption/decryption than asymmetric keys. Asymmetric keys use a key pair to accomplish their purpose. Only the owner of the asymmetric key has the private-key part; the outside world has the public-key part. Public keys are so public that they can be published in key directories. One use of asymmetric key pairs is to encrypt a hash of some data (such as a legal document) with your private key. A user who possesses your public key can recalculate the hash and decrypt the encrypted hash with your public key, and be assured that it came from you because only you have the private key used to encrypt it. This is called *signing*. The outside world can use your public key to encrypt data to send to you; only you have the correct private key to decrypt it. This is known as *sealing the data*. Asymmetric keys are slower to encrypt and decrypt data, but are often used to generate or protect a symmetric "session key" for use in a single data-encryption session. *Certificates* are simply asymmetric keys with additional metadata: a key issuer, expiration date, and so on. SQL Server supports X509.V1 certificates; it can store but cannot use the V3-specific fields in a X509.V3 certificate. To summarize, there are three general rules of encryption to remember:

- Symmetric keys are faster than asymmetric keys.
- The greater the amount of data,[4] the longer it takes to encrypt and decrypt.
- In general, the longer the key used for encryption, the safer the encryption is, but the longer it takes to encrypt and decrypt.

Let's use the set of keys we defined in the preceding section to encrypt some data in a table. We'll show the scenario in which two users can each see only their own data. In addition, there is an administrator who can see both users' data. First, we'll define a table that will hold an encrypted field:

```
-- The primary key and name data are public
-- The secret_data column is encrypted

CREATE TABLE dbo.secret_table (
  id INT PRIMARY KEY IDENTITY,
  first_name VARCHAR(20),
  last_name VARCHAR(50),
  secret_data VARBINARY(8000)
)
GO
GRANT INSERT, SELECT ON dbo.secret_table TO User1, User2
GO
```

---

4. Note that in SQL Server 2005 asymmetric-key encryption, the ciphertext data (data after encryption) is limited to one block.

Note that this table definition does not specify anywhere that secret_data is to be used to store encrypted data. In fact, the same column can be used to store both encrypted and unencrypted data, though this might lead to some unwieldy SQL statements. The column is defined as VARBINARY (which is a requirement) but doesn't support the new data type VARBINARY(MAX). But how big does the column actually have to be? And how much encrypted data can be stored? The minimum amount of room needed for storage can be calculated using the algorithm in Listing 6-3. The encryption algorithms use "normal" VARCHAR data types rather than the new VARCHAR(MAX) data type, so the maximum amount of encrypted data is just under 8,000 bytes.[5] Attempting to encrypt any bigger data will result in a truncation error.

LISTING 6-3: Algorithm to calculate field size needed for encrypted data

```
CREATE FUNCTION dbo.CalculateCipherLen(
  @KeyName sysname, @PTLen int, @UsesHash int = 0 )
RETURNS int
as
BEGIN
    declare @KeyType        nvarchar(2)
    declare @RetVal int
    declare @BLOCK int
    declare @IS_BLOCK      int
    declare @HASHLEN       int

    -- Hash length that
    SET @HASHLEN    = 20
    SET @RetVal     = NULL
    -- Look for the symmetric key in the catalog
    SELECT @KeyType = key_algorithm
       FROM sys.symmetric_keys WHERE name = @KeyName

    -- If parameters are valid
    IF( @KeyType is not null AND @PTLen > 0)
      BEGIN
         -- If hash is being used. NOTE: as we use this value to
         -- calculate the length, we only use 0 or 1
    IF( @UsesHash <> 0 ) SET @UsesHash = 1

    -- 64 bit block ciphers
    IF( @KeyType = N'R2' OR @KeyType = N'D'
        OR @KeyType = N'D3' OR @KeyType = N'DX' )
```

---

5. Actually, the ciphertext limit is 8,000 bytes, including padding with SQL Server-specific headers, so the plaintext limit is a little lower.

```
      BEGIN
        SET @BLOCK = 8
        SET @IS_BLOCK    = 1
      END
  -- 128 bit block ciphers
  ELSE IF( @KeyType = N'A1' OR @KeyType = N'A2' OR @KeyType = N'A3' )
      BEGIN
        SET @BLOCK = 16
SET @IS_BLOCK     = 1
      END
      -- Stream ciphers, only RC4 is supported as a stream cipher
      ELSE
        BEGIN
          SET @IS_BLOCK    = 0
        END

      -- Calculate the expected length.
      -- The formula is different for block ciphers & stream ciphers
      IF( @IS_BLOCK = 1 )
        BEGIN
        SET @RetVal =
          ( FLOOR( (8 + @PTLen + (@UsesHash * @HASHLEN) )/@BLOCK)+1 ) *
            @BLOCK + 16 + @BLOCK
        END
        ELSE
    BEGIN
            SET @RetVal = @PTLen + (@UsesHash * @HASHLEN) + 28
          END
        END
        RETURN @RetVal
END
GO
```

Now let's put some data into our table. Also be aware of the fact that encrypting data makes the column essentially useless as an index or with the UNIQUE, PRIMARY KEY, and FOREIGN KEY column constraints.

To use symmetric keys, a user must not only have permission to use them, but also must explicitly open the key. To open a key, you have to supply the appropriate secret for the key; this depends on how the key was secured with the CREATE and ALTER DDL statements. If the key was secured by using the database master key, only access to the key is needed. The database master key itself can be automatically opened, as long as it's stored in the master database as described earlier in this chapter (protected by the service master key); this is the default. Keys need to be open for both encryption and decryption. Let's put an encrypted row into the database for each user, as shown in Listing 6-4.

LISTING 6-4: Encrypting data while inserting it into a table

```
-- insert rows into secret_table, using encryption
EXECUTE AS USER='user1'
OPEN SYMMETRIC KEY Key1 DECRYPTION BY CERTIFICATE user1cert;
INSERT dbo.secret_table VALUES('Joe', 'User',
  EncryptByKey(Key_GUID('Key1'),'some secret number1'))
CLOSE SYMMETRIC KEY Key1
GO
REVERT
GO

EXECUTE AS USER='user2'
OPEN SYMMETRIC KEY Key2 DECRYPTION BY CERTIFICATE user2cert;
INSERT dbo.secret_table VALUES('Jill', 'Smith',
  EncryptByKey(Key_GUID('Key2'),'some other secret number2'))
CLOSE SYMMETRIC KEY Key2
GO
REVERT
GO
```

Keys should be closed when you are through with them, although all open keys (known as the *keyring*) are automatically closed on session termination. This is true even when connection pooling is used. The keyring is per-session, however, and unrelated to the execution context. Now let's fetch the data.

If you attempt to fetch a column that contains encrypted data without using the appropriate decrypt function, the encrypted data is returned whether or not you have the appropriate encryption key open. To fetch the unencrypted data, you must use an encryption algorithm in the SELECT statement. An ease-of-use alternative is to encapsulate this in a VIEW. When the decrypt function is specified as part of a SELECT statement, SQL Server attempts decryption using all the keys that you have open. If any key is successful, the correct data is returned; otherwise, the decrypt function returns NULL. This is illustrated in Listing 6-5.

LISTING 6-5: Only users with access to the keys can access data

```
EXECUTE AS USER='user1'
OPEN SYMMETRIC KEY Key1 DECRYPTION BY CERTIFICATE user1cert
-- you get the encrypted value
SELECT id, first_name, last_name, secret_data
  FROM secret_table
```

```
-- you either get the unencrypted value or NULL
SELECT id, first_name, last_name,
       cast(decryptByKey(secret_data) AS VARCHAR(256))
  FROM secret_table
CLOSE SYMMETRIC KEY Key1
GO
REVERT
GO


EXECUTE AS USER='user2'
OPEN SYMMETRIC KEY Key2 DECRYPTION BY CERTIFICATE user2cert
-- you get the encrypted value
SELECT id, first_name, last_name, secret_data
  FROM secret_table
-- you either get the unencrypted value or NULL
SELECT id, first_name, last_name,
       cast(decryptByKey(secret_data) AS VARCHAR(256))
  FROM secret_table
CLOSE SYMMETRIC KEY Key2
GO
REVERT
GO


EXECUTE AS USER='admin1'
OPEN SYMMETRIC KEY Key1 DECRYPTION BY CERTIFICATE user1cert
OPEN SYMMETRIC KEY Key2 DECRYPTION BY CERTIFICATE user2cert
-- cyphertext
SELECT id, first_name, last_name, secret_data
  FROM secret_table
-- sees both rows decrypted
SELECT id, first_name, last_name,
       cast(decryptByKey(secret_data) AS VARCHAR(256))
  FROM secret_table
CLOSE ALL SYMMETRIC KEYS
GO
REVERT
GO
```

In addition to the encrypt/decrypt functions for every key type and even pass phrase–based encryption/decryption, there are automatic decryption functions when using certificates or asymmetric keys. These functions are provided as a convenience if a single certificate or asymmetric key is used to encrypt all the data in a table, as shown in Listing 6-6. In this case, you can use a VIEW to read the table, and key management is taken care of automatically.

LISTING 6-6: Using the DecryptByKeyAutoCert function in a VIEW

```
-- Generate a certificate owned by DBO
CREATE CERTIFICATE somecert
    AUTHORIZATION DBO WITH SUBJECT = 'Cert for Encrypted column'
GRANT CONTROL ON CERTIFICATE::somecert TO lowpriv_user
GO
CREATE SYMMETRIC KEY somekey AUTHORIZATION DBO
  WITH ALGORITHM = TRIPLE_DES ENCRYPTION BY CERTIFICATE somecert
GRANT VIEW DEFINITION ON SYMMETRIC KEY::somekey TO lowpriv_user
GO
CREATE TABLE dbo.secret_col_table (
  id INT PRIMARY KEY IDENTITY,
  secret_col VARBINARY(8000)
)
GO
OPEN SYMMETRIC KEY somekey DECRYPTION BY CERTIFICATE somecert
INSERT dbo.secret_col_table VALUES(
  EncryptByKey(Key_GUID('somekey'), 'more secret data'))
CLOSE SYMMETRIC KEY somekey
GO
CREATE VIEW dbo.public_view AS
 SELECT id, convert(varchar(100),
   DecryptByKeyAutocert(cert_id('somecert'), null, secret_col))
     AS dbo.secret_col
 FROM dbo.secret_col_table
GO
-- now the lowpriv_user can access the column
GRANT SELECT ON dbo.public_view TO lowpriv_user
GO
```

Note that when using a VIEW defined using an automatic decryption function, the low-privileged user requires not only access to the view, but also access to the certificate (CONTROL) and the ability to "see" (VIEW DEFINITION) the encryption key. You can use a helper function that uses the EXECUTE AS OWNER feature to further simplify this; we'll be looking at EXECUTE AS later in this chapter.

Separation of Users and Schemas

SQL:1999 defines the concept of a database schema as a named group of data that is owned by a particular authorization ID. Schemas are scoped to the database (called CATALOG in SQL:1999 and the information schema views), and one database can contain one or more schemas. Schema objects—such tables, views, and stored procedures, live in a schema—and the two-part name of a database object is actually `schemaname.objectname`.

Prior to SQL Server 2005, the concept of a schema was tied to a particular user. Any objects created by a user were owned by that user, and SQL Server really defined the two-part name of a database object as `ownername.objectname` rather than `schemaname.objectname`. There was a CREATE SCHEMA DDL statement, but you did not have the option of naming your schema, only its owner, as shown here:

```
-- SQL Server 2000 create schema, no schema name
CREATE SCHEMA AUTHORIZATION fred
    CREATE VIEW v1 as SELECT au_id, au_lname FROM authors
    GRANT SELECT ON v1 to public
GO

-- SQL Server 2005 create schema with name
CREATE SCHEMA fredstuff AUTHORIZATION fred
```

This pre–SQL Server 2005 CREATE SCHEMA statement actually was a convenient way to create objects that belonged to a specific user (like `fred`, in this case) and grant permissions to them in a single DDL statement batch. The problem of having database objects tied to a particular user was that to drop the user, the database administrator had to reassign or drop and re-create all that user's database objects.

SQL Server 2005 introduces the concept of named schemas as separate from users. When you use the new CREATE USER DDL statement to create a user, you can assign a default schema for that user. If a default schema is not assigned, the DBO (database owner) schema is the default, as shown here:

```
-- user's default schema is uschema
CREATE USER u1 FOR LOGIN u1 WITH DEFAULT_SCHEMA = 'uschema'
go

-- user's default schema is dbo
CREATE USER u2 FOR LOGIN u2
go
```

A schema can be owned not only by a specific user (created with a SQL Server login or Windows login), but also by a database role or an application role defined in that database. The new CREATE APPLICATION ROLE

DDL statement permits assignment of a default schema, but because many users can be assigned to a role (an ordinary role, not an application role), CREATE ROLE does not assign a default schema for roles, Windows groups mapped as users, or symmetric and asymmetric keys mapped as users. Note that the legacy procedures sp_adduser and sp_addapprole have been changed first to create a schema with the same name of the user or application role and then to call the appropriate CREATE statement, specifying that schema as the default schema. Use of the new CREATE statements is preferred; the behavior of the stored procedures is kept only for backward compatibility.

The owner of a schema (a single user or multiple users) can create database objects within that schema if he has CREATE privilege on the object and also grant schema-level privileges to others. The schema owner does have to be granted permission to create the database objects, but the grant permission exists on a database level, not on a schema level. Here's an example of a user that has an associated schema and is also the owner of that schema:

```
USE demo1
GO


CREATE LOGIN alogin1 WITH password = 'password1',
DEFAULT_DATABASE = demo1
GO


-- default named schema
CREATE USER auser1 FOR LOGIN alogin1
WITH DEFAULT_SCHEMA = aschema1
GO


CREATE SCHEMA aschema1 AUTHORIZATION auser1
GRANT CREATE TABLE TO auser1
GO


EXECUTE AS USER='auser1'
GO
-- this works and creates aschema1.table1
CREATE TABLE table1 (theid INTEGER)
GO
```

In this case, if we did not set a default_schema for the auser1 user, his default_schema would be dbo. Because auser1 is not a member of the dbo database role, the CREATE TABLE statement would fail.

What this means to the database administrator is that because schemas (and the objects they contain) can be owned by a role, when a user is dropped from the database, the database objects she has created do not have to be reassigned or dropped and re-created. Listing 6-7 shows an example using a SQL Server role for a payroll system.

LISTING 6-7: Managing access by inclusion in a role

```
USE payrolldb
GO
CREATE ROLE payroll
GO
CREATE SCHEMA prschema AUTHORIZATION payroll
GO
CREATE LOGIN janet WITH PASSWORD = 'StrongPW#',
DEFAULT_DATABASE = payrolldb
GO
- default named schema
CREATE USER janet FOR LOGIN janet
WITH DEFAULT_SCHEMA = prschema
GO
-- add janet to payroll and let her create tables
sp_addrolemember 'payroll', 'janet'
GRANT CREATE TABLE TO janet
GO
```

Now user janet can create tables, and they will be contained within the prschema schema. If Janet is reassigned, the user janet can be dropped from the database without affecting any of the tables she has created.

Having named schemas affects the way database object names are resolved. If user janet issues the SQL statement SELECT * from benefits, SQL Server will attempt to resolve the table name benefits in this order:

1. sys.benefits (only for system objects; in this case, benefits is not a system object)
2. prschema.benefits (using the default schema)
3. dbo.benefits

One further special case needs to be mentioned. It is possible that a database user will have a default schema that she does not own (such as DBO) but will have the ability to create database objects in a different schema.

In that case, the database object in the CREATE DDL statement must use the two-part name explicitly. If user janet were defined without a DEFAULT_SCHEMA keyword,[6] for example, her default schema would be dbo. Because she does not have permission on the dbo schema, any attempt to create a database object with a one-part name would fail:

```
-- this statement would fail
CREATE TABLE benefits2003 (empid INT) -- other columns elided

-- this statement would succeed
CREATE TABLE prschema.benefits2003 (empid INT)
```

Schemas have their own sets of permissions. You can grant or deny permissions like SELECT, EXECUTE, or VIEW DEFINITION on a schemawide basis. The following SQL statement prohibits the role payroll from seeing any database objects in the bob schema using the system views:

```
DENY VIEW DEFINITION ON SCHEMA::bob TO payroll
```

Synonyms

SQL Server 2005 introduces support for a database object known as a *synonym*. A synonym is just an alternative name for an existing database object that keeps a database user (more likely, a database programmer) from having to use a multipart name for an object. Synonyms can be defined on a two-part, three-part, or four-part SQL Server object name. A synonym can be defined by the following database objects:

- Table
- View
- Stored procedure
- User-defined function
- Extended stored procedure
- Replication filter procedure

---

6. Note that as defined in the example above, janet does have a default schema, prschema.

Although synonyms can be created on a multipart object name, they are scoped to the database that they are created in. Listing 6-8 shows some examples of creating and using synonyms.

LISTING 6-8: CREATE-ing and using SYNONYMs

```
USE AdventureWorks
GO

CREATE SYNONYM dbo.Customers_East ON Eastserver.Northwind.dbo.Customers
GO

CREATE SYNONYM dbo.Contact FOR Person.Contact
GO

-- use the one-part or two-part name
SELECT * FROM Contact
SELECT * FROM dbo.Customers_East
GO

USE Northwind
GO

-- use the three-part name
SELECT * FROM AdventureWorks..Contact
```

An interesting feature of synonyms is that a synonym itself belongs to a schema. Although you can create a synonym for a user-defined function, because a user-defined function must always be referred to using a two-part name, even if a synonym is defined, you must use the function's two-part synonym name.

Specifying Execution Context for Procedural Code

In previous versions of SQL Server, catalogued procedural code always ran within the security context of the caller, as explained earlier in this chapter in the section on ownership chaining. This is a good strategy for the most common case—for example, when you want to allow users access to tables through stored procedures without giving them access to the base tables. Ownership chaining won't work in two cases, however. The first case is where the owner of the procedure and the owner of the database object that the procedure accesses are not the same. The second case is where you use dynamic SQL, as shown in Figure 6-6.

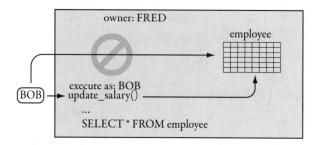

FIGURE 6-6: Dynamic SQL will always break an ownership chain.

Dynamic SQL usually shouldn't be used if you can accomplish the same result using a different construct. As an example, in Listing 6-9, we'll use a stored procedure that executes the following dynamic SQL composed by concatenating strings. (Note: We'll cover the new T-SQL PIVOT syntax in Chapter 8.)

LISTING 6-9: Dynamic SQL with string concatenation is a security risk

```
-- this should get a dynamic list of properties
CREATE FUNCTION products.get_property_names()
RETURNS VARCHAR(1000)
AS
BEGIN
-- hardcode for now
RETURN '[color], [size], [fabric]'
END
GO
-- CALLER needs SELECT permission on products.properties

CREATE PROCEDURE products.get_property_values
AS
DECLARE @stmt VARCHAR(8000)
DECLARE @col_list VARCHAR(1000)
SET @col_list = products.get_property_names()
-- NOTE: that this is subject to SQL injection
-- "col_list" must be validated properly
SET @stmt='SELECT * FROM products.properties
  PIVOT (MAX(value)
  FOR name IN ('+@col_list+')) AS P'
EXECUTE(@stmt)
go
```

SQL Server 2005 now allows you to specify that procedural code execute in a different execution context. There are four reasons you might want to do this:

- You want dynamic SQL to execute in the context of the creator of the stored procedure, as static T-SQL would.

- Because data access code in CLR procedures (through the `SqlClient` data provider discussed in Chapter 4) is effectively dynamic SQL, you might want this code to execute in the context of the creator of the stored procedure as well.

- You want to evaluate ownership chains in the context of the creator of the stored procedure rather than the caller of the procedure, although it's a good idea not to rely on ownership chains at all.

- You need an execution principal for code, like Service Broker activation procedures, that don't have a caller in the traditional sense. (Service Broker is discussed in Chapter 11.)

You choose the execution context on a per-procedure basis when you create the procedure, using the EXECUTE AS parameter. Execution context can also be set on triggers and user-defined functions, except for inline table-valued user-defined functions. An example is shown in the following code:

```
-- this will execute as the owner of the stored procedure
-- if properties table and get_property_names() have the same owner,
-- ownership chain is not broken
CREATE PROCEDURE products.get_property_values
WITH EXECUTE AS OWNER
AS
DECLARE @col_list VARCHAR(1000)
SET @col_list = products.get_property_names()
-- NOTE: that this is subject to SQL injection
-- "col_list" must be validated property
SET @stmt='SELECT * FROM products.properties
  PIVOT (MAX(value)
  FOR property_names IN ('+@col_list+')) AS P'
EXECUTE( @stmt)
go
```

You can also use EXECUTE AS with batches. In fact, we've been using it with the examples in this chapter. It replaces and supersedes the functionality of

SETUSER in previous versions of SQL Server. You go back to the previous identity by using the REVERT statement. EXECUTE AS enhances SETUSER in its ability to impersonate a login as well as a user and in the fact that EXECUTE AS blocks can be nested. You can also specify a cookie with EXECUTE AS used for batches; the cookie is required in the REVERT statement to revert to the previous security context.

There are different EXECUTE AS options with procedural code and SQL batches, as listed in Table 6-3.

EXECUTE AS CALLER is still the default behavior in SQL Server 2005. EXECUTE AS SELF or EXECUTE AS OWNER can be used in the definition of the stored procedure so that even though permission will be checked when dynamic SQL is used, it will be checked against the procedure owner's permissions. The distinction between the two is that the owner of a procedure might be the schema owner and may not necessarily be the principal who created the procedure. The procedure creator may not be the same as the schema owner, who is the owner of every object created in the schema by default. Figure 6-7 shows using EXECUTE AS SELF to make dynamic SQL behave the same as static SQL.

Special care must be taken to guard against SQL *injection* (that is, piggybacking of dangerous code after "normal" parameters) when EXECUTE

TABLE 6-3: EXECUTE AS Options

Option	Usable in Modules?	Usable in Batches?
EXECUTE AS CALLER	Yes	No
EXECUTE AS OWNER	Yes	No
EXECUTE AS SELF	Yes	No
EXECUTE AS 'principal name'	Yes	No
EXECUTE AS USER= 'user name'	No	Yes
EXECUTE AS LOGIN= 'login name'	No	Yes

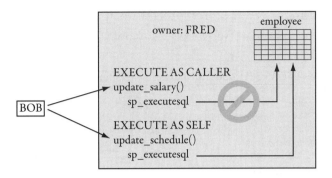

FIGURE 6-7: Using **EXECUTE AS SELF** with dynamic SQL

AS is used. Although counting the rows in a table is pretty mundane code, the fact is that any dynamically constructed code in a stored procedure can be potentially dangerous. EXECUTE AS also can be used to create applications that won't depend on ownership chaining without necessarily using dynamic SQL at all. The purpose is to give flexibility to the application writers. Say that you have a procedure that looks like this:

```
-- this will execute as DBO
CREATE PROCEDURE count_rows_as_dbo(@name NVARCHAR(50)
  WITH EXECUTE AS 'DBO'
AS
EXECUTE('SELECT COUNT(*) FROM ' + @name)
go
```

Given the count_rows_as_dbo stored procedure in the preceding example, if the procedure was catalogued by the DBO, the following code will execute as DBO, regardless of the user who calls it:

```
DECLARE @s varchar(50)
-- DO NOT fill in this variable from user input!!!
SET @s = 'authors;drop table customers'
-- count the rows and drop the table!
count_rows_as_dbo @s
```

Although EXECUTE AS SELF looks interesting, it should be used with care because it can make ownership chains more complex. When a stored procedure with EXECUTE AS SELF accesses any table that the current owner does not own, an ownership chain will be broken, and permissions on the underlying object will be checked. In addition, when a different stored procedure uses this stored procedure, it is possible that ownership chains could be broken at two levels, as shown in Listing 6-10.

LISTING 6-10: EXECUTE AS SELF does not bypass ownership checks

```
-- table FOO_TABLE is owned by DBO.
-- using a procedure count_rows_as_me
CREATE PROCEDURE count_rows_as_me(@name NVARCHAR(50)
  WITH EXECUTE AS SELF
AS
EXECUTE('SELECT COUNT(*) FROM ' + @name)
go

SETUSER JAY
go
-- this checks permissions if JAY is not DBO
count_rows_as_me 'foo_table'
--
--
SETUSER 'fred'
go

CREATE PROCEDURE select_and_count
AS
SELECT * FROM customers
count_rows_as_me 'foo_table'
go

-- this does two ownership checks
-- even if FRED is DBO
EXECUTE select_and_count
go
```

By default, procedural code that uses a nondefault execution context can access only resources in the current database—that is, you may not use three-part names at all. This is to prevent a user with DBO privilege in one database from gaining access to data in another database. If you need to access resources in another database or system-level resources, you must grant appropriate permissions to the executor of the code. Another option is to sign the code with a certificate, map the certificate to a login, and grant permissions to the certificate. We'll see this option later in this chapter.

Administrators and auditors will be concerned about the use of EXECUTE AS, because the function SUSER_NAME() returns the current identity, not the original caller's identity. Auditors can keep track of this by auditing identity changes using SQL Profiler events, Event Notifications, or Windows Management Instrumentation (WMI) events. In addition, a new `ORIGINAL_LOGIN()` function retrieves the name of the login of the session. There is no function that returns the original user name, however. In addition to using `ORIGINAL_LOGIN()`, it is possible to call `EXECUTE AS CALLER` to revert to the original caller (go back to the default behavior). It is highly recommended to use `EXECUTE AS CALLER` on all the operations that are not required to be executed by the module's context whenever possible.

Code Signing

A slightly different way to approach procedural execution context is to use certificates or asymmetric keys to sign a procedure. This is possible for T-SQL stored procedures, user-defined functions, and triggers. Adding a signature to procedural code must be accompanied by defining a database user corresponding to the certificate or asymmetric key that signed the code. Then permissions are granted to that user. When the procedure executes, after verifying the signature, the certificate or asymmetric key–mapped user will be used to modify the current execution context. It will always be added as a secondary identity to the execution context (think of it as a role for the duration of the executing code). Additionally, if the module was marked by `EXECUTE AS`, it will also be added to the authenticators list. Listing 6-11 shows an example.

LISTING 6-11: Signing a stored procedure with a certificate

```
-- signed modules
CREATE CERTIFICATE signing_cert
   AUTHORIZATION DBO WITH SUBJECT = 'Cert for Signing Procs'
GO

CREATE USER signing_user FOR CERTIFICATE signing_cert
GO

CREATE SCHEMA user1_schema AUTHORIZATION user1
GRANT CREATE PROCEDURE TO user1
GO

-- this table is in DBO schema
```

```
-- no access granted to user1
CREATE TABLE signing_table (
 id INTEGER PRIMARY KEY,
 thedata VARCHAR(100)
)
GO
INSERT signing_table VALUES(1, 'data1')
INSERT signing_table VALUES(2, 'data2')
GO

EXECUTE AS USER='user1'
GO
CREATE PROCEDURE user1_schema.get_signing_table
AS
SELECT * FROM signing_table
GO
-- attempt to execute it, fails
EXECUTE user1_schema.get_signing_table
GO
REVERT
GO

-- sign the procedure with the cert
ADD SIGNATURE TO user1_schema.get_signing_table
  BY CERTIFICATE signing_cert
-- then give the cert's user access to table
GRANT SELECT ON signing_table TO signing_user
GO

EXECUTE AS USER='user1'
GO
-- attempt to execute it, works now
EXECUTE user1_schema.get_signing_table
GO
REVERT
GO
```

Even though the example doesn't show this, it is also possible to specify that a certificate's private key should not be maintained by the database after signing the modules with ALTER CERTIFICATE signing_cert REMOVE PRIVATE KEY. The private key is necessary only for signing, not for authorization.

As a general rule, EXECUTE AS is good only in the database in which the procedure is defined. This is useful in cases when a Web-hosting service runs a single instance of SQL Server and assigns a different database to each client. Clients shouldn't be able to access data in others' databases in the same instance, even (or especially) under the DBO identity. If access to the target database using impersonated credentials is desired, it can be accomplished by allowing the source database's DBO AUTHENTICATE privilege and setting the foreign database as TRUSTWORTHY. This can be accomplished only by someone with CONTROL SERVER privilege (sysadmin). An alternative uses code signing and the TRUSTWORTHY database property by giving the DBO permission to authenticate and marking the trustworthy bit ON. It should be pointed out that by granting AUTHENTICATE, the DBO on the SOURCE database can easily become DBO on the TARGET database, and if the authenticate has been granted to a server scope, the DBO can become sysadmin. Because of this, TRUSTWORTHY really refers to the trustworthiness of the database administration chain and should be set properly. The details of impersonation in foreign databases and instances are outside the scope of this book.

SQL Server Permissions and SQLCLR Objects

We have six new kinds of SQL Server objects in the managed world of SQL Server 2005. Three of these objects are managed-code variations on SQL Server objects:

- Stored procedures
- User-defined functions
- Triggers

Three of the objects are new in SQL Server 2005:

- Assemblies
- User-defined types
- User-defined aggregates

The reason that all these objects are new is that they all run executable code rather than have SQL Server run the code. In previous versions of SQL Server, extended stored procedures or COM objects using COM automation to run code always ran that code in the context of the Windows user account that was running the SQL Server service process. With the introduction of a managed environment that can control aspects of code loading (through the assembly loading policy mentioned in Chapter 2) and code execution through Host Protection Attributes (HPAs) that work through code access security, execution of .NET Framework assembly code catalogued in SAFE assemblies is as safe, security-wise, as running vanilla T-SQL code from inside SQL Server. From a SQL Server object-security point of view, all SQLCLR code is safer than the equivalent extended stored procedure.

When SQL Server is used as a host for the .NET Framework runtime:

- Managed user code does not gain unauthorized access to user data or other user code in the database.
- There are controls for restricting managed user code from accessing any resources outside the server and using it strictly for local data access and computation.
- Unless impersonation is specifically coded into the procedure, managed user code can access only resources that the SQL server identity can access.
- SQL Server uses .NET Framework code access security (CAS) and provides three distinct permission sets for managed user code.
- CLR procedures and functions are a way to provide security wrappers similarly to the way T-SQL procedures and functions do, by using SQL Server permissions.

We'll first look at the extension of the traditional SQL Server object security to the new objects and then go on to describe .NET Framework–specific considerations.

Assembly Permissions: Who Can Catalog and Use an Assembly?

To catalog assembly code to SQL Server, a user must have the ability to execute the CREATE ASSEMBLY DDL statement. ALTER ASSEMBLY and DROP ASSEMBLY are related DDL statements. By default, only members of the sysadmin server role and the db_owner and ddl_admin database

roles have the permission to execute the assembly-related DDL statements. The permission can be granted to other users. The user or role executing the statement becomes the owner of the assembly. In addition, it
is possible to assign an assembly to another role using the AUTHORIZA-
TION parameter of CREATE ASSEMBLY or ALTER AUTHORIZATION, as
shown in Listing 6-12. The reason that you might want to change an
assembly's owner is that there is a separate AppDomain created per
database and per assembly owner. If you need to call directly (not using
T-SQL) into another assembly's methods, it must be owned by the same
owner.

LISTING 6-12: Using ASSEMBLY DDL

```
--
-- create an assembly owned by fred
--
CREATE ASSEMBLY SomeTypes
  AUTHORIZATION fred
  FROM 'c:\types\SomeTypes.dll'
GO

-- create an assembly owned by DBO
-- while logged on as sysadmin
CREATE ASSEMBLY SomeMoreTypes
  AUTHORIZATION dbo
  FROM 'c:\types\SomeMoreTypes.dll'

-- alter the first assembly to be owned by DBO
ALTER AUTHORIZATION ON assembly::SomeTypes TO dbo
```

In the most common scenario, CREATE ASSEMBLY reads bytes from the
Windows file system, although if you use CREATE ASSEMBLY specifying
the hexadecimal bytes that make up the assembly as part of the CREATE
ASSEMBLY DDL statement, no file system access of any kind is required.
The preceding example reads bytes from a network share. ALTER ASSEMBLY
may also read bytes from the file system if the options of ALTER ASSEM-
BLY that reload code or load debugging symbols are used. Some Windows
security principal must have the permission to read the required files. But
what security principal is used? This depends on the privilege of the user
running the SQL Server service process and whether the SQL Server user

is using Windows integrated security or SQL Server security to log in to the server.

If the user is logged in using a SQL Server security login, the access to the remote file system will fail. When a Windows security login is used, access to the bits is obtained through impersonation. That means file system access will fail if the user running the SQL Server service process does not have the (Windows) right to perform impersonation—that is, to change the currently executing thread so that it executes as a different user. If the user running the SQL Server service process has impersonation authority, and the user is logged in to SQL Server as a Windows user, the request to read bytes executes using an impersonation token of the currently logged-on user.

One final piece of the puzzle is needed for CREATE ASSEMBLY and ALTER ASSEMBLY. We can define three different levels of code access security for a specific assembly: SAFE, EXTERNAL_ACCESS, and UNSAFE, listed in order of decreasing code safety. Although these levels relate to code access security, additional permissions are required to execute CREATE and ALTER ASSEMBLY and to give the resulting assembly any permission set other than SAFE. To CREATE or ALTER EXTERNAL_ACCESS or UNSAFE assemblies, you have two choices:

- The LOGIN has the appropriate permission (UNSAFE ASSEMBLY or EXTERNAL ACCESS) in the master database, and the user database has the TRUSTWORTHY property on.
- The ASSEMBLY is signed with an asymmetric key or certificate that has a LOGIN with UNSAFE ASSEMBLY or EXTERNAL ACCESS permission.

Here's an example of how the second choice would work:

1. Create a strong-named key in c:\temp\assm.snk.
2. Sign the assembly unsafe1.dll with this strong-named key.
3. Make a SQL Server LOGIN for the key.
4. Give LOGIN the appropriate permissions.
5. Catalog the unsafe assembly.

In code, it looks like Listing 6-13.

LISTING 6-13: Creating an UNSAFE assembly without marking the user database TRUSTWORTHY

```
-- master key in master database
USE master
go


CREATE MASTER KEY ENCRYPTION BY PASSWORD = 'StrongPassword1'
go


-- keyfile generated by Visual Studio 2005
-- or .NET Framework command line utilities
-- this is the keyfile that the assembly is signed with
CREATE ASYMMETRIC KEY assm FROM FILE='c:\temp\assm.snk'
GO


CREATE LOGIN snk FROM ASYMMETRIC KEY assm
GO
-- this is in the master database
GRANT UNSAFE ASSEMBLY TO snk
GO


USE userdb
GO


CREATE ASSEMBLY unsafeassemblyex FROM 'c:\temp\unsafe1.dll'
  WITH PERMISSION_SET = UNSAFE
GO
```

That's only one variation of it. You can also use the key stored in the assembly (CREATE ASYMMETRIC KEY FROM EXECUTABLE FILE=...) or an assembly already catalogued inside the database (CREATE ASYMMETRIC KEY FROM ASSEMBLY...). You can do the same thing using certificates rather than asymmetric keys.

Some of the permissions that relate to an assembly are based on the user's identity—that is, normal SQL Server authorization. In general, access to all the .NET Framework–based SQL Server objects is predicated on the checking of three different types of interobject links. These are known as invocation links, schema-bound links, and table-access links.

Invocation links refer to invocation of code and are enabled by the EXECUTE permissions. The code may be managed or T-SQL code, such as a stored procedure.

Examples of this could be a user calling a database object (for example, a user calling a stored procedure) or one piece of code calling into another piece of code (for example, an assembly calling another assembly or a procedure accessing a UDT column).

Schema-bound links are always between two database objects and are enabled by the REFERENCES permission. The presence of the schema-bound link causes a metadata dependency in SQL Server that prevents the underlying object from being modified or dropped as long as the object that references it is present. You cannot drop an assembly if it contains a user-defined type that has been catalogued, for example, and you cannot drop a user-defined type that is in use as a column in a table.

Table-access links correspond to retrieving or modifying values in a table, a view, or a table-valued function. They are similar to invocation links except that they have a finer-grained access control. You can define separate SELECT, INSERT, UPDATE, and DELETE permissions on a table or view.

REFERENCES permission gives a user the ability to create objects that reference SQLCLR assemblies or specific objects such as stored procedures, user-defined functions, or user-defined types that reside in assemblies; REFERENCES on a UDT, for example, gives a user permission to create tables that use the UDT as a column. REFERENCES permission allows the grantee to define schema-bound links to that object.

EXECUTE permission on an assembly allows a user to invoke methods or instantiate public classes within that assembly. Granting a user EXECUTE permission on an assembly does not automatically give him access to the stored procedures, user-defined functions, and UDTs that are defined within an assembly as SQL Server objects. Permissions to the specific object to be accessed must also be granted. Interassembly invocation links between assemblies owned by different users are controlled by the fact that a separate AppDomain is created for each assembly owner, rather than by the EXECUTE permission on assemblies. It is highly recommended that if you need to call between classes in different assemblies, those assemblies should have the same owner.

A user-defined type must be defined in the SQL Server catalog to be visible to SQL Server stored procedures and other T-SQL procedural code, just as an assembly is. When a UDT is defined in the SQL Server catalog, users need the appropriate permission to invoke it, just as they do for any other database object.

A UDT that is catalogued to SQL Server with CREATE TYPE is secured through permissions like any other SQL Server object. As with assemblies, you can grant REFERENCES and EXECUTE permissions on a UDT; with a UDT, however, the meaning is slightly different. Schema-bound links, in the context of a UDT, consist of:

- Creating a table with the UDT as a column
- Defining a stored procedure, UDF, or trigger on the static method of a UDT
- Defining a view using the WITH SCHEMABINDING option that references the UDT

EXECUTE permission on a UDT is defined at the class level, not at the method level. Granting EXECUTE permission on a UDT does not automatically grant permission on every stored procedure or user-defined function in the UDT through T-SQL. This must be granted by granting permission to the stored procedure or UDF SQL Server object directly. EXECUTE permission is also required to fetch a UDT or execute its methods from code inside the server using the SqlClient data provider.

User-defined aggregates follow the same rules. A schema-bound link to a user-defined aggregate would consist of:

- Creating a table with the user-defined aggregates used in a constraint
- Defining a stored procedure, UDF, or trigger that uses the user-defined aggregate
- Defining a view using the WITH SCHEMABINDING option that uses the user-defined aggregate

REFERENCES permission would be required to create any of the database objects listed earlier.

Ownership chains apply when using user permissions with SQL Server objects, just as they do when using other SQL objects, such as tables and views. Following are a few examples that will illustrate the concepts:

- User bob attempts to execute CREATE ASSEMBLY for bobsprocs. The bobsprocs assembly has a method that references another assembly, timsprocs, that is already catalogued in the database. User bob needs to have REFERENCES permission to the timsprocs assembly, because a schema-bound link will be set up between the two assemblies.

- If user bob creates a procedure, bobproc1, that is based on a method in the bobsprocs assembly, no permissions are checked. If user fred creates the bobproc1 procedure, however, this will set up a schema-bound link. User fred needs to have REFERENCES permission to the bobsprocs assembly.

- The procedure bobproc1 in bobsprocs is specified as execution_context = caller. When user alice attempts to execute bobproc1, she must have EXECUTE permissions on the procedure, but the code runs as bob.

- User alice then defines a table, atable, using the UDT bobtype, which is part of the assembly bobsprocs. To do this, she needs REFERENCES permission on the bobproc assembly and on the bobtype UDT.

- User joe attempts to execute a SELECT statement that contains the UDT bobtype in the table atable. To do this, he needs SELECT permission on atable and EXECUTE permission on bobtype.

What .NET Framework Code Can Do from within SQL Server: Safety Levels

SQL Server permissions take care of dealing with security from a SQL Server–centric point of view. But if a .NET Framework stored procedure can load arbitrary assemblies from the file system or the network, the security of the SQL Server process could be compromised. The first concern is taken care of by the new .NET Framework hosting APIs. Aside from a specific subset of the .NET Framework base class libraries (BCL), SQL Server handles all assembly-loading requests. You cannot instruct SQL Server to load arbitrary assemblies from the local file system or the Internet. In addition, the IL code in each .NET Framework assembly is checked for validity when CREATE ASSEMBLY is run. On a more granular level, the .NET Framework uses not only SQL Server user-based permissions, but also .NET Framework code access security.

Introduction to Code Access Security

.NET Framework code access security is meant to check the permissions of code before executing it, rather than checking the permissions of the user principal who executes the code. Code access security determines how trustworthy code is by mapping pieces of evidence—such as where the code was loaded from, whether the code was signed with a digital signature, and even which company wrote the code—to permissions. This evidence is collected and inspected when the code is loaded. Code access security matches evidence against the security policy to produce a set of permissions. Security policy is a combination of enterprise security policy, machine policy, user-specific policy, and AppDomain security policy. The general concept of determining permissions from evidence and security policy is discussed in the .NET Framework documentation.

Code access security works by taking the intersection of the privileges at four different runtime security policy levels:

- Enterprise
- Machine
- User
- Host

SQL Server 2005 honors the policies set at other policy levels, so you can effectively subset the three well-defined levels by restricting the privileges at, for example, the machine level.

In most ordinary .NET Framework programs, code access security is used when code is loaded to determine the location (most likely, the file system or network) of the code. .NET Framework assemblies loaded from SQL Server, however, can be loaded from only two places:

- The SQL Server database itself (user code must be catalogued and stored in the database)
- The global assembly cache (Framework class libraries only)

When CREATE ASSEMBLY is run, the code is analyzed, and any outside code that it calls (dependent assemblies) is also catalogued and stored inside SQL Server. Code location evidence means very little for SQL Server assemblies, because .NET Framework code is never loaded from the Internet or the local file system. SQL Server enforces a stronger security policy, using HPAs as well as three levels of security that are declared when the assembly is catalogued. If SQL Server determines that the assembly contains code it shouldn't be allowed to execute, CREATE ASSEMBLY simply fails. The .NET Framework class libraries are the only code loaded from the global assembly cache, and they are subject to strong constraints, which we will discuss later in this chapter.

Code access security enforces permission-based security through HPAs at execution time as well. With each access to any resource that requires a permission (such as a file or DNS resolver), the code access security inspects the call stack to ensure that every piece of code, up to the original caller, has the appropriate permission. This is known as the *stack walk*.

Between code analysis at create assembly time and the execution-time stack walk, the .NET Framework code access security system and SQL Server's extensions to strengthen it ensure that no SAFE code is called that could compromise the stability and security of the system in unforeseen ways. This is a big improvement over pre–SQL Server 2005 compiled code, which consisted of extended stored procedures and COM-based components.

Code Access Security and .NET Framework Assemblies

Because SQL Server controls assembly loading, as well as facets of .NET Framework code execution, it can also assign a custom "safety level" to an assembly. Safety levels determine what non–SQL Server resources .NET Framework assemblies can access. There are three safety levels: SAFE,

EXTERNAL_ACCESS, and UNSAFE. These are specified on CREATE ASSEMBLY and changed by using ALTER ASSEMBLY under the control of the database administrator. The different safety levels approximately correspond to the following:

- SAFE—Can access computational .NET Framework classes and local data access using the SqlClient data provider. Safety is equivalent to a T-SQL procedure.
- EXTERNAL_ACCESS—Can access all code that SAFE mode can and, in addition, items such as the file system, the Registry, and other databases through ADO.NET. It is approximately equivalent to a T-SQL procedure that can access some of the system extended stored procedures.
- UNSAFE—Can access most (but not all) code in a subset of the base class libraries. It is approximately equivalent to a user-written extended stored procedure, but it also has the advantage of memory management unless unmanaged memory and pointers are used.

What these different levels can do is enforced by a permission set. SQL Server provides each assembly with decorating methods with HPAs. These HPAs are enforced at execution time (or possibly during Just-in-Time compilation), based on the code's security level. Because SQL Server HPAs and permission sets are documented, third-party library writers are free to instrument their libraries to be sensitive to SQL Server's permissions. Table 6-4 shows a summary of the general behavior of each of the named permission sets.

TABLE 6-4: General Behavior of SQL Server Permission Sets

Permission Set	Guarantees Against Information Leakage	Guarantees Against Elevation Attack (Against Malicious Code)	Guarantees for Reliability (for Nonmalicious Code)
SAFE	Yes	Yes	Yes
EXTERNAL_ACCESS	No	No	Yes
UNSAFE	No	No	No

Following is a more comprehensive list of the permissions afforded assemblies on a permission-set basis. Unless otherwise noted, the assemblies can obtain the `Permission` initialized with `PermissionState.Unrestricted`. Note that this list is subject to change in Service Packs and could be affected by the underlying operating system and .NET Framework. Windows XP SP2, for example, forbade almost all use of the managed classes that created raw sockets.

- Permission set for SAFE assemblies
  - `SecurityPermission(SecurityPermissionFlag.Execute)`
- Permission set for EXTERNAL_ACCESS assemblies
  - Permission set for SAFE assemblies, plus:
  - `ConfigurationPermission`
  - `DnsPermission`
  - `EnvironmentPermission`
  - `EventLogPermission`
  - `FileIOPermission`
  - `OleDbPermission`
  - `RegistryPermission`
  - `SocketPermission`
  - `SqlClientPermission`
  - `WebPermission`
- Permission set for UNSAFE assemblies
  - `Unrestricted`

Let's go through an example of how safety levels would work in practice. The short program in Listing 6-14 accesses a search service on the Web. This code uses the classes in the `System.Web` namespace directly.

LISTING 6-14: Assembly must be catalogued as EXTERNAL_ACCESS work for this to work

```
private static String WebSearch(String subject) {
String url =
 "http://www.websearch.com/search?hl=en&lr=&ie=UTF-8&oe=UTF-8&q=";

//Submit Web request and get response
url = String.Concat(url, subject);
WebRequest req = WebRequest.Create(url);
```

```
WebResponse result = req.GetResponse();

//Load response stream into string
StreamReader sr = new StreamReader(result.GetResponseStream());
string outstring = sr.ReadToEnd();
sr.Close();
return outstring;
}
```

We'll use it as part of a class that is compiled into an assembly. Now we define the assembly to SQL Server, using two CREATE ASSEMBLY statements and two symbolic names with different safety levels:

```
--Register the unrestricted access privileged assembly
-- Create assembly with external access
CREATE ASSEMBLY searchEA
FROM 'c:\types\searchEA.dll'
WITH PERMISSION_SET =  EXTERNAL_ACCESS
GO


-- Create assembly without external access
-- Must make this strong-named assembly with difference version
-- See chapter 2
CREATE ASSEMBLY searchSafe
FROM  'c:\types\searchSafe.dll'
WITH PERMISSION_SET = SAFE
GO
```

Then use the symbolic names to define two versions of the same user-defined function, as shown in Listing 6-15.

LISTING 6-15: Invoking the network-accessing function in T-SQL

```
-- Create function on assembly with external access
CREATE FUNCTION WebSearchEA(@sym NVARCHAR(4000))
RETURNS REAL
EXTERNAL NAME searchEA.SearchEngine.WebSearch
GO

-- Create function on assembly with no external access
CREATE FUNCTION WebSearchSafe(@sym NVARCHAR(4000))
RETURNS REAL
EXTERNAL NAME searchSafe.SearchEngine.WebSearch
GO

-- now, attempt to use them
```

```
DECLARE @a REAL

-- this will work properly
SET @a = dbo. WebSearchEA('SQL+Server+2005')
PRINT @a

-- this fails with a code access security violation
SET @a = dbo.WebSearchSafe('SQL+Server+2005')
PRINT @a
```

What happens when a stored procedure that has limited access (SAFE) attempts to call a stored procedure that is declared as UNSAFE? Because of the way the stack walk works, this enforces security in a way that is even more restrictive than SQL Server ownership chains. Remember that an ownership chain is checked only when it is broken—that is, when the caller is not the owner of the object she attempts to access. The stack walk checks permissions all the way up the stack; failing permission at any level will cause the call to fail. This may also have some performance impact, because it implies that every stack walk normally goes all the way up to the top, although an assembly marked as UNSAFE has ability to assert a privilege and stop the stack walk. Code access security provides an additional level of security regardless of the user principal who executes the code.

One final piece of the code access security framework is the AllowPartiallyTrustedCallers assembly-level attribute. This attribute is used to indicate that the assembly can be called by other assemblies that are not fully trusted according to the rules of the code access security system. If a partially trusted assembly (for example, a SQL Server assembly catalogued as SAFE or EXTERNAL_ACCESS) attempts to access a strong-named assembly that is not marked with the AllowPartiallyTrustedCallers attribute, a SecurityException is thrown. Assemblies of subroutines catalogued to SQL Server and used only within SQL Server should, therefore, be marked with the AllowPartiallyTrustedCallers[7] attribute to ensure that they can be called by other SAFE or EXTERNAL ACCESS assemblies.

---

7. In general, marking assemblies as AllowPartiallyTrustedCallers is a glaring security hole unless you know that this is really an acceptable thing to do. Loading an assembly as SAFE or EXTERNAL_ACCESS, however, already protects against the things that AllowPartiallyTrustedCallers=false is supposed to protect against, so in this case, it is reasonable. But care must be used if the assembly is used outside SQL Server.

Where Are We?

In Chapter 2, we started by declaring that the most important aspect of any database's execution is security. SQL Server 2005, like every new version of SQL Server, includes features that make the system more secure. SQL Server 2005 mandates password-policy enforcement for SQL Server–based logins, providing equivalent safety to Windows integrated logins. SQL Server 2005 metadata uses access control like the rest of SQL Server, to prohibit arbitrary access without permission. SQL Server 2005 permits procedural code to specify its execution context, making properly written dynamic SQL safer. Finally, it improves on extended stored procedures with verifiable custom hosted .NET Framework code.

Because .NET Framework code cannot only access SQL Server objects, but also call out to the .NET Framework base class libraries, .NET Framework code inside SQL Server is subject to three levels of checking. The base class libraries are classified to determine which are safe to use, and SQL Server will refuse to load any library deemed to be inapplicable or unsafe. .NET Framework procedural code, including assemblies and user-defined types and aggregates, is subject to normal SQL Server user authorization checks. Finally, SQL Server defines three different security levels for .NET Framework code that can be specified at CREATE ASSEMBLY time. Each of the base class libraries was outfitted with custom permissions that mandate what the assembly will be able to do at each level. This is enforced via .NET Framework code access security.

■7■
SQL Engine Enhancements

S QL SERVER 2005 includes new SQL engine functionality. The enhancements span the range from an alternative mechanism for transaction isolation to a new way of using query hints. And statement-level recompilation even improves existing SQL applications that were written before 2005.

Improvements to the SQL Engine

Microsoft has continually improved the Transact-SQL (T-SQL) language and the infrastructure of SQL Server itself. In brief, the improvements in SQL Server 2005 include the following:

- SNAPSHOT isolation—Additional isolation level that does not use write locks
- Statement-level recompile—More efficient recompilation of stored procedures
- Event Notifications—Integration of Data Definition Language (DDL) and trace event operations with Service Broker
- Large data types—New data types that deprecate TEXT, NTEXT, and IMAGE
- DDL triggers—Triggers that fire on DDL operations
- Additional query hints
- Plan guides for deployment of query hints

SNAPSHOT Isolation

SQL Server changes the state of a database by performing a transaction on it. Each transaction is a unit of work consisting of one or more steps. A "perfect" transaction is *ACID*, meaning that it is *atomic, consistent, isolated, and durable*. In short, this means that the result of performing two trans-actions on a database, even if they are performed simultaneously by inter-leaving some of the steps that make them up, will not corrupt the database.

Atomic means that a transaction will perform all its steps or fail and per-form none of its steps. *Consistent* means that the transaction must not leave the results of a partial calculation in the database; if a transaction is to move money from one account to another, for example, it must not terminate after having subtracted money from one account but not having added it to the other. *Isolated* means that none of the changes a transaction makes to a data-base becomes visible to other transactions until the transaction making the changes completes; then they all appear simultaneously. *Durable* means that changes made to the database by a transaction that completes are per-manent, typically by being written to a medium like a disk.

A transaction need not always be perfect with respect to the ACID properties. The isolation level of a transaction determines how close to perfect it is. Prior to SQL Server 2005, SQL Server provided four levels of isolation: READ UNCOMMITTED, REPEATABLE READ, READ COMMITTED, and SERIALIZABLE.

A SERIALIZABLE transaction is a perfect transaction. Functionally, a database could always use SERIALIZABLE—that is, perfect—transactions, but doing so typically affected performance adversely. Judicious use of isolation levels other than SERIALIZABLE, when analysis of an applica-tion shows that it does not require perfect transactions, will improve performance.

SQL Server uses the isolation level of a transaction to control concurrent access to data through a set of read and write locks. It applies these locks pessimistically—that is, the locks prevent any access to data that might compromise the required isolation level. In some cases, this will delay a transaction as it waits for a lock to be freed or may even cause it to fail because of a timeout waiting for the lock.

SQL Server 2005 adds SNAPSHOT isolation that in effect provides alternative implementations of SERIALIZABLE and READ COMMITTED levels of isolation that use versioned concurrency control rather than pessimistic locking to control concurrent access. For some applications, SNAPSHOT isolation may provide better performance than pre–SQL Server 2005 implementations did. In addition, SNAPSHOT isolation makes it much easier to port database applications to SQL Server from database engines that make extensive use of SNAPSHOT isolation.

SQL Server 2005 has two kinds of SNAPSHOT isolation: transaction level and statement level. *Transaction-level* SNAPSHOT isolation makes transactions perfect, the same as SERIALIZABLE does. *Statement-level* SNAPSHOT isolation results in transactions that have the same degree of isolation as READ COMMITTED does. SNAPSHOT isolation just achieves these isolation levels differently.

Transaction-level SNAPSHOT isolation optimistically assumes that if a transaction operates on an image of that database's committed data when the transaction started, the result will be the same as a transaction run at the SERIALIZABLE isolation level. Sometime before the transaction completes, the optimistic assumption is tested, and if it proves to be false, the transaction is rolled back.

Transaction-level SNAPSHOT isolation works by in effect making a virtual copy of the database by taking a snapshot of it when a transaction starts. Figure 7-1 shows this.

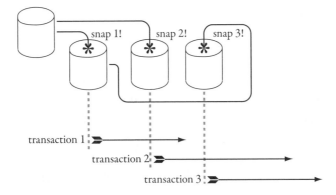

FIGURE 7-1: Snapshot versioning

There are three transactions in Figure 7-1: transaction 1, transaction 2, and transaction 3. When transaction 1 starts, it is given a snapshot of the initial database. Transaction 2 starts before transaction 1 finishes, so it is also given a snapshot of the initial database. Transaction 3 starts after transaction 1 finishes but before transaction 2 does. Transaction 3 is given a snapshot of the initial database plus all the changes committed by transaction 1.

The result of using SERIALIZABLE or transaction-level SNAPSHOT isolation is the same; some transactions will fail and have to be retried, and may fail again, but the integrity of the database is always guaranteed.

SQL Server can't actually make a snapshot of the entire database, of course, but it achieves the same effect by tracking all changes made to the database while one or more transactions are incomplete. This technique is called *row versioning*.

The row-versioning model is built upon having multiple copies of the data. When data is read, the read happens against the copy of the data, and no locks are held. When data is written, the write happens against the "real" data, and it is protected with a write lock. In a system implementing row versioning, for example, user A starts a transaction and updates a column in a row. Before the transaction is committed, user B wants to read the same column in the same row. He is allowed to do the read but will read an older value. This is not the value that user A is in the process of updating the column to, but the value user A originally read.

In statement-level SNAPSHOT isolation, the reader always reads the last committed value of a given row, just as READ COMMITTED does in a versioning database. Let's say we have a single-row table (called tab) with two columns: ID and name. Table 7-1 shows a versioning database at READ COMMITTED isolation.

The other transaction isolation level in a versioning database, SERIALIZABLE, is always implemented by the behavior that the reader always reads the row as of the beginning of the transaction, regardless of whether other users' changes are committed during the duration of the transaction. Table 7-2 shows a specific example of how two transactions interoperate when the SERIALIZABLE isolation level of a versioning database is used.

The difference between this table and Table 7-1 occurs at step 5. Even though user 2 has updated a row and committed the update, user 1, using

TABLE 7-1: Versioning Database at READ COMMITTED Isolation

Step	User 1	User 2
1	BEGIN TRAN SELECT name FROM tab WHERE id = 1 **value is 'Name'	
2		BEGIN TRAN UPDATE tab SET name = 'NewName' WHERE id = 1
3	SELECT name FROM tab WHERE id = 1 **value is 'Name'	
4		COMMIT
5	SELECT name FROM tab WHERE id = 1 **value is 'NewName'	
6	COMMIT	
7	SELECT name FROM tab WHERE id = 1 **value is 'NewName'	

the SERIALIZABLE transaction isolation level, does not "see" the next value until user 1 commits his transaction. He sees the new value only in step 7. In SQL Server 2005, this is called transaction-level SNAPSHOT isolation.

Transaction-level SNAPSHOT isolation requires that SNAPSHOT be enabled by using the SNAPSHOT isolation option of the ALTER DATABASE command. The following SQL batch does this for the pubs database:

```
ALTER DATABASE pubs
SET ALLOW_SNAPSHOT_ISOLATION ON
```

SNAPSHOT isolation can be turned on or off as needed. If a session attempts to use SNAPSHOT isolation where it is not available, it receives an

TABLE 7-2: Versioning Database at SERIALIZABLE Isolation

Step	User 1	User 2
1	BEGIN TRAN SELECT name FROM tab WHERE id = 1 **value is 'Name'	
2		BEGIN TRAN UPDATE tab SET name = 'NewName' WHERE id = 1
3	SELECT name FROM tab WHERE id = 1 **value is 'Name'	
4		COMMIT
5	SELECT name FROM tab WHERE id = 1 **value is 'Name'	
6	COMMIT	
7	SELECT name FROM tab WHERE id = 1 **value is 'NewName'	

error message: "Snapshot isolation transaction failed accessing database '[Your database]' because snapshot isolation is not allowed in this database." For more information about the state transitions possible when changing the snapshot isolation setting, as well as the effects on DDL statements, reference the whitepaper "SQL Server 2005 Beta 2 Snapshot Isolation," by Kimberly L. Tripp, on the MSDN Web site (http://msdn.microsoft.com).

When SNAPSHOT isolation has been enabled, transaction-level isolation is used by specifically setting the transaction isolation level to SNAPSHOT. The SQL batch in Listing 7-1 does this.

LISTING 7-1: Setting and using the SNAPSHOT isolation level

```
ALTER DATABASE pubs
SET ALLOW_SNAPSHOT_ISOLATION ON
GO
USE pubs
GO
SET TRANSACTION ISOLATION LEVEL SNAPSHOT
BEGIN TRANS
-- SQL Expressions
COMMIT TRANS
```

The SQL expressions in the preceding batch will be executed, in effect, against a snapshot of the database that was taken when BEGIN TRANS was executed.

Statement-level SNAPSHOT isolation requires the use of a different database option, READ_COMMITTED_SNAPSHOT. If this database option is ON, all transactions done at the READ COMMITTED level will be executed as READ COMMITTED–level transactions using versioning instead of locking. The transaction shown in the SQL batch in Listing 7-2 will be executed as READ COMMITTED using versioning.

LISTING 7-2: Setting and using the READ_COMMITTED_SNAPSHOT option

```
-- alter the database
ALTER DATABASE pubs SET READ_COMMITTED_SNAPSHOT ON
GO
USE pubs
GO
SET TRANSACTION ISOLATION LEVEL READ COMMITTED
BEGIN TRAN
-- SQL expression will be executed as READ COMMITTED using versioning
END TRAN
```

Whether or not READ_COMMITTED_SNAPSHOT or ALLOW_SNAPSHOT_ISOLATION is ON can be checked for a particular database by using the sys.databases metadata view. The columns to check are snapshot_isolation_state, snapshot_isolation_state_desc, and is_read_committed_snapshot_on.

As stated earlier, SQL Server does not actually make a copy of a database when a SNAPSHOT transaction is started. Whenever a record is updated,

SQL Server stores a copy (version) of the previously committed value in TEMPDB and maintains these changes in the database as usual. All the versions of a record are marked with the system change number when the change was made, and the versions are chained in TEMPDB using a linked list. The newest record value is stored in a database page and linked to the version store in TEMPDB. For read access in a SNAPSHOT isolation transaction, SQL Server first accesses from the data page the last committed record. Then it retrieves the record value from the version store by traversing the chain of pointers to the specific record version of the data.

The code in Table 7-3 shows an example of how SNAPSHOT isolation works. The example uses a table, snapTest, looking like this:

```
--it is necessary to run
--SET ALLOW_SNAPSHOT_ISOLATION ON
--if that's not done already
CREATE TABLE snapTest ([id] INT IDENTITY,
                       col1 VARCHAR(15))

--insert some data
INSERT INTO snapTest VALUES(1,'Niels')
```

The steps in Table 7-3 do the following:

1. User 1 starts a transaction under SNAPSHOT isolation and updates one column in one row. This causes SQL Server to store a copy of the original value in TEMPDB. Notice that User 1 does not commit or roll back at this stage, so locks are held. If we were to run sp_lock, we would see an exclusive lock on the primary key.

2. User 2 starts a new transaction under a new session and tries to read from the same row that is currently being updated. This is the row with an exclusive lock. If this had been a previous version of SQL Server (running under at least READ COMMITTED), we would be locked out. Running in SNAPSHOT mode, however, SQL Server looks in the version store in TEMPDB to retrieve the latest committed value and returns 'Niels'.

3. User 1 commits the transaction, so the value is updated in the database, and another version of the row is put into the version store.

TABLE 7-3: Example of SNAPSHOT Isolation

Step	User 1	User 2

1	`SET TRANSACTION ISOLATION`
	`LEVEL SNAPSHOT`
	`BEGIN TRAN`
	`UPDATE snapTest`
	`SET col1 = 'NewNiels'`
	`WHERE id = 1`	

2		`SET TRANSACTION`
		`ISOLATION LEVEL`
		`SNAPSHOT`
		`BEGIN TRAN`
		`SELECT col1 FROM`
		`snapTest`
		`WHERE id = 1`
		`** receives value`
		`'Niels'`

3	`COMMIT TRAN`	

4		`SELECT col1`
		`FROM snapTest`
		`WHERE id = 1`
		`** receives value`
		`'Niels'`

5		`COMMIT TRAN`

6		`SELECT col1`
		`FROM snapTest`
		`WHERE id = 1`
		`** receives value`
		`'NewNiels'`

4. User 2 does a new SELECT (from within his original transaction) and will now receive the original value, `'Niels'`.

5. User 2 finally commits the transaction.

6. User 2 does a new SELECT (after his transaction commits) and will now receive the new value, `"NewNiels"`.

SNAPSHOT isolation is useful for converting an application written for a versioning database like Oracle or Borland's InterBase to SQL Server. When an application is developed for a versioning database, the developer does not need to be concerned with locking. Converting such an application to SQL Server may result in diminished performance because SQL Server does more locking than these other databases. Prior to SQL Server 2005, this sort of conversion may have required rewriting the application. In version 2005, in many cases the only thing that will have to be done is enable SNAPSHOT isolation and READ_COMMITTED_SNAPSHOT.

SNAPSHOT isolation is also beneficial for applications that mostly read and do few updates. It is also interesting to note that when SQL Server 2005 is installed, versioning is enabled in the MASTER and MSDB databases by default. This is because it is used for some internal features of SQL Server 2005, such as the online index rebuilding feature.

Drawbacks of Versioning

Versioning has the capability to increase concurrency but does come with a few drawbacks of its own. Before you write new applications to use versioning, you should be aware of these drawbacks. Then you can assess the value of locking against the convenience of versioning.

Versioning can be costly because row versions need to be maintained even if no read operations are executing. This has the potential to cause contention in TEMPDB or even fill up TEMPDB. If a database is set up for versioning, versions are kept in TEMPDB whether or not anyone is running a SNAPSHOT isolation-level transaction. Although a garbage-collector algorithm will analyze the older versioning transaction and clean up TEMPDB eventually, you have no control over how often that cleanup is done. Plan the size of TEMPDB accordingly; it is used to keep versions for all databases with SNAPSHOT enabled. If you run out of space in TEMPDB, long-running transactions may fail.

In addition, reading data sometimes costs more because of the need to traverse the version list. If you are doing versioning at the READ COMMITTED isolation level, the database may have to start at the beginning of the version list and read through it to attempt to read the last committed version.

There is also the possibility of update concurrency problems. Let's suppose that in Table 7-1, User 1 decides to update the row also. Table 7-4 shows how this would look.

In this scenario, User 1 reads the value 'Name' and may base his update on that value. If User 2 commits his transaction before User 1 commits his, and User 1 tries to update, he bases his update on possibly bad data (the old value he read in step 1). Rather than allow this to happen, SQL Server raises an error. The error message in this case is as follows:

```
Msg 3960, Level 16, State 1, Line 1. Cannot use snapshot isolation to
access table 'tab' in database 'pubs'. Snapshot transaction aborted due to
update conflict. Retry transaction.
```

Obviously, retrying transactions often enough will slow the overall throughput of the application. In addition, the window of time for a concurrency violation to occur increases the longer a transaction reads old values. Because at the SNAPSHOT isolation level the user always reads the old value

TABLE 7-4: Versioning Database at SNAPSHOT Isolation, Concurrent Updates

Step	User 1	User 2
1	BEGIN TRAN SELECT name FROM tab WHERE id = 1 **value is 'Name'	
2		BEGIN TRAN UPDATE tab SET name = 'Newname' WHERE id = 1
3		COMMIT
4	UPDATE tab SET name = 'Another name' WHERE id = 1 ** produces concurrency violation	
5	ROLLBACK (and try update again?)	

until he commits the transaction, the window is much bigger—that is, concurrency violations are statistically more likely to occur. In fact, vendors of versioning databases recommend against using SNAPSHOT isolation in most cases. READ COMMITTED is a better choice with versioning.

Finally, as we said before, in versioning databases readers don't block writers, which might be what we want. In a versioning database, there must be a way, when it is needed to ensure consistency, to insist on a lock on read that lasts for the duration the transaction. Ordinarily, this is done by doing a SQL SELECT FOR UPDATE. But SQL Server does not support SELECT FOR UPDATE with the appropriate semantic. There is a solution, however. Even when READ_COMMITTED_SNAPSHOT is on, you can ensure a read lock by using SQL Server's REPEATABLE READ isolation level, which never does versioning. The SQL Server equivalent of ANSI's SELECT FOR UPDATE is SELECT with (REPEATABLEREAD). This is one place where programs written for versioning databases may have to change their code in porting code from a versioning database to SQL Server 2005.

Monitoring Versioning

Allowing versioning to achieve concurrency is a major change. We've already seen how it can affect monitoring and capacity planning for TEMPDB. Therefore, all the tools and techniques that we've used in the past must be updated to account for this new concurrency style. Here are some of the enhancements that make this possible.

The following is a list of some new T-SQL system metadata views and dynamic management views that assist in this area:

- sys.databases—Contains information about the state of snapshot isolation and whether read-committed SNAPSHOT is on
- sys.dm_tran_top_version_generators—Tables with most versions
- sys.dm_tran_transactions_snapshot—Transaction and SNAPSHOT sequence numbers when a SNAPSHOT transaction started
- sys.dm_tran_active_snapshot_database_transactions— Includes information about SNAPSHOT transaction (or not), if SNAPSHOT includes information about version chains and SNAPSHOT timestamps
- sys.dm_tran_version_store—Displays information about all records in the version store

There are new performance-monitor counters for the following:

- Average version store data-generation rate (kilobytes per minute)
- Size of current version store (kilobytes)
- Free space in TEMPDB (kilobytes)—this is not new but is more important now
- Space used in the version store for each database (kilobytes)
- Longest running time in any SNAPSHOT transaction (seconds)

By using the new dynamic management views for versioning in conjunction with the views for locking and blocking, and the new performance-monitor counter, you should be able to minimize SNAPSHOT isolation-related problems, as well as diagnose any that do occur.

Data Definition Language Triggers

A *trigger* is a block of SQL statements that is executed based on the fact that there has been a change (INSERT, UPDATE, or DELETE) to a row in a table or view. In previous versions of SQL Server, the statements had to be written in T-SQL, but in version 2005, as we saw in Chapter 3, they can also be written using .NET Framework languages. As we mentioned, the triggers are fired based on action statements (Data Manipulation Language, or DML, statements) in the database.

What about changes based on DDL statements—changes to the schema of a database or database server? It has not been possible to use triggers for that purpose—until SQL Server 2005. In SQL Server 2005, you can create triggers for DDL statements as well as DML.

The syntax for creating a trigger for a DDL statement is shown in Listing 7-3. As with a DML trigger, DDL triggers can be written using .NET Framework languages.

LISTING 7-3: Syntax for a DDL trigger

```
CREATE TRIGGER trigger_name
ON { ALL SERVER | DATABASE }
[ WITH <ddl_trigger_option> [ ,...n ] ]
{ FOR | AFTER } { event_type | event_group } [ ,...n ]
AS {
  sql_statement  [ ; ] [ ,...n ] |
```

```
        EXTERNAL NAME < method specifier >  [ ; ] }

<ddl_trigger_option> ::=
    [ ENCRYPTION ]
    [ EXECUTE AS Clause ]

< method_specifier > ::=
    assembly_name.class_name.method_name
```

The syntax for a DML trigger is almost identical to that for a DDL trigger. There are, however, some differences:

- The ON clause in a DDL trigger refers to either the scope of the whole database server (ALL SERVER) or the current database (DATABASE).
- A DDL trigger cannot be an INSTEAD OF trigger.
- The event for which the trigger fires is defined in the event_type argument, which for several events is a comma-delimited list. You can also use event_groups.

As an alternative to specifying a particular event_type, you can use the blanket argument DDL_DATABASE_LEVEL_EVENTS or any defined level of subevents from the DDL_DATABASE_LEVEL_EVENTS hierarchy. This hierarchy is the same one used by the WMI (Windows Management Interface) provider for server events. SQL Server Books Online has more information about the event hierarchy, as well as the full list of DDL statements that can be used in the event_type argument and also are included in the DDL_DATABASE_LEVEL_EVENTS by default. A typical use of DDL triggers is for auditing and logging. Listing 7-4 shows a simple example where we create a trigger that writes to a log table.

LISTING 7-4: Creating and using a DDL trigger

```
--first create a table to log to
CREATE TABLE dbo.ddlLog (id INT PRIMARY KEY IDENTITY,
    logTxt XML)
GO


--create our test table
CREATE TABLE dbo.triTest (id INT PRIMARY KEY)
GO


-- create the trigger
```

```
CREATE TRIGGER ddlTri
ON DATABASE
AFTER DROP_TABLE
AS
INSERT INTO dbo.ddlLog VALUES('table dropped')
```

You may wonder what the XML is all about in creating the first table. We cover the XML data type in detail in Chapter 9; for now, it's enough to realize that XML is a new built-in data type in SQL Server 2005. The trigger is created with a scope of the local database (ON DATABASE), and it fires as soon as a table is dropped in that database (ON DROP_TABLE). Run the following code to see the trigger in action:

```
-- cause the trigger to fire
DROP TABLE triTest
-- check the trigger output
SELECT * FROM dbo.ddlLog
```

The DROP TABLE command fires the trigger and inserts one record into the ddlLog table. The record is later retrieved by the SELECT command.

As mentioned previously, DDL triggers can be very useful for logging and auditing. We do not get very much information from the trigger we just created, however. In DML triggers, we have the inserted and deleted tables, which allow us to get information about the data affected by the trigger. So clearly, we need a way to get more information about events when a DDL trigger fires. The way to do that is through the EVENTDATA function.

The EVENTDATA system function returns information about what event fired a specific DDL trigger. The return value of the function is XML, and the XML is typed to a particular XML schema. Depending on the event type, the XML instance includes different information. The following four items, however, are included for any event type:

- The time of the event
- The server process ID (SPID) of the connection that caused the trigger to fire
- The login name and user name of the user who executed the statement
- The type of the event

The additional information included in the result from EVENTDATA is covered in SQL Server Books Online, so we will not go through each item here. For our trigger, however, which fires on the DROP TABLE command, the additional information items are as follows:

- Database
- Schema
- Object
- ObjectType
- TSQLCommand

In Listing 7-5, we change the trigger to insert the information from the EVENTDATA function into the ddlLog table. Additionally, we change the trigger to fire on all DDL events.

LISTING 7-5: Alter trigger to use EVENTDATA

```
-- alter the trigger
ALTER TRIGGER ddlTri
ON DATABASE
AFTER DDL_DATABASE_LEVEL_EVENTS
AS
INSERT INTO ddlLog VALUES(EVENTDATA())
```

From the following code, we get the output in Listing 7-6:

```
--delete all entries in ddlLog
DELETE ddlLog

--create a new table
CREATE TABLE evtTest (id INT PRIMARY KEY)

--select the logTxt column with the XML
SELECT logTxt
FROM ddlLog
```

LISTING 7-6: Output from EVENTDATA

```
<EVENT_INSTANCE>
  <EventType>CREATE_TABLE</EventType>
  <PostTime>2005-11-17T09:35:04.617</PostTime>
  <SPID>56</SPID>
  <ServerName>ZMV03</ServerName>
  <LoginName>ZMV03\Administrator</LoginName>
```

```
<UserName>dbo</UserName>
<DatabaseName>pubs</DatabaseName>
<SchemaName>dbo</SchemaName>
<ObjectName>evtTest</ObjectName>
<ObjectType>TABLE</ObjectType>
<TSQLCommand>
  <SetOptions ANSI_NULLS="ON" ANSI_NULL_DEFAULT="ON"
      ANSI_PADDING="ON" QUOTED_IDENTIFIER="ON" ENCRYPTED="FALSE" />
  <CommandText>CREATE TABLE evtTest (id int primary key)
  </CommandText>
</TSQLCommand>
</EVENT_INSTANCE>
```

Because the data returned from the function is XML, we can use XQuery queries to retrieve specific item information. This can be done both in the trigger and from the table where we store the data. Listing 7-7 illustrates how to retrieve information about the EventType, Object, and Command-Text items in the EVENTDATA information stored in the table ddlLog. Notice that we store it in an XML data type variable before we execute the XQuery statement against it.

LISTING 7-7: Using XQuery to SELECT items in the EVENTDATA

```
DECLARE @data XML
SELECT @data = logTxt FROM ddlLog
WHERE id = 11

SELECT
@data.value('(EVENT_INSTANCE/EventType)[1]','NVARCHAR(50)')
  AS 'EventType',
@data.value('(EVENT_INSTANCE/ObjectName)[1]','NVARCHAR(128)')
  AS 'Object',
@data.value('
 (EVENT_INSTANCE/TSQLCommand/CommandText)[1]','NVARCHAR(4000)')
  AS 'CommandText'
```

If the syntax in the previous code snippet seems strange, that's because it is using XML and XQuery; read Chapters 9 and 10, where the XML data type and XQuery are covered in detail. If you don't want to use inline XQuery to pick pieces out of the EVENTDATA XML each time you use it, Listing 7-8 produces a rowset from the EVENTDATA document. Bear in mind that not every instance of EVENTDATA contains the same elements as every other instance. Missing elements will result in NULL values in the rowset.

LISTING 7-8: Using XQuery to create a rowset from EVENTDATA information

```
DECLARE @x XML
SET @x = EVENTDATA()
SELECT Tab.Col.value('./EventType[1]','NVARCHAR(50)') AS 'EventType',
 Tab.Col.value('./PostTime[1]','datetime') AS  'PostTime',
 Tab.Col.value('./SPID[1]','NVARCHAR(50)') AS  'SPID',
 Tab.Col.value('./ServerName[1]','NVARCHAR(50)') AS  'ServerName',
 Tab.Col.value('./LoginName[1]','NVARCHAR(50)') AS 'LoginName',
 Tab.Col.value('./UserName[1]','NVARCHAR(50)') AS 'UserName',
 Tab.Col.value('./DatabaseName[1]','NVARCHAR(128)') AS 'DatabaseName',
 Tab.Col.value('./SchemaName[1]','NVARCHAR(128)') AS 'SchemaName',
 Tab.Col.value('./ObjectName[1]','NVARCHAR(128)') AS 'ObjectName',
 Tab.Col.value('./ObjectType[1]','NVARCHAR(50)') AS 'ObjectType',
 Tab.Col.value('./TSQLCommand[1]/CommandText[1]','NVARCHAR(4000)')
   AS 'CommandText',
 Tab.Col.value('./TSQLCommand[1]/SetOptions[1]/@ANSI_NULLS',
   'NVARCHAR(3)') AS 'ANSI_NULLS_OPTION',
 Tab.Col.value('./TSQLCommand[1]/SetOptions[1]/@ANSI_NULL_DEFAULT',
   'NVARCHAR(3)') AS 'ANSI_NULL_DEFAULT_OPTION',
 Tab.Col.value('./TSQLCommand[1]/SetOptions[1]/@ANSI_PADDING',
   'NVARCHAR(3)') AS 'ANSI_PADDING_OPTION',
 Tab.Col.value('./TSQLCommand[1]/SetOptions[1]/@QUOTED_IDENTIFIER',
   'NVARCHAR(3)') AS 'QUOTED_IDENTIFIER_OPTION',
 Tab.Col.value('./TSQLCommand[1]/SetOptions[1]/@ENCRYPTED_OPTION',
   'NVARCHAR(4)') AS 'ENCRYPTED_OPTION'
FROM @x.nodes('/EVENT_INSTANCE') AS Tab(Col)
```

The programming model for both DML and DDL triggers is a synchronous model, which serves well when the processing that the trigger does is relatively short running. This is necessary because DDL and DML triggers can be used to enforce rules and can roll back transactions if these rules are violated. If the trigger needs to do longer-running processing tasks, the scalability inevitably suffers. Bearing this in mind, we can see that for certain tasks, it would be beneficial to have an asynchronous event model. Therefore, in SQL Server 2005, Microsoft has included a new asynchronous Event Notification model that works asynchronously: *Event Notifications.*

Event Notifications

Event Notifications differ from triggers in that the actual notification does not execute any code. Instead, information about the event is posted to a SQL Server Service Broker (SSB) service and is placed on a message queue where it can be read by other processes.[1] Another difference between triggers and Event Notifications is that the Event Notifications execute in response not only to DDL statements, but also to many trace events. This is a superset of the events that can be specified in DDL triggers.

Listing 7-9 shows the syntax for creating an Event Notification.

LISTING 7-9: Syntax for an EVENT NOTIFICATION

```
CREATE EVENT NOTIFICATION event_notification_name
ON { SERVER | DATABASE | QUEUE queue_name }
[ WITH FAN IN ]
FOR { event_type | event_group } [ ,...n ]
TO 'broker_service', { broker_instance | 'current database' }
```

The syntax looks a little like the syntax for creating a DDL trigger, and the arguments are as follows:

- event_notification_name—This is the name of the Event Notification. It must be a valid SQL identifier.
- SERVER—The scope of the Event Notification is the current server.
- DATABASE—The scope of the Event Notification is the current database.
- QUEUE—Using an EVENT NOTIFICATION on a Service Broker QUEUE is used for external activation. See Chapter 11 for more information.
- WITH FAN IN—This reduces the number of events sent if the same event is specified with multiple EVENT NOTIFICATIONS.
- event_type or event_group—This is the name of an event that, after execution, causes the Event Notification to execute. SQL Server Books Online has the full list of events included in event_type and event_groups.
- broker_service—This is the SSB service to which SQL Server posts the data about an event. You must also specify whether the service exists on the current database or specify a Service Broker SERVICE ID. Service Broker IDs are unique even across databases and SQL Servers. You can find the ID for a particular database in the sys.databases table; it's the value in service_broker_guid column for the appropriate database.

---

1. SQL Server Service Broker is a new technology in SQL Server 2005 that facilitates sending messages in a secure and reliable way. It is covered in Chapter 11.

The Event Notification contains the same information received from the EVENTDATA function mentioned previously. When the Event Notification fires, the notification mechanism executes the EVENTDATA function and posts the information to a Service Broker SERVICE. For an Event Notification to be created, an existing SQL Server Service Broker instance needs to be located either locally or remotely. The steps to create the SQL Server Service Broker are shown in Listing 7-10. Chapter 11 covers SSB in detail.

LISTING 7-10: Steps to create a service broker SERVICE

```
--first we need a queue
CREATE QUEUE evtDdlNotif
WITH STATUS = ON

--then we can create the service
CREATE SERVICE evtDdlService
ON QUEUE evtDdlNotif
--this is a built-in contract
--which uses an existing message type
--http://schemas.microsoft.com/SQL/Notifications/EventNotification
([http://schemas.microsoft.com/SQL/Notifications/PostEventNotification]
)
```

First, the message queue that will hold the EVENTDATA information is created. Typically, another process listens for incoming messages on this queue, or another process will kick off when a message arrives. Then a service is built on the queue. When a SQL Server Service Broker service is created, there needs to be a contract to indicate what types of messages this service understands. In a SQL Server Service Broker application, the developer usually defines message types and contracts based on the application's requirements. For Event Notifications, however, Microsoft has a predefined message type, http://schemas.microsoft.com/SQL/Notifications /EventNotification and a contract, http://schemas.microsoft.com /SQL/Notifications/PostEventNotification.

The following code shows how to create an Event Notification for DDL events scoped to the local database, sending the notifications to the evtDdlService:

```
CREATE EVENT NOTIFICATION ddlEvents
ON DATABASE
```

```
FOR DDL_DATABASE_LEVEL_EVENTS
TO SERVICE 'evtDdlService', 'current database'
```

With both the Event Notification and the service in place, a new process can be started in SQL Server Management Studio, using the WAITFOR and RECEIVE statements (more about this in Chapter 11) as in the following code:

```
WAITFOR(
RECEIVE * FROM evtDdlNotif
)
```

Now you can execute a DDL statement, switch to the process with the WAITFOR statement, and view the result. Running CREATE TABLE evt NotifTbl (id INT) shows in the WAITFOR process a one-row resultset, where the row has a message_type_id of 20. This is the http://schemas. microsoft.com/SQL/Notifications/EventNotification message type. The EVENTDATA information is stored as a binary value in the message_body column. To see the actual data, we need to change the WAITFOR statement a little bit, as shown in Listing 7-11.

LISTING 7-11: Reading EVENT NOTIFICATION information from the QUEUE

```
DECLARE @msgtypeid INT
DECLARE @msg XML

WAITFOR(
RECEIVE TOP(1)
@msgtypeid = message_type_id,
@msg = CONVERT(XML, message_body)
FROM evtDdlNotif
)
--check if this is the correct message type
IF @msgtypeid = 4
--do something useful WITH the message
--here we just select it as a result
  SELECT @msg
```

You may wonder what happens if the transaction that caused the notification is rolled back. In that case, the posting of the notification is rolled back as well. If for some reason the delivery of a notification fails, the original transaction is not affected.

Large Value Data Types

In SQL Server 2000 (and 7), the maximum size for VARCHAR and VARBINARY was 8,000, and for NVARCHAR, 4,000. If you had data that potentially exceeded that size, you needed to use the TEXT, NTEXT, or IMAGE data type (known as large object data types, or LOBs). These data types were more challenging to use because they required special retrieval and manipulation statements.

This situation changes in SQL Server 2005 with the introduction of three new data types that use the MAX specifier. This specifier allows storage of up to 2^{31} bytes—that is, 2^{31} single-byte ASCII characters or 2^{30} double-byte ASCII characters. When you use the VARCHAR(MAX) or NVARCHAR(MAX) data type, the data is stored as character strings, whereas for VARBINARY(MAX), it is stored as bytes. These three data types are commonly known as large value data types or the MAX data types. Listing 7-12 shows how you can use these types to store large values in a table. Note that in SQL Server 2005, all these columns can be used together in a single row; we'll get back to this point later in this chapter.

LISTING 7-12: Table using the large value types

```
CREATE TABLE largeValues (
  id INT IDENTITY,
  long_document VARCHAR(MAX),
  long_unicode_document NVARCHAR(MAX),
  large_picture VARBINARY(MAX)
)
```

We mentioned earlier that LOBs are challenging to use. Additionally, they cannot, for example, be used as variables in a procedure or a function. The large value data types do not have these restrictions, as we can see in Listing 7-13, which shows a large value data type being used as function parameter. It also shows how a VARCHAR literal can be concatenated with a variable of type VARCHAR(MAX), creating a larger VARCHAR (max) value.

LISTING 7-13: (N)VARCHAR supports most T-SQL string handling functions

```
CREATE FUNCTION dovmax(@in VARCHAR(MAX))
RETURNS VARCHAR(MAX)
AS
BEGIN
--supports concatenation
RETURN @in + '12345'
END
```

SQL Server's string handling functions can be used on VARCHAR(MAX) and NVARCHAR(MAX) columns. So instead of having to read in and parse an entire large value string, SUBSTRING can be used. By storing the data as character strings (or bytes), the large value data types are similar in behavior to their smaller counterparts VARCHAR, NVARCHAR, and VARBINARY, and offer a consistent programming model. Using the large value data types instead of LOBs is recommended; in fact, the LOBs are deprecated in this release.

It should be noted that the MAX data types are distinct from the existing varying character and binary data types that specify a length. The VARCHAR(MAX) data type, for example, is not the same type as VARCHAR(n) but a different data type. When you use string functions with the MAX data types, all input variables must be MAX data types or must be explicitly CAST/CONVERTed to the appropriate data type. Listing 7-14 shows an example using the REPLICATE function.

LISTING 7-14: Using large value types with the REPLICATE function

```
DECLARE @x VARCHAR(MAX)
SET @x = REPLICATE('a', 9000) -- first operand is only VARCHAR
PRINT DATALENGTH(@x)  -- prints 8000
SET @x = REPLICATE(CAST('a' as VARCHAR(MAX)), 9000)
PRINT DATALENGTH(@x)  -- prints 9000
```

The MAX data types are stored differently from the way the old LOB data types TEXT, NTEXT, and IMAGE are. The MAX data types are stored in row by default. The exact number of characters that can be stored in row is determined by the length of the fixed-length columns in the same table, up to 8,000 bytes; after 8,000 bytes, the data is stored in separate data pages. This behavior can be changed by using sp_tableoption and setting the 'large value types out of row' option on. The older LOB data types are stored out of row by default; you can change this by using the 'text in row' option with sp_tableoption. When the old or new LOB types are stored out of row, a 16-byte reference to their storage location is stored in row. Fetching and updating the data through the reference is managed by SQL Server.

The MAX character and binary data types have a WRITE method that allows you to update the data partially or to extend the data. The syntax used for this method is instance.WRITE. Although this is the same syntax used in invoked methods on a .NET Framework UDT, the MAX data types are not implemented using .NET Framework. Because WRITE is a distinct data type method rather than a function, however, attempting to invoke the method on a NULL instance of the type will raise an error. This is consistent with the SQL:1999/SQL:2003 standard behavior. You invoke the method and specify a starting character index and number of characters/bytes to be written. If the starting character/byte number is equal to the length of the instance, or if the value would cause the instance to be extended, additional characters/bytes are appended to the instance. Specifying a length greater than the number of characters/bytes in the value is not an error, but attempting to specify an offset greater than the length of the instance raises an error. Listing 7-15 shows an example.

LISTING 7-15: Using the WRITE method

```
DECLARE @x NVARCHAR(MAX)
DECLARE @y NVARCHAR(MAX)
SET @y = REPLICATE(cast('b' as NVARCHAR(MAX)), 500)
SET @x.WRITE(@y, 0, 500)        -- error, can't write to NULL instance
SET @x = REPLICATE(cast('a' as NVARCHAR(MAX)), 5000)
PRINT LEN(@x)                   -- prints 5000
SET @x.WRITE(@y, 5000, 500)
PRINT LEN(@x)                   -- prints 5500
SET @x.WRITE(@y, 5000, 995)     -- not an error, replaces 500
PRINT LEN(@x)                   -- prints 5500
SET @x.WRITE(@y, 5200, 995)     -- not an error, replaces 300, appends 200
PRINT LEN(@x)                   -- prints 5700
SET @x.WRITE(@y, 5800, 500) -- error, offset larger than last character
GO
```

In addition to the introduction of the three new large object data types, the restrictions on having a table that contains rows longer than 8,060 bytes (the amount of data that can be stored on a single data page) have been relaxed. In previous versions of SQL Server, if you had a table with rows of greater than 8,060 bytes, you would receive a warning at table-creation time, and attempting to store data longer than 8,060 bytes would succeed but silently truncate the data. You can have rows in which the total size of variable-length columns is greater than 8,060 types, and all of the data will be stored. If the size of the fixed-length columns exceeds 8,060 bytes, an error is raised. The example in Listing 7-16 illustrates this.

LISTING 7-16: A table's fixed-length fields must total 8,060 characters or less

```
CREATE TABLE largeValues2 (
  COLUMN1 VARCHAR(MAX), COLUMN2 VARCHAR(MAX)      -- OK
)
GO
CREATE TABLE largeFixedLengthValues (
  COLUMN1 CHAR(80),    COLUMN2 CHAR(8000))        -- error
GO
```

Loading Data with the New BULK Provider

SQL Server 2005 provides an alternative to the BULK INSERT statement for loading data from a file. The new functionality is accessed by using a new OLE DB BULK rowset provider with the INSERT INTO SELECT ... FROM OPENROWSET syntax. This provider allows a more flexible syntax than BULK INSERT because all the flexibility of the SQL SELECT statement is available while loading from a file. Using the BULK provider allows you to select a subset of columns in the input file and permits data conversion using the CONVERT function within the SELECT statement.

Using the provider gives you the flexibility of loading a single large data value into either a data column or a SQL variable by using the SINGLE_BLOB, SINGLE_CLOB, or SINGLE_NCLOB keyword. Here's a simple example:

```
DECLARE @d VARCHAR(MAX)

SET @d = (SELECT * FROM  OPENROWSET
   (BULK 'c:\mylargedocument.txt', SINGLE_CLOB) AS A
PRINT @d
GO
```

We'll have more to say about the BULK provider in Chapter 9, because you can also use the BULK provider to load XML into the database from a file.

Statement-Level Recompilation

SQL Server must compile an execution plan for a query before it can be executed. The execution plan is cached for later use so that the overhead of compiling it will not be incurred when the query is executed in the future. The execution plan is compiled the first time the query is used, and its optimization is based on information available to SQL Server at that time. Indexes available, table schema, and even the amount of data in a table can affect what kind of plan is compiled.

Several things can cause a cached execution plan to become nonoptimal. An index useful to the execution of the query may have been added since the execution plan was compiled and cached, for example. SQL Server detects these kinds of changes to a database and marks any queries that could be affected by the change to be recompiled the next time the query is executed.

This change detection and marking for recompilation is automatic and keeps the execution plan up to date with the current state of the database, but sometimes, it is a mixed blessing because of the overhead of compiling the execution plan. SQL Server 2005 has improved the efficiency of the recompilation process by recompiling only those parts of the query that will likely be improved by the recompilation. You need not do anything to enable this; even your existing stored procedures will take advantage of this feature when they are run on SQL Server 2005.

Figure 7-2 shows an example of where SQL Server would recompile a stored procedure. It shows a stored procedure (1), GetPubAuth, being created. This stored procedure accesses two different tables: the Publishers and Authors tables in the pubs database.

The execution plan is compiled the first time GetPubAuth is executed (2). The execution plan is based on the tables accessed by GetPubAuth and the value of the @state parameter—in this case, 'UT'.

```
① CREATE PROCEDURE GetPubAuth(@state CHAR(2))
  AS
  SELECT * FROM pubs..Publishers WHERE State = @state;
  SELECT * FROM pubs..Authors WHERE State = @state;

② exec GetPubAuth 'UT'

③ CREATE INDEX pub _ state ON pubs..Publishers(state)

④ exec GetPubAuth 'CA'

⑤
```

```
Untitled - 2 (CANOPUS5)
EventClass          TextData
Trace Start
SP:Recompile        SELECT * FROM pubs..Publishers WHERE State = @state;
SQL:StmtRecompile   SELECT * FROM pubs..Publishers WHERE State = @state;
```

FIGURE 7-2: Recompile

After the execution of the `GetPubAuth` stored procedure, an index is added (3) that indexes the `State` column of the `Publishers` table. This causes SQL Server to mark the `GetPubAuth` stored procedure for recompilation because it accesses the `Publishers` table.

The `GetPubAuth` stored procedure is executed again (4), but this time with `'CA'` as a parameter. The recompilation appears in the SQL Server Profiler tool (5) as two events. One event, which was in previous versions of SQL Server, is `SP:Recompile`. The second event, added to SQL Server 2005, is `SQL:StmtRecompile`.

Only one line of the `GetPubAuth` stored procedure is recompiled: the one that accesses the `Publishers` table instead of the entire stored procedure. The execution plan for this line is optimized for a `@state` value equal to `'CA'`. Note that this does not change the fact that the execution plan for the statement that accesses the `Authors` table is optimized for a `@state` value equal to `'UT'`. If you need more fine-tuned or direct control over the compilation of execution plans, you may need to use query hints or even force SQL Server 2005 to use a specific plan.

Query Hints, Plan Guides, and Plan Forcing

One of the biggest advances of the relational database was the declarative SQL language. Rather than write code to navigate the database directly, you describe your query in SQL, and the query processor determines how to execute the query for best performance. As the query processor and engine get "smarter," your queries run faster without major programmatic rewrites. On the other hand, programmers now spend a great deal of time trying to understand exactly how the query engine works and sometimes even second-guess the query processor on a rare occasion when it picks a suboptimal plan. Although you should rarely need to use them, query hints permit you to instruct the query engine how to execute your query. I've actually needed to use query hints only a few times in my career: once because the same query was used for two use cases that needed different plans, and once when a Service Pack changed a query's plan to one that I thought was suboptimal. SQL Server will cache only one query plan per query, and improvements in the query engine that make 99 percent of the queries run faster may make 1 percent of queries run slower.

SQL Server 2005 comes with three major improvements that make query hints easier to use and manage:

- Enhanced presentation of query plans for review
- New query hints
- A new feature called *plan guides* that makes query hints easier to use and to remove when they are no longer needed

Before we launch into describing these improvements, we're required to include the following disclaimer: "Query hints are generally evil, because you're telling the query processor what to do rather than allowing it to decide what to do. This could negate the work of over 20 years of query optimization and means you might as well be using imperative programming. Using hints makes your system more cumbersome to maintain, because you must retest all your previous query assumptions each time you make a change. Overhinting will be likely to make your system run slower overall."

Now that we've gotten that out of the way, let's describe the new plan-reading and -hinting features and how they work.

The way that you figure out what the query processor is doing to process your query and exactly how many rows are being processed is to turn on showplan and showplan statistics. In SQL Server 2000, there are two styles of showplan; they capture mostly the same data but present it differently. With the Query Analyzer utility, you can turn on the ability to show the actual or estimated execution plan. You receive the information in a nice graphical format; the statistics and specifics are available by hovering over the relevant plan step. Even the thicknesses of the lines between the graphics convey information. The only drawback to looking at query plans this way is that you can't bundle up this information and send it to a friend (or to tech support) for assistance. The interactive graphics don't even lend themselves well to screenshots. After a few screenshots, everyone reverts to the tried-and-true method of analyzing this information: the text-based showplan. Although the information is not formatted as nicely, it is text format, so you can send it in e-mail without information loss. You can even write string-parsing code to automate analysis of the plan, though this is fairly complex to write.

SQL Server 2005 introduces XML-based showplan. The text-based showplan is still there to support programmers who use it. The XML-based showplan is a bit wordy but has some additional capabilities. First, the graphic showplan in SQL Server Management Studio (SSMS) is now (most likely) an XML stylesheet. You can capture your XML showplan output in either SSMS or in SQL Profiler, save the XML to a file, and send it to a friend. You must save the XML itself with the `.sqlplan` extension, but double-clicking or loading this file into either utility produces a graphical showplan, hover-over statistics and all. Also, because lots of tools are available (including SQL Server 2005) that deal with XML queries, it is easier to write code that analyzes an XML showplan than to write code that performs string parsing of a textual showplan. There's even an XML schema for the showplan provided in a subdirectory of the Tools directory. Finally, XML showplan output can be used to do plan forcing. We'll discuss plan forcing later in this chapter.

Many query hints are available for SQL Server. You specify them using an `OPTION` keyword and the hint in parentheses at the end of the query. Listing 7-17 shows an example of the syntax, forcing the query processor to use a `MERGE JOIN` to accomplish the join between the `Store` and `Sales OrderHeader` tables.

LISTING 7-17: Using a query hint on the SELECT statement

```
USE AdventureWorks;
GO
SELECT Name, SalesOrderNumber, OrderDate, TotalDue
FROM Sales.Store AS S
    JOIN Sales.SalesOrderHeader AS SO ON S.CustomerID = SO.CustomerID
ORDER BY Name, OrderDate
OPTION (MERGE JOIN);
GO
```

Query hints exist to override many query processor behaviors. Some examples are

- Degrees of parallelism
- Query recompilation
- Join styles and join order
- Optimization for first N rows

There are a few new query hints in SQL Server 2005. One of them, `OPTIMIZE FOR`, allows you to tell the optimizer the value of a parameter to use in optimization for a parameterized query. This value will override the value actually submitted to the query in the current statement. If we knew, for example, that most of the rows had a state value of 'CA', we could have the optimizer use 'CA' as the parameter value, even though it is not the current parameter. Listing 7-18 shows an example.

LISTING 7-18: Using the OPTIMIZE FOR query hint

```
DECLARE @state_name CHAR(2)
SET @state_name = 'CA'
SELECT * FROM Person.Address AS A
  JOIN Person.StateProvince AS S
  ON A.StateProvinceID = S.StateProvinceID
WHERE S.StateProvinceCode = @state_name
OPTION ( OPTIMIZE FOR (@state_name = 'CA') )
```

Another new query hint, MAXRECURSION, is used to set the maximum number of times the recursive portion of a recursive common table expression will be executed. We'll discuss this in Chapter 8.

The final new hint is the most interesting one. It's called *plan forcing*. If you had a query that worked differently in a previous release of SQL Server, or even a query plan (within limits) that you'd like the query processor to try because you believe it will be faster, you can force SQL Server to use that plan by providing a USE PLAN query hint along with an XML-format plan. You can get the XML plan by using XML showplan as described above or even hand-edit the plan within some tightly enforced limits. This plan exactly directs the query processor how to proceed. The query processor now has no role in deciding how the query is to be executed. This might be necessary in certain well-defined situations.

There is a potential problem with using XML plans as query hints; in SQL Server, if the entire text of the query exceeds 8,000 bytes, the query hint will not be used. Because the XML plan is quite wordy, we will likely be exceeding this limit. Enter plan guides.

A *plan guide* is a SQL Server 2005 database object that associates a query hint with a SQL statement. The statement can be either part of a stored procedure or a stand-alone statement. When you have defined a plan guide, you can turn the hint to which the plan guide refers on or off with a system stored procedure. In addition, the DBA can turn off all plan guides for a specific database with an ALTER DATABASE statement. Creating a plan guide for the statement in Listing 7-19 and using it would look like this.

LISTING 7-19: Creating and enabling a plan guide

```
-- create plan guide for our query hint
sp_create_plan_guide
  @name = N'PortlandGuide',
  @stmt = N'SELECT * FROM Person.Address WHERE City = @city_name',
  @type = N'SQL',
  @module_or_batch = NULL,
  @params = N'@city_name NVARCHAR(30)',
  @hints = N'OPTION (OPTIMIZE FOR (@city_name = N''Portland''))'
GO
sp_control_plan_guide N'ENABLE', N'PortlandGuide'
GO
```

A plan guide dissociates the query hint from the query text itself. One key advantage of using plan guides is that you can force a plan in a query that you don't have access to. You can change the way a query in a third-party packaged application works, for example, even though you have no way to add a hint to the text. Plan guides also make it unnecessary to track all the places where a hint has been used. If a hotfix (or, more likely, the next Service Pack or release of SQL Server) makes your hint unnecessary, just turn the plan guide off. In previous releases, you'd have to search through all your T-SQL source code or application for every occurrence of the hint and replace the code—a time-consuming and potentially error-prone process. You can create a plan guide for any SQL statement, including server cursor processing. Plan guides can also be used in conjunction with plan forcing, discussed earlier in this chapter. This solves the 8,000-byte-limit problem described earlier. To use plan guides together with plan forcing, you would

1. Run the query or stored procedure in SQL Server Management Studio after selecting the Include Actual Execution Plan option from the Query menu. This produces a graphical execution plan.

2. Capture to XML showplan to a file by using the Save Execution Plan As context-menu item.

3. Construct a plan guide with the last parameter (the query hint) being set to `"OPTION (USE PLAN '[your XML showplan from step 1 here]')"`. Don't forget to escape any single quotes in the XML showplan text.

Figure 7-3 shows the steps in this procedure using a fairly simple query. Bear in mind that this is just one method that you can use to capture an execution plan as an XML file in XML showplan format. You can also use "SET SHOWPLAN_XML ON" from the query window directly, use the option in SQL Profiler that allows you to save all XML showplan output to a single file, or save each query's showplan output to a separate file. In addition, if the XML showplan output is saved in a file with the .sqlplan extension, it can be opened in SQL Server Management Studio in graphical mode. This is a very handy option, because it allows you to share an XML showplan with a colleague or e-mail it to technical support. The recipient of the file still has the ability to view it in graphical mode.

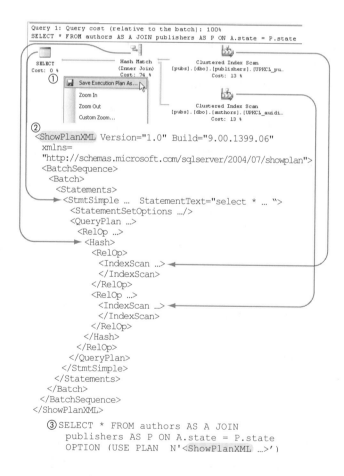

FIGURE 7-3: Capturing an XML showplan for use with plan forcing

Where Are We?

Transaction isolation is one of the features that define a database product. SQL Server has supported all the transaction isolation levels in the ANSI standard by using locking; SQL Server 2005 adds support for transaction isolation by using versioning as well. This extends the reach of SQL Server to behaviors that are possible only when using a versioning database while retaining locking of its default transaction isolation mechanism.

New large value data types make writing T-SQL code that handles large data easier, because they act in a manner consistent with the rest of the data types in SQL Server. In addition, the restriction that data rows cannot span pages has been relaxed, making it easier to use these multiple long variable-length columns in a single row without worrying about page overflow. This makes the logical structure of the database less dependent on the physical structure.

Database triggers and Event Notifications make SQL Server 2005 a more active database by allowing synchronous control over DDL and asynchronous ability to react to DDL events or even control reaction to trace events. Event notifications use SQL Server Service Broker; we'll be discussing this feature in depth in Chapter 11.

Procedure-level recompiles take CPU cycles; this has always affected how programmers write stored procedures. SQL Server 2005 increases a programmer's choices by doing recompiles at a statement level rather than a procedure level. In addition, there are new plan hints and the ability to force a particular plan for a particular SQL statement. This is useful if the query processor isn't choosing the right plan but should be used with caution. With plan guides, there is also the ability to separate hints from statements in programs and to provide hints in situations where the programmer can't change package source code.

In addition to internal engine features like the ones we've seen in this chapter, there are a plethora of enhancements to the T-SQL language itself. We'll discuss these enhancements in Chapter 8.

8

T-SQL Language Enhancements

S QL SERVER 2005 includes new Transact-SQL (T-SQL) functionality. SQL Server 2005 represents a major enhancement to SQL Server. Even if you ignore major additions such as hosting the CLR, Common Language Runtime, in process in SQL Server and support of XML as a first-class native data type, the T-SQL enhancements alone are enough to consider this a major update of SQL Server.

The enhancements span the range from more support of SQL:1999 syntax for SQL to enhanced error handling.

Improvements to Transact-SQL

In brief, the improvements include the following:

- Error handling—TRY/CATCH syntax for handling errors
    - INTERSECT and EXCEPT
    - TOP—Row count based on an expression
    - ON DELETE and ON UPDATE
    - APPLY—New JOIN syntax made for use with user-defined functions and XML
    - Common table expressions—Declarative syntax that makes a reusable expression part of a query

- Table sampling
- Hierarchical queries—Declarative syntax for tree-based queries
- PIVOT—Declarative syntax aggregations across columns and converting columns to rows
- Ranking functions and partitioning

This chapter uses the pubs and AdventureWorks database for its examples.

Error Handling

Prior to SQL Server 2005, handling of errors was tedious at best; some of the pieces of information associated with the error were not readily available; and some errors could be handled only on the client. SQL Server 2005 adds a TRY/CATCH syntax that allows all errors to be handled in T-SQL. It is similar to exception handling in a number of languages where TRY marks a section of code to be monitored for errors and CATCH marks a section of code to be executed if an error occurs. Some of these languages also support marking a section of code, called the *finally block,* to be executed in spite of an error occurring. SQL Server 2005 does not provide this capability.

Prior to SQL Server 2005, errors were handled by reading the session variable @@ERROR read immediately after a statement was executed without knowing in advance whether that statement produced an error. An error was indicated by a nonzero value of @@ERROR. If the severity of the error was of interest, it would have to be looked up in the sysmessages table in the master database.

Figure 8-1 shows a way of handling errors using @@ERROR. The error number must be captured (1) after each statement and then tested (2). If the error number is not zero, control is transferred to an error handler (3). The error handler extracts the severity of the error (4) from the sysmessages table based on the error number. Some of this could be factored out into a stored procedure, of course, but this would still require that two lines of code be added to every statement to capture and then test the error number.

There are a couple of issues with using @@ERROR. One is that certain types of errors terminate the execution of the batch, so the code that tests

```
    DECLARE @myError INT
    BEGIN TRAN
    INSERT INTO pubs..jobs
        VALUES('fix fonts', 10, 20)
①  SET @myError = @@ERROR
②  IF @myError <> 0 GOTO ErrorOccurred
    INSERT INTO pubs..jobs
        VALUES('add headlines', 3, 20)
    SET @myError = @@ERROR
    IF @myError <> 0 GOTO ErrorOccurred
    COMMIT TRAN
    GOTO Done
③  ErrorOccurred:
    DECLARE @severity int
④  SELECT @severity = severity
        FROM master..sysmessages
    WHERE error = @myError
    IF @@TRANCOUNT > 0 ROLLBACK TRAN
    PRINT 'Error ' +
    CAST(@myError as VARCHAR(5)) +
    ' occurred with severity ' +
    CAST(@severity as varchar(3))
    Done:
```

FIGURE 8-1: @@ERROR error handler

@@ERROR is never run. Another issue is that @@ERROR depends on your never forgetting to add those capture and test lines. When you miss doing this, you introduce a very hard-to-find bug when, for example, a transaction that should be rolled back is not. Code would be much more robust if you could just declare, "If something goes wrong, do this," where "this" is an arbitrary error hander that you provide.

In fact, SQL Server does provide a limited way to do this, by setting the XACT_ABORT=ON. In this case, an error will cause an existing transaction to be rolled back automatically without any coding on your part. This is all you can do with this feature, though; you cannot specify that a particular error handler be used.

SQL Server 2005 adds a feature to T-SQL that allows you to specify declaratively an arbitrary error handler. This feature is called *exception handling*. To use it, you mark an area of code that you want to TRY to execute and mark another area of code to CATCH any error that occurs in the code you tried to execute. This technique works for most errors, even deadlock errors, which prior to SQL Server 2005 could be handled only on the client. Note that this technique will not work for syntax errors or fatal errors that end the connection to the user.

The code in Figure 8-2 is equivalent to that in Figure 8-1, but it uses the new exception syntax. The code you want to try to execute (1) is put between BEGIN TRY and END TRY phrases. The error handler (2) immediately follows it and is between BEGIN CATCH and END CATCH phrases. A BEGIN TRY/END TRY must always be followed immediately by a BEGIN CATCH/END CATCH. There is a lot less typing in Figure 8-2 than in Figure 8-1, which is always a plus, but the real value is that you cannot "forget" to add the error capture and error test after each statement, and it catches almost all errors.

Besides being a more robust and less tedious way to write code, SQL Server 2005 exceptions provide more information than @@ERROR does. In fact, the @myError variable shown in Figure 8-2 is really superfluous; there is no need to capture @@ERROR any more. Table 8-1 shows functions that SQL Server 2005 has to pass on error information to an error handler. Note that these functions are valid only inside a BEGIN CATCH/END CATCH clause.

The ERROR_NUMBER(), ERROR_SEVERITY(), ERROR_STATE, and ERROR_MESSAGE() functions return the corresponding values from the RAISERROR that was used to report the error—that is, caused the exception. ERROR_LINE() and ERROR_PROCEDURE() identify the T-SQL that caused the error. XACT_STATE() indicates whether a transaction is in progress or whether the transaction is in an uncommittable state. Uncommittable transactions are something new that we will be looking at later in this chapter.

Figure 8-3 and Figure 8-4 show the usage of all the error functions except XACT_STATE(). Figure 8-3 shows a stored procedure (1), BadInsert,

```
  BEGIN TRY
① DECLARE @myError int
  BEGIN TRAN
  INSERT INTO pubs..jobs
     VALUES('fix fonts', 10, 20)
  INSERT INTO pubs..jobs
     VALUES('add headlines', 3, 20)
  COMMIT TRAN
  END TRY
  BEGIN CATCH
② IF XACT _ STATE() <> 0 ROLLBACK TRAN
  PRINT 'Error ' +
  CAST(ERROR _ NUMBER() AS VARCHAR(4)) +
  ' with severity ' +
  CAST(ERROR _ SEVERITY() AS VARCHAR(5))
  END CATCH
```

FIGURE 8-2: TRY/CATCH error handler

TABLE 8-1: Error Functions

Error Function	Returns
ERROR_NUMBER()	Number of error from RAISERROR
ERROR_SEVERITY()	Severity of error from RAISERROR
ERROR_STATE()	State of error from RAISERROR
ERROR_MESSAGE()	Message from RAISERROR
ERROR_LINE()	Line on which error occurred
ERROR_PROCEDURE()	Procedure in which error occurred
XACT_STATE()	Transaction state

which attempts to insert an illegal value into the jobs table of the pubs database. The min_lvl column in the jobs table has a check constraint on it that requires it to be at least 10.

The batch in Figure 8-4 executes (1) the BadInsert stored procedure inside a BEGIN TRY/END TRY clause. The error handler (3) prints out the values of the various error functions.

Figure 8-5 shows the output produced by the error handler in Figure 8-3. Note that the error message (1) produced is the actual error output message, not the template of the error message that is stored in master..sysmessages. There was no need to capture @@ERROR; the error number is available in the handle through the ERROR() function. Also included are the name (2) of the stored procedure and the line number in the stored procedure that produced the error.

```
①CREATE PROCEDURE BadInsert
AS
DECLARE @myError int
BEGIN TRAN
INSERT INTO pubs..jobs VALUES('headlines', 3, 20)
COMMIT TRAN
```

FIGURE 8-3: BadInsert stored procedure

```
  BEGIN TRY
① EXEC BadInsert;
  END TRY
  BEGIN CATCH
  IF XACT _ STATE() <> 0 ROLLBACK TRAN
② PRINT 'error ' + CAST(ERROR _ NUMBER() AS VARCHAR(4))
  PRINT 'severity '
  + CAST(ERROR _ SEVERITY() AS VARCHAR(5))
  PRINT 'state ' + CAST(ERROR _ STATE() AS VARCHAR(5))
  PRINT ERROR _ MESSAGE()
  PRINT 'procedure '
     + CAST(ISNULL(ERROR _ PROCEDURE(), 'BATCH')
     AS VARCHAR(5))
  PRINT 'line ' + CAST(ERROR _ LINE() as VARCHAR(5))
  END CATCH
```

FIGURE 8-4: Catching error

The XACT_STATE() indicates the state of the transaction when the error occurred; its possible return values are summarized in Table 8-2. There are three possible states: no transaction, committable transaction, and uncommittable transaction. The first two are ones we typically deal with. The uncommittable transaction means that the transaction cannot be committed, and the batch may not take any action that causes something to be written to the transaction log—for example, rolling back a transaction to a savepoint.

Prior to SQL Server 2005, you never had to deal with an uncommittable transaction yourself in T-SQL. The reason you do now is that some errors in a BEGIN TRY/END TRY clause transfer control to the BEGIN CATCH/END CATCH clause before SQL Server 2005 has a chance to clean up all the things that it normally would. Probably the most common uncommittable transaction is produced by a trigger that raises an error inside a BEGIN TRY clause. Note that the behavior of triggers outside a BEGIN TRY clause is unchanged from previous versions SQL Server. Also, in some cases an error

```
  error 547
  severity 16
  state 0
  The INSERT statement conflicted with the CHECK constraint
①    "CK__jobs__min_lvl__1920BF5C"...
②procedure BadInsert
  line 5
```

FIGURE 8-5: Error handler output

TABLE 8-2: Possible Values of XACT_STATE

XACT_STATE( ) Return Value	Indicates
0	There is no current transaction. Do not roll back transaction, as that will cause an error. You may continue processing.
1	There is a transaction in progress. You may roll it back, roll back to a savepoint, commit it, or just continue processing.
−1	There is a transaction in progress, but it is uncommittable. It must be rolled back completely—that is, ROLLBACK TRAN must be used. You may not do any action that causes the transaction log to be written—for example, rolling back to a savepoint.

in a distributed transaction can lead to an uncommittable transaction, and whenever an error occurs and XACT_ABORT is ON, the transaction will be uncommittable in the error handler.

It is important that the error handler in a BEGIN CATCH/END CATCH clause check for an uncommittable transaction and roll it back. If the error handler does anything—for example an INSERT, which requires the transaction log to be written—before rolling back an uncommittable transaction, the batch will be terminated, and the rest of the handler will not be run.

Figure 8-6 shows a T-SQL batch that attempts to do an INSERT during an uncommittable transaction. It starts (1) by setting XACT_ABORT ON. Next, it does an INSERT (2) into the jobs table that violates a check constraint on that table. This transfers control to the error handler in the BEGIN CATCH/END CATCH phrase with an uncommittable transaction pending. The error handler attempts do to a valid INSERT (3) into the jobs table. This terminates the batch, rolls back the transaction, and sends the client a 3930 error. The PRINT instruction (4) is never executed.

Figure 8-7 shows a T-SQL batch whose intention is to commit all inserts into the jobs table of the pubs database up to the point at which an error occurs. It starts by setting XACT_ABORT ON (1).

The second insert (2) in the script will produce an error because it will violate a check constraint on the min_lvl column of the jobs table.

```
① SET XACT _ ABORT ON
   BEGIN TRY
   BEGIN TRANSACTION
   INSERT INTO pubs..jobs
②     VALUES('fix fonts', 3, 20)
   COMMIT TRANSACTION
   END TRY
   BEGIN CATCH
③ INSERT INTO pubs..jobs
      VALUES('add headlines', 10, 20)
④ PRINT 'We got to here'
   END CATCH

Msg 3930, Level 16, State 1, Line 9
The current transaction cannot be committed and
cannot support operations that write to the log
file. Roll back the transaction.
```

FIGURE 8-6: Uncommittable transaction

The intention of the batch, however, is to commit the INSERT previous to this one if possible.

The first thing the error handler does is to check (3) to see if the transaction is in an uncommittable state. If so, it rolls back the transaction; otherwise, it commits it. In this script, the entire transaction will be rolled back, because when XACT_ABORT is ON, an error will always leave a transaction in an uncommittable state if there is an error. Note that if this T-SQL script were executed with XACT_ABORT OFF, the 'adverts1' job would have been committed and the 'adverts2' job would not have been committed, as was the intention of the batch.

```
① SET XACT _ ABORT ON

   BEGIN TRY
   BEGIN TRAN
   INSERT INTO pubs..jobs
      VALUES('adverts1', 10, 20)
   INSERT INTO pubs..jobs
②     VALUES('adverts2', 3, 20)
   COMMIT TRAN
   END TRY
   BEGIN CATCH
③ IF XACT _ STATE() = -1 ROLLBACK TRAN
   ELSE COMMIT TRAN
   END CATCH
```

FIGURE 8-7: Handling uncommittable
transaction

At first glance, it might seem that the new TRY/CATCH is somehow taking away capabilities that versions previous to SQL Server 2005 had, because it forces us to roll back a transaction. It seems that the option of committing everything up to the point of an error has been taken away from us. If error handling for the T-SQL batch in Figure 8-7 were done as was shown in Figure 8-1—that is, using the @@ERROR variable—neither row would have been inserted; the entire transaction would have been rolled back automatically because of XACT_ABORT ON.

The difference is that if the batch in Figure 8-1 were executed with XACT_ABORT ON, we would never even see the error—that is, its error handler would never have been executed, because XACT_ABORT would not only have rolled back the transaction, but also terminated the batch. The batch in Figure 8-7 will have the opportunity to process the error even if XACT_ABORT is ON, but it will also have the responsibility to roll back any uncommittable transaction.

A feature of some languages that catch errors is the ability to rethrow an error. In SQL, Server you can do the equivalent by using a RAISERROR statement. The new functions, such as ERROR_NUMBER and ERROR_STATE, in SQL Server 2005 make it possible to do this more easily than could be done in the past.

Figure 8-8 shows the part of an error handler that reraises an error. The RAISERROR statement can take only literal values or variables as input, so

```
     BEGIN CATCH
① DECLARE @error_message NVARCHAR(MAX)
     SET @error_message = ERROR_MESSAGE()
     DECLARE @error_severity INT
     SET @error_severity = ERROR_SEVERITY();
     DECLARE @error_state INT
     SET @error_state = ERROR_STATE();
② IF @error_state = 0 SET @error_state = 1
     IF XACT_STATE() <> 0 ROLLBACK TRAN
     -- do error handling here

     -- pass error back to client
     -- if it cannot be handled
③ RAISERROR (@error_message,
         @error_severity,
         @error_state)
     END CATCH
```

FIGURE 8-8: Reraising error

it is necessary to capture error information in variables (1) in the handler so that RAISERROR can use them.

SQL Server can raise some errors that have an error state of zero, for example—a check-constraint violation. The RAISERROR statement does not allow an error state of zero, so this must be checked for and changed (2) to a value greater than zero. You will have to decide your own convention for this.

If, after processing the error, the error handler decides that it cannot handle the error, it can reraise the error using the RAISERROR statement (3) and the error values captured at the beginning of the error handler.

One kind of error that, at least in theory, should not be passed back to the client application is a deadlock error. A client application doesn't cause a deadlock, and typically, it will have no idea how to handle it. Prior to SQL Server 2005, there was no choice but to pass a deadlock error, and many other errors, back to the client for handling.

We will look at handling a deadlock error in T-SQL as an example of how, in general, all these errors can be handled in T-SQL. Note that SQL Server does not produce timeout errors; clients do. A client can choose to terminate a batch if the batch seems to be taking to long to complete. TRY/CATCH clauses will not catch timeout errors; they must still be handled on the client.

Prior to SQL Server 2005, SQL Server would roll back one of the transactions involved when a deadlock occurs. It would also terminate the batch involved and send a 1205 message to the client on that connection, saying that the batch had been terminated and the transaction rolled back. The batch that is terminated is not given the opportunity to process the error by, for example, retrying the transaction.

Client and middle-tier applications often don't realize that they are responsible for retrying queries terminated due to deadlock. They view the deadlock error as fatal, because they don't know a 1205 error can be retried, and just pass back an incomprehensible error message that says they were "chosen as a deadlock victim." This is compounded by the fact that under normal circumstances, deadlock don't often occur. The result is that the occasional deadlock can lead to at best the appearance of flakiness in an application and at worst can cascade into a real problem. The retry logic for deadlocks prior to SQL Server 2005 had to reside in the client, but now TRY/CATCH provides an alternative; it can be encapsulated inside the server.

One of the things that must be considered is that in general, it makes sense to retry only some errors—that is, 1205 errors. Other errors should be sent back to the caller or otherwise handled. A second consideration is that retrying a transaction in T-SQL takes this ability away from the client and centralizes it in the server. This lets the server use a standard way across all applications to retry transactions and even log that fact so that retries can be monitored, but because it is a very different way of handling things, it could have an unexpected effect on existing applications that currently handle retry themselves.

When a transaction in a BEGIN TRY/END TRY clause is terminated because of a deadlock, control is transferred to the BEGIN CATCH/END CATCH clause, just like any other error, with an ERROR_NUMBER of 1205. The typical response to a 1205 error should be just to retry the query—a couple of times, if need be. Even a completely correctly designed database can occasionally experience a deadlock. In SQL Server 2005, the client can be insulated, to a large extent, from this event by implementing this response in T-SQL itself.

Note that retrying deadlocks from T-SQL is not a solution for a database that is having frequent deadlocks. In this case, the underlying cause should be found and fixed.

Figure 8-9 shows a batch that retries transactions that are aborted due to deadlock. Obviously, there are many variations on this, including logging, but this example covers the main points. The first thing the batch does is make a variable (1), @retryCount, that is used to limit the number of retries.

The work the transaction is to do (2) is put inside a labeled BEGIN TRY/END TRY clause.

The BEGIN CATCH/END CATCH clause starts by capturing the error information (3) so that it can be reraised later, if necessary. Next, it checks to see whether a deadlock error occurred (4). If that was the case, it checks to see whether there are any retries left (5). If there are any retries left, it decrements the retry count, rolls back the transaction if necessary, and then goes to the Retry label (6).

If there are no retries left, or the error was not due to a deadlock, the transaction does normal error cleanup and then reraises (7) the error if necessary.

```
   DECLARE @retryCount INT
①SET @retryCount = 3
   Retry: BEGIN TRY
   BEGIN TRAN
②-- do work here
   COMMIT TRAN
   END TRY
   BEGIN CATCH
③DECLARE @error_message NVARCHAR(MAX)
   SET @error_message = ERROR_MESSAGE()
   DECLARE @error_severity INT
   SET @error_severity = ERROR_SEVERITY();
   DECLARE @error_state INT
   SET @error_state = ERROR_STATE();
   IF @error_state = 0 SET @error_state = 1
④IF ERROR_NUMBER() = 1205 BEGIN
⑤IF @retryCount > 0
      SET @retryCount = @retryCount - 1
   IF XACT_STATE() <> 0 ROLLBACK TRAN
⑥GOTO Retry
   END
   -- do error processing here
⑦RAISERROR (@error_message,
      @error_severity, @error_state)
   END CATCH
```

FIGURE 8-9: Retrying transaction

Listing 8-1 is an example that puts together some of the things we have been discussing about BEGIN TRY/BEGIN CATCH. It is meant only as a simple example of how BEGIN TRY/BEGIN CATCH works, not as a standard idiom. It starts by making a couple of error messages: 50001 for an error that should be retried and 50002 for a garden-variety error for which retry isn't useful.

It is often useful to be able to reraise an error in a BEGIN CATCH phrase. You can't just reraise the same error; you don't have enough information to duplicate the original RAISERROR. The example adds a new message, 60000, for reraising errors. The text for the message will have the information about the underlying error.

The ReRaise stored procedure makes it easy to format the text for the 60000 messages. Note that this stored procedure is useful only inside a BEGIN CATCH phrase, because it uses functions like ERROR_NUMBER() that are useful only inside a BEGIN CATCH phrase.

The Retry stored procedure encapsulates the information about what errors can be retried and how many times they should be retried. Note that the ERROR_NUMBER() is checked against a list of retryable errors; it includes the concurrency error 1206 and the error we arbitrarily said was retryable (50001). The status returned by Retry is zero if the error is not retryable— that is, it is an ordinary error.

It returns a status of two when no more retries are left. You could encapsulate the logging of failed retries here. It returns a status of one if another retry should be done. You could encapsulate the logging of retries here.

Note that this stored procedure assumes that the parameter @retryCount is NULL when it is first called.

The ErrorTestW stored procedure is a stored procedure used to try out the Retry and ReRaise stored procedures. The local variable @status will capture the result of executing the Retry stored procedure. As long as @status is NULL or greater than zero, the BEGIN TRY phrase of the ErrorTestW will be run, over and over. All the BEGIN TRY phrase does is raise the error number passed into it; we will pass in 50001 and 50002 to see how it behaves for retryable errors and those that are not.

The result of the RAISERROR in the BEGIN TRY phrase, of course, will be to pass control to the BEGIN CATCH phrase. The BEGIN CATCH phrase executes the Retry stored procedure and checks the status it returns. If the status returned is two, the retry count has expired, and there is nothing left to do except do cleanup and maybe reraising the error, which it does by executing ReRaise. A returned status of zero indicates a garden-variety error so it just cleans up and reraises the error. A return status of one just repeats the BEGIN TRY.

LISTING 8-1: TRY/CATCH usage

```
EXEC sp_addmessage 50001,
    16,
    N'retryable error %s'


EXEC sp_addmessage 50002,
    16,
    N'error %s'

EXEC sp_addmessage 60000,
    10,
N'Reraised Error %d, Level %d, State %d, Procedure %s, Line %d,
Message: %s';
```

```
CREATE PROC ReRaise
AS
DECLARE @error_message NVARCHAR(MAX)
SET @error_message = ERROR_MESSAGE();
DECLARE @error_number INT
SET @error_number = ERROR_NUMBER()
DECLARE @error_severity INT
SET @error_severity = ERROR_SEVERITY();
DECLARE @error_state INT
SET @error_state = ERROR_STATE();
IF @error_state < 1 SET @error_state = 1
DECLARE @error_procedure NVARCHAR(200)
SET @error_procedure = ISNULL(ERROR_PROCEDURE(), '?');
DECLARE @error_line INT
SET @error_line = ERROR_LINE()
RAISERROR(60000,
@error_severity,
1,
@error_number,
@error_severity,
@error_state,
@error_procedure,
@error_line,
@error_message
)
GO


CREATE
PROC Retry(@retryCount INT OUTPUT)
AS
PRINT 'retry'
IF ERROR_NUMBER() in (1206, 50001)
BEGIN
  IF @retryCount IS NULL SET @retryCount = 3
    IF @retryCount > 0
    BEGIN
      -- add logging as appropriate
      SET @retryCount = @retryCount - 1
      RETURN 1 -- retry expression
    END
    ELSE
      -- add logging as appropriate
      RETURN 2 -- retry expired
END
RETURN 0 -- not retryable
GO


CREATE PROC ErrorTestW(@error INT)
AS
```

```
DECLARE @status INT
WHILE ISNULL(@status, 1) > 0
BEGIN TRY
-- simulate an error
RAISERROR (@error, 16, 1, 'oops')
END TRY
BEGIN CATCH
DECLARE @retryCount INT
EXEC @status = Retry @retryCount OUTPUT
IF @status = 2
BEGIN
-- retry expired, do cleanup
-- just so you can see it happening
print 'do retry'
EXEC ReRaise
RETURN
END
IF @status = 0
BEGIN
-- if you get to here it is
-- not retryable, clean up as
-- for other errors
PRINT 'cleanup'
-- if you want to
EXEC ReRaise
END
END CATCH
GO


EXEC ErrorTestW 50001
EXEC ErrorTestW 50002
```

Figure 8-10 shows the results of the ErrorTestW stored procedure for 50001 and 50002. Note that the 50001 error gets retried a number of times and then is reraised. You can see that the text of the first 60000 message tells you the underlying error was 50001.

The 50002 error failed on the first try because it was not on the list of retryable errors.

Note that system errors would be rethrown immediately, the same way as these user errors, if they were not on the list of retryable errors. Their information is wrapped up in the error message, and the recipient of the error would know it was a retry error because the error code was 60000.

```
EXEC ErrorTestW 50001
EXEC ErrorTestW 50002
```

```
Messages
retry
retry
retry
retry
do retry
Msg 60000, Level 16, State 1, Procedure ReRaise, Line 21
Reraised Error 50001, Level 16, State 1, Procedure ErrorTestW, Line 8, Message: retryable error oops
retry
cleanup
Msg 60000, Level 16, State 1, Procedure ReRaise, Line 21
Reraised Error 50002, Level 16, State 1, Procedure ErrorTestW, Line 6, Message: error oops
```

FIGURE 8-10: Testing reraise

INTERSECT and EXCEPT

The strength of T-SQL lies in its ability to operate efficiently on sets of
entities—for example, rows in a table. A common set operation is to make
a new set that contains all the entities common to both sets. Another is to
remove from a set those entities that are contained in some other set. Previous to SQL Server 2005, these operations could be performed using the
EXISTS keyword. SQL Server 2005 introduces two operators, INTERSECT
and EXCEPT, that perform the operations in a more straightforward manner.

The INTERSECT and EXCEPT operators connect two SELECT expressions—
that is, there is an individual SELECT expression to the left and right of the
operator. Each of the SELECT expressions must produce the same number
of columns, and the corresponding columns must be of data types that are
comparable. Note that anything that can be done using INTERSECT and
EXCEPT can be done using EXISTS, but in some cases, the new operators are
more straightforward.

The query in Figure 8-11 finds all the states that have a publisher but no
author. The expression selects all the states (1) from the publishers table and

FIGURE 8-11: Publisher states with no authors

then removes from it any states (2) found in the authors table. What are left are the states that have publishers but no authors. This leaves five states and a NULL. There is a NULL because the publishers table contains some non-U.S. publishers that have a NULL for their state code, but there are no authors that have NULL for their state code.

INTERSECT and EXCEPT are part of what makes SQL Server 2005 more compliant with the SQL:1999 standard. SQL Server 2005 does not support the CORRESPONDING BY clause, however, and INTERSECT and EXCEPT always produce distinct results, which is optional in SQL:1999.

Figure 8-12 shows a query that produces the same result as the one in Figure 8-11. Note the use of the DISTINCT (1) keyword. INTERSECT and EXCEPT in SQL Server 2005 never produce duplicates, so this is needed to purge duplicates. WHERE NOT EXISTS (2) is the equivalent of EXCEPT in this case. Likewise, WHERE EXISTS would be the equivalent of INTERSECT. Note that an OR clause (3) must be added so that NULL values will compare as equal. INTERSECT and EXCEPT consider the equality comparison of two NULL values to be true.

The order of the SELECT statements in an EXCEPT expression is significant. The states that have publishers but no authors are not the same as the states that have authors but no publishers. Figure 8-13 shows the result of reversing the order of the SELECT statements in Figure 8-11.

INTERSECT can be used to find all the states that have both an author and a publisher. Figure 8-14 shows an example of this.

It is a bit more work if you want to find the names of the publishers that are in states that have no authors, rather than the names of states. Figure 8-15 shows some ways you might try to get the publisher names. A SELECT (1) on the left of the EXCEPT operator may not include the pub_name column (1) unless there is a corresponding column in the SELECT on the right of the EXCEPT operator. The SQL:1999 standard CORRESPONDING BY (2) is a

```
              ①
      SELECT DISTINCT state from pubs..publishers AS P
②WHERE NOT EXISTS
      (SELECT * FROM pubs..authors AS A
      WHERE P.state = A.state
③OR (A.state is NULL and P.state is NULL)
```

FIGURE 8-12: Equivalent EXCEPT syntax

FIGURE 8-13: Author states with no publishers

straightforward way to do what we want, but it cannot be used, because it is not supported by SQL Server 2005. CORRESPONDING BY allows you to specify the columns used for intersection or exception as a subset of the columns that are selected in the left expression.

Figure 8-16 shows some queries that will find the names of publishers in states that do not have authors. One way is to use an EXCEPT expression (1) as a subquery that is part of an IN clause. Another way is to use the WHERE NOT EXISTS equivalent (2) of the EXCEPT expression (1) to find the publishers. Note that both queries are complicated by the fact that the publishers and authors tables allow NULL in the state column.

In some cases, the latter query in Figure 8-16 will produce a better execution plan. You will have to look at the execution plan on a case-by-case basis to decide which form to use. Figure 8-17, for example, shows the relative query costs for the execution plans for the two queries shown in Figure 8-16. Also keep in mind that execution plans depend not only on the query itself, but also on the indexes and other resources that are available.

FIGURE 8-14: States with an author and publisher

```
① SELECT pub_name, state FROM pubs..publishers
   EXCEPT
   SELECT state FROM pubs..authors

② SELECT pub_name, state from pubs..publishers
   INTERSECT CORRESPONDING BY (state)
   SELECT state FROM pubs..authors
```

FIGURE 8-15: Wrong ways to find publisher names

An INTO clause can be used with INTERSECT or EXCEPT as shown in Figure 8-18. It must appear in the left SELECT expression (1) if it is used.

There some limits and other considerations when using INTERSECT or EXCEPT. ORDER BY can be used only to order the overall results; it cannot be used with the individual SELECT statements. GROUP BY and HAVING may be used in the individual select statements but not with the overall results.

TOP

Prior to SQL Server 2005, the TOP clause required its value to be a literal value and could be used only in a SELECT statement. In SQL Server 2005, the value can be an expression, and it can be used in DELETE, UPDATE, and INSERT in addition to SELECT.

The fact that the value of a TOP clause can be an expression means you can now use TOP in places that previously would have required dynamic SQL.

```
① SELECT P.pub_name FROM pubs..publishers P
   WHERE ISNULL(P.state, '__') IN
   (
   SELECT ISNULL(state, '__') FROM pubs..publishers
   EXCEPT
   SELECT ISNULL(state, '__') FROM pubs..authors
   )

② SELECT P.pub_name FROM pubs..publishers P
   WHERE NOT EXISTS
   (SELECT * from pubs..authors A
   WHERE A.state = P.state
   OR (A.state IS NULL AND P.state IS NULL))
```

FIGURE 8-16: Publisher names from states without authors

FIGURE 8-17: Relative execution plans

Figure 8-19 compares parameterizing the top rows returned by a SELECT statement using the new TOP syntax with the technique used in SQL Server before SQL Server 2005. The first stored procedure (1) in Figure 8-19 parameterizes the top number of best-selling titles to be selected from the titles table in the pubs database. The new TOP syntax uses an expression inside parentheses that follow the TOP keyword (2) instead of a literal numeric value without parentheses. The old syntax for SELECT is still supported, too.

The second stored procedure (3) in Figure 8-19 produces the same results as the first stored procedure (1) but uses SET ROWCOUNT instead. SET ROWCOUNT in earlier versions of SQL Server was the only way, in effect, to parameterize TOP, but it had some limitations. One of the limitations was that a SET ROWCOUNT–based expression was not composable—that is, it could not be used as a subquery or derived table.

The stored procedure TopPublishers in Figure 8-20 selects the publishers of the @count top best-selling titles. The TOP clause is part of a subquery (1) and is parameterized by @count (2). SET ROWCOUNT would not be very useful here, because it would apply to both the main query and the subquery. It would be possible to implement TopPublishers using SET ROWCOUNT, but it would be a more complicated stored procedure and probably would have a temporary table or variable.

Another limitation of SET ROWCOUNT is that it exactly limits the number of rows returned. TOP, in SQL Server 2005, and previous versions, supports

```
                        ①
SELECT   state INTO #states FROM pubs..publishers
EXCEPT
SELECT state FROM pubs..authors
```

FIGURE 8-18: Using INTO clause

```
①CREATE PROC TopTitles(@count INT)
  AS          ②
  SELECT TOP (@count) title FROM pubs..titles
  ORDER BY ytd _ sales DESC


③CREATE PROC TopTitles2(@count INT)
  AS          ④
  SET ROWCOUNT @count
  SELECT title FROM pubs..titles
  ORDER BY ytd _ sales DESC
  SET ROWCOUNT 0
```

FIGURE 8-19: TOP value as a parameter

the WITH TIES phrase. WITH TIES must be used in conjunction with an ORDER BY clause and causes SQL Server to count rows with the same value as a single item for the purposes of counting for TOP. Figure 8-21 shows the TopTitlesTies stored procedure, which produces a different list of top titles by using the WITH TIES phrase (1).

When ties are included, there are five top titles when four are asked for (2) in the titles table in the pubs database. Note that TopTitles2 (3), which uses SET ROWCOUNT, finds only four top titles.

SQL Server 2005 now supports the use of TOP in DELETE, INSERT, and UPDATE expressions. Note that the TOP syntax, when used with these commands, must include parentheses, even if a literal value is used.

One of the uses of TOP is to reduce contention that can be caused when an expression accesses a large number of rows. A DELETE expression is always a single transaction, even if it spans a large number of rows. This can result in many locks being held for a long time, which impacts overall performance because of contention for the locks and retaining rows in the transaction log for a long time. The use of locks can be minimized by

```
CREATE PROC TopPublishers(@count INT)
AS
SELECT pub _ name FROM pubs..publishers
WHERE pub _ id IN
            ②
①(SELECT TOP(@count) pub _ id FROM pubs..titles
  ORDER BY ytd _ sales DESC)
```

FIGURE 8-20: Selecting top publishers

```
    CREATE PROC TopTitlesTies(@count INT)
    AS
①  SELECT TOP (@count) WITH TIES
    title FROM pubs..titles
    ORDER BY ytd_sales
```

②EXEC TopTitlesTies 4   ③EXEC TopTitles2 4

	title
1	The Psychology of C
2	Net Etiquette
3	Life Without Fear
4	Computer Phobic AND
5	Onions, Leeks, and

	title
1	The Psychology of Computer
2	Net Etiquette
3	Life Without Fear
4	Computer Phobic AND Non-Ph

FIGURE 8-21: Top titles, including ties

repeatedly executing the DELETE expression on a small number of rows until all the desired rows have been deleted.

Figure 8-22 shows the TestData table (1) being filled (2) with some data. Then all the rows where data is greater than 500 are deleted, in blocks of ten, to minimize the use of locks. The block size is parameterized in the @block, which is then used in a TOP phrase (3). If any rows were successfully deleted (4), the DELETE (3) command is repeated.

```
①CREATE TABLE TestData
  (
  data int
  )

②DECLARE @rows INT
  SET @rows = 10000
  WHILE @rows > 0
  BEGIN
  INSERT INTO TestData VALUES (@rows)
  SET @rows = @rows - 1
  END

  DECLARE @blockSize INT
  SET @blockSize = 10
  DECLARE @rcount INT
  SET @rcount = 1
④WHILE @rcount > 0
  BEGIN
③DELETE TestData WHERE data > 500
  SET @rcount = @@ROWCOUNT
  END
```

FIGURE 8-22: Delete in blocks

This is a trivial table, of course, and the rows involved could have easily been deleted in a single expression with no impact on the server, but this example is meant just to show the technique. This technique is useful when a large number of rows must be deleted.

Note that the technique shown Figure 8-22 is not deleting the rows in a single transaction. This means that a failure will leave some rows deleted and some rows not deleted. If the operation were done in a single transaction, all the rows would have been deleted, or none would have been deleted. This is a tradeoff you will have to make, but the technique shown in Figure 8-22 will have less negative impact on the running server when a large number of rows is involved and requires a smaller number of entries in the transaction log to be rolled forward in the event of a failure and restart of SQL Server.

SET ROWCOUNT could have been used, of course, and would have produced the same effect as TOP in Figure 8-22, but it certainly would have led to a more complicated T-SQL script. Moreover, some future version of SQL Server is slated to drop support for the use of SET ROWCOUNT with INSERT, UPDATE, and SELECT commands. If you are using SET ROWCOUNT with these commands in your T-SQL scripts, you will not have to update them for SQL Server 2005, but at some point in the future, you will.

ON DELETE and ON UPDATE

The ON DELETE and ON UPDATE clauses of the CREATE TABLE expression give you another way to manage columns that have foreign keys. Figure 8-23 shows some tables that keep track of departments and employees in a company. The Departments table has a column named Manager that, to ensure that the manager is an employee, has a foreign key that references the Employees table.

A simple query will show that Joe is the manager of department 1999. If Joe leaves the company, he will have to be deleted from the Employees table, but that will not be possible until the Departments table is updated with a new manager or the department itself is deleted from the Departments table. In the case where deleting the department is not an option, the Departments table will have to be updated with a new manager.

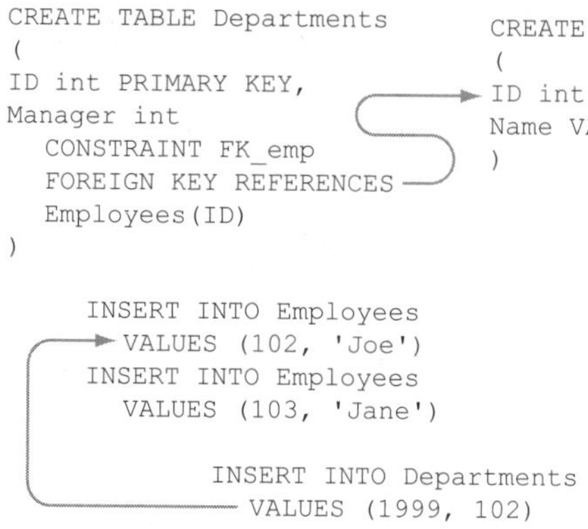

```
CREATE TABLE Departments          CREATE TABLE Employees
(                                 (
ID int PRIMARY KEY,                 ID int PRIMARY KEY,
Manager int                         Name VARCHAR(20)
   CONSTRAINT FK_emp                )
   FOREIGN KEY REFERENCES
   Employees(ID)
)
```

```
INSERT INTO Employees
VALUES (102, 'Joe')
INSERT INTO Employees
   VALUES (103, 'Jane')

         INSERT INTO Departments
         VALUES (1999, 102)
```

FIGURE 8-23: Departments and employees

This is an example of a typical parent–child relationship. You can think of the Employees table as holding the parents and the Departments table as holding the children, though not every employee has a department as a child. The general problem is that a change to a parent may require a change to its children.

A couple of conventions can be used if Joe leaves on short notice and no new manager has been selected for the department. One is to replace the manager of the department with a NULL, and the other is to replace the manager with a well-known ID from the Employee tables that is used to indicate that no employee exists for the position. The latter convention is useful if you would rather not have to deal with NULL values in your database.

The ON DELETE clause can be added to the column definition of a table to specify which of these conventions to use when a corresponding row in the table being referenced is deleted. The same issue can come up with the same conventions possible when the table being referenced is updated, of course. The ON UPDATE clause also can be added to a column definition to specify which convention to use in this case.

Figure 8-24 shows the Departments table defined using the ON DELETE and ON UPDATE clauses. In the case of a delete, the "replace with NULL" convention is being used. In the case of update, the "replace with well-known value" convention is being used. It is unlikely that you would want to use different conventions for delete and update on the same column, of course, but it is done in this case so the example can show how each works.

```
CREATE TABLE Departments          CREATE TABLE Employees
(                                 (
ID int PRIMARY KEY,              ID int PRIMARY KEY,
Manager int DEFAULT 0            Name VARCHAR(20)
   FOREIGN KEY REFERENCES        )
   Employees(ID)
   ON DELETE SET NULL
   ON UPDATE SET DEFAULT
)
         INSERT INTO Employees
           VALUES (0, '%NO EMPLOYEE')
         INSERT INTO Employees
          VALUES (102, 'Joe')
         INSERT INTO Employees
           VALUES (103, 'Jane')

            INSERT INTO Departments
             VALUES (1999, 102)
```

FIGURE 8-24: Using ON UPDATE and ON DELETE

If the row being referenced by the Manager column is deleted, the value for the manager column will be replaced with NULL. If the row being referenced by the Manager column is updated, and its ID is changed, the value for the Manager column is replaced with the default value for the column, which in this case is zero.

Figure 8-25 shows the effect of the ON DELETE and ON UPDATE clauses. The Employees table is updated (1), and the ID of employee 102—Joe, the manager of department 1999—is changed to 110. This causes the "replace with well-known value" convention to be used to update the Departments table so that employee 0 becomes the manager of department 1999.

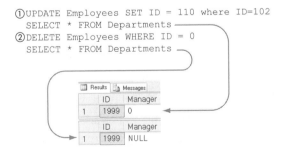

```
①UPDATE Employees SET ID = 110 where ID=102
  SELECT * FROM Departments
②DELETE Employees WHERE ID = 0
  SELECT * FROM Departments
```

	ID	Manager
1	1999	0

	ID	Manager
1	1999	NULL

FIGURE 8-25: Effects of ON UPDATE and ON DELETE

Next, employee 0 is deleted (2) from the Employees table. The causes the "replace with NULL" convention to be used to update the Departments table so that NULL becomes the manager of department 1999.

The ON DELETE and ON UPDATE clauses make it easy to specify declaratively the use of the "replace with NULL" or "replace with well-known value" conventions for handling the cases where foreign keys change. There are some caveats, of course. In no case will these clauses let any constraints be violated. If an ON DELETE/UPDATE SET DEFAULT clause is used, the default value for the column must exist in the column being referred to when a row in a referenced table is deleted or updated. Likewise, an ON DELETE/UPDATE SET DEFAULT clause may be used only on a column that allows NULLs.

OUTPUT

Prior to SQL Server 2005, the only way to observe, after the fact, the results of an INSERT, DELETE, or UPDATE command was through a trigger. From within a trigger, you get to see the state of a row before and after the execution of the command. SQL Server 2005 adds an optional OUTPUT clause to the INSERT, UPDATE, and DELETE commands that in effect lets you capture the information you would see inside a trigger, but see it in a T-SQL script or stream it back to a client.

The INSERT, UPDATE, and DELETE commands use a common syntax for the OUTPUT clause itself but differ in its placement in the command. The OUTPUT clause can be used as though it were a SELECT command that returns results to the client or with an INTO clause that adds rows to a table.

One of the uses of OUTPUT is to obtain the value of an identity column that was assigned to a row by an INSERT command.

Figure 8-26 shows the use of OUTPUT as though it were a SELECT. It creates the table TestData (1) to hold some data that might result from a testing process. It does an INSERT command (2) to add a value to the data. The INSERT command includes an OUTPUT clause (3) that returns (4) both the data value and its new identity. The SCOPE_IDENTITY() function could have been used to get the new identity in this example, but later, we will see that this technique can be used when multiple rows are added and SCOPE_IDENTITY() would not be useful.

```
①CREATE TABLE TestData
  (
  id INT IDENTITY PRIMARY KEY,
  data INT
  )

②INSERT INTO testdata
      OUTPUT INSERTED.id AS [Inserted id],
    ③ INSERTED.data AS [Inserted data]
  VALUES (20)
```

④ Results | Messages

	Inserted id	Inserted data
1	14	20

FIGURE 8-26: Obtaining identity

The part of the OUTPUT clause syntax that is common to all OUTPUT clauses is the OUTPUT keyword followed by comma-separated column names, optionally aliased. The columns can come from the INSERTED or DELETED table.

The INSERTED and DELETED tables are logical tables, not physical ones. The INSERTED table will contain all the columns of the table being processed. The columns will contain the values of the rows changed or added after processing—that is, after the INSERT or UPDATE has taken place. The DELETED table will contain the values of the rows changed or removed prior to processing—that is, prior to the DELETE or UPDATE command's being executed.

An INSERT command produces only an INSERTED table. A DELETE command produces only a DELETED table. An UPDATE command produces both tables.

Figure 8-27 shows some typical usages of OUTPUT. The UPDATE statement at the top of the figure uses both the DELETED (1) and INSERTED (2) tables. It aliases the data columns from the INSERTED and DELETED tables to distinguish the old and new data in output. The OUTPUT clause comes immediately after the SET clause and before any FROM or WHERE clause in an UPDATE command.

The values returned by an OUTPUT clause reflect the values after the INSERT, UPDATE, or DELETE has been executed but before any triggers have fired. For an INSTEAD OF trigger, the values will reflect what would have

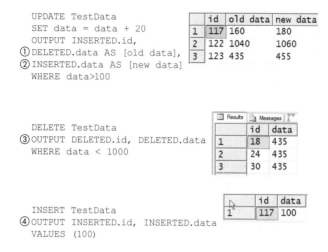

```
UPDATE TestData
SET data = data + 20
OUTPUT INSERTED.id,
① DELETED.data AS [old data],
② INSERTED.data AS [new data]
WHERE data>100
```

	id	old data	new data
1	117	160	180
2	122	1040	1060
3	123	435	455

```
DELETE TestData
③ OUTPUT DELETED.id, DELETED.data
WHERE data < 1000
```

	id	data
1	18	435
2	24	435
3	30	435

```
INSERT TestData
④ OUTPUT INSERTED.id, INSERTED.data
VALUES (100)
```

	id	data
1	117	100

FIGURE 8-27: Typical usage of OUTPUT

been in the table if there was no INSTEAD OF trigger, but of course, the INSTEAD OF trigger will still fire.

The DELETE statement in the middle of the figure uses the DELETED (3) table. The OUTPUT clause comes immediately after the table name and before any WHERE clause.

The INSERT statement at the bottom of the figure uses the INSERTED (4) table. The OUTPUT clause comes immediately before any values in an INSERT command.

The identity in Figure 8-26 could have also been obtained using the SCOPE_IDENTITY function without the use of the OUTPUT clause, of course. But SCOPE_IDENTITY isn't useful if more than one row is processed in a single statement. Note that neither @@IDENTITY nor SCOPE_IDENTITY should be used in an OUTPUT clause; either will return the value of the identity as it was before the expression was executed.

Figure 8-28 shows using an INSERT/SELECT statement to insert multiple rows of data. It uses the same OUTPUT clause (1) as the example in Figure 8-26 does. The data is selected from a subquery that just unions some sample data. The client receives (3) a row for each value inserted that includes the value itself and its identity.

```
INSERT Scratch.dbo.TestData
    ① OUTPUT INSERTED.id AS [Inserted id],
         INSERTED.data AS [Inserted data]
② SELECT * FROM
  (SELECT 3 AS D
  UNION SELECT 5 AS D
  UNION SELECT 23 AS D
  UNION SELECT 4 AS D
  UNION SELECT 1000 AS D
  ) AS A
```

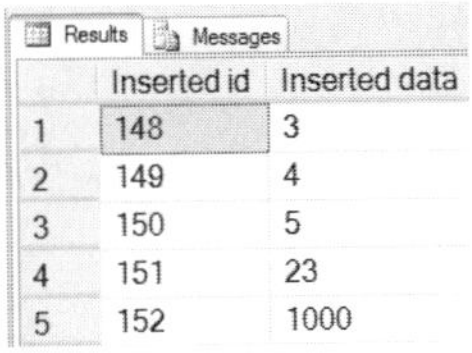

		Inserted id	Inserted data
③	1	148	3
	2	149	4
	3	150	5
	4	151	23
	5	152	1000

FIGURE 8-28: Obtaining identities from bulk insert

The * wildcard can be used with either the INSERTED or DELETED table. This is shown (1) in Figure 8-29.

The OUTPUT cause can also be used to insert into a table instead of returning a rowset. It supports inserting into a permanent, temporary, or variable table. It does not support the SELECT/INTO syntax that creates a table and then inserts data into it. The example in Figure 8-30 creates a table variable (1). It uses an OUTPUT clause (2) in the same way that Figure 8-28 did but adds an INTO clause (3) to it to insert the newly added data into the table variable @newData. The INTO clause always comes after the last column specified in the OUTPUT clause.

```
INSERT Scratch.dbo.TestData
OUTPUT INSERTED.* ①
SELECT *
   SELECT * FROM
  (SELECT 3 AS D
  UNION SELECT 5 AS D
  UNION SELECT 23 AS D
  UNION SELECT 4 AS D
  UNION SELECT 1000 AS D
  ) AS A
```

FIGURE 8-29: Wildcard usage

```
①DECLARE @newData TABLE(id INT, data INT)
 INSERT Scratch.dbo.TestData
  ②OUTPUT INSERTED.id AS [Inserted id],
    INSERTED.data AS [Inserted data]
  ③INTO @newData
 SELECT *
   SELECT * FROM
 (SELECT 3 AS D
 UNION SELECT 5 AS D
 UNION SELECT 23 AS D
 UNION SELECT 4 AS D
 UNION SELECT 1000 AS D
 ) AS A
 SELECT * FROM @newData
```

FIGURE 8-30: Using OUTPUT INTO

APPLY Operators

SQL Server 2005 adds two specialized join operators: CROSS APPLY and OUTER APPLY. Both act like a CROSS JOIN operator in that they join two sets and produce their Cartesian product, except that no ON clause is allowed in a CROSS or OUTER APPLY. They are distinguished from a CROSS JOIN in that the expression on the right side of a CROSS or OUTER APPLY can refer to elements of the expression on the left side. This functionality is required to make use of the nodes function, which is discussed in Chapter 10 and can also be useful in queries that do not involve XML.

Figure 8-31 shows the mechanics of using CROSS APPLY (2). Here, it is used to produce a Cartesian product of two sets. The first set (1) is the

```
SELECT title _ id, au _ id FROM
   ①(SELECT TOP 2 title _ id FROM pubs..titles) AS T
②CROSS APPLY
   ③(SELECT TOP 3 au _ id FROM pubs..authors) AS A
```

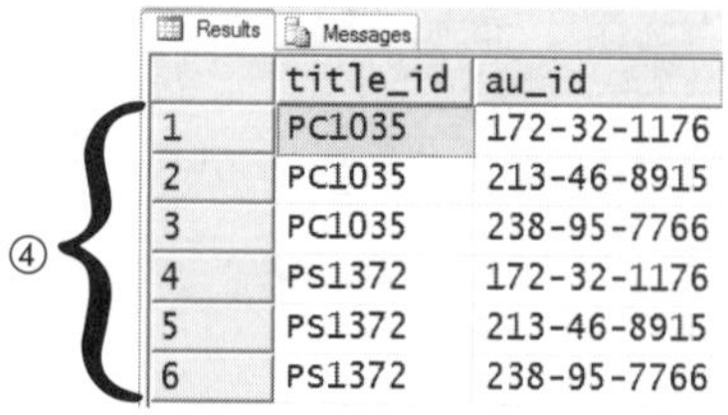

	title_id	au_id
1	PC1035	172-32-1176
2	PC1035	213-46-8915
3	PC1035	238-95-7766
4	PS1372	172-32-1176
5	PS1372	213-46-8915
6	PS1372	238-95-7766

④

FIGURE 8-31: Cartesian product

unqualified top two titles in the `titles` table in the pubs database. The second set (3) is likewise the unqualified top three authors in the `authors` table in the pubs database. The result (4) is six rows of data—that is, the Cartesian product—that includes every combination of the results of the `SELECT` statements.

You can get the same result with `CROSS JOIN` as you can with `CROSS APPLY` and `OUTER APPLY`. Figure 8-32 shows a query that is equivalent to the one in Figure 8-31. The `CROSS JOIN` (1) replaces the `CROSS APPLY`.

It is pretty rare that you would want the Cartesian product, and if you did, you would probably use `CROSS JOIN`, not `CROSS APPLY`; it is typically an intermediate result that is further reduced by the associated `WHERE` clause. There are some cases where this kind of result is useful, though, in particular if the expression on the right side always returns a single row or is dependent on the left side.

Figure 8-33 shows a query that uses `CROSS APPLY` (1) to find the least expensive book for each publisher in the pubs database. The left side is the `publishers` table in the pubs database. The right side of the `CROSS APPLY` is a subquery that depends on the `pub_id` (2) from the left side. The right side produces a row only if the publisher publishes at least one book. `CROSS APPLY` produces an output only when both sides are non-null, just as a `CROSS JOIN` does. Note that the query in Figure 8-33 would not work if `CROSS JOIN` were substituted for `CROSS APPLY`, because the right side makes a reference to the `pub_id` on the left side, and `CROSS JOIN` does not allow this.

Note that when you are using the `APPLY` operator, the expression to the right of the operator can reference columns from the expression to the left of the operator, but the expression on the left of the operator may not reference columns from the right of the operator.

Figure 8-34 is the same query as that in Figure 8-33 except that it uses an `OUTER APPLY` (1) instead of `CROSS APPLY`. The `OUTER APPLY`, just like an

```
SELECT title _ id, au _ id FROM
 (SELECT TOP 2 title _ id FROM pubs..titles) AS T
①CROSS JOIN
 (SELECT TOP 3 au _ id FROM pubs..authors) AS A
```

FIGURE 8-32: JOIN cartesian product

```
SELECT T.title, P.pub_name FROM
pubs..publishers P
①CROSS APPLY
 (SELECT TOP 1 title from pubs..titles
 where P.pub_id = pub_id②
 ORDER BY Price
 ) AS T
```

	title	pub_name
1	You Can Combat Computer Stress!	New Moon Books
2	The Psychology of Computer Cooking	Binnet & Hardley
3	Net Etiquette	Algodata Infosystems

FIGURE 8-33: CROSS APPLY

OUTER JOIN, includes all rows produced with NULLs for the values of non-existent rows.

The right side of a CROSS or OUTER APPLY is a rowset, which in the previous example was produced by a subquery. The right side could, of course, have been a table-valued function. Figure 8-35 shows a table-valued function, LeastExpensiveTitle (1), that returns a single row that contains the least expensive title from the publisher specified by the @pub_id passed into it. This function is essentially the subquery that was used on the right side of the CROSS APPLY in Figure 8-33.

This function is used (2) on the right side of a CROSS APPLY. This query produces the same output as Figure 8-33. The nodes function, which is

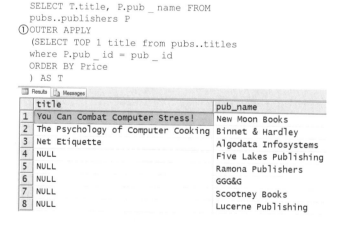

```
SELECT T.title, P.pub_name FROM
pubs..publishers P
①OUTER APPLY
 (SELECT TOP 1 title from pubs..titles
 where P.pub_id = pub_id
 ORDER BY Price
 ) AS T
```

	title	pub_name
1	You Can Combat Computer Stress!	New Moon Books
2	The Psychology of Computer Cooking	Binnet & Hardley
3	Net Etiquette	Algodata Infosystems
4	NULL	Five Lakes Publishing
5	NULL	Ramona Publishers
6	NULL	GGG&G
7	NULL	Scootney Books
8	NULL	Lucerne Publishing

FIGURE 8-34: OUTER APPLY

```
①CREATE FUNCTION LeastExpensiveTitle(
  @pub_id CHAR(4)
  )
  RETURNS TABLE
  RETURN SELECT TOP 1 title FROM pubs..titles
  WHERE pub_id = @pub_id
  ORDER BY PRICE

  SELECT T.title, P.pub_name FROM
  pubs..publishers AS P
  CROSS APPLY
②LeastExpensiveTitle(P.pub_id) AS T
```

FIGURE 8-35: Using a table-valued function with **CROSS APPLY**

discussed in Chapter 10, is also a table-valued function and likewise will be used on the right side of a CROSS or OUTER APPLY.

Common Table Expressions

A *common table expression* (CTE) is an expression that is referred to by name within the context of a single query. CTEs are part of the SQL:1999 standard and extend the syntax of SELECT, INSERT, DELETE, and UPDATE statements by adding a preface to them that can define one or more common table expressions.

Figure 8-36 illustrates the general syntax for a CTE. The preface for a CTE is always introduced by a WITH keyword. The CTE must be the first

```
         introduces CTE
name ──▶ WITH
         TreData (number)◀── column names
         AS
      ⎧ (
body ⎨ SELECT data FROM TestData WHERE data % 3 = 0
      ⎩ ),
         OddData ◀── second CTE
         AS
         (
         SELECT id, data FROM TestData
         WHERE data % 2 <> 0          references
         )
         SELECT id, data FROM OddData
         WHERE data IN (select number from TreData)
```

FIGURE 8-36: CTE syntax

statement in a batch or be preceded by a semicolon (;). Each CTE has a name used to reference the expression that makes up its body. A CTE may optionally name the columns returned by the expression in its body. Consecutive CTEs are separated by commas. The SQL expression that follows the last CTE makes references to the names of the CTEs that preceded it.

The syntax of a CTE makes it appear that it will build a temporary table for each CTE, and then the statements that reference the CTEs will use those tables. This is not the case. A CTE is an alternative syntax for a subquery. Figure 8-37 shows in effect how the statement in Figure 8-36 will be used. In other words, a CTE will be evaluated as a whole, just as any other SQL statement is, and an execution plan will be built for it as a whole. So any statement that contains subqueries can be converted to a CTE, and vice versa.

Figure 8-38 shows a SQL script with a trivial CTE just to give you a feeling for its usage. The `WITH` (1) clause in effect defines an expression named `MathConst` that has two columns (2) named `PI` and `Avogadro`. The body of the CTE is in parentheses (3) and contains a `SELECT` statement (3). The `SELECT` statement that follows the body of the CTE references (4) the `Math-Const` expression and returns the single row that it contains.

Figure 8-39 shows the subquery-based statement that is the equivalent of the CTE-based statement in Figure 8-38. The CTE referenced in Figure 8-38 is reduced to a subquery (1) in Figure 8-39.

We will use the `Sales.SalesPerson`, `Sales.SalesHeader`, and `Sales.SalesDetail` tables from the AdventureWorks database to illustrate the use of CTEs. The `SalesPerson` table lists each salesperson who works for AdventureWorks. Each salesperson has a SalesPersonID that

```
         SELECT id, data FROM
         (
OddData  SELECT id, data FROM TestData
         WHERE data % 2 <> 0
         ) as OddData
         WHERE data IN
         (
TreData   SELECT data AS number FROM TestData
         WHERE data % 3 = 0
         )
```

FIGURE 8-37: Expanded CTE

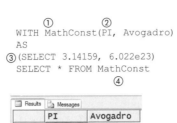

FIGURE 8-38: CTE usage

identifies him or her. A sales header is inserted into the SalesHeader for each sale that is made at AdventureWorks. The header includes the Sales-PersonID of the salesperson making the sale. A line item is inserted into the `SalesDetail` table for each product that was sold in that sale. The line item includes the `ProductID` of the product sold and the `SalesHeaderID` of the header to which it belongs.

The stock room has just called the Big Boss and told him that it is out of part number 744. The Big Boss calls you and wants you to make a report that lists the `SalesPersonID` of each salesperson. Also, the Big Boss wants the text "Make Call" listed along with the `SalesPersonID` if a salesperson made a sale that depends on part number 744 to be completed. Otherwise, he wants the text `'Relax'` printed next to the salesperson's ID.

Before we actually use the CTE, let's write a query that finds all the IDs of salespeople who have sales that depend on part number 744. Figure 8-40 shows a query that finds all the `SalesOrderHeaders` that have at least one `SalesOrderDetail` for `ProductID` 744. This query could be used to make the report for the Big Boss.

Figure 8-41 shows a statement that uses the query (1) from Figure 8-40 as a subquery to make the report the Big Boss wants. Notice that there is a subquery with a subquery. The outer one gets `SalesOrderHeaders` (1) provided

```
       SELECT * FROM
   ① (SELECT 3.14159 AS PI, 6.022e23 AS Avogadro)
       AS MathConst
```

FIGURE 8-39: Equivalent subquery

```
SELECT SalesPersonID FROM Sales.SalesOrderHeader
WHERE SalesOrderID in
(
    SELECT SalesOrderID FROM Sales.SalesOrderDetail
    WHERE ProductID = 744
)
```

	SalesPersonID
1	268
2	275
3	276
4	279
5	280
6	282
7	283

FIGURE 8-40: Salesperson IDs for orders for ProductID 744

that it contains a 744 ProductID (2) in one of its SalesOrderDetails. The CASE clause outputs 'Make Call!' if the SalesPersonID is in one of the SalesOrderHeaders that contain ProductID 744.

Figure 8-42 shows using a CTE to implement a query equivalent to the one in Figure 8-41 and the output it produces. The DetailsFor744 (1) CTE is an expression that finds all the SalesOrderIDs that contain a ProductID of 744 in their SalesOrderDetails.

The MakeCall (2) CTE makes reference to the DetailsFor744 (3) CTE. Note that a CTE can always make a reference to a preceding CTE in the same expression. It finds the SalesPersonIDs from SalesOrderHeaders that have a ProductID of 744 in their SalesOrderDetails.

```
SELECT SalesPersonID ,
CASE
WHEN SalesPersonID in
(
  ①SELECT SalesPersonID FROM   Sales.SalesOrderHeader
    WHERE SalesOrderID in
    (
      ②SELECT SalesOrderID FROM Sales.SalesOrderDetail
        WHERE ProductID = 744
    )
)
THEN 'Make Call!'
ELSE 'Relax'
END AS Message
FROM Sales.SalesPerson;
```

FIGURE 8-41: Big Boss report using subquery

```
WITH DetailsFor744 AS①
(
SELECT SalesOrderID FROM
Sales.SalesOrderDetail
WHERE ProductID=744
),
MakeCall AS②
(
SELECT SalesPersonID FROM
Sales.SalesOrderHeader
WHERE SalesOrderID in       ③
(SELECT SalesOrderID FROM DetailsFor744)
)
SELECT SalesPersonID,
CASE
WHEN SalesPersonID in        ④
(SELECT SalesPersonID FROM MakeCall)
THEN 'Make Call!'
ELSE 'Relax'
END AS Message
FROM Sales.SalesPerson;
```

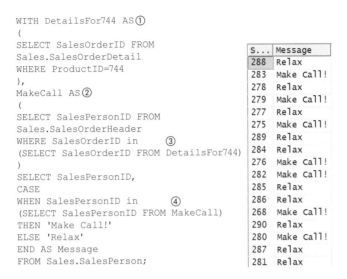

S...	Message
288	Relax
283	Make Call!
278	Relax
279	Make Call!
277	Relax
275	Make Call!
289	Relax
284	Relax
276	Make Call!
282	Make Call!
285	Relax
286	Relax
268	Make Call!
290	Relax
280	Make Call!
287	Relax
281	Relax

FIGURE 8-42: Report for Big Boss using a CTE

The SELECT statement that follows the last CTE makes a reference to the MakeCall (4) CTE to distinguish the salespeople who have orders depending on ProductID 744.

As you can see in this case, the CTE is just an alternative syntax for a derived table and, in this case, a more verbose one. In fact, you might find the query in Figure 8-41 easier to read than the one in Figure 8-42. But both have the same query plan.

But let's make things more interesting. Just as you finish the query for the Big Boss's report, you get another call. The Big Boss wants something a bit different. He says he doesn't want any salespeople wasting time making extra phone calls if all their orders that use part 744 have a value less than the average value of all the orders that depend on part 744. He says he wants the salespeople to make a call only if they have an "expensive" order.

There are many ways to make this "expensive" report, but Figure 8-43 shows a way to do it with several subqueries. It starts in a way similar to the preceding queries in that it uses a subquery (1) to find all the SalesOrder-Headers that depend on ProductID 744. This has to be qualified further by calculating the value of the order (2), which is the sum of the extended price—that is, units times cost—for all the SalesOrderDetail rows associated with that SalesOrderHeader.

```
SELECT SalesPersonID,
CASE
WHEN SalesPersonID in
(
SELECT OH.SalesPersonID FROM Sales.SalesOrderHeader OH
WHERE OH.SalesOrderID in
(
SELECT SalesOrderID FROM Sales.SalesOrderDetail OD
①WHERE ProductID = 744
  AND
  (
  ②SELECT SUM(UnitPrice * OrderQty) FROM Sales.SalesOrderDetail
    WHERE OH.SalesOrderID = SalesOrderID
  )
  >
  (
  ③SELECT AVG(Total) FROM
    (
      SELECT SUM(UnitPrice * OrderQty) AS Total
        FROM Sales.SalesOrderDetail
        WHERE SalesOrderID in
          (SELECT SalesOrderID FROM Sales.SalesOrderDetail
            WHERE ProductID = OD.ProductID)
      ④GROUP BY SalesOrderID
      ) d
    )
  )
)
THEN 'Make Call!'
ELSE 'Relax'
END
FROM Sales.SalesPerson
```

FIGURE 8-43: Expensive orders using subquery

The value of the order has to be greater than the average value of all the orders that depend on ProductID 744. Average value is calculated (3) by averaging the total value of the orders that depend on ProductID 744 when grouped by (4) the SalesOrderID. Whew!

Figure 8-44 shows the result of running the query shown in Figure 8-43. Note that two fewer salespeople have to make calls. What we are going to do next is repeat this query, but we'll use a CTE instead and see whether it is anything more than a syntactic difference.

The query in Figure 8-45 is the equivalent of that in Figure 8-43 except that it uses CTEs to do the subqueries. The OrdersFor744 (1) CTE finds the SalesOrderIDs for the orders that depend on part 744. The Order-TotalsFor744 (2) CTE uses the GROUP BY SalesOrderID to calculate the value of each of the orders found by the OrdersFor744 CTE. The AvgOrdersFor744 CTE (3) finds the overall average of the totals found by the OrderTotalsFor744 CTE.

The AboveAvgOrdersFor744 (4) CTE finds the orders whose total is greater than the overall average of the orders that depended on part 744.

SalesPersonID	Message
288	Relax
283	Relax
278	Relax
279	Make Call!
277	Relax
275	Relax
289	Relax
284	Relax
276	Make Call!
282	Make Call!
285	Relax
286	Relax
268	Make Call!
290	Relax
280	Make Call!
287	Relax
281	Relax

FIGURE 8-44: Expensive
order report

Note that the CROSS APPLY operator is used here, because AvgOrdersFor744 returns only a single row, and it is used to do a magnitude comparison.

The MakeCall (5) CTE gets the SalesOrderIDs for all the above-average orders from the AboveAvgOrderFor744 CTE. The final expression

```
WITH
OrdersFor744 AS (①)
SELECT SalesOrderID FROM Sales.SalesOrderHeader
WHERE SalesOrderID in (SELECT SalesOrderID FROM
Sales.SalesOrderDetail WHERE ProductID=744)
),
OrderTotalsFor744 AS (②)
SELECT SalesOrderID, SUM(UnitPrice * OrderQty) AS Total
From Sales.SalesOrderDetail
WHERE SalesOrderID in (SELECT SalesOrderID FROM OrdersFor744)
GROUP BY SalesOrderID
),
AvgOrdersFor744 AS (③)
SELECT Avg(Total) AS Average FROM OrderTotalsFor744
),
AboveAvgOrdersFor744 AS (④)
SELECT OT.SalesOrderID FROM OrderTotalsFor744 OT
CROSS APPLY AvgOrdersFor744 AS A WHERE A.Average < OT.Total
),
MakeCall AS (⑤)
SELECT SalesPersonID FROM Sales.SalesOrderHeader
WHERE SalesOrderID in
(SELECT SalesOrderID FROM AboveAvgOrdersFor744)
)
SELECT SalesPersonID,
CASE
WHEN SalesPersonID in (SELECT SalesPersonID FROM MakeCall)
THEN 'Make Call!'
ELSE 'Relax'
END
FROM Sales.SalesPerson;
```

FIGURE 8-45: Expensive orders using CTE

works the same way as the one in Figure 8-42, but this time, the `MakeCall` CTE returns a different set of `SalesPersonIDs`.

Comparing the query in Figure 8-45 with the one in Figure 8-43, you will see that the one in Figure 8-45 is a bit more verbose. Some might find following the query in Figure 8-45 easier because each subquery has a name, but if you are used to writing subqueries, that might not be the case. There is more to this comparison than syntax, however.

If you run both queries in the same batch and look at the actual execution plan for them, you will see that the CTE-based query (1) in Figure 8-45 is about one-fifth the cost of the subquery-based query (2) in Figure 8-43 as shown in Figure 8-46, with the database as configured as installed. If you use the database engine tuning advisor and add the indexes it recommends for these queries, the CTE-based query will be about one-ninth the cost of the subquery-based one. In either case, the CTE-based query costs noticeably less. Like any performance metric, of course, this has to be tested in your actual usage environment to see which is better suited to your needs.

The reason for this is that the CTE gives the query engine more information. The subquery-based query doesn't realize that the calculation of the average value of the order needs to be run only once and runs it once per row. With the CTE-based query, it is easy for the query engine to see that it needs to calculate this aggregate only once.

If you had to make this report in a version of SQL Server before SQL Server 2005, you probably would have calculated the average value into a variable and then used that, rather than letting the query engine calculate it once per row. What you lose by doing this is composability. The CTE-based query can be used to define a view or an inline table-valued function, and the solution that declares a variable cannot.

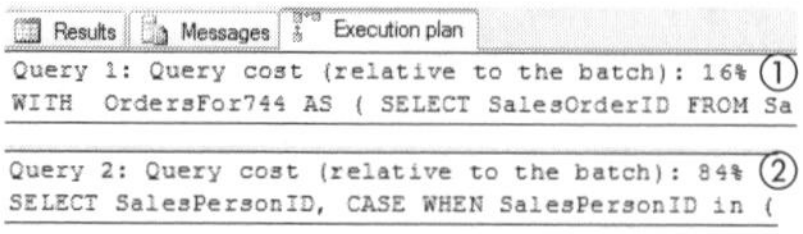

FIGURE 8-46: Execution plan comparison

Recursive Queries

The CTE is the basis of another feature of SQL Server 2005 that is also part of the SQL:1999 standard: a recursive query. This is especially useful for a chart of accounts in an accounting system or a parts explosion in a bill of materials. Both of these involve tree-structured data. In general, a recursive query is useful any time tree-structured data is involved. We will start by looking at an example of a chart of accounts to see how recursive queries work.

Figure 8-47 shows a diagram of a simple chart of accounts containing two kinds of accounts: detail accounts and rollup accounts. Detail accounts have an actual balance associated with them; when a posting is made to an accounting system, it is posted to detail accounts. In Figure 8-47, account 4001 is a detail account that has a balance of $12.

Rollup accounts are used to summarize the totals of detail accounts that descend from them. Every account, except for the root account, has a parent. The total of a rollup account is the sum of the detail accounts that descend from it. In Figure 8-47, account 3002 is a rollup account, and it represents the sum of its two children: accounts 4001 and 4002. Rollup account 2001 represents the total of detail accounts 3001, 4001, and 4002.

One of the ways to represent a chart of accounts is to have two tables: one for detail accounts and the other for rollup accounts. A detail account has an account number, a parent account number, and a balance for columns. A rollup account has an account number and a parent but no balance associated with it.

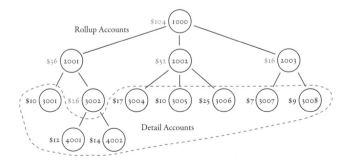

FIGURE 8-47: Chart of accounts

A SQL batch that builds and populates the two tables for the accounts is shown in Figure 8-48. Note that referential integrity is not included just for simplicity.

One question you might ask of a chart of accounts is "What is the balance of account xxxx?", where "xxxx" is an account number. For example, "What is the balance of account 1000?" Note that because 1000 is the root of all the accounts, we could just add up all the detail accounts, but we will do this using a recursive query and then build on it to find the balance of any account.

In a typical recursive query, there are three parts: an anchor, which initializes the recursion; a recursion member; and a final query. Figure 8-49 shows a recursive query named Rollup that calculates the balance of account 1000. A recursive query is a CTE that includes a UNION ALL (2) operator. The statement that precedes the UNION ALL operator is the anchor (1) and is executed just once.

The statement that follows the UNION ALL operator is the recursion (3) query. It joins the CTE itself—that is, joins Rollup. It always joins the result of the previous query until it produces no results. Note that the term *rollup* is a bit overloaded. T-SQL supports a ROLLUP option on GROUP BY clauses. Here, we are discussing rollup in the bookkeeping sense that it is used in a

```
CREATE TABLE DetailAccount(
    id INT PRIMARY KEY,
    parent INT,
    balance FLOAT)
CREATE TABLE RollupAccount(
    id INT PRIMARY KEY,
    parent INT)
INSERT INTO DetailAccount VALUES (3001, 2001, 10)
INSERT INTO DetailAccount VALUES(4001, 3002, 12)
INSERT INTO DetailAccount VALUES(4002, 3002, 14)
INSERT INTO DetailAccount VALUES(3004, 2002, 17)
INSERT INTO DetailAccount VALUES(3005, 2002, 10)
INSERT INTO DetailAccount VALUES(3006, 2002, 25)
INSERT INTO DetailAccount VALUES(3007, 2003, 7)
INSERT INTO DetailAccount VALUES(3008, 2003, 9)

INSERT INTO RollupAccount VALUES(3002, 2001)
INSERT INTO RollupAccount VALUES(2001, 1000)
INSERT INTO RollupAccount VALUES(2002, 1000)
INSERT INTO RollupAccount VALUES(2003, 1000)
INSERT INTO RollupAccount VALUES(1000, NULL)
```

FIGURE 8-48: Building a chart of accounts

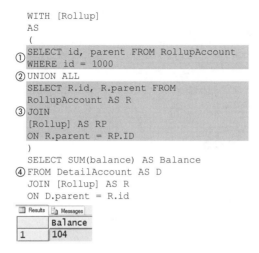

```
WITH [Rollup]
AS
(
①  SELECT id, parent FROM RollupAccount
    WHERE id = 1000
②  UNION ALL
    SELECT R.id, R.parent FROM
    RollupAccount AS R
③  JOIN
    [Rollup] AS RP
    ON R.parent = RP.ID
)
    SELECT SUM(balance) AS Balance
④  FROM DetailAccount AS D
    JOIN [Rollup] AS R
    ON D.parent = R.id
```

Results	Messages

	Balance
1	104

FIGURE 8-49: Account 1000 balance

chart of accounts as shown in Figure 8-47, not the ROLLUP option for a GROUP BY clause.

The statement that follows the CTE is the final query (4). It also uses the CTE—that is, Rollup—to produce its result. In the final query, the CTE contains all the results produced by the initialization query and every recursion query. In the case of this example, it contains the IDs of all the rollup accounts, so this query sums all accounts.

The calculation done in Figure 8-49 can be thought of as being done in phases, as is shown in Figure 8-50. The first phase is the initialization (1) by execution of the anchor. In this example, it produces a single row from the RollupAccount table: the row with account 1000.

The second phase is produced the first time the recursion member is executed (2). It selects all the child accounts of account 1000 by joining the RollupAccount table with the results of the first phase using a parent–child relationship.

Because the second phase produced results, the recursion member is executed (3) again, but this time, the RollupAccount table is joined with the results of the second phase (2) to produce all the children of the rows produced by the second phase.

An attempt is made to execute the recursion query one more time. The RollupAccountTable is joined with the single row produced by

Rollup CTE

	id	parent
1	1000	0
2	2001	1000
3	2002	1000
4	2003	1000
5	3002	2001

① SELECT id, parent FROM
   RollupAccount where id = 1000

② SELECT R.id, R.parent FROM
   RollupAccount AS R JOIN
   [Rollup] AS RP ON R.parent = RP.ID ③

	id	parent	Balance
1	3001	2001	10
2	3004	2002	17
3	3005	2002	10
4	3006	2002	25
5	3007	2003	7
6	3008	2003	9
7	4001	3002	12
8	4002	3002	14

④ SELECT SUM(balance) AS Balance
   FROM DetailAccount AS D
   JOIN
   [Rollup] AS R ON
   R.id = D.parent

FIGURE 8-50: Phases of calculation

the second phase. There are no rows in the `RollupAccountTable` that contain 3000 in their parent column, so this join produces no results. This is sometimes called the *fix point,* as subsequently executing the recursion query will produce no different results. This terminates the recursion phase.

The final query (4) executes when the recursion phases have terminated. It joins the DetailAccount table to all the results produced by all the first three phases—that is, the initialization and recursion phases—using a parent–child relationship.

In summary, the recursive member always joins with only the results of the previous query, which is either the anchor or a recursion member. The final query joins the results of all the preceding phases.

Figure 8-49 shows the basic syntax and usage of a recursive query. It is a CTE with two statements separated by a `UNION ALL` operator. The statement before the `UNION ALL` operator is executed once, and the statement after the `UNION ALL` is executed repeatedly, joined against the results of the previous statement execution, until it produces no more rows. Finally, the statement that follows the CTE is joined against all the results produced recursively by the CTE.

It is possible to design a recursive query that would repeatedly execute the recursion member a large or infinite number of times. You can limit this in two ways. First, by default SQL Server 2005 will limit it to 100 recursions. You can change this limit by using the MAXRECURSION query hint, as shown in Figure 8-51. The example shown in Figure 8-51 uses (MAXRECURSION 1) to limit recursion to one. When (MAXRECURSION 0) is used, no recursion limit is imposed. Exceeding the recursion limit produces a 530 error (2).

In some cases, you will want to limit the recursion but instead of producing an error just use the result obtained up to that point. Your CTE will have to keep track of the depth of recursion to do this. Figure 8-52 executes the recursion query just once. To do this, it adds a depth column (1) to the anchor query with a value of zero. It also adds a depth column to the recursion member and increments it by one (2) every time the recursion query is executed. Last, it does a test of the depth column (3) in the recursion query itself to decide when to terminate the recursion.

The examples of recursive queries shown so far are a bit limited because the anchor has had a literal id in it. A recursive query, however, like any CTE, can be part of an inline table-valued function so that the id for the anchor can be parameterized. There are several ways to do this, but one way that will get a reasonable amount of reuse is to make a table-valued function that produces a table with three columns.

```
WITH [Rollup]
AS
(
SELECT id, parent FROM RollupAccount
WHERE id = 1000
UNION ALL
SELECT R.id, R.parent FROM
RollupAccount AS R
JOIN
[Rollup] AS RP
ON R.parent = RP.ID
)
SELECT SUM(balance) AS Balance
FROM DetailAccount
JOIN
Rollup
ON DetailAccount.parent = [Rollup].id
①OPTION (MAXRECURSION 1)

②Msg 530, Level 16, State 1, Line 1
  The statement terminated. The maximum recursion
  1 has been exhausted before statement completion.
```

FIGURE 8-51: MAXRECURSION

```
WITH [Rollup]
AS
(                      ①
SELECT id, parent, 0 AS depth FROM RollupAccount
WHERE id = 1000
UNION ALL                      ②
SELECT R.id, R.parent, depth + 1 AS depth FROM
RollupAccount AS R
JOIN
[Rollup] AS RP
ON R.parent = RP.ID
③WHERE depth < 1
)
SELECT SUM(balance) AS Balance
FROM DetailAccount
JOIN
[Rollup]
ON DetailAccount.parent = Rollup.id
```

FIGURE 8-52: Limiting recursion

In the case of the `HumanResources.Employee table`, one column would have the `EmployeeID`; the next, the `ManagerID`; and finally, a depth column that indicates the depth of the employee in the hierarchy. You pass an id into the function, and you get back a tree with the employee whose id you passed at the root. You can't actually return a tree, of course; you can return only a table. But the table includes all the members of the tree.

```
  CREATE FUNCTION AWEmpTree(@startAt INT)
①RETURNS TABLE
  RETURN
  WITH Rollup AS (
  SELECT EmployeeID, ManagerID,
     0 AS depth
     FROM AdventureWorks.HumanResources.Employee
     WHERE EmployeeID = @startAt
  UNION ALL
  SELECT E.EmployeeID,
     E.ManagerID, depth + 1 AS depth
     FROM AdventureWorks.HumanResources.Employee E
     JOIN
   ②Rollup AS R ON R.EmployeeID = E.ManagerID
  )
③SELECT EmployeeID, ManagerID, depth FROM Rollup
```

FIGURE 8-53: Tree rollup function

Figure 8-53 shows an inline table-valued function that does this for the HumanResources.Employee table in the AdventureWorks sample database. You pass in the id for an employee, and it returns the row for that employee, all the employees who have that id as a parent, and so on. The AWEmpTree table returns a table (1), and that table contains (3) an EmployeeID with its ManagerID and depth in the tree. Note that the recursion member joins with the Rollup CTE (2) where the EmployeeID of the Rollup CTE equals the ManagerID of the employee.

Figure 8-54 shows the AWEmpTree function from Figure 8-53 used to find all the employees who report to employee 273. You can see that employee 273 is at the root of the tree because that employee has a depth of zero. You can also see that employees 268, 284, and 288 directly report to employee 273 and have a depth of one. The rest indirectly report to employee 273 and have a depth as appropriate.

Besides being able to roll up an entity with its descendents, it is useful to find the ancestors of an entity. A recursive query can be used to do this, too. Figure 8-55 shows an AWEmpAncestors function that is the

```
SELECT * FROM dbo.AWEmpTree(273)
ORDER BY depth
```

	EmployeeID	ManagerID	depth
1	273	109	0
2	268	273	1
3	284	273	1
4	288	273	1
5	275	268	2
6	276	268	2
7	277	268	2
8	278	268	2
9	279	268	2
10	280	268	2
11	281	268	2
12	282	268	2
13	283	268	2
14	285	284	2
15	286	284	2
16	287	268	2
17	289	284	2
18	290	288	2

FIGURE 8-54: Rollup for employee 273

```
CREATE FUNCTION AWEmpAncestors(@startAt INT)
RETURNS TABLE
RETURN
WITH Rollup
AS
(
SELECT EmployeeID, ManagerID, 0 AS distance
    FROM AdventureWorks.HumanResources.Employee
    WHERE EmployeeID = @startAt
UNION ALL
SELECT E.EmployeeID, E.ManagerID,
    distance + 1 AS distance
    FROM AdventureWorks.HumanResources.Employee E
JOIN
 ①Rollup AS R ON E.EmployeeID = R.ManagerID
)
SELECT EmployeeID, ManagerID, distance FROM Rollup
```

FIGURE 8-55: Ancestor function

complement of the AWEmpTree function. This is done simply by reversing the parent-child relationship (1) that is used in the join in the AWEmpTree function.

Figure 8-56 shows the results of using the AWEmpAncestors function from Figure 8-55.

When you have tree and ancestor inline table-valued functions, you can use them in other queries to answer the typical kinds of questions made of trees. Figure 8-57 shows a query that lists all the direct reports (1) for employee 140. The other query counts the number of employees (2) who report to employee 140.

```
SELECT * FROM dbo.AWEmpAncestors(287)
ORDER BY distance
```

	EmployeeID	ManagerID	distance
1	287	268	0
2	268	273	1
3	273	109	2
4	109	NULL	3

FIGURE 8-56: Employee ancestors

```
① SELECT EmployeeID AS [Direct Reports]
   FROM dbo.AWEmpTree(140)
   WHERE depth = 1
```

	Direct Reports
1	30
2	71
3	103
4	139

```
② SELECT COUNT(*) - 1 [Number of Reports]
   FROM dbo.AWEmpTree(140)
```

	Number of Reports
1	28

FIGURE 8-57: Using tree functions

PIVOT and UNPIVOT Operators

SQL Server 2005 adds the PIVOT operator to T-SQL, so named because it can create a new table by swapping the rows and columns of an existing table. In general, the PIVOT operator is used to create an analytical view of some data.

PIVOT

A typical analytical use of the PIVOT operator is to convert temporal data to categorized data so as to make the data easier to analyze. Consider a table used to record each sale made as it occurs; each row represents a single sale and includes the quarter that indicates when it occurred. This sort of view makes sense for recording sales but is not easy to use if you want to compare sales made in the same quarter, year over year.

Figure 8-58 shows the SalesByQuarter table (1) and a sample of some of the entries in it. Each sale is recorded as the amount of the sale, the year, and the quarter in which the sale was made. Notice that it shows two of the sales (2) made in Q2 of 2005.

You might want to analyze this data to see changes in total sales between Q1 quarters in two different years. Figure 8-59 shows an aggregate calculation of the sum of amounts (2) in the SalesByQuarter table for each

```
① CREATE TABLE SalesByQuarter
   (year INT,
   quarter CHAR(2),
   amount MONEY
   )
```

	year	quarter	amount
1	2005	Q1	1748.7419
2	2005	Q2	1030.7885
3	2005	Q2	8477.0647
4	2005	Q3	3377.1457
5	1985	Q2	6420.7386
6	1985	Q1	218.6107
7	1985	Q4	7451.2315
8	1985	Q3	8864.0221
9	1986	Q2	7890.7177
10	1986	Q3	1418.7956

FIGURE 8-58: Sales recorded as entered

year for Q1. Note that only sales having a quarter of Q1 (1) are aggregated. This is a good start, because it makes it easy to see that sales in Q1 of 2005 were better than in Q1 of 2004.

But we really need three more columns; we would like results for Q1, Q2, Q3, and Q4 in the same table. In Figure 8-60, the SELECT (3) statement groups the sum of the sales in a quarter (2) with its corresponding year (3).

Figure 8-61 shows the results of running the query in Figure 8-60. Now we can compare any quarterly results year over year. The query in Figure 8-60 is a bit complicated. The PIVOT operator is a much easier and more efficient way to get the same results.

Figure 8-62 shows a query that produces the same results as the query in Figure 8-60. It selects all the columns (1) from the SalesByQuarter table.

```
SELECT Year, SUM(amount) AS Q1
From SalesByQuarter GROUP BY Year, Quarter
HAVING quarter='Q1' ①
ORDER BY Year DESC
```

	Year	Q1
1	2005	1095529.6258
2	2004	922501.7944
3	2003	864787.3271
4	2002	928155.9357
5	2001	941655.7496
6	2000	829940.6428

FIGURE 8-59: Q1 results, year over year

```
① SELECT year
  ,SUM (
  ② CASE WHEN quarter = 'Q1'
     THEN amount ELSE 0 END) Q1
  ,SUM (
     CASE WHEN quarter = 'Q2'
     THEN amount ELSE 0 END) Q2
  ,SUM (
     CASE WHEN quarter = 'Q3'
     THEN amount ELSE 0 END) Q3
  ,sum (
     CASE WHEN quarter = 'Q4'
     THEN amount ELSE 0 END) Q4
  FROM
  SalesByQuarter
  ③ GROUP BY year
     ORDER BY year DESC
```

FIGURE 8-60: Query for quarterly results

It applies the PIVOT operator (2) to the result of the SELECT statement. The PIVOT operator is always followed by an aliased clause in parentheses.

The first part of the clause is always an aggregate function (3)—in this example, SUM—on one of the columns produced by the SELECT statement. Note that in the general case, an aggregate function can have an expression as a parameter, but when it is used in the clause that follows the PIVOT operator, the parameter can be only the literal name of one of the columns produced by the SELECT statement.

The aggregate function is always followed by a FOR/IN clause. Immediately following the FOR term of the clause is the literal name of one of the columns produced by the SELECT statement. This is the column to be pivoted (4)—that is, the unique values in the column are to become the column headings of the result produced by the PIVOT operator.

	year	Q1	Q2	Q3	Q4
1	2005	1095529.6258	891892.7717	1055729.9663	870690.2878
2	2004	922501.7944	905762.0179	1017514.297	941077.6756
3	2003	864787.3271	916230.6115	970573.6317	1012399.6143
4	2002	928155.9357	963277.7359	998392.0994	872686.5949
5	2001	941655.7496	934636.3164	1023157.5254	968357.5139

FIGURE 8-61: All quarterly results

```
          ①
     SELECT * FROM SalesByQuarter
 ② PIVOT
     (
 ③ SUM (amount)
              ④              ⑤
     FOR quarter IN (Q1, Q2, Q3, Q4)
     ) AS P
     ORDER BY YEAR DESC
```

FIGURE 8-62: PIVOT operator

Following the name of the column to be pivoted is a comma-separated list of values enclosed in parentheses (5). These values are the column heading names that the PIVOT operator will produce and also correspond to values, cast as strings, from the column to be pivoted (4).

Last, the PIVOT operator in effect adds a GROUP BY clause that includes all the columns produced by the SELECT statement except the column named in the aggregate function and the column being pivoted. In this example, year is the only column not used by the PIVOT operator.

The syntax for PIVOT is a bit compact, but it is in effect doing what the query in Figure 8-60 does. Figure 8-63 compares the syntax of a PIVOT operator with the hand-built query shown in Figure 8-60.

The Q1 value listed in the FOR/IN clause produces a column (2) of output, as do Q2, Q3, and Q4. The aggregate (1)—SUM, in this case—is applied

```
     SELECT * FROM SalesByQuarter
     PIVOT
     (
     SUM (amount)
 ①   FOR quarter IN (Q1, Q2, Q3, Q4)) AS P
     ORDER BY YEAR DESC


     SELECT year                        ②
     , SUM (
        CASE WHEN quarter = 'Q1'
        THEN amount ELSE 0 END) Q1
     , SUM
     ...
     FROM
     SalesByQuarter
        GROUP BY year
        ORDER BY year DESC
```

FIGURE 8-63: PIVOT comparison with hand-built query

to the amount only if the amount comes from a row that corresponds to a particular quarter.

The table used in the preceding example didn't have a primary key or even anything that might be used as a primary key, which makes it a rather unlikely table to find in a relational database. Let's look at what happens if we make a new table, `SalesByQuarterId` (1), by adding an identity column to the original table, as shown in Figure 8-64. In real life, this id column could be the sales order number that would be used to identify the order.

If we use the `PIVOT` operator on this new table (2) the same way we did on the previous table, the results produced (3) are not all that useful. The problem is that the id is not used in the `SUM` aggregate function, of course, so it is added to the `GROUP BY` clause in all subqueries. This results in one row for each row in the `SalesByQuarterId` table—something that is not all that useful. What you would like to do is ignore the id column in the `SalesByQuarterId` table.

The net effect of the * in the `SELECT` statement that precedes the `PIVOT` operator is shown in Figure 8-65. It is expanded by adding all the columns from the table that are not mentioned in the aggregate or the `FOR` clause (1) and all the values (2) from the `IN` clause as column names. You can literally

```
CREATE TABLE SalesByQuarterId ①
(
id int identity primary key,
year INT,
quarter CHAR(2),
amount MONEY
)

 SELECT * FROM SalesByQuarterID ②
 PIVOT
 (
 SUM (amount)
 FOR quarter IN (Q1, Q2, Q3, Q4)
 ) AS P
 ORDER BY YEAR DESC
```

	id	year	Q1	Q2	Q3	Q4
1	81	2005	NULL	NULL	NULL	6635.5885
2	82	2005	NULL	NULL	129.0074	NULL
3	83	2005	NULL	8476.6649	NULL	NULL
4	84	2005	NULL	1563.6068	NULL	NULL

FIGURE 8-64: PIVOT with id

```
         ①
SELECT id, year, Q1, Q2, Q3, Q4 FROM SalesByQuarterID
PIVOT
(                            ②
SUM (amount)
FOR quarter IN (Q1, Q2, Q3, Q4)
) AS P
ORDER BY YEAR DESC
```

FIGURE 8-65: Expanded PIVOT

type these column names yourself and not use the * if you want to, but if you don't include the id column, you will get a syntax error, so that will not improve on the results shown in Figure 8-64.

You must remove the id column, and the way to do that is with a subquery. Figure 8-66 shows a CTE (1) used to make a subquery that removes the id column. The CTE is referenced (2) in the PIVOT expression. Given that SalesByQuarter and SalesByQuarterID have the same data in them, the query in Figure 8-66 produces the same results as the query in Figure 8-62.

There is one last thing you might like to do when using the PIVOT operator; you might want to rename the columns. You might want the column name for Q1 to be Quarter 1, for example. Figure 8-67 shows how to do this. You expand the * in the SELECT that uses the PIVOT operator, as was shown in Figure 8-66 and alias the values (1) from the IN clause. The output produced by this PIVOT (2) is also shown in Figure 8-67. If the table had a primary key in it, as SalesByQuarterID did, of course you would have to use a CTE or derived table to remove that column.

```
        ①
WITH orders
AS
(
SELECT year, quarter, amount FROM SalesByQuarterID
)              ②
SELECT * FROM orders
PIVOT
(
SUM (amount)
FOR quarter in (Q1, Q2, Q3, Q4)
) AS P
ORDER BY year
```

FIGURE 8-66: PIVOT with extra columns

```
SELECT year,
Q1 as [Quarter 1], ①
Q2 as [Quarter 2],
Q3 as [Quarter 3],
Q4 as [Quarter 4]
FROM SalesByQuarter
PIVOT
(
SUM (amount)
FOR quarter IN (Q1, Q2, Q3, Q4)
) AS P
ORDER BY YEAR DESC
```

②

	year	Quarter 1	Quarter 2	Quarter 3	Quarter 4
1	2004	140598.3087	173985.2988	99712.4225	119822.2872
2	2003	121749.2219	114236.73	147660.7842	161563.4964
3	2002	217148.5916	77355.0454	85075.9293	79056.359
4	2001	121442.9099	159543.9006	98018.1326	137272.8686

FIGURE 8-67: PIVOT with headings

UNPIVOT

The UNPIVOT operator is complementary in operation to the PIVOT opera-tor in that it tries to undo what the PIVOT operator did. It is not comple-mentary in the sense that it completely reverses the effect of the PIVOT operator. It can't do that; an aggregated value cannot be broken into its con-stituent parts. What it does is take column headings and turn them into val-ues in a single column.

Figure 8-68 shows a table variable, @pivoted (1), that is filled by pivot-ing SalesByQuarter as was done in previous examples. The contents of the @pivoted table are the same as those shown in Figure 8-61. This table is used to illustrate how the UNPIVOT operator works.

The UNPIVOT clause follows a SELECT statement, just as the PIVOT clause does. The body of the UNPIVOT clause is in parentheses and contains a FOR/IN phrase, just as the PIVOT clause does. An UNPIVOT operator does not contain an aggregate function, however.

The UNPIVOT operator produces a table with all the columns of the input table except the columns mentioned in parentheses (4) to the right of the IN phrase. It adds two columns to this: one whose name is the name to the left (2) of the FOR phrase, and the other whose name is to the right (3) of the

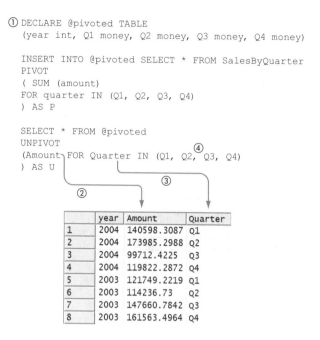

FIGURE 8-68: UNPIVOT operator

`FOR` phrase. In the example shown in Figure 8-68, these are the `Amount` and `Quarter` columns, respectively.

Figure 8-69 illustrates the effect of the `UNPIVOT` operator on a single row of the `@pivoted` table. The year (1) is repeated once for each of the other columns in the `@pivoted` table into rows in the output table. The column heading is copied (1) into the `Quarter` column of the output table, and the value in that column is copied into the Amount column. The net effect is to put all the non-null values aggregated by the `PIVOT` operator into a single column, each tagged with the name of its source column.

Ranking and Partitioning

SQL Server 2005 adds support for the SQL:1999 standard ranking functions and partitioning operations. Ranking functions in effect add a numeric column to the output of a query that represents the rank a row would have

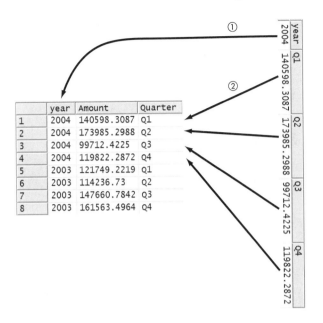

FIGURE 8-69: UNPIVOTing a row

when sorted according to some criterion. Partitioning is used to apply ranking operations or aggregate functions to subsets of a table produced by partitioning it in a way that is similar to the use of GROUP BY to apply aggregate functions to subsets of a table. The ranking functions are ROW_NUMBER, RANK, DENSE_RANK, and NTILE; all require an OVER clause following them.

The ROW_NUMBER function is one of the most straightforward to look at. The rank it assigns to a row is the position that the row would hold according to a specified sorting criterion. Figure 8-70 shows ROW_NUMBER being used to find the position of a row from the SalesOrderDetail table from AdventureWorks database if it were sorted by its ProductID column.

The ROW_NUMBER function (1), like all ranking functions, is always followed by an OVER (2) clause. The OVER clause must contain an ORDER BY phrase when used with the ROW_NUMBER or any ranking function. The ORDER BY phrase is followed by a comma-separated list of column names, as it would be if it were being used to sort a SELECT statement.

```
        ①              ②      ③
SELECT ROW _ NUMBER() OVER (ORDER BY ProductID)
AS [Row Number],
SalesOrderDetailID AS [Detail ID], ProductID
FROM Sales.SalesOrderDetail
ORDER BY SalesOrderDetailID
```

④

Row Number	Detail ID	ProductID
1	32572	1	776
2	32800	2	777
3	33042	3	778
4	31439	4	771
5	31680	5	772
6	31901	6	773
7	32134	7	774

FIGURE 8-70: ROW_NUMBER function

ROW_NUMBER

The ROW_NUMBER function, in the example in Figure 8-70, produces (4) the position the row would fall in if the overall expression were ordered by the ProductID column. Note that in this example, the overall expression is ordered by the SalesOrderDetailID column. This is done to illustrate that the ORDER BY phrase used in an OVER clause is evaluated independently of any other ORDER BY phrase used in another OVER clause or used to sort the overall results of a query.

The ranking functions produce a column of output and may be aliased, as shown in Figure 8-70. The alias may not be referred to from a predicate in the expression. The alias maybe referred to from an ORDER BY clause for the overall query, however. Figure 8-71 shows an attempt to select the rows from the query in Figure 8-70 that are between 200 and 300. It does this by making a reference to the [Row Number] alias. This produces a 207 error (2).

An alias of a ranking function may be referenced only through a subquery. Figure 8-72 shows a row number being referenced via a subquery. A CTE named Rows contains the subquery. The Rows CTE selects both the row number (1) aliased as [Row Number], and the primary key (2)—that is, the SalesOrderDetailID column—from the SalesOrderDetail table. The SELECT that follows the CTE joins the CTE itself with the SalesOrderDetail

```
SELECT ROW _ NUMBER() OVER (ORDER BY ProductID)
AS [Row Number],
SalesOrderDetailID AS [Detail ID],
ProductID
FROM Sales.SalesOrderDetail
① WHERE [Row Number] BETWEEN 200 and 300
```

② Messages
```
Msg 207, Level 16, State 1, Line 6
Invalid column name 'Row Number'.
Msg 207, Level 16, State 1, Line 6
Invalid column name 'Row Number'.
```

FIGURE 8-71: Referencing a ROW_NUMBER directly

table on its primary key (3). It adds a predicate (4) that can reference the row number via the CTE so that it can be used as part of the BETWEEN clause. Note that using the ROW_NUMBER function typically produces a more performant result than other techniques that might be used for this purpose.

RANK

The ROW_NUMBER function always gives each row a different rank. The RANK gives each row a rank according to a criterion that you specify. If that criterion produces the same result for two rows, however, those rows will be given the same rank.

The SalesOrderHeader table of the AdventureWorks database has a DueDate column that represents the day by which an order must be shipped. If these rows are ranked by shipping priority, two rows that have

```
WITH Rows
AS (
SELECT ROW _ NUMBER() OVER (ORDER BY ProductID)
① AS [Row Number],
② SalesOrderDetailID AS [Detail ID]
FROM Sales.SalesOrderDetail
)
SELECT
O.SalesOrderDetailID AS [Detail ID],
O.ProductID,
Rows.[Row Number]
FROM Sales.SalesOrderDetail AS O
③ JOIN Rows on Rows.[Detail ID] = O.SalesOrderDetailID
④ WHERE Rows.[Row Number] BETWEEN 100 AND 200
```

FIGURE 8-72: Referencing a ROW_NUMBER via subquery

the same DueDate could be given the same shipping priority, because there would be about the same amount of time available to finish putting together the order. And when two rows have different DueDate values, the one with the later DueDate would have a lower shipping priority, because there would be more time to get that order together.

Figure 8-73 shows a query (1) that prioritizes orders in the SalesOrderHeaderTable. The RANK function is used to rank rows in order of their DueDate, with the lowest number [Ship Priority] being the most important. The first two rows of output (1) have the same DueDate and in fact have the same priority—that is, 1. Examining the 43rd and 44th rows (3) shows that they have different DueDates and in fact have different [Ship Priority]s, with the later DueDate having a higher number.

DENSE_RANK

The RANK function does not guarantee that it will produce contiguous numbers—only that the numbers will be the same when the sort criterion produces the same result. If the sort criterion produces different results, the row that would be later in the sort will have a higher number. The DENSE_RANK function produces the same results as the RANK function except that it adds the additional guarantee that the numbers it produces are contiguous. Figure 8-74 shows a query (1) that is the same as the one in Figure 8-73 except that it uses DENSE_RANK instead of RANK. Examining the

```
① SELECT SalesOrderID,
   RANK() OVER (ORDER BY DueDate)
   AS [Ship Priority],
   DueDate
   FROM Sales.SalesOrderHeader
   ORDER BY DueDate
```

② Results | Messages

	SalesOrderID	Ship Priority	DueDate
1	43659	1	2001-07-13
2	43660	1	2001-07-13
3	43661	1	2001-07-13
4	43662	1	2001-07-13

③ Results | Messages

	SalesOrderID	Ship Priority	DueDate
43	43701	1	2001-07-13
44	43702	44	2001-07-14
45	43703	44	2001-07-14

FIGURE 8-73: Shipping priority

```
① SELECT SalesOrderID,
   DENSE _ RANK() OVER (ORDER BY DueDate)
   AS [Ship Priority],
   DueDate
   FROM Sales.SalesOrderHeader
   ORDER BY duedate
```

② Results Messages

	SalesOrderID	Ship Priority	DueDate
43	43701	1	2001-07-13
44	43702	2	2001-07-14
45	43703	2	2001-07-14
46	43704	2	2001-07-14
47	43705	2	2001-07-14
48	43706	3	2001-07-15

FIGURE 8-74: DENSE_RANK

results (2) shows that the numbers produced by DENSE_RANK are contiguous. Keep in mind that there is more overhead in using the DENSE_RANK function than the RANK function.

NTILE

Another way to rank results is in sets of approximately equal size. You might want to break a table into ten sets of rows such that none of the rows in the second set will sort before any row in the first set, and so on. Each of these sets is called a *tile*.

The query (1) in Figure 8-75 uses the NTILE function to break the SalesOrderHeader table into 5,000 tiles. The SalesOrderHeader sample

```
① SELECT SalesOrderID,
   NTILE(5000) OVER (ORDER BY DueDate) AS [Ship Tile],
   DueDate
   FROM Sales.SalesOrderHeader
   ORDER BY duedate
```

② Results Messages

	SalesOrderID	Ship Tile	DueDate
1	43659	1	2001-07-13
2	43660	1	2001-07-13
3	43661	1	2001-07-13
4	43662	1	2001-07-13
5	43663	1	2001-07-13
6	43664	1	2001-07-13
7	43665	1	2001-07-13
③ 8	43666	2	2001-07-13
9	43667	2	2001-07-13

FIGURE 8-75: NTILE

database in this example has about 32,000 rows in it. Each tile should then have about six rows in it. NTILE does not guarantee that each tile will have exactly the same number of rows in it—only that they will have approximately the same number of rows. The results (2) of the query show that the first tile has seven rows (3) in it.

Also, NTILE guarantees only that items in a higher-numbered tile will not sort before items in a lower-numbered tile. Items in two consecutive tiles might sort in the same position.

The criterion used for the ranking function examples shown so far has used a column name in the ORDER BY clause. The ORDER BY clause, however, can use an expression or even a subquery.

Figure 8-76 shows a query that ranks a row from the SalesOrder-Header table from the AdventureWorks database according to the number of line items it contains. The line items are contained in the SalesOrderDetail table and use a foreign key that relates it to the SalesOrderID column of the SalesOrderHeader table. The DENSE_RANK function is used, and its ORDER BY clause uses a subquery (1) as the criterion for ranking. This subquery returns a single scalar that is the number of line items associated with a row from the SalesOrderHeader table. The result is that all SalesOrderHeaders that have the same number of line items have the same [Line Item Rank].

The query in Figure 8-76 includes the actual Line Item Count (2) for reference. The results (3) show that SalesOrderIDs with the same number of line items do, in fact, have the same Line Item Rank.

```
SELECT SalesOrderID,
DENSE _ RANK() OVER (ORDER BY
① (SELECT COUNT(*) FROM Sales.SalesOrderDetail WHERE
SalesOrderID = O.SalesOrderID)) AS [Line Item Rank],
② (SELECT COUNT(*) FROM Sales.SalesOrderDetail WHERE
SalesOrderID = O.SalesOrderID) AS [Line Item Count]
FROM Sales.SalesOrderHeader O
```

	SalesOrderID	Line Item Rank	Line Item Count
③ 31460	46981	64	65
31461	51751	64	65
31462	55297	65	66
31463	47355	67	68
31464	53465	68	71
31465	51160	68	71

FIGURE 8-76: DENSE_RANK via subquery

PARTITION BY

The ranking functions can be applied on a by-partition basis. Each partition in effect restarts the ranking process.

Figure 8-77 shows a query that calculates a row number on the Sale-sOrderDetail table that is partitioned by the SalesOrderID. The calculation of the row number is based on the LineTotal column of the SalesOrderDetail table. This means that the row number will restart at one for each sales order.

The PARTITION BY clause, when it is used, must precede the ORDER BY clause. This means that the row number is calculated as though each set of rows that has the same SalesOrderID were a separate table. Note that any of the ranking functions could have been used where ROW_NUMBER was used.

The PARTITION BY (1) clause in Figure 8-77 selects the SalesOrderID column to partition the table. The ORDER BY (2) clause specifies that the row number should be calculated based on the value of the LineTotal Column. The LineTotal and SalesOrderDetailID are included in the results for reference only, to show that the row number is being calculated as expected.

The results (4) in Figure 8-77 show that the row numbers for SalesOrderID 75119 start at one. Likewise, the row numbers for SalesOrderID

```
SELECT SalesOrderID,
ROW _ NUMBER() OVER
(
① PARTITION BY SalesOrderID
② ORDER BY LineTotal
) [Row Number],
   LineTotal,
③ SalesOrderDetailID
FROM Sales.SalesOrderDetail
ORDER BY SalesOrderID, LineTotal
```

④ Results | Messages

SalesOrderID	Row Number	LineTotal	SalesOrderDetailID
1. 75119	1	2.290000	121306
1. 75119	2	4.990000	121304
1. 75119	3	35.000000	121305
1. 75120	1	8.990000	121309
1. 75120	2	21.980000	121307
1. 75120	3	53.990000	121308
1. 75121	1	4.990000	121310
1. 75121	2	34.990000	121312

FIGURE 8-77: Ranking within an order

75120 start at one, and so on for the rest of the SalesOrderIDs. In other words, the SalesOrderDetail table was partitioned by its SalesOrderID column, and then the row numbers were calculated for each partition independently of the other partitions.

Aggregate Partitions

Aggregate functions, including user-defined aggregate functions (see Chapter 5), can be applied to partitions of a table by following the aggregate function with an OVER clause, similar to the way that it is used for a ranking function. The results it produces can be the same as those produced by a GROUP BY clause, but as we will see, aggregate partitions are a bit more flexible and may provide a different execution plan. When an OVER clause follows an aggregate function, it may not contain an ORDER BY clause.

Figure 8-78 shows a query that calculates a sum across partitions. It uses the SUM aggregate function (1) over partitions (2) based on the value in the SalesOrderID column. The SalesOrderID column is included for reference only, so the effect of the partitioned sums can be seen. Note that all the SalesOrderDetailIDs from SalesOrderID 75115 have the same Total. In other words, the Total column represents the sum of the LineTotals for all the rows of the SalesOrderDetailIDs whose SalesOrderID column is 75115.

Aggregate functions used with an OVER clause provide functionality similar to that provided by GROUP BY and in fact can be used to yield the same results. Figure 8-79 shows two queries that produce the same results. The first query (1) uses the SUM aggregate function with an OVER clause, and

```
  Select SalesOrderDetailID,
① SUM(LineTotal)
② OVER(PARTITION BY SalesOrderID)
  AS [Total],
③ SalesOrderID
  FROM AdventureWorks.Sales.SalesOrderDetail
  ORDER BY SalesOrderID
```

④

SalesOrderDetailID	Total	SalesOrderID
12... 121293	21.490000	75114
12... 121294	80.470000	75115
12... 121295	80.470000	75115
12... 121296	80.470000	75115
12... 121297	4.990000	75116

FIGURE 8-78: Sum across partitions

```
① SELECT DISTINCT SalesOrderID,
    SUM(LineTotal)
    OVER(PARTITION BY SalesOrderID)
    AS [Total]
    FROM Sales.SalesOrderDetail
    ORDER BY SalesOrderID
② Query 1: Query cost (relative to the batch): 89%
    Select DISTINCT SalesOrderID, SUM(LineTotal) OVER

③ SELECT SalesOrderID,
    SUM(LineTotal) AS [Total]
    FROM Sales.SalesOrderDetail
    GROUP BY SalesOrderID
    ORDER BY SalesOrderID
④ Query 2: Query cost (relative to the batch): 11%
    SELECT SalesOrderID, SUM(LineTotal) AS [Total] FROM
```

FIGURE 8-79: PARTITION/GROUP BY
comparison

the second (3) uses it with a GROUP BY clause. Note that the first query must use the DISTINCT phrase to get the same result as the second query. Also note that the second query has a significantly better execution plan (4) than the execution plan (2) for the first query. As with any performance metric, you must evaluate these queries in the context of your own applications to decide which is the better choice for your purposes.

Another difference between the OVER clause and the GROUP BY clause is that the OVER clause has no restrictions on what columns may be specified in the query, unlike the GROUP BY clause, which limits columns to those listed in the GROUP BY expression itself or as a parameter of an aggregate functions. Figure 8-80 shows a query that specifies a column (1) that is not

```
    SELECT
① SalesOrderDetailID,
    SalesOrderID,
② SUM(LineTotal) OVER (PARTITION BY SalesOrderID)
    AS [Total]
    FROM Sales.SalesOrderDetail
```

	SalesOrderDetailID	SalesOrderID	Total
1	1	43659	20565.620600
2	2	43659	20565.620600
3	3	43659	20565.620600
4	4	43659	20565.620600
5	5	43659	20565.620600

FIGURE 8-80: No column restrictions with OVER

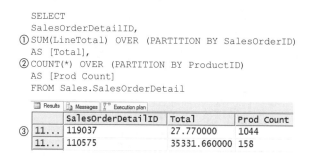

FIGURE 8-81: Multiple partitions

used by the aggregate function (2) or in the PARTITION BY clause. The results (3) repeat some values.

Aggregate calculations may be made over different partitions in a single query. Note that when GROUP BY is used, there can be only a single group. Figure 8-81 shows a query that does a SUM (1) partitioned over SalesOrderID and a COUNT (2) partitioned over ProductID. The results (3) show that the sum of all the LineTotals for the rows from the SalesOrderDetail table that have the same SalesOrderID as that for SalesOrderDetailID 119037 is 27.77. It also shows that the ProductID used by SalesOrderDetail 119037 appears in 1,044 rows of the SalesOrderDetail table.

TABLESAMPLE

Sometimes, you have a very large table and want some information from it that is approximate in nature. An example of this would be the average price of a line item in a purchase order or the average number of line items in a purchase order. There is no need to incur the overhead of reading all the rows in the table just to get an approximate value. The TABLESAMPLE clause in a SELECT statement lets you randomly sample a set of rows to be processed.

Figure 8-82 shows a query that calculates the approximate average value of a line item from an order in the AdventureWorks sample database. The AVG aggregate function is used with extended price of a line item (1)—that is, unit price times the quantity—as its parameter. The TABLESAMPLE clause (2) always immediately follows a table name.

```
                    ①
SELECT AVG(UnitPrice * OrderQty) AS [Avg Line Item]
FROM Sales.SalesOrderDetail
TABLESAMPLE SYSTEM (10)②
```

③

	Avg Line Item
1	1010.746

④

	Avg Line Item
1	835.8079

FIGURE 8-82: Approximate calculation

The SYSTEM phrase is optional and comes before the percentage, in parentheses, of the table that is to be sampled. The SYSTEM phrase specifies that the sampling algorithm that TABLESAMPLE uses is a proprietary one implemented by SQL Server 2005. The SQL:1999 standard lists some standard sampling algorithms that can be specified, but SYSTEM is the only one supported by SQL Server 2005.

Two different results of running the query are shown in Figure 8-82. Note that one run (3) yielded 1010.746, and the other (4) yielded 835.8079. This is due to the nature of the sampling algorithm. Sampling 10 percent of a table means that the probability that a given page of a table—that is, of the pages SQL Server uses to store the information in the table—will be used in the calculation is 10 percent. Each page is sampled anew each time the query is run.

This method of sampling has a number of implications. This first implication is that the results from two executions of a TABLESAMPLE may, as we have seen, be different. Each time the query is run, possibly a different set of pages will be sampled.

Another implication is that the number of rows used in the calculation can vary from run to run. TABLESAMPLE does not sample rows; it samples pages. The probability that a page will be used from run to run changes, and the number of rows contained in a page may also vary from page to page. Figure 8-83 shows a query that counts (1) the number of rows returned by TABLESAMPLE for two different (2) (3) executions of the query.

Because the selection of a page is probabilistic, there is always the possibility that either all or none of the pages that make up a table will be selected.

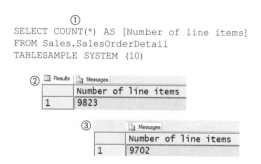

```
     ①
SELECT COUNT(*) AS [Number of line items]
FROM Sales.SalesOrderDetail
TABLESAMPLE SYSTEM (10)
```

② Results | Messages

	Number of line items
1	9823

③ Messages

	Number of line items
1	9702

FIGURE 8-83: Row count variance

The chances of this happening go up as the table becomes smaller. Note that in general, TABLESAMPLE is not very useful for small tables.

TABLESAMPLE selects only pages, not rows, so it can be used only on physical tables, not derived tables, and the sampling is done before any predicate is evaluated in a query. Figure 8-84 shows an attempt to use TABLESAMPLE on a derived table, which cannot work because a derived table has no pages. The query uses a CTE (1) to make a subquery and then attempts to use a TABLESAMPLE clause on that CTE. This results in a 494 error (3).

Figure 8-85 shows two queries that at first glance appear to be equivalent. One query (1) selects rows from the SalesOrderDetail table and counts them. The other query (3) self-joins the SalesOrderDetail table on its primary key; keep in mind that a self-join on the primary key essentially produces the original table. If TABLESAMPLE were not used, each of these queries would produce the same number of rows. The result (2) of the first query, however, is about ten times the size of the result (4) of the second query.

```
①WITH BigLineItems
  AS
  ( SELECT * FROM Sales.SalesOrderDetail
  WHERE UnitPrice > 10)
  SELECT * FROM
②BigLineItems TABLESAMPLE(10)
```

Messages

```
Msg 494, Level 16, State 1, Line 1
The TABLESAMPLE clause can only be used with local tables.
        ③
```

FIGURE 8-84: TABLESAMPLE on derived table

① `SELECT COUNT(*) FROM`
`Sales.SalesOrderDetail AS D1 TABLESAMPLE(10)`

②

	Count
1	12518

③ `SELECT COUNT(*) FROM`
`Sales.SalesOrderDetail AS D1 TABLESAMPLE(10)`
`JOIN`
`Sales.SalesOrderDetail D2 TABLESAMPLE(10)`
`ON D2.SalesOrderDetailID = D1.SalesOrderDetailID`

④

	Count
1	1078

FIGURE 8-85: Count discrepancy

The pages used on the right side of the join are a different random selection from those on the left because TABLESAMPLE is used. The count produced by the second query (3) reflects the probability of the same page's being selected in both the left and right random selection. Because the probability is 10 percent for each selection, the probability of the same page's being selected on both sides of the join is 1 percent. This is one-tenth the probability of a page's being used in the first query—hence, the approximately factor-of-ten difference in the results produced.

In general, a TABLESAMPLE used on both sides of a join can easily produce unexpected results.

The algorithm that TABLESAMPLE uses to sample pages is based on a pseudorandom sequence that you can control by using a REPEATABLE clause. The REPEATABLE clause is optional; it immediately follows the TABLESAMPLE and requires an integer parameter called the seed. It doesn't really matter what the value of the seed is except that it must be greater than zero. The same sequence is produced when the same seed is used. The use of the REPEATABLE clause (1) is shown in Figure 8-86. Executing the query shown in Figure 8-86 twice (2) (3) produces the same results, unlike the similar query shown in Figure 8-82 that did not use a REPEAT-ABLE clause. Note that this example assumes that the content of the SalesOrderDetail table does not change between executions of the query.

```
SELECT COUNT(*) AS [Number of line items]
FROM Sales.SalesOrderDetail
TABLESAMPLE SYSTEM (10)
① REPEATABLE(1)
```

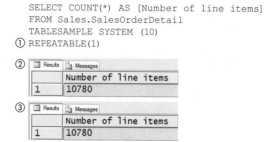

FIGURE 8-86: Repeatable TABLESAMPLE

The TABLESAMPLE clause has optional unit phrases that can be included with its parameter. The default unit is specified by the PERCENT phrase following the quantity, somewhat as it is used in a TOP clause. The optional unit of rows is specified by a ROWS phrase following the quantity.

Figure 8-87 shows the usage of the unit specifications. The ROWS phrase is somewhat misleading. It does not sample the number of rows specified; it is used to calculate a percentage. The SalesOrderDetail table contains 121,317 rows (1), as shown in Figure 8-87. A query that asks for a TABLE-SAMPLE of 12,132 rows (2)—that is, about one-tenth of the rows in the SalesOrderDetail table—produces the same results as a query that asks for a TABLESAMPLE of 10 percent (3) of the SalesOrderDetail table. When the ROWS phrase is used, you are not guaranteed that the exact number (4) of rows specified will be used.

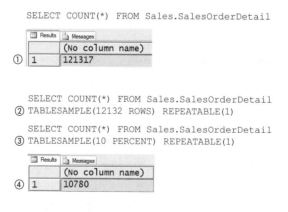

FIGURE 8-87: ROWS clause

Note that the TABLESAMPLE queries in Figure 8-87 use a REPEATABLE clause to ensure that the same pages are sampled just illustrate how the ROWS phrase is interpreted.

Where Are We?

Even if the only thing you use in SQL Server is T-SQL itself, you will find many new features. Some of these new features add SQL:1999 standard syntax; some provide alternative representations for queries that may be easier to read and produce better execution plans; and some do both.

The BEGIN TRY clause is a more convenient way to handle errors; it allows more errors to be encapsulated within T-SQL and passed back to the client only if the needs of the application require it. The row numbering and partitioning capabilities make it possible to implement in a much more straightforward and efficient way than was previously possible. Common table expressions provide a cleaner syntax (your mileage may vary) and sometimes a more efficient way to use derived tables. OUTPUT lets us minimize the number of round trips needed to determine which rows were modified by a query.

All in all, the T-SQL enhancements in SQL Server 2005 represent another step in adding SQL:1999 compliance to T-SQL and give us more straightforward and efficient ways to manipulate data.

▛ 9 ▄
XML in the Database:
The XML Data Type

S QL SERVER 2005 introduces a new scalar data type, the XML data type.
XML is a first-class data type in SQL Server now, and this has a wide-
ranging impact on the use of XML.

The XML Data Type

A new type of data has gained popularity in recent years: XML. XML has
evolved from a simple data transfer format to a data model that includes its
own schema-definition vocabulary, XSD, as well as query languages. In this
chapter, we'll look at the XML data type and see how it differs from conventional CLOB (character large object field, called TEXT field in SQL Server)
storage of an XML document.

You can use the XML data type like any other data type in SQL Server. It
can be used in the following ways:

- As a column in a table
- As a variable in Transact-SQL (T-SQL)
- As a stored procedure or user-defined function parameter
- As a user-defined function return value

The XML type is quite similar, but not identical, to the distinct type defined by SQL:1999 and discussed in Chapter 1. Although the serialized form of XML is similar in appearance to a CLOB (VARCHAR(MAX)), you convert it to and from a VARCHAR type, rather than assign it. Like distinct types, the XML data type cannot be compared with other data types without being cast or converted, but unlike distinct types, two instances of an XML data type cannot be compared at all.

Like a SQL:1999 distinct type, the XML type has its own methods; these methods enable the use of an alternative query language, XQuery. The data in an XML type does not follow the relational data model but is based on an extended XML Infoset model, which is used to model structured—that is, hierarchical—data.

A column that is defined as being of type XML stores its data in the database itself. The column is not a pointer to an XML document on the file system. This means that XML data is included in the backup and restore process; is subject to ordinary SQL Server security (and some extensions to security, as we'll mention later); and participates in transactions, constraints, and logging. Having XML data inside a relational database may offend some relational purists, but it means that your data lives in a single repository for reasons of administration, reliability, and control.

Using XML Data Type in Tables

Let's begin by using the XML data type to define a column in a table. The following DDL statement creates a table:

```
CREATE TABLE xml_tab (
   the_id INTEGER PRIMARY KEY,
   xml_col XML)
```

Note that you can also have a table that consists of only a single XML data type column; the XML data type cannot be used itself as a primary key, however. Later, we will see that you can create an XML-specific index on this column, but this index will not be used in SQL comparisons; it will be used to improve the performance of the functions associated with an XML data type. In addition to the previous example that created a single XML type column in a table, you can have tables that contain more than one XML data type column. You can create a table with an XML column in local or global temporary tables as well as ordinary tables. An XML data type column can be used in a VIEW as well.

XML data type columns have certain limitations when used in tables:

- They may not be declared as a PRIMARY KEY in a table.
- They may not be declared as a FOREIGN KEY in a table.
- They may not be declared with a UNIQUE constraint.
- They may not be declared with the COLLATE keyword.

These first three limitations exist because individual instances of the XML data type may not be compared with one another. Although it would not be difficult to perform a string comparison with XML data, it would be an order of magnitude more difficult to perform a comparison at the Infoset level. The two XML documents in the following example are Infoset equivalent but not lexically equivalent:

```
<!-- These two documents are equivalent -->
<doc1>
    <row au_id="111-11-1111"/>
</doc1>

<doc1>
    <row au_id='111-11-1111'></row>
</doc1>
```

The XML data type cannot use the COLLATE keyword, because XML provides its own encoding via the encoding attribute on the XML document declaration. The following code is an example of using encoding. If the document uses an encoding that is unknown or unsupported, SQL Server will return an error. An error will also result if the content does not match the specified encoding. The encoding specifies UTF-8 but contains characters encoded as Unicode, for example.

```
-- This works correctly
INSERT xml_tab VALUES(1,

'<?xml version="1.0" encoding="utf-8"?>
<doc1>
    <row au_id="111-11-1111"/>
</doc1>')
```

```
-- This fails, cannot switch encoding
-- encoding does not match character type (Unicode) being converted
INSERT xml_tab VALUES(1,

N'<?xml version="1.0" encoding="utf-8"?>
<doc1>
    <row au_id="111-11-1111"/>
</doc1>')


-- This fails with an unknown encoding error
INSERT xml_tab VALUES(1,

'<?xml version="1.0" encoding="i-bogus"?>
<doc1>
    <row au_id='111-11-1111'></row>
</doc1>')
```

Although the encoding specified in the XML document declaration is taken into consideration when storing the document, documents are always physically stored as UTF-16. The XML data type's internal format is an opaque binary format. XML is tokenized before being stored, producing a certain amount of compression, although compression is not the primary purpose of the binary format. The XML data type column has the same size limit as the MAX data types discussed in Chapter 7; it can be up to 2GB. Because of the tokenization, you may be able to store more than 2GB of XML text in the column and, in rare instances, less than 2GB of text. You can obtain the actual length, in bytes, of an XML data type instance by using the DATALENGTH system function. Columns of the XML data type are stored in-row by default like the MAX data types, and this option is may be overridden by the "large value types out of row" option on the table. The XML data can also reside on a different physical filegroup from the rest of the data in the table.

XML data type columns can have NULL constraints (the default nullability is the current default of your SQL Server session) and DEFAULT values. Column- and table-level CHECK constraints based on the XML Infoset model are supported, although constraints using methods that are specific to the XML type must be wrapped in a UDF. Although we'll talk about the methods in more detail in Chapter 10, a typical CHECK constraint on an XML type is shown in Listing 9-1.

LISTING 9-1: XML CHECK constraints must be encapsulated in a UDF

```
-- pdoc must have a person element
-- as a child of the people root
-- create the wrapper UDF
CREATE FUNCTION check_for_person (@thedoc XML)
RETURNS BIT
AS
BEGIN
-- function that uses XQuery, see next chapter
RETURN @thedoc.exist('/people/person')
END
GO
CREATE TABLE xmltab(
  id INTEGER PRIMARY KEY,
  pdoc XML CHECK(dbo.check_for_person(pdoc)=1)
)
```

Because XML data types follow the XML Infoset data model, they are usually not constrained by relational constraints but by a collection of one or more XML schemas. SQL Server's XML data type supports schema validation. We will explore this in detail in the next section.

The XML data type supports an implicit conversion from any character or national character data type, including CHAR, VARCHAR, NCHAR, and NVARCHAR, but not from other SQL Server data types. You can use CAST or CONVERT to convert from BINARY, VARBINARY, TEXT, NTEXT, and data types to the XML data type for storage as well. Casting from TEXT and NTEXT is permitted to enable forward compatibility for users who stored their XML data in these data types in previous versions of SQL Server. Casting from the BINARY data types is useful for features like SQL Server Service Broker that can communicate using binary or XML. In addition, you can store a SQL_VARIANT data type in an XML data type table after casting it to a character-based type. Listing 9-2 shows inserting rows into a table containing an XML data type.

LISTING 9-2: Inserting rows into a table with an XML data type

```
CREATE TABLE xml_tab(
  the_id INTEGER PRIMARY_KEY IDENTITY,
  xml_col XML)
GO

-- these work fine
```

```
INSERT INTO xml_tab VALUES('<doc1></doc1>')
INSERT INTO xml_tab VALUES(N'<doc1></doc1>')

-- so does this (if first cast to varchar/nvarchar)
DECLARE @v SQL_VARIANT
SET @v = N'<someotherdoc></someotherdoc>'
INSERT INTO xml_tab VALUES(CAST(@v AS varchar(max)))

-- this fails at the insert statement
DECLARE @SOMENUM FLOAT
SET @SOMENUM = 3.1416
INSERT INTO xml_tab VALUES(CAST(@SOMENUM as XML))
```

Although we've stored only well-formed XML documents in the XML data type column so far, we can also use this column to store document fragments or top-level text nodes. This is useful because we can store the results of a SELECT...FOR XML query or XQuery results, which may not be complete documents, in an XML data type column. The documents or fragments must abide by XML well-formedness rules, however. Listing 9-3 shows some examples.

LISTING 9-3: Inserting XML data into a table

```
CREATE TABLE xml_tab(
  the_id INTEGER PRIMARY_KEY IDENTITY,
  xml_col XML)
GO

-- ok, complete document
INSERT INTO xml_tab VALUES('<doc2></doc2>')

-- ok, document fragment
-- though it's not a single well-formed document
-- (two root elements)
INSERT INTO xml_tab VALUES('<doc1></doc1><doc2></doc2>')

-- ok, text node/atomic value
INSERT INTO xml_tab VALUES('The Window and Shade Store')

-- error, not well-formed
INSERT INTO xml_tab VALUES('The Window & Shade Store')

-- error, not well-formed
INSERT INTO xml_tab VALUES('<doc1><doc2></doc1></doc2>')
```

There is no implicit conversion from the XML data type to any other data types, but the CAST and CONVERT operators do convert between any of the character or National character data types, as well as BINARY and VARBINARY. When you cast from BINARY and VARBINARY, you can either specify the encoding in the XML itself or include the beginning byte-order mark (0xFFFE) if the format is Unicode. When you cast to BINARY or VARBINARY, the XML will be cast to UTF-16 with the byte-order mark present. You can cast a TEXT or NTEXT data type instance to an instance of the XML type, but you cannot cast an instance of the XML type to TEXT or NTEXT. Using one of the special methods of the XML data type (the value method, discussed later in this chapter) can produce different SQL data types. Listing 9-4 shows retrieving data from an XML data type column.

LISTING 9-4: Returning data from an XML data type column

```
CREATE TABLE xml_tab(
  the_id INTEGER PRIMARY_KEY IDENTITY,
  xml_col XML)
GO

INSERT INTO xml_tab VALUES('<doc2></doc2>')
INSERT INTO xml_tab VALUES(N'<doc2></doc2>')
GO

-- both rows' values are cast to the same data type
SELECT CAST(xml_col as NCHAR(2000)) FROM xml_tab
GO

-- illegal, no cast to SQL_VARIANT
SELECT CAST(xml_col as SQL_VARIANT) FROM xml_tab
GO
```

Because the values of two XML data type instances cannot be compared (except by using IS NULL), you cannot use the XML data type in SQL predicates or SQL clauses that require comparison, such as GROUP BY and ORDER BY. The XML data type also cannot be used in any scalar function or aggregate where comparison is required. Because the XML data type is castable to any character-based type, however, this functionality will work if CAST (or CONVERT) is used. This behavior is exactly the behavior specified for a distinct data type by the SQL:1999 specification. Although comparison of the XML document type as a string is risky, notice that in the preceding example, both `'<doc2/>'` and `'<doc2></doc2>'` are "converted" to the same lexical form, `'<doc2/>'`, when the CAST or CONVERT function is used. The XML data type does retain Infoset fidelity but does not guarantee lexical fidelity. Listing 9-5 illustrates what you can and cannot do with the XML data type in SQL statements.

LISTING 9-5: Using the XML data type in SQL statements

```
-- assume the same xml_tab as in previous examples

-- comparison to NULL works
SELECT the_id FROM xml_tab
  WHERE xml_col IS NULL

-- illegal
SELECT xml_col FROM xml_tab
  GROUP BY xml_col

SELECT xml_col FROM xml_tab
  ORDER BY xml_col

SELECT xml_col FROM xml_tab
  WHERE xml_col = '<doc2/>'

-- fails, no implicit conversion to character type
SELECT SUBSTRING(xml_col,1,2) FROM xml_tab

-- casting to string allows this to work
SELECT xml_col from xml_tab
  WHERE CAST(xml_col AS VARCHAR) = '<doc2/>'
```

Using XML Data Variables and Parameters

SQL Server 2005 allows you to use the XML data type as a normal scalar variable in T-SQL. You can assign XML documents or fragments to the variable as you would any other variable, as shown in this example:

```
-- declare a variable of XML data type
DECLARE @x XML

-- implicit cast (must be a valid XML document or fragment)
SET @x = '<doc1><name>Bob</name></doc1>'

-- use it
INSERT  xml_tab VALUES(@x)
```

Just as with an XML column, variables of the XML data type can be used as input to an assignment statement. Variables of the XML data type have the same processing limits as columns of the XML data type; they may not be used in place of a string in scalar functions such as SUBSTRING, in comparisons, in ORDER BY or GROUP BY clauses in dynamic SQL, or as parameters without first being cast or converted to a character data type. Stored procedures or user-defined function parameters and user-defined function return codes may be XML types. This allows you to return dynamic XML to the user based on logical operations, such as in the following example:

```
-- create the user-defined function
CREATE FUNCTION my_business_logic(
  @in_dept INTEGER
)
RETURNS XML
AS
BEGIN
  DECLARE @x XML
  -- do some business logic that produces an XML document
  RETURN @x
END
GO

-- now call it, using dept 10
SELECT dbo.my_business_logic(10)
```

Note that the XML return code is a scalar type rather than a TABLE type.

As with XML data type columns and variables, procedure parameters and return codes can be declared with a schema collection name and used to ensure schema validity. Although being able to schema-validate input parameters may obviate the requirement for a lot of domain-checking of input, we can still use the fact that we can do processing inside procedures to make the XML a lot more dynamic.

Later in this chapter, we'll see how using and producing XML based on dynamic rules and being able to pass in XML as just another data type can be used in conjunction with the new extended features of the composition and decomposition functions, SELECT...FOR XML and OpenXML.

Typed and Untyped XML: Cataloguing and Using XML SCHEMA COLLECTIONs

In addition to storing untyped XML documents or fragments in an XML data type column, you can use SQL Server to validate your XML data type column, variable, or parameter by associating it with an XML SCHEMA COLLECTION. Therefore, you can think of XML data types as being either schema-validated (containing data types defined by a specific set of XML schemas) or untyped (containing any well-formed XML). Whether your XML type is typed or untyped, it can still contain documents or fragments, because fragments can also be schema valid. In addition, when you define an XML type to be schema validated, you can also specify that it can contain only XML documents, or XML documents or fragments (known as *XML content*).

XML schemas define a series of data types that exist in a particular namespace. Schemas are themselves well-formed schema-compliant XML documents, just as relational table definitions and other DDL are valid T-SQL. Although there can be more than one schema definition document for a particular namespace, a schema definition document defines types in only one namespace. The XML Schema Definition language (XSD) defines a standard set of base types that are supported as types in XML documents, just as the SQL:1999 standard defines a set of base types that relational databases must support. The XSD base data types are shown in Figure 9-1.

Schema documents may also import types from other namespaces using the import element. There are also some special namespaces that are "imported" by default when using SQL Server's XML type. Two of the most important ones are

- The *http://www.w3.org/2001/XMLSchema namespace*. This namespace defines the constructs (elements and attributes) used in XML schema documents.
- The *http://www.w3.org/2001/XMLSchema-instance namespace*. This namespace defines the constructs to be used in XML documents that are not schemas.

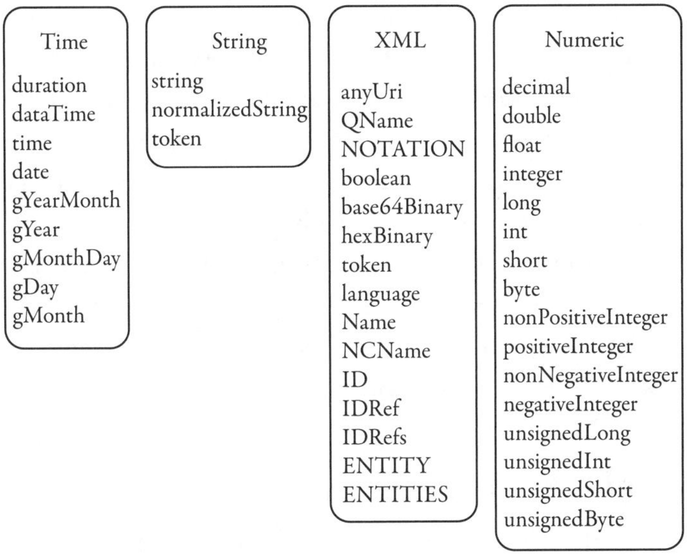

FIGURE 9-1: XSD base data types

These usually are assigned the namespace prefixes xs and xsi, respectively, although a lot of other schema-manipulating products will use the xsd prefix rather than xs. A complete explanation of the XML Schema specification is beyond the scope of this book, but Listing 9-6 illustrates the main concept.

LISTING 9-6: A simple XML schema

```
<!-- defines types for the namespace "http://example.org/People"
     This is known as the targetNamespace but does not indicate
     The location of the schema document -->
<xsd:schema xmlns:xsd="http://www.w3.org/2001/XMLSchema"
         xmlns:tns="http://example.org/People"
         targetNamespace="http://example.org/People" >

   <xsd:simpleType name="personAge" >
     <xsd:restriction base="xsd:float" >
       <xsd:maxInclusive value="120" />
       <xsd:minExclusive value="0" />
     </xsd:restriction>
   </xsd:simpleType>

   <xsd:element name="age" type="tns:personAge" />

</xsd:schema>
```

Note that an XSD schema includes some schema elements, such as `max-Inclusive` and `minExclusive`, that serve to constrain or restrict the base data types. This constraint process is known as *derivation by restriction,* and the schema elements and attributes that act as constraints are known as *facets.*

Although there is an `xsi:schemaLocation` attribute that can be helpful in locating arbitrary schema documents in an instance document, the XML schema specification does not mandate an algorithm by which an XML document locates its schema. SQL Server 2005 stores schema documents inside the database and keeps track of them based on the schema collection; it doesn't use `xsi:schemaLocation`.

SQL Server XML SCHEMA COLLECTIONs

Schema documents are catalogued in SQL Server as part of a named XML SCHEMA COLLECTION by means of the CREATE XML SCHEMA COLLECTION DDL statement:

```
USE pubs
GO

CREATE XML SCHEMA COLLECTION peoplecoll AS
' <xsd:schema xmlns:xsd="http://www.w3.org/2001/XMLSchema">
    <!-- other types omitted -->
    <xsd:simpleType name="personAge" >
      <xsd:restriction base="xsd:float" >
        <xsd:maxInclusive value="120" />
        <xsd:minExclusive value="0" />
      </xsd:restriction>
    </xsd:simpleType>
    <xsd:element name="age" type="personAge" />
</xsd:schema>
<xsd:schema xmlns:xsd="http://www.w3.org/2001/XMLSchema"
            xmlns:tns="http://example.org/LogansRun"
            targetNamespace="http://example.org/LogansRun" >
    <!-- other types omitted -->
    <xsd:simpleType name="personAge" >
      <xsd:restriction base="xsd:float" >
        <xsd:maxInclusive value="30" />
        <xsd:minExclusive value="0" />
      </xsd:restriction>
    </xsd:simpleType>
    <xsd:element name="age" type="tns:personAge" />
</xsd:schema>'
```

Note that an XML SCHEMA COLLECTION has a SQL Server object name (dbo.peoplecoll, in this case, because XML SCHEMA COLLECTIONs are scoped within a SQL schema) and consists of one or more XML schemas, defining the permitted types in one or more XML namespaces. It cannot be referenced outside the database it is defined in or by using a three-part object name, like pubs.dbo.peoplecoll. An XML schema that will be used to validate XML content also can have no associated namespace, like the first schema in the previous collection. This is known as the *no-namespace schema* and is distinguished by the fact that its schema element has no targetNamespace attribute. You are restricted to one no-namespace schema per XML schema collection.

Typed XML

XML data type columns, parameters, and variables may be typed or untyped—that is, they may conform to a schema or not. To specify that you are using a typed column, you would specify the schema collection name in parentheses as a qualifier on XML data type specification, like this:

```
CREATE TABLE xml_tab (
    the_id INTEGER,
    xml_col XML(peoplecoll)
)
```

By doing this, you've just defined a series of integrity constraints with respect to what can appear in the XML that makes up that column! Typing the XML data in a column by using an XML schema collection not only serves as an integrity constraint, but also is an optimization for SQL Server's XQuery engine because you are using typed data in the query. It also allows the XQuery engine to know the data type of its intermediate and final results. If the XML data is not strongly typed, XQuery treats everything as a weakly typed "string" value, xdt:untypedAtomic.

The integrity checking for a typed XML column happens each time a new value is set into it. This would occur when you are inserting or updating the column in a table. As an example, creating the following table and adding some rows to it will cause each instance of the XML data type to be schema validated at insert time:

```
CREATE TABLE person_tab(
 id INT IDENTITY PRIMARY KEY,
 -- the person column can only contain
 -- Infoset items that are defined in the schema collection
 -- defined above
 person XML(peoplecoll))
GO

-- this works, person between 0 and 30 years old
INSERT INTO person_tab VALUES(
'<age xmlns="http://example.org/LogansRun">11</age>')

-- so does this, using the no-namespace schema
INSERT INTO person_tab VALUES(
'<age>75</age>')

-- this insert fails
INSERT INTO person_tab VALUES(
'<age xmlns="http://example.org/LogansRun">31</age>')
```

You can precede your schema collection identifier with the keyword DOCUMENT or CONTENT. If you do not use one of these keywords, the default is equivalent to specifying CONTENT. If DOCUMENT is specified, the column can contain only XML documents (a document is defined as having a single root element), but if you specify CONTENT, the column can contain documents or fragments, as long as all the elements match an element in one of the schemas. Here's an example that illustrates the difference:

```
CREATE TABLE person_docs(
 id INT IDENTITY primary key,
 person XML(DOCUMENT peoplecoll))
GO

CREATE TABLE person_content(
 id INT IDENTITY PRIMARY KEY,
 person XML(CONTENT peoplecoll))
GO

-- this works with either table, a single root element
INSERT INTO person_docs VALUES(
'<age xmlns="http://example.org/LogansRun">11</age>')
INSERT INTO person_content VALUES(
'<age xmlns="http://example.org/LogansRun">11</age>')
```

```
-- this fails, more than one root element
INSERT INTO person_docs VALUES(
'<age xmlns="http://example.org/LogansRun">5</age>
 <age xmlns="http://example.org/LogansRun">5</age>
')
GO

-- this works because it's a valid fragment
INSERT INTO person_content VALUES(
'<age xmlns="http://example.org/LogansRun">5</age>
 <age xmlns="http://example.org/LogansRun">5</age>
')
GO
```

XML variables can also be schema validated by declaring them with a name of an already-defined schema collection:

```
-- this document or fragment must correspond to this schema collection
DECLARE @x XML(accountingcoll)

-- input is validated here
SET @x =
'<po xmlns="urn:com-develop:purchaseorder">
   <orderid>4321</orderid>
   <customerid>10753</customerid>
   <items>
      <itemno>987-65</itemno>
      <qty>5</qty>
   </items>
</po>'
```

There are three ways to specify the type of an XML element in an XML document. You can define an XML namespace prefix for a particular namespace and use the prefix on the element in question, use a default XML namespace definition, or use xsi:type to specify the data type.

Management of XML Schemas and Schema Collections

When an XML schema collection is stored in SQL Server, its schemas are not stored directly as XML documents. Instead, they are shredded into a proprietary format that is useful for optimizing schema validation. Although you can extract your XML schemas using the system function xml_schema_namespace(), as shown in the following example, comments and schema annotations are not recovered:

```
-- this returns a single XML schema document
-- for the 'http://example.org/LogansRun' namespace
-- if it occurs in the XML schema collection 'dbo.peoplecoll'
SELECT xml_schema_namespace(
   N'dbo', N'peoplecoll', N'http://example.org/LogansRun')
GO


-- this returns all of the XML schema documents
-- in the peoplecoll XML schema collection
-- multiple schema documents are separated by a space
SELECT xml_schema_namespace(N'dbo', N'peoplecoll')
GO
```

The exact signature of xml_schema_namespace is

```
DECLARE FUNCTION xml_schema_namespace (
  @relational_schema NVARCHAR(4000),
  @xml_schema_collection_name NVARCHAR(4000),
  [,@namespace NVARCHAR(4000)]
)
RETURNS XML
```

where @relational_schema is the relational schema that contains the collection. It returns a schema document (as an XML data type instance) representing the content of the XML schema namespaces associated with the SQL XML schema collection identifier.

If you need to keep track of an original schema in its exact text format, you should store it separately. A convenient way to keep track of your schemas is to insert them into a table with an XML column:

```
CREATE TABLE xml_schema_save_tab (
  the_id INTEGER PRIMARY KEY,
  xml_schema_col XML)
GO

INSERT INTO xml_schema_save_tab VALUES(1,
N'<xsd:schema xmlns:xsd="http://www.w3.org/2001/XMLSchema"
            xmlns:tns="http://example.org/LogansRun"
            targetNamespace="http://example.org/LogansRun" >
   <!-- this schema defines a single data type, personAge,
        and I want to save this comment as well as the schema -->
   <xsd:simpleType name="personAge" >
     <xsd:restriction base="xsd:float" >
```

```
            <xsd:maxInclusive value="30" />
            <xsd:minExclusive value="0" />
        </xsd:restriction>
    </xsd:simpleType>
    <xsd:element name="age" type="tns:personAge" />
</xsd:schema>')
GO
```

XML schema collections are tied to a specific SQL schema within a specific database; they are first-class SQL Server database objects that can be referenced with a one- or two-part name by users with the appropriate permission. Because many XML documents use types from multiple XML namespaces, an XML schema collection can contain multiple unrelated schemas. In addition, many XML schemas import types from other schemas; you can use the XML schema `<import>` statement to import another XML schema namespace that you use in a second schema definition for a different namespace. In addition to defining all the schemas in a collection by using the `CREATE XML SCHEMA COLLECTION` DDL statement, you can add more schemas to a collection after it's been created using `ALTER XML SCHEMA COLLECTION`. If we first define the following `XML SCHEMA COLLECTION`,

```
CREATE XML SCHEMA COLLECTION mytrees AS
'<xsd:schema xmlns:xsd="http://www.w3.org/2001/XMLSchema"
            xmlns:tns="http://example.org/Trees"
            targetNamespace="http://example.org/Trees" >
    <xsd:simpleType name="treeAge" >
        <xsd:restriction base="xsd:float" >
            <xsd:maxInclusive value="1000" />
            <xsd:minExclusive value="0" />
        </xsd:restriction>
    </xsd:simpleType>
    <xsd:element name="treeage" type="tns:treeAge" />
</xsd:schema>'
```

it is permissible to import that schema definition into another schema definition for a different namespace, as the following code shows:

```
ALTER XML SCHEMA COLLECTION mytrees ADD
'<xsd:schema xmlns:xsd="http://www.w3.org/2001/XMLSchema"
            xmlns:tns="http://example.org/Trees2"
            targetNamespace="http://example.org/Trees2" >
    <xsd:import namespace="http://example.org/Trees"/>
    <xsd:simpleType name="treeAge2" >
        <xsd:restriction xmlns:t2="http://example.org/Trees"
                    base="t2:treeAge" >
```

```
        <xsd:maxInclusive value="500" />
      </xsd:restriction>
    </xsd:simpleType>
    <xsd:element name="treeage2" type="tns:treeAge2" />
</xsd:schema>'
```

Notice that the `simpleType treeAge2` in the namespace `http://example.org/Trees2` is derived by restriction from the base type `t2:treeAge` in a different namespace. We could also have defined both schemas in the collection with a single CREATE XML SCHEMA COLLECTION DDL statement.

An XML schema collection is dropped from the database like any other SQL Server object and is subject to the same constraints. You may not drop an XML schema collection, for example, if it is being used to type an XML data type column:

```
-- this would fail if the XML schema collection
-- was used to type an XML data type column
DROP XML SCHEMA COLLECTION peoplecoll
```

Security for XML SCHEMA COLLECTIONS and Strongly Typed Instances

Security for XML SCHEMA COLLECTIONS and strongly typed instances is applied on the database objects and is analogous to security on native SQL Server data. XML schema collections are scoped to the SQL schema within a database, so you can permit users or roles to define XML schemas:

```
GRANT CREATE XML SCHEMA COLLECTION TO public
```

When a specific XML schema collection is catalogued, permissions must be granted to reference the schema or use strongly typed columns or parameters:

```
GRANT REFERENCES ON XML SCHEMA COLLECTION::people
   TO FRED
```

The permissions that can be granted on a specific schema collection are as follows:

- REFERENCES—Gives permission to define tables and views that reference a schema collection
- EXECUTE—Gives permission to use strongly typed columns, parameters, or variables that refer to a given schema collection

Creating an Index on an XML Column

You can create indexes on an XML column, using approximately the same syntax that you use for a SQL index. Four kinds of XML indexes can be created. Before you can create any kind of XML index, the table must have an ordinary SQL data type primary key column. First, you must create the *primary index;* this creates a node table and an index of the node table. Note that a *node table* is a relational table that contains one row for every node in an XML document, this can get fairly large. We'll discuss the exact structure of the node table in Chapter 10. This index associates each node with the SQL key column and is useful for ad hoc queries. You can create an XML index over only the document structure, using the FOR PATH keyword. This is similar to the concept of creating a "key" in XSLT; this type of index helps in XQuery path statements. You can also create an index over the values of the elements and attributes in the XML data type column with the FOR VALUE keyword. This type of index can help in XQuery content searches. The FOR PROPERTY keyword creates an index that is most usable when your XML consists of a shallow hierarchy with many elements or attributes that are really name–value pairs. Additional XML index types may be defined in the future. You create an XML index on the entire column, and you cannot index subsets of the document content. The syntax is shown in Listing 9-7.

LISTING 9-7: Creating XML indexes

```
CREATE TABLE xml_tab(
  the_id INTEGER PRIMARY KEY IDENTITY,
  xml_col XML)
GO

CREATE PRIMARY XML INDEX xmlidx1 ON xml_tab(xml_col)
GO

-- structural index
CREATE XML INDEX xmls1 ON xml_tab(xml_col)
 USING XML INDEX xmlidx1 FOR PATH
GO

-- property index
CREATE XML INDEX xmlp1 ON xml_tab(xml_col)
 USING XML INDEX xmlidx1 FOR PROPERTY
GO
```

```
-- value index
CREATE XML INDEX xmlv1 ON xml_tab(xml_col)
 USING XML INDEX xmlidx1 FOR VALUE
GO
```

Although this is similar to an "ordinary" SQL primary key and index creation statement with an extra XML keyword, the actual effect of the statement is much different from creating a SQL Server index. What you are creating in the case of an XML column is an index over the internal representation or structure of the column whose purpose is to optimize XQuery queries rather than SQL queries. Remember that the SQL comparison operators cannot be used on an XML column. Because the index contains the (SQL) primary key of the table, however, it can assist in queries that use XQuery criteria and a primary key value in a SQL WHERE clause. Though the internal representation of the XML index is an internal implementation detail, suffice it to say that creating such an index will not help optimize queries that cast or convert the XML data to character types first.

Because the XML index is not a "normal" SQL index, some limitations apply to these indexes:

- You cannot create an XML composite index—that is, an index on more than one XML column or an XML column and a non-XML column.
- You cannot create an XML index as a clustered index or use it as a partitioning criterion.

In addition, because all XML indexes and SQL indexes share the same value space in a database, you cannot create an XML index (of any kind) and a SQL index with the same index name, or two different kinds of XML indexes with the same name. Although an XML type can also be used with full-text search, this is outside of the scope of this book.

XML Type Functions

In addition to being used as a table or view column, variable, or parameter in its entirety, the XML data type contains a variety of type-specific methods. These are invoked by using the SQL:1999 instance.method syntax, similar to the WRITE method of the VARCHAR(max) type.

The XML type methods encompass a few different groups of functionality:

- Determining whether a node or nodes exist that satisfy a given XQuery expression (exist method)
- Selecting a single value using XQuery and returning it as a SQL data type (value method)
- Querying the value of the XML type via XQuery (query method)
- Creating a table with one row per node that matches an XQuery (nodes method) for use with the other XQuery methods
- Modifying the value of the XML type via XQuery DML (modify method)

The modify method is a mutator method, like VARCHAR(MAX).WRITE; all the other methods are accessor methods. As with the WRITE and UDT mutators, the modify method may not be used with a NULL instead of an XML data type.

Because all the current methods on an XML data type are built around using XQuery to query an instance of the type, we'll defer these until the next chapter. Other methods—for example, validating an instance of an XML type on demand—that have nothing to do with XQuery may be added to the XML data type in future releases. Currently, you can validate an instance of an XML data type against an XML SCHEMA COLLECTION by attempting to assign it to a typed XML variable or insert it into a typed XML column.

SELECT . . . FOR XML Enhancements

SQL Server 2000 provides an enhancement to T-SQL permitting composition of XML document fragments using SQL queries against relational tables. This is the SELECT...FOR XML syntax. This syntax can produce fragments in element or attribute normal form XML and can even produce a combination of elements and attributes. There are three "dialects" of FOR XML queries:

- FOR XML RAW—Produces one XML element for each row in the result, no matter how many tables participate in the query. There is an attribute for each column, and the names of attributes reflect the column names or aliases. FOR XML RAW has been enhanced in SQL Server 2005 to allow element normal form XML.

- FOR XML AUTO—Produces one XML element by row in the result but produces nested XML elements if there is more than one table in the query. The order of nesting is defined by the order of the columns in the SELECT statement.

- FOR XML EXPLICIT—Produces XML by means of SQL UNION queries. Each arm of the UNION query produces a different level of XML. This is by far the most flexible dialect and can produce element or attribute normal form and nesting XML exactly as you like. This is also by far the most complex dialect to program.

Listings 9-8, 9-9, and 9-10 show the results of FOR XML SELECT statements against the pubs database.

LISTING 9-8: FOR XML RAW syntax and results

```
-- this query:
SELECT Customers.CustomerID, Orders.OrderID
FROM Customers
   JOIN Orders ON Customers.CustomerID = Orders.CustomerID
ORDER BY Customers.CustomerID
FOR XML RAW


-- produces this XML output document fragment
  <row CustomerID="ALFKI" OrderID="10643" />
  <row CustomerID="ALFKI" OrderID="10692" />
  <row CustomerID="ALFKI" OrderID="10703" />
  <row CustomerID="ALFKI" OrderID="10835" />
  <row CustomerID="ANATR" OrderID="10308" />
```

LISTING 9-9: FOR XML AUTO syntax and results

```
-- this query:
SELECT Customers.CustomerID, Orders.OrderID
FROM Customers
   JOIN Orders ON Customers.CustomerID = Orders.CustomerID
ORDER BY Customers.CustomerID
FOR XML AUTO


-- produces the following XML document fragment
  <Customers CustomerID="ALFKI">
    <Orders OrderID="10643" />
    <Orders OrderID="10692" />
    <Orders OrderID="10702" />
    <Orders OrderID="10835" />
```

```
  </Customers>
  <Customers CustomerID="ANATR">
    <Orders OrderID="10308" />
  </Customers>
```

LISTING 9-10: FOR XML EXPLICIT syntax and results

```
-- this query:
SELECT      1 as Tag, NULL as Parent,
            Customers.CustomerID as [Customer!1!CustomerID],
            NULL as [Order!2!OrderID]
FROM        Customers
UNION ALL
SELECT      2, 1,
            Customers.CustomerID,
            Orders.OrderID
FROM Customers
  JOIN Orders ON Customers.CustomerID = Orders.CustomerID
ORDER BY [Customer!1!CustomerID]
FOR XML EXPLICIT

-- produces this output document fragment
<Customer CustomerID="ALFKI">
    <Order OrderID="10643"/>
    <Order OrderID="10692"/>
    <Order OrderID="10702"/>
</Customer>
```

In SQL Server 2005, there are quite a few refinements and enhancements to FOR XML queries:

- There is a new dialect of FOR XML query called FOR XML PATH.
- FOR XML can produce an instance of an XML type.
- FOR XML is able to prepend the XML result with an inline schema in XSD schema format. The previous version of FOR XML could prepend only an inline XDR (XML Data Reduced) schema.
- You can select the namespace for the inline XSD schema referred to earlier.
- You can nest FOR XML queries.
- You can produce element-centric XML using FOR XML RAW.
- You can choose to generate xsi:nil for NULL database values rather than leave that element out of the XML result entirely.

- You can produce a root element for the XML fragment, making it an XML document.

- There is improved whitespace handling through entitization—that is, representing characters as XML entity references, using the numeric value for the character.

- There are subtle improvements to the algorithm for determining nesting in FOR XML AUTO.

Let's explore some of these features to see how they would be useful.

FOR XML PATH Mode

SQL Server 2005's choices of XML output are rich and varied. FOR XML RAW and FOR XML AUTO produce two well-known but "static" XML documents. There is a maximum of one level of nesting with FOR XML RAW; FOR XML AUTO requires that all columns selected from the same table occur at the same nesting level. With RAW and AUTO modes, you must choose either element normal form or attribute normal form. Mixing elements and attributes in the same document requires FOR XML EXPLICIT, which is quite a bit more complex to write. FOR XML PATH is a new mode that gives you more control over nesting levels and mixing attributes and elements. It combines the ease of coding of AUTO and RAW modes with the power of EXPLICIT mode. In fact, it should be possible to code almost all the document formats that require EXPLICIT mode (or postquery XML transformation) using FOR XML PATH mode.

With PATH mode, you shape the XML document by using column aliases that contain XPath expressions. When PATH mode sees an alias that contains a forward slash, it creates another level of hierarchy in the output document. Listing 9-11 shows an example using the authors table that combines the first and last name into a single name element and makes au_id an attribute by using PATH mode.

LISTING 9-11: FOR XML PATH syntax and results

```
WITH XMLNAMESPACES('http://example.org/person/names' as nam)
SELECT au_id AS [@authorid],
       au_fname AS [nam:name/nam:firstname],
       au_lname AS [nam:name/nam:lastname]
```

```
  FROM authors
  WHERE au_id > '998'
  FOR XML PATH
GO

-- this produces the following document fragment:
<row xmlns:nam="http://example.org/person/names" authorid="998-72-3567">
  <nam:name>
    <nam:firstname>Albert</nam:firstname>
    <nam:lastname>Ringer</nam:lastname>
  </nam:name>
</row>
```

In addition to being able to mix elements and attributes and create new hierarchy levels, you can use the following XPath node test functions:

- `node()`—The content is inserted as a text node. If the content is a complex UDT, the entire tree is inserted. You can also use `*` (asterisk) as a shortcut for `node()`.
- `text()`— The content is inserted as a text node, but this produces an error if the column's data type is UDT or XML.
- `data()`—The content is inserted as an atomic value followed by a single space. This allows you to produce lists of element and attribute values.
- `comment()`—This produces an XML comment using the value.
- `processing-instruction()`—This produces an XML processing instruction using the value.

You can also specify namespaces in your output document by using namespace-to-namespace prefix mappings and the SQL:2003 standard `"WITH XMLNAMESPACES"` syntax. Long pathnames are subject to the limitation that SQL Server aliases can be up to 128 Unicode characters long.

Producing an XML Data Type

It is now possible to use the XML fragments or the documents produced by FOR XML to populate an XML data type column in a table or an XML variable or procedure parameter. This can be done via a few different methods.

First, we can set the result of a SELECT...FOR XML query to a variable of XML data type, like this:

```
-- declare a variable of type XML
DECLARE @x XML
-- now, write to it,
-- NOTE: parentheses around the SELECT statement are required
SET @x = ( SELECT * FROM authors FOR XML AUTO, TYPE )
```

You can also use FOR XML queries to produce input to a table using INSERT INTO ... SELECT syntax, like this:

```
-- create a table
CREATE TABLE xml_tab(id INT IDENTITY PRIMARY KEY, xml_col XML)
GO

-- populate it with a FOR XML query
DECLARE @x XML
SET @x = ( SELECT * FROM authors FOR XML AUTO, TYPE )
INSERT INTO xml_tab VALUES (@x)
GO
```

Finally, because the XML type is a distinct type, you may want to return it to the caller as a VARCHAR or NVARCHAR data type. You can use the result of a FOR XML query for this. Here's an example:

```
DECLARE @x NVARCHAR(max)
-- it is implement important NOT to use TYPE qualifier here
-- or else a conversion will be required
SET @x = (SELECT * FROM pubs.dbo.authors FOR XML RAW)
```

Using a VARCHAR or NVARCHAR data type differs from using the TYPE qualifier in FOR XML in that the TYPE qualifier will raise errors if invalid characters and non–well-formed fragments are created.

Producing an XML data type column drastically affects how the data is presented to clients. When you leave out the TYPE specifier, FOR XML queries produce a rowset of data that is made into a single stream in the client libraries rather than appearing as a one-column, one-row rowset. The .NET Framework library Microsoft.Data.SqlXml, introduced with the SQLXML 3.0 Web release, is a .NET Framework wrapper around the unmanaged OLE DB code to enable .NET Framework clients to process the

XML stream. Although this stream of data appeared in Query Analyzer as though it were a one-column rowset with a single column named with a specific GUID, this was only a limitation of Query Analyzer. The special GUID was an indication to the client libraries that the data actually should appear as a stream.

When the `TYPE` specifier is used, a `FOR XML` query does produce a one-row, one-column rowset. This should reduce the confusion for client-side programmers who were never quite comfortable with a SQL statement that produced a stream of XML. SQL Server 2005 can now produce an `XML` data type column that can be consumed with "ordinary" rowset-handling code. See Chapter 13 for examples of handling `XML` data type columns from the client.

Producing an Inline XSD Format Schema

`FOR XML` queries now can include an inline schema that describes the resultset in XML Schema Definition format. This works only with `RAW` and `AUTO` modes. At the time that SQL Server 2000 was released, the XSD schema was not yet a W3C standard. Rather than support an intermediate version of XSD, SQL Server 2000 was able to prepend an XDR format schema. XDR is a Microsoft-specific precursor of the XSD schema specification designed around OLE DB; it was submitted to the W3C as a note prior to the standardization of XSD. XDR is still used by products like BizTalk and APIs like ADO classic. XDR is supported, though deprecated, in ADO.NET as well. Listing 9-12 shows how to prepend an XDR schema or XSD schema to a `SELECT . . . FOR XML` result.

LISTING 9-12: Prepending schemas to FOR XML results

```
-- prepend an XDR schema
SELECT * FROM authors
  FOR XML AUTO, XMLDATA

-- prepend an XSD schema (new in SQL Server 2005)
SELECT * FROM authors
  FOR XML AUTO, XMLSCHEMA
```

ADO classic supports XDR schemas when used inline with `ADODB.Recordsets`; however, ADO is very picky about the exact dialect of

XDR supported, requires specific XDR annotations, and is not compatible with FOR XML, XMLDATA. BizTalk did support using FOR XML, XMLDATA queries to describe its data, although BizTalk 2000 and later can support XSD schemas in addition to XDR. Schema generation is supported with the FOR XML RAW and FOR XML AUTO dialects.

ADO.NET 1 exposes a method, SqlCommand.GetXmlReader, that returns a document fragment from a SELECT...FOR XML query. In version 1, using the XMLDATA option to generate an inline schema was a requirement for using the returned XmlReader correctly to populate a System.Data.DataSet. Using the new FOR XML, XMLSCHEMA version should provide much better results, because the XSD support in .NET Framework (including ADO.NET) far outstrips XDR support. You should be able to use FOR XML, XMLSCHEMA queries in BizTalk and other Microsoft products as well. The instance schema produced includes a schema import for the "http://schemas.microsoft.com/sqlserver/2004/sqltypes" built-in namespace and indicates that it can be found at "http://schemas.microsoft.com/sqlserver/2004/sqltypes/sqltypes.xsd". This schema contains the mapping of SQL Server's type system to XML schema types. These "instance schema plus rowset" elements can be wrapped in SOAP packets and used manually in a Web Service; we'll discuss Web Services support in SQL Server 2005 in more detail in Chapter 12.

For producing interoperable XML in this manner, the picture is a little less rosy. The XML schema specification does not mandate the way in which an XML document locates its schema during validation. Although the XSD specification provides the attribute xsi:schemaLocation (in the XSI namespace described earlier), XML processors are not required to support even this mechanism, and the location of a schema is completely implementation defined. SQL Server uses a set of precatalogued system and user schemas when doing its own validation.

What we're getting to is that very few non-Microsoft XML processors or tools recognize inline schemas and will use them to do schema validation. The XML editor XML Spy is a notable exception. So although inline schemas are fine in an environment where they will be consumed by Microsoft tools, they are not interoperable. Although it would be inconvenient to use, a generic XSLT or XQuery program could be used to split out the inline schema.

NULL Database Values

The XML model, especially XML schema, handles missing or unknown values differently from SQL. SQL specifies that both missing and unknown values are represented as NULL. In an XML schema, the definition for an attribute that could be missing is specified as use="optional"; therefore, in FOR XML queries, NULL attribute values are simply omitted. When FOR XML AUTO, ELEMENTS, or FOR XML RAW, ELEMENTS is specified, though, there are two choices for the XML representation. By default, when the database contains a NULL value, the element in the FOR XML result is simply omitted. In an XML schema, this representation format would be defined in XML as an element with the "maxOccurs=1" and "minOccurs=0" facets.

With elements, in the SQL Server 2005 version of FOR XML, we have a different choice. Rather than leave an element corresponding to a NULL database value out entirely, we can also specify that the FOR XML query use xsi:nil="1" to indicate an XML nil value. An example should clarify the choices. We have created and populated a simple table as follows:

```
CREATE TABLE students (
  id INTEGER, name VARCHAR(50), major VARCHAR(20) NULL)

INSERT students VALUES(1, 'Bob Smith', 'Chemistry')
INSERT students VALUES(2, 'Fred Jones', NULL)
```

Using the query SELECT * FROM students for XML AUTO, ELEMENTS in SQL Server Management Studio yields the following result:

```
<students>
  <id>1</id>
  <name>Bob Smith</name>
  <major>Chemistry</major>
 </students>
 <students>
  <id>2</id>
  <name>Fred Jones</name>
 </students>
```

Note that Fred Jones's major element is simply missing. Using the query `SELECT * FROM students FOR XML AUTO, ELEMENTS XSINIL` yields the following results:

```
<students xmlns:xsi="http://www.w3.org/2001/XMLSchema-instance">
  <id>1</id>
  <name>Bob Smith</name>
  <major>Chemistry</major>
 </students>
 <students xmlns:xsi="http://www.w3.org/2001/XMLSchema-instance">
  <id>2</id>
  <name>Fred Jones</name>
  <major xsi:nil="1" />
 </students>
```

Using `xsi:nil="1"` indicates that the value of Fred Smith's major is nil. Because some Web Service toolkits use `xsi:nil` (and expect it in SOAP messages that are sent to them), this is a nice option to have when generating XML.

Producing a Root Element

By default, `FOR XML` queries produce XML fragments—that is, otherwise-well-formed XML that lacks a root element. APIs that expect an XML document, such as `XmlDocument.Load`, will fail in attempting to load the fragment. The reason for this behavior is that output from multiple `FOR XML` queries can be composed into a single document; the client-side data access API (such as `Microsoft.Data.SqlXml` in SQLXML 3.0 and above) is expected to add the root element. For users and libraries that do not expose a method to add the root element, now you can add it using the `ROOT` directive of a `FOR XML` query. You are allowed to name the root element anything you want. The syntax is shown here:

```
-- this query:
SELECT Customers.CustomerID, Orders.OrderID
FROM Customers, Orders
WHERE Customers.CustomerID = Orders.CustomerID
ORDER BY Customers.CustomerID
FOR XML AUTO, ROOT('NorthwindCustomers')

-- produces the following XML document (not a fragment)
<NorthwindCustomers>
  <Customers CustomerID="ALFKI">
```

```
    <Orders OrderID="10643" />
    <Orders OrderID="10692" />
    <Orders OrderID="10702" />
    <Orders OrderID="10835" />
  </Customers>
  <Customers CustomerID="ANATR">
    <Orders OrderID="10308" />
  </Customers>
  <!-- some rows omitted -->
</NorthwindCustomers>
```

Other Features

Two features that may need more explanation are whitespace entitization and nested XML queries. Whitespace entitization is an improvement on the way in which the SQL Server 2000 FOR XML generation algorithm treats carriage returns and line feeds in the output XML. SQL Server 2000 renders carriage returns and line feeds as their native hexadecimal characters, causing problems with parsers that expect these characters to be XML entities. In SQL Server 2005, the carriage return, for example, is encoded as  this improves fidelity on the client side when processing the XML but is incompatible with your current FOR XML applications. To retain SQL Server 2000 compatibility for whitespace compatibility, use the version of CONVERT that acts like xml:space="preserve" has been specified. Here's an example:

```
-- CONVERT a string to XML then CONVERT it back to NVARCHAR(10)

SELECT CONVERT(NVARCHAR(10), CONVERT(XML, '<b>  </b>', 1), 1)

→ <b>  </b>  -- retain whitespace, no entitization
SELECT CONVERT(NVARCHAR(10), CONVERT(XML, '<b>  </b>', 0), 0)
→ <b/>        -- don't retain whitespace
SELECT CONVERT(NVARCHAR(10), CONVERT(XML, '<b>  </b>', 0), 1)
→ <b/>        -- don't retain whitespace
SELECT CONVERT(NVARCHAR(10), CONVERT(XML, '<b>  </b>', 1), 0)
→ <b> &#x20;</b> -- retain whitespace, SQL Server 2005 entitization
```

In SQL Server 2005's FOR XML processing, you can use nested queries to produce levels of nesting in your XML. These are similar to subqueries in SQL, except that the resultset is not flat but produces multiple nested levels of hierarchy. Using the stores and discounts tables in the pubs database, the following query

```
SELECT stor_id, stor_name, state,
 (SELECT discounttype, discount FROM discounts d
    WHERE d.stor_id = s.stor_id
    FOR XML AUTO, ELEMENTS, TYPE)
FROM stores s
ORDER BY s.stor_id
FOR XML AUTO, ELEMENTS
```

will yield the following nested XML:

```
<s>
  <stor_id>6380</stor_id>
  <stor_name>Eric the Read Books</stor_name>
  <state>WA</state>
</s>
<!-- some elements omitted here -->
<s>
  <stor_id>8042</stor_id>
  <stor_name>Bookbeat</stor_name>
  <state>OR</state>
  <d>
   <discounttype>Customer Discount</discounttype>
   <discount>5.00</discount>
  </d>
</s>
```

Mapping SQL and XML Data Types

Throughout this chapter, we've been able, through the new XML data type, to mix XML and relational types at will, sometimes even in the same query. SQL types can be used in the production of XML data types, and XML data types and XML queries against these types can return output that is usable in T-SQL, perhaps even as input to complex .NET Framework types. At this point, before we discuss the composition and decomposition functionality, it behooves us to realize that we are actually dealing with two different type systems. These are the SQL type system, as defined by SQL:1999; and the XML type system, as defined by the XML 1 and Namespaces, the XPath 2 and XQuery 1 data model, and XML Schema specifications. We are mostly concerned with the XML Schema specification, because this is the heart of the XML type system definitions.

XML Schema is a rich type system, encompassing simple types (similar to SQL types), XML types (from XML's SGML roots), complex types using object-oriented type principles like the .NET Framework type system, and SQL:1999 OBJECT data types. Some of the constructs go beyond the bounds of the current SQL type system, even when SQL:1999 complex types are included. An XML facet, for example, can indicate that an array of elements always consists of exactly five or six elements (minOccurs=5, maxOccurs=6); nothing in SQL:1999 is analogous. In this section, we go over the idiosyncrasies and edge cases in mappings showing mappings from SQL types to XML types, and vice versa. We'll also defer the subject of mapping XML data types to SQL types until Chapter 10, because this is used in XQuery and to a lesser extent in OpenXML.

Mapping SQL Types to XML Types

You can produce XML types from the underlying SQL types when using these features of SQL Server 2005:

- FOR XML queries
- sql:variable and sql:column in server-side XQuery functions on the XML data type (discussed in Chapter 10)
- Producing SOAP messages from SQL Server (discussed in Chapter 12)

SQL Server defines a specific XML Schema to codify the mapping, using http://schemas.microsoft.com/sqlserver/2004/sqltypes as a namespace, which is close to the SQL:2003 Part 14 ANSI standard (more on the standard later). This schema provides a direct mapping of SQL Server types to XML types; therefore, it refers to SQL Server data types that are not explicitly mentioned in the spec and leaves out types that SQL Server does not support. In general, this schema defines an XML SimpleType named after the corresponding SQL Server type but derived by restriction in XML. The SQL Server CHAR data type, for example, is represented as follows:

```
<xsd:simpleType name="char">
    <xsd:restriction base="xsd:string"/>
</xsd:simpleType>
```

String, Binary, and Decimal Types

Character-based data types in SQL Server are mapped to the xsd:string data type. Each column in a SQL Server table or a SELECT statement can have character types of a different length (CHAR(x)) or maximum length (VARCHAR(x)). In the SQL Server specific sqltypes schema, these types are mapped to an xsd:string with no xsd:maxLength or xsd:length facet:

```
<!-- other data types elided for clarity -->
<!-- from http://schemas.microsoft.com/sqlserver/2004/
sqltypes -->
<xsd:simpleType name="varchar">
          <xsd:restriction base="xsd:string"/>
</xsd:simpleType>
<xsd:simpleType name="nvarchar">
          <xsd:restriction base="xsd:string"/>
</xsd:simpleType>
```

In specific resultsets or columns, you would add the maxLength facet or, in the case of CHAR, the xsd:length and xsd:length facets, just as you would in SQL Server:

```
<!-- a column that is defined as NVARCHAR(40) -->
<xsd:element name="first_name" minOccurs="0">
          <xsd:simpleType>
                  <xsd:restriction base="sqltypes:nvarchar">
                          <xsd:maxLength="40"/>
                  </xsd:restriction>
          </xsd:simpleType>
</xsd:element>
```

It seems odd at first glance to group binary and decimal data types with the character data types. The reason for doing this is that binary data types can have a maximum length but can be variable. Decimal data types can have a variable precision and scale. In mapping to SQL Server, these are approached the same way that character data types are. In general, the binary data types (binary, varbinary, and image in SQL Server) are defined as xsd:base64Binary. The decimal data type maps to xsd:decimal. When specific instances are referred to in resultset schemas, the correct maxLength, precision, and scale facets are added.

Other General Data Types

The integral data types, bit data type, and float data types have almost exact mappings to XSD data types. In the case of integral types, they will have restrictions based on the value space. The SQL Server data type INT, for example, has a value space that is slightly different from xsd:integer. Another case is the SQL Server MONEY and SMALLMONEY data types, which map to decimal types with specific maxInclusive and minInclusive facets:

```
<xsd:simpleType name="smallmoney">
    <xsd:restriction base="xsd:decimal">
        <xsd:totalDigits value="10"/>
        <xsd:fractionDigits value="4"/>
        <xsd:maxInclusive value="214748.3647"/>
        <xsd:minInclusive value="-214748.3648"/>
    </xsd:restriction>
</xsd:simpleType>
```

Date Data Type

The SQL:2003 standard maps date data types directly to XSD-equivalent data types—that is, types like xs:date, xs:time, and xs:timestamp. Many implementations (including SQL Server) actually store date values as a number of seconds since a "magic date" and time values with a given precision. The standard for SQL data types does specify the range of the date data type and the precision of the time data type, although SQL Server's SQL datetime data type does not implement either standard. The XSD-to-SQL type mappings accommodate specifying different ranges by using annotations; SQL Server's implementation of mapping uses the xs:pattern, xs:minOccurs, and xs:maxOccurs facets.

Note that although SQL:2003 Part 14 is straightforward in its mapping of date, time, and datetime data types, XQuery 1 and XPath have different representations of these types that must include a time-zone specifier. The two data models are not aligned. This complicates matters when using SQL Server datetime with SQL Server XQuery.

Pattern-Based Data Types

Some SQL Server data types do not have an exact, or even an approximate, value-space–based relationship to any corresponding XSD data type. Examples of this include SQL Server's GUID data type and SQL Server's date-based data types, which are not based at all on the ISO8601 standard date used by XSD. These types are mapped to XSD by using the XSD pattern facet and considered a derivation by restriction of either xsd:string (in the case of GUID) or `xsd:dateTime`. As an example, here is the mapping of a GUID:

```
<xsd:simpleType name="uniqueidentifier">
  <xsd:restriction base="xsd:string">
     <xsd:pattern value="([0-9a-fA-F]{8}-[0-9a-fA-F]{4}-[0-9a-fA-F]
{4}-[0-9a-fA-F]{4}-[0-9a-fA-F]{12})|(\{[0-9a-fA-F]{8}-[0-9a-fA-F]{4}-
[0-9a-fA-F]{4}-[0-9a-fA-F]{4}-[0-9a-fA-F]{12}\})"/>
            </xsd:restriction>
        </xsd:simpleType>
</xsd:simpleType>
```

Wildcard Data Types

The two SQL Server types that must be represented as wildcards are `SQL_VARIANT` and the SQL Server `XML` type. `SQL_VARIANT` must map to `xsd:any` because there is no simple combination of restrictions that would cover all the different possibilities. SQL Server's `XML` type would map to `xsd:any` with a possible wildcard schema region—that is, any in a specific namespace. This is even more straightforward in the case of typed XML instances.

Nullability

SQL Server type instances, when defined as columns in tables, can be defined as `NULL` or `NOT NULL`. `NOT NULL` is the default in XSD schemas, as represented by the default facets `maxOccurs=1` and `minOccurs=1`. Data types that are declared `NULL` in SQL Server tables must be represented as `minOccurs=0`. `NULL` values in XML can be represented simply by omitting the element or by specifying an empty element with the attribute `xsi:type=nil`. When using SQL Server's `FOR XML`, you can choose either option using the new `ELEMENTS XSINIL` directive discussed earlier in this chapter. Note that there is also a new column directive, `!xsinil`, for the `FOR XML EXPLICIT` mode.

OpenXML Enhancements

SQL Server 2000 provides a system-defined function, `OpenXML`, that creates `Rowsets` from XML documents. This allows an XML document to be decomposed into possibly multiple `Rowsets`. These `Rowsets` can be exposed as resultsets or used with the `INSERT INTO...SELECT` statement to insert rows into one or more relational tables. This is also known as *shredding* an XML document. SQL Server 2005 provides an alternative, preferred way to produce a rowset from XML: the xml.nodes function. We'll talk about the xml.nodes function in Chapter 10.

OpenXML requires an XML document handle as input; this handle is produced by using a system stored procedure, sp_xml_preparedocument. OpenXML uses a subset of XPath 1 to indicate which nodes to select as rows and also to indicate which elements and attributes correspond to columns in the Rowset. An example of using OpenXML is shown in Listing 9-13.

LISTING 9-13: Using OpenXML to insert rows

```
DECLARE @h int
DECLARE @xmldoc VARCHAR(1000)

SET @xmldoc =
'<root>
<stores stor_id="8888" stor_name="Bob''s Books"
    stor_address="111 Somewhere" city="Portland"
    state="OR" zip="97225">
</stores>
<stores stor_id="8889"
    stor_name="Powell''s City Of Books"
    stor_address="1005 W Burnside" city="Portland"
    state="OR" zip="97209">
</stores>
</root>'

EXEC sp_xml_preparedocument @h OUTPUT, @xmldoc

INSERT INTO stores
SELECT * FROM OpenXML(@h,'/root/stores')
WITH stores

EXEC sp_xml_removedocument @h
```

There are two changes to OpenXML for SQL Server 2005:

- The XML data type is also supported as an output column or an overflow column in the OpenXML WITH clause.
- You can pass an XML data type variable directly into sp_xml_preparedocument as long as it contains an XML document (not a fragment).

Another improvement in SQL Server 2005 that should assist in OpenXML processing is the introduction of the VARCHAR(MAX) and XML data types. In SQL Server 2000, although you could pass in TEXT fields as procedure parameters, you could not operate on them or generate them inside the procedure. Because in SQL Server 2005, you can have parameters of VARCHAR(MAX) and XML data types, you can process these types before using them in OpenXML processing. In addition, because SELECT...FOR XML now produces variables of the XML data type with a root element, you can generate the input to OpenXML from a FOR XML query.

You must take care when using OpenXML, because it produces Rowsets from an XML DOM (document object model). The integer returned from sp_xml_preparedocument is actually a pointer to an instance of an XML DOM. This object (a COM object in the current implementation) is very memory intensive. SQL Server will produce errors if a serverwide memory limit for XML processing is exceeded. Using the XML data type as input to sp_xml_preparedocument produces a DOM even though the XML data type may already be parsed.

Loading XML into the Database from Files

For loading large XML documents into the database, parsing the documents into a DOM just to use OpenXML is very memory intensive. Users are encouraged to use the XML Bulk Load facility on the client side. This Bulk Load facility works by reading the XML and producing SQL statements on the client side, which are sent to SQL Server as a batch.

In SQL Server 2005, you can also insert XML data stored in flat files directly into XML data type columns by using SQL BULK INSERT–type functionality on the server. This saves on network traffic because you specify the exact SQL statement to be used rather than have client Bulk Load shred an XML document into relational tables by using a mapping schema.

Loading XML on the server is accomplished by using the system rowset provider function OPENROWSET and specifying the new BULK provider. The BULK provider can also load multiple rows of XML data into XML columns from a single file. Given a file that looks like this

```
1              <Root><Invoice InvoiceID="12345" /></Root>
2              <Root><Invoice InvoiceID="13579" /></Root>
```

and a two-column table defined in SQL Server as follows,

```
CREATE TABLE invoices (rowid INTEGER PRIMARY KEY, invoicedoc XML)
```

this SQL Server statement uses the BULK provider to populate the invoices table:

```
INSERT invoices
 SELECT *
 FROM  OPENROWSET
  (Bulk 'c:\myinvoices.txt', formatfile = 'c:\bcpformat.xml') AS X
GO
```

As with other BULK INSERT operations, the new syntax requires a format file. Here's a format file for the simple example:

```
<BCPFORMAT
  xmlns="http://schemas.microsoft.com/sqlserver/2004/bulkload/format"
  xmlns:xsi="http://www.w3.org/2001/XMLSchema-instance">
 <RECORD>
  <FIELD ID="1" xsi:type="CharTerm" TERMINATOR="\t" MAX_LENGTH="12" />
  <FIELD ID="2" xsi:type="CharTerm" TERMINATOR="\r\n" />
 </RECORD>
 <ROW>
  <COLUMN SOURCE="1" NAME="IntCol" xsi:type="SQLINT" />
  <COLUMN SOURCE="2" NAME="XmlCol" xsi:type="SQLCHAR" />
 </ROW>
</BCPFORMAT>
```

If your table contains only a single XML column to be inserted (for example, if the rowid in the previous invoices table is an identity column), you can use the bulk copy SINGLE_CLOB or SINGLE_BLOB option, like this:

```
INSERT invoices2
 SELECT *
 FROM  OPENROWSET
  (Bulk 'c:\invoice1.xml', SINGLE_BLOB) AS X
go
```

Usage of SINGLE_BLOB is like SINGLE_CLOB or SINGLE_NCLOB, but it does not have conflicting codepage encoding issues. When your flat file, which might be obtained from a customer using BizTalk, is loaded into a

SQL Server data type column, it can be parsed into relational tables by using OpenXML. A temporary table with an XML column might be used as a way to load large documents for later processing.

ANSI SQL Standard Compliance

In addition to the prolific specifications for everything XML guided by the W3C, the ANSI/ISO SQL committee has gotten into the act with an effort to standardize the integration of XML and relational databases. This series of specifications was started under the auspices of the SQLX committee of database vendors but has been subsumed as Part 14 of the SQL:2003 specification. A committee that includes representatives from Microsoft, Oracle, and IBM, among others, is working on this part of the SQL spec. This specification touches on a number of subjects that we've discussed in this chapter, and it's interesting to look at how the implementation relates to the specification.

XML Data Type

The XML data type in SQL Server 2005 conforms to the SQL:2003 specification. In fact, one of the architects on the SQL Server XML team is a member of the SQL:2003 standardization committee. The XML type is defined as a new scalar data type that can be used in variables, procedure parameters, and columns in tables. The limitations of SQL Server's XML data type (for example, two instances of the XML data type cannot be compared for equality) are specification compliant. Casting and converting to and from other data types differs from the spec, which mandates the XMLPARSE and XMLSERIALIZE methods.

The data model of the XML data type defined by Part 14 is based on a slightly extended XML information set model, where the document information item is replaced by a root information item that roughly corresponds to the document node in the XPath 2/XQuery 1 data model. This data model permits an XML data type to contain XML documents, document fragments, and top-level text elements. The SQL Server XML data type adheres to this standard, but this standard is not the same as the XPath 2.0/XQuery 1.0 data model. The XML Schema specification permits "lax" validation of its instances—that is, for an instance of the XML, if you can find the schema definition for an element, you do strict validation and throw an error if it doesn't validate correctly, but if you can't find the definition, you "skip" validate. When using schema validation, SQL Server does not permit "lax" validation and allows only "strict" or "skip" validation. The SQL:2003 spec distinguishes two variations of the XML data type: XML document with prolog and XML content. The difference between the two is used in defining how concatenating two XML types should behave. SQL Server allows you to make a similar distinction (document versus content) between schema-validated XML data types but does not allow concatenation of two XML data type instances directly, though you can cast each one to a character data type, concatenate the character types, and cast the result to the XML data type:

```
DECLARE @x1 XML, @x2 XML, @x3 XML

SELECT @x1 = '<doc1></doc1><doc2></doc2>'
SELECT @x2 = '<doc3/>'

-- this is permitted by the spec
-- but produces an error in SQL Server
SELECT @x3 = @x1 + @x2

-- this works
DECLARE @v1 VARCHAR(MAX)
SET @v1 = (CAST(@x1 AS VARCHAR(MAX))) + (CAST(@x2 AS VARCHAR(MAX)))
SET @x3 = @v1
```

The ANSI SQL spec indicates that XML data type values probably will be stored in either UTF-8 or UTF-16, although alternative encodings will be permitted. The spec also defines that XML data type columns cannot use the SQL COLLATION keyword or functions; this is consistent with SQL Server 2005 behavior.

Finally, the ANSI SQL specification defines a series of XML data type constructor functions, such as XmlForest and XmlElement. SQL Server 2005 currently does not support these functions. SQL Server's FOR XML TYPE keyword syntax, however, can be used to construct an XML data type; this syntax in SQL Server predates the specification and is easier to use.

In addition, in SQL Server 2005, XQuery constructor functions can be used to create an instance of an XML data type from SQL content using the XQuery `sql:column` function, as we'll see in Chapter 10.

Mapping SQL Catalogs and Tables to XML

The ANSI SQL spec defines mappings of SQL catalogs, schemas, and tables to a virtual XML document, which can then be used to produce instances of an XML data type. The ANSI standard provides for both a table-as-document and a table-as-forest mapping. The ANSI standard mapping to a document is roughly equivalent to SQL Server's `SELECT * FROM table FOR XML RAW, ELEMENTS, ROOT('tablename')`, where `tablename` is the actual name of the table. Mapping as a forest is roughly equivalent to SQL Server's `SELECT * FROM table FOR XML AUTO, ELEMENTS`. SQL Server's `FOR XML` capability provides a rich superset of the ANSI standard for in-the-database XML generation. The following example shows the table-as-document and table-as-forest documents that result when the standard is applied with a simple SQL table:

```
<!-- Mapping of a table in the ANSI spec -->
<!-- Also, it's the result of
<!-- "SELECT * FROM EMPLOYEE
      FOR XML RAW,ELEMENTS ROOT('EMPLOYEE')" -->
<!-- in SQL Server -->

<EMPLOYEE>
 <ROW>
  <EMPNO>000010</EMPNO>
  <FIRSTNAME>CHRISTINE</FIRSTNAME>
  <LASTNAME>HAAS</LASTNAME>
  <BIRTHDATE>1933-08-24</BIRTHDATE>
  <SALARY>52750.00</SALARY>
 </ROW>
 <ROW>
  <EMPNO>000020</EMPNO>
  <FIRSTNAME>MICHAEL</FIRSTNAME>
  <LASTNAME>THOMPSON</LASTNAME>
  <BIRTHDATE>1948-02-02</BIRTHDATE>
  <SALARY>41250.00</SALARY>
 </ROW>
 .
 .
 .
```

```
</EMPLOYEE>

<!-- ANSI mapping as an XmlForest -->

<!-- Also the result of -->
<!-- "SELECT * FROM EMPLOYEE FOR XML AUTO,ELEMENTS -->
<!-- in SQL Server -->

<EMPLOYEE>
  <EMPNO>000010</EMPNO>
  <FIRSTNAME>CHRISTINE</FIRSTNAME>
  <LASTNAME>HAAS</LASTNAME>
  <BIRTHDATE>1933-08-24T00:00:00</BIRTHDATE> <!-- ISO 8606 -->
  <SALARY>52750.00</SALARY>
</EMPLOYEE>
<EMPLOYEE>
  <EMPNO>000020</EMPNO>
  <FIRSTNAME>MICHAEL</FIRSTNAME>
  <LASTNAME>THOMPSON</LASTNAME>
  <BIRTHDATE>1948-02-02T00:00:00</BIRTHDATE>
  <SALARY>41250.00</SALARY>
</EMPLOYEE>
```

In addition, the ANSI spec provides a method to convert SQL names to XML names. Many names that are valid (for tables and columns) in SQL are not valid XML names. The XML specification forbids certain constructs in names (such as names that begin with XML or contain spaces) that are valid SQL names, for example. The specification mandates replacing characters that are illegal in XML with "_xHHHH_," where "HHHH" is the hexadecimal characters that make up the Unicode code point; for example, "hire date" in SQL becomes "hire_x0020_date" in XML. In addition, any SQL name that begins with "XML" is prefixed by "_xFFFF_"; for example, "xmlcol" becomes "_xFFFF_xmlcol". SQL Server 2005's FOR XML extension completely complies with the specification.

Mapping SQL Data Types to XML Data Types

The ANSI SQL standard also establishes a mapping of ANSI SQL types, which do not have a one-to-one correspondence to SQL Server data types. This has a namespace http://standards.iso.org/iso/9075/2003/sqlxml. Other than the set of types covered, there are a few differences between the ANSI specification and SQL Server's implementation and the "http://schemas.microsoft.com/sqlserver/2004/sqltypes" schema.

The ANSI SQL spec permits both `xsd:base64Binary` and `xsd:hexBinary` as choices for representing a `VARBINARY` type. SQL Server chose `xsd:base64Binary`. The spec also allows representing nullable data as `xsd:nillible=true` and using `xsi:nil` on the empty element. SQL Server 2005 supports either type.

Finally, the ANSI SQL spec suggests the use of `xsd:annotations` (XSD comments) to indicate SQL constructs that cannot be described (such as data-specific types) or that have no meaning in XSD. For example:

```
<!-- annotation for database-specific SMALLINT data type in ANSI SQL -->
<xsd:annotation>
  <xsd:appinfo>
    <sqlxml:sqltype kind="PREDEFINED" name="SMALLINT"/>
  </xsd:appinfo>
</xsd:annotation>
```

The specification also states that "it is implementation defined whether these annotations are generated." The SQL Server `sqltypes` schema does not use these annotations and instead adds attributes to schema elements to capture other SQL info. It is permitted to add attributes to an xml schema element, as long as they are not in the xsd namespace. Here is an example:

```
<xsd:simpleType>
  <xsd:restriction base="sqltypes:nvarchar" sqltypes:localeId="1033"
      sqltypes:sqlCompareOptions="IgnoreCase IgnoreKanaType IgnoreWidth"
      sqltypes:sqlSortId="52">
    <xsd:maxLength value="10"></xsd:maxLength>
  </xsd:restriction>
</xsd:simpleType>
```

Where Are We?

In this chapter, we looked closely at the new XML data type, which provides integration of relational and XML functionality, in addition to permitting XML data to be stored in the database. This XML data can be security protected, can be XSD schema–validated, can take part in transactions, can be operated on by SQL utilities, and in general is a great step forward from storing XML in files on the file system.

We've also seen how SQL Server's XML functionality adheres closely to XML standards and is an implementation of most of the new SQL:2003 Part 14 standard. This allows interoperability among not only Microsoft products, but also those from third-party and other large vendors.

In Chapter 10, we'll investigate the newest XML query languages, XQuery 1.0 and XPath 2.0, and see how these work inside SQL Server.

10

XML Query Languages: XQuery and XPath

X ML BRINGS WITH it some powerful query languages for dealing with the hierarchical format that is typical of an XML document. This chapter covers XQuery from the perspective of its definition in a series of W3C standards. After looking at the standards, we describe the SQL Server 2005–specific implementation of the XQuery standards. The implementation consists of five SQL Server–specific methods on the XML data type that use XQuery to allow you to query or mutate XML data.

What Is XQuery?

In Chapter 1, we describe the components and uses of XML, and in Chapter 9, we cover the XML native data type in SQL Server 2005. The XML data type typically is a complex type—that is, a type that almost always contains more than one data value. We can use XML data type columns in two distinct ways:

- Query the data and perform actions on it as though it were a simple data type. This is analogous to the way we would treat an XML file in the file system; we read the entire file or write the entire file.
- Run queries and actions on the XML data in the column, using the fact that the XML Infoset model allows the concrete data to be exposed as a sequence of data values or nodes. For this, we need an XML query language.

Currently, the most-used query language in XML is XPath. XPath 1.0 is a mature W3C recommendation. XPath uses a syntax for queries that is similar to the syntax you'd use to locate files on a file system (using forward slashes to indicate levels of hierarchy). XPath queries are used to select data from an XML document in XSLT, the XML stylesheet language. XSLT 1.0 is also a mature W3C recommendation. XSLT operates on a data model defined in the XPath recommendation, which is a somewhat different view of XML than that provided by the Infoset. XPath 1.0 and XSLT 1.0 are supported in the .NET Framework base class libraries as part of the `System.Xml` namespace.[1]

XQuery 1.0, XPath 2.0, and XSLT 2.0 are in the midst of the W3C standardization process. As of late 2005, they are at "Candidate Recommendation," which is the last step before becoming a final Recommendation. Both XQuery 1.0 and XSLT 2.0 use XPath 2.0 to select subsets of data to operate on. XQuery is a query language designed to be SQL-like in its appearance and to be optimizable. A native XQuery 1.0 engine and XPath 2.0 parser live inside the SQL Server 2005 and work in conjunction with the relational engine. This will change the diagram of SQL Server internals presented in Chapter 1 to look like Figure 10-1.

Because you can load .NET Framework classes from the `System.Xml.dll` assembly inside SQL Server 2005, it is also possible to use the client-side XML APIs inside the server.

The SQL Server 2005 internal implementation of XQuery implements a stable subset of the entire XQuery 1.0 language specification. It differs from most other implementations of XQuery in where it gets it data. In the most common implementations of XQuery, the data comes from one or more instances in one or more files, perhaps by using the SAX (Simple API for XML) or DOM (Document Object Model)[2] API to produce an XML Infoset. In SQL Server's

---

1. Although XML and the .NET Framework use the concept of namespace for approximately the same thing, to disambiguate similarly named data (classes in the .NET Framework; attributes and elements in XML), *namespace* is an overloaded term. We'll try to use *XML namespace* to refer to namespaces as defined by the XML Namespaces specification and *.NET Framework namespace* to refer to .NET Framework namespaces when the meaning could be unclear.
2. For further information about the DOM API, refer to the specifications on the W3C Web site. For a simple description of the SAX API, reference the information on the XML.org Web site at http://www.xml.org/xml/resources_focus_sax.shtml.

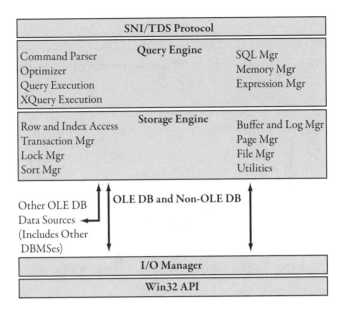

SNI/TDS Protocol		
Query Engine		
Command Parser Optimizer Query Execution XQuery Execution		SQL Mgr Memory Mgr Expression Mgr
Storage Engine		
Row and Index Access Transaction Mgr Lock Mgr Sort Mgr		Buffer and Log Mgr Page Mgr File Mgr Utilities

Other OLE DB
Data Sources
(Includes Other
DBMSes)

OLE DB and Non-OLE DB

I/O Manager
Win32 API

FIGURE 10-1: SQL Server 2005 internals

implementation, the query is tied to an instance of an XML data type or an XML type variable with the option of using SQL columns or variables as well.

We'll start by describing XQuery from the latest W3C standards documents without making direct reference to the implementation inside SQL Server. Note that SQL Server 2005 does not implement the entire specification; we'll have more to say about this later. Remember as we go that SQL Server implements a useful subset of the specification. We'll continue by comparing XQuery with SQL, the language used by every SQL Server developer. After you are comfortable with the XQuery language, we'll look at the implementation of XQuery in SQL Server 2005, pointing out differences from the spec whenever they are relevant. SQL Server implements some XQuery extension functions to allow integration of SQL and XML data inside the XQuery query itself.

An Introduction to XQuery

The XQuery specification consists of a series of specification documents and some related documents. The specification describes not only the query language semantics, but also the underlying data model, the XPath 2.0 path expression language used in XQuery expressions, a formal algebra, and a way to represent XQuery queries in an XML format. The names of the specifications follow. To see the most current versions of these specifications, browse to http://www.w3.org/XML/Query.

- XML Query Requirements
- XML Query Use Cases
- XQuery 1.0 and XPath 2.0 Data Model
- XSLT 2.0 and XQuery 1.0 Serialization
- XQuery 1.0 and XPath 2.0 Formal Semantics
- XQuery 1.0, an XML Query Language
- XQuery 1.0 and XPath 2.0 Functions and Operators
- XML Syntax for XQuery 1.0 (XQueryX)
- XPath Requirements Version 2.0
- XML Path Language (XPath) 2.0
- XML Query and XPath Full-Text Requirements
- XML Query and XPath Full-Text Use Cases
- XML Query and XPath 2.0 Full-Text
- XQuery Update Facility Requirements
- Building a Tokenizer for XPath or XQuery

The documents that you may be going back to most often if you use them for reference will probably be "XQuery 1.0, an XML Query Language" and "XQuery 1.0 and XPath 2.0 Functions and Operators," but the key concept document is "XQuery 1.0 and XPath 2.0 Data Model," because you can't understand how to use XQuery if you don't understand the model of the data you are querying. The data model used by SQL Server 2005 (and the ISO/ANSI SQL:2003 specification) is slightly different from the XQuery Data Model. The next version of the ISO/ANSI SQL spec may align with the XQuery 1.0/XPath 2.0 data model.

The main building block of the XQuery Data Model is the sequence. A *sequence* is an ordered collection of zero or more items. *Items* in a sequence are either *nodes* or *atomic values*. There are seven types of XML nodes: document, element, attribute, text, namespace, processing instruction, and comment.

Atomic values are instances of values of XML Schema or XQuery 1.0/XPath 2.0 atomic data types. This model includes types defined in the XML Schema specification, Part 2, Datatypes, and some additional types (including `xdt:untyped`, `xdt:untypedAtomic` and `xdt:anyAtomicType`) that are specific to the XQuery 1.0/XPath 2.0 data model.

Another way to say this is that XQuery language uses the XML Schema type system; instances of XML Schema types are recognized as first-class items in XQuery sequences. XQuery sequences can consist of only items that are nodes, only items that are atomic values, or a combination of both. To demonstrate quickly, here is an XML fragment that consists of two element nodes, each with an attribute node and a text node:

```
<hello color="green">world</hello>
<hello color="red">world</hello>
```

And here are a few atomic values:

```
42          (an instance of the value of an xs:integer)
hello world (an instance of the value of an xs:string)
2003-08-06  (an instance of the value of an xs:date)
```

One thing to notice here is that `world` in the node example is a text node of type `string` and the `hello world` in the atomic value example is an atomic value, not a node. The difference is subtle. Input sequences in queries are represented using comma-separated values surrounded by parentheses, like this:

```
(1,2,3)
(4,5,<root/>)
```

Sequences are serialized as space-separated values, without the parentheses, like this:

```
1 2 3
4 5 <root/>
```

The XQuery Data Model is a closed data model, meaning that the value of every expression is guaranteed to be an instance of the data model. In other words, each expression will yield a sequence, even if it is a sequence containing no items or only a single item. Sequences are flat, not nested; a sequence cannot contain another sequence. In SQL Server 2005's implementation, sequences must be homogeneous (that is, all nodes or all atomic values); the (4,5,<root/>) sequence above would be disallowed.

According to the specification, the data model, like XML itself, is a node-labeled, tree-structured graph, although sequences are flat. Two main concepts of the data model are *node identity* and *document order*. Nodes (but not atomic values or sequences) have a unique identity that is assigned when the node constructor is used to construct a node or when data containing nodes is parsed by the query. No two nodes share the same node identity. In the XQuery Data Model, order is significant, and an algorithm for determining the order of nodes in an XML document or fragment is defined in the specification. Here is the document order algorithm defined in the XPath 2.0 specification, which is illustrated in Figure 10-2:

1. The root node is the first node.
2. The relative order of siblings is determined by their order in the XML representation of the tree. A node N1 occurs before a node N2 in document order if, and only if, the start tag node of N1 occurs before the start of N2 in the XML representation.
3. Attribute nodes immediately follow the namespace nodes of the element with which they are associated. The relative order of attribute nodes is stable but implementation dependent.
4. Element nodes occur before their children; children occur before following siblings.
5. Namespace nodes immediately follow the element node with which they are associated. The relative order of namespace nodes is stable but implementation dependent.[3]

Finally, the XQuery Data Model extends the XML Information Set (Infoset) after schema validation, known as the Post Schema Validation

---

3. Namespace nodes are not shown in our diagram. Although the XPath 2.0 specification that we are citing supports namespace nodes, XQuery does not support them specifically.

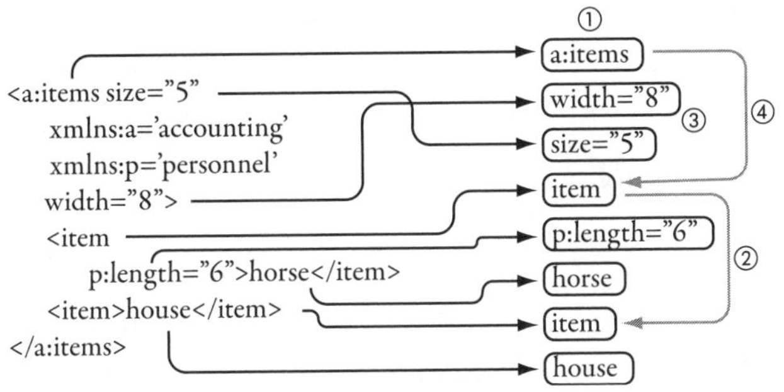

FIGURE 10-2: XML document illustrating document order

Infoset (PSVI). Some of the items defined in the PSVI definition are not used in the XQuery Data Model, however, and the XQuery language itself does not use all the information yielded by schema validation either. The data model supports well-formed XML documents defined in terms of the XML 1.0 and Namespaces specification, as well as the following types of XML documents:

- Well-formed documents conforming to the Namespaces and XML specs
- DTD-valid documents conforming to the Namespaces and XML specs
- XML Schema validated documents

The data model goes beyond the XML Infoset to support data that does not conform to the Infoset as well. As we showed in the examples earlier, this data can consist of the following:

- Well-formed document fragments (XML with multiple top-level nodes)
- Sequences of document nodes
- Sequences of atomic values
- Top-level atomic values (top-level text, for example)
- Sequences mixing nodes and atomic values

Now that we know what we are querying, let's look at the structure of the query itself. XQuery, like XML itself, is case sensitive. Keywords are all lowercase. The query consists of two parts: an optional *query prolog,* followed by the *query body.*

The XQuery Prolog

The query prolog sets up part of the "environment" in which to query. A simple example of this environment would be the default XML Namespace to which elements without a namespace prefix belong, as shown here:

```
(: This is an XQuery comment. Query Prolog begins here :)
declare default element namespace = http://example.org;

(: XQuery body begins here :)
(: looking for somelement in namespace "http://example.org" :)
//somelement
```

Items that can be declared in the XQuery prolog include the following, though this is not an exhaustive list:

- Default element namespace
- Default namespace for functions
- Namespace declarations with a corresponding namespace prefix
- XML Schema `import` statements
- `XMLSpace` declarative (that is, whether boundary whitespace is preserved)
- Default collation
- User-defined function definitions

SQL Server 2005's implementation allows only namespace mappings in the prolog. Note also that if you do not define a default element, attribute, or function namespace, the default is "no namespace." In addition to the namespace prefixes that you define yourself, there are five namespace prefix/namespace pairs that are built in and never need to be declared in the query prolog:

- `xml = http://www.w3.org/XML/1998/namespace`
- `xs = http://www.w3.org/2001/XMLSchema`
- `xsi = http://www.w3.org/2001/XMLSchema-instance`

- `fn = http://www.w3.org/2004/07/xpath-functions`
- `xdt = http://www.w3.org/2004/07/xpath-datatypes`

SQL Server's implementation also includes:

- `(no prefix) = urn:schemas-microsoft-com:xml-sql`
- `(no prefix) = http://schemas.microsoft.com/sqlserver/` `2004/SOAP`
- `sqltypes = http://schemas.microsoft.com/sqlserver/` `2004/sqltypes`

Finally, XQuery has a rich set of built-in functions and operators, defined in the "XQuery 1.0 and XPath 2.0 Functions and Operators Version 1.0" document. In addition, you can define user-defined functions in the query prolog. We'll look at system-defined and user-defined functions in the context of SQL Server's implementation later in the chapter.

The XQuery Body

Now we'll move on to the query body—the part of the query that actually produces the output that we want. An XQuery query consists of expressions; expressions can contain data and variables. There are many different types of expressions, the simplest being the literal expression, which is a simple string or numeric literal. The expression `'Hello World'` is an example of a valid (though fairly useless) XQuery query. The query result consists of that same string, `Hello World`. XQuery variables are named by variable name. The `let` expression assigns a value to a variable. The following query declares a variable, `$a` (XQuery variables begin with a dollar sign), assigns the value of a string literal to it, and returns the variable's value as the result of the query:[4]

```
let $a := 'Hello World'
return $a
```

You can also declare variables in the prolog.

Because you'll probably want to do something more with your query than emit "Hello World," you'll need to provide some XML input to the

---

4. The fact that the `let` assignment construct is not supported by SQL Server 2005's implementation of XQuery is discussed later in the chapter.

query. XQuery has the concept of an execution context for its queries, and part of the execution context is the input sequence. In general, the way that the input sequence is provided is implementation defined, but XQuery defines some functions that can be used in conjunction with input: `fn:doc` and `fn:collection`. `fn:doc`, in its simplest form, can be used to return a document node, given a string URI that references an XML document. It also may be used to address multiple documents or document fragments. `fn:collection` returns a sequence of nodes pointed to by a collection that is named by a URI. Note that you can always implicitly set the context node or provide data via externally bound variables. Now we have input! The following query echoes the content of a file containing an XML document using the `fn:doc` function:[5]

```
let $a := doc("data/test/items.xml")
return $a
```

Notice that this query illustrates two items that are implementation dependent. The parser that uses this query allows the use of the document function without the namespace prefix, because it is a built-in system function. Also, the parser allows the use of a relative pathname rather than strictly requiring a URI; the current part used to resolve the relative pathname is part of the environment. This is just an example of possible parser implementation-dependent behavior.

Two of the most important constructs of the XQuery language are path expressions and FLWOR expressions. Path expressions refer to XPath, the selection language portion of XQuery. XPath expressions consist of a series of evaluation steps, separated by forward slashes. Each evaluation step selects a sequence of nodes, each item of which is input to the next evaluation step. The result of the final evaluation step in the output is the final result of the XPath expression. If any location step returns an empty sequence, the XPath expression stops (because there are no items for the next step to process) and returns an empty sequence. XPath expressions can

---

5. Note that SQL Server 2005's implementation of XQuery does not support the `doc` function; you cannot query from a file directly.

be used as stand-alone queries. In fact, if all you want to do is simply select a sequence of nodes in document order, this may be all you need. Let's assume we have a simple document that looks like the following:

```
<items>
  <item status="sold">
    <itemno>1234</itemno>
    <seller>Fanning</seller>
    <description>Antique Lamp</description>
    <reserve-price>200</reserve-price>
    <end-date>12-31-2002</end-date>
  </item>
  <item status="sold">
    <itemno>1235</itemno>
    <seller>Smith</seller>
    <description>Rugs</description>
    <reserve-price>1000</reserve-price>
    <end-date>2-1-2002</end-date>
  </item>
</items>
```

The XQuery

```
doc("data/test/items.xml")/items/item/itemno
```

produces the following output, a sequence of nodes:

```
<itemno>1234</itemno>
<itemno>1235</itemno>
```

Because XML documents are hierarchical, XPath expression steps can operate on different axes of data. Although the XPath specification defines 13 different axes, an XQuery implementation has to support only 6 of them, though implementations may choose to support more:

- The child axis contains the children of the context node.
- The descendant axis contains the descendants of the context node. A descendant is a child or a child of a child and so on; thus, the descendant axis never contains attribute or namespace nodes.
- The parent axis contains the parent of the context node, if there is one.
- The attribute axis contains the attributes of the context node; the axis will be empty unless the context node is an element.

- The self axis contains just the context node itself.
- The descendant-or-self axis contains the context node and the descendants of the context node.

Figure 10-3 shows the nodes that make up the main XPath axes for a particular document, given a particular context node.

The context node that we are referring to here is the starting point of the evaluation step. In our earlier simple XPath expression, the starting point of the first evaluation step, the document node, is a concrete node. In the XQuery Data Model, this is the root node. The root node is the parent `items` node in this example document. In the second evaluation step, the `items` node would be the context node; in the third evaluation step, each `item` node would be the context node in turn; and so on. Each evaluation step can also filter the resulting sequence using a *node test* that can filter by name or by node type. In the last evaluation step, for example, only children of `item` named `itemno` will be selected. If we wanted to select all the children of `item` nodes, including `seller` nodes, `description` nodes, and all others, we could change the path expression to the following:

```
doc("data/test/items.xml")/items/item/*
```

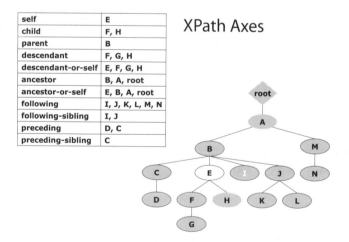

self	E
child	F, H
parent	B
descendant	F, G, H
descendant-or-self	E, F, G, H
ancestor	B, A, root
ancestor-or-self	E, B, A, root
following	I, J, K, L, M, N
following-sibling	I, J
preceding	D, C
preceding-sibling	C

XPath Axes

FIGURE 10-3: XPath axes

Each evaluation step has an axis; in our simple query, we have let the axis default to "child" by leaving it out. The same query could be expressed this way:

```
doc("data/test/items.xml")/child::items/child::item/child::*
```

Any other valid axis could also be used. Another common abbreviation is to abbreviate the attribute axis to @. The evaluation step /attribute: :status in a query against the document above could be abbreviated to /@status.

Although XPath has much more functionality and a function library of its own (that can be used in path expressions in XQuery), in addition to being able to use the XPath and XQuery operators and functions, we'll finish by discussing XPath predicates. After you filter any evaluation step by using a node test, you can filter the results further by using a *query predicate*. Query predicates follow the node test in square brackets. This predicate filters item elements whose itemno subelement has a text subelement with a value less than 1,000:

```
doc("data/test/items.xml")/items/item[itemno/text() < 1000]
```

A predicate can be as simple or complex as you want, but it must evaluate to a boolean value. More exactly, it is evaluated using the Effective Boolean Value (essentially, the rules for fn:Boolean). /a[1], for example, would evaluate to true for the first node named "a" in no namespace at the root; other nodes named "a" would evaluate to false. You can even have multiple predicates on the same evaluation step, if you want.

The heart of XQuery expressions—what forms most of the "selection logic" in an XQuery query—is called the FLWOR expressions. FLWOR (pronounced "flower") is an acronym for the five main expression keywords: for, let, where, order by, and return. We've already seen the let expression, used to assign a value to a variable, and the return expression, for returning the value of a variable in the query:

```
let $a := doc("data/test/items.xml")
return $a
```

We'll briefly define the use of each expression.

The `for` and `let` keywords are used to set up a stream of tuples, each tuple containing one or more bound variables. The `for` keyword is used for iteration. In the following query,

```
for $p in doc("mydocument.xml")/people/person
let $a := $p/age
where $a > 50
return $p/name/firstName/text()
```

the `for` statement uses an XPath expression to select a sequence of items. The `for` statement iterates over all the items that match the XPath expression, assigning a different item to the variable $p, one value for each time around the loop. If the sequence produced is (`<person name='joe'/>` `<person name='bob'/>`, `<person name='phil'/>`), the loop is executed three times, with $p assigned to one node for each iteration. The `let` keyword performs an assignment. The expression on the right side of the assignment is assigned to the variable in its entirety. The assignment takes place whether the value is a single item (as in the `let $a := $p/age` statement in the preceding query) or an entire sequence. To show the difference between iteration and assignment, consider the following two queries:

```
for $p in (1,2), $q in (A,B)
let $a := (7,8,9)
return ($p, $q, $a)
(: this returns: 1 A 7 8 9 1 B 7 8 9 2 A 7 8 9 2 B 7 8 9 :)

for $p in (1,2)
let $a := (7,8,9), $q := (A,B)
return ($p, $q, $a)
(: this returns: 1 A B 7 8 9 2 A B 7 8 9 :)
```

You can use the `where` keyword to filter the resulting tuples. You can filter based on the value based on any XQuery expression. Interestingly, in many situations you could use an XPath predicate in the `for` statement to achieve the same effect as using a `where` keyword. The earlier query that looks for people using the FLWOR `where` clause could be expressed just as easily like this:

```
for $p in doc("mydocument.xml")/people/person[age > 50]
return $p/name/firstName/text()
```

XQuery supports five types of comparison operators in the `where` clause:

1. General (existential) comparison
2. Value comparison
3. Node comparison
4. Type comparison
5. Document position comparison

General comparison can compare a sequence with another sequence or with a value. If any of the items in the sequence match using the comparison operator (the general comparison operators are symbols like =, >, and <), the comparison is true. For example:

```
(1,2,3) = 1         (: this is true :)
(1,2,3) != 1        (: this is also true :)
(1,2,3) = (4,5,6)   (: this is not true, none of the values compare :)
```

Value comparison compares an expression to an atomic value, and the expression must resolve to an atomic value, or the comparison produces an error. The value comparison operators are letter abbreviations like eq, gt, and lt. Here are some value comparisons:

```
given the sequence: <doc num="1"/>
number(/doc/@num) lt 2       (: this is true :)
number(/doc/@num) lt "2"     (: this will work too :)
count(/doc) eq 4             (: this is false :)
(1,2,3) ne (4,5,6)   (: this is an error, sequences are not comparable :)
```

Node comparison compares node identity; this is accomplished by using the XQuery `is` operator. Each node (including a constructed node) has a unique identity. The `is` operator compares two expressions that return a node for equality. `is` cannot be used with sequences. Type comparison looks at the data type of a node or atomic value. Document position comparison operators test whether one node is before or after another node in document order.

The `order by` keyword changes the order of the returned tuples. Usually, tuples are returned in the order of the input, which often is the document

order (which we defined earlier in this chapter). The expression after the
`order by` clause must resolve to a single atomic value; node sets and
sequences are not orderable. The following query orders the returned items
by the text of the `givenName` subelement of the name:

```
for $p in doc("mydocument.xml")/people/person[age > 50]
order by $p/name/givenName/text() descending
return $p/name/firstName/text()
```

The `return` keyword defines what the sequence that constitutes the
return value will look like. In the last few queries, we have been returning
only information derived from tuples as simple items. But items can be
composed from scratch or from existing tuple information using node constructors. Node constructors can use simple literal strings with individual
items separated by commas, but they can also use calculated values
enclosed in curly braces. An example follows:

```
<descriptive-catalog>
   {
     for $i in doc("catalog.xml")//item,
         $p in doc("parts.xml")//part[partno = $i/partno],
         $s in doc("suppliers.xml")//supplier[suppno = $i/suppno]
     order by $p/description, $s/suppname
     return
         <item>
            {
            $p/description,
            $s/suppname,
            $i/price
            }
         </item>
   }
</descriptive-catalog>
```

Notice that this example uses construction twice. The `<descriptive-
catalog>` element is constructed by simply using it as a literal. The
`<item>`s in the return clause are constructed with a literal, but all `<item>`
subelements are constructed by evaluation of the expressions between the
curly braces; this is called a direct constructor. In addition to literal constructors and direct constructors, you can use computed constructors; these
begin with the name of the node type to be constructed, followed by the
content in curly braces. Here's an example of computed constructors:

```
element person
{
  attribute name
    {$p/name[1]/givenName[1]/text()[1])}
}
```

That's a brief introduction, and here's a list of some of the other types of expressions available in XQuery:

- Function calls
- Expressions combining sequences
- Arithmetic and logic expressions
- Comparisons—content, identity, and order based
- Quantified expressions—where one element satisfies a condition
- Expressions involving types—cast, instance of, treat, and typeswitch

Finally, let's explore the question "With what types of data [XML can represent many different data models] is XQuery useful?" Some authors have attempted to make a distinction between XQuery and XSLT based on the premise that although XSLT and XQuery can be used for almost all the same functions (at least if you compare XSLT 2.0 and XQuery 1.0), XSLT, with its template mechanism, is better for data-driven transformations, whereas XQuery is better suited for queries. We find it instructive to look at the XQuery use-cases document to see what the inventors of XQuery had in mind. The use cases mention many different kinds of data:

- Experiences and exemplars—general XML
- Tree—queries that preserve hierarchy
- Sequence—queries based on document ordering
- Relational—relational data (representing tables as XML documents)
- SGML—queries against SGML data
- String—string search (aka full-text search)
- Queries using namespaces
- Parts explosion—usually done well by object and CODASYL databases
- Strong types—queries that exploit strongly typed data
- Full-text use cases (separate specification)

So it appears that XQuery can be useful with all kinds of data; particular implementations, however, may not implement certain features that their data types cannot take advantage of. We'll see this point when we look at the XQuery implementation inside SQL Server.

Comparing and Contrasting XQuery and SQL

SQL is the native language of SQL Server. SQL Server programmers have used it exclusively with Transact-SQL (T-SQL) until the CLR language became available in SQL Server 2005. These same programmers probably were not familiar with XQuery, and it is instructive to compare the two languages to make SQL programmers more at home.

SQL currently is a more complete language than XQuery with regard to its capabilities. SQL can be used for data definition (DDL), data manipulation (INSERT, UPDATE, and DELETE), and queries (SELECT). XQuery delegates its DDL to XML Schema, and the rest of XQuery equates to the SQL SELECT statement. Microsoft and others have proposed data manipulation extensions to XQuery, and the W3C has begun research and produced the "XQuery Update Facility Requirements" document. XQuery-based data manipulation is part of SQL Server 2005. But for now, we'll just compare SQL's SELECT and XQuery's FLWOR expressions.

The clauses of a SQL SELECT statement have an almost one-to-one correspondence in function to the clauses of a FLWOR statement, as shown in Figure 10-4.

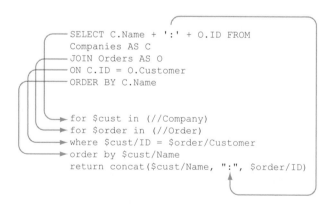

```
SELECT C.Name + ':' + O.ID FROM
Companies AS C
JOIN Orders AS O
ON C.ID = O.Customer
ORDER BY C.Name


for $cust in (//Company)
for $order in (//Order)
where $cust/ID = $order/Customer
order by $cust/Name
return concat($cust/Name, ":", $order/ID)
```

FIGURE 10-4: SQL SELECT and FLWOR

Both SQL's SELECT clause and XQuery FLWOR's return clause enumerate data to be returned from the query. SELECT names columns in a resultset to be returned, whereas return names a sequence of items to be returned. Fairly complex nodes can be returned using, for example, element constructors and nested elements, but items in a sequence are what are being returned nevertheless. Another similarity is that both return and SELECT can be nested in a single statement.

SQL's FROM clause lists the tables from which the data will be selected. Each row in each table is combined with each row in other tables to yield a Cartesian product of tuples, which make up the candidate rows in the resultset. XQuery FLWOR's for clause works exactly the same way by defining variables. Multiple clauses in a for statement, separated by commas, produce a Cartesian product of candidate tuples as well. Because a for clause in XQuery can contain a selection using XPath, for also has some of the functionality of a SQL WHERE clause; this is especially noticeable when the XPath predicate is used. Both SQL and XQuery do support WHERE and ORDER BY, although the XQuery WHERE clause can be based on general (this is known as existential comparison), value comparison, and other types of comparison, whereas SQL is based on value comparison.

Both XQuery FLWOR's let clause and SQL's SET clause can be used for assignment, though let brings variables into scope inside an XQuery FLWOR expression like for does. SET in SQL is often a clause in a SQL UPDATE statement, or a stand-alone statement in a SQL batch or a stored procedure. In fact, in T-SQL, SELECT can also be used for assignment.

Though some of the matches are not 100 percent exact, it should not be a big stretch for SQL users to learn XQuery. The ease of adoption by SQL programmers, rather than data models served, is probably the reason for relational database vendors (or, for that matter, OODBMS (Object Oriented Database Management System) vendors, because XQuery also resembles OQL, the Object Query Language in object-oriented databases) to embrace XQuery over the functionally equivalent XSLT language.

SQL and XQuery differ with respect to their data models. Attributes (column values) in SQL usually have two possible value spaces: an atomic value or NULL. Having NULL complicates some of the SQL operations;

NULLs are not included by default in aggregate operations, for example. XQuery has the NULL sequence (a sequence with zero items), which has some of the same semantics (and complications) as the SQL NULL, as well as the xsi:nil = true attribute that denotes a nil value. In addition, XQuery has to deal with complications of nodes versus atomic values, as well as the complications of possibly hierarchical nodes or multivalue sequences. This makes some of the rules for XQuery quite complex. As an example, value comparisons between unlike data types in SQL are not possible without casting (although SQL Server performs implicit casting in some cases). Comparing a value with NULL (including NULL) is always undefined. This rule could be stated in two sentences with two cases. Contrast this with the rules for value comparison in XQuery:

1. Atomization is applied to each operand. If the result is not an empty sequence or a single atomic value, a type error is raised.

2. If either operand is an empty sequence, the result is an empty sequence.

3. If either operand has the most specific type xdt:untypedAtomic, that operand is cast to a required type, which is determined as follows:

4. If the type of the other operand is numeric, the required type is xs:double.
   - If the most specific type of the other operand is xdt:untyped Atomic, the required type is xs:string.
   - Otherwise, the required type is the type of the other operand.

5. If the cast fails, a dynamic error is raised.

6. The result of the comparison is true if the value of the first operand is (equal, not equal, less than, less than or equal, greater than, or greater than or equal) to the value of the second operand; otherwise, the result of the comparison is false. The "B.2 Operator Mapping" section of the specifications describes which combinations of atomic types are comparable and how comparisons are performed on values of various types. If the value of the first operand is not comparable with the value of the second operand, a type error is raised.

Quite a bit more complex, don't you agree? This rule is not presented here for your memorization—only to point out that the XQuery rules are more complex than the equivalent SQL rules.

Both SQL and XQuery are strongly typed languages. *Strong typing* refers to the fact that all of the functions and operators require the correct data type, although a language is allowed to do implicit typecasting and type promotion. SQL implementations do static type checking; in XQuery, static type checking is optional, although SQL Server's implementation of XQuery implements it. *Static type checking* refers to the fact that a language has a type-checking phase of the query in which the expressions are checked for type-correctness and cardinality; this type checking does not use the data. When static type checking is used, having schemas assists optimization. Both SQL and XQuery are declarative languages; T-SQL is a procedural extension, however, especially considering modules like stored procedures that can contain SQL statements and procedural logic.

While we're mentioning stored procedures, the XQuery equivalents to SQL's stored procedures and user-defined functions (Persistent Stored Modules, as they are called in ANSI SQL) are user-defined functions. These can either be defined in the query prolog or in separate modules. XQuery allows for implementation-dependent extensions to store and access modules in libraries. XQuery's functions are supposed to be side effect free. SQL stored procedures and triggers are not guaranteed to be side effect free, although SQL user-defined functions can make this guarantee.

In conclusion, the SQL SELECT statement has a lot in common with the XQuery language, though XQuery is more complex because of the underlying data model. XQuery has some of the functionality of data manipulation through the use of constructors but no way to affect the underlying data. It more reflects the querying and reporting functionality of SQL SELECT and stored procedures.

Using XQuery with the XML Data Type

SQL Server 2005's implementation of XQuery is aligned with the July 2004 version of the XQuery specification. It's an implementation of a stable subset of the specification.

SQL Server supports XQuery on the XML data type directly. It does this through four of the XML data type's methods:

- `xml.query` takes an XQuery query as input and returns an XML data type as a result.
- `xml.value` takes an XQuery query as input and returns a SQL type as a scalar value.
- `xml.exist` takes an XQuery query as input and returns zero or one, depending on whether the query returns an empty sequence (zero) or a sequence with at least one item (one).
- `xml.nodes` takes an XQuery query as input and returns a one-column rowset that contains references to XML documents with the XQuery context set at the matching node.

Any of these accessor functions can also return NULL if the input value is NULL. XQuery usually gets its input from the XQuery function `doc` or `collection` in dealing with documents from the file system or input from a stream. XQuery can also use a user-defined context document. In SQL Server 2005, though, the XML functions refer to a specific instance of the XML data type, and input will come from that instance's value; this is the context document.

Although the XQuery language itself can be used to produce complex documents, as we've seen, this functionality is really used to a great extent in SQL Server only in the `xml.query` function. When using `xml.value` and `xml.exist`, we'll almost always be using simple XPath 2.0 expressions rather than complex XQuery with sequences, constructors, formatting information, and so on. Although we could use more complex XQuery, the reason for this is that `xml.value` can return only a sequence containing a single scalar value (it cannot return an XML data type), and `xml.exist` is used to check for existence. So let's cover them first.

xml.exist(string xquery-text)
The `xml.exist` function applies an XQuery query to an instance of the XML data type. If the query returns an empty sequence, `xml.exist` returns false (0); if the query returns anything other than an empty sequence, `xml.exist`

returns true (1). Null input returns a NULL answer. Here's a simple example using an untyped XML variable:

```
DECLARE  @x XML
SELECT @x.exist('/people/person')    -- returns NULL

SET @x = '<people><person>fred</person></people>'
SELECT @x.exist('/people/person')    -- returns 1

SET @x = '<person>sam</person>'
SELECT @x.exist('/people/person')    -- returns 0
```

You can also use a SQL SELECT statement that uses the xml.exist function on an XML data type column in a table. If we define the following table,

```
CREATE TABLE xml_tab(
  the_id INTEGER PRIMARY KEY IDENTITY,
  xml_col XML)
```

and fill the table with some rows, using the xml.exist function in the column list of a SQL SELECT statement will search the xml_col value in each row, looking for data that matches the given XQuery expression. For each row, if the row contains matching data in the specified column, the function returns true (1). If the rows inserted look like this,

```
INSERT xml_tab VALUES('<people><person name="curly"/></people>')
INSERT xml_tab VALUES('<people><person name="larry"/></people>')
INSERT xml_tab VALUES('<people><person name="moe"/></people>')
GO
```

the XQuery xml.exist expression to see if any row in the table contains a person named "moe" would look like this:

```
SELECT xml_col.exist('/people/person[@name="moe"]') AS is_there_moe
  FROM xml_tab
```

The result will be a three-row rowset containing the values, 0 ("False"), 0 ("False"), and 1 ("True") in the is_there_moe column. Notice that if we add just a single row containing a single XML document with multiple <person> elements,

```
-- insert one row containing an XML document with 3 persons
-- rather than 3 rows each containing an XML document with 1 person
INSERT xml_tab VALUES(
 '<people>
    <person name="curly"/>
    <person name="larry"/>
    <person name="moe"/>
  </people>')
```

the result of the SELECT statement above is a one-row rowset containing the value 1 ("True") , not one row for each person in the XML document. The rows are the rows of a SQL rowset, rather than XML results.

Because the xml.exist function returns bit, a SQL data type, it could also be used as a predicate in a SQL statement—that is, in a SQL WHERE clause. This SQL statement would select only rows that had an XML document containing a person named "moe":

```
SELECT the_id FROM xml_tab
  WHERE xml_col.exist('/people/person[@name="moe"]') = 1
```

A good use for xml.exist is in a selection predicate in a query that then produces complex XML for the same or another XML column by using the xml.query function. In this case, the xml.query function operates only on the subset of rows selected by xml.exist, rather than on all the rows in the table. We'll come back to this when we discuss xml.query.

xml.value(string xquery-text, string SQLType)

The xml.value function takes a textual XQuery query as a string and returns a single scalar value. The SQL Server type of the value returned is specified as the second argument, and the value is cast to that data type. The data type can be any SQL Server type except the following:

- XML data type
- TIMESTAMP data type
- UNIQUEIDENTIFIER data type
- SQL_VARIANT data type
- IMAGE, TEXT, or NTEXT data type
- A CLR UDT

You wouldn't need to have xml.value to return a single XML data type, because a different method, xml.query, does exactly that. The xml.value function must be guaranteed to return a single scalar value, or else an error is thrown. SQL Server's implementation of XQuery static type checking works according to the specification: Query execution is divided into a static type-checking phase and a dynamic execution phase. Static type checking does not use the data to determine if the query is guaranteed to return a singleton value. If the query fails static type checking, it's as though you misspelled the word SELECT (as, for example, SELEC) in a SQL query. The query is not executed, and an error is thrown. If this static-type-checking error occurs in a stored procedure definition, CREATE PROCEDURE fails.

Using our overly simple document from the xml.exist section,

```
CREATE TABLE xml_tab(
  the_id INTEGER PRIMARY KEY IDENTITY,
  xml_col XML)
GO


INSERT xml_tab VALUES('<people><person name="curly"/></people>')
INSERT xml_tab VALUES('<people><person name="larry"/></people>')
INSERT xml_tab VALUES('<people><person name="moe"/></people>')
GO
```

the following SQL query using xml.value

```
SELECT the_id,
  xml_col.value('/people[1]/person[1]/@name', 'varchar(50)') AS name
  FROM xml_tab
```

would produce a single row containing the_id and name columns for each row. The result would look like this:

```
the_id      name
------  ----------------------------
1           curly
2           larry
3           moe
```

Note that we've had to use the subscript [1] in every XPath evaluation step to ensure that we're getting a singleton answer (strictly speaking, the cardinality must be zero-or-one). This is because of SQL Server XQuery's static type checking. If we didn't use the subscript, the engine would have to assume that the document permits multiple `person` elements and would fail with this error message: `XQuery [value()]: 'value()' requires a singleton (or empty sequence), found operand of type 'xdt:untypedAtomic *'`. Using the subscript predicate ensures that the query returns `'xdt:untypedAtomic ?'`.

The `xml.value` function is good for mixing data extracted from the `XML` data type in the same query with columns returned from SQL Server, which by definition contain a single value. In addition, it can be used as a predicate in a SQL `JOIN` clause or in a SQL `WHERE` clause, as in the following query:

```
SELECT the_id
  FROM xml_tab
  WHERE xml_col.value(
    '/people[1]/person[1]/@name', 'VARCHAR(50)') = 'curly'
```

xml.query(string xquery-text)

Although all the functions of the `XML` data type do invoke the internal XQuery engine, the function that returns an instance of the `XML` data type is `xml.query`. This function takes the XQuery text, which can be as simple or complex as you like, as an input string and returns an instance of `XML` data type. The result is always an XQuery sequence as the specification indicates, except when your input instance is `NULL`; then the result is `NULL`. The resulting instance of `XML` data type can be returned as a SQL variable, used as input to an `INSERT` statement that expects an XML type, or returned as an output parameter from a stored procedure. The instance is always untyped XML. To check for schema-validity, you can assign the returned XML to an XML variable typed with an `XML SCHEMA COLLECTION`. SQL Server's XQuery does not implement the XQuery `validate` function.

The simplest XQuery query might be one that consists only of an XPath 2.0 expression. This would return a sequence containing zero or more nodes or atomic values. Given our previous document, a simple XQuery query like this

```
SELECT xml_col.query('/people/person') AS persons
  FROM xml_tab
```

would return an XML instance with a value that is a sequence containing a single node for each row:

```
persons
----------------------
<person name="curly"/>
<person name="larry"/>
<person name="moe"/>
```

The query does not have to return a single node or a well-formed document, however. If the following row is added to the table, the results are different:

```
INSERT xml_tab VALUES(
 '<people>
    <person name="laurel"/>
    <person name="hardy"/>
  </people>')
GO

SELECT xml_col.query('/people/person') AS persons
  FROM xml_tab
```

These are the results:

```
persons
--------------------------------------------
<person name="curly"/>
<person name="larry"/>
<person name="moe"/>
<person name="laurel"/><person name="hardy"/>
```

Note that the result from the last row is a multinode sequence, and though it is not a well-formed XML document, it does adhere to the XQuery 1.0 Data Model.

In addition to simple XQuery statements consisting of a simple XPath expression, you can use the FLWOR expressions that we saw at the beginning of this chapter. (Note that at this time, SQL Server's implementation of XQuery does not support the let FLWOR operator.) This query uses FLWOR expressions and produces the same result as the previous query:

```
SELECT xml_col.query('
    for $b in /people/person
    return ($b)
 ')
 FROM xml_tab
```

You can subset the results with an XQuery predicate and the WHERE clause, as well as with an XPath predicate. For example, these two queries return the same results.

```
-- XQuery WHERE clause
SELECT the_id, xml_col.query('
   for $b in /people/person
   where  $b/@name = "moe"
   return ($b)
 ') AS persons
 FROM xml_tab

-- XPath predicate
SELECT the_id, xml_col.query('/people/person[@name="moe"]') AS persons
   FROM xml_tab
```

Note that for the columns in which `"moe"` did not occur, the result is an empty sequence rather than an empty string or a NULL value. That's because the output from xml.query is an XML data type. If you cast or convert the XML empty sequence to a VARCHAR data type, it is an empty string, not the value NULL:

```
the_id        persons
---------------------------
1
2
3             <person name="moe"/>
4
```

You can also return literal content interspersed with query data by using the XQuery standard curly brace notation. The following query returns a series of results surrounded by XHTML list tags (`<li>`). Note that this uses an element normal form version of the XML in the table, rather than the attribute normal form we've been using thus far:

```
CREATE TABLE xml_tab(
   the_id INTEGER PRIMARY KEY IDENTITY,
   xml_col XML)
GO

INSERT xml_tab
VALUES('<people><person><name>curly</name></person></people>')
INSERT xml_tab
VALUES('<people><person><name>larry</name></person></people>')
```

```
INSERT xml_tab
VALUES('<people><person><name>moe</name></person></people>')

INSERT xml_tab VALUES(
 '<people>
    <person><name>curly</name></person>
    <person><name>larry</name></person>
    <person><name>moe</name></person>
    <person><name>moe</name></person>
  </people>')
GO

-- literal result element and
-- constructor with curly braces
SELECT xml_col.query('
   for $b in //person
   where  $b/name="moe"
   return <li>{ string($b/name[1]) }</li>
 ') as query_for_moe
 FROM xml_tab
GO
```

This returns

```
query_for_moe
-------------


<li>moe</li>
<li>moe</li><li>moe</li>
```

This query also uses the XQuery string function, which leads us to talking about XQuery standard functions. We'll talk about XQuery standard functions and operators later in this chapter.

xml.nodes(string xquery-text)

The `xml.nodes` XML data type function produces a single-column rowset from the contents of an XML data type column or variable. This function takes an XQuery expression and produces zero or more rows that contain a single column that is an opaque reference to a special type of XML document. This reference is special because the context node for future XQuery functions is set at the node that matches the XQuery statement in the `xml.nodes` clause. This document must be used with other XQuery functions, like `query` or `value`, and can even be used as input to another `nodes` function.

Because `xml.nodes` produces a context node other than the root node, relative path expressions can be used with the resultant document reference. Because the column in the table produced by `xml.nodes` is of data type XML, you can use XML functions on it to extract pieces of its content. Here's a simple example that uses an XML variable containing a small document:

```
DECLARE @x XML
SET @x = '
<customers>
  <customer>
    <givenName>Jill</givenName><givenName>Rodgers</givenName>
    <country>US</country>
  </customer>
  <customer>
    <givenName>Juan</givenName><givenName>Rodriguez</givenName>
    <country>Costa Rica</country>
  </customer>
</customers>'
SELECT
  tab.col.value('givenName[1]', 'VARCHAR(20)') AS FirstName,
  tab.col.value('givenName[1]', 'VARCHAR(20)') AS GivenName,
  tab.col.value('country[1]', 'VARCHAR(20)') AS Country,
  tab.col.exist('country/text()[.="US"]') AS Local
FROM
@x.nodes('//customer') tab(col)
```

That produces this output:

```
LastName FirstName   Country      Local
---------------------------------------
Jill       Rodgers     US            1
Juan       Rodriguez   Costa Rica    0
```

Note that the table produced by `xml.nodes` must be aliased in the form `tablename(columnname)`. In this example, we call it `tab(col)` though the names themselves are irrelevant. Note also that the table produced by `xml.nodes` cannot be returned directly to the caller, because there isn't a good way to visualize what it contains.

If you use `xml.nodes` with an instance of a column in a table, the function must be used in conjunction with the CROSS APPLY or OUTER APPLY clause of a SELECT statement, because the table that contains the XML data type column must be part of the left side of an APPLY clause. Here's a simple example that shows its usage. Starting with the simple XML data type table of `people`,

```
CREATE TABLE xml_tab(
  the_id INTEGER PRIMARY KEY IDENTITY,
  xml_col XML)
GO

INSERT xml_tab
VALUES('<people><person><name>curly</name></person></people>')
INSERT xml_tab
VALUES('<people><person><name>larry</name></person></people>')
INSERT xml_tab
VALUES('<people><person><name>moe</name></person></people>')
INSERT xml_tab values('
  <people>
     <person><name>laurel</name></person>
     <person><name>hardy</name></person>
  </people>')
GO
```

we can use the `xml.nodes` method to extract a series of rows, one for each person's name:

```
xml_col.nodes('/people/person[1]') AS result(a)
```

This produces a four-row, one-column rowset of abstract document references (meaning that the entire document in the table-valued function does not take up the same amount of memory as the original document in the table), with each abstract document pointing at a different XML context node. Then we can use the `xml.value` function to extract values:[6]

```
SELECT the_id, tab.col.value('text()[1]', 'VARCHAR(20)') AS name
  FROM xml_tab
  CROSS APPLY
    xml_col.nodes('/people/person/name') AS tab(col)
```

This produces a rowset that looks like this:

```
the_id      name
-------     ---------
1           curly
2           larry
3           moe
4           laurel
4           hardy
```

---

6. For more information about the T-SQL CROSS APPLY operator, refer to Chapter 8.

Notice that we could not have produced the same result by using either the `xml.value` function or the `xml.query` function alone. The `xml.value` function would produce an error, because it needs to return a scalar value. The `xml.query` function would return only four rows, a single row for the "laurel and hardy" person.

There are a few interesting features to note about this syntax:

- The `xml.nodes` method produces a table, which must be given an alias in the form `tablename(columnname)`.

- The `xml.value` method on the left side of the CROSS APPLY keyword refers to the table and column from the `xml.nodes` method.

- The `xml.nodes` statement on the right side of the CROSS APPLY keyword refers to the `xml_col` column from the `xml_tab` table. The `xml_tab` table appears on the left side of the CROSS APPLY keyword.

- The SELECT statement can also refer to the other columns in the `xml_tab` table—in this case, the `the_id` column.

You could use OUTER APPLY instead of CROSS APPLY. In this case, because all the row values contain a matching <name> node, the result will be the same, but if we added a "nameless person" as follows,

```
INSERT xml_tab VALUES('<people><person></person></people>')
```

the CROSS APPLY version would produce five rows, and the OUTER APPLY version would produce six rows with the name as a NULL value. A similar condition occurs even if the part of the query that uses the `value` method against the `noderefs` returns NULL. Suppose that we look for a node in the `xml.value` portion (`l_name`) that doesn't exist in any of the `noderefs`:

```
SELECT the_id,
       tab.col.value('l_name[1]/text()[1]', 'varchar(20)') AS l_name
  FROM xml_tab
  CROSS APPLY
    xml_col.nodes('/people/person/name') AS tab(col)
```

CROSS APPLY still produces five rows, and OUTER APPLY produces six rows, all with NULL values for `l_name`.

Although the syntax for producing the table may seem strange at first, this equates to the second parameter in the `OpenXML` function, which also produces one row for each node selected by the expression in the second parameter. You use each reference node produced by the `xml.nodes` function as a starting node (context node) for the `XML` data type accessor functions `xml.query`, `xml.value`, `xml.nodes`, and `xml.exist`. These functions are used to produce additional columns in the final rowset, analogous to the `WITH` clause in `OpenXML`. When used in conjunction with the `XML` data type functions, the `xml.nodes` function is a less-memory-intensive version of `OpenXML`. It uses less memory because the table contains references to data in the `XML` data type column; we get similar results to using `OpenXML` without the overhead of having a DOM in memory.

XQuery Standard Functions and Operators

The XQuery standard includes two companion specifications that describe the data model and its standard functions and operators. These standards apply not only to XQuery, but also to XPath 2.0 and indirectly to XSLT 2.0, which uses XPath 2.0 as its query language. The first specification, "XQuery 1.0 and XPath 2.0 Data Model," lays the groundwork for both specifications and defines the data model as being based on the XML Information Set data model, with some extensions. It also describes functions that each XQuery processor should implement internally. Note that although these are described using functional notation, they are meant to be implemented inside the parser and should not be confused with the standard SQL function library. We discussed the data model in Chapter 9, along with its implementation in the SQL Server 2005 `XML` data type.

The second companion spec is more relevant to XQuery and XPath as query languages. It is called "XQuery 1.0 and XPath 2.0 Functions and Operators Version 1.0," and it describes a standard function library and a standard set of operators for XQuery engine implementers. This would be similar to the standard function library in SQL:1999. The XQuery engine in SQL Server 2005 implements some of the standard functions, concentrating on the ones that make the most sense for a database or where the functionality is similar to a T-SQL function.

The functions and operators are grouped in the spec according to the data type that they operate on or their relationship to other functions and operators. The complete list of groups is as follows:

- Accessors
- Error function
- Trace function
- Constructors
- Functions and operators on numerics
- Functions on strings
- Functions and operators on boolean values
- Functions and operators on durations, dates, and times
- Functions related to `QNames`
- Functions and operators for `anyURI`
- Functions and operators on `base64Binary` and `hexBinary`
- Functions and operators on `NOTATION`
- Functions and operators on nodes
- Functions and operators on sequences
- Context functions
- Casting

Some of these categories require further explanation.

Accessors get information about a specific node. Examples include `fn:node-kind`, `fn:node-name`, and `fn:data`, which obtain the kind of node, the `QName`, and the data type.

The error function is called whenever a nonstatic error (that is, an error at query execution time) occurs. It can also be invoked from XQuery or XPath applications and is similar to a .NET Framework exception. SQL Server 2005 XQuery does not implement this function.

Constructors are provided for every built-in data type in the XML Schema, Part 2, Datatypes, specification. These are similar to constructors in .NET Framework classes and may be used to create nodes dynamically at runtime.

Context functions can get information about the current execution context—that is, the document, node, and number of items in the current sequence being processed. These are similar to environment variables in a program or the current environment (SET variables) in a SQL query.

Casting functions are used to cast between different data types, similar to casting in a programming language, the CType function in Visual Basic .NET, or the CAST function in SQL:1999. A specific casting function is defined for each legal cast among the XML Schema primitive types.

SQL Server XQuery Functions and Operators

The SQL Server engine's implementation of XQuery provides a subset of the XQuery and XPath functions and operators. The functions that are implemented are listed in the sidebar "XQuery Functions Supported by SQL Server."

XQuery Functions Supported by SQL Server

Data Accessor Functions

```
string
data
```

Functions on Numeric Values

```
floor
ceiling
round
```

Functions on String Values

```
concat
contains
substring
string-length
```

Constructors and Functions on Booleans

```
not
```

Functions on Nodes

```
number
local-name
namespace-uri
```

Context Functions

```
position
last
```

Functions on Sequences

```
empty
id
distinct-values
```

Aggregate Functions

```
count
avg
min
max
sum
```

Functions Related to QNames

```
expanded-QName
local-name-from-QName
namespace-uri-from-QName
```

Constructor Functions

To create instances of any of the XSD types (except QName, xs:NMTOKEN, xs:NOTATION, xdt:yearMonthDuration, xdt:dayTimeDuration, and subtypes of xs:duration)

The sidebar "XQuery Operators Supported by SQL Server" lists all the operators supported by SQL Server 2005's implementation of XQuery.

XQuery Operators Supported by SQL Server

Numeric operators: +, -, *, div, mod

Value comparison operators: eq, ne, lt, gt, le, ge

General comparison operators: =, !=, <, >, <=, >=

Note also that although the specification defined that each function (including built-in functions) lives in a specific namespace, SQL Server's XQuery engine does not require the namespace prefix for the built-in functions.

In addition to the fact that not all the functions and operators are implemented, there are some usage limits. Some of the limits you might run into are

- Use of a positional variable with the for clause of FLWOR using the at keyword is not supported.
- The context functions (last and position) are allowed only in predicates.

- Queries and some functions (like the `data` function) are not allowed over constructed sequences.
- You cannot use an `ORDER BY` clause that compares multiple iterators.
- You cannot construct the name of an element or attribute using expressions.
- Some filter expressions are not allowed in path expressions.

Here are examples of some of these constructs:

```
(: A query over a constructed sequence :)
for $i in (for $j in //a return <row>{ $j }</row>)
return $i

(: A filter expression with a filter in a path expression :)
/a/b/attribute()
(: This is allowed :)
/a/b/@*

(: Using order by with multiple iterators :)
for $x in //a
for $y in //b
order by $x > $y
return $x, $y
```

SQL Server's implementation does not allow XQuery user-defined functions or modules, but some built-in extension functions permit using SQL variables and table data inside the XQuery statement. Let's look at them now.

SQL Server XQuery Extended Functions

Because the XQuery engine is executing in the context of a relational database, it is convenient to provide a standard way to use non-XML data (that is, relational data) inside the XQuery query itself. SQL Server provides two extension functions for exactly this purpose: `sql:column` and `sql:variable`. These keywords allow you to refer to relational columns in tables and T-SQL variables, respectively, from inside an XQuery query. Because an XQuery eventually uses the relational query processor with some XQuery-specific functions and optimizations, you can use the `sql:variable` XQuery function to parameterize your XQuery queries in a way similar to parameterizing SQL queries.

These functions can be used anywhere an XQuery query can be used—namely, `xml.exist`, `xml.value`, `xml.query`, and `xml.modify`. `xml.modify` is discussed in the next section.

The functions can refer to any SQL data type, with the following exceptions:

- The XML data type
- User-defined data types
- TIMESTAMP
- UNIQUEIDENTIFIER
- TEXT and NTEXT
- IMAGE

sql:column

This function refers to a column in the current row of the current SQL query. The column can be in the same table as the XML data type column, or it can be included in the result as part of a join. The table must be in the same database and owned by the same schema owner, and is specified using a two-part name in the format Tablename.Columnname Here's an example, using the table with name as a subelement that we've been using in the XQuery xml.nodes examples:

```
CREATE TABLE xml_tab(
   the_id INTEGER PRIMARY KEY IDENTITY,
   xml_col XML)
GO

INSERT xml_tab
VALUES('<people><person><name>curly</name></person></people>')
INSERT xml_tab
VALUES('<people><person><name>larry</name></person></people>')
INSERT xml_tab
VALUES('<people><person><name>moe</name></person></people>')

INSERT xml_tab VALUES(
  '<people>
     <person><name>curly</name></person>
     <person><name>larry</name></person>
     <person><name>moe</name></person>
     <person><name>moe</name></person>
  </people>')
GO
SELECT xml_col.query('
   for $b in //person
   where  $b/name="moe"
```

```
   return <li>{ $b/name/text() } in record number
          {sql:column("xml_tab.the_id")}</li>
')
FROM xml_tab
```

This returns the following result. (Note: The first two rows in the result are empty, and some extra whitespace appears between the word `number` and the value of the `id` field because of the way the query text is formatted.)

```
---------------------------------



<li>moe in record number 3</li>
<li>moe in record number 4</li><li>moe in record number 4</li>
```

sql:variable

The `sql:variable` function allows you to use any T-SQL variable that is in scope at the time the XQuery query is executed. This will be a single value for the entire query, as opposed to the `sql:column`, where the column value changes with every row of the result. This function is subject to the same data type limitations as `sql:column`. An example of using `sql:variable` in an XQuery query would look like this:

```
DECLARE @occupation VARCHAR(50)
SET @occupation = ' is a stooge'
SELECT xml_col.query('
   for $b in //person
   where $b/name="moe"
   return <li>{ $b/name/text() } { sql:variable("@occupation") }</li>
')
 FROM xml_tab
```

This statement uses the value of a T-SQL variable, `@occupation`, in the returned sequence in the XQuery query.

This returns the following result. (Note: The first two rows in the result are empty.)

```
----------------------------------------------------



<li>moe is a stooge</li>
<li>moe is a stooge</li><li>moe is a stooge</li>
```

Multiple-Document Query in SQL Server XQuery

As we saw in the XQuery specification discussion earlier in this chapter, queries can encompass more than one physical XML document by using the `doc` or `collection` function. In SQL Server's implementation of XQuery, however, the functions that allow input are not implemented. This is because the XQuery functions are implemented as instance functions that apply to a specific instance of the `XML` data type. Using the instance functions (`xml.query`, `xml.exist`, and `xml.value`), the XQuery query is a single document only. So what if you want to combine more than one document—the XQuery equivalent of a SQL `JOIN`?

One way to combine multiple documents to produce a single XQuery sequence as a result is to perform the query over each document separately and concatenate the results. This can be easily accomplished using the `SELECT...FOR XML...TYPE` syntax, although this is an `XML` data type instance subject to the `XML` data type size limit (at least 2GB). This may not always be what you want, however. Some multidocument queries are based on using one document to "join" another in a nested `for` loop. These types of queries cannot be accomplished by using sequence concatenation. Another way to accomplish multidocument queries is to use the `xml.query` function on different types, combined with the SQL `JOIN` syntax. This doesn't deal with the nested-tuple problem, either.

XML DML:[7] Updating XML Columns

The XQuery 1.0 specification does not currently include an XQuery syntax for mutating XML instances or documents in place. A data manipulation language (DML) is not planned for the first version of XQuery, but a working draft is under development. A working draft of the first specification in the series, "XQuery Update Facility Requirements," was released in April 2005.

---

7. Although technically, the word *DML* refers to data manipulation language and includes the SELECT statement in SQL, SQL Server 2005 Books Online uses this to refer to the XML data type mutator method, which does not include SELECT-like functionality.

Because SQL Server 2005 will use XQuery as the native mechanism for querying the XML data type inside the server, it is required to have some sort of manipulation language. The alternative would be replacing the instance of the XML data type only as an entire entity. Because changes to XML data type instances should participate in the current transaction context, this would be equivalent to using SELECT and INSERT in SQL without having a corresponding UPDATE statement. Therefore, SQL Server 2005 introduces an implementation of XML DML.

XML DML is implemented using XQuery-like syntax with SQL-like extensions. This emphasizes the fact that manipulating an XML instance inside SQL Server is equivalent to manipulating a complex type or, more accurately, a graph of complex types. You invoke XML DML by using the xml.modify mutator function on a single XML data type column, variable, or procedure parameter. You use XML DML within the context of a SQL SET statement, using either UPDATE...SET on an XML data type column or using SET on an XML variable or parameter. As a general rule, it would look like this:

```
-- change the value of XML data type column instance
-- note: the string 'some XML DML' is NOT valid XML DML
UPDATE some_table
  SET xml_col.modify('some XML DML')
  WHERE id = 1

-- change the value of an XML variable
DECLARE @x XML
-- initialize it
SET @x = '<some>initial XML</some>'
-- now, mutate it
-- in this case delete all of the some nodes at the root
SET @x.modify('delete /some')
```

As with the VARCHAR(MAX).WRITE mutator, attempting to call modify() on a NULL XML instance will cause a SQL exception. Note that this syntax is used only to modify the XML nodes contained in an existing instance of an XML data type. To change a value to or from NULL, you must use the normal XML data type construction syntax. With the xml.modify function, you can use XQuery syntax with the addition of three keywords: insert, delete, and replace value of. Only one of these keywords may be used in a single XML DML statement.

xml.modify('insert ...')

You use the XML DML `insert` statement to insert a single node or an ordered sequence of nodes into the XML data type instance as children or siblings of another node. The node or sequence to be inserted can be an XML or XQuery expression, as can the "target node" that defines the position of the insert. The general format of the `insert` statement is as follows,

```
insert
    Expression1
       {as first | as last} into | after | before
    Expression2
```

where `Expression1` is the node or sequence to be inserted and `Expression2` is the insert target. Any of the seven node types and sequences of those types may be inserted as long as they do not result in an instance that is malformed XML. Remember that well-formed document fragments are permitted in XML data types.

The keywords `as first`, `as last`, and `into` are used to specify inserting child nodes. Using the `into` keyword inserts the node or sequence specified in `Expression1` as a direct descendant, without regard for position. It usually is used to insert child nodes into an instance where no children currently exist. Using `as first` or `as last` ensures that the nodes will be inserted at the beginning or end of a sequence of siblings. These usually are used when you know that the node already contains child nodes. These keyword are ignored and do not cause an error when attribute nodes are being inserted. When processing-instruction or comment nodes are being inserted, "child" refers to the position in the document rather than a real parent–child relationship.

Let's start with an instance of an XML invoice and mutate the invoice. Here's our starting point:

```
-- declare XML variable and set its initial value
DECLARE @x xml
SET @x =
'<Invoice>
   <InvoiceID>1000</InvoiceID>
   <CustomerName>Jane Smith</CustomerName>
   <LineItems>
      <LineItem>
```

```
            <Sku>134</Sku>
            <Quantity>10</Quantity>
            <Description>Chicken Patties</Description>
            <UnitPrice>9.95</UnitPrice>
        </LineItem>
        <LineItem>
            <Sku>153</Sku>
            <Quantity>5</Quantity>
            <Description>Vanilla Ice Cream</Description>
            <UnitPrice>1.50</UnitPrice>
        </LineItem>
    </LineItems>
</Invoice>'
```

You could insert a new `InvoiceDate` element as a child of the `Invoice` element by using the following statement:

```
SET @x.modify('insert <InvoiceDate>2002-06-15</InvoiceDate>
              into /Invoice[1]')

SELECT @x
```

This statement would insert the `InvoiceDate` element as the last child of `Invoice`, after `LineItems`. To insert it as the first child of `Invoice`, simply change the statement to the following:

```
SET @x.modify('insert <InvoiceDate>2002-06-15</InvoiceDate>
              as first
              into /Invoice[1]')

SELECT @x
```

Here's an example of inserting an attribute, `status="backorder"`, on the `Invoice` element:

```
SET @x.modify('insert attribute status{"backorder"}
              into /Invoice[1]')

SELECT @x
```

Notice that this uses the constructor evaluation syntax (curly braces) to define the value of the attribute (`backorder`). You can also insert an entire series of elements using the `insert` statement. If you wanted to add a new `LineItem`, you would do the following:

```
SET @x.modify('insert
      (
      <LineItem>
         <Sku>154</Sku>
         <Quantity>20</Quantity>
         <Description>Chocolate Ice Cream</Description>
         <UnitPrice>1.50</UnitPrice>
      </LineItem>
       )
       into /Invoice[1]/LineItems[1]')
SELECT @x
```

The `after` and `before` keywords are used to insert siblings at the same level of hierarchy in the document. These keywords cannot be used in the same statement as `into`; this produces an error. It is also an error to use the `after` and `before` keywords when inserting attributes.

Following our earlier example, if you want to set the `InvoiceDate` at a specific position in the `Invoice` element's set of children, you need to use the `before` or `after` keyword and have an XPath expression that points to the appropriate sibling:

```
SET @x.modify('insert <InvoiceDate>2002-06-15</InvoiceDate>
  before /Invoice[1]/CustomerName[1]')

— this works too, and equates to the same position
SET @x.modify('insert <InvoiceDate>2002-06-15</InvoiceDate>
  after /Invoice[1]/InvoiceID[1]')
```

The key to understanding the `insert` statement is that although `Expression1` can be any of the seven node types and can contain multiple nodes in a sequence or even hierarchical XML, `Expression2` must evaluate to a single node. If `Expression2` evaluates to a sequence of nodes and no node, the `insert` statement will fail. In addition, `Expression2` cannot refer to a node that has been constructed earlier in the query; it must refer to a node in the original XML instance. This is what the variable looks like after all the previous modifications. Although `InvoiceDate` was used multiple times in multiple examples, we've chosen to show only the insert position from the last example (ignoring the first two examples, where `InvoiceDate` was inserted in a different position):

```
-- value in the variable @x after modifications
'<Invoice status="backorder">
   <InvoiceID>1000</InvoiceID>
   <InvoiceDate>2002-06-15</InvoiceDate>
   <CustomerName>Jane Smith</CustomerName>
   <LineItems>
      <LineItem>
         <Sku>134</Sku>
         <Quantity>10</Quantity>
         <Description>Chicken Patties</Description>
         <UnitPrice>9.95</UnitPrice>
      </LineItem>
      <LineItem>
         <Sku>153</Sku>
         <Quantity>5</Quantity>
         <Description>Vanilla Ice Cream</Description>
         <UnitPrice>1.50</UnitPrice>
      </LineItem>
      <LineItem>
         <Sku>154</Sku>
         <Quantity>20</Quantity>
         <Description>Chocolate Ice Cream</Description>
         <UnitPrice>1.50</UnitPrice>
      </LineItem>
   </LineItems>
</Invoice>'
go
```

xml.modify('delete . . .')

The `delete` XML DML command, as input to the `modify` function, deletes zero or more nodes that are identified by the output sequence of the XQuery query following the keyword `delete`. As in SQL, you can qualify the `delete` statement with a `where` clause. The general syntax of `delete` is

```
delete Expression
```

Each node returned by `Expression` is deleted. Returning a sequence of zero nodes just deletes zero nodes; it is not an error. As with the `insert` command, attempting to delete a constructed node (a node that was produced earlier in the query, rather than a node in the original document) will cause an error. Attempting to delete a value rather than a node will result in an error. Also, attempting to delete a metadata attribute, such as a namespace declaration, will result in an error. To delete all the `LineItem` elements in our example, you could execute the following statement:

```
SET @x.modify('delete /Invoice/LineItems/LineItem')
```

xml.modify('replace value of . . .')

Unlike a searched `UPDATE` in SQL and also unlike `xml.modify` (`'delete...'`), `xml.modify('replace value of...')` modifies the value of a single node. It is not a searched `UPDATE` that uses a `WHERE` clause to select a sequence of nodes. The general syntax for `replace value of` follows:

```
replace value of
    Expression1
with
    Expression2
```

`Expression1` must return a single node; if a sequence of zero nodes or multiple nodes is returned, an error is produced. Note that again, this is unlike a searched `UPDATE` statement in SQL, where returning zero rows to update is not an error. It is more similar to `UPDATE WHERE CURRENT OF` in SQL when using a cursor. `Expression1` is used to find the current node.

`Expression2` must be a sequence of atomic values. If it returns nodes, they are atomized. The sequence in `Expression2` completely replaces the node in `Expression1`. Here's an example that updates the `CustomerName` element's `text` child element from "Jane Smith" to "John Smith":

```
SET @x.modify('replace value of
        /Invoice[1]/CustomerName[1]/text()[1]
      to "John Smith"
       ')
```

General Conclusions and Best Practices

XML DML can be used to update portions of an XML data instance in place. The insert, update, and delete can be composed as part of a transaction. This is a unique ability for XML; although XML is often compared to databases and complex types, the usual pattern was to retrieve the XML, update the corresponding XML DOM (or, in .NET Framework's `XPathNavigator`), and then write the entire document back to the file system. XML DML treats

XML more like a complex type or a database and as similar to functionality found in XML-specific databases.

When you use XML DML to update a small piece of a large instance of an XML data type, it is a "sparse update" as far as the database is concerned—that is, usually, only the portion of the XML that is changed is actually updated in the database and written to the transaction log. In the best-case scenario, only the page containing the individual value replaced by a `replace value of` DML statement is logged. In the worst case, if you insert a node as the leftmost sibling of the root, most of the document may have to be logged.

There are a few general rules to remember when using XML DML:

- The nodes referenced by `modify` operations must be nodes in the original document.
- XML DML is not analogous to SQL DML. Although `insert` and `delete` are similar, position is all important. For SQL programmers, it is the equivalent of using an updatable cursor. Multiple `insert` or `replace value of` operations can be accomplished by invoking the `modify` function within a T-SQL loop, once for each node to be inserted/replaced.
- The resulting XML document or fragment cannot be malformed, or the `xml.modify` operation will fail.
- If the XML instance is validated by an XML schema, the `xml.modify` operation cannot interfere with schema validation.

Special Considerations When Using XQuery Inside SQL Server

XML Schemas and SQL Server 2005 XQuery

Unlike XPath 1.0, XPath 2.0 and XQuery 1.0 are strongly typed query languages. This is quite evident in the wide range of constructors and casting functions for different data types. The reasoning behind this is that XQuery is built to be optimized, and using strong types rather than using every element and attribute as type `string` or inferring/converting between types allows the query engine to do a better job of optimizing and executing the query. Imagine that the T-SQL query parser had to infer the coercion of every piece of data or deal with everything as a single data type!

Every XML data type column, XML variable, and XML procedure parameter can be strongly typed by reference to an XML schema or can be untyped. When typed XML is used in an XQuery, the query parser has more information to work with, and this prevents unnecessary type conversions. If untyped XML is used, the query engine must start with the premise that every piece of data is type string; infer the data type required by the query, based on the rules of the language; and convert to the appropriate type. As an example, the following query

```
SELECT invoice_id  FROM xml_invoice
WHERE invoice.value('sum(//amount)', 'decimal(9,2)') > 150.00
```

must convert amount element content to decimal before doing the summarization if the XML column named invoice is untyped. When this XQuery is integrated into the relational query plan, this is the equivalent of a non-SARGable query (a query in SQL that doesn't use a search argument)—that is, it can't use indexes on the content, if you've created them, because each value must be converted first by using a type conversion function. This is one instance where the effect of having a typed column is observable.

XQuery supports static type checking, meaning that every expression will be checked at parse time. In addition, strong typing permits the XQuery language to syntax-check the input based on types at parse time, as T-SQL can, so fewer runtime errors occur. XQuery also allows the query processor to reorder the queries; although this is a performance optimization, this could lead to runtime errors on occasion.

You've seen a very noticeable example of SQL Server XQuery's static type checking in almost all the example queries in this chapter. In these queries, whenever a function or return value requires a singleton, we must use the [1] subscript to ensure that it's really a singleton; otherwise, a parse-time error results. Almost all other XQuery processors (without static type checking) will execute the query and produce a runtime error if the value is not actually a singleton. If we had a strongly typed XML column instead, in which the schema defined the elements we're referring to as maxOccurs=1 minOccurs=1 (the default), a query without the subscript would succeed, because the parser "knows" that the element in question is a singleton. Having a schema-validated column permits you to do the type checking at column insert/update time, rather than take the extra measure of requiring a subscript to enforce it at XQuery parse time.

Even though the XML instance that is input to an XML function can be typed or untyped, remember that the result of an `xml.query` function is always an untyped XML instance. Typed XML should always be used, if possible, to give the XQuery engine a chance to use its knowledge of the data type involved. This also makes the resulting query run faster, as well as producing more accurate results and fewer runtime errors.

XML Indexes Usage in XQuery

As we mentioned in Chapter 9, you can create four different types of XML indexes on the XML data type, these are used to speed XQuery processing. The index types are:

- `XML PRIMARY INDEX`—that is, node table and its associated clustered index
- PATH index
- PROPERTY index
- VALUE index

The `PRIMARY XML INDEX` is almost always useful when you're using the XQuery functions; the three possible secondary indexes are useful for different types of queries. A key point to remember is that when the query processor evaluates the SQL query, it uses the SQL (relational) query engine. This applies to the XML portion of the query as well as the SQL portion. Because the same query processor is used for the entire query, the query produces a single query plan, as SQL queries always do. And that's where indexes come in.

Data in an `XML` data type column is always stored in a special binary format. Although the query engine could work by fetching the entire BLOB into an internal buffer and processing the content, SQL Server benefits by having as little data in memory as possible at a given time. That's where the node table and indexes come in. The node table is an alternative representation, similar in concept to a materialized view, of the XML document. It contains 12 columns; the primary XML index actually refers to an index over a column in the node table and the primary key of the base table. Table 10-1 lists the columns in the node table.

TABLE 10-1: Columns in the Node Table

Column Name	Column Description	DataType
id	node identifier in ordpath format	varbinary(900)
nid	node name (tokenized)	int
tagname	tag name	nvarchar(4000)
taguri	tag uri	nvarchar(4000)
tid	node data type (tokenized)	int
value	first portion of the node value	sql_variant
lvalue	long node value (pointer)	nvarchar(max)
lvaluebin	long node value in binary (pointer)	varbinary(max)
hid	path (tokenized)	varchar(900)
xsinil	is it NULL (xsi:nil)	bit
xsitype	does it use xsi:type	bit
pk1	primary key of the base table	int

The PRIMARY XML INDEX is a relational index on the columns pk1 and id. The three other indexes are indexes on other columns in the node table. For more information about XML Indexes, reference the paper "XQuery Indexes in a Relational Database System," by Shankar Pal, et al., at http://www.vldb2005.org/program/paper/thu/p1175-pal.pdf.

The execution plan of a SQL query that uses XQuery inside the XML data type functions looks for the most part like a "normal" relational execution plan. There are a few XML-specific operations, but one of the indexes is almost always used if they exist. Just as in SQL, different types of indexes are useful for different styles of XML queries.

XML PATH index is useful for indexes involving paths. It may not always be the index selected for every expression involving a path (most XQuery queries will use at least one path expression), but the XML PATH index is

useful when you're using explicit paths (no // in the path) and most useful when the XML is highly nested and the path is long.

XML VALUE index is useful when you are using inexact paths (// somewhere in the path) or attribute wildcards (@*) or if your values are different in each text node. Having many different values (rather than some
repeating values) would make the XML VALUE index highly selective.

XML PROPERTY index is most useful when you are using many XML
data type methods (that use XQuery) in the same SQL expression, and
each function selects a different property from the same set of XML
instances. Remember that the entire SQL query (which may contain multiple XML data type methods) is evaluated and optimized into a single
query plan. Another use for XML PROPERTY index is when the data is semistructured, and the same values and elements may appear at different levels of hierarchy.

The PRIMARY XML INDEX is the fallback index; it's used if none of the
other indexes is selective enough. The SQL query engine will look at the statistics distributions for an XQuery index just as it will with a SQL index.
This is totally unrelated to the XQuery (or SQL) static type checking, so that
the general order of events, given a SQL query with one or more XML data
type methods using XQuery, is

1. Static analysis and object resolution of the SQL query
2. Static type checking of all XQuery code in XML data type functions
3. Consultation of node table and other SQL table statistics to choose
   the optimum overall query plan

For more information on XQuery in SQL query plans, consult the
paper "XML Indexes in SQL Server 2005," by Bob Beauchemin, at
http://msdn.microsoft.com/library/default.asp?url=/library/en-
us/dnsql90/html/xmlindexes.asp.

Early SQL parsers were unoptimized; this was one of the reasons that
early relational databases ran slowly. The performance improvement in
relational databases since their inception is due, in no small way, to the optimization of SQL query processors, including static type analysis as well as
to other, physical optimizations, such as types of indexes. With an XML data
type, indexing and strong typing through XML schemas, and a query

language that allows optimizations based on strong typing, XQuery users will most likely experience the same improvements in performance as the data type and query language mature. Programmers (and especially data center managers) like the idea of the same code running faster as vendors improve their parser engines, with minimal changes to the query code itself.

Where Are We?

SQL Server 2005 not only introduces XML as a new scalar data type, but also introduces a query language and a data manipulation language to operate on it. The query language selected for operation inside SQL Server is XQuery, a new query language that is still in standardization. (At this writing, XQuery is in W3C Working Draft at Candidate Recommendation status.) The XQuery implementation inside the database makes some simplifications and optimizations when compared with the entire specification. The subsetting is done to allow the queries to be optimizable and fast. This is a goal of XQuery itself, although the specification does not define implementable subsets.

Because XQuery does not specify a data manipulation language, SQL Server provides a proprietary language that uses XQuery expressions to produce sequences to mutate, known as XML DML. The standardization of XML DML is being considered, because every implementation by relational or XML database vendors is different. This is reminiscent of the early days of SQL.

◼ 11 ◼
SQL Server Service Broker

S QL SERVER SERVICE BROKER (SSB) is part of SQL Server and is used to build reliable, scalable, asynchronous, distributed data applications. With Service Broker, the developers of these applications can concentrate their efforts on the issues of the problem space in which they are going to be applied. The system-level details of implementing a messaging application are delegated to Service Broker itself.

Messaging Applications

Messaging applications are nothing new. Almost all large-scale enterprise applications use at least some messaging infrastructure. In general, messaging applications take a different approach from applications based on calling functions that return a result. When you use a message-based application, you send it a message and go on about your business. If you care, you might check some time later to see what, if any, effect the message you sent had, or you might become the recipient of a message that informs you of the status or effect of your message.

The technique of "send a message and go on about your business" has been around for a really long time. It used to be that you would walk to the computer-center window and drop off a message in the form of a tray of punch cards or magnetic tapes. A few hours later, you would check back at the window and probably receive a message in the form of a printout. Even today, many applications work by sending a file to a well-known network share and then check back later to see whether the file has been processed.

The "send a message and go on about your business" technique is the core of Service Broker for the same reason that it was used in providing computing services: It decouples the use of system resources from the overhead of allocating them.

Let's do a quick thought experiment with the computer-center window that works the way applications that call a function and get a result work. Imagine that you go to the window after waiting in line for quite a while and hand your magnetic tape to the operator, who mounts it, runs your job, dismounts the tape, gets your printout and hands it to you, and then does that all over again for the next person in line. The usage of the computer center grows at some point to where the line of people waiting to hand the operator their jobs just keeps getting longer and longer. Adding another computer to the computer center won't do any good, because the operator runs just one job at a time. The problem with this way of running the computer-center window is that the allocation of the resource—the computer system—is tightly coupled to its use.

Even applications that are not message based often have some message-based aspects to them. A simple example of this is an application that runs once a day and processes all the files in a particular directory. Messaging has been the original model for processing business data ever since there have been modern businesses. The interoffice mailing envelope used to send forms from one clerk to another for processing is an example. Over time, this was updated to send boxes of punch cards from one office to another, and then magnetic tapes. Now we send messages to services over networks. Services have replaced clerks, and messages have replaced forms, but the basic model and the applicability of decoupling data from the resources used to process it haven't changed.

Two of the compelling features for using message-based services—and interoffice envelopes and forms, for that matter—are deferred processing and distributed processing. They are compelling because real-life business applications implicitly depend on these features:

- Deferred processing—It may not be possible, or even desirable, to perform all the work associated with a particular task at one time. A work order submitted to fix a piece of broken equipment can't be fully processed until a work crew is assigned to it, has gone to the site of the equipment, fixed it, and then reported back. In fact, when the work order is received, the only thing it might make sense to do is to assign an order number to it and wait until the end of the day to assign a work crew to it, so that the assignment of work crews can be optimized over all the work orders.

- Distributed processing—The work associated with a task must be completed in a timely manner. Often, however, it is quite difficult to predict how many tasks there will be at a given time and how many resources each will take to be completed. Distributed systems allow processing resources to be applied where they are needed and to be expanded incrementally without changing the applications that use them.

Service Broker is a framework that manages the deferred processing of business tasks and allows system administrators to apply the resources in a distributed system so that the application can be developed as though all the resources it needs are available to it at all times. Deferred and distributed processing are compelling because they allow the development of an application to concentrate on the application's problem domain and decouple it from the system details.

Figure 11-1 diagrams the typical process followed to fix a piece of broken equipment. A large company has its facilities spread out over several buildings that are known by their nicknames: Building 5, Parker Street, and

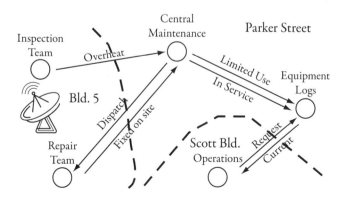

Figure 11-1: Business transaction

the Scott Building. An equipment inspector in Building 5 finds that a satellite link is overheating. The inspector in Building 5 and sends a work order to Central Maintenance at the Parker Street building, requesting that the satellite link be repaired. At that point, the inspector immediately goes on to check other equipment; the inspector does not need to wait for a response from Central Maintenance. At the end of the day, the inspector might check to see whether the message he sent was processed.

The Parker Street building maintains all the equipment logs that keep track of the status of equipment. Central Maintenance immediately updates the logs to show that the use of the satellite link in Building 5 is limited because of equipment problems. This isn't an emergency as long as the rest of the company knows that the use of the satellite link is limited. Later, in the evening, Central Maintenance prepares the next day's work assignments for the repair teams. The next morning, it sends a work assignment to one of the repair teams on site at Building 5 to fix the satellite link.

Later that day, the repair team in Building 5 sends a completed work assignment to Central Maintenance that says the satellite link is fully operational. When Central Maintenance receives this message, it updates its equipment logs to show that the satellite link is fully operational again.

While all this was going on, the Operations group in the Scott Building was checking to see whether the satellite link in Building 5 is fully operational so they could use it instead of going to an outside vendor for the service.

Figure 11-1 shows a business process for fixing things that are broken that has been used in various forms since before computers, though the satellite link might be a bit of an anachronism. Forms, interoffice mail, and log books were used to implement the process. Each of the circles in Figure 11-1 would be a clerk who processed forms sent by interoffice mail. An equipment log would be a book or maybe a box of forms with current equipment status. Note that in its heyday, interoffice mail was being picked up and delivered hourly or even more often for critical operations like these.

The work order process shown in Figure 11-1 could be implemented in many ways today, of course. The "in" thing today would be to make the Central Maintenance, Equipment Logs, and Operations circles in Figure 11-1 Web Services and have the Inspection and Repair Team circles use Web applications to access them.

Web Services, queuing technologies, DCOM (Microsoft's distributed component object model), or any of several other technologies provide reasonably straightforward ways of moving messages between services. What they don't provide, but Service Broker does, is a straightforward way to manage deferred and distributed processing.

"Wait a second," you might say. "Isn't a queue the archetype for deferred processing and distributed systems?" Well, yes and no. The devil is in the "straightforward way to manage" details.

Almost certainly, any of these implementations would involve databases. Central Maintenance would keep track of work orders and equipment status in databases. The Operations group would also have kept track of its ongoing projects in a database. Even today, though, it's quite possible that the Inspection and Repair teams might still be running on paper and wouldn't have their own databases, but just use file-based applications to keep track of what they are doing. But in the end, the messages they send to Central Maintenance are used to update data in some databases.

The first step on the road to understanding what Service Broker brings to the table is the fact that virtually all business applications use databases, though possibly indirectly. Queuing technologies, DCOM, and so on end up acting as an intermediary between databases. In simplest terms, Service Broker cuts out the intermediaries and lets databases talk directly to one another.

Does this mean that Server Broker replaces all these other technologies? If all business operations could be reduced to the simple kind of diagram shown in Figure 11-1, the answer would be yes. But real-life business applications are much larger and have many more requirements to meet than that diagram implies, so the answer is no. Service Broker probably will be the best choice, however, for those operations that require deferred processing among databases located on different machines. Let's start by looking at what Service Broker actually can do so you can decide on its applicability to your enterprise.

To get things started, we will send a message from the Inspection Team to Central Maintenance. Before we can do anything, we need a database to work with, so we will create one and name it `Company`. We should make sure that the database has a master key. A `CREATE MASTER KEY WITH ENCRYPTION BY PASSWORD = 'P@ssw0rd'` expression while `Company` is the database in use will do this. Chapter 6 discusses keys in more detail.

In Service Broker, messages are sent only from one service to another. A *service* is a new kind of database object that is created by the CREATE SERVICE statement. Every service must be associated with a queue. A *queue* is another new kind of database object created by a CREATE QUEUE statement. Messages sent to a service are stored in a queue associated with a service until they are processed.

Figure 11-2 shows the InspectionQueue being created (1) and then the InspectionService being created (2) and associated with the InspectionQueue. Messages sent to the InspectionService will be stored in the InspectionQueue.

The metadata for services, queues, and other Service Broker objects can be seen in system views in the database they were created in; sys.services and sys.service_queues are the views used to see the metadata associated with service and queues. Figure 11-3 shows a query that joins sys.services (1) with sys.service_queues (2). The service we created previously and its associated queue (3) are shown in the results. Note also that some other services are shown in the results. The Event and Query Notification features of SQL Server 2005 are implemented using Service Broker.

Service Broker handles messaging a bit differently from many other messaging frameworks. The primary messaging construct in Service Broker is not a message; it is a conversation. The BEGIN DIALOG CONVERSATION statement is used to initiate a conversation between two services. As the name implies, messages between services are sent via a conversation. Conversations are not meant to be used as static paths between services, though they could be viewed that way. Typically, a conversation is created for a particular task; then, when it is no longer needed, it is ended using the END CONVERSATION statement. In typical usage, there may be many simultaneous conversations between a given pair of services.

A message in Service Broker is a sequence of bytes. The size of a message is limited to 2GB. These bytes might be bitmaps, text encoded as bytes, or

FIGURE 11-2: Creating InspectionService

```
  SELECT S.name AS Service, Q.name AS Queue
① FROM sys.services AS S
② JOIN sys.service_queues AS Q
  ON Q.object_id = S.service_queue_id
```

	Service	Queue
1 ③	InspectionService	InspectionQueue
2	http://schemas.microsoft.com/SQL/Notifications/Eve...	EventNotificationErrorsQueue
3	http://schemas.microsoft.com/SQL/Notifications/Qu...	QueryNotificationErrorsQueue
4	http://schemas.microsoft.com/SQL/ServiceBroker/S...	ServiceBrokerQueue

FIGURE 11-3: Services and queues metadata

anything else that can be represented as a stream of bytes. Service Broker provides some extra capabilities when the bytes represent XML documents. In general, XML is the preferred way to send text, because it eliminates the need for the service at one end of the conversation to know what text encoding was used by the service at the other end of the conversation. Note that the encoding and collation used in XML are independent of any configuration setting in SQL Server 2005. Chapter 9 covers the XML data type, which is how Service Broker manages XML.

Figure 11-4 shows a Transact-SQL (T-SQL) batch that builds a conversation from the Inspection service to the Central Maintenance service. Each end of a conversation is identified by its conversation handle, which is a UNIQUEIDENTIFIER. In SQL Server, a UNIQUEIDENTIFIER is a globally unique identifier (GUID). Note that a GUID is just a 128-bit number that is generated by a randomizing algorithm.

The BEGIN DIALOG CONVERSATION expression (1) builds a conversation between a "from" and a "to" service. Every conversation has two endpoints,

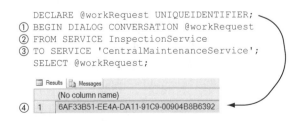

```
  DECLARE @workRequest UNIQUEIDENTIFIER;
① BEGIN DIALOG CONVERSATION @workRequest
② FROM SERVICE InspectionService
③ TO SERVICE 'CentralMaintenanceService';
  SELECT @workRequest;
```

	(No column name)
④ 1	6AF33B51-EE4A-DA11-91C9-00904B8B6392

FIGURE 11-4: BEGIN DIALOG CONVERSATION

each identified by a conversation handle. One endpoint is attached to the "from" service. and the other is attached to the "to" service. The conversation handle for one endpoint of a conversation is used to send a message to the service attached to the other endpoint of the conversation.

BEGIN DIALOG CONVERSATION puts the conversation handle for the endpoint of the conversation attached to the "from" service into the variable that follows it; in this batch, that is @workRequest (4). Later, we will see where the conversation handle for the "to" endpoint is found and used.

The FROM SERVICE phrase (2) identifies the "from" service at one end of the conversation. Services do not have multipart names. The service identified InspectionService in this batch must already exist in the database in use.

The name of a service is stored as an NVARCHAR(128), but regardless of how collation is configured in the server, the name of a service is always case sensitive. Compares to and lookups of services are done with the exact bytes in the name of the service, not the characters. As we will see later, the name of a service may be passed between instances of SQL Server 2005. Byte-by-byte comparison of service names eliminates the need for one instance of SQL Server 2005 to know the collation of another instance of SQL Server 2005.

The TO SERVICE clause (3) in Figure 11-4 identifies the service at the other end of the conversation. At this point, you might think that the batch shown in Figure 11-4 would produce an error if it were run, because we have not yet created the CentralMaintenanceService, let alone identified its location. It is easy to think of a distributed application as being distributed in space; after all, the whole point of a distributed system is that it is spread out over many locations.

But distributed systems, like all real systems, are also distributed in time. The way a system looks today is not necessarily the way it will look a month from now, when a new office is added or a new server comes online. Service Broker does not expect a TO SERVICE to be in existence at the time a conversation is started or even, as we will see shortly, accessible when a message is sent to it. This is why the TO SERVICE name is a literal string—that is, in quotes. This makes it much easier to roll out or reconfigure a system because you do not have to synchronize perfectly the changes in all parts of the system. It is possible, of course, that the "other" system will never exist or is in error, but later in this chapter, we will look at several techniques an application can use to detect this.

Each database in an instance of SQL Server 2005 keeps track of the conversation endpoints associated with the services in that database. The sys.conversation_endpoints view, as shown in Figure 11-5, lists the conversations in the Company database. There is only one: the one we created in Figure 11-4.

The SEND ON CONVERSATION statement (2) shown in Figure 11-6 sends a message. Messages are sent "on" the conversation handle that follows the ON CONVERSATION phrase—in this example, @workRequest. The message will be put into the queue of the service at the other end of the conversation. At this point, of course, the service at the other end of the conversation does not exist, but we will get to that soon.

A SEND expression is required either to be the first statement in a batch or to be separated from the previous statement with a semicolon. Notice that the SET statement (1) in Figure 11-6 is terminated with a semi-colon.

Typically, the first message sent on a conversation is sent immediately after the BEGIN DIALOG CONVERSATION expression, but we have built the conversation in a different batch. The @workRequest variable (1) in Figure 11-6 is set with the conversation handle we found in Figure 11-5. This is an example; in typical usage, it is unlikely that you would want to hard-code a conversation handle.

The message itself (3) in the batch in Figure 11-6 is enclosed in parentheses after the conversation handle and must be of data type VARBINARY(MAX), but a string or XML will automatically be converted to VARBINARY(MAX).

Note that the message we are sending is an ASCII string that has been converted to VARBINARY (MAX). We could have chosen to send a Unicode string by using the N prefix on the literal string. As long as the other end of the

```
select conversation_handle
from Company.sys.conversation_endpoints
```

FIGURE 11-5: Conversation endpoints

```
   DECLARE @workRequest UNIQUEIDENTIFIER;
①  SET @workRequest =
        '6AF33B51-EE4A-DA11-91C9-00904B8B6392';
②  SEND ON CONVERSATION @workRequest
③     ('<WorkRequest>
       <Equipment>2-37-BK</Equipment>
       <Reason>Overheat</Reason>
       </WorkRequest>'
       );
```

FIGURE 11-6: Sending message

conversation interprets the VARBINARY(MAX) byte stream it receives as XML, we need not worry about how the string is encoded, because XML can always detect and properly interpret the encoding of a stream of bytes. There are some caveats to this, but none is of any significance for SQL Server 2005.

We still are playing a bit fast and loose with the way we are moving data from one service to another without defining what it should look like, but only to keep this example as simple as possible. Later, we will see that we can define MESSAGE TYPEs and CONTRACTs to put much tighter constraints on the formats of messages sent between services.

The batch in Figure 11-6 appears to be like the one in Figure 11-4, in that it seems like it should not work because the service at the other end of the conversation, CentralMaintenanceService, does not exist. Whenever a message is sent to a service that cannot be found, or that can be found but exists on a different instance of SQL Server 2005, the message is sent to the transmission queue in the database of the service that tries to send the message. This is an important feature, because it means that Service Broker does not depend on having connections available when messages are sent.

The transmission queue is visible through the sys.transmission_queue system view in the database of the "from" service of the conversation. The SELECT expression (1) shown in Figure 11-7 shows that the transmission queue is holding a message that was sent from InspectionService to CentralMaintenanceService (2) because CentralMaintenance Service could not be found.

Note that when the system does not seem to be behaving properly, you might consider running as a diagnostic a job that checks the transmission queue to see whether it is unduly full.

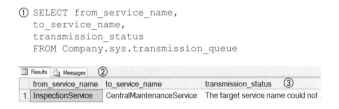

```
① SELECT from_service_name,
   to_service_name,
   transmission_status
   FROM Company.sys.transmission_queue
```

from_service_name	to_service_name	transmission_status ③
1. InspectionService	CentralMaintenanceService	The target service name could not .

FIGURE 11-7: Contents of sys.transmission_queue

Internally, a Service Broker queue is a table, but it is handled in a special way. A SELECT expression can be used to look at the content of a queue, and a new kind of expression in SQL Server 2005, the RECEIVE expression, can be used to take things out of a queue. Even though a queue is internally a table, using INSERT, UPDATE, or DELETE on one will raise an error. Note that sys.transmission_queue is a queue in the architectural sense, but it was not created using CREATE QUEUE and may not be used to RECEIVE expressions.

So even though there is no CentralMaintenanceService, at least Service Broker hasn't lost our message, but it didn't tell us that the TO SERVICE wasn't there either. Let's think again about what would happen if a SEND expression raised an error when it could not find the TO SERVICE. If you ran a batch to SEND a message, and it raised an error saying that it couldn't find the TO SERVICE, what would you do? You probably would retry the SEND. After all, it may have failed due to some sort of intermittent network issue.

Service Broker has a built-in algorithm for retrying anything that is in the sys.transmission_queue. If the transmission to the TO SERVICE fails, it will try it again in about 4 seconds and then again about 8 seconds after that. It will keep on doubling the time intervals between attempts to transmit the message until the interval becomes about 60 seconds. Then it will continue to retry once a minute until you stop it. Service Broker will never lose a message and never stop you from sending one.

Now we will add the Central Maintenance service and see what happens to the message stored in sys.transmission_queue. Figure 11-8 shows a batch to make the Central Maintenance service. It is almost the same as the one that we used to make the Inspection service. First, we create the CentralMaintenanceQueue (1). Then we create the CentralMaintenance Service (2) on that queue.

```
① CREATE QUEUE CentralMaintenanceQueue

② CREATE SERVICE CentralMaintenanceService
   ON QUEUE CentralMaintenanceQueue
③ ([DEFAULT])
```

FIGURE 11-8: CentralMaintenanceService

The difference for CentralMaintenanceService is that a service that is used as the TO SERVICE in a BEGIN DIALOG CONVERSATION expression must specify the format of the messages it is willing to accept. The messages a service is willing to accept are specified in a CONTRACT. We will look at the details of using CONTRACTs later in this chapter, but for now, we will use the built-in DEFAULT CONTRACT which says in effect that the service will accept any sequence of bytes as a message. Technically, it says that it will accept messages of the DEFAULT type, but we will cover message types when we get to CONTRACTs.

In Figure 11-8, the name of the contract (3) is in parentheses just after the name of the queue associated with the service. The CentralMaintenance Service accepts messages that comply with the DEFAULT contract—that is, any message of the DEFAULT type. Note that the name of the contract is in square brackets, because DEFAULT is a keyword in T-SQL and DEFAULT happens to be the name of the contract that CentralMaintenance Service uses.

It won't happen right away, but eventually, Service Broker will try to send the message in the transmission queue for CentralMaintenance Service as part of the retry algorithm explained earlier in this chapter, and it will be successful. A message sent to a service is put into the queue associated with that service. One of the columns of a queue is the message_body column, which is of type VARBINARY(MAX) and contains the actual message. The query in Figure 11-9 casts the message_body (1) from the CentralMaintenanceQueue (3) as XML. The results (3) show the message that was sent to the CentralMaintenanceService by the InspectionService.

One of the often-unrecognized values of XML is that the encoding of its text is embedded in the XML itself. This means that the recipient of an XML-based message never needs to be told what the encoding is. If, however,

```
① SELECT CAST(message_body as XML)
   AS Message
② FROM CentralMaintenanceQueue
```

Results | Messages

Message
③ 1 | `<WorkRequest><Equipment>2-37-BK</Equipment><Reason>Overheat</F`

FIGURE 11-9: CentralMaintenanceQueue

the message body is one of the character types from SQL Server 2005—that is, CHAR, NCHAR, VARCHAR, or NVARCHAR—there is no way for the recipient of the message to know how to cast the message body to read it. This means that enterprisewide conventions, configuration messages, or some other means will have to be used and maintained so that recipients of character-based messages will know how to cast them to turn them back into characters.

On the other hand, always using XML for text messages, even when they don't need the structure that can be added by XML, means that the recipient of the message need not know what the SQL Server 2005 character type is or, in the case of CHAR and VARCHAR, what code page was used in that message. Figure 11-10 shows the kind of error that can occur when the recipient of a message chooses to cast it to the wrong character type. Note that the example in Figure 11-9 did not need to know anything about the encoding of the message to turn it into text.

Service Broker is used to build distributed system, and using XML for all text messages means that one system will not have to tell other systems what encoding or code page to use to read the messages it sends. That information will be part of the XML itself.

```
① SELECT CAST(message_body as NVARCHAR(MAX))
   AS Message
   FROM CentralMaintenanceQueue
```

Results | Messages

Message
② 1 |

FIGURE 11-10: NVARCHAR(MAX) message_body

Processing Messages

We have seen that we can send messages from one service to another and not have to worry very much about intermittent faults or whether the service has been configured yet. The next thing to do is process the message. The act of processing a single message is fairly straightforward, and we will do that now to illustrate the syntax and operation of the RECEIVE expression and the typical way it is used.

But before we write the code to process the message, we should define the processing requirement for it. To keep things simple, we will do two things: move the message into a table that keeps track of pending work orders, and send a message back to the sender with a timestamp added to it so the sender will know when the work order was processed.

We do not need to design a proper database just to show how messages are processed, so the pending work table will have just a single XML column to store messages. A simple CREATE TABLE PendingWork (work XML) is sufficient for our example.

Syntactically, RECEIVE is the similar to SELECT in that it has a list of columns, a FROM clause, and an optional WHERE predicate. Like a SELECT statement, it can also use a TOP expression to limit the number of rows returned. The FROM clause of a RECEIVE must specify a queue. It cannot be used with a table.

The columns the RECEIVE specifies come from a queue. A queue has 15 columns, but 4 are enough to do simple message processing, conversation_ group_id, conversation_handle, message_body, and message_type columns. This example will use only two of them, but all the columns are documented in Books Online. We will make use of the other columns in later examples.

Figure 11-11 shows a batch that processes a single message from the CentralMaintenanceQueue. The first thing to note is that the RECEIVE expression and the processing of the message are run under a common transaction (1). This is not necessary, but processing of messages is typically done this way. Queues are transactional; after all, they are tables. This batch is not doing any error checking, which it should, but doing so would not keep the example as simple. If the batch did detect an error, it could roll back the transaction, which would put the message back into the queue so that the message could be processed later.

```
① BEGIN TRAN
   DECLARE @message XML;
② DECLARE @conv UNIQUEIDENTIFIER;
   DECLARE @ts VARCHAR(MAX);
   SET @ts = CAST(GETDATE() AS VARCHAR(MAX));
③ RECEIVE TOP (1)
       @message = CAST(message_body AS XML),
       @conv = conversation_handle
       FROM CentralMaintenanceQueue;
   IF @@ROWCOUNT = 1
   BEGIN
④ SET @message.modify('insert (
       attribute received{sql:variable(''@ts'')}
       ) into (/*[1])');
⑤ SEND ON CONVERSATION @conv
       (@message)
       INSERT INTO PendingWork VALUES (@message)
   END
   COMMIT TRAN
```

FIGURE 11-11: Receiving a single message

The two columns of interest for this batch are the `message_body` and `conversation_handle` columns. The `message_body` is, of course, the message itself, and it is captured by the `@message` variable. The conversation handle is for the endpoint of the conversation that is attached to the `CentralMaintenanceService`.

The conversation handle is captured in the `@conv` variable (2) and is later used to send a reply (5) to the sender of the message the batch is processing. This is an important feature of Service Broker; the batch that processes a message does not need to know the identity or location of the service that sent the message it's processing to send a reply to that service.

The batch in Figure 11-11 reads the message out of the `CentralMaintenanceQueue` using a `RECEIVE` statement (3). Service Broker guarantees that messages that are sent on a given conservation will be received exactly once and received in the order in which they were sent. Note that this guarantee applies only to messages within a given conversation, not across multiple conversations.

A `RECEIVE` is also similar to a `SELECT` in that it sets the `@@ROWCOUNT` variable with the number of rows received. The `RECEIVE` expression, as it is written in this batch, will return immediately with `@@ROWCOUNT = 0` if the queue is empty.

A timestamp is applied to the message when it is received. The @ts variable in the batch contains the current time as a string. The XQuery modify
function is applied to the @message variable to insert a "received" attribute
into the document element of the message. See Chapter 9 for details on
using the XML data type and XQuery in SQL Server 2005. In brief, the /*
always means the documents element of an XML document—that is, the
first element in the document, which is sometimes called the root element.
The insert attribute in the modify function says to add the timestamp as an
attribute named 'received' to this element.

After the message has a timestamp, it is sent (5) as a reply back to its
sender; last, the message itself is inserted into the PendingWork table.

We can see the results of the batch from Figure 11-11 in Figure 11-12.
The InspectionQueue (1) has the original message with a timestamp in it.
The message appeared in the InspectionQueue because the Central-
MaintenanceService sent a reply to the message sent by the Inspection
Service.

The conversation_handle for the message is the same one that was originally used to send the message from InspectionService to Central-
MaintenanceService in Figure 11-6 and can be used to correlate messages
if need be. Note that the conversation_handle identifies the endpoint of a
conversation, not the conversation itself. Each endpoint of a conversation
has a different conversation_handle. The PendingWork (2) table also has
the message that was inserted into it.

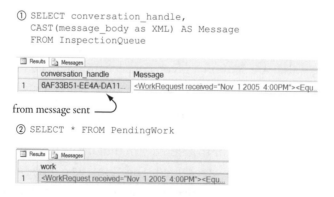

FIGURE 11-12: Results of processing messages

So far, we have looked at the basics of using Service Broker. To recap where we are now, we have made two services, `InspectionService` and `CentralMaintenanceService`, in a single database named Company. Each service has an associated queue, InspectionQueue and `Central-MaintenanceQueue`, respectively. We can build a conversation between two services and use that conversation to send messages, with guaranteed delivery and order, between them.

Messages sent to a service are put into the queue associated with that service. All messages include a conversation handle that can be used to send a reply to the sender of the message. The conversation handle can be used to correlate messages. We saw that sending messages is asynchronous and that connectivity is not required to build conversations or send messages. Listing 11-1 puts together all the elements we have just covered.

Before going further, consider a general note on syntax. SQL Server 2005 and Service Broker in particular introduce several new expressions to T-SQL. Some of the expressions used for Service Broker require a semicolon (;) to separate them from preceding statements if they are not the first statement in a batch. The expressions that require this are SEND, RECEIVE, MOVE CONVERSATION, and GET CONVERSATION GROUP.

Also, the part of Listing 11-1 from Figure 11-6 shows a hard-coded GUID. It is from the part from Figure 11-4 that uses BEGIN DIALOG CONVERSATION to get a conversation endpoint.

LISTING 11-1: Messages between services

```
CREATE DATABASE Company
GO


ALTER DATABASE Company
SET ENABLE_BROKER
CREATE MASTER KEY ENCRYPTION BY PASSWORD = 'P@ssw0rd'
GO



use Company
GO


-- Figure 11-3
CREATE QUEUE InspectionQueue
CREATE SERVICE InspectionService
ON QUEUE InspectionQueue
GO
```

```
-- Figure 11-3
SELECT S.name AS Service, Q.name AS Queue
FROM sys.services AS S
JOIN sys.service_queues AS Q
ON Q.object_id = S.service_queue_id
GO


-- Figure 11-4
DECLARE @workRequest UNIQUEIDENTIFIER;
BEGIN DIALOG CONVERSATION @workRequest
FROM SERVICE InspectionService
TO SERVICE 'CentralMaintenanceService';
SELECT @workRequest;
GO


--   Figure 11-5
SELECT conversation_handle FROM Company.sys.conversation_endpoints
GO


-- Figure 11-6
DECLARE @workRequest UNIQUEIDENTIFIER;
SET @workRequest = '6AF33B51-EE4A-DA11-91C9-00904B8B6392';
SEND ON CONVERSATION @workRequest
('<WorkRequest>
<Equipment>2-37-BK</Equipment>
<Reason>Overheat</Reason>
</WorkRequest>'
);
GO


-- Figure 11-7
SELECT from_service_name,
to_service_name,
transmission_status
FROM Company.sys.transmission_queue


-- Figure 11-8
CREATE QUEUE CentralMaintenanceQueue

CREATE SERVICE CentralMaintenanceService
ON QUEUE CentralMaintenanceQueue
([DEFAULT])
GO


-- Figure 11-9
SELECT CAST(message_body as XML)
AS Message
FROM CentralMaintenanceQueue
GO
```

```
-- Figure 11-10
SELECT CAST(message_body as NVARCHAR(MAX))
AS Message
FROM CentralMaintenanceQueue
GO

CREATE TABLE PendingWork
(
work XML
)
GO

-- Figure 11-11
BEGIN TRAN
DECLARE @message XML;
DECLARE @conv UNIQUEIDENTIFIER;
DECLARE @ts VARCHAR(MAX);
SET @ts = CAST(GETDATE() AS VARCHAR(MAX));
RECEIVE TOP (1)
    @message = CAST(message_body AS XML),
    @conv = conversation_handle
    FROM CentralMaintenanceQueue;
IF @@ROWCOUNT = 1
BEGIN
    SET @message.modify('insert (
    attribute received{sql:variable(''@ts'')}
    ) into (/*[1])');
    SEND ON CONVERSATION @conv
    (@message)
    INSERT INTO PendingWork VALUES (@message)
END
COMMIT TRAN
GO

-- Figure 11-12
SELECT * FROM PendingWork

SELECT CAST(message_body as XML) FROM InspectionQueue
GO
```

Business Transactions

The preceding example and discussion deliberately skipped many of the
features of Service Broker so that its basic mechanics would be clear. In fact,
from what we have seen so far, Service Broker is not a whole lot different
from any other form of messaging framework. The additional features we

are going to look at now show the main strength of Service Broker: its ability to manage business transactions.

A *business transaction* is an activity that has been part of the business process since long before computers existed. An example of a business transaction is the purchase of parts by a manufacturer from a vendor. The business transaction starts when the vendor receives a purchase order. Some work is required to ensure that the manufacturer's credit is good and that the items ordered are still being sold. Then there might be some work to set up a manufacturing process, followed by other work to ship the parts, send a bill, and so on. Almost all these pieces of work take time. A business transaction usually has a long, indeterminate lifetime, stretching into days, months, or even years. Typically, many independent people and databases are involved in it. In other words, a business transaction consists of many somewhat-independent pieces of work spread out over time and space.

SQL Server 2005, like all relational databases, supports database transactions. A database transaction is different from a business transaction. A *database transaction* is sometimes called a *unit of work,* and this term is a bit more descriptive of what a database transaction is. A transaction is some work that is done as a single unit. Everything the transaction does is described in a single place in the transaction.

A database transaction has the properties of being atomic, consistent, isolated, and durable—that is, the ACID properties. We will not discuss what each of these properties means, but taken together, they ensure that database transactions are guaranteed, by mathematics, to maintain the integrity of a relational database. In practice, this typically means that a database transaction must be finished in a fraction of a millisecond, and at its completion, it will either be committed or rolled back.

A business transaction is implemented as a series of related database transactions. Each database transaction is, of course, independent of other database transactions. This series of database transactions is sometimes called a *long-running transaction* or sometimes a *saga* to distinguish it from a database transaction. The term *long-running transaction* is a bit conflicted; there is no way that a series of independent transactions can be ACID, and for this reason, some will object to this term. For clarity, this chapter will use the term *transaction* to mean to a database transaction and the term *saga,* rather than *long-running transaction*, for the series of database transactions that makes up a business transaction.

A transaction is easier to deal with than a saga. A transaction starts and then finishes by either committing or rolling back; then you are done with it. A saga will do a transaction when it starts—to insert a new purchase order into a database, for example. Many systems would assume, for the sake of efficiency, that the purchase order would be approved and do some other transactions that might, for example, take out of inventory some parts the vendor will need to fulfill the purchase order.

The saga that implements a business transaction can fail. The customer might cancel the order after the saga has started, for example. Unlike a transaction, which can be rolled back and undo everything it did, a saga cannot be undone. A saga must be designed so that if it fails, its effects can be compensated. Compensation is not the same as rolling back a transaction. A failed saga for a purchase order that initially took parts out of inventory could compensate by putting those parts back into inventory. It could not compensate, however, for the fact that another purchase order was rejected because the parts needed to fulfill it were not available from inventory, so the order subsequently was canceled.

Service Broker provides straightforward solutions to several programming issues that usually crop up in implementing a business transaction as a saga. The design of the application has to take these issues into account; in general, they are managed in Service Broker with little or no coding on the part of the application:

- Concurrent processing—An application often runs more than one thread of execution at the same time to use system hardware more effectively; to manage independent items of work logically; or to allow some work to progress while other work is blocked, such as waiting for a disk access to complete. Increasing the concurrency of applications can lead to doing more work in less time.

  Resources, such as queues and other pieces of state, are shared among all the threads of execution in the application and, if not properly managed, will lead to corrupting a shared resource. This is sometimes called the *synchronizer problem* and is very difficult to prevent. Databases manage this problem through the use of transactions by automatically applying locks as needed to achieve a desired level of transaction isolation. Transaction isolation ensures the integrity of the database but also has the undesirable effect of decreasing the concurrency of an application.

Service Broker manages the issues associated with concurrent processing with minimal negative impact on concurrency.

- Preserving message order—It usually is much easier to write an application that receives messages in the order in which they were sent to it. In general, messages cannot be depended on to arrive in the order in which they were sent, and they may not arrive at all. Applications must somehow take this into account. Service Broker ensures that messages are received, and received in the order in which they were sent in a conversation.

- Correlating messages—Applications often receive replies to messages that they have sent. The replies to these messages may be delayed, occurring even weeks or years later, and they rarely arrive in the order in which the messages that caused them were sent. The message the application receives may be related to a specific message that it sent or just in general to a particular saga it is working on.

  An application, while processing a business transaction, might send many messages, one of which says, "Order part 123." Later, it might receive a message that says, "Part 123 no longer available." The application needs some way to determine whether this message is related to the "Order part 123" message, some other message, or to a saga. Service Broker can be used to manage the correlation of replies with the messages and sagas that caused them.

- Processing serialization—Receiving messages in the order in which they were sent is not the same as processing messages in the order in which they were sent. In a multithreaded environment, for example, it is possible for one thread to receive a message but not complete its processing until after a second thread finishes processing a message received after the first message.

  Sometimes, processing messages in the order in which they are received is not important, and sometimes, it is. An application may receive a message that says, "Start a new purchase order," followed by several messages that say, "Add this line item to the purchase order." The "Start a new purchase order" message must be processed before any line items can be added to it. Service Broker can guarantee the serial processing of messages over a reasonably arbitrary set of messages.

- Compensation—*Compensation* is the process of undoing the effects of a business transaction that fails. There are several ways to implement compensation. One way is for each transaction in a saga, in addition to its other work, to add an instruction to a list of "undo" instructions. If the saga fails, the application runs the list of undo instructions to compensate for the effects of the failed saga.

  Service Broker takes a different approach to compensations. Optionally, it will retain all the messages associated with a saga until the saga is finished. If the saga finishes by failing, the applications can leverage the fact that Service Broker can preserve message order, correlate messages, and ensure the serial processing of messages to implement compensation. In effect, the "undo" list is a list of all the messages in the saga that were processed, in the order in which they were processed, up to the point of failure.

Next, we are going to look at the features of Service Broker that make these issues fairly easy to deal with. Note that the order of explanation of these features that follows is not necessarily the order in which they would be used to build a system. The listings that follow these discussions illustrate the use of the topics in an appropriate operational order.

Service Programs

Messages that end up in a queue must at some point be read and processed. The code that processes them is generically called a *service program*. It can be a stored procedure that is executed, though it could be an ad hoc script or even a program running outside SQL Server 2005 that has a connection to it.

The service program may be executed on an ad hoc basis, on a regular schedule, or in response to other events in the overall system. In some cases, the same service program is always used with a given queue, and sometimes, several service programs are used with a given queue.

The main difference among these service programs is what causes them to be executed. It might be that, using the work-order-processing system discussed at the beginning of this chapter as an example, a clerk might run a particular stored procedure as he left work for the day. The stored procedure would read all the new work orders out of the `CentralMaintenanceQueue` and put together the work crews for the next day. And of course SQL Server Agent could be used to automatically schedule the stored procedure to run on a regular basis.

In other cases, events in the system might trigger a service program to read and process the messages in queue. Some companies that deal with equipment that must sit outside in the weather, for example, have systems that automatically respond to computer-based weather reports. Part of the response might be to execute a service program to read and process the messages in the `CentralMaintenanceQueue` as part of preparation for a storm.

Theses are all examples of batch processing. At some time of day or in response to an event, queues are read, and their messages are processed; Service Broker supports this, of course. Another way to process messages is to do the processing continuously—that is, process the messages as they arrive. Service Broker supports this, too. Service Broker activation procedures are a mechanism for processing messages continuously. Sometimes, this is called *internal activation* because the activation procedure is a stored procedure inside the database that is executed by Service Broker. Later, we will look at external activation where a Service Broker is used to activate a program that is outside SQL Server 2005. Most systems will have a mixture of batch processing and continuous processing.

We processed messages in the example that started in Figure 11-2 and was illustrated in Listing 11-1 by executing a batch that read a single message from a queue. To get the effect of continuous processing, we could put the batch in Figure 11-11 inside a loop and just let it run forever, or we could have it submitted by SQL Agent on some schedule to process messages as they arrive.

Though functionally, these solutions would work, both would add a large amount of unnecessary overhead; batches would run when there was nothing in a queue for them to read, taking away resources from batches that had messages to process. And neither would adapt to changing load by giving more resources to queues that were filling up faster than others. Both of these techniques would have trouble scaling to process a large number of messages because of the unnecessary overhead they would incur.

Ideally, for continuous processing, we would like the batch that processed messages for a queue to be executed magically when messages appeared and to not be running at all when the queue was empty. In fact, we would like multiple instances of the batch to start up when a single instance could not process messages in the queue fast enough. In other words, we would like our batches to be running only where there are messages in queues and otherwise to be completely out of the way. Activation procedures have exactly this behavior.

An *activation procedure* is a stored procedure invoked by Server Broker to process messages as they appear in a queue. Later in this chapter, we will look at the way Service Broker uses activation procedures, but first, we will look at the syntax for associating an activation procedure with a queue.

Note that a queue is not required to have an activation procedure, but it is the preferred technique when continuous processing of messages is required. A queue may have at most one activation procedure, but a stored procedure may be used as the activation procedure for more than one queue. Later, we will see that the information in a message is sufficient for a stored procedure to know which queue a message came from.

An activation procedure can be associated with a queue when the queue is created or altered. Figure 11-13 shows the CREATE QUEUE expression being used to create a queue with an activation procedure. The CREATE QUEUE expression has an optional WITH ACTIVATION (1) clause that designates a stored procedure as the activation procedure for the queue being created. The PROCEDURE_NAME clause (2) must specify an existing stored procedure. The MAX_QUEUE_READERS clause (2) specifies the maximum number of instances of the activation procedure that Service Broker is allowed to run at the same time for this queue. In general, the higher the MAX_QUEUE_READERS setting, the more throughput there will be in reading messages from the queue, at the cost of using more system resources. Note that the ALTER QUEUE statement, described in Books Online, can be used to change this number while an application is running, meaning that

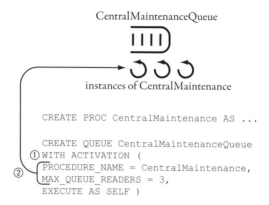

FIGURE 11-13: Activation procedure

maximum concurrency associated with processing messages in this queue can be increased or decreased dynamically as needed.

Figure 11-14 diagrams a queue with messages flowing into it and an associated activation procedure. Service Broker can detect that a message has been put into a queue; after all, it put the message there. When Service Broker puts a message into a queue, if it has not already done so, it will execute the activation procedure associated with that queue, with no parameters. Service Broker expects that the activation procedure will read the message from the queue.

In effect, Service Broker monitors the depth of the queue—that is, the number of messages in it—over time. If it sees that the queue isn't being empted by the activation procedure it previously executed, it executes the activation procedure again, with no parameters, provided that there are fewer than MAX_QUEUE_READERS instances of the activation procedure for that queue already running.

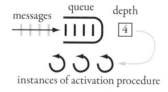

FIGURE 11-14: Continuous
message processing

It's a reasonable model to think of Service Broker executing more and more copies of an activation procedure until the depth of the queue stops growing. In fact, Service Broker does not actually measure the depth of the queue; that would be inefficient. Instead, it monitors events that happen to queues—a message being put into a queue, a conversation group being unlocked, and a RECEIVE expression returning no rows—to determine whether the queue requires the execution of another instance of the activation procedure. Note that conversation groups are a construct related to conversations that we will be discussing later in this chapter.

Service Broker does not manipulate the queue itself in any way; it expects that the activation procedure will do that. All Service Broker does is keep on executing more instances of the activation procedure as long as it sees that messages in the queue are not being processed fast enough, up to a limit configured for the queue. Service Broker is in effect automatically increasing the processing concurrency of the queues that need more concurrency.

The algorithm that Service Broker uses to monitor queues is not exposed, and there is no way to configure it. Every few seconds, it checks the queues to see whether any activation procedures need to be executed. The result is that an application can adapt automatically to the message load presented to it.

An activation procedure can be enabled or not. Disabling an activation procedure prevents Service Broker from executing it. By default, the WITH ACTIVATION clause of the CREATE QUEUE statement enables the activation procedure. The STATUS clause of the WITH ACTIVATION clause determines whether the activation procedure is enabled. Figure 11-15 shows a queue

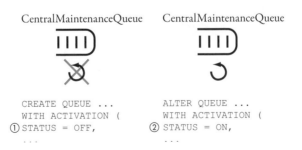

FIGURE 11-15: Enabling activation procedure

that is initially created with an activation procedure disabled (1). Later, an ALTER QUEUE expression can be used to enable (2) the activation procedure.

Note that because ALTER QUEUE can be used while an application is running, processing of messages for a particular queue can be turned on or off as needed. Turning off the processing of messages in effect leaves more computing resources for other queues.

When an activation procedure for a queue is turned off, the activation procedure is not executed, and messages just pile up in the queue until the activation procedure is turned back on or some other batch reads the queue. Sometimes, it is useful to turn off the queue itself and not allow any message to enter it. By default, when a queue is created, it is enabled. Figure 11-16 shows the use of the STATUS option for a queue to create it in an off (1) state. The queue can be enabled or disabled at any time by using the ALTER QUEUE expression with a STATUS option (2).

It might seem that turning off a queue is a drastic thing to do; will messages be lost? Service Broker does not lose messages even when queues are turned off. In Figure 11-6, we saw that we could send a message to a service and queue that did not even exist and not lose the messages. When a queue is turned off, messages destined for it will wait in transmission queues, as we saw in Figure 11-7.

Almost all database applications adjust computing resource usage based on time of day or other events, sometimes automatically and sometimes manually. The simplest form of this kind of control is to submit at night a batch that you don't want using resources in the daytime. Sometimes, you have to make adjustments manually by stopping some

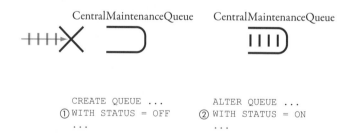

FIGURE 11-16: Enabling queue

batches and starting others due to unforeseen events. Activation procedures give you a way to use all available resources automatically without giving up the ability to make manual or automatic adjustments to resource usage.

What we have just looked at is sometimes called internal activation because the code that processes the messages in a stored procedure inside the database. It is also possible to use external activation to process messages that use a procedure outside the database to process messages. When a queue needs to be processed, Service Broker generates a QUEUE_ACTIVATION event. An Event Notification created with a CREATE EVENT NOTIFICATION expression can be used to handle this event. See Chapter 7 for a discussion of Event Notifications. Search for "Event-Based Activation" in Books Online for a discussion of using Event Notifications in external applications.

Conversations

In Figure 11-4, we began a conversation and then proceeded to use that conversation to send messages. Service Broker uses conversations to preserve message order—which is to guarantee that messages are received in the order in which they were sent—in a conversation.

A conversation is begun between services. Every conversation has two endpoints; each endpoint is associated with a service and, indirectly, with its associated queue. Messages are sent on a conversation, not to a queue or services, as shown in Figure 11-6. Specifically, the ON CONVERSATION clause in a SEND expression specifies a conversation_handle, which is a GUID that represents a conversation endpoint. Messages sent on a conversation endpoint appear in the queue at the opposite endpoint of the conversation in the order in which they were sent.

Figure 11-17 illustrates a conversation preserving message order. The left endpoint of the conversation is identified by a GUID that starts with F93B, and the right endpoint of the conversation is identified by a GUID that starts with 0A8F. The batch shown on the left side of the illustration uses the SEND expression to send, in order, messages M1, M2, M3, M4, and M5 on conversation endpoint F93B. They appear in the queue at the other end of the conversation in the order in which they were sent. Likewise, the

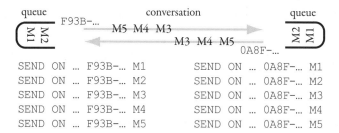

<figure><figcaption>**FIGURE 11-17: Conversation preserving order**</figcaption></figure>

batch on the right side of the illustration sends five messages that appear in the queue on the right side of the illustration in the order in which they were sent.

We saw in Figure 11-5 that conversation endpoints are visible in the sys.conversation_endpoints system view in a database. The conversation_handle specified in the ON CONVERSATION clause are scoped to the database in use and must be in the conversation_handle column of the sys.conversation_endpoints system view for the database in use when the SEND expression is executed; otherwise, an error will be raised.

Conversations are meant to have a limited lifetime, even though that lifetime might be measured in months or years. The END CONVERSATION expression is used to end a conversation.

A conversation may be active or inactive. A conversation is active from the time it is begun until an END CONVERSATION expression has been used on both ends of the conversation, at which point it becomes inactive.

The END CONVERSATION expression may used to end an active conversation only by the owner of the conversation, a user in the role of the owner of the database, or a user in the sysadmin role. Note that a conversation is just another database object and is owned by the identity that created it using a BEGIN DIALOG CONVERSATION expression.

There are three reasons to end a conversation. One is the normal end of conversation that occurs when the conversation is no longer necessary. A second reason is that an error has been detected, and it is not possible to continue the conversation.

The third reason to end a conversation is as a maintenance operation performed because a conversation that should have ended has not, and it must be cleaned up, administratively, to free system resources. Note that conversations that are not active do not take up memory resources, but they do take up nonmemory resources, such as disk and backup systems. Typically, a conversation is cleaned up administratively because there is reason to believe that it will never end, in which case it is a resource leak.

To bring a normal end to a conversation, the END CONVERSATION expression is used with the conversation_handle (2) of the conversation being ended, as shown in Figure 11-18. This example starts a conversation, sends (1) a message on that conversation, and then ends (2) the conversation. In this case, any pending messages for the other end of the conversation—those sent with SEND (1) before the END CONVERSATION—are sent to the other end of the conversation, followed by a message with a NULL message_body and a message type of http://schemas.microsoft.com/SQL/ServiceBroker/EndDialog (3). Any messages still in the queue from the other end of the conversation are deleted with no warning. In addition,

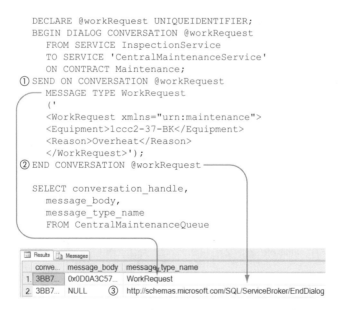

FIGURE 11-18: Normal END CONVERSATION

any messages that subsequently arrive from the other end of the conversation will be silently thrown away.

The recipient of an http://schemas.microsoft.com/SQL/ServiceBroker/EndDialog message must in turn use END CONVERSATION to end its side of the conversation. This allows Service Broker to clean up the database resources associated with the conversation.

A conversation can be ended with an indication that an error has occurred. Figure 11-19 shows an END CONVERSATION expression that includes a WITH ERROR clause (1). The WITH ERROR clause requires an error number, which must be positive, and an error description. Negative error numbers are reserved for Service Broker itself to use. This works in the same way as an END CONVERSATION expression without a WITH ERROR clause, except that the message to the other end of the conversation (2) is of message type http://schemas.microsoft.com/SQL/ServiceBroker/Error, and the message body contains the error information. The recipient of this message should respond to it with an END CONVERSATION, as it would for a normal end of conversation. Note that this example shows a hard-coded GUID being used for @workRequest. In normal practice, this would not be done, but it is done in this example just to make it complete.

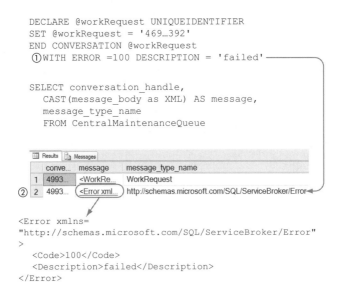

FIGURE 11-19: END CONVERSATION with error

To clean up completely all the resources associated with a conversation, both ends of the conversation must use the END CONVERSATION statement. Sometimes, due to an equipment failure or programming error, this does not happen, and the resources associated with a conversation must be cleaned up forcibly. Adding a WITH CLEANUP phrase to the end of an END CONVERSATION expression will forcibly clean up the resources associated with a conversation and not send any messages to the other end of the conversation and will drop all pending messages from the other end of the conversation. This is not the recommended way to end a conversation and should be used only as a last resort. An END CONVERSATION expression that includes the WITH CLEANUP phrase may be executed only by a user in the role of sysadmin or owner of the database that contains the conversation.

Note that typically, equipment failure is handled by Service Broker by just waiting for the broken equipment to come back online, at which time conversation can go on running. In some cases, when the equipment never comes back online, the WITH CLEANUP phrase will be needed to free up resources.

Sometimes, there is a need to clean up forcibly all resources associated with all conversations in a database. The ALTER DATABASE <database> SET NEW_BROKER expression will do this. Note that this expression will not complete as long as there are any users of the database being altered. This empties all queues, ends all conversations, drops any pending messages without sending any messages to the other end of the conversations that are dropped, and creates a new GUID to identify the broker instance. We have not yet discussed the broker-instance GUID, but this is used by conversations to communicate with services across databases, and creating a new broker-instance GUID will doom any conversation from another database. SET NEW_BROKER can be quite useful during development, but it should be used only as a last resort in a production setting.

The SEND expression, by design, is asynchronous. A byproduct of this is that it does not inform the sender whether the message was delivered to the other end of the conversation. Timeouts are used with asynchronous messages both as part of normal message processing (sending a message like "I'll accept bids for the next 20 minutes," for example) and to detect errors and failures. Service Broker provides two kinds of timeouts: the lifetime of a dialog and a conversation timer.

All dialogs have a lifetime, which optionally may be specified by the use of a LIFETIME clause (1) appended to the BEGIN DIALOG CONVERSATION expression, as shown in Figure 11-20. The LIFETIME clause specifies the lifetime of the dialog in seconds. If the LIFETIME clause is not used, the lifetime is the maximum value of the int type, in seconds. If the dialog has not been ended by both ends of the conversation using END CONVERSATION before the lifetime expires, a message (2) is sent to both ends of the conversation indicating that the lifetime of the dialog has expired.

When the lifetime of a dialog has expired, it may no longer be used. Attempts to send messages using it will fail with an error. The conversation for the dialog still exists, however, until both ends of the conversation have executed an END CONVERSATION expression for the conversation.

The lifetime of a dialog is a big hammer; when it has expired, you can no longer use the dialog. An alternative to the lifetime of a dialog is the conversation timer. A *conversation timer* is a timer that sends a message to the conversation endpoint that set it when it expires. It has no other effect on the conversation.

```
DECLARE @workRequest UNIQUEIDENTIFIER;
BEGIN DIALOG CONVERSATION @workRequest
  FROM SERVICE InspectionService
  TO SERVICE 'CentralMaintenanceService'
  ON CONTRACT Maintenance
①WITH LIFETIME = 1;

SELECT conversation_handle,
  CAST(message_body AS XML) AS message
  FROM InspectionQueue
```

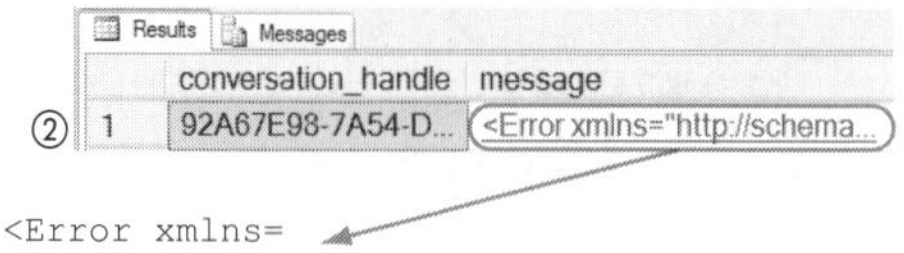

Results	Messages
conversation_handle	message
② 1	92A67E98-7A54-D...	<Error xmlns="http://schema...

```
<Error xmlns=
"http://schemas.microsoft.com/SQL/ServiceBroker/Error">
  <Code>-8489</Code>
  <Description>
     The dialog has exceeded the specified LIFETIME.
  </Description>
</Error>
```

FIGURE 11-20: Dialog lifetime

The purpose of a conversation timer is to act as a reminder that a dialog has been inactive for longer than you typically expect it to be. When you receive a message that a conversation timer has expired, you take some sort of corrective action. You might send a message to the service, saying, "Auction has begun and will end in 10 minutes," and also set a conversation time for ten minutes. If you receive a conversation timeout message, your corrective action might be just to end the conversation.

Figure 11-21 shows the use of a conversation timer. The BEGIN CONVERSATION TIMER expression (1) specifies a conversation_handle in parentheses, followed by a TIMEOUT phrase, which sets the timeout in seconds. When the time expires, the endpoint specified in the BEGIN CONVERSATION TIMER expression receives a message (2) with a NULL message_ body of type http://schemas.Microsoft.com/SQL/ServiceBroker/Messages/DialogTimer.

If you are familiar with the way that timers are built in Windows or .NET Framework, you might think that a conversation timer requires a lot of system resources. SQL Server 2005 does not manage timers the same way that Windows or .NET Framework does. Timers are internally just some data, and an appropriate-size instance of SQL Server 2005 can support millions of timers. Keep in mind, though, that a conversation timer is only approximate.

Note that a conversation timer is specific to an end of a conversation; each end can have a different timer. There is only one conversation time at each end of the conversation.

FIGURE 11-21: Conversation timer

Conversation Groups

Service Broker uses conversation groups to correlate messages and, if required by the application, to serialize the processing order of messages.

A business transaction typically involves more than a single message. A business transaction involving a purchase order, for example, might involve a message requesting a purchase order number and other messages checking stock levels, customer credit, and so on. In most cases, messages associated with one business transaction can be processed independently of those associated with other business transactions.

Conversation groups, in conjunction with activation procedures, are a core aspect of Service Broker's ability to process messages in a scalable and efficient manner. It does so by allowing an application to leverage the fact that some messages are related to others. A conversation group identifies a set of conversations whose messages must be processed serially but that may be processed in parallel with messages in conversations from other conversation groups.

Every conversation belongs to a conversation group. Optionally, multiple conversations may be put into the same conversation group. A message is said to belong to a conversation group if the conversation that sends or receives it belongs to that conversation group.

Every message includes a `conversation_handle` and a `conversation_group_id`. The `conversation_handle` can be used to correlate messages within a conversation. Likewise, the `converstation_group_id` can be used to correlate messages within a conversation group.

Messages in a given conversation group can be, and often are, processed serially. This means that messages are processed in a way similar to the way rows in a table are processed in a transaction when the transaction isolation level is serializable. Processing the messages in a transaction gives that transaction exclusive access to all messages in that conversation group, in all dialogs, until the transaction commits or rolls back.

A conversation group can be locked, and when it is, the lock is held until the transaction under which it was obtained finishes by a commit or rollback. While the lock is held, only expressions running in the scope of the transaction that obtained the lock can read messages from any queue belonging to that conversation group. Note that this is done by Service

Broker without using any locks on the queue itself. Note that it is possible to add more conversation groups to the transaction.

There is no way to lock a conversation group directly, as there is in some T-SQL statements that allow locking hints. Several expressions will lock a conversation group when executed: RECEIVE, SEND, MOVE CONVERSATION, END CONVERSATION, and GET CONVERSATION GROUP. In typical usage, there is a BEGIN TRAN before using one of these statements, followed by a COMMIT or ROLLBACK TRAN after the processing of the messages involved has been completed. This is why the example Figure 11-11 starts with a BEGIN TRAN before it executes a RECEIVE expression.

There is a difference in guaranteeing that messages in a conversation will be received in the order in which they are sent and guaranteeing that messages are processed in the order in which they are received. Service Broker guarantees the former but not the latter. Figure 11-22 shows a queue with messages flowing into it. In this example, assume that all the messages in the queue are from the same conversation. There are two batches in the illustration, each using RECEIVE to read the queue. The batches are executed at almost the same time. Batch 1 is executed (1) first; it uses RECEIVE to read the first message, message 1, from the queue and begins to process it. If there were no locking for conversation groups, when batch 2 is executed (2), it would read the next message in the conversation, message 2.

Now there are two batches running at the same time, and each is processing a different message from the same conversation. It may just so happen that batch 2 finishes before batch 1, even though it started later, which would result in the second message being processed before the first.

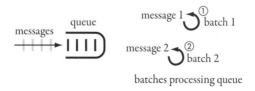

batches processing queue

FIGURE 11-22: Preserving processing order

RECEIVE, like SELECT and similar T-SQL statements, is always executed under a transaction. In other words, even if you don't write it that way, in effect RECEIVE always looks like this:

```
BEGIN TRAN
RECEIVE ...
COMMIT TRAN
-- more T-SQL expressions
```

This is not enough to ensure that messages are processed in the order in which they are received; that is the problem shown in Figure 11-22.

A programming convention is required to ensure that messages in a conversation group are processed in the order in which they are received. The RECEIVE expression that reads a queue must be inside an explicit transaction, as shown in Figure 11-11, and the transaction may not be committed or rolled back until all processing for the message has been completed. If this programming convention is followed, all messages in a conversation group will be processed in the order in which they were received.

The specific conversation group a conversation belongs to is determined by the BEGIN DIALOG CONVERSATION expression when the conversation is begun or later by a MOVE CONVERSATION statement. By default, a new conversation group is created for a new conversation. There are some limits on which existing conversation group a new conversation can join. Likewise, a conversation can be moved from one conversation group to another, again with some limitations. The conversation_group_id in a message identifies the conversation group for the message, and the conversation_ handle identifies its conversation.

There are four ways a conversation can become part of a conversation group. The conversation begun in Figure 11-4 did not specify a particular conversation group to join, so a new conversation group was created, and the conversation was added to that conversation group. Optionally, a new conversation can be added to an existing conversation group, added to a specified new conversation group, or added to the conversation group of another conversation.

Figure 11-23 shows three ways a conversation can be made part of a conversation group. In these cases, a WITH clause is appended to the BEGIN DIALOG CONVERSATION expression. Specifying an existing conversation_group_id

```
    DECLARE @otherGroup UNIQUEIDENTIFIER
    DECLARE @workRequest UNIQUEIDENTIFIER;
    BEGIN DIALOG CONVERSATION @workRequest
①  FROM SERVICE InspectionService
    TO SERVICE 'CentralMaintenanceService'
    ON CONTRACT Maintenance
    WITH RELATED_CONVERSATION_GROUP @otherGroup;

    DECLARE @newGroup UNIQUEIDENTITIER
    SET @newGroup = NEWID()
    DECLARE @workRequest UNIQUEIDENTIFIER;
    BEGIN DIALOG CONVERSATION @workRequest
②  FROM SERVICE InspectionService
    TO SERVICE 'CentralMaintenanceService'
    ON CONTRACT Maintenance
    WITH RELATED_CONVERSATION_GROUP @newGroup;

    DECLARE @otherConversation UNIQUEIDENTIFIER
    DECLARE @workRequest UNIQUEIDENTIFIER;
    BEGIN DIALOG CONVERSATION @workRequest
③  FROM SERVICE InspectionService
    TO SERVICE 'CentralMaintenanceService'
    ON CONTRACT Maintenance
    WITH RELATED_CONVERSATION @otherConversation;
```

FIGURE 11-23: Adding conversation to conversation group

(1) in WITH RELATED_CONVERSATION_GROUP clause will add the new conversation to that conversation group.

A conversation_group_id is a UNIQUEIDENTIFIER—that is, a GUID. If the UNIQUEIDENTIFIER used in the WITH RELATED_CONVERSATION_GROUP clause does not specify an existing conversation group (2), the new conversation will be added to a new conversation group with that UNIQUEI-DENTIFIER as its conversation_group_id.

A new conversation can be added to the conversation group of an existing conversation by using the WITH RELATED_CONVERSATION clause (3) and passing it the conversation_handle of the existing conversation. The new conversation will be added to the conversation group of the related conversation.

A new conversation may not be added to an arbitrary existing conversation group. All conversations in a conversation group must have the service specified in the FROM clause as either the initiator or the target of the conversation.

Figure 11-24 illustrates how access to queues is managed internally by Service Broker. There are two tables for managing conversations; they can be seen through the system views sys.conversation_groups and sys.conversation_endpoints. Service Broker in effect locks a conversation_group_id in sys.conversation_groups (1). Each conversation is related

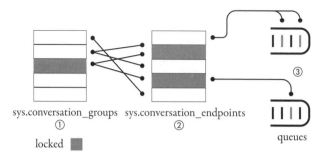

sys.conversation_groups   sys.conversation_endpoints

①   ②

locked ■   queues

FIGURE 11-24: Conversation group locking

to its conversation group by the `conversation_group_id`. Each message
(3) is related to its conversation by its `conversation_id`. The result of this
technique is that Server Broker can add messages to queues and read via
`RECEIVE` at a much greater rate than if it implemented queues as ordinary
tables accessed under an isolation-level serializable transaction.

Note that this explanation of locking of conversation groups is just infor-
mational. The actual implementation is hidden. `sys.conversation_groups`
and `sys.conversation_endpoints` are views, not physical tables, but are
used to show the concept. Scalability and performance were important goals
for Service Broker, and the internal design makes sure that the overhead of
using queues is minimized.

The effect of locking on conversation groups is illustrated in the diagram
in Figure 11-25. It has a queue (1) with messages entering the queue at the
left and leaving it at the right. Conversations and conversation groups are
identified in SQL Server 2005 by a `UNIQUEIDENTIFIER`, but to simplify
referring to them in this diagram, conversations are identified with an integer,

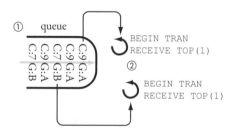

FIGURE 11-25: Conversation message
processing

and conversation groups are identified with a letter. The next message ready to leave the queue is from conversation C:9 and conversation group G:A—that is, the message farthest to the right.

There are two RECEIVE expressions (2) executing at about the same time. Before they start, no conversation groups are locked. The semantics of RECEIVE are to read the next message ready to leave the queue that is not in a conversation group locked by a transaction different from the one it is running under. The RECEIVE in the top part of the diagram starts just before the one in the bottom part.

When the top RECEIVE in Figure 11-25, starts none of the conversation groups is locked, so it gets the next message ready to leave the queue—that is, the one farthest to the right—and locks conversation group A. When the bottom RECEIVE starts to execute, the next message ready to leave the queue is the second one from the right, but it is from conversation group A, which was locked by the top RECEIVE. The bottom RECEIVE instead gets the third message from the right, because it is the next message ready to leave the queue that is in a different conversation group, B, from the one that the top RECEIVE read.

Figure 11-25 shows the locking behavior of conversation groups in a single queue. In fact, the locking behavior extends across all queues, and the locking is determined only by conversation group. Figure 11-26 shows the

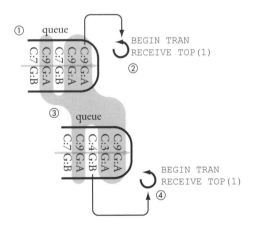

FIGURE 11-26: Conversation groups across multiple queues

same two batches that were shown in Figure 11-25, but in this case, each batch is working with a different queue. The top queue (1) in Figure 11-26 is being read by the top RECEIVE expression (2). Likewise, the bottom queue (3) is being read by the bottom RECEIVE expression(4). The top RECEIVE expression executes first and reads the first message in the top query, which is from conversation C:9 and conversation group G:A. This locks all the messages in conversation group G:A. When the bottom RECEIVE expression is executed, the G:A conversation group is already locked, so it reads the third message in the bottom queue—that is, the first message in that queue that is not in conversation group G:A.

Note that this locking behavior extends only to queues in the same database.

A SEND expression locks the conversation group of the message it is sending. This means that there will be no processing of messages in the conversation group of the message until the transaction under which the SEND expression was executed has finished.

So far, we have been using the RECEIVE expression with a TOP (1) clause. A RECEIVE expression is similar to a SELECT expression in that it returns a set of rows and the TOP (1) clause is limiting the number of rows returned to a single row. If RECEIVE is used without a TOP clause, or a TOP(n) where n is greater than one, it may return multiple rows in the same way that SELECT does, with some limitations.

A RECEIVE expression without a TOP(1) clause will potentially return multiple rows, with each row representing a message from the queue it is reading. A RECEIVE expression does not attempt to return all the messages in a queue, however. The messages returned from a single execution of a RECEIVE expression will always be from the single conversation group.

The rows that a RECEIVE expression returns will be sent back to the client of the connection that executed the RECEIVE expression if there are no INTO clause or variables to capture the results, just as a SELECT expression returns rows when there are no INTO clause or variables.

An INTO clause can be added to a RECEIVE expression to capture the returned rows. The target of the INTO clause must be a table variable; it cannot be an actual table, because RECEIVE supports a table variable only in an INTO clause. Figure 11-27 shows a RECEIVE expression used in this way. The INTO clause comes immediately after the queue name (2), similar to

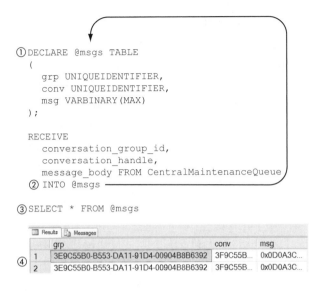

```
①DECLARE @msgs TABLE
  (
      grp UNIQUEIDENTIFIER,
      conv UNIQUEIDENTIFIER,
      msg VARBINARY(MAX)
  );

  RECEIVE
      conversation_group_id,
      conversation_handle,
      message_body FROM CentralMaintenanceQueue
  ② INTO @msgs

③SELECT * FROM @msgs
```

grp	conv	msg
1 3E9C55B0-B553-DA11-91D4-00904B8B6392	3F9C55B...	0x0D0A3C...
2 3E9C55B0-B553-DA11-91D4-00904B8B6392	3F9C55B...	0x0D0A3C...

FIGURE 11-27: RECEIVE returning multiple rows

placing it after the table name in a SELECT expression. The target of the INTO expression must be a table variable (1). The rows of the table variable are selected (3), and the results show that all the messages returned are from the same conversation group.

A RECEIVE expression may also have a predicate, but the predicate may do an equals test only on the conversation_handle or conversation_group_id column.

An application often needs to store state between the processing of its messages. One message in a conversation might say, "Create a new purchase order." Then another message in the same conversation might arrive hours later, saying, "Cancel." Processing the second message would require finding the purchase order created by the first message. This problem could be solved by requiring all messages about purchase orders to contain a purchase order number, of course. Many times, however, this is not really convenient, and sometimes, it is not possible. The client that sent the "Create new purchase order" message might want to send the "Cancel" message before it knows the purchase order number.

A straightforward way to store state for a Service Broker application is to put it into tables and identify it by the conversation_group_id of the message being processed. Every message includes its `conversation_group_id`. In addition, assuming that the application follows the convention of doing all message and state processing inside a transaction, there will never be the issue of two parts of an application trying to process the state at the same time. The message processing will in effect be given exclusive access to the state for the messages' conversation group without using locks on the tables that hold the state, by leveraging the lock on the conversation group.

Message Types

In Figure 11-6, we sent an XML message. Later, in Figure 11-9, we saw that the message was stored in the queue in as a `VARBINARY(MAX)` in the Message column, and we had to cast back to XML to read it. Messages are in fact just a sequence of bytes, and the `SEND` in Figure 11-6 could have sent any sequence of bytes we wanted. Often, an application will want tighter control over what gets sent in a conversation. The `CREATE MESSAGE TYPE` and `CREATE CONTRACT` expressions are used to specify the format of messages and the direction in which they can be sent in a conversation.

The `CREATE MESSAGE TYPE` expression defines the format of a message, which is the content of the `message_body` column in the queue. Figure 11-28 shows the usage of the `CREATE MESSAGE TYPE` (1) statement. All message names—WorkRequest, in Figure 11-28—are case sensitive, just as service names are, regardless of the collation of the SQL Server instance.

Every database contains a built-in message type named `DEFAULT`. The example in Listing 11-1 used the message type even though it did not specify it. The `DEFAULT` message type allows any message content because its data type is `VARBINARY(MAX)`. The `DEFAULT` message type cannot be changed or dropped.

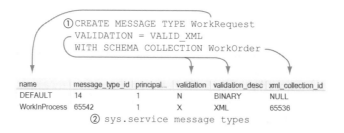

```
① CREATE MESSAGE TYPE WorkRequest
   VALIDATION = VALID_XML
   WITH SCHEMA COLLECTION WorkOrder
```

name	message_type_id	principal...	validation	validation_desc	xml_collection_id
DEFAULT	14	1	N	BINARY	NULL
WorkInProcess	65542	1	X	XML	65536

② `sys.service message types`

FIGURE 11-28: CREATE MESSAGE TYPE

Message types are stored in a database and can be seen via a `sys.service_message_types` (2) view for that database, as shown in Figure 11-28. Message types have a one-part name and cannot be referenced outside the database that is in use.

Every message type is associated with a VALIDATION. The VALIDATION specifies how the content of the message must be validated. Message validation is done only on the target. There are four kinds of validation: NONE, EMPTY, WELL_FORMED_XML, and VALID_XML.

NONE is the validation associated with the DEFAULT message type and specifies that no validation is to be done, which means that any content is allowed.

EMPTY specifies that there may be no message content. This type of message can be thought of as a marker message, where the name of the message type indicates the meaning of the message, and no message body is required.

WELL_FORMED_XML, from its name, implies that the message must conform to the Extensible Markup Language (XML) Recommendation from the World Wide Web Consortium, because the term "well-formed XML" comes from this recommendation. This recommendation specifies what is commonly known as an XML document, WELL_FORMED_XML in Service Broker, however, does not mean quite the same thing that "well-formed XML" does in the XML Recommendation.

The WELL_FORMED_XML validation does not allow a DTD to be part of the document, even though the recommendation does. It also allows what are commonly called document fragments, which the recommendation does not. *Document fragments* are documents that have more than one root element or maybe no elements at all. A document fragment is essentially a document that can be represented by the data model described in the XPath 1.0 Recommendation of the World Wide Web Consortium. These recommendations are available at http://www.w3.org/TR/2004/REC-xml11-20040204/ and http://www.w3.org/TR/1999/REC-xpath-19991116, respectively.

Coverage of the XML and XPath 1.0 recommendations are beyond the scope of this book except by way of the example that follows. Figure 11-29 shows two XML documents. The first document has a DTD (1) and is well-formed XML according to the XML Recommendation. However it may not be used when the validation for the message type is either WELL_FORMED_XML or VALID_XML. This document shows a common idiom used in XML

```
<!DOCTYPE WorkRequst [   ①
<!ENTITY R1 "Overheat">
]>
<WorkRequest xmlns="urn:maintenance">
<Equipment>2-37-BK</Equipment>
<Reason>&R1;</Reason>
</WorkRequest>
```

```
<WorkRequest xmlns="urn:maintenance">   ②
<Equipment>42-3-L</Equipment>
<Reason>Fuse</Reason>
</WorkRequest>
```
```
<WorkRequest xmlns="urn:maintenance">   ③
<Equipment>2-37-BK</Equipment>
<Reason>Overheat</Reason>
</WorkRequest>
```

FIGURE 11-29: XML documents

where the DTD contains ENTITYs that are essentially used as macros to be expanded elsewhere in the document. The T-SQL CONVERT function, using style 2, can be used to remove the DTD and expand the ENTITYs that they can be used as a message. The usage of CONVERT will be covered later.

The second document is not well formed according to the XML Recommendation because there are two root elements in it: one WorkRequest (2) followed by another WorkRequest (3). Even though this document is not well formed, it may be used as a message when the validation WELL_FORMED_XML is used.

VALID_XML specifies the content is well-formed XML as specified in the XML recommendation, except that no DTD is allowed. But documents like the second one in Figure 11-29, with more than one root element, are not allowed. In addition, this specifies that the message can be validated against an XML Schema from the XML schema collection specified in the WITH SCHEMA COLLECTION clause. XML Schema is specified in the XML Schema 1.0 Recommendation from the World Wide Web Consortium. It can be found at http://www.w3.org/TR/2004/REC-xmlschema-1-20041028/ and http://www.w3.org/TR/2004/REC-xmlschema-2-20041028/. XML, the XML data type, and XML Schema in SQL Server 2005 are discussed in Chapter 9. Note that SQL Server 2005 does not support all the features of the XML Schema Recommendation. See Chapter 9 for a discussion of what is supported.

Using the validation VALID_XML in a message type puts the tightest constraints on a message but also has the most overhead, as it completely specifies all parts of a message. An explanation of XML Schema is beyond the scope of this book, but an introductory tutorial that covers the parts used in this example can be found at http://www.w3.org/TR/2004/REC-xmlschema-0-20041028/.

Figure 11-30 shows the XML Schema (1) and a message (2) that is valid according to this XML Schema. This schema specifies that the document element—that is, the outermost element—of the message will be named WorkRequest. The WorkRequest element will contain two other elements: in order, Equipment and Reason. The WorkRequest element has a time-stamp attribute. All the elements will be in the 'urn:maintenance' name-space. As you can see, an XML Schema allows for fairly fine-grained control over the format of a message.

The example in Listing 11-1 used the DEFAULT message type, which uses validation NONE. Figure 11-31 shows the three other message types to illustrate the other types of validation. The WorkInProcess (1) message type uses VALID_XML validate. The WITH SCHEMA COLLECTION clause references

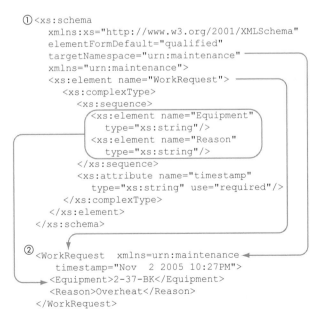

FIGURE 11-30: XML Schema and message

```
CREATE XML SCHEMA COLLECTION WorkOrder
AS
'<xs:schema …
 xmlns="urn:maintenance">
…
</xs:schema>'
① CREATE MESSAGE TYPE WorkInProcess
    VALIDATION = VALID_XML
    WITH SCHEMA COLLECTION WorkOrder

② CREATE MESSAGE TYPE WorkRequest
    VALIDATION = WELL_FORMED_XML

③ CREATE MESSAGE TYPE WorkComplete
    VALIDATION  = EMPTY
```

FIGURE 11-31: Message types

an XML SCHEMA COLLECTION that contains the XML schema shown in Figure 11-30. WorkInProgress will look like the typical message shown in Figure 11-30. Chapter 9 covers the use of the CREATE XML SCHEMA COLLECTION expression.

The WorkRequest (2) message type in Figure 11-31 uses WELL_FORMED_ XML, so messages of this type may be any XML message, even a document fragment. The WorkComplete (3) message uses EMPTY validation. A Work-Complete message may have no content; the name of the message type itself indicates the meaning of the message.

Contracts

A contract specifies a set of messages and the endpoints of a conversation that can use them. Contracts are used in a BEGIN DIALOG CONVERSATION expression to constrain the messages used in a conversation. Figure 11-32

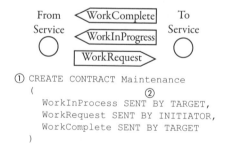

```
① CREATE CONTRACT Maintenance
  (                           ②
      WorkInProcess SENT BY TARGET,
      WorkRequest SENT BY INITIATOR,
      WorkComplete SENT BY TARGET
  )
```

FIGURE 11-32: Contract

shows a CREATE CONTRACT expression (1) creating the Maintenance contract. The name of a contract is case sensitive regardless of the collation for the SQL Server instance. Message types are used in two places: SEND expressions and contracts. Contracts may be used in two places: BEGIN DIALOG CONVERSATION and CREATE SERVICE expressions.

The CREATE CONTRACT expression specifies, in parentheses, a comma-separated list of message types. A SENT BY (2) clause with each message type specifies the direction in which that message can be sent in a conversation. There are three choices for direction: ANY, TARGET, and INITIATOR. ANY specifies that the message may be sent from either endpoint in a conversation. TARGET specifies that the message may be sent only by the conversation endpoint associated with the TO SERVICE, as specified in the BEGIN DIALOG CONVERSATION expression. INITIATOR specifies that the message may be sent only from the endpoint associated with the FROM SERVICE.

Message types have only one-part names, so any message type specified in a CREATE CONTRACT expression must exist in the database in use when the CREATE CONTRACT expression is executed. The database and schema prefixes used when referring to other database objects may not be used on message type names.

Note that a contract specifies only message types and direction. It does not specify a message protocol—that is, it does not specify the sequence of or when a particular message should be used.

Contracts are stored in the database in use when the CREATE CONTRACT statement is executed. There is a built-in contract named DEFAULT in every database. It specifies the DEFAULT message type with a SENT BY ANY clause. The DEFAULT contract cannot be dropped or changed. The sys.service_contracts view (1), shown in Figure 11-33, can be used to see (2) the contracts in a database. Note that besides the DEFAULT contract, several other contracts are used by applications built into SQL Server 2005.

The CREATE SERVICE expression may optionally specify that it supports one or more contracts. The CentralMaintenanceService in the preceding example specified the built-in DEFAULT contract, as shown in Figure 11-8. The InspectionService did not specify any contract, as shown in Figure 11-2.

Figure 11-34 shows a CREATE SERVICE expression (2) that supports two contracts: DEFAULT and Maintenance. A service can support only a contract (2) that has been created in the same database as the one in which

①
```
select * from sys.service_contracts
```

②

	name	service_contract_id	principal_id
1	DEFAULT	6	1
2	Maintenance	65536	1
3	http://schemas.microsoft.com/SQL/Notifications/Pos...	2	1
4	http://schemas.microsoft.com/SQL/Notifications/Pos...	1	1
5	http://schemas.microsoft.com/SQL/ServiceBroker/B...	3	1
6	http://schemas.microsoft.com/SQL/ServiceBroker/S...	5	1
7	http://schemas.microsoft.com/SQL/ServiceBroker/S...	4	1

FIGURE 11-33: Contracts view

it was created. Note that the DEFAULT contract is not supported by default; if it is not specified, the service will not support it.

Every conversation uses a contract to constrain the messages that will be sent on it. If a contract is not specified in the BEGIN DIALOG CONVERSATION expression, as it was not in Figure 11-4, the DEFAULT contract is used by the conversation. The ON CONTRACT clause (2), shown in Figure 11-35, specifies the contract to use. The contract specified must be one of the contracts (1) that is supported by the TO SERVICE.

There is a corollary to the fact that the TO SERVICE must support the contract a conversation will use. A service that does not specify any contracts may not be used as a TO SERVICE. The InspectionService in Figure 11-2, for example, could not be used as a TO SERVICE.

Send and Message Type

We have already seen that a message always includes a conversation handle, which is in the conversation_handle column of the queue, which

```
① CREATE CONTRACT Maintenance
  (
  WorkInProcess SENT BY TARGET,
  WorkRequest SENT BY INITIATOR,
  WorkComplete SENT BY TARGET
  )

② CREATE SERVICE CentralMaintenanceService
  ON QUEUE CentralMaintenanceQueue
  ([DEFAULT], Maintenance)
```

FIGURE 11-34: Supporting contracts

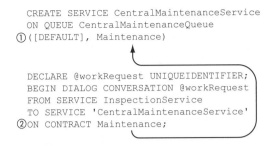

```
CREATE SERVICE CentralMaintenanceService
ON QUEUE CentralMaintenanceQueue
① ([DEFAULT], Maintenance)


DECLARE @workRequest UNIQUEIDENTIFIER;
BEGIN DIALOG CONVERSATION @workRequest
FROM SERVICE InspectionService
   TO SERVICE 'CentralMaintenanceService'
② ON CONTRACT Maintenance;
```

FIGURE 11-35: Conversation contract

can be used to send a reply to the sender of the message. Messages also always include the names of the service contract being used and the message type of the message. Figure 11-36 shows the `conversation_handle`, `service_contract_name`, and `message_type_name` columns of the `CentralMaintenanceQueue` (1). You can see that the queue contains the `WorkRequest` message that was sent using the `Maintenance` contract.

The message type name is added to the message by the `SEND` expression (1) with an optional `MESSAGE TYPE` clause, as shown in Figure 11-37. When a `SEND` expression does not specify a message type, such as the `SEND` expression in Figure 11-6, the `DEFAULT` message type is used.

The SEND expression will not block or raise an error if a message that does not comply with the validation chosen for the messages is attempted to be sent. Instead, at some point it will receive an error message in its queue. Figure 11-38 shows an example of sending a malformed message. The message being sent is a `WorkRequest` message, which was specified as using validation `WELL_FORMED_XML` in Figure 11-31.

Note that executing a `SEND` expression specifying a message type that is not part of the contract will raise an error.

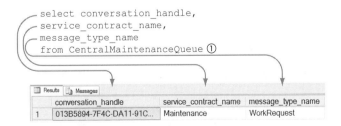

FIGURE 11-36: Message types in queue

FIGURE 11-37: SEND and message type

The problem with the message in Figure 11-38 is that there is a string(1) that must be enclosed in single or double quotes to be in compliance with the XML Recommendation. Even though the message is malformed, the SEND expression will be executed successfully.

The service associated with the other end of the @workRequest conversation in this example is the InspectionService. The result of sending the malformed message will be that an error message will be put into the InspectionQueue (2). The message (3) will be an XML description of the error that was found. The message is from Service Broker, and it can be identified as such because the document element is "Error" in the http://schemas.microsoft.com/SQL/ServiceBroker/Error namespace.

```
SEND ON CONVERSATION @workRequest
MESSAGE TYPE WorkRequest                    ①
('<WorkRequest xmlns=urn:maintenance>
<Equipment>2-37-BK</Equipment>
<Reason>Overheat</Reason>
</WorkRequest>');

-- some time passes ...                      ②
select CAST(message_body as XML) from InspectionQueue

<Error xmlns= ③
"http://schemas.microsoft.com/SQL/ServiceBroker/Error">
   <Code>-9615</Code>
   <Description>A message of type 'WorkRequest'
   failed XML validation on the target service.
   XML parsing: line 1, character 20, A string literal
   was expected This occurred in the message with
   Conversation ID '669044DD-7D17-4563-98CB-AE076EE2AA72',
   Initiator: 1, and Message
   sequence number: 0.</Description>
</Error>
```

FIGURE 11-38: Sending malformed message

The message that caused the error will be lost. When a service receives an error, any subsequent message sent on the conversation on which the error occurred will be lost. In other words, when an error occurs on a conversation, an application will no longer be able to send messages on that conversation. Note that even though it will no longer be possible to send messages on that conversation, it still will be possible to read messages from it. Also, as we will discuss in more detail later in this chapter, if retention is enabled in the queue, it is possible to recover the message that caused the error.

This response to an error, basically turning off the conversation, fits in with the Service Broker view that the primary programming element in Service Broker is the conversation, not the message. In other words, the message in error was lost; therefore, any message that followed it would be out of order. A conversation is by definition a sequence of messages received in the order in which they were sent, so the conversation is broken, and it makes no sense to carry it on any further.

Many queuing technologies view the message as the primary programming element; they will automatically send a bad message to a special queue and continue to process subsequent messages. Imagine if the intent of the bad message was to say, "Do not process any of the funds-transfer messages that follow me." Service Broker's approach to error handling is quite different from this; it stops further processing in the conversation.

There are a couple of important points to note about XML documents that contain a DTD. The first message shown in Figure 11-29 contains a DTD. This message does not comply with the WELL_FORMED_XML validation. If SQL Server 2005 detects a WELL_FORMED_XML message that has DTD in it, however, it will not send an error message. In other words, the application will not know that a malformed message was sent if the problem was due to a DTD.

This is not correct operation and may be corrected in some future Service Pack for SQL Server 2005 release. The conversation will be shut down as with any error, though, and the message itself will be stored in the sys.transmission_queue and never be sent, but no error message will be sent to inform the application.

It turns out that the idiom shown in the message (2), as shown in Figure 11-39, is a fairly common one, where an ENTITY is used like a simple replacement macro. If some of the messages in your application are from sources outside SQL Server, it is possible that they use this idiom. The

```
         DECLARE @x XML
①  SET  @x = CONVERT(XML,
         '
②  <!DOCTYPE WorkRequst [
         <!ENTITY R1 "Overheat">
         ]>
         <WorkRequest xmlns="urn:maintenance">
         <Equipment>2-37-BK</Equipment>
         <Reason>&R1;</Reason>
         </WorkRequest>',
         2);
         SELECT @x

③  <WorkRequest xmlns="urn:maintenance">
            <Equipment>2-37-BK</Equipment>
            <Reason>Overheat</Reason>
         </WorkRequest>
```

FIGURE 11-39: Using CONVERT with DTD

T-SQL CONVERT function (1) has been enhanced in SQL Server 2005 to do the macro replacements and strip out the DTD when the expression it is converting is a string or VARBINARY, the desired type is XML, and the style is 2. The result (3) of using the CONVERT function in this way is an XML document that complies the XML_WELL_FORMED validation.

Processing Loop

We saw in the ad hoc batch in Figure 11-11 how to read a single message from a queue with a RECEIVE expression and then process it within a transaction. We also saw in Figure 11-13 that a queue can be configured with an activation procedure that Service Broker will start whenever the queue seems to be becoming deeper. This gives us the ability to process messages in the queue as they appear.

Some overhead is required to start a stored procedure, so in general, it is best to process all the messages in a queue in a single execution of a stored procedure. In fact, the overhead is sufficient that waiting a short time to see whether any more messages appear after the queue is emptied before returning from the stored procedure is best practice.

Typically, the procedure that processes messages will dispatch the messages based on their message type before processing them. This procedure must also take into account the fact that some of the messages it receives may not be part of a contract; they may be error or status messages from Service Broker.

Figure 11-40 shows a simple message-processing loop. This loop could be used to process messages for the CentralMaintenanceService. The loop

```
WHILE 1 = 1
BEGIN
  BEGIN TRAN
  WAITFOR (①
  RECEIVE TOP (1)
    @message = message_body,
    @conv = conversation_handle,
    @group = conversation_group_id,
    @type = message_type_name
    FROM CentralMaintenanceQueue
  ), TIMEOUT 5000;②
  IF @@ROWCOUNT = 1
  BEGIN
    -- process message ③
    EXEC ProcessCentralMaintanence
      @message, @conv, @group, @type
    COMMIT TRAN
  END
  ELSE
    ROLLBACK TRAN
    BREAK④
  END
END
```

FIGURE 11-40: Message processing loop

runs until a BREAK (4) is executed when no messages have been read by the RECEIVE expression. A WAITFOR (1) clause is wrapped around a RECEIVE expression and specifies a TIMEOUT (2) in milliseconds. This makes the RECEIVE expression wait for up to 5 seconds to see whether something appears in the queue. If there is nothing in the queue after 5 seconds of waiting, the RECEIVE will end with @@ROWCOUNT = 0, which will execute the BREAK (4) instruction and roll back the outstanding transaction.

If there is anything in the queue within 5 seconds of the RECEIVE being executed, the RECEIVE ends with @@ROWCOUNT = 1; the variables used to capture the columns from the queue are set with appropriate values; and the message is processed (3) by a stored procedure, ProcessCentralMaintenance. When the message has been processed, the transaction is committed; then a BEGIN TRAN is executed, followed by the RECEIVE expression. The RECEIVE will again wait for up to 5 seconds for another message and will keep doing this until the queue is empty and stays empty for 5 seconds.

The RECEIVE and the processing that follows are done under the same transaction. It is important that each RECEIVE/processing step be under a different transaction. Each RECEIVE has the potential of locking a different conversation group. If all the RECEIVE/processing steps were done under the same transaction, they could unnecessarily prevent processing loops from running. There is one exception to this that we will look at later in this chapter: multiple RECEIVE/processing steps done under the same transaction and the same conversation group.

The message-processing (3) part of the processing loop in Figure 11-40 must take into account all the messages it might receive. The processing loop itself doesn't really know what conversation it will be part of, so we will assume that it is going to be in the activation procedure for the CentralMaintenanceQueue that was created in Figure 11-34. This means that the processing loop will have to support the DEFAULT and Maintenance contracts, along with the END CONVERSATION and error messages that Service Broker might send to it.

Listing 11-2 shows the stored procedure, ProcessCentralMaintenance, that dispatches messages based on their message_type_name. It handles the four possible message types that the CentralMaintenanceService might receive: DEFAULT, WorkRequest, http://schemas.microsoft.com/SQL/ServiceBroker/EndDialog, and http://schemas.microsoft.com/SQL/ServiceBroker/Error.

We have not defined the processing for the DEFAULT, so the processing for it just selects the message itself as a placeholder.

We will process the WorkRequest the same way we did in Figure 11-11— send back a reply that is timestamped and add the request to the WorkInProgress table—but with a few differences. We used the XQuery modify function in Figure 11-11 to add the timestamp to the incoming message, so we could use it as a reply. But in Figure 11-11, we received the message as an XML type. The ProcessCentralMaintenance stored procedure, however, receives the message as a VARBINARY(MAX) so that it can handle any of the possible message types it could receive. The XQuery modify method may not be used on a VARBINARY(MAX), even if it contains XML. So we have to convert the message to XML by copying it into an XML variable and then use the XQuery modify method on that variable.

We also have changed the WorkInProgress table by adding a group column to hold the conversation_group_id of the message. This is the typical way state is stored in a Service Broker application. When another message is processed by ProcessCentralMaintenance, it can use that message's conversation_group_id to look up the data in the WorkInProgress table.

When an http://schemas.microsoft.com/SQL/ServiceBroker/EndDialog message is processed, the ProcessCentralMaintenance stored procedure just executes an END CONVERSATION expression to clean up its end of the conversation.

When an http://schemas.microsoft.com/SQL/ServiceBroker/Error message is processed, the ProcessCentralMaintenance stored procedure removes all entries in the WorkInProgress table for the conversation group of the error message and then executes an END CONVERSATION expression to clean up its end of the conversation.

Note the processing that is done when an http://schemas.microsoft.com/ SQL/ServiceBroker/EndDialog or http://schemas.microsoft.com/SQL/ ServiceBroker/Error is not dictated by Service Broker. The application must plan for responding to these messages in a way that makes sense for the overall application. In most cases, though, both messages will execute an END CONVERSATION, and an error may require any state to be cleaned up.

Note that there a number of ways to dispatch on message type. A case statement could be used, for example. Also notice that the names of the message types from Service Broker are rather long. In fact, they are uniform resource identifiers as are typically used on the Web. These are not the URLs for Web sites, however. Uniform resource identifiers are specified in the Uniform Resource Identifier RFC (2396). A URL is a kind of uniform resource identifier. The examples in this chapter have used short, simple names for Service Broker objects to make it easier to follow the explanation. It is best practice to use a uniform resource identifier for the name of a Service Broker object, as that will make it easier to maintain them in a large enterprise.

Note that at the end of the ProcessCentralMaintenance stored procedure simply removes the work in progress from the WorkInProgress table when an error is detected. An actual application would have to have a more sensible way to handle errors; the purpose of this example is just to show that errors must be handled in some way.

LISTING 11-2: Message dispatch

```
CREATE
PROC ProcessCentral Maintenance
(
@message VARBINARY(MAX),
@conv UNIQUEIDENTIFIER,
@group UNIQUEIDENTIFIER,
@type NVARCHAR(256)
)
```

```
AS
IF @type = 'DEFAULT'
BEGIN
 --process default message
 SELECT @message
END
IF @type = 'WorkRequest'
BEGIN
 DECLARE @ts VARCHAR(MAX);
 SET @ts = CAST(GETDATE() AS VARCHAR(MAX));
 DECLARE @xmlMsg XML
 SET @xmlMsg = @message
 SET @xmlMsg.modify('insert (
 attribute timestamp{sql:variable(''@ts'')}
 ) into (/*[1])');
 SELECT @message, @conv;
 SEND ON CONVERSATION @conv
 Message Type WorkInProcess
 (@message)
 INSERT INTO PendingWork VALUES (@group, @message)
END
IF @type =
'http://schemas.microsoft.com/SQL/ServiceBroker/EndDialog'
BEGIN
 END CONVERSATION @conv
END
IF @type =
'http://schemas.microsoft.com/SQL/ServiceBroker/Error'
BEGIN
 —handle error
 DELETE WorkInProgress WHERE group = @group
 END CONVERSATION @conv
END
```

The message-processing loop shown in Figure 11-40 and Listing 11-2 processes one message at a time. Even though it is processing one message at a time, it is still very efficient, because it processes as many messages as possible each time the loop is called.

There is an enhancement to this loop that in some cases will make it even more efficient. The principle is to process messages one conversation group at a time instead of one message at a time. This can be more efficient, because the cost of getting the state for the conversation group can be amortized over many messages.

The GET CONVERSATION GROUP expression gets the conversation_group_id for the next available message—that is, the next message in an unlocked conversation group—in the queue and locks the corresponding conversation group.

The implementation of the conversation-group-at-a-time processing is shown in Listing 11-3. It is a loop within a loop. The outer loop uses a GET CONVERSATION GROUP expression to get and lock the next conversation group. A GET CONVERSATION GROUP expression can use a WAITFOR clause, shown in bold, in the same way that a RECEIVE expression can. If no conversation group is available after a few seconds, the transaction is rolled back, and the lock is released.

A conversation group is available; then the loop from Listing 11-3 is run. But the RECEIVE expression uses a predicate that looks only for messages in the conversation group that were found by the GET CONVERSATION GROUP expression.

LISTING 11-3: Conversation group at a time

```
WHILE 1 = 1
BEGIN
DECLARE @message VARBINARY(MAX);
DECLARE @conv UNIQUEIDENTIFIER;
DECLARE @group UNIQUEIDENTIFIER;
DECLARE @type NVARCHAR(256)
BEGIN TRAN
WAITFOR (
  GET CONVERSATION GROUP @conv
  FROM CentralMaintenanceQueue
  ), TIMEOUT 5000
IF @ROWCOUNT = 0
BEGIN
  ROLLBACK TRAN
  BREAK
END
-- get state
WHILE 1=1
BEGIN
RECEIVE TOP (1)
  @message = message_body,
  @group = conversation_group_id,
  @type = message_type_name
  FROM CentralMaintenanceQueue
  WHERE conversation_group_id = @conv;
-- process message
EXEC ProcessCentralMaintenance
END
COMMIT TRAN
END
```

Poison Messages

Message processing, as shown in Listing 11-2 and Listing 11-3, is done under a transaction, and queues themselves are transactional. If, in the course of processing a message, the transaction is rolled back, the message will be put back into the queue. At some point—in fact, in most cases immediately, because the message will be at the beginning of the queue—the message will be read again, and during its processing, the transaction might again be rolled back. A message whose processing always causes the transaction that wraps it to be rolled back is called *a poison message.*

One of the strategies for managing poison messages is to move the message to a special queue after it causes some small number of rolled-back transactions and then continue processing the messages that follow it. The "poison message" queue is processed at some later time, possibly by hand. Some queuing frameworks will automatically implement this strategy, relieving the application code of having to track the number of times a transaction is rolled back.

Service Broker provides no special support to continue processing automatically when a poison message is received. Service Broker treats the conversation as the fundamental unit of information, not the message. Imagine a conversation that produced a message that said, "Ignore all following funds transfers," but that could not be processed because of other data it contained. Moving this message to a poison-message queue and then processing the ones that follow would not be a good thing to do.

Service Broker provides no automatic support for bypassing poison messages. It does allow for the fact that in the course of normal processing of a message, something unexpected might happen—for example, the transaction that wraps the processing might become the victim of a deadlock.

The processing loop for a queue must process all messages it receives. If a poison-message queue makes sense for the application, the processing loop will have to implement it.

Service Broker does provide last-resort protection for poison messages, so it will never get into an infinite loop of rolling back a transaction and reprocessing a message. Whenever a queue has a message put back into it five times in a row, due to a rolled-back transaction, Service Broker disables the queue—that is it, in effect executes ALTER QUEUE WITH STATUS = OFF, as shown in Figure 11-16. Note that this is truly a last-resort protection, as it stops not only messages from the conversation involved, but also messages in all conversations that use the queue that it turned off. This means that `sys.transmission_queues` trying to send messages on these conversations will be filling up until the queue is enabled.

When Service Broker uses the last-resort protection, it also raises a SQL Event named `Broker_Queue_Disabled`. This event can be found in Books Online under `BROKER_QUEUE_DISABLE` and "designing Event Notifications," SQL Events are discussed in Chapter 8. The handler for this event may be able to clean up the problem automatically, or it may have to notify a person to clean things up manually.

Compensation

Service Broker is a framework that can be used to implement business transactions as sagas—a series of independent database transactions that may go on for a long time, even years. Compensation is a way to undo the effects of a saga in a way analogous to a rollback of a database transaction. A saga is not a database transaction, however; there is no "guaranteed by mathematics" way to clean up what has been done by a saga when it fails. It is up to the application to design a compensation strategy for when a saga fails.

An example of a saga that fails is one for a purchase order that was canceled by the customer who issued it. Between the time the purchase order was received and the time that it was canceled, the saga associated with it may have taken parts out of inventory or even, as a side effect, started up a manufacturing process. When a cancellation is received, the saga must compensate for the changes it has made—for example, return parts to inventory and cancel production runs. Note that unlike database transactions, compensation does not actually put things back exactly as they were.

Queues optionally may be configured to retain messages for the life of a conversation. Note that an error will not end the life of a conversation; both ends of the conversation must call END CONVERSATION to do that, even when an error is involved. The retained messages include both those sent by the service associated with the queue and those received by the queue.

By default, retention is not enabled for a queue. Figure 11-41 shows a CREATE QUEUE expression that uses a WITH RETENTION option (1) to enable

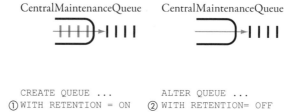

FIGURE 11-41: Retention

retention for the queue. Retention may be enabled or disabled at any time by using `ALTER QUEUE` expression (2).

The example in Figure 11-42 has retention enabled for both the Central-MaintenanceQueue, which is associated with the `CentralMaintenance-Service`, and the `InspectionQueue`, which is associated with the InspectionService. It sends a message (1) from the `InspectionService` to the `CentralMaintenanceService`. The message, however, appears (2) in the `InspectionQueue`—that is, the queue for the `FROM SERVICE`.

Even though this message is in the `InspectionQueue`, it cannot be read using a `RECEIVE` expression. The `RECEIVE` expression will always skip any

```
DECLARE @workRequest UNIQUEIDENTIFIER;
BEGIN DIALOG CONVERSATION @workRequest
    FROM SERVICE InspectionService
    TO SERVICE 'CentralMaintenanceService'
    ON CONTRACT Maintenance;
① SEND ON CONVERSATION @workRequest
    MESSAGE TYPE WorkRequest
    ('
    <WorkRequest xmlns="urn:maintenance">
    <Equipment>1ccc2-37-BK</Equipment>
    <Reason>Overheat</Reason>
    </WorkRequest>');

SELECT status,
    CAST(message_body AS XML) AS message
    from InspectionQueue
```

	status	message
② 1	3	<WorkRequest xmlns="urn:maintenance"><Equipment>...

FIGURE 11-42: Retention of sent message

retained messages. The status column of a queue indicates why the message is there. A status of 0 indicates that the message is ready to be read. The RECEIVE will read only messages whose status is 0.

A status of 3 indicates that the message was sent by a service associated with the queue, which is the case for the message we can see in the InvoiceQueue (2) in Figure 11-42. A status of 1 means that the message has already been read but is being retained.

Figure 11-43 shows a queue retaining a message that was received. A RECEIVE expression is used to read (1) the CentralMaintenanceQueue. After the message has been read, it is still in (2) the CentralMaintenanceQueue but with a status of 1, indicating that it has been read.

When a saga fails, the application can go back to all the queues involved, use a SELECT * WHERE STATUS = 1 expression to find the messages that have been retained for it, and use those messages to determine how to compensate for the effects of the saga.

There is no way to remove retained messages directly. The retained messages will remain in the queue until the conversation they belong to has been ended. When using retention to implement compensation, you must keep conversations involved with a saga active until the retained messages associated with them are no longer needed.

Retention is not the only way to implement compensation. The main disadvantage of retention is that if sagas are long or involve many messages, queues will become large and impact overall performance. Retention not only requires more storage to hold the messages, in effect each message is sent twice, once to put it back into the queue it was read from and then again to send it to its destination.

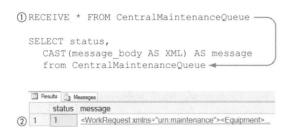

FIGURE 11-43: Retention of received message

Compensation can be implemented without using retention. If possible, it is best to implement a compensation strategy based on some simple state rather than on all the messages processed to get to that state. A saga that processes a purchase order, for example, might add a column for each line item that says whether that part has been reserved from inventory for that purchase order. If the saga fails, the compensation could use the purchase order to determine what to return to inventory. This technique would almost certainly require less storage than all the messages used to process the purchase order.

Distribution

So far, all the discussions and examples of using Service Broker have been with services that are all in the same database. This has been done to make the explanations of how services, queues, and the like work easier to follow. A typical Service Broker application will be distributed over many databases and many servers. Now we are going to look at how this is done.

The example shown in Figure 11-6 that sends a message to a non\existent service shows that Service Broker manages services through their names, not directly by their locations. Service Broker maps the name of a service to its location. If it can find no location for the name when a message is sent, it puts the message into the `sys.transmission_queue` and keeps it there until it can.

There are two separate topics to cover. One is how Service Broker maps the name of a service to the location of that service, and the other is how Service Broker manages security for a conversation between two different instances of SQL Server on different machines. You may find it easier to try the examples that follow by using two instances of SQL Server on the same machine. Sometimes, the order in which things are set up is important. Listing 11-6 and Listing 11-7, later in this chapter, summarize the points that follow with things set up in an appropriate order.

Figure 11-44 diagrams two instances of SQL Server 2005 that contain the services we have been working with, `CentralMaintenanceService` and `InspectionService`, in a single database. The instance on the left, Bismark, contains a database, Company, that contains the `CentralMaintenance-Service`. Service Broker does not use the name of a database to identify the location of a service. It uses a `UNIQUEIDENTIFIER`, which it assigns, called a broker instance. In Figure 11-44, the `CentralMaintenanceService` is

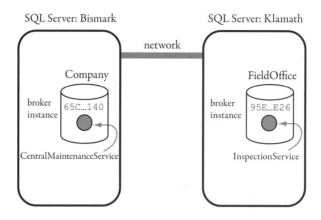

FIGURE 11-44: Service broker instances

located in the 65C9E167-0DE0-4B12-9E14-A0DAEB2B4140 broker instance in the SQL Server 2005 Bismark instance.

On the right side of Figure 11-44 is an instance of SQL Server 2005 named Klamath. It contains the `FieldOffice` database, which contains the InspectionService.

The two instances of SQL Server communicate by using the network and the Adjacent Broker Protocol, which is implemented by Service Broker. Note that the connection between SQL Server 2005 instances shown in Figure 11-44 is not a static connection; it is made only as required.

Every database in a SQL Server 2005 instance is a Service Broker and has a unique `broker_instance` in the form of a GUID. The broker instance for a database is in the `service_broker_guid` column of the `sys.databases` system view. Figure 11-45 shows a `SELECT` expression used to find the broker instance for the Company database in the Bismark SQL Server 2005 instance. Note that terms *Service Broker GUID* and *broker instance* are synonyms, and both terms appear in Books Online and various system views.

Sometimes, you need to know the broker instance for a database. In those cases, you have to look it up in the `sys.databases` view of the appropriate instance of SQL Server 2005. Figure 11-45 shows a `SELECT` expression used to find the service instance of the Company database.

`BEGIN DIALOG CONVERSATION` optionally allows the `TO SERVICE` to specify a broker instance. When it is not specified, the broker instance of the database in use when the `BEGIN DIALOG CONVERSATION` is executed is used.

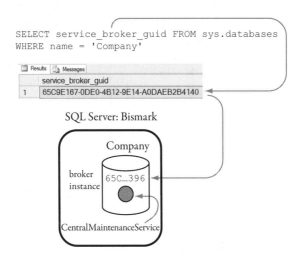

FIGURE 11-45: Service broker instance

In the previous examples, all the services were in the same database, so we didn't have to deal with the broker instance. It is possible to have two services with the same name in different databases of the same instance of SQL Server 2005. In this case, the broker instance can be used to specify one of these two services.

Listing 11-4 shows a BEGIN DIALOG CONVERSATION that specifies the broker instance, shown in bold, for CentralMaintenanceService. When the broker instance is used, it follows the name of the TO SERVICE after a comma. A special broker instance, 'CURRENT DATABASE', may also be used to specify the current database explicitly.

LISTING 11-4: Specifying broker instance

```
DECLARE @workRequest UNIQUEIDENTIFIER;
BEGIN DIALOG CONVERSATION @workRequest
FROM SERVICE InspectionService
TO SERVICE 'CentralMaintenanceService',
'65C9E167-0DE0-4B12-9E14-A0DAEB2B4140'
ON CONTRACT Maintenance;
SELECT @workRequest;
SEND ON CONVERSATION @workRequest
MESSAGE TYPE WorkRequest
('
<WorkRequest xmlns="urn:maintenance">
<Equipment>1ccc2-37-BK</Equipment>
<Reason>Overheat</Reason>
</WorkRequest>');
```

Service Broker always uses a routing table to determine the instance of SQL Server 2005 that a message should be sent to. Each database in a SQL Server 2005 instance has a routing table. The routing table can be seen though the sys.routes system view in that database. The routing table from the database in use when the SEND expression is executed is used to determine the instance of SQL Server 2005 that a message should be sent to.

A routing table includes several pieces of information, all of which are documented in Books Online. There are three key pieces of information used to route messages, and they are in the `remote_service_name`, `broker_instance`, and `address` columns of the `sys.routes` system view. The routing table maps the remote_service_name of a service and its broker instance, from the TO SERVICE in BEGIN DIALOG CONVERSATION expression, to an instance of SQL Server 2005.

When SQL Server 2005 is installed, it includes a route named `AutoCreatedLocal` in the routing table for the model database. As a result, unless this is changed, all new databases include this route in their routing table. Figure 11-46 shows the contents of the initial routing table for a database. The `AutoCreatedLocal` route is used as a wildcard for those services that do not match any other entry in the routing table. The NULL for the `remote_service_name` (1) and `broker_instance` (2) are wildcards that match any service name or broker instance. LOCAL (3) means that the message should be sent to the instance of SQL Server 2005 that the SEND command is running on—that is, the local instance.

Routes are managed using the CREATE ROUTE, ALTER ROUTE, and DROP ROUTE expressions. CREATE ROUTE specifies the three key pieces of information that were previously mentioned, along with a LIFETIME for the route. Listing 11-5 shows the typical usage of CREATE ROUTE. The SERVICE_NAME

```
SELECT name,
    remote_service_name,
    broker_instance,
    address
    FROM model.sys.routes
```

	name	remote_service_name	broker_instance	address
1	AutoCreatedLocal	NULL	NULL	LOCAL
		①	②	③

FIGURE 11-46: Default routing table

option corresponds to the remote_service_name shown in the sys.routes system view. The BROKER_INSTANCE and ADDRESS options correspond to the like-named columns in the sys.routes system view.

The only required parts of the CREATE ROUTE expression are the name of the route—CentralMaintenance, in this case—and the ADDRESS option. Unspecified options will be entered into the routing table as NULL. The address in this example, N'TCP://192.168.226.138:4030', is the IP address of an instance of SQL Server 2005 and the port on which it is listening for Service Broker messages. Alternatively, the address may be a host name and port. The port used is unrelated to the port SQL Server 2005 listens on for TDS client connections; an instance of SQL Server 2005 has to be configured to listen for Service Broker messages, and later in this chapter, we see how to do that. The BROKER_INSTANCE is from the sys.databases table in the instance of SQL Server 2005 that has the CentralMaintenanceService, as was shown in Figure 11-45.

LISTING 11-5: Create route

```
CREATE ROUTE CentralMaintenance
WITH SERVICE_NAME = 'CentralMaintenanceService',
BROKER_INSTANCE = '65C9E167-0DE0-4B12-9E14-A0DAEB2B4140',
ADDRESS = N'TCP://192.168.226.138:4030'
```

The SQL Server 2005 instance referenced in a CREATE ROUTE or ALTER ROUTE expression does not have to be enabled to listen for Service Broker messages or even exist when the route is created or changed. Similar to what we saw in Figure 11-6, when we sent a message to a nonexistent service, the sys.transmission_queue will hold messages until the instance of SQL Server 2005 referred to by the ADDRESS option exists and is ready to accept messages. Also, creating a route does not cause a connection to be made to the ADDRESS specified at that time; Service Broker uses the routing table to make connections as needed by SEND expressions. The CREATE ROUTE expression can succeed with a completely fictitious address.

If there are entries where remote_service_name and broker_instance match exactly, they are used. It is possible to have more than one route for a given service name. If there is no remote_service_name that exactly matches the name of the service, the entries in the routing table with a NULL remote_service_name are used. If there are entries that match the service name, and the `TO SERVICE` of the conversation involved did not specify a broker instance, those entries are used. The full details of the matching algorithm are in Books Online. Keep in mind that route names are always binary matched, not by characters, so they are case sensitive regardless of how SQL Server is configured.

If only one route is found, it is used to find the address of the SQL Server 2005 instance for that service. Figure 11-47 shows a routing table with two routes that could match the `TO SERVICE` of a conversation.

Whenever there is more than one match for a service, Service Broker uses one of them based on a simple algorithm that uses the modulus of the handle of the dialog. This is a very useful feature of Service Broker. It provides a sort of load for parts of Service Broker applications. The load balancing is "sort of" because the load balancing is done with no real load information and is done on a per-conversation basis, not a per-message basis. Nonetheless, this simple feature of Service Broker can be used to make a Service Broker application a lot more robust without having to make any changes to the application itself.

In fact, we have covered only half the routing story. Service Broker has to use a routing table when a `SEND` expression is used to figure out where a service is located. What happens when a message arrives at an endpoint? Remember that a Service Broker endpoint is associated with an instance of SQL Server 2005, not a particular database. When a message arrives at an

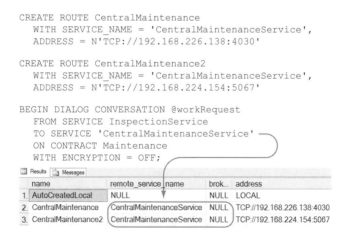

FIGURE 11-47: Route assignment

endpoint, Service Broker uses the routing table that is in msdb to find the location of the service.

The implication of this is that all conversations that go between instances of SQL Server 2005 require four routing tables to be configured: one routing table in the database that sends a message on the conversation, a second in msdb of the instance of SQL Server 2005 that receives the message, a third in the database of the service that sends a reply to the message, and a fourth in msdb of the instance of SQL Server 2005 that sent the message. The third and fourth routing tables are needed so that the service that receives the message will be able to send a reply.

Figure 11-48 shows how msdb would be set up in the Bismark instance of SQL Server 2005. Note that Service Broker assigns the broker instance to a database, so you will have to look it up in `sys.databases`. Note that this route specifies a `SERVICE_NAME` for a service that is in Bismark.

SQL Server 2005 is secure by design and default, so several things are required to enable Service Broker conversations between SQL Server 2005 instances. Each SQL Server 2005 instance must be configured to listen for other SQL Server 2005 instances using the Adjacent Broker Protocol. There must also be a way for each server to authenticate the other so it can decide whether to authorize the connection. Service Broker can use Windows authentication to do this.

When the service, sqlservr.exe, that implements SQL Server 2005 starts running, it logs onto Windows with a Windows identity. You configure this identity when you install SQL Sever 2005, as shown in Figure 11-49. Corp, in this diagram, is a domain, and SQLID is a member of it.

The identity that an instance of SQL Server 2005 uses to log onto Windows must be a SQL login on any instance of SQL Server 2005 that it will

```
use msdb
SELECT service_broker_guid
   FROM sys.databases WHERE name='Company'

CREATE ROUTE Central
   WITH SERVICE_NAME = 'CentralMaintenanceService',
   ADDRESS = N'LOCAL',
   BROKER_INSTANCE =
      '65C9E167-0DE0-4B12-9E14-A0DAEB2B4140'
```

FIGURE 11-48: Routing in msdb

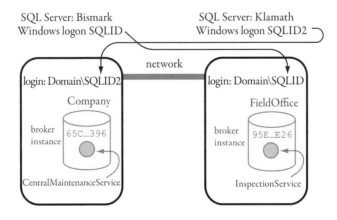

Figure 11-49: Windows logon

be sending a Service Broker message to. Figure 11-50 shows two SQL Server instances. The Klamath instance, on the right, logged onto Windows using the identity Domain\SQLID2 when it started running. It you are trying out the examples with two instances of SQL Server on a single machine, Domain would be the name of the machine. This means that the Windows identity used run an instance of SQL Server must also be a login on every instance of SQL Server that it will be connecting to with Service Broker.

The Bismark instance on the left has a SQL Windows login for Domain\SQLID2. Likewise, the Klamath instance has a login for Domain\ SQLID. These logins do not require a user in any database.

Figure 11-50: Connections identities

Figure 11-51 shows a batch that will create the Service Broker endpoint for the Klamath instance of SQL Server 2005 that can be accessed by the Bismark instance of SQL Server 2005. It starts by creating a login (1) based on a Windows identity used by the Bismark instance when it logs onto Windows. Then it creates an endpoint (2). SQL Server supports several kinds of endpoints, but Service Broker supports only a single Service Broker endpoint in an instance of SQL Server 2005, and it must be a TCP endpoint. The AS TCP clause must specify the port that it will listen on. The actual port number is not important, but it must not be in use already.

An endpoint has a name, so it can be referenced. This endpoint is created in the STARTED state, but by default, an endpoint is created in the STOPPED state. There is an ALTER ENDPOINT expression, documented in Books Online, that can be used to change the state of an endpoint. This endpoint is configured as a Service Broker endpoint, and it uses Windows authentication.

This login is granted CONNECT (3) permission on the Service Broker endpoint. This permission is required for the Bismark instance to send messages to the Klamath instance. Note that the master database must be in use to be able to GRANT CONNECT to an endpoint. You cannot GRANT CONNECT to an endpoint from any other database.

The data saved by CREATE ENDPOINT for a Service Broker endpoint can be seen in two system views, sys.endpoints and sys.tcp_endpoints. Figure 11-52 shows a join of these views from the Klamath instance of SQL Server 2005. It shows that there is a Service Broker endpoint named Inspection (1) that is in the STARTED state (2) and listens on port 4030 (4) using the TCP (3) protocol.

Listing 11-6 and Listing 11-7 are batches for setting Klamath and Bismark, respectively. The batches assume that both instances are set up on the same

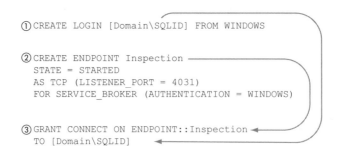

```
① CREATE LOGIN [Domain\SQLID] FROM WINDOWS

② CREATE ENDPOINT Inspection
   STATE = STARTED
   AS TCP (LISTENER_PORT = 4031)
   FOR SERVICE_BROKER (AUTHENTICATION = WINDOWS)

③ GRANT CONNECT ON ENDPOINT::Inspection
   TO [Domain\SQLID]
```

FIGURE 11-51: Endpoint for Klamath

```
select E.name,
  E.state_desc,
  E.protocol_desc,
  T.port
  from sys.endpoints E
  JOIN sys.tcp_endpoints T
  ON E.endpoint_id = T.endpoint_id
  WHERE E.type_desc = 'SERVICE_BROKER'
```

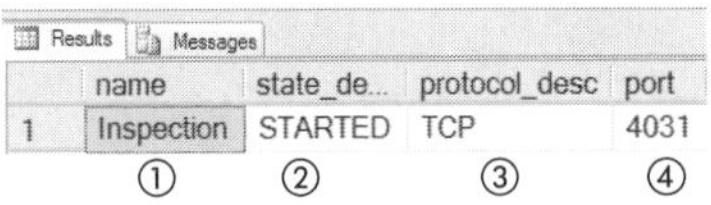

	name	state_de...	protocol_desc	port
1	Inspection	STARTED	TCP	4031
	①	②	③	④

FIGURE 11-52: Endpoints

machine and that the machine's name is DANAL-BASE. The IP addresses, ports, and broker instances used are machine dependent and will have to be changed to match the machine they are run on. It is recommended that you run each statement in the batch separately and look at how it affects the data in the various system views we have been discussing.

Note that the GUIDs in the `CREATE ROUTE` expression near the ends of Listing 11-6 and Listing 11-7 had to be looked up using the technique shown in Figure 11-45.

LISTING 11-6: Klamath setup

```
use master
-- Figure 11-51
CREATE LOGIN [DANAL-BASE\SQLID] FROM WINDOWS

CREATE DATABASE FieldOffice
ALTER DATABASE FieldOffice
SET ENABLE_BROKER
USE FieldOffice
CREATE MASTER KEY ENCRYPTION BY PASSWORD = 'P@ssw0rd'
use master

CREATE ENDPOINT Inspection
STATE = STARTED
AS TCP (LISTENER_PORT = 4031)
FOR SERVICE_BROKER (AUTHENTICATION = WINDOWS)

GRANT CONNECT ON ENDPOINT::Inspection
TO [DANAL-BASE\SQLID]


use FieldOffice
 GRANT SEND ON Service::InspectionService
```

```
TO PUBLIC

-- Listing 11-5

CREATE ROUTE CentralMaintenance
WITH SERVICE_NAME = 'CentralMaintenanceService',
ADDRESS = N'TCP://192.168.226.138:4030'

-- Figure 11-48
use msdb

SELECT service_broker_guid FROM sys.databases WHERE name='FieldOffice'
CREATE ROUTE Inspection
WITH SERVICE_NAME = 'InspectionService',
ADDRESS = N'LOCAL',
BROKER_INSTANCE = '424D4331-B382-49C7-81A0-D2B82D81350F'

use FieldOffice

CREATE ROUTE CentralMaintenance
WITH SERVICE_NAME = 'CentralMaintenanceService',
ADDRESS = N'TCP://192.168.226.138:4030'
```

LISTING 11-7: Bismark setup

```
CREATE DATABASE Company
ALTER DATABASE Company
SET ENABLE_BROKER
USE Company
CREATE MASTER KEY ENCRYPTION BY PASSWORD = 'P@ssw0rd'

use master
CREATE LOGIN [DANAL-BASE\SQLID2] FROM WINDOWS

CREATE ENDPOINT Central
AS TCP (LISTENER_PORT = 4030)
FOR SERVICE_BROKER (AUTHENTICATION = WINDOWS)

ALTER ENDPOINT Central STATE = STARTED

GRANT CONNECT ON ENDPOINT::Central
TO [DANAL-BASE\SQLID2]

use Company

GRANT SEND ON Service::CentralMaintenanceService
TO PUBLIC

CREATE ROUTE Inspection
```

```
WITH SERVICE_NAME = 'InspectionService',
ADDRESS = N'TCP://192.168.226.138:4031'


use msdb
SELECT service_broker_guid FROM sys.databases WHERE name='Company'

CREATE ROUTE Central
WITH SERVICE_NAME = 'CentralMaintenanceService',
ADDRESS = N'LOCAL',
BROKER_INSTANCE = '1A245923-86D3-4B52-BCAD-0713E0C4F7FC'
```

One of the nice things about a Service Broker application is that when you distribute it across systems, the application code doesn't change. In fact, the code we used at the beginning of the chapter, where the services were both in the same database, will still work; we just have to move it to the servers we want it to work on, configure the routes, and add the endpoints.

Listing 11-8 has the application that would run on the Bismark instance of SQL Server 2005, and Listing 11-9 has the application that would run on the Klamath instance of SQL Server 2005. The results of using these applications would be the same as when we used the `CentralMaintenanceService` and `InspectionService` at the beginning of this chapter.

One important thing to note about moving a Service Broker application: All the XML schemas, message types, and contracts used must be copied to any database the application gets moved to.

LISTING 11-8: Bismark application

```
CREATE XML SCHEMA COLLECTION WorkOrder
AS
'<xs:schema xmlns:xs="http://www.w3.org/2001/XMLSchema"
elementFormDefault="qualified"
targetNamespace="urn:maintenance"
 xmlns="urn:maintenance">
  <xs:element name="WorkRequest">
    <xs:complexType>
      <xs:sequence>
        <xs:element name="Equipment" type="xs:string"/>
        <xs:element name="Reason" type="xs:string"/>
      </xs:sequence>
        <xs:attribute name="timestamp" type="xs:string" use="required"/>
    </xs:complexType>
  </xs:element>
```

```
</xs:schema>
'



CREATE MESSAGE TYPE WorkInProcess
VALIDATION = VALID_XML WITH SCHEMA COLLECTION WorkOrder

CREATE MESSAGE TYPE WorkRequest
VALIDATION = WELL_FORMED_XML

CREATE MESSAGE TYPE WorkComplete
VALIDATION  = EMPTY


CREATE CONTRACT Maintenance
(
WorkInProcess SENT BY TARGET,
WorkRequest SENT BY INITIATOR,
WorkComplete SENT BY TARGET
)



CREATE QUEUE CentralMaintenanceQueue
WITH ACTIVATION (
PROCEDURE_NAME = CentralMaintenance,
MAX_QUEUE_READERS = 2,
EXECUTE AS SELF )

CREATE SERVICE CentralMaintenanceService
ON QUEUE CentralMaintenanceQueue
([DEFAULT], Maintenance)



CREATE TABLE PendingWork
(
work XML
)
GO



CREATE
PROC CentralMaintenance
AS
WHILE 1 = 1
BEGIN
DECLARE @message VARBINARY(MAX);
DECLARE @conv UNIQUEIDENTIFIER;
```

```
DECLARE @group UNIQUEIDENTIFIER;
DECLARE @type NVARCHAR(256)
BEGIN TRAN
WAITFOR (
 GET CONVERSATION GROUP @conv
 FROM CentralMaintenanceQueue
 ), TIMEOUT 5000
IF @conv IS NULL
BEGIN
 ROLLBACK TRAN
 BREAK
END
-- get state
WHILE 1=1
BEGIN
WAITFOR (
RECEIVE TOP (1)
 @message = message_body,
 @group = conversation_group_id,
 @type = message_type_name
 FROM CentralMaintenanceQueue
 WHERE conversation_group_id = @conv
), TIMEOUT 5000;
IF @@ROWCOUNT = 1
-- process message
EXEC ProcessCentralMaintenance
END
END
GO


CREATE
PROC ProcessCentralMaintenance
(
@message VARBINARY(MAX),
@conv UNIQUEIDENTIFIER,
@group UNIQUEIDENTIFIER,
@type NVARCHAR(256)
)
AS
IF @type = 'DEFAULT'
BEGIN
--process default message
SELECT @message
END
IF @type = 'WorkRequest'
BEGIN
DECLARE @ts VARCHAR(MAX);
SET @ts = CAST(GETDATE() AS VARCHAR(MAX));
DECLARE @xmlMsg XML
SET @xmlMsg = @message
```

```
SET @xmlMsg.modify('insert (
attribute timestamp{sql:variable("@ts")}
) into (/*[1])');
SELECT @message, @conv;
SEND ON CONVERSATION @conv
Message Type WorkInProcess
(@message)
INSERT INTO PendingWork VALUES (@message)
END
IF @type =
'http://schemas.microsoft.com/SQL/ServiceBroker/EndDialog'
BEGIN
END CONVERSATION @conv
END
IF @type =
'http://schemas.microsoft.com/SQL/ServiceBroker/Error'
BEGIN
-- handle error
SELECT @message
END
GO



CREATE QUEUE CentralMaintenanceQueue
WITH ACTIVATION (
PROCEDURE_NAME = CentralMaintenance,
MAX_QUEUE_READERS = 2,
EXECUTE AS SELF )

CREATE SERVICE CentralMaintenanceService
ON QUEUE CentralMaintenanceQueue
([DEFAULT], Maintenance)
```

LISTING 11-9: Klamath application

```
CREATE XML SCHEMA COLLECTION WorkOrder
AS
'<xs:schema xmlns:xs="http://www.w3.org/2001/XMLSchema"
elementFormDefault="qualified"
targetNamespace="urn:maintenance"
 xmlns="urn:maintenance">
  <xs:element name="WorkRequest">
    <xs:complexType>
      <xs:sequence>
        <xs:element name="Equipment" type="xs:string"/>
        <xs:element name="Reason" type="xs:string"/>
      </xs:sequence>
        <xs:attribute name="timestamp" type="xs:string" use="required"/>
```

```
       </xs:complexType>
   </xs:element>
</xs:schema>
'

CREATE MESSAGE TYPE WorkInProcess
VALIDATION = VALID_XML WITH SCHEMA COLLECTION WorkOrder

CREATE MESSAGE TYPE WorkRequest
VALIDATION = WELL_FORMED_XML

CREATE MESSAGE TYPE WorkComplete
VALIDATION  = EMPTY

CREATE CONTRACT Maintenance
(
WorkInProcess SENT BY TARGET,
WorkRequest SENT BY INITIATOR,
WorkComplete SENT BY TARGET
)


CREATE QUEUE InspectionQueue

CREATE SERVICE InspectionService
ON QUEUE InspectionQueue


DECLARE @workRequest UNIQUEIDENTIFIER;
BEGIN DIALOG CONVERSATION @workRequest
FROM SERVICE InspectionService
TO SERVICE 'CentralMaintenanceService'
ON CONTRACT Maintenance
WITH ENCRYPTION = OFF;
SEND ON CONVERSATION @workRequest
MESSAGE TYPE WorkRequest
('
<WorkRequest xmlns="urn:maintenance">
<Equipment>1ccc2-37-BK</Equipment>
<Reason>Overheat</Reason>
</WorkRequest>');
```

Where Are We?

SQL Server Service Broker is a platform that deeply integrates messaging
into the database architecture and provides a framework for implementing
business transactions as sagas—a series of related database transactions
that may be distributed across time and systems.

We started this chapter by building some services that were contained in a single database; later, albeit with some configuration, we were able to move these applications to different servers without changing them.

Distributed applications introduce several other issues that applications that run on a single server do not have. Authentication is required for remote communication, and Service Broker leverages Windows authentication to handle this. Service Broker also can use X509 Certificates to do authentication when there is no common Windows domain between servers. Service Broker supports doing next-hop routing so that virtual networks can be implemented. Service Broker supports both point-to-point encryption, when message confidentiality is required, and end-to-end encryption, when message confidentiality is required across a virtual network. Space constraints limit this chapter from covering all these topics, but they are covered in Books Online. Search for "Service Broker Routing" and "Service Broker Dialog Security" for more discussion of these topics.

▃ 12 ▪

SQL Server As a Platform
for Web Services

W EB SERVICES ARE directly integrated into SQL Server 2005. Web
Services do not require a library to be distributed to clients and are
widely supported across all languages and platforms commonly in use today.
Prior to SQL Server 2005, the only way to communicate with SQL Server was
with Microsoft-supplied libraries that had to be distributed to clients.

Mixing Databases and Web Services

SQL Server 2005 adds another protocol that clients can use to communicate
directly with SQL Server: SOAP over HTTP, which is Web Services.

Prior to SQL Server 2005, a proprietary protocol, TDS (Tabular Data
Stream), was used by clients to communicate directly with SQL Server. TDS
is a proprietary and undocumented protocol, and requires a set of client
network libraries. These libraries are the SQL Server network libraries, and
Microsoft distributes them only on Windows operating systems.

SQL Server supports using old versions of the TDS protocol for compatibility purposes, but only with limited functionality. Even the libraries
distributed by Sybase for its database system will work with SQL Server
because Sybase also uses TDS; SQL Server and Sybase at one time used a
common codebase. Access to the full functionality of SQL Server 2005 via
TDS requires the latest network libraries that are distributed by Microsoft.

Web Services expose a standard mechanism for communication that uses standard protocols and message formats. The network protocol most often used is HTTP, and the message format is known as SOAP. SOAP is described in a set of recommendations from the World Wide Web Consortium. A primer is available at http://www.w3.org/TR/2003/REC-soap12-part0-20030624/.

SOAP over HTTP has become a popular means of communication because it does not depend on particular libraries being distributed to clients and can even be used between applications running on different operating systems. The systems involved need only to support HTTP and XML, which is the case for virtually all languages and operating systems in common use today.

In practice, it is possible to connect to SQL Server using TDS through a firewall, and it is not all that uncommon. But the techniques for this are not as familiar as the ones for letting HTTP connections go through a firewall. SQL Server 2005 includes many new features that extend its utility far beyond being a repository for corporate data. These new features, along with the fact that Web Services are integrated directly into SQL Server 2005, will lead to use cases for SQL Server we would never have thought of before.

Web Services integrated directly into SQL Server 2005 are very useful, even if we ignore the capability to punch through a firewall. They offer connectivity to SQL Server without the requirement to deploy a client library and keep it up to date, even when those "clients" are middle-tier servers. Web Services themselves are being widely deployed. With SQL Server 2005, middle-tier servers can relay on a Web Service message directly to SQL Server without having to process it. And, of course, those middle-tier servers might not even be running Windows as an operating system.

It's a bit of a red herring to think of Web Services integrated directly into SQL Server 2005 as just providing a standard of punching through a firewall, because it adds much more than that. In the past, SQL Server has supported connectivity though Banyan Vines and Novell Netware because at the time, they were in wide use. Think of Web Services integrated directly into SQL Server 2005 as just another networking technology that is supported by SQL Server.

SQL Server 2000 also allowed communication via HTTP and Web Services, but it depended on Internet Information Server (IIS) for HTTP and SOAP support. It did this by adding a custom ISAPI (Internet Server Application Program Interface) filter and extensions to IIS; in other words, it created an ISAPI application, which is the standard way to extend IIS.

This ISAPI application could be configured by an MMC (Microsoft Management Console) snap-in to add virtual directories to IIS and map those virtual directories to functionality in SQL Server. The ISAPI application would listen for appropriately formatted HTTP requests, convert them to TDS commands, send the commands to SQL Server, and return the results in the form of XML as the HTTP response. It provided access to SQL Server through user-configured batches, called templates, and arbitrary SQL expressions—all with appropriate levels of security, of course.

Over time, this functionality was improved and distributed though Web releases and called SQLXML. These releases added features that allowed XML to be used to update SQL Server and to map stored procedures and function to Web Services. In effect, this turned SQL Server into a Web Service.

SQLXML and the ISAPI filter and extensions needed to make it work are not distributed with SQL Server 2005, but all the capabilities of SQLXML 3.0 are available in SQL 2005. This means that applications that currently use SQLXML will not have to be upgraded to use SQL Server 2005. They will operate as they always did, although through IIS.

SQL Server 2000 depended on IIS to implement the HTTP protocol for it. Windows Server 2003 and Windows XP with Service Pack 2 (SP2) include a driver, http.sys, that fully implements the HTTP protocol. SQL Server 2005 uses http.sys to implement the HTTP protocol, which means that it has no dependency on IIS but does require Windows Server 2003 or Windows XP with SP2 as a host to support Web Services.

For a number of reasons, http.sys is a more efficient implementation of HTTP than the previous implementation used in Windows—for example, the implementations in IIS prior to IIS6. One of the key reasons is that http.sys fully implements HTTP in a kernel mode driver. Typically, applications will make fewer round trips between user and kernel mode with http.sys. Also, because http.sys is a driver, a single implementation can be used by multiple applications at the same time. This means that if appropriately configured, two applications can listen on port 80 at the same time. In general, http.sys is a better implementation of HTTP overall than previous versions.

HTTP Endpoint Declaration

In SQLXML 3.0, we could expose any stored procedure or function or allow a Transact-SQL (T-SQL) script to be executed over HTTP. We have the same capabilities in SQL Server 2005 by using an HTTP endpoint to implement a Web Service. In SQLXML 3.0, the procedures and functions were exposed as Web Services, and the query string of an HTTP GET command could be passed to SQL Server as a T-SQL script. In SQL Server 2005, all these are exposed as Web Services.

The way that we defined an HTTP endpoint with SQLXML 3.0 was to use either a COM object model that wrote to the IIS metabase and the Windows Registry or to use an MMC snap-in that provided a graphic interface to configure it. This functionality is now built directly into SQL Server 2005. The information itself is stored in SQL Server, not in an external file or the Windows Registry. T-SQL expressions are used to define, drop, and alter it. The relevant DDL statements are CREATE ENDPOINT, ALTER ENDPOINT, and DROP ENDPOINT. You can use these DDL statements to define endpoints for protocols other than HTTP (for example, SQL Server Service Broker endpoints) and for features other than Web Services, but in this chapter, we'll cover only using them to define HTTP endpoints for Web Services. We'll discuss them here and at the same time correlate these DDL statements with the COM object model that you use in SQLXML 3.0. Listing 12-1 shows the complete syntax for defining an HTTP endpoint in T-SQL.

LISTING 12-1: Syntax for Web Service

```
CREATE ENDPOINT endPointName [AUTHORIZATION <login>]
 [ STATE = { STARTED | STOPPED | DISABLED } ]
 AS HTTP
( [ SITE = {'*' | '+' | 'webSite' } ,]
PATH = ' url'
, PORTS = ({CLEAR | SSL} [,... n])
[, CLEAR_PORT = clearPort ]
[, SSL_PORT = SSLPort ]
, AUTHENTICATION =({BASIC | DIGEST |
NTLM | KERBEROS | INTEGRATED} [,...n])
[, AUTH_REALM = { 'realm' | NONE } ]
[, DEFAULT_LOGON_DOMAIN = {'domain' | NONE } ]
```

```
[, COMPRESSION = { ENABLED | DISABLED } ]
)
[ FOR SOAP (
[ { WEBMETHOD ['namespace' .] 'methodalias' (
NAME = three.part.name
[, SCHEMA = { NONE | STANDARD | DEFAULT }]
[, FORMAT = { NONE | ALL_RESULTS | ROWSETS_ONLY }])
} [,... n] ]
[ BATCHES = { ENABLED | DISABLED } ]
[ , WSDL = { NONE | DEFAULT | 'sp_name' } ]
[ , SESSIONS = { ENABLED | DISABLED } ]
[ , SESSION_TIMEOUT = {int | NEVER}]
[ , DATABASE = { 'database_name' | DEFAULT } ]
[ , NAMESPACE = { 'namespace' | DEFAULT } ]
[ , SCHEMA = { NONE | STANDARD } ]
[, CHARACTER_SET = { SQL | XML } ]
[, HEADER_LIMIT = int ]
)
```

This syntax, seen in its entirety, may seem imposing at first, but it is broken into two major sections. The AS HTTP section specifies the characteristics of the endpoint itself. The FOR SOAP section specifies the characteristics of the Web Service hosted at that endpoint.

We will start by looking a simple example of a Web Service so we can see how the major parts work. This example will expose a stored procedure, RepairEstimate, as a Web Service. Given a car model as input, RepairEstimate will return an estimate of the cost to repair it. There are several things besides creating an HTTP endpoint that we will need to do to make a working Web Service. Listing 12-2 shows a batch that creates this Web Service.

LISTING 12-2: RepairPoint Web Service

```
CREATE DATABASE Repairs
use Repairs

CREATE LOGIN [Canopus5\MiniDan] FROM WINDOWS

CREATE Function RepairEstimate(@model NVARCHAR(10))
RETURNS INT
AS
BEGIN
RETURN 12
END

CREATE USER [Canopus5\MiniDan]
```

```
GRANT EXECUTE ON RepairEstimate TO [Canopus5\MiniDan]

EXEC  sp_reserve_http_namespace
 N'http://*:80/Repairs/req'

CREATE ENDPOINT RepairPoint
STATE  = Started
AS HTTP
(
 PATH = '/Repairs/req',
 PORTS = (CLEAR),
 SITE = '*',
 AUTHENTICATION = (INTEGRATED)
)
FOR SOAP
(
 WEBMETHOD 'urn:autos'.'GetEstimate'
 (NAME = 'Repairs.dbo.RepairEstimate',
 SCHEMA=STANDARD),
 WSDL=DEFAULT,
 SCHEMA=STANDARD,
 DATABASE = 'Repairs',
 NAMESPACE = 'urn:other'
)

use master
GRANT CONNECT ON ENDPOINT::RepairPoint
 TO [Canopus5\MiniDan]
```

The batch in Listing 12-2 starts by creating a database named `Repairs` and then makes it the database in use.

Just because we are using HTTP doesn't mean security goes out the window, so to speak. In this example, we are going to use Windows security to authenticate the use of our Web Service. That will make this Web Service the equivalent of what we would have if we used Windows authentication in SQL Server for TDS connections. So a client using this Web Service is no more insecure or dangerous than a client that connects to SQL Server using TDS and Windows authentication. In fact, you actually have greater control over an HTTP endpoint than TDS; HTTP endpoints can be individually enabled, and an identity connecting to the HTTP endpoint must have connect permission for that endpoint, so access to it can be managed in the same way that access to any other database object is.

Because we are going to use Windows authentication, we will need a Windows user to access our Web Service. We gave the Windows user

MiniDan a SQL Windows login for our test. MiniDan is from the Canopus5 domain.

The implementation of `RepairEstimate` follows. Note that `RepairEstimate` is a bogus function, in that it always returns 12. We are going to expose `RepairEstimate` through a Web Service, but this of itself does not give anyone the right to execute it or to use any of the objects in SQL Server 2005. A user executing a Web Service needs the same permission that he would if he connected via TDS and tried to execute the underlying function or stored procedure.

We create a `Canopus5\MiniDan` user in the `Repair` database and then grant that user execute permission on `RepairEstimate`. We might have made `Canopus5\MiniDan` a member of a role that had execute permission or a member of a group that owned the schema for `RepairEstimate`. The important point is that we manage permissions for a user of Web Services in exactly the same way that we do for users who connect with TDS.

A Web Service lives at a Web address. In SQLXML 3.0, we used either the COM object model or the MMC snap-in to create a virtual directory in IIS for our Web Service. HTTP commands sent to this virtual directory would be directed to our Web Service. SQL Server 2005 uses http.sys to accomplish the same thing.

The platform SDK provides an API for the http.sys driver. This API allows an application to say, in effect, "From now on, listen for HTTP requests that arrive for 'http://canopus5:80/Repairs/req' and send them to me." The `CREATE ENDPOINT` expression uses this API under the covers to listen on the appropriate URL.

Access to http.sys is controlled on a by-URL basis. A Windows administrator can access any URL, but in general, other Windows identities must be registered in advance. The http.sys driver maintains a list of registered URLs; each URL is associated with an ACL, which is an access control token. The ACL is in effect a list of Windows identities that are allowed to listen on that URL. Whenever an application attempts to use http.sys to listen on a URL, the identity of the user running the application is checked against the ACL. If that user identity or the identity of a group the user belongs to is not in the ACL, the application will not be allowed to listen on that URL.

For SQL Server 2005, this means that the identity that SQL Server 2005 runs under will be checked against the ACL for any URL used in a `CREATE`

ENDPOINT expression for an HTTP endpoint. If SQL Server 2005 is running as the local system, it will have access to all possible URLs. If it is running under any other identity, the identity probably will have to have the identity registered in advance of using CREATE ENDPOINT.

SQL Server 2005 does not provide a way to see what URLs already have identities registered. If an identity is already registered for SQL Server 2005, it is unlikely that that URL will be available for use by CREATE ENDPOINT. There is a utility, httpcfg.exe, that is part of the Windows XP Support Tools. These tools can be found in the support\tools directory of either the Windows Server 2003 or Windows XP Professional SP2 distribution.

We would like our Web Service to have http://Canopus5:80/Repairs/req for a URL. Figure 12-1 shows the httpcfg utility being used to find the HTTP endpoints that are already registered. We can see the three endpoints on port 80 that are assigned an ACL, and none of them uses the URL we want, so the URL http://Canopus5:80/Repairs/req is available to us.

The httpcfg utility can also be used to reserve an endpoint, but it is easier to do that using T-SQL. The sp_reserve_http_namespace stored procedure can be used to reserve the URL. Figure 12-3, later in this chapter, shows the sp_reserve_http_namespace being used just before CREATE ENDPOINT to reserve an HTTP endpoint. Note that the CREATE ENDPOINT will itself attempt to reserve the namespace if necessary, but in some cases, this will fail, because the identity that uses the CREATE ENDPOINT expression does not have the permission required to register an endpoint.

Even in those cases where it is not required to reserve a URL, it is best practice to use sp_reserve_http_namespace just for clarity. A URL reservation can be removed by using the sp_delete_http_namepace_reservation.

```
Visual Studio 2005 Command Prompt

C:\Temp>httpcfg QUERY urlacl
    URL : http://*:2869/
    ACL : D:(A;;GX;;;LS)
---------------------------------------------------------------
    URL : http://Canopus5:80/Repairs/Hours/
    ACL : D:(A;;GA;;;S-1-5-21-636068366-2924379638-3822972120-1016)
---------------------------------------------------------------
    URL : http://Canopus5:80/Accounting/
    ACL : D:(A;;GA;;;S-1-5-21-636068366-2924379638-3822972120-1016)
---------------------------------------------------------------
    URL : http://canopus5:80/test/
    ACL : D:(A;;GA;;;S-1-5-21-636068366-2924379638-3822972120-1016)
---------------------------------------------------------------
C:\Temp>
```

FIGURE 12-1: httpcfg

Reservation and deletion of reservations of URL for http.sys may be done only by a Windows administrator. When `sp_reserve_http_namespace` and `sp_delete_http_namespace_reservation` are executed, they impersonate the current user. This means that the current user must be a Windows login and must be a Windows administrator, or the stored procedures will fail. Likewise, the stored procedures will fail if the user has an SQL Server login instead of a Windows login.

CREATE ENDPOINT

A `CREATE ENDPOINT` expression for an HTTP endpoint has two major sections. The first section defines the parameters associated with an HTTP endpoint, and the second section defines the Web Service being hosted on that endpoint.

Every endpoint has a name. Figure 12-2 shows the `CREATE ENDPOINT` expression for the endpoint named `RepairPoint` (1). Note that an endpoint is scoped to the instance of SQL Server 2005, not to a particular database, so there can be no other `RepairPoint` endpoint in this instance of SQL Server.

This endpoint is created in the `Started` (2) state, which is the default if it is not specified. We will discuss the `STATE` option in more detail later in this chapter.

SQL Server 2005 supports several endpoints, and the `AS` clause specifies the type. In this case, the endpoint is an `AS HTTP` (3) endpoint. The parameters for an HTTP endpoint are defined within the `AS HTTP` clause. This endpoint will use `INTEGRATED` (4) authentication, so it will operate in the same way as when a client using TDS connects to SQL Server 2005 using integrated security.

```
                          ①
CREATE ENDPOINT RepairPoint
STATE  = Started②
AS HTTP③
(
PATH = '/Repairs/req',
PORTS = (CLEAR),
SITE = '*',
AUTHENTICATION = (INTEGRATED)④
)
...
```

FIGURE 12-2: CREATE ENDPOINT

Endpoint URL

Parts of the AS HTTP clause are mapped into the parts of a URL, which is defined in the Uniform Resource Identifiers RFC (2396). This RFC breaks a URL into three parts: the scheme, the authority, and the path. The *scheme* for HTTP is "http://". The *authority* is the part that follows the scheme, up to the first following /. The authority in this example is Canopus5:80. The authority typically is the name of the machine and port, or the domain name and port. What follows it is the *path.*

In Figure 12-3, the authority is made from the values of the SITE and PORTS options of the AS HTTP phrase. The PORTS option doesn't specify a port, which means that port 80 should be used.

An asterisk (*) for the SITE means that any HTTP requests for any authority—for port 80, in this case—will be handled by this endpoint. The HTTP protocol allows for multiple authorities to occupy the same IP address. In this example, however, the only authority being listened for is Canopus5:80.

The value of the PATH option is the path for the URL.

The URL that was created from the AS HTTP clause should be, and in some cases must be, reserved before the CREATE ENDPOINT expression is executed. The result of running httpcfg.exe after the sp_reserve_http_namespace stored procedure is executed, as it is in Listing 12-2 earlier in this chapter, is shown in Figure 12-4. Here, we can see that http://Canopus5:80//Repairs/req has been reserved. Note that httpcfg.exe always shows the canonical form of the URL, no matter how it was reserved, so it will always contain a / at the end.

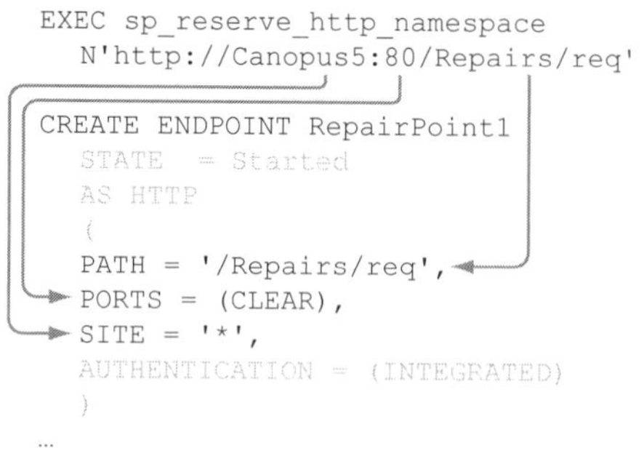

```
EXEC sp_reserve_http_namespace
    N'http://Canopus5:80/Repairs/req'

CREATE ENDPOINT RepairPoint1
    STATE   = Started
    AS HTTP
    (
    PATH = '/Repairs/req',
    PORTS = (CLEAR),
    SITE = '*',
    AUTHENTICATION = (INTEGRATED)
    )
    ...
```

FIGURE 12-3: Mapping of AS HTTP to URL

```
Visual Studio 2005 Command Prompt

c:\Temp>httpcfg QUERY urlacl
    URL : http://*:2869/
    ACL : D:(A;;GX;;;LS)
------------------------------------------------------------------
    URL : http://Canopus5:80/Repairs/Hours/
    ACL : D:(A;;GA;;;S-1-5-21-636068366-2924379638-3822972120-1016)
------------------------------------------------------------------
    URL : http://canopus5:80/Accounting/
    ACL : D:(A;;GA;;;S-1-5-21-636068366-2924379638-3822972120-1016)
------------------------------------------------------------------
    URL : http://canopus5:80/test/
    ACL : D:(A;;GA;;;S-1-5-21-636068366-2924379638-3822972120-1016)
------------------------------------------------------------------
    URL : http://Canopus5:80/Repairs/req/
    ACL : D:(A;;GA;;;S-1-5-21-636068366-2924379638-3822972120-1016)
```

FIGURE 12-4: URL reserved by SQL Server

Endpoint State

It is important to note that only users who are members of the sysadmin role or who have been granted CREATE ENDPOINT permission can use a CREATE ENDPOINT expression. There are no HTTP endpoints defined by default. When you install a fresh version of SQL Server on a system, you have no HTTP connectivity. Someone with appropriate privileges must use CREATE ENDPOINT to make an HTTP endpoint.

An important property of an endpoint is that it has a state. The endpoint state can be set to STARTED, STOPPED, or DISABLED using a CREATE ENDPOINT or ALTER ENDPOINT expression.

When the state of an HTTP endpoint is STARTED, it is listening for HTTP requests and will process them as appropriate. When the state is STOPPED, the HTTP endpoint will return an error message, "HTTP status 503: Service Unavailable," to all requests sent to that endpoint. When the state is DISABLED, the endpoint will not be visible to a client making an HTTP request—that is, the client will time out trying to connect to the end-point. Note that when the state is changed from DISABLED to any other value, SQL Server 2005 must be restarted for the change to take effect. Other changes take effect immediately.

The Surface Area Configuration tool that ships with SQL Server 2005 also can be used to start and stop, but not disable, HTTP endpoints. HTTP endpoints are managed as a Surface Area Connection Feature. Figure 12-5 shows the Surface Area Configuration Tool. An HTTP endpoint used for a Web Service is called a Native XML Web Service feature (1). Figure 12-5 shows the RepairPoint (2) Web Service being stopped (3).

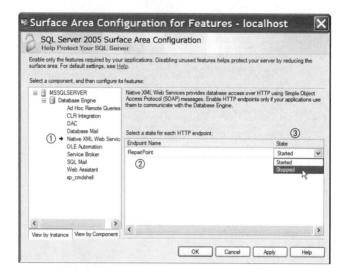

FIGURE 12-5: Surface area configuration tool

Endpoint Metadata

The data that defines an HTTP endpoint can be seen in two system views: sys.endpoints and sys.http_endpoints. Figure 12-6 shows a SELECT expression (1) that retrieves some of the metadata for the HTTP endpoints in this instance of SQL Server 2005. The views do duplicate some of the metadata but are divided into generic endpoint data (2) and endpoint data specific to HTTP (3). Roughly, the content of sys.http_endpoints comes from the information in the AS HTTP clause.

```
①SELECT E.name, E.type_desc,
    E.state_desc, H.site,
    H.url_path, H.clear_port
    FROM sys.endpoints AS E
    INNER JOIN sys.http_endpoints AS H
    ON E.endpoint_id = H.endpoint_id
```

FIGURE 12-6: Endpoint metadata

You might notice that this query did not list the same HTTP endpoints shown in Figure 12-5 that illustrated the use of httpcfg. Those HTTP endpoints were not reserved by this instance of SQL Server 2005; they were reserved by some other application. The `sys.endpoints` and `sys.http_endpoints` views show only the endpoints created by `CREATE ENDPOINT`.

Webmethods

The first section of the `CREATE ENDPOINT` expression defines the characteristics of an HTTP endpoint in an `AS HTTP` clause. The second section is a `FOR SOAP` clause that defines the Webmethods available to this endpoint. The term *Webmethod* comes from ASP.NET and in ASP.NET means a .NET Framework method that is mapped to a Web Service. Likewise, in SQL Server 2005, a Webmethod maps a SQL Server function or stored procedure to an HTTP endpoint.

The `FOR SOAP` clause from the batch in Listing 12-2 earlier in this chapter is shown in Figure 12-7. It defines a single `WEBMETHOD` that maps the `Repairs.dbo.RepairEstimate` to the `GetEstimate` Webmethod. Note that the three-part name of the stored procedure or function is required. The database specified by the `DATABASE` phrase is the database that will be in use when the stored procedure or function is executed.

Most development environments make it very straightforward to use a Web Service. Visual Studio 2005 has an Add Web Reference wizard that makes using a Web Service no different from using any class from a .NET Framework assembly. Other development environments for Windows and other platforms have similar capabilities.

Web Services work by receiving, and possibly replying with, SOAP messages using HTTP POST commands. The SOAP message format is described in SOAP Version 1.2 Part 0: Primer, at http://www.w3.org/TR/2003/REC-soap12-part0-20030624/, and the Simple Object Access Protocol (SOAP) 1.1,

```
FOR SOAP
(
  WEBMETHOD 'urn:autos'.'GetEstimate'
  (NAME = 'Repairs.dbo.RepairEstimate',
    SCHEMA=STANDARD),
  WSDL=DEFAULT,
  SCHEMA=STANDARD,
  DATABASE = 'Repairs',
  NAMESPACE = 'urn:other'
)
```

FIGURE 12-7: Mapping Webmethod to function

located at http://www.w3.org/TR/2000/NOTE-SOAP-20000508/. It is beyond the scope of this book to discuss SOAP messages fully, but we will look at a few examples of them.

Note that HTTP supports numerous commands; GET and POST are the most common. The GET command is what a Web browser typically uses to browse a site. It includes just the URL for the site and possibly a query string but no other information. The POST command is similar but may also include a message body. Web browsers use the POST command to send a form to a Web site for processing, for example. Likewise, SOAP uses POST commands so that it can send its message in the body of the POST command.

The use of SOAP and HTTP by Web Services means that any application that can support both HTTP and XML can use a Web Service hosted in SQL Server 2005. In practice, most applications do not attempt to use HTTP or XML directly but instead use a tool that produces a proxy class that the application uses. Then, to the application, the Web Service appears as an object with methods that represent the Webmethods in the Web Service. In other words, the Web Service appears as just another class the program uses.

The Visual Studio 2005 Add Web Reference wizard will build a proxy for a Web Service. Figure 12-8 shows a console application in Visual Studio 2005 that is adding a Web reference so that it can use a Web Service. Appendix C contains an introduction to using Visual Studio 2005.

The Add Web Reference wizard brings up a dialog box like the one in Figure 12-9. You fill in the URL for the Web Service, and the wizard builds

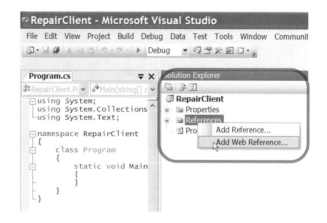

FIGURE 12-8: Visual studio adding Web Reference

```
EXEC sp_reserve_http_namespace
    N'http://Canopus5:80/Repairs/req'
                      ①
```

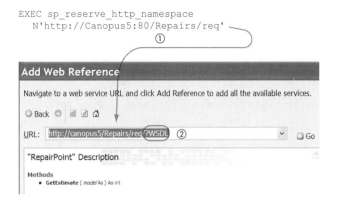

FIGURE 12-9: Visual studio making proxy

a proxy class for the Web Service. The URL that it wants is the one that was reserved (1) for the CREATE ENDPOINT expression, but with a ?WSDL query string (2) appended. Under the covers, the Add Web Reference wizard is using an HTTP GET command in exactly the same way that a Web browser would. In effect, SQL Server is returning a Web page that Visual Studio 2005 reads to get the information it needs to create a proxy. Note that SQL Server 2005 Web Services are not required to support the ?WSDL query string, but doing so simplifies the development of applications that use that Web Service.

When the proxy has been generated by clicking the Add Reference button in the Add Web Reference dialog box, it can be used by the program. Figure 12-10 shows the proxy in a program. The wizard named the proxy class RepairPoint, which corresponds to the name of the endpoint that hosts the Web Service. The program makes an instance (1) of the RepairPoint class. This Web Service requires Windows authentication, so the credentials of the user running this program are added (2) to the RepairPoint object.

Then the program uses the GetEstimate method (3) of the RepairPoint object to get an estimate of the repair cost for a B-990 model automobile. The result of running the program is shown in Figure 12-11 and, not surprisingly, is 12.

To the developer of the application in Figure 12-10, the Web Service in SQL Server 2005 appears as just another class she used to write her code.

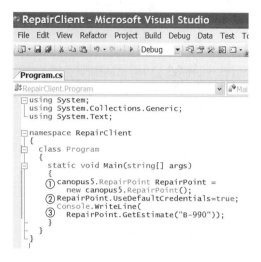

FIGURE 12-10: Using a proxy

Note that the developer did not have to use ADO.NET or the SQL language to access SQL Server 2005.

Behind the scenes, the `GetEstimate` method of the `Repair` class is creating a SOAP message and using HTTP to send it to SQL Server 2005. The SOAP message generated by the GetEstimate method in Figure 12-10 is shown in Listing 12-3. This is a SOAP message. Every SOAP message has a Body element inside an Envelope element. The contents of the Body element are considered to be the payload of the message. Here, we can see that the payload of the message is the `GetEstimate` method call and parameter converted to XML.

LISTING 12-3: SOAP request

```
<soap:Envelope xmlns:soap=
"http://schemas.xmlsoap.org/soap/envelope/"
xmlns:xsi="http://www.w3.org/2001/XMLSchema-instance"
xmlns:xsd="http://www.w3.org/2001/XMLSchema">
  <soap:Body>
    <GetEstimate xmlns="urn:autos">
      <model>B-990</model>
    </GetEstimate>
  </soap:Body>
</soap:Envelope>
```

```
ᴄⁿ Visual Studio 2005 Command Prompt
C>RepairClient.exe
12

C>
```

FIGURE 12-11: Estimate

What comes back as a response to the `GetEstimate` method is also a SOAP message and is shown in Listing 12-4. There is a lot more gobbledy-gook in the response than in the request; later in this chapter, we will see why that is. The payload, at the end of this message, is just the return value, 12, for the `GetEstimate` function converted to XML.

LISTING 12-4: SOAP response

```
<SOAP-ENV:Envelope xml:space="preserve"
xmlns:xsd=
"http://www.w3.org/2001/XMLSchema"
xmlns:xsi=
"http://www.w3.org/2001/XMLSchema-instance"
xmlns:SOAP-ENV=
"http://schemas.xmlsoap.org/soap/envelope/"
xmlns:sql=
"http://schemas.microsoft.com/sqlserver/2004/SOAP"
xmlns:sqlsoaptypes=
"http://schemas.microsoft.com/sqlserver/2004/SOAP/types"
xmlns:sqlrowcount=
"http://schemas.microsoft.com/sqlserver/2004/SOAP/types/SqlRowCount"
xmlns:sqlmessage=
"http://schemas.microsoft.com/sqlserver/2004/SOAP/types/SqlMessage"
xmlns:sqlresultstream=
"http://schemas.microsoft.com/sqlserver/2004/SOAP/types/SqlResultStream"
xmlns:sqltransaction=
"http://schemas.microsoft.com/sqlserver/2004/SOAP/types/SqlTransaction"
xmlns:sqltypes=
"http://schemas.microsoft.com/sqlserver/2004/sqltypes"
xmlns:msdata="urn:schemas-microsoft-com:xml-msdata"
xmlns:method="urn:autos">

<SOAP-ENV:Body>
  <method:GetEstimateResponse>
    <method:GetEstimateResult>12</method:GetEstimateResult>
  </method:GetEstimateResponse>
</SOAP-ENV:Body>
</SOAP-ENV:Envelope>
```

Sometimes, when working on a SQL Server 2005 application, you will use the SQL Profiler utility to watch what SQL Server is doing. To do a similar sort of thing when SQL Server 2005 is hosting a Web Service, you will need to monitor the HTTP commands and response going to and from SQL Server 2005. Numerous tools for doing this are available. One that is particularly useful is Fiddler, written by Eric Lawrence from Microsoft. It is available as a free download from http://www.fiddlertool.com.

WSDL Web Service Definition Language

As you can see, it is fairly easy for a developer using Visual Studio 2005 to build applications that use Web Services that are hosted in SQL Server 2005. What about developers using other development environments on other platforms?

In fact, virtually all development environments on all platforms in common use today have tools similar to the one in Visual Studio 2005 and are about as easy to use. All these development environments, including Visual Studio 2005, depend on being able to access the Web Service Definition Language (WSDL) file that defines the Web Service.

A WSDL file is an XML file that defines everything you need to know to access a Web Service. Several versions of WSDL are available. WSDL 1.1 is described in the WSDL 1.1 note of the World Wide Web Consortium at http://www.w3.org/TR/wsdl#_wsdl. WSDL 1.2 is described in the WSDL Version 1.2 working draft at http://www.w3.org/TR/2003/WD-wsdl12-20030303/. A new version of WSDL is being developed and is described in WSDL Version 2.0 working draft at http://www.w3.org/TR/wsdl20/. It is beyond the scope of this book to discuss WSDL files in detail, but we will cover some of the basics.

All these specifications are somewhat detailed because they are designed to accommodate a wide range of definitions of what is considered to be a Web Service. The later versions make it easier to be more specific and less ambiguous about what is in a Web Service and what kind of data it can consume and produce. WSDL 2.0, for example, probably will provide a standard way to manage versions of a Web Service.

In practice today, all development environments support WSDL 1.1, and some that support WSDL 1.2. SQL Server 2005 will automatically produce a WSDL 1.1 file based on the definition of the Web Service in the CREATE

ENDPOINT expression. It does this in response to an HTTP GET command with a ?WSDL query string appended to the URL. The Add Web Reference wizard, shown in Figure 12-9 got back a WSDL file and then used the information in that WSDL to build a proxy class for the application.

The WSDL option in the FOR SOAP clause in Figure 12-7 specified that a DEFAULT WSDL file should be generated. This means that SQL Server 2005 will automatically create the WSDL file for this Web Service. It uses the system stored procedure sp_http_generate_wsdl_defaultcomplexorsimple to do this. We can see this in the metadata stored for a Web Service,

The information about Web Services can be seen in the sys.soap_endpoints system view. The information about the Webmethods in Web Services can be seen in the sys.endpoint_Webmethods view. Figure 12-12 shows a SELECT expression (1) that retrieves the wsdl_generator_procedure column from the sys.soap_endpoints view. You can see that the WSDL=DEFAULT option puts (2) the sp_http_generate_wsdl_defaultcomplexorsimple into the wsdl_generator_procedure column.

When a Web Service receives an HTTP GET command, it invokes the wsdl_generator_procedure for the endpoint. This is how the Add Web Reference wizard in Visual Studio 2005, shown in Figure 12-9 earlier in this chapter, was able to get the WSDL file needed to create the proxy for the application. Listing 12-5 shows the WSDL file that SQL Server 2005 generated

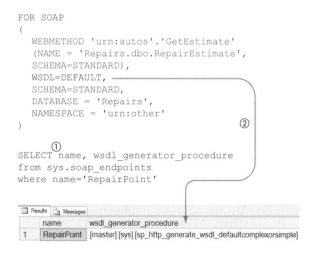

```
FOR SOAP
(
    WEBMETHOD 'urn:autos'.'GetEstimate'
    (NAME = 'Repairs.dbo.RepairEstimate',
    SCHEMA=STANDARD),
    WSDL=DEFAULT, ──────────
    SCHEMA=STANDARD,
    DATABASE = 'Repairs',
    NAMESPACE = 'urn:other'
)                                              ②

      ①
SELECT name, wsdl_generator_procedure
from sys.soap_endpoints
where name='RepairPoint'
```

	name	wsdl_generator_procedure
1	RepairPoint	[master].[sys].[sp_http_generate_wsdl_defaultcomplexorsimple]

FIGURE 12-12: WSDL generator

for the `RepairPoint` Web Service. As you can see, it contains quite a lot of information. Two key pieces of information it contains are the formats for the payloads of the SOAP messages that are used by the `RepairPoint` Web Service.

LISTING 12-5: RepairPoint WSDL

```
<wsdl:definitions xmlns:wsdl="http://schemas.xmlsoap.org/wsdl/"
xmlns:soap="http://schemas.xmlsoap.org/wsdl/soap/"
xmlns:sqloptions="http://schemas.microsoft.com/sqlserver/2004/SOAP/Options"
xmlns:s0="urn:autos" xmlns:tns="urn:other"
                    targetNamespace="urn:other">
  <wsdl:types>
    <xsd:schema xmlns:xsd="http://www.w3.org/2001/XMLSchema"
targetNamespace="http://schemas.microsoft.com/sqlserver/2004/sqltypes"
attributeFormDefault="qualified"
xmlns:sqltypes="http://schemas.microsoft.com/sqlserver/2004/sqltypes">
      <xsd:annotation>
        <xsd:documentation xml:lang="en">&#xD;&#xA;XML Schema describing
the base types to which SQL Server types are being mapped. For more
information, please consult the documentation.&#xD;&#xA;&#xD;&#xA;(c)
Copyright 2004, Microsoft Corporation&#xD;&#xA;&#xD;&#xA;The following
schema for Microsoft SQL Server is presented in XML format and is for
informational purposes only. Microsoft Corporation ("Microsoft") may have
trademarks, copyrights, or other intellectual property rights covering
subject matter in the schema.&#xD;&#xA;&#xD;&#xA;Microsoft does not make
any representation or warranty regarding the schema or any product or
item developed based on the schema. The schema is provided to you on an
AS IS basis. Microsoft disclaims all express, implied and statutory
warranties, including but not limited to the implied warranties of
merchantability, fitness for a particular purpose, and freedom from
infringement. Without limiting the generality of the foregoing, Microsoft
does not make any warranty of any kind that any item developed based on
the schema, or any portion of the schema, will not infringe any
copyright, patent, trade secret, or other intellectual property right of
any person or entity in any country. It is your responsibility to seek
licenses for such intellectual property rights where
appropriate.&#xD;&#xA;&#xD;&#xA;MICROSOFT SHALL NOT BE LIABLE FOR ANY
DAMAGES OF ANY KIND ARISING OUT OF OR IN CONNECTION WITH THE USE OF THE
SCHEMA, INCLUDING WITHOUT LIMITATION, ANY DIRECT, INDIRECT, INCIDENTAL,
CONSEQUENTIAL (INCLUDING ANY LOST PROFITS), PUNITIVE OR SPECIAL DAMAGES,
WHETHER OR NOT MICROSOFT HAS BEEN ADVISED OF SUCH
DAMAGES.&#xD;&#xA;</xsd:documentation>
      </xsd:annotation>
      <!-- Global types and attributes that can be used for schema
annotations. -->
      <xsd:simpleType name="sqlDbTypeEnum">
        <xsd:restriction base="xsd:string">
          <xsd:enumeration value="BigInt"/>
```

```
          <xsd:enumeration value="Binary"/>
          <xsd:enumeration value="Bit"/>
          <xsd:enumeration value="Char"/>
          <xsd:enumeration value="DateTime"/>
          <xsd:enumeration value="Decimal"/>
          <xsd:enumeration value="Float"/>
          <xsd:enumeration value="Image"/>
          <xsd:enumeration value="Int"/>
          <xsd:enumeration value="Money"/>
          <xsd:enumeration value="NChar"/>
          <xsd:enumeration value="NText"/>
          <!-- The sqlDbTypeEnum aligns with the .Net System.Data.SqlDbType
enum and does not provide an entry for Numeric (which is mapped to
Decimal). -->
          <xsd:enumeration value="NVarChar"/>
          <xsd:enumeration value="Real"/>
          <xsd:enumeration value="SmallDateTime"/>
          <xsd:enumeration value="SmallInt"/>
          <xsd:enumeration value="SmallMoney"/>
          <xsd:enumeration value="Text"/>
          <xsd:enumeration value="Timestamp"/>
          <xsd:enumeration value="TinyInt"/>
          <xsd:enumeration value="Udt"/>
          <xsd:enumeration value="UniqueIdentifier"/>
          <xsd:enumeration value="VarBinary"/>
          <xsd:enumeration value="VarChar"/>
          <xsd:enumeration value="Variant"/>
          <xsd:enumeration value="Xml"/>
        </xsd:restriction>
      </xsd:simpleType>
      <xsd:simpleType name="sqlCompareOptionsEnum">
        <xsd:restriction base="xsd:string">
          <xsd:enumeration value="Default"/>
          <xsd:enumeration value="None"/>
          <xsd:enumeration value="IgnoreCase"/>
          <xsd:enumeration value="IgnoreNonSpace"/>
          <xsd:enumeration value="IgnoreKanaType"/>
          <xsd:enumeration value="IgnoreWidth"/>
          <xsd:enumeration value="BinarySort"/>
          <xsd:enumeration value="BinarySort2"/>
        </xsd:restriction>
      </xsd:simpleType>
      <xsd:simpleType name="sqlCompareOptionsList">
        <xsd:list itemType="sqltypes:sqlCompareOptionsEnum"/>
      </xsd:simpleType>
      <xsd:attribute default="NVarChar" name="sqlDbType"
type="sqltypes:sqlDbTypeEnum"/>
      <xsd:attribute name="clrTypeName" type="xsd:string"/>
      <xsd:attribute default="1" name="maxLength" type="xsd:long"/>
      <xsd:attribute default="-1" name="localeId" type="xsd:int"/>
      <xsd:attribute default="Default" name="sqlCompareOptions"
```

```
type="sqltypes:sqlCompareOptionsList"/>
      <xsd:attribute default="0" name="sqlCollationVersion"
type="xsd:int"/>
      <xsd:attribute default="0" name="sqlSortId" type="xsd:int"/>
      <xsd:attribute default="0" name="scale" type="xsd:unsignedByte"/>
      <xsd:attribute default="18" name="precision" type=
"xsd:unsignedByte"/>
      <xsd:attribute name="xmlSchemaCollection" type="xsd:string"/>
      <xsd:attribute name="sqlTypeAlias" type="xsd:string"/>
      <!-- Global types that describe the base SQL types. -->
      <xsd:simpleType name="char">
        <xsd:restriction base="xsd:string"/>
      </xsd:simpleType>
      <xsd:simpleType name="nchar">
        <xsd:restriction base="xsd:string"/>
      </xsd:simpleType>
      <xsd:simpleType name="varchar">
        <xsd:restriction base="xsd:string"/>
      </xsd:simpleType>
      <xsd:simpleType name="nvarchar">
        <xsd:restriction base="xsd:string"/>
      </xsd:simpleType>
      <xsd:simpleType name="text">
        <xsd:restriction base="xsd:string"/>
      </xsd:simpleType>
      <xsd:simpleType name="ntext">
        <xsd:restriction base="xsd:string"/>
      </xsd:simpleType>
      <xsd:simpleType name="varbinary">
        <xsd:restriction base="xsd:base64Binary"/>
      </xsd:simpleType>
      <xsd:simpleType name="binary">
        <xsd:restriction base="xsd:base64Binary"/>
      </xsd:simpleType>
      <xsd:simpleType name="image">
        <xsd:restriction base="xsd:base64Binary"/>
      </xsd:simpleType>
      <xsd:simpleType name="timestamp">
        <xsd:restriction base="xsd:base64Binary">
          <xsd:maxLength value="8"/>
        </xsd:restriction>
      </xsd:simpleType>
      <xsd:simpleType name="timestampNumeric">
        <!-- The timestampNumeric type supports a legacy format of
timestamp. -->
        <xsd:restriction base="xsd:long"/>
      </xsd:simpleType>
      <xsd:simpleType name="decimal">
        <xsd:restriction base="xsd:decimal"/>
      </xsd:simpleType>
```

```xml
<xsd:simpleType name="numeric">
  <xsd:restriction base="xsd:decimal"/>
</xsd:simpleType>
<xsd:simpleType name="bigint">
  <xsd:restriction base="xsd:long"/>
</xsd:simpleType>
<xsd:simpleType name="int">
  <xsd:restriction base="xsd:int"/>
</xsd:simpleType>
<xsd:simpleType name="smallint">
  <xsd:restriction base="xsd:short"/>
</xsd:simpleType>
<xsd:simpleType name="tinyint">
  <xsd:restriction base="xsd:unsignedByte"/>
</xsd:simpleType>
<xsd:simpleType name="bit">
  <xsd:restriction base="xsd:boolean"/>
</xsd:simpleType>
<xsd:simpleType name="float">
  <xsd:restriction base="xsd:double"/>
</xsd:simpleType>
<xsd:simpleType name="real">
  <xsd:restriction base="xsd:float"/>
</xsd:simpleType>
<xsd:simpleType name="datetime">
  <xsd:restriction base="xsd:dateTime">
    <xsd:pattern value="((000[1-9])|(00[1-9][0-9])|(0[1-9][0-9]
{2})|([1-9][0-9]{3}))-((0[1-9])|(1[012]))-((0[1-9])|([12][0-9])|
(3[01]))T(([01][0-9])|(2[0-3]))(:[0-5][0-9]){2}(\.[0-9]{2}[037])?"/>
    <xsd:maxInclusive value="9999-12-31T23:59:59.997"/>
    <xsd:minInclusive value="1753-01-01T00:00:00.000"/>
  </xsd:restriction>
</xsd:simpleType>
<xsd:simpleType name="smalldatetime">
  <xsd:restriction base="xsd:dateTime">
    <xsd:pattern value="((000[1-9])|(00[1-9][0-9])|(0[1-9][0-9]
{2})|([1-9][0-9]{3}))-((0[1-9])|(1[012]))-((0[1-9])|([12][0-9])|
(3[01]))T(([01][0-9])|(2[0-3]))(:[0-5][0-9])(:00)"/>
    <xsd:maxInclusive value="2079-06-06T23:59:00"/>
    <xsd:minInclusive value="1900-01-01T00:00:00"/>
  </xsd:restriction>
</xsd:simpleType>
<xsd:simpleType name="money">
  <xsd:restriction base="xsd:decimal">
    <xsd:totalDigits value="19"/>
    <xsd:fractionDigits value="4"/>
    <xsd:maxInclusive value="922337203685477.5807"/>
    <xsd:minInclusive value="-922337203685477.5808"/>
  </xsd:restriction>
</xsd:simpleType>
```

```
<xsd:simpleType name="smallmoney">
  <xsd:restriction base="xsd:decimal">
    <xsd:totalDigits value="10"/>
    <xsd:fractionDigits value="4"/>
    <xsd:maxInclusive value="214748.3647"/>
    <xsd:minInclusive value="-214748.3648"/>
  </xsd:restriction>
</xsd:simpleType>
<xsd:simpleType name="uniqueidentifier">
  <xsd:restriction base="xsd:string">
    <xsd:pattern value="([0-9a-fA-F]{8}-[0-9a-fA-F]{4}-[0-9a-fA-F]
{4}-[0-9a-fA-F]{4}-[0-9a-fA-F]{12})|(\{[0-9a-fA-F]{8}-[0-9a-fA-F]{4}-
[0-9a-fA-F]{4}-[0-9a-fA-F]{4}-[0-9a-fA-F]{12}\})"/>
  </xsd:restriction>
</xsd:simpleType>
<!-- sql_variant directly maps to xsd:anyType -->
<xsd:complexType name="xml" mixed="true">
  <xsd:sequence>
    <xsd:any minOccurs="0" maxOccurs="unbounded"
processContents="skip"/>
  </xsd:sequence>
</xsd:complexType>
<!-- the following type is for FOR XML binary URL results only -->
<xsd:simpleType name="dbobject">
  <xsd:restriction base="xsd:anyURI"/>
</xsd:simpleType>
</xsd:schema>
<xsd:schema xmlns:xsd="http://www.w3.org/2001/XMLSchema"
attributeFormDefault="qualified" elementFormDefault="qualified"
targetNamespace="http://schemas.microsoft.com/sqlserver/2004/
SOAP/types">
  <xsd:annotation>
    <xsd:documentation xml:lang="en">&#xD;&#xA;(c) Copyright 2004,
Microsoft Corporation&#xD;&#xA;&#xD;&#xA;The following schema for
Microsoft SQL Server is presented in XML format and is for informational
purposes only. Microsoft Corporation ("Microsoft") may have trademarks,
copyrights, or other intellectual property rights covering subject matter
in the schema.&#xD;&#xA;&#xD;&#xA;Microsoft does not make any representation
or warranty regarding the schema or any product or item developed based
on the schema. The schema is provided to you on an AS IS basis.
Microsoft disclaims all express, implied and statutory warranties,
including but not limited to the implied warranties of merchantability,
fitness for a particular purpose, and freedom from infringement. Without
limiting the generality of the foregoing, Microsoft does not make any
warranty of any kind that any item developed based on the schema, or any
portion of the schema, will not infringe any copyright, patent, trade
secret, or other intellectual property right of any person or entity in
any country. It is your responsibility to seek licenses for such intel-
lectual property rights where appropriate.&#xD;&#xA;&#xD;&#xA;MICROSOFT
SHALL NOT BE LIABLE FOR ANY DAMAGES OF ANY KIND ARISING OUT OF OR IN
```

```
CONNECTION WITH THE USE OF THE SCHEMA, INCLUDING WITHOUT LIMITATION, ANY
DIRECT, INDIRECT, INCIDENTAL, CONSEQUENTIAL (INCLUDING ANY LOST PROFITS),
PUNITIVE OR SPECIAL DAMAGES, WHETHER OR NOT MICROSOFT HAS BEEN ADVISED OF
SUCH DAMAGES.&#xD;&#xA;</xsd:documentation>
      </xsd:annotation>
      <xsd:complexType name="SqlRowSet">
        <xsd:sequence maxOccurs="unbounded">
          <xsd:element ref="xsd:schema"/>
          <xsd:any/>
        </xsd:sequence>
      </xsd:complexType>
      <xsd:complexType name="SqlXml" mixed="true">
        <xsd:sequence>
          <xsd:any processContents="skip"/>
        </xsd:sequence>
      </xsd:complexType>
      <xsd:simpleType name="SqlResultCode">
        <xsd:restriction base="xsd:int">
          <xsd:minInclusive value="0"/>
        </xsd:restriction>
      </xsd:simpleType>
      <xsd:attribute name="IsDataSetWithSchema" type="xsd:boolean"/>
    </xsd:schema>
    <xsd:schema xmlns:xsd="http://www.w3.org/2001/XMLSchema"
attributeFormDefault="qualified" elementFormDefault="qualified"
targetNamespace="http://schemas.microsoft.com/sqlserver/2004/SOAP/
types/SqlTransaction">
      <xsd:annotation>
        <xsd:documentation xml:lang="en">&#xD;&#xA;(c) Copyright 2004,
Microsoft Corporation&#xD;&#xA;&#xD;&#xA;The following schema for
Microsoft SQL Server is presented in XML format and is for informational
purposes only. Microsoft Corporation ("Microsoft") may have trademarks,
copyrights, or other intellectual property rights covering subject matter
in the schema.&#xD;&#xA;&#xD;&#xA;Microsoft does not make any representa-
tion or warranty regarding the schema or any product or item developed
based on the schema. The schema is provided to you on an AS IS basis.
Microsoft disclaims all express, implied and statutory warranties,
including but not limited to the implied warranties of merchantability,
fitness for a particular purpose, and freedom from infringement. Without
limiting the generality of the foregoing, Microsoft does not make any
warranty of any kind that any item developed based on the schema, or any
portion of the schema, will not infringe any copyright, patent, trade
secret, or other intellectual property right of any person or entity in any
country. It is your responsibility to seek licenses for such intellectual
property rights where appropriate.&#xD;&#xA;&#xD;&#xA;MICROSOFT SHALL NOT
BE LIABLE FOR ANY DAMAGES OF ANY KIND ARISING OUT OF OR IN CONNECTION
WITH THE USE OF THE SCHEMA, INCLUDING WITHOUT LIMITATION, ANY DIRECT,
INDIRECT, INCIDENTAL, CONSEQUENTIAL (INCLUDING ANY LOST PROFITS),
PUNITIVE OR SPECIAL DAMAGES, WHETHER OR NOT MICROSOFT HAS BEEN ADVISED OF
SUCH DAMAGES.&#xD;&#xA;</xsd:documentation>
```

```
      </xsd:annotation>
      <xsd:complexType name="SqlTransaction">
        <xsd:sequence minOccurs="1" maxOccurs="1">
          <xsd:element name="Descriptor" type="xsd:base64Binary"/>
          <xsd:element name="Type">
            <xsd:simpleType>
              <xsd:restriction base="xsd:string">
                <xsd:enumeration value="Begin"/>
                <xsd:enumeration value="Commit"/>
                <xsd:enumeration value="Rollback"/>
                <xsd:enumeration value="EnlistDTC"/>
                <xsd:enumeration value="Defect"/>
              </xsd:restriction>
            </xsd:simpleType>
          </xsd:element>
        </xsd:sequence>
      </xsd:complexType>
    </xsd:schema>
    <xsd:schema xmlns:xsd="http://www.w3.org/2001/XMLSchema"
attributeFormDefault="qualified" elementFormDefault="qualified"
targetNamespace="http://schemas.microsoft.com/sqlserver/2004/SOAP/
types/SqlRowCount">
      <xsd:annotation>
        <xsd:documentation xml:lang="en">&#xD;&#xA;(c) Copyright 2004,
Microsoft Corporation&#xD;&#xA;&#xD;&#xA;The following schema for
Microsoft SQL Server is presented in XML format and is for informational
purposes only. Microsoft Corporation ("Microsoft") may have trademarks,
copyrights, or other intellectual property rights covering subject matter
in the schema.&#xD;&#xA;&#xD;&#xA;Microsoft does not make any representation
or warranty regarding the schema or any product or item developed based
on the schema. The schema is provided to you on an AS IS basis. Microsoft
disclaims all express, implied and statutory warranties, including but
not limited to the implied warranties of merchantability, fitness for a
particular purpose, and freedom from infringement. Without limiting the
generality of the foregoing, Microsoft does not make any warranty of any
kind that any item developed based on the schema, or any portion of the
schema, will not infringe any copyright, patent, trade secret, or other
intellectual property right of any person or entity in any country. It is
your responsibility to seek licenses for such intellectual property
rights where appropriate.&#xD;&#xA;&#xD;&#xA;MICROSOFT SHALL NOT BE
LIABLE FOR ANY DAMAGES OF ANY KIND ARISING OUT OF OR IN CONNECTION WITH
THE USE OF THE SCHEMA, INCLUDING WITHOUT LIMITATION, ANY DIRECT,
INDIRECT, INCIDENTAL, CONSEQUENTIAL (INCLUDING ANY LOST PROFITS),
PUNITIVE OR SPECIAL DAMAGES, WHETHER OR NOT MICROSOFT HAS BEEN ADVISED OF
SUCH DAMAGES.&#xD;&#xA;</xsd:documentation>
      </xsd:annotation>
      <xsd:complexType name="SqlRowCount">
        <xsd:sequence minOccurs="1" maxOccurs="1">
          <xsd:element name="Count" type="xsd:long"/>
        </xsd:sequence>
```

```
         </xsd:complexType>
      </xsd:schema>
      <xsd:schema xmlns:xsd="http://www.w3.org/2001/XMLSchema"
xmlns:sqlmessage="http://schemas.microsoft.com/sqlserver/2004/SOAP/types/
SqlMessage" attributeFormDefault="qualified" elementFormDefault="qualified"

targetNamespace="http://schemas.microsoft.com/sqlserver/2004/SOAP/
types/SqlMessage">
         <xsd:annotation>
           <xsd:documentation xml:lang="en">&#xD;&#xA;(c) Copyright 2004,
Microsoft Corporation&#xD;&#xA;&#xD;&#xA;The following schema for
Microsoft SQL Server is presented in XML format and is for informational
purposes only. Microsoft Corporation ("Microsoft") may have trademarks,
copyrights, or other intellectual property rights covering subject matter
in the schema.&#xD;&#xA;&#xD;&#xA;Microsoft does not make any representa-
tion or warranty regarding the schema or any product or item developed
based on the schema. The schema is provided to you on an AS IS basis.
Microsoft disclaims all express, implied and statutory warranties,
including but not limited to the implied warranties of merchantability,
fitness for a particular purpose, and freedom from infringement. Without
limiting the generality of the foregoing, Microsoft does not make any
warranty of any kind that any item developed based on the schema, or any
portion of the schema, will not infringe any copyright, patent, trade
secret, or other intellectual property right of any person or entity in any
country. It is your responsibility to seek licenses for such intellectual
property rights where appropriate.&#xD;&#xA;&#xD;&#xA;MICROSOFT SHALL NOT
BE LIABLE FOR ANY DAMAGES OF ANY KIND ARISING OUT OF OR IN CONNECTION
WITH THE USE OF THE SCHEMA, INCLUDING WITHOUT LIMITATION, ANY DIRECT,
INDIRECT, INCIDENTAL, CONSEQUENTIAL (INCLUDING ANY LOST PROFITS),
PUNITIVE OR SPECIAL DAMAGES, WHETHER OR NOT MICROSOFT HAS BEEN ADVISED OF
SUCH DAMAGES.&#xD;&#xA;</xsd:documentation>
         </xsd:annotation>
         <xsd:simpleType name="nonNegativeInteger">
           <xsd:restriction base="xsd:int">
             <xsd:minInclusive value="0"/>
           </xsd:restriction>
         </xsd:simpleType>
         <xsd:complexType name="SqlMessage">
           <xsd:sequence minOccurs="1" maxOccurs="1">
             <xsd:element name="Class" type="sqlmessage:
nonNegativeInteger"/>
             <xsd:element name="LineNumber" type="sqlmessage:
nonNegativeInteger"/>
             <xsd:element name="Message" type="xsd:string"/>
             <xsd:element name="Number" type="sqlmessage:
nonNegativeInteger"/>
             <xsd:element name="Procedure" type="xsd:string" minOccurs="0"/>
             <xsd:element name="Server" type="xsd:string" minOccurs="0"/>
             <xsd:element name="Source" type="xsd:string"/>
             <xsd:element name="State" type="sqlmessage:
```

```
nonNegativeInteger"/>
        </xsd:sequence>
      </xsd:complexType>
    </xsd:schema>
    <xsd:schema xmlns:xsd="http://www.w3.org/2001/XMLSchema" xmlns:
sqlsoaptypes="http://schemas.microsoft.com/sqlserver/2004/SOAP/types"
xmlns:sqlmessage="http://schemas.microsoft.com/sqlserver/2004/SOAP/types/
SqlMessage"

xmlns:sqlrowcount="http://schemas.microsoft.com/sqlserver/2004/SOAP/types
/SqlRowCount"
xmlns:sqltransaction="http://schemas.microsoft.com/sqlserver/2004/SOAP/
types/SqlTransaction" attributeFormDefault="qualified"
                elementFormDefault="qualified"
targetNamespace="http://schemas.microsoft.com/sqlserver/2004/SOAP/types/
SqlResultStream">
      <xsd:annotation>
        <xsd:documentation xml:lang="en">&#xD;&#xA;(c) Copyright 2004,
Microsoft Corporation&#xD;&#xA;&#xD;&#xA;The following schema for
Microsoft SQL Server is presented in XML format and is for informational
purposes only. Microsoft Corporation ("Microsoft") may have trademarks,
copyrights, or other intellectual property rights covering subject matter in
the schema.&#xD;&#xA;&#xD;&#xA;Microsoft does not make any representation or
warranty regarding the schema or any product or item developed based on
the schema. The schema is provided to you on an AS IS basis.  Microsoft
disclaims all express, implied and statutory warranties, including but
not limited to the implied warranties of merchantability, fitness for a
particular purpose, and freedom from infringement. Without limiting the
generality of the foregoing, Microsoft does not make any warranty of any
kind that any item developed based on the schema, or any portion of the
schema, will not infringe any copyright, patent, trade secret, or other
intellectual property right of any person or entity in any country. It is
your responsibility to seek licenses for such intellectual property
rights where appropriate.&#xD;&#xA;&#xD;&#xA;MICROSOFT SHALL NOT BE
LIABLE FOR ANY DAMAGES OF ANY KIND ARISING OUT OF OR IN CONNECTION WITH
THE USE OF THE SCHEMA, INCLUDING WITHOUT LIMITATION, ANY DIRECT, INDI-
RECT, INCIDENTAL, CONSEQUENTIAL (INCLUDING ANY LOST PROFITS), PUNITIVE
OR SPECIAL DAMAGES, WHETHER OR NOT MICROSOFT HAS BEEN ADVISED OF SUCH
DAMAGES.&#xD;&#xA;</xsd:documentation>
      </xsd:annotation>
      <xsd:import
namespace="http://schemas.microsoft.com/sqlserver/2004/SOAP/types"/>
      <xsd:import
namespace="http://schemas.microsoft.com/sqlserver/2004/SOAP/types/
SqlMessage"/>
        <xsd:import namespace="http://schemas.microsoft.com/sqlserver/2004/
SOAP/types/SqlRowCount"/>
      <xsd:import
namespace="http://schemas.microsoft.com/sqlserver/2004/SOAP/types/
SqlTransaction"/>
```

```
      <xsd:complexType name="SqlResultStream">
        <xsd:choice minOccurs="1" maxOccurs="unbounded">
          <xsd:element name="SqlRowSet" type="sqlsoaptypes:SqlRowSet"/>
          <xsd:element name="SqlXml" type="sqlsoaptypes:SqlXml"/>
          <xsd:element name="SqlMessage" type="sqlmessage:SqlMessage"/>
          <xsd:element name="SqlRowCount" type="sqlrowcount:
SqlRowCount"/>
          <xsd:element name="SqlResultCode" type="sqlsoaptypes:
SqlResultCode"/>
          <xsd:element name="SqlTransaction" type="sqltransaction:
SqlTransaction"/>
        </xsd:choice>
      </xsd:complexType>
    </xsd:schema>
    <xsd:schema xmlns:xsd="http://www.w3.org/2001/XMLSchema"
attributeFormDefault="qualified" elementFormDefault="qualified"
targetNamespace="http://schemas.microsoft.com/sqlserver/2004/SOAP/Options">
      <xsd:annotation>
        <xsd:documentation xml:lang="en">&#xD;&#xA;(c) Copyright 2004,
Microsoft Corporation&#xD;&#xA;&#xD;&#xA;The following schema for
Microsoft SQL Server is presented in XML format and is for informational
purposes only. Microsoft Corporation ("Microsoft") may have trademarks,
copyrights, or other intellectual property rights covering subject matter
in the schema.&#xD;&#xA;&#xD;&#xA;Microsoft does not make any representa-
tion or warranty regarding the schema or any product or item developed
based on the schema. The schema is provided to you on an AS IS basis.
Microsoft disclaims all express, implied and statutory warranties,
including but not limited to the implied warranties of merchantability,
fitness for a particular purpose, and freedom from infringement. Without
limiting the generality of the foregoing, Microsoft does not make any
warranty of any kind that any item developed based on the schema, or any
portion of the schema, will not infringe any copyright, patent, trade
secret, or other intellectual property right of any person or entity in any
country. It is your responsibility to seek licenses for such intellectual
property rights where appropriate.&#xD;&#xA;&#xD;&#xA;MICROSOFT SHALL NOT
BE LIABLE FOR ANY DAMAGES OF ANY KIND ARISING OUT OF OR IN CONNECTION
WITH THE USE OF THE SCHEMA, INCLUDING WITHOUT LIMITATION, ANY DIRECT,
INDIRECT, INCIDENTAL, CONSEQUENTIAL (INCLUDING ANY LOST PROFITS),
PUNITIVE OR SPECIAL DAMAGES, WHETHER OR NOT MICROSOFT HAS BEEN ADVISED OF
SUCH DAMAGES.&#xD;&#xA;</xsd:documentation>
      </xsd:annotation>
      <xsd:element name="initialDatabase">
        <xsd:annotation>
          <xsd:documentation>Set initial database on login.</xsd:
documentation>
        </xsd:annotation>
        <xsd:complexType>
          <xsd:attribute name="value" type="xsd:string"
form="unqualified" use="required">
            <xsd:annotation>
```

```
                    <xsd:documentation>The name of the initial database to
attach to.</xsd:documentation>
                </xsd:annotation>
            </xsd:attribute>
            <xsd:attribute name="optional" default="false"
type="xsd:boolean" form="unqualified">
                <xsd:annotation>
                    <xsd:documentation>Whether the initial database is optional
or not.</xsd:documentation>
                </xsd:annotation>
            </xsd:attribute>
            <xsd:attribute name="filename" type="xsd:string"
form="unqualified">
                <xsd:annotation>
                    <xsd:documentation>The filename of the database to attach
to.</xsd:documentation>
                </xsd:annotation>
            </xsd:attribute>
        </xsd:complexType>
    </xsd:element>
    <xsd:element name="initialLanguage">
        <xsd:annotation>
            <xsd:documentation>Set initial language to set.</xsd:
documentation>
        </xsd:annotation>
        <xsd:complexType>
            <xsd:attribute name="value" type="xsd:string"
form="unqualified" use="required">
                <xsd:annotation>
                    <xsd:documentation>The name of the initial language to
set.</xsd:documentation>
                </xsd:annotation>
            </xsd:attribute>
            <xsd:attribute name="optional" default="false"
type="xsd:boolean" form="unqualified">
                <xsd:annotation>
                    <xsd:documentation>Whether the initial language is optional
or not.</xsd:documentation>
                </xsd:annotation>
            </xsd:attribute>
        </xsd:complexType>
    </xsd:element>
    <xsd:element name="environmentChangeNotifications">
        <xsd:annotation>
            <xsd:documentation>Receive environment change
notifications.</xsd:documentation>
        </xsd:annotation>
        <xsd:complexType>
            <xsd:attribute name="databaseChange" default="false"
type="xsd:boolean" form="unqualified">
```

```
            <xsd:annotation>
              <xsd:documentation>Receive notifications of database
changes.</xsd:documentation>
            </xsd:annotation>
          </xsd:attribute>
          <xsd:attribute name="languageChange" default="false"
type="xsd:boolean" form="unqualified">
            <xsd:annotation>
              <xsd:documentation>Receive notifications of language
changes.</xsd:documentation>
            </xsd:annotation>
          </xsd:attribute>
          <xsd:attribute name="transactionBoundary" default="false"
type="xsd:boolean" form="unqualified">
            <xsd:annotation>
              <xsd:documentation>Receive notifications of transaction
boundaries.</xsd:documentation>
            </xsd:annotation>
          </xsd:attribute>
        </xsd:complexType>
      </xsd:element>
      <xsd:element name="applicationName">
        <xsd:annotation>
          <xsd:documentation>Set the application name for the
login.</xsd:documentation>
        </xsd:annotation>
        <xsd:complexType>
          <xsd:attribute name="value" type="xsd:string"
form="unqualified" use="required">
            <xsd:annotation>
              <xsd:documentation>The application name to set for the
login.</xsd:documentation>
            </xsd:annotation>
          </xsd:attribute>
        </xsd:complexType>
      </xsd:element>
      <xsd:element name="hostName">
        <xsd:annotation>
          <xsd:documentation>Set the host name for the login.</xsd:
documentation>
        </xsd:annotation>
        <xsd:complexType>
          <xsd:attribute name="value" type="xsd:string" form="unqualified"
use="required">
            <xsd:annotation>
              <xsd:documentation>The host name to set for the
login.</xsd:documentation>
            </xsd:annotation>
          </xsd:attribute>
        </xsd:complexType>
```

```
        </xsd:element>
        <xsd:element name="clientPID">
          <xsd:annotation>
            <xsd:documentation>Set the client process ID for the
login.</xsd:documentation>
          </xsd:annotation>
          <xsd:complexType>
            <xsd:attribute name="value" type="xsd:long"
form="unqualified" use="required">
              <xsd:annotation>
                <xsd:documentation>The client process ID to set for the
login.</xsd:documentation>
              </xsd:annotation>
            </xsd:attribute>
          </xsd:complexType>
        </xsd:element>
        <xsd:element name="clientNetworkID">
          <xsd:annotation>
            <xsd:documentation>Set the client network ID for the
login.</xsd:documentation>
          </xsd:annotation>
          <xsd:complexType>
            <xsd:attribute name="value" type="xsd:base64Binary"
form="unqualified" use="required">
              <xsd:annotation>
                <xsd:documentation>The client network ID to set for the
login.</xsd:documentation>
              </xsd:annotation>
            </xsd:attribute>
          </xsd:complexType>
        </xsd:element>
        <xsd:element name="clientInterface">
          <xsd:annotation>
            <xsd:documentation>Set the client interface for the
login.</xsd:documentation>
          </xsd:annotation>
          <xsd:complexType>
            <xsd:attribute name="value" type="xsd:string"
form="unqualified" use="required">
              <xsd:annotation>
                <xsd:documentation>The client interface to set for the
login.</xsd:documentation>
              </xsd:annotation>
            </xsd:attribute>
          </xsd:complexType>
        </xsd:element>
        <xsd:element name="notificationRequest">
          <xsd:annotation>
            <xsd:documentation>Requests query notifications for the
request.</xsd:documentation>
```

```xml
        </xsd:annotation>
        <xsd:complexType>
          <xsd:attribute name="notificationId" type="xsd:string"
form="unqualified" use="required">
            <xsd:annotation>
              <xsd:documentation>The notification identifier.</xsd:
documentation>
            </xsd:annotation>
          </xsd:attribute>
          <xsd:attribute name="deliveryService" type="xsd:string"
form="unqualified" use="required">
            <xsd:annotation>
              <xsd:documentation>The delivery service.</xsd:
documentation>
            </xsd:annotation>
          </xsd:attribute>
          <xsd:attribute name="timeout" type="xsd:integer"
form="unqualified">
            <xsd:annotation>
              <xsd:documentation>The timeout value.</xsd:documentation>
            </xsd:annotation>
          </xsd:attribute>
        </xsd:complexType>
      </xsd:element>
      <xsd:element name="sqlSession">
        <xsd:annotation>
          <xsd:documentation>SQL Server SOAP Session</xsd:documentation>
        </xsd:annotation>
        <xsd:complexType>
          <xsd:attribute name="initiate" default="false"
type="xsd:boolean" form="unqualified">
            <xsd:annotation>
              <xsd:documentation>Set to 'true' to request to start a new
session.</xsd:documentation>
            </xsd:annotation>
          </xsd:attribute>
          <xsd:attribute name="terminate" default="false"
type="xsd:boolean" form="unqualified">
            <xsd:annotation>
              <xsd:documentation>Set to 'true' to request to terminate an
existing session.</xsd:documentation>
            </xsd:annotation>
          </xsd:attribute>
          <xsd:attribute name="sessionId" type="xsd:base64Binary"
form="unqualified">
            <xsd:annotation>
              <xsd:documentation>The ID of a session.</xsd:documentation>
            </xsd:annotation>
          </xsd:attribute>
          <xsd:attribute name="timeout" type="xsd:int" form="unqualified">
```

```
              <xsd:annotation>
                 <xsd:documentation>The timeout in seconds before the
session expires.</xsd:documentation>
                 </xsd:annotation>
              </xsd:attribute>
              <xsd:attribute name="transactionDescriptor"
type="xsd:base64Binary" form="unqualified">
                 <xsd:annotation>
                    <xsd:documentation>The descriptor of a transaction to
enlist to.</xsd:documentation>
                    </xsd:annotation>
                 </xsd:attribute>
           </xsd:complexType>
        </xsd:element>
      </xsd:schema>
      <xsd:schema xmlns:xsd="http://www.w3.org/2001/XMLSchema" xmlns:
sqlparameter="http://schemas.microsoft.com/sqlserver/2004/SOAP/types/
SqlParameter"
xmlns:sqltypes="http://schemas.microsoft.com/sqlserver/2004/sqltypes"

targetNamespace="http://schemas.microsoft.com/sqlserver/2004/SOAP/types/
SqlParameter" elementFormDefault="qualified" attributeFormDefault=
"qualified">
        <xsd:annotation>
           <xsd:documentation xml:lang="en">&#xD;&#xA;(c) Copyright 2004,
Microsoft Corporation&#xD;&#xA;&#xD;&#xA;The following schema for
Microsoft SQL Server is presented in XML format and is for informational
purposes only. Microsoft Corporation ("Microsoft") may have trademarks,
copyrights, or other intellectual property rights covering subject matter
in the schema.&#xD;&#xA;&#xD;&#xA;Microsoft does not make any representa-
tion or warranty regarding the schema or any product or item developed
based on the schema. The schema is provided to you on an AS IS basis.
Microsoft disclaims all express, implied and statutory warranties,
including but not limited to the implied warranties of merchantability,
fitness for a particular purpose, and freedom from infringement. Without
limiting the generality of the foregoing, Microsoft does not make any
warranty of any kind that any item developed based on the schema, or any
portion of the schema, will not infringe any copyright, patent, trade
secret, or other intellectual property right of any person or entity in any
country. It is your responsibility to seek licenses for such intellectual
property rights where appropriate.&#xD;&#xA;&#xD;&#xA;MICROSOFT SHALL NOT
BE LIABLE FOR ANY DAMAGES OF ANY KIND ARISING OUT OF OR IN CONNECTION
WITH THE USE OF THE SCHEMA, INCLUDING WITHOUT LIMITATION, ANY DIRECT,
INDIRECT, INCIDENTAL, CONSEQUENTIAL (INCLUDING ANY LOST PROFITS), PUNITIVE
OR SPECIAL DAMAGES, WHETHER OR NOT MICROSOFT HAS BEEN ADVISED OF SUCH
DAMAGES.&#xD;&#xA;</xsd:documentation>
        </xsd:annotation>
        <xsd:import
namespace="http://schemas.microsoft.com/sqlserver/2004/sqltypes"/>
        <xsd:simpleType name="ParameterDirection">
```

```xml
      <xsd:restriction base="xsd:string">
        <xsd:enumeration value="Input"/>
        <xsd:enumeration value="InputOutput"/>
      </xsd:restriction>
    </xsd:simpleType>
    <xsd:complexType name="ArrayOfSqlParameter">
      <xsd:sequence>
        <xsd:element minOccurs="0" maxOccurs="unbounded"
name="SqlParameter" type="sqlparameter:SqlParameter"/>
      </xsd:sequence>
    </xsd:complexType>
    <xsd:complexType name="SqlParameter">
      <xsd:sequence>
        <xsd:element minOccurs="1" maxOccurs="1" name="Value"
nillable="true"/>
      </xsd:sequence>
      <xsd:attribute name="name" type="xsd:string" use="required"
form="unqualified"/>
      <xsd:attribute default="NVarChar" name="sqlDbType" type=
"sqltypes:sqlDbTypeEnum" use="optional" form="unqualified"/>
      <xsd:attribute default="Input" name="direction" type=
"sqlparameter:ParameterDirection" use="optional" form="unqualified"/>
      <xsd:attribute default="1" name="maxLength" type="xsd:long"
use="optional" form="unqualified"/>
      <xsd:attribute default="18" name="precision" type="xsd:
unsignedByte" use="optional" form="unqualified"/>
      <xsd:attribute default="0" name="scale" type="xsd:unsignedByte"
use="optional" form="unqualified"/>
      <xsd:attribute default="" name="clrTypeName" type="xsd:string"
use="optional" form="unqualified"/>
      <xsd:attribute default="Default" name="sqlCompareOptions"
type="sqltypes:sqlCompareOptionsList" use="optional" form="unqualified"/>
      <xsd:attribute default="-1" name="localeId" type="xsd:int"
use="optional" form="unqualified"/>
      <xsd:attribute default="0" name="sqlCollationVersion"
type="xsd:int" use="optional" form="unqualified"/>
      <xsd:attribute default="0" name="sqlSortId" type="xsd:int"
use="optional" form="unqualified"/>
      <xsd:attribute default="" name="xmlSchemaCollection"
type="xsd:string" use="optional" form="unqualified"/>
    </xsd:complexType>
  </xsd:schema>
  <xsd:schema xmlns:xsd="http://www.w3.org/2001/XMLSchema"
attributeFormDefault="qualified" elementFormDefault="qualified"
targetNamespace="urn:autos"
xmlns:sqltypes="http://schemas.microsoft.com/sqlserver/2004/sqltypes"

xmlns:sqlsoaptypes="http://schemas.microsoft.com/sqlserver/2004/SOAP/ types"
xmlns:sqlrowcount="http://schemas.microsoft.com/sqlserver/2004/SOAP/
types/SqlRowCount"
```

```
xmlns:sqlmessage="http://schemas.microsoft.com/sqlserver/2004/SOAP/types/
SqlMessage"
xmlns:sqlresultstream="http://schemas.microsoft.com/sqlserver/2004/SOAP/
types/SqlResultStream"

xmlns:sqlparameter="http://schemas.microsoft.com/sqlserver/2004/SOAP/
types/SqlParameter">
      <xsd:import
namespace="http://schemas.microsoft.com/sqlserver/2004/sqltypes"/>
      <xsd:import
namespace="http://schemas.microsoft.com/sqlserver/2004/SOAP/types/
SqlResultStream"/>
      <xsd:element name="GetEstimate">
        <xsd:complexType>
          <xsd:sequence>
            <xsd:element minOccurs="1" maxOccurs="1" name="model"
nillable="true">
              <xsd:simpleType>
                <xsd:restriction base="sqltypes:nvarchar"
sqltypes:localeId="1033" sqltypes:sqlCompareOptions="IgnoreCase
IgnoreKanaType IgnoreWidth" sqltypes:sqlSortId="52">
                  <xsd:maxLength value="10"></xsd:maxLength>
                </xsd:restriction>
              </xsd:simpleType>
            </xsd:element>
          </xsd:sequence>
        </xsd:complexType>
      </xsd:element>
      <xsd:element name="GetEstimateResponse">
        <xsd:complexType>
          <xsd:sequence>
            <xsd:element minOccurs="1" maxOccurs="1" name=
"GetEstimateResult" type="sqltypes:int" nillable="true"></xsd:element>
          </xsd:sequence>
        </xsd:complexType>
      </xsd:element>
    </xsd:schema>
  </wsdl:types>
  <wsdl:message name="s0MsgGetEstimateSoapIn">
    <wsdl:part name="parameters" element="s0:GetEstimate"></wsdl:part>
  </wsdl:message>
  <wsdl:message name="s0MsgGetEstimateSoapOut">
    <wsdl:part name="parameters"
element="s0:GetEstimateResponse"></wsdl:part>
  </wsdl:message>
  <wsdl:portType name="RepairPointSoap">
    <wsdl:operation name="GetEstimate">
      <wsdl:input name="s0MsgGetEstimateSoapIn" message="tns:
s0MsgGetEstimateSoapIn"></wsdl:input>
      <wsdl:output name="s0MsgGetEstimateSoapOut"
message="tns:s0MsgGetEstimateSoapOut"></wsdl:output>
```

```
      </wsdl:operation>
    </wsdl:portType>
    <wsdl:binding name="RepairPointSoap" type="tns:RepairPointSoap">
      <soap:binding transport="http://schemas.xmlsoap.org/soap/http"
style="document"/>
      <wsdl:operation name="GetEstimate">
        <soap:operation soapAction="urn:autosGetEstimate"
style="document"></soap:operation>
        <wsdl:input name="s0MsgGetEstimateSoapIn">
          <soap:body use="literal"/>
        </wsdl:input>
        <wsdl:output name="s0MsgGetEstimateSoapOut">
          <soap:body use="literal"/>
        </wsdl:output>
      </wsdl:operation>
    </wsdl:binding>
    <wsdl:service name="RepairPoint">
      <wsdl:port name="RepairPoint" binding="tns:RepairPointSoap">
        <soap:address
location="http://canopus5/Repairs/req"></soap:address>
      </wsdl:port>
    </wsdl:service>
</wsdl:definitions>
```

Note that one way to see that actual WSDL for a Web Service hosted in SQL Server 2005 is to use Internet Explorer to access the endpoint instead of the Visual Studio 2005 Add Web Reference wizard, as shown in Figure 12-13.

The format of the payloads for SOAP messages is defined in terms of the XML Schema 1.0 recommendation. A primer for this recommendation is available at http://www.w3.org/TR/2004/REC-xmlschema-0-20041028/.

FIGURE 12-13: Using Internet Explorer

It is beyond the scope of this book to discuss XML Schema in detail, but we will look at some simple aspects of it.

Listing 12-3 earlier in this chapter showed the SOAP message that was sent to SQL Server 2005 when the application called the GetEstimate method of the RepairPoint object. The Add Web Reference wizard in Visual Studio 2005 figured out the format for the payload of that SOAP message from the WSDL file shown in Listing 12-5. Figure 12-14 shows a fragment of that file: that part that defines the GetEstimate element, which is the payload of the SOAP message. It says the payload should be an element named "GetEstimate" (1) and that it should contain an element named "model" (2).

The content of the model element is defined by a restriction (3). Restriction is an element from XML Schema 1.0 that allows you to refine a type definition further. In this case, the restriction contains a maxLength element, which says that the string contained in the model may not have more than ten characters.

If you look closely, you will see what appears to be the metadata that SQL Server 2005 uses to define a string. In this case, it says that the content of the model element should be a NVARCHAR; then it goes on to list things

```
                             ①
<xsd:element name="GetEstimate">
 <xsd:complexType>
  <xsd:sequence>
   <xsd:element
    minOccurs="1"
    maxOccurs="1"
    name="model" ②
    nillable="true">
    <xsd:simpleType>
     <xsd:restriction   ③
      base="sqltypes:nvarchar"
      sqltypes:localeId="1033"
      sqltypes:sqlCompareOptions="IgnoreCase
      IgnoreKanaType IgnoreWidth"
      sqltypes:sqlSortId="52">
       <xsd:maxLength value="10"></xsd:maxLength>
      </xsd:restriction>
     </xsd:simpleType>
    </xsd:element>
   </xsd:sequence>
  </xsd:complexType>
 </xsd:element>
```

FIGURE 12-14: GetEstimate schema

like the locale for the string. What SQL Server 2005 has done is map the metadata it uses for the @model parameter of the RepairEstimate stored procedure to XML.

Visual Studio 2005 has some idea of how to interpret the fact that model (2) is a NVARCHAR; Visual Studio 2005 was designed with support of SQL Server 2005 in mind. It is unlikely that other platforms and development environments will be able to interpret nvarchar. As shown in Figure 12-15, however, another part of the WSDL file defines NVARCHAR (1) in terms of a standard XML schema type, string. All platforms understand how to interpret an XML Schema 1.0 string.

By default, SQL Server 2005 will define data types in terms of their SQL type and then redefine the SQL type in terms of standard XML Schema 1.0 types. In fact, most of the WSDL files shown in Listing 12-5 earlier in this chapter consist of definitions of SQL types in terms of standard XML Schema 1.0 types.

SQL Server 2005 can create a WSDL file that defines data types directly in standard XML Schema types. Three possible query strings can be used. The ?WSDL one (2) is shown in Figure 12-9, to obtain a WSDL file from SQL Server 2005, WSDL, WSDLComplex, and WSDLSimple. By default, WSDL and WSDLComplex will produce the WSDL file shown in Listing 12-5. WSDLSimple will produce a similar WSDL file except that data types will be defined directly with XML Schema types.

Figure 12-16 shows the fragment of the WSDL file produced when WSDLSimple is used, which defines the format of the model parameter of the GetEstimate Webmethod. You can see here that the content of model is defined as the standard XML Schema 1.0 type string without the level of

```
<xsd:simpleType name="nvarchar">
  <xsd:restriction base="xsd:string"/>   ①
</xsd:simpleType>

              ②
<xsd:element  name="model">
  <xsd:restriction base="sqltypes:nvarchar"
    sqltypes:localeId="1033"
    sqltypes:sqlCompareOptions="IgnoreCase
    IgnoreKanaType IgnoreWidth"
    sqltypes:sqlSortId="52">
    <xsd:maxLength value="10"></xsd:maxLength>
  </xsd:restriction>
</xsd:element>
```

FIGURE 12-15: Definition of nvarchar

```
<xsd:element name="GetEstimate">
  <xsd:complexType>
    <xsd:sequence>
      <xsd:element minOccurs="1" maxOccurs="1"
        name="model" type="xsd:string"
        nillable="true">
      </xsd:element>
    </xsd:sequence>
  </xsd:complexType>
</xsd:element>
```

FIGURE 12-16: Element for GetEstimate

indirection through a NVARCHAR, which itself is defined as a string, as shown in Figure 12-15.

The choice of ?WSDLComplex or ?WSDLSimple depends on the needs of the client that will be using the Web Service, as well as the platform and environment used to develop the client.

In the case of the Add Web Reference wizard in Visual Studio 2005, when ?WSDLComplex is used, the proxy class will use data types from the System.Data.SqlTypes namespace. These are the data types that represent the corresponding data types found in SQL Server 2005—that is, they can be null. Figure 12-17 shows the IntelliSense provided by Visual Studio 2005 for the GetEstimate method for an application that used ?WSDLComplex to build the RepairPoint proxy class. You can see here that the SqlInt32 type was used for the return value and that the SqlString type was used for the input parameter. The SqlTypes are discussed in Chapter 3.

When ?WSDLSimple is used with the Add Web Reference wizard in Visual Studio 2005, the proxy class will use data types from the System namespace—in other words, data types commonly used in .NET Framework applications that do not use ADO.NET. In some cases, these will be value types.

CLR value types are discussed in Appendix A and in the MSDN documentation for Visual Studio 2005 for .NET Framework; look for "value types"

```
class Program
{
  static void Main(string[] args)
  {
    RepairPoint rp = new RepairPoint();
    rp.UseDefaultCredentials = true;
    rp.GetEstimate("
  }                System.Data.SqlTypes.SqlInt32 RepairPoint.GetEstimate (System.Data.SqlTypes.SqlString model)
}
```

FIGURE 12-17: Proxy for ?WSDLComplex

in the index. In brief, they are basically the primitive data types used for numerics, such System.Int32 and int in C#.

Two choices are available for each value, or primitive, type in .NET Framework 2.0. Prior to .NET Framework 2.0, there was no way to represent a null value for a value type like a `System.Int32`, but .NET Framework 2.0 added support for nullable types through the `System.Nullable<>` template class. `System.Nullable<Int32>`, for example, is an `Int32` that can represent a null. Whether a nullable type is in the proxy class is determined by information in the XML Schema that defines the message.

Nullable types are discussed in the MSDN documentation for Visual Studio 2005 for .NET Framework; look for "Nullable<T>" in the index.

Just as the WSDL file includes an XML Schema 1.0 definition for the format of messages sent to it, as shown in Figure 12-14, it includes one for the messages it sends back to the client. Figure 12-18 shows the XML Schema 1.0 definition for `GetEstimateResponse`, which is in the payload of the SOAP message sent back to the client. It says that the `GetEstimateResponse` element should contain a GetEstimateResult element that contains the return value. Note that the return type is sqltypes:int, which is redefined as an int from XML Schema 1.0, just as the nvarchar was redefined as a string.

We can see the information that the Add Web Reference wizard uses in the definition for `GetEstimateResult`, shown in Figure 12-18; it has an attribute nillable="true". As the name implies, it means that the GetEstimateResult element is nillable. The nillable="true" attribute is added whether ?WSDLSimple or ?WSDLComplex is used, but later, we will look at creating a custom XML Schema where this might not be the case.

```
<xsd:element name="GetEstimateResponse">
  <xsd:complexType>
    <xsd:sequence>
      <xsd:element
        minOccurs="1"
        maxOccurs="1"
        name="GetEstimateResult"
        type="xsd:int"
        nillable="true">
      </xsd:element>
    </xsd:sequence>
  </xsd:complexType>
</xsd:element>
```

FIGURE 12-18: GetEstimateResponse schema

There is no "NULL" defined in XML Schema 1.0, as there is in most databases, but the nillable="true" attribute says in effect that the element represents a value that comes from a database and might be NULL. INTs in SQL Server 2005 can be NULL, which is why the GetEstimateResult is attributed in this way. This is not the only way this might be done, but the underlying reasons for this choice involve a discussion of how an XML document is validated against an XML Schema and is not part of the scope of this book.

The nillable="true" attribute allows a message like the one shown in Listing 12-6 to be returned to the client. Note that the GetEstimateResult element has no content—that is, it contains no number, as the message in Listing 12-4 did, but it does have an attribute xsi:nil="1", which typically would be interpreted as meaning the GetEstimateResult is NULL. If the XML Schema shown in Figure 12-18 did not have the nillable="true" attribute, this message would be invalid according to that XML Schema definition.

In short, SQL Server 2005 adds the nillable="true" attribute to data type definitions for both ?WSDLComplex and ?WSDLSimple to indicate that a value for one of these data types might be NULL. It also marks null values with a xsi:nil="1" attribute so that clients recognize a null value.

LISTING 12-6: Return of NULL value

```
<SOAP-ENV:Envelope xml:space="preserve"
xmlns:xsd=
"http://www.w3.org/2001/XMLSchema"
xmlns:xsi=
"http://www.w3.org/2001/XMLSchema-instance"
xmlns:SOAP-ENV=
"http://schemas.xmlsoap.org/soap/envelope/"
xmlns:sql=
"http://schemas.microsoft.com/sqlserver/2004/SOAP"
xmlns:sqlsoaptypes=
"http://schemas.microsoft.com/sqlserver/2004/SOAP/types"
xmlns:sqlrowcount=
"http://schemas.microsoft.com/sqlserver/2004/SOAP/types/SqlRowCount"
xmlns:sqlmessage=
"http://schemas.microsoft.com/sqlserver/2004/SOAP/types/SqlMessage"
xmlns:sqlresultstream=
"http://schemas.microsoft.com/sqlserver/2004/SOAP/types/SqlResultStream"
xmlns:sqltransaction=
"http://schemas.microsoft.com/sqlserver/2004/SOAP/types/SqlTransaction"
xmlns:sqltypes=
"http://schemas.microsoft.com/sqlserver/2004/sqltypes"
xmlns:msdata="urn:schemas-microsoft-com:xml-msdata"
xmlns:method="urn:autos">
```

```
<SOAP-ENV:Body>
  <method:GetEstimateResponse>
      <method:GetEstimateResult xsi:nil="1"/>
  </method:GetEstimateResponse>
</SOAP-ENV:Body>
</SOAP-ENV:Envelope>
```

The way client code makes use of nillable and xsi:nil depends on the platform and development environment that created the proxy code the client will use to access the Web Service. In this case, the Add Web Reference wizard in Visual Studio 2005 interprets these data types as nullable types when they are directly specified as XML Schema numeric types by ?WSDLSimple.

The result is that client code that uses a proxy made with ?WSDLSimple must use the nullable types provided by the .NET Framework instead of SqlTypes types, as was done for ?WSDLComplex shown in Figure 12-18. Figure 12-19 shows the IntelliSense for a proxy created using ?WSDLSimple. Note that the GetEstimate function returns a int? type. int? is an alias for Nullable<Int32>, which is a type in .NET Framework. Most languages provide a set of aliases for the nullable types in .NET Framework 2.0; for C#, a ? is added as a suffix to the non-nullable version of the type.

In many cases, the .NET Framework will hide the difference between a nullable and a non-nullable type. In some cases, however, the exact nullable type must be used. If the code in Figure 12-19 were changed as follows, it would not compile because of a mismatch between the return type of GetEstimate and the type of i2:

```
int i2 = rp.GetEstimate("asdf");
```

Remember all the things people have said about supporting null values making programming more complicated? They're true!

```
class Program
{
  static void Main(string[] args)
  {
    RepairPoint rp = new RepairPoint();
    rp.UseDefaultCredentials = true;
    Nullable<Int32> i = rp.GetEstimate("asdf");
    int? i2 = rp.GetEsti int? RepairPoint.GetEstimate (string model)
    Console.WriteLine(i);
  }
}
```

FIGURE 12-19: Proxy for ?WSDLSimple

XML Namespaces

Namespaces are part of both SOAP messages and WSDL files. Namespaces are defined in the Namespaces in XML Recommendation at http://www.w3.org/TR/2004/REC-xml-names11-20040204/. A full discussion of namespaces is beyond the scope of the book, but in simple terms, a namespace is used to prevent clashes between items that have the same name but different definitions. Two people might want to make a definition of what an account is, for example. The definitions will be different, because the accounts will be used in different environments. Each person would choose a namespace for the names for his items. One might choose the namespace urn:big-company-com:bookkeeping and the urn:small-company-com:book-keeping. The account from the urn:big-company-com:bookkeeping would have a different definition from that from the urn:little-company-com:book-keeping, even though they have the same name.

A WSDL file has a `targetNamespace`, and the schema for the payload of a SOAP message also has a `targetNamespace`. The `targetNamespace` for the WSDL file is defined by the NAMESPACE option FOR SOAP clause, and the `targetNamespace` for the payload of a SOAP message is defined in the WEBMETHOD clause.

Figure 12-20 shows a fragment of the FOR SOAP clause (1) from Listing 12-2 that defines the RepairPoint Web Service. The "urn:autos" in the

```
① FOR SOAP
    (
    WEBMETHOD 'urn:autos'.'GetEstimate'
    (NAME = 'Repairs.dbo.RepairEstimate' …),
    …
    NAMESPACE = 'urn:other'
    )

② <wsdl:definitions
    xmlns:wsdl="http://schemas.xmlsoap.org/wsdl/"
    targetNamespace="urn:other"
    …
    >

③ <soap:Body>
        <GetEstimate xmlns="urn:autos">
```

FIGURE 12-20: Namespaces

WEBMETHOD clause is the targetNamespace for the payload of the SOAP message for the Webmethod, which means that it is the namespace of the GetEstimate element (3).

Figure 12-20 shows the beginning of the WSDL file for the RepairPoint Web Service. The complete file is shown in Listing 12-15 later in this chapter. The targetNamespace of the wsdl:definitions element (2) in Figure 12-20 is "urn:other", which was defined in the NAMESPACE option of the FOR SOAP (1) clause for the RepairPoint Web Service.

WSDL Generation

Figure 12-12 earlier in this chapter showed the FOR SOAP clause using the WSDL=DEFAULT option, and all that this does is configure the Web Service to use the sp_http_generate_wsdl_defaultcomplexorsimple stored procedure to generate the WSDL file. There are two other possible values for the WSDL option: NONE and the name of a stored procedure.

The WSDL=NONE option prevents access to the WSDL file for the Web Service. This may be useful if the WSDL file is considered to be valuable intellectual property, and you want to ensure that it can be obtained only through some kind of business channel.

You can also use the WSDL option to specify a particular stored procedure to be used to generate the WSDL file. You might want a simple WSDL file to be generated when the ?WSDL query string is used instead of the complex one. SQL Server 2005 provides a stored procedure that will do this; it is named sp_http_generate_wsdl_defaultsimpleorcomplex. If you set the WSDL='sp_http_generate_wsdl_defaultsimpleorcomplex' for your WSDL option in the FOR SOAP clause, ?WSDL and ?WSDLSimple will return a simple WSDL file, and ?WSDLComplex will return the complex one.

In some cases, you will want to return a custom WSDL file of your own design. In Web Services, it usually is best to keep things as simple as possible, and even the WSDLSimple file that SQL Server 2005 produced for the GetEstimate contains definitions for many SQL types, even though it did not use them. Listing 12-7 shows a custom WSDL file for the RepairPoint Web Service that does not include any of the XML Schema definitions for SQL types.

LISTING 12-7: Custom WSDL file

```
<wsdl:definitions xmlns:wsdl="http://schemas.xmlsoap.org/wsdl/"
xmlns:soap="http://schemas.xmlsoap.org/wsdl/soap/" xmlns:sqloptions=
"http://schemas.microsoft.com/sqlserver/2004/SOAP/Options"
xmlns:s0="urn:autos"
xmlns:tns="urn:other"
targetNamespace="urn:other">
  <wsdl:types>
    <xsd:schema xmlns:xsd="http://www.w3.org/2001/XMLSchema"
        attributeFormDefault="qualified"
        elementFormDefault="qualified"
        targetNamespace="urn:autos">
      <xsd:element name="GetEstimate">
        <xsd:complexType>
          <xsd:sequence>
            <xsd:element minOccurs="1" maxOccurs="1"
              name="model" type="xsd:string"
              nillable="true">
            </xsd:element>
          </xsd:sequence>
        </xsd:complexType>
      </xsd:element>
      <xsd:element name="GetEstimateResponse">
        <xsd:complexType>
          <xsd:sequence>
            <xsd:element minOccurs="1" maxOccurs="1"
              name="GetEstimateResult" type="xsd:int"
              nillable="true">
            </xsd:element>
          </xsd:sequence>
        </xsd:complexType>
      </xsd:element>
    </xsd:schema>
  </wsdl:types>
  <wsdl:message name="s0MsgGetEstimateSoapIn">
    <wsdl:part name="parameters"
      element="s0:GetEstimate">
    </wsdl:part>
  </wsdl:message>
  <wsdl:message name="s0MsgGetEstimateSoapOut">
    <wsdl:part name="parameters"
      element="s0:GetEstimateResponse">
    </wsdl:part>
  </wsdl:message>
  <wsdl:portType name="RepairPointSoap">
    <wsdl:operation name="GetEstimate">
      <wsdl:input name="s0MsgGetEstimateSoapIn"
        message="tns:s0MsgGetEstimateSoapIn">
      </wsdl:input>
      <wsdl:output name="s0MsgGetEstimateSoapOut"
```

```
        message="tns:s0MsgGetEstimateSoapOut">
      </wsdl:output>
    </wsdl:operation>
  </wsdl:portType>
  <wsdl:binding name="RepairPointSoap"
     type="tns:RepairPointSoap">
    <soap:binding
        transport="http://schemas.xmlsoap.org/soap/http"
        style="document"/>
    <wsdl:operation name="GetEstimate">
      <soap:operation soapAction="urn:autosGetEstimate"
          style="document">
      </soap:operation>
      <wsdl:input name="s0MsgGetEstimateSoapIn">
        <soap:body use="literal"/>
      </wsdl:input>
      <wsdl:output name="s0MsgGetEstimateSoapOut">
        <soap:body use="literal"/>
      </wsdl:output>
    </wsdl:operation>
  </wsdl:binding>
  <wsdl:service name="RepairPoint">
    <wsdl:port name="RepairPoint"
       binding="tns:RepairPointSoap">
      <soap:address location=
       "http://canopus5/Repairs/req"></soap:address>
    </wsdl:port>
  </wsdl:service>
</wsdl:definitions>
```

You could deploy a custom WSDL file by setting the WSDL=NONE option in the FOR SOAP clause and putting the WSDL file up on a share somewhere or in a UDDI (Universal Description, Discover and Integration) server. A discussion of UDDI is beyond the scope of this book, but it is discussed in the MSDN documentation; look for "UDDI" in the index.

You can also write your own WSDL generator procedure and use the WSDL option in the FOR SOAP clause to configure SQL Server 2005 to use it.

A WSDL generator procedure is a stored procedure that returns a rowset that has a single row with a single column of type NVARCHAR(MAX) named [XML_F52E2B61-18A1-11d1-B105-00805F49916B]. Note that this column name is used to indicate that the column contains XML. The value of the column is the WSDL file. Listing 12-8 shows the signature of the stored procedure.

When SQL Server 2005 calls a WSDL generator procedure, the @end-pointID parameter gets the key you can use to look up the endpoint in the `sys.http_endpoints` view. The `@isSSL` parameter is 0 if this is a clear port and 1 if it is an SSL port. The `@host` parameter has the name of the host—that is, the name of the machine hosting the Web Service. The `@queryString` contains the query string from the URL that was used to request the WSDL file. The `@userAgent` contains the user agent header from the HTTP GET command that was used to get the WSDL file.

LISTING 12-8: WSDL generator signature

```
CREATE
PROCEDURE GenerateRepairWSDL
(@endpointID as int,
@isSSL as bit,
@host as nvarchar(256),
@queryString as nvarchar(256),
@userAgent as nvarchar(256)
)
```

You will not know several pieces of information at the time you write a WSDL generator procedure. One of these is the name of the machine that the Web Service is hosted on. The WSDL file in Listing 12-7 earlier in this chapter hard-coded the machine name to Canopus5. This Web Service may be deployed on another system. The result is that at least some of the WSDL file will have to be generated dynamically when the WSDL generator procedure is called. Later, we will see that this is easy to do using XQuery.

In spite of the simplicity of the WSDL file shown in Listing 12-7, some applications still will prefer to use the WSDLComplex or WSDLSimple form, so any WSDL generator procedure should preserve access to them. To do this, the Web server should accept an extra query string to specify that the minimal WSDL file be produced. The Web Service should accept a ?WSDLMinimal query string in addition to the ?WSDL, ?WSDLSimple, and ?WSDLComplex query strings. Note that the choice of ?WDSLMinimal was arbitrary; you can use anything you want.

One of the things we have not discussed is the fact that a Web Service may be hosted on a Secure Sockets Layer (SSL) port and then accessed using HTTPS instead of HTTP. We won't be discussing the details of using SSL due to space considerations. The use of SSL, however, is configured in the `AS HTTP` clause of the `CREATE ENDPOINT` expression. The `AS HTTP` clause shown in Listing 12-9 shows a Web Service configured to accept requests both in the clear and with SSL. The port used for HTTP in the clear is different from the one that uses SSL, and the WSDL file will have to reflect this.

LISTING 12-9: Web Service using SSL

```
CREATE ENDPOINT RepairPoint
STATE  = Started
AS HTTP
(
PATH = '/Repairs/req',
PORTS = (CLEAR, SSL),
SITE = '*',
AUTHENTICATION = (INTEGRATED)
)
```

A key problem in making a WSDL generator procedure is creating the proper URL from the WSDL generator procedure input parameters. When SQL Server 2005 calls a WSDL generator procedure, the @endpointID parameter specifies which endpoint the WDSL file must be created for. Some of the information we will need is in the sys.http_endpoints view and is shown in the results of the SELECT expression in Figure 12-21.

Note that the sys.http_endpoints view lists both a clear_port and an ssl_port. The @isSSL parameter shown in Listing 12-8 earlier in this chapter will be 0 if the WSDL file should be generated for the clear port and 1 if it should be generated for the SSL port. The ssl_port in Figure 12-21 is 0 because the AS HTTP clause used to make the RepairPoint Web Service, shown in Figure 12-3 earlier in this chapter, does not specify the use of SSL.

The @host parameter shown in Listing 12-8 passes in the name of the host machine, and the @queryString passes in the query string from the URL that requested the WSDL file.

You can implement a WSDL generator procedure completely in a single stored procedure, but in general, several things can be reused, so the example

```
SELECT endpoint_id, clear_port,
   ssl_port, url_path FROM sys.http_endpoints
```

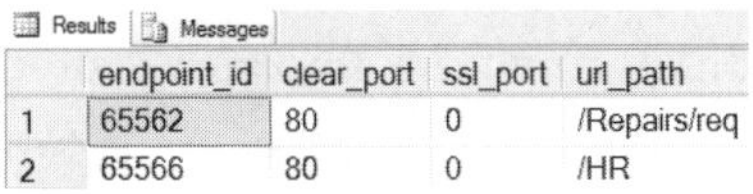

	endpoint_id	clear_port	ssl_port	url_path
1	65562	80	0	/Repairs/req
2	65566	80	0	/HR

FIGURE 12-21: HTTP Endpoint information

that follows will factor the implementation in three parts. One part will compose the proper URL for the Web Service; one will compose the WSDL file itself; and the last will dispatch the generation of the WSDL to the appropriate stored procedure.

Listing 12-10 shows a helper function named `GetWSDLUrl`. This function composes the URL for the endpoint and returns it as an `NVARCHAR`. The `@endpointID` is used to look up the endpoint information in the `sys.http_endpoints` view. The `@isSSL` parameter is used to put the proper scheme at the beginning of the URL and select either the clear or ssl port. The `@host` parameter is the machine name.

LISTING 12-10: URL function

```
CREATE FUNCTION GetWSDLUrl(
@endpointID as INT,
@host NVARCHAR(256),
@isSSL as bit
)
RETURNS NVARCHAR(MAX)
AS
BEGIN
DECLARE @vdir NVARCHAR(MAX);
DECLARE @clear_port NVARCHAR(5);
DECLARE @ssl_port NVARCHAR(5);
DECLARE @url_path NVARCHAR(MAX);
SELECT @clear_port = CAST(clear_port AS NVARCHAR(5)),
 @ssl_port = CAST(ssl_port AS NVARCHAR(5)), @url_path = url_path
FROM sys.http_endpoints WHERE endpoint_id = @endpointID
IF @isSSl = 0
SELECT @vdir ='http://' + @host + ':' + @clear_port + @url_path;
ELSE
SELECT @vdir ='https://' + @host + ':' + @ssl_port + @url_path;
RETURN @vdir;
END
```

Figure 12-22 shows how the `GetWSDLUrl` function composes the URL from an endpoint_id, a host, and an SSL indicator. The appropriate port and path from the sys.http_endpoints view are put together with the hostname passed into the `GetWSDLUrl` stored procedure.

Listing 12-11 shows a helper function, `RepairWSDL`, that will create a WSDL file for the `RepairPoint` Web Service. Most of the function is the literal WSDL file. This might be better stored in a table but is done this way to make the example complete in a single place. The function starts by using

```
SELECT endpoint_id, clear_port,
   ssl_port, url_path FROM sys.http_endpoints
   WHERE endpoint_id = 65562
```

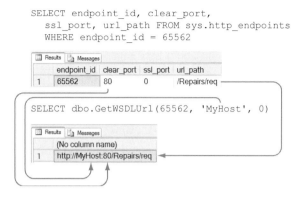

FIGURE 12-22: Using URL function

the GetWSDLUrl function, shown in Listing 12-10, to get the URL that should be in the WSLD file.

The literal WSDL file is set into the @wsdl variable. Near the end of the function, an XQuery modify instruction is used to insert the URL made by the GetWSDLUrl into the address attribute of the soap:address element. It returns the @wsdl variable as an NVARCHAR(MAX). See Chapter 10 for a discussion of XQuery and the modify instruction.

LISTING 12-11: RepairWSDL function

```
CREATE FUNCTION RepairWSDL
(@endpointID as int,
@isSSL as bit,
@host as nvarchar(256)
)
RETURNS NVARCHAR(MAX)
AS
BEGIN
DECLARE @vdir NVARCHAR(MAX);
SELECT @vdir = dbo.GetWSDLUrl(@endpointID, @host, @isSSL);
DECLARE @wsdl XML;
SET @wsdl =
'<wsdl:definitions xmlns:tns="urn:other" xmlns:soap="http://schemas.
xmlsoap.org/wsdl/soap/" xmlns:s0="urn:autos" targetNamespace="urn:other"
xmlns:wsdl="http://schemas.xmlsoap.org/wsdl/">
  <wsdl:types>
    <schema xmlns:xsd="http://www.w3.org/2001/XMLSchema"
attributeFormDefault="qualified" elementFormDefault="qualified"
targetNamespace="urn:autos" xmlns="http://www.w3.org/2001/XMLSchema">
      <xsd:element name="GetEstimate">
        <xsd:complexType>
```

```xml
              <xsd:sequence>
                <xsd:element minOccurs="1" maxOccurs="1" name="model"
nillable="true">
                  <xsd:simpleType>
                    <xsd:restriction base="xsd:string">
                      <xsd:maxLength value="10" />
                    </xsd:restriction>
                  </xsd:simpleType>
                </xsd:element>
              </xsd:sequence>
            </xsd:complexType>
          </xsd:element>
          <xsd:element name="GetEstimateResponse">
            <xsd:complexType>
              <xsd:sequence>
                <xsd:element minOccurs="1" maxOccurs="1"
name="GetEstimateResult" nillable="true" type="xsd:int" />
              </xsd:sequence>
            </xsd:complexType>
          </xsd:element>
        </schema>
      </wsdl:types>
      <wsdl:message name="s0MsgGetEstimateSoapIn">
        <wsdl:part name="parameters" element="s0:GetEstimate" />
      </wsdl:message>
      <wsdl:message name="s0MsgGetEstimateSoapOut">
        <wsdl:part name="parameters" element="s0:GetEstimateResponse" />
      </wsdl:message>
      <wsdl:portType name="RepairPointSoap">
        <wsdl:operation name="GetEstimate">
          <wsdl:input name="s0MsgGetEstimateSoapIn"
message="tns:s0MsgGetEstimateSoapIn" />
          <wsdl:output name="s0MsgGetEstimateSoapOut"
message="tns:s0MsgGetEstimateSoapOut" />
        </wsdl:operation>
      </wsdl:portType>
      <wsdl:binding name="RepairPointSoap" type="tns:RepairPointSoap">
        <soap:binding transport="http://schemas.xmlsoap.org/soap/http" />
        <wsdl:operation name="GetEstimate">
          <soap:operation soapAction="urn:autosGetEstimate" style="document" />
          <wsdl:input name="s0MsgGetEstimateSoapIn">
            <soap:body use="literal" />
          </wsdl:input>
          <wsdl:output name="s0MsgGetEstimateSoapOut">
            <soap:body use="literal" />
          </wsdl:output>
        </wsdl:operation>
      </wsdl:binding>
      <wsdl:service name="RepairPoint">
        <wsdl:port name="RepairPoint" binding="tns:RepairPointSoap">
          <soap:address location="url" />
        </wsdl:port>
```

```
   </wsdl:service>
</wsdl:definitions>'
SET @wsdl.modify('
declare namespace soap="http://schemas.xmlsoap.org/wsdl/soap/";
replace value of (//soap:address[1]/@location)[1] with
sql:variable("@vdir")');
RETURN CAST(@wsdl AS NVARCHAR(MAX));
END
```

Now we have the pieces we need to make a WSDL generator procedure, GenerateRepairWSDL, shown in Listing 12-12. If the query string passed in via @queryString is ?WSDLMinimal, GenerateRepairWSDL uses the RepairWSDL function to make a single-row, single-column rowset that contains the WSDL. If the query string is not ?WSDLMinimal, it delegates the creation of the WSDL file to the sp_http_generate_wsdl_defaultcomplexorsimple stored procedure—the stored procedure that SQL Server 2005 uses to create WSDL files. Note that using this technique, you could, if necessary, support several formats for your WSDL file.

Note that the SELECT statement that returns the XML for the WSDL file is aliased to [XML_F52E2B61-18A1-11d1-B105-00805F49916B]. As mentioned earlier in this chapter, this must be the name of the column returned by the stored procedure that creates the WSDL file.

LISTING 12-12: WSDL generator procedure

```
CREATE PROCEDURE GenerateRepairWSDL
(@endpointID as int,
@isSSL as bit,
@host as nvarchar(256),
@queryString as nvarchar(256),
@userAgent as nvarchar(256)
) AS
BEGIN
IF @queryString = 'WSDLMinimal'
BEGIN
SELECT dbo.RepairWSDL(@endpointID, @isSSl, @host) AS
[XML_F52E2B61-18A1-11d1-B105-00805F49916B];
RETURN
END
ELSE
BEGIN
EXEC sp_http_generate_wsdl_defaultcomplexorsimple
@endpointID, @isSSL, @host, @queryString, @userAgent;
RETURN
END
END
```

Listing 12-13 shows a FOR SOAP clause configured to use the GenerateRepairWSDL stored procedure to generate the WSDL file for a Web Service.

LISTING 12-13: FOR SOAP configured to use custom WSDL

```
FOR SOAP
(
WEBMETHOD 'urn:autos'.'GetPersonel'
(NAME = 'Repairs.dbo.Names', SCHEMA=STANDARD),
WSDL= 'Repairs.dbo.GenerateRepairWSDL',
SCHEMA=STANDARD,
DATABASE = 'Repairs',
NAMESPACE = 'urn:other'
)
```

Stored Procedure in Web Service

The RepairPoint Web Service we have been working with will look familiar to developers who have been using Web Services, but it will look a bit different to developers who have been using ADO.NET and connecting to SQL Server 2005 using TDS. It is common in ADO.NET-based applications to issue arbitrary SQL queries or to call stored procedures and collect the rowsets produced in a System.Data.DataSet. SQL Server 2005 Web Services support this programming idiom, albeit with a programming model that is a bit different from that in ADO.NET. Note that this programming model was also supported in SQLXML 3.0.

By default, the payload of the SOAP message returned by SQL Server 2005 Web Service is in effect, the same as what would be returned in TDS, but in the form of XML.

To illustrate this, we are going to host the stored procedure Test5, shown in Listing 12-14, in a SQL Server 2005 Web Service. The stored procedure has an output parameter, prints a message, raises an error, and does a SELECT that returns a rowset with two rows in it. In other words, it does a lot of things you might expect a stored procedure to do.

LISTING 12-14: Test5 stored procedure

```
CREATE PROC Test5 (@data INT output)
AS
SET @data = 5
PRINT 'This is the Test5 message'
RAISERROR ('Test5 error', 10, 1)
```

```
SELECT * FROM
(SELECT 1 AS ID, 'Joe' AS NAME
UNION
SELECT 2 AS ID, 'Jane' AS NAME)
AS A
```

Listing 12-15 shows the CREATE ENDPOINT expression used to make a Web Service that has the Test5 stored procedure as a Webmethod. It is essentially the same as the CREATE ENDPOINT expression used to make the RepairPoint Web Service shown in Listing 12-2 earlier in this chapter, except that the Web method is GetTest5, and it executes the Test5 stored procedure.

LISTING 12-15: Test Web Service

```
CREATE ENDPOINT Test5
STATE = Started
AS HTTP
(
PATH = '/Test5',
PORTS = (CLEAR),
SITE = '*',
AUTHENTICATION = (INTEGRATED)
)
FOR SOAP
(
WEBMETHOD 'urn:autos'.'GetTest5'
(NAME = 'Repairs.dbo.Test5', SCHEMA=DEFAULT),
WSDL=DEFAULT,
SCHEMA=STANDARD
DATABASE = 'Repairs',
NAMESPACE = 'urn:other'
)
```

We saw in Figure 12-15 earlier in this chapter that a SQL Server 2005 Web Service defines SQL Server scalar types in terms of XML Schema 1.0 types; in that case, it defined an NVARCHAR as an XML Schema 1.0 string. Likewise, a SQL Server 2005 Web Service defines the data typically found in a TDS stream in terms of SQL XML 1.0 types.

A SQL Server 2005 Web Service defines an XML Schema type name, SqlResponseStream, as the type of the payload of the SOAP message it returns for a stored procedure or an arbitrary SQL query. A SqlResultStream

contains a collection of elements representing the items you would expect to
be returned from an SQL query. The elements are enumerated below:

SqlRowSet	A rowset from a query
SqlXml	The xml from an FOR XML statement or other XML
SqlMessage	The result of a RAISERROR or a PRINT statement
SqlRowCount	The number of rows
SqlResultCode	The result code of a stored procedure

Listing 12-16 shows the SOAP message that would be sent in response
to a client that used the GetTest5 Webmethod.

LISTING 12-16: SOAP message response for Test5

```
<SOAP-ENV:Envelope
xml:space="preserve"
xmlns:xsd="http://www.w3.org/2001/XMLSchema"
xmlns:xsi="http://www.w3.org/2001/XMLSchema-instance"
xmlns:SOAP-ENV="http://schemas.xmlsoap.org/soap/envelope/"
xmlns:sql="http://schemas.microsoft.com/sqlserver/2004/SOAP"
xmlns:sqlsoaptypes="http://schemas.microsoft.com/sqlserver/2004/SOAP/types"
xmlns:sqlrowcount="http://schemas.microsoft.com/sqlserver/2004/SOAP/types/
SqlRowCount"
xmlns:sqlmessage="http://schemas.microsoft.com/sqlserver/2004/SOAP/types/
SqlMessage"
xmlns:sqlresultstream="http://schemas.microsoft.com/sqlserver/2004/SOAP/
types/SqlResultStream"
xmlns:sqltransaction="http://schemas.microsoft.com/sqlserver/2004/SOAP/
types/SqlTransaction"
xmlns:sqltypes="http://schemas.microsoft.com/sqlserver/2004/sqltypes"
xmlns:msdata="urn:schemas-microsoft-com:xml-msdata"
xmlns:method="urn:autos">
  <SOAP-ENV:Body>
    <method:GetTest5Response>
      <method:GetTest5Result xmlns="">
        <sqlresultstream:SqlRowCount xsi:type="sqlrowcount:SqlRowCount">
          <sqlrowcount:Count>1</sqlrowcount:Count>
        </sqlresultstream:SqlRowCount>
        <sqlresultstream:SqlMessage xsi:type="sqlmessage:SqlMessage">
          <sqlmessage:Class>0</sqlmessage:Class>
          <sqlmessage:LineNumber>5</sqlmessage:LineNumber>
          <sqlmessage:Message>This is the Test5 message</sqlmessage:
Message>
          <sqlmessage:Number>0</sqlmessage:Number>
          <sqlmessage:Procedure>Test5</sqlmessage:Procedure>
          <sqlmessage:Server>CANOPUS5</sqlmessage:Server>
```

```
    <sqlmessage:Source>Microsoft-SQL/9.0</sqlmessage:Source>
    <sqlmessage:State>1</sqlmessage:State>
  </sqlresultstream:SqlMessage>
  <sqlresultstream:SqlMessage xsi:type="sqlmessage:SqlMessage">
    <sqlmessage:Class>0</sqlmessage:Class>
    <sqlmessage:LineNumber>6</sqlmessage:LineNumber>
    <sqlmessage:Message>Test5 error</sqlmessage:Message>
    <sqlmessage:Number>50000</sqlmessage:Number>
    <sqlmessage:Procedure>Test5</sqlmessage:Procedure>
    <sqlmessage:Server>CANOPUS5</sqlmessage:Server>
    <sqlmessage:Source>Microsoft-SQL/9.0</sqlmessage:Source>
    <sqlmessage:State>1</sqlmessage:State>
  </sqlresultstream:SqlMessage>
  <sqlresultstream:SqlRowSet
  xsi:type="sqlsoaptypes:SqlRowSet"
  msdata:UseDataSetSchemaOnly="true"
  msdata:UDTColumnValueWrapped="true">
    <xsd:schema xmlns:xsd="http://www.w3.org/2001/XMLSchema"

targetNamespace="http://schemas.microsoft.com/sqlserver/2004/sqltypes">
      <xsd:simpleType name="int">
        <xsd:restriction base="xsd:int"/>
      </xsd:simpleType>
      <xsd:simpleType name="varchar">
        <xsd:restriction base="xsd:string"/>
      </xsd:simpleType>
    </xsd:schema>
    <xsd:schema
    targetNamespace="urn:schemas-microsoft-com:sql:SqlRowSet1"
    xmlns="" xmlns:xsd="http://www.w3.org/2001/XMLSchema"

xmlns:sqltypes="http://schemas.microsoft.com/sqlserver/2004/sqltypes"
    elementFormDefault="qualified">
      <xsd:import
namespace="http://schemas.microsoft.com/sqlserver/2004/sqltypes"/>
      <xsd:element
      name="SqlRowSet1"
      msdata:IsDataSet="true"
      msdata:DataSetNamespace="urn:schemas-microsoft-com:sql:
SqlDataSet"
        msdata:DataSetName="SqlDataSet">
        <xsd:complexType>
          <xsd:sequence>
            <xsd:element name="row" minOccurs="0"
maxOccurs="unbounded">
              <xsd:complexType>
                <xsd:sequence>
                  <xsd:element name="ID" type="sqltypes:int"/>
                  <xsd:element name="NAME">
                    <xsd:simpleType>
                      <xsd:restriction
```

```
                                base="sqltypes:varchar"
                                sqltypes:localeId="1033"
                                sqltypes:sqlCompareOptions="IgnoreCase
IgnoreKanaType IgnoreWidth"
                                sqltypes:sqlSortId="52">
                                  <xsd:maxLength value="4"/>
                                </xsd:restriction>
                              </xsd:simpleType>
                            </xsd:element>
                          </xsd:sequence>
                        </xsd:complexType>
                      </xsd:element>
                    </xsd:sequence>
                  </xsd:complexType>
                </xsd:element>
              </xsd:schema>
              <diffgr:diffgram
                xmlns:diffgr="urn:schemas-microsoft-com:xml-diffgram-v1">
                <SqlRowSet1
                  xmlns="urn:schemas-microsoft-com:sql:SqlRowSet1">
                  <row>
                    <ID>1</ID>
                    <NAME>Joe</NAME>
                  </row>
                  <row>
                    <ID>2</ID>
                    <NAME>Jane</NAME>
                  </row>
                </SqlRowSet1>
              </diffgr:diffgram>
            </sqlresultstream:SqlRowSet>
            <sqlresultstream:SqlRowCount
            xsi:type="sqlrowcount:SqlRowCount">
              <sqlrowcount:Count>2</sqlrowcount:Count>
            </sqlresultstream:SqlRowCount>
            <sqlresultstream:SqlResultCode
            xsi:type="sqlsoaptypes:SqlResultCode">0</sqlresultstream:
SqlResultCode>
        </method:GetTest5Result>
        <method:data>5</method:data>
      </method:GetTest5Response>
    </SOAP-ENV:Body>
  </SOAP-ENV:Envelope>
```

Figure 12-23 reduces the SOAP message shown in Listing 12-16 to its bare minimum and shows the correspondence of its elements to the Test5 stored procedure that produced it. The first thing it returns is a SqlRowCount with a value of 1, which indicates that the output parameter was set. Next come two SqlMessages: one for the PRINT statement and one for the

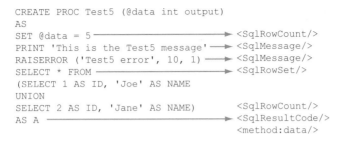

```
CREATE PROC Test5 (@data int output)
AS
SET @data = 5 ──────────────────────► <SqlRowCount/>
PRINT 'This is the Test5 message' ──► <SqlMessage/>
RAISERROR ('Test5 error', 10, 1) ──► <SqlMessage/>
SELECT * FROM ──────────────────────► <SqlRowSet/>
(SELECT 1 AS ID, 'Joe' AS NAME
UNION
SELECT 2 AS ID, 'Jane' AS NAME)        <SqlRowCount/>
AS A ───────────────────────────────► <SqlResultCode/>
                                       <method:data/>
```

FIGURE 12-23: SqlResultStream

error that was raised. Next comes a `SqlRowSet` that represents the rowset returned by the `SELECT` statement, followed by another `SqlRowCount` with a value of 2, for the two rows in the rowset. Next comes the `SqlResultCode`, with a value of 0, which is the result code returned by the stored procedure. Last is the value of the data output parameter, 5. If you have worked on the client side with ADO.NET, you know that output parameters always come at the end of the TDS stream.

Listing 12-17 shows a C# console program that processes the `SqlResultStream` returned by the `Test5` Webmethod. It was created with Visual Studio 2005 and used the Add Web Reference wizard, via http://canopus5/Test5?WSDL, to make the `Test5` proxy class used to access the Web Service. Note that canopus5 is the machine hosting SQL Server 2005.

A Webmethod that is implemented by a stored procedure returns an array of objects. Each object in the array is an object from the `SqlResultStream` returned by the Web Service. The beginning of the message in Listing 12-16 has XML Schema 1.0 type definitions for a `SqlRowCount`, `SqlMessage`, and a `SqlResultCode`. The Add Web Reference wizard uses these definitions to create .NET Framework classes with corresponding names. All these classes, along with the proxy class, `Test5`, are in the `Test5Client.canopus5` namespace, and they are used in a .NET Framework program to represent the corresponding elements from the `SqlResultStream`.

In Figure 12-23, one of the things in the `SqlResultStream` is a `SqlRowSet` that represents the result of a query. The Add Web Reference wizard does not build a .NET Framework class for the `SqlResultStream`. The format of a `SqlRowSet` is something that can be read directly by a `System.Data.DataSet`. As a result, the `SqlRowSet` is returned as a `DataSet`.

A discussion of the `System.Data.DataSet` class is beyond the scope of this book, but in simple terms, it is a container of tables, and although it isn't, it can be thought of as an in-memory database. `DataSet`s are documented in the MSDN documentation for .NET Framework.

So the array of objects that is returned by the `GetTest5` method is the TDS stream from SQL Server 2005 that the Web Service turned into XML and that the Add Web Reference wizard turned into objects. The program in Listing 12-17 processes the objects by checking the type of each one and then printing out a short description of what it is and its value.

LISTING 12-17: SqlResultStream client program

```
using System;
using System.Collections.Generic;
using System.Text;
using System.Data.SqlTypes;
using System.Data;
using Test5Client.canopus5;

class Program
{
  static void Main(string[] args)
  {
    canopus5.Test5 test5 =
      new Test5Client.canopus5.Test5();
    test5.UseDefaultCredentials = true;
    SqlInt32 data = 0;
    Object[] results = test5.GetTest5(ref data);
    foreach (object result in results)
    {
      if (result is Int32)
      {
        Console.WriteLine("Result code {0}", (Int32)result);
      }
      if (result is SqlRowCount)
      {
        Console.WriteLine(
          "Row count {0}",
          (result as SqlRowCount).Count);
      }
      if (result is SqlMessage)
      {
        Console.WriteLine(
          "Message {0}",
          (result as SqlMessage).Message);
      }
```

```
    if (result is DataSet)
    {
      Console.WriteLine("DataSet");
      (result as DataSet).WriteXml(Console.Out);
      Console.WriteLine();
    }
  }
 }
}
```

Figure 12-24 shows the results produced by the program in Listing 12-17.

In some cases, the only things of interest in the `SqlResultStream` are the `SqlRowSets` it contains, and things like `SqlRowCounts` and `SqlMessages` can be ignored. The `FORMAT` option of the `WEBMETHOD` clause can be used to restrict the `SqlResultStream` to returning only `SqlRowSets`. There are two possible values for the `FORMAT` option: `ALL_RESULTS` and `ROWSETS_ONLY`. `ALL_RESULTS` is the default and produces the results in Listing 12-16. `ROWSETS_ONLY` restricts the `SqlResultStream` to `SqlRowSets`. Listing 12-18 shows the `FOR SOAP` clause configured for `ROWSETS_ONLY`.

LISTING 12-18: ROWSETS_ONLY

```
FOR SOAP
(
WEBMETHOD 'urn:autos'.'GetTest5'
(NAME = 'Repairs.dbo.Test5',
  SCHEMA=DEFAULT,
  FORMAT=ROWSETS_ONLY),
WSDL=DEFAULT,
SCHEMA=STANDARD
DATABASE = 'Repairs',
NAMESPACE = 'urn:other'
)
```

When `ROWSETS_ONLY` is specified, the Webmethod returns a `System.Data.DataSet` instead of an array of objects. Listing 12-19 shows the `GetTest5` method of the preceding example as it would be written if the `Test5` Web Service were configured for `ROWSETS_ONLY` only.

LISTING 12-19: DataSet return value

```
    DataSet results;
    results = test5.GetTest5(ref data);
```

```
C:\WINDOWS\system32\cmd.exe
Row count 1
Message This is the Test5 message
Message Test5 error
DataSet
<SqlDataSet xmlns="urn:schemas-microsoft-com:sql:SqlDataSet">
  <row xmlns="urn:schemas-microsoft-com:sql:SqlRowSet1">
    <ID>1</ID>
    <NAME>Joe</NAME>
  </row>
  <row xmlns="urn:schemas-microsoft-com:sql:SqlRowSet1">
    <ID>2</ID>
    <NAME>Jane</NAME>
  </row>
</SqlDataSet>
Row count 2
Result code 0
Press any key to continue . . .
```

FIGURE 12-24: Result of processing SqlResultStream

SQL Batches

Setting `FORMAT=ROWSETS_ONLY` ignores all other results, such as a message and errors, that would be produced by the execution of the stored procedure associated with the Web Service. With ADO.NET, of course, an application cannot only call a stored procedure, but also execute an arbitrary SQL batch. SQL Server 2005 Web Services also can provide this capability, but it must be enabled in the Web Service. At first glance, it might seem to be folly to have a Web Service that allows arbitrary SQL to be executed. But keep in mind that the HTTP and Web Services are just alternatives to using TDS to connect to SQL Server 2005. All users are still authenticated and allowed to do only what they are authorized to do, just as is the case with a TDS connection.

Listing 12-20 shows a `CREATE ENDPOINT` expression that makes a Web Service named SQLServer that will accept arbitrary SQL as input. There are two possible values for the `BATCHES` option of the `FOR SOAP` clause: `ENABLED` and `DISABLED`. `DISABLED` is the default. When `BATCHES = ENABLED`, the Web Service will accept arbitrary SQL.

LISTING 12-20: Batch-Enabled Web Service

```
CREATE ENDPOINT SQLServer
STATE  = Started
AS HTTP
(
PATH = '/SQL',
PORTS = (CLEAR),
```

```
SITE = '*',
AUTHENTICATION = (INTEGRATED)
)
FOR SOAP
(
WSDL=DEFAULT,
SCHEMA=STANDARD,
DATABASE = 'Repairs',
NAMESPACE = 'urn:other',
BATCHES=ENABLED
)
```

Adding `BATCHED=ENABLED` to the `CREATE ENDPOINT` expression creates a Webmethod named sqlbatch. Its definition is in the WSDL file that SQL Server 2005 creates for the Web Service. This WSDL is similar to the one for the RepairPoint Web Service, shown in Listing 12-5, in that it begins with the XML Schema 1.0 type definition for the data types that SQL Server uses. The main difference is in the XML Schema 1.0 that defines the payload of the messages.

Listing 12-21 shows the part of the WSDL that defines the payload of the SOAP messages sent to and from the SQLServer Web Service. The sqlbatch element is used to send a command to a Web Service and contains two other elements: BatchCommands and Parameters. BatchCommands, as its name implies, is used to send a SQL batch to the Web Service. The parameters for the batch are in the Parameters element. If you are used to working the service side of things, this is sort of like using `sp_executesql`. If you are used to working on the client side of things, this is very similar to the ADO.NET `System.Data.SqlClient.SqlCommand` class.

The second element in the sqlBatchResponse is used to send results back to the client. It also contains two elements. The first is a `SqlResultStream`—the same thing that was used in the previous example Web Service, `Test5`, to return the results of a stored procedure. As was the case in `Test5` Web Service example, the `SqlResultStream` will be returned as a `DataSet`. It also contains a Parameters element that is used to return any output parameters.

LISTING 12-21: sqlbatch payload formats

```
<xsd:element name="sqlbatch">
  <xsd:complexType>
    <xsd:sequence>
```

```
        <xsd:element minOccurs="1" maxOccurs="1"
          name="BatchCommands" type="xsd:string"/>
          <xsd:element minOccurs="0" maxOccurs="1"
            name="Parameters"
            type="sqlparameter:ArrayOfSqlParameter"
            nillable="true"/>
      </xsd:sequence>
    </xsd:complexType>
  </xsd:element>
  <xsd:element name="sqlbatchResponse">
    <xsd:complexType>
      <xsd:sequence>
        <xsd:element minOccurs="1" maxOccurs="1"
          name="sqlbatchResult"
          type="sqlresultstream:SqlResultStream"
          nillable="false"/>
        <xsd:element minOccurs="0" maxOccurs="1"
          name="Parameters"
          type="sqlparameter:ArrayOfSqlParameter"
          nillable="true"/>
      </xsd:sequence>
    </xsd:complexType>
  </xsd:element>
```

Listing 12-22 shows a C# console program that processes the sql-
BatchResponse returned by sending a SQL batch to the SQLServer Web Services. It was created with Visual Studio 2005 and used the Add Web
Reference wizard, via http://canopus5/SQLServer?WSDL, to make a
proxy SQLServer class used to access the Web Service. Note that canopus5
is the machine hosting SQL Server 2005.

The proxy class generated by the Add Web Reference wizard,
SQLServer, has a method named sqlbatch. It takes two parameters. The
first is a string, which is the SQL batch. The second is a SqlParameter
array.

Note that this SqlParameter class was generated by the Add Web
Reference wizard, is not the same as the System.Data.SqlClient.
SqlParameter class, and may cause name ambiguities that will prevent
a program from compiling. There are various techniques to get rid of
ambiguous names; the program in Listing 12-22 aliases the
System.Data namespace because the program needs only the DataSet
from it.

LISTING 12-22: BATCHES=ENABLED client

```csharp
using System;
using System.Collections.Generic;
using System.Text;
using ConsoleApplication2.canopus5;
using d=System.Data;

class Program
{
  static void Main(string[] args)
  {
    SQLServer s = new SQLServer();
    s.UseDefaultCredentials = true;
    SqlParameter[] parameters = new SqlParameter[2];
    parameters[0] = new SqlParameter();
    parameters[0].direction = ParameterDirection.Input;
    parameters[0].Value = 3;
    parameters[0].name = "P1";
    parameters[0].sqlDbType = sqlDbTypeEnum.Int;
    parameters[1] = new SqlParameter();
    parameters[1].direction = ParameterDirection.Input;
    parameters[1].Value = 4;
    parameters[1].name = "P2";
    parameters[1].sqlDbType = sqlDbTypeEnum.Int;
    object[] results = s.sqlbatch(
     @"Select @P1 AS FIRST;
     PRINT 'hello';
     SELECT @P2 AS SECOND;", ref parameters);
    foreach (object result in results)
    {
      if (result is SqlRowCount)
      {
        Console.WriteLine(
        "Row count {0}",
        (result as SqlRowCount).Count);
      }
      if (result is SqlMessage)
      {
        Console.WriteLine(
         "Message {0}",
         (result as SqlMessage).Message);
      }
      if (result is d.DataSet)
      {
        Console.WriteLine("DataSet");
        (result as d.DataSet).WriteXml(Console.Out);
        Console.WriteLine();
      }
    }
  }
}
```

Figure 12-25 shows the results produced by the program in Listing 12-22.

We have looked at three different Web Services: `RepairPoint`, which hosted a SQL Server 2005 user-defined function; `Test5`, which hosted a SQL Server 2005 stored procedure; and `SQLServer`, which hosted the `sqlbatch` Web method. Each was done in a separate Web Service just for simplicity; there is no requirement to do this. A single Web Service in SQL Server 2005 can host as many Webmethods as you want; just include a `WEBMETHOD` clause for each one in the `FOR SOAP` clause. Likewise, the `FOR SOAP` clause may have `BATCHES=ENABLED` even when it includes several `WEBMETHOD` clauses.

Other Features

There are several other features of Web Services in SQL Server 2005 to mention, but we will not discuss them in detail because of space limitations.

All the Web Services we have looked at so far have used Windows authentication. If your clients and/or middle-tier servers are using Windows authentication, there will be no issue in having them use it to use SQL Server 2005 Web Services.

When SQL Server 2005 is hosting a Web Service, it is acting as a Web server, just like IIS. Web servers can be configured to allow unauthenticated clients to use them; the client is said to be anonymous in this case, and the Web server provides an identity for a client that accesses it this way. SQL Server 2005 does not allow anonymous clients for Web Services—ever.

Web Services also support HTTP basic authentication. With basic authentication, a client sends a name and a password to the server, and the server uses that to authenticate the client. SQL Server 2005 will allow only basic authentication to be used if the connection is made using SSL. When basic

```
C:\WINDOWS\system32\cmd.exe
DataSet
<SqlDataSet xmlns="urn:schemas-microsoft-com:sql:SqlDataSet">
   <row xmlns="urn:schemas-microsoft-com:sql:SqlRowSet1">
      <FIRST>3</FIRST>
   </row>
</SqlDataSet>
Row count 1
Message hello
DataSet
<SqlDataSet xmlns="urn:schemas-microsoft-com:sql:SqlDataSet">
   <row xmlns="urn:schemas-microsoft-com:sql:SqlRowSet2">
      <SECOND>4</SECOND>
   </row>
</SqlDataSet>
Row count 1
Press any key to continue . . .
```

FIGURE 12-25: Result of processing sqlBatchResponse

authentication is used in conjunction with SSL, with an https:// scheme in the URL, the password is passed to the server in an encrypted form, so its confidentiality is preserved. When basic authentication is used, the name and password are authenticated against a Windows identity.

For SQL Server to use SSL, it must be configured with an SSL certificate. The httpcfg.exe utility mentioned earlier in this chapter, and shown being used to find registered URLs in Figure 12-1, is used to do this. The SSL topic in Books Online discusses how this is done.

Web Services, like Web servers, support the concept of a session. HTTP is a sessionless protocol, but by various conventions, it can support a session—that is, a series of requests from a specific client that saves state between requests. Sessions are not enabled by default; the SESSIONS clause in the CREATE ENDPOINT and ALTER ENDPOINT must be used to enable sessions. Likewise, the SESSION_TIMEOUT clause is used to set the timeout for a session—the maximum amount of time allowed between SOAP messages in the same session. Search for "Working with SOAP Sessions" in MSDN for more discussion of using sessions in Web Services.

SQL Server 2005 can also use a SQL Server login to authenticate a Web Service client. The WS-Security specification, which is maintained by OASIS (http://www.oasis-open.org), specifies a format for including a name and password as part of a SOAP message. SQL Server 2005 supports this format, provided that the server is configured for MIXED authentication—that is, the server supports both Windows and SQL Server authentication, and the connection is made using HTTPS. The WS-Security specification specifies ways to send a password in an encrypted form, but SQL Server 2005 does not support this. If HTTPS is used, however, the entire message will be encrypted by HTTPS. Search MSDN for "SQL Server Authentication over SOAP" for a discussion of using SQL authentication with Web Services.

SQLXML 4.0 Functionality and SQL Server 2005

SQLXML is a term that was used even before SQL Server 2000 to refer to XML functions usable with SQL Server. Some of the SQLXML functionality executes code inside the SQL Server process; some of it executes out of process, using middle-tier or client code through the OLE DB provider paradigm. As an example, "SELECT...FOR XML" queries transform relational rowsets into XML; the transformation can happen in OLE DB or in the server process itself.

After the release of SQL Server 2000, additional client-side/OLE DB functionality for using XML with SQL Server was provided through a series of Web releases. These were released via Microsoft's Web site and officially supported. Soon after SQL Server 2000's release, SQLXML Web Release 1.0 appeared on the scene, followed shortly thereafter by Web Release 2.0 and 3.0. Each release added more ways to integrate XML with SQL Server using IIS and client-side functions. In this section, we'll use the term *SQLXML* to refer to the out-of-process functions only. The total amount of functionality in SQLXML 3.0 Service Pack 3 (the current release) is impressive. The features included are

- A SQL XML Bulk Loader, using annotated XSD schemas to map XML to relational data.
- Support of legacy XDR-mapping schemas, including a program to convert annotated XDR to annotated XSD.
- A SQLXMLOLEDB provider—a OLE DB service provider
- Client-side XML processing (FOR XML on client).
- RAW, EXPLICIT, and NESTED modes.
- Client-side XSLT postprocessing built into the model.
- A query dialect to submit SQL queries embedded in XML elements, known as template queries.
- A way to submit XPath queries to SQL Server using mapping schemas and a variation of the template query dialect.
- A set of ADO.NET data classes that exposes the same functionality as SQLXMLOLEDB in .NET Framework.
- Template and XPath queries that also are available directly through the SQLOLEDB provider.
- Updategrams that use annotated XSD schemas to map XML to SQL and accomplish multiple, possibly transacted, updates against relational tables.
- Diffgrams that use XML-specific format to perform multiple updates. These are similar to the diffgrams generated by the .NET Framework DataSet.
- An ISAPI application that encapsulated that functionality. This application enables using the functionality through templates or specially constructed URLs. In addition, it allows stored-procedure

or template-query output to be formatted into SOAP packets, allowing support for Web Services.

* A MMC snap-in to configure the ISAPI application.

In SQL Server 2005, some of the SQLXML features have been superseded
by equivalent or better functionality inside the database itself. See the article
"XML in Yukon: New Version Showcases Native XML Type and Advanced
Data Handling," by Bob Beauchemin, in *MSDN* magazine, for an early feature
list, and "XML Support in Microsoft SQL Server 2005," by Shankar Pal, Mark
Fussel, and Irwin Dolobowsky, for a more recent update. The inclusion of a
native XML data type in SQL Server 2005 means that SQL Server no longer has
to stream XML to clients. The XML data type can be used as a column in an
ordinary SQL rowset. We'll have more to say about that later in this chapter.
SQLXML 3.0 can still be used with a SQL Server 2005 database at the SQL
Server 2000 level of XML functionality. But in addition, there is a SQLXML 4.0
feature, included with SQL Server 2005, that supports and updates most of the
old functionality to work with the new data types, such as the native XML data
type and the new large value types—that is, VARCHAR(MAX), NVARCHAR(MAX),
and VARBINARY(MAX). SQLXML 4.0 is used by SQL Server Notification Services, and this part of SQL Server 2005 benefits from the ability to support
those new data types. Users of SQLXML 3.0 can upgrade their programs too.

How SQLXML Works

SQLXML provides similar functionality as in-database XML but it can work
on the middle-tier or client. It can use an adjunct to the in-database functionality to distribute the XML processing. You use the SQLXMLOLEDB
provider in the "provider=" operand of the connection string and use the
underlying provider in the "data provider=" operand of the connection
string. All the SQLXML functionality included in the .NET Framework
managed wrapper works both in version 3.0 and 4.0 by making calls to OLE
DB providers, using a slightly different connection string. The OLE DB
provider for SQL Server 2000 and earlier releases is SQLOLEDB. In SQL
Server 2005, this provider was superseded by the SQL Native Client OLE
DB provider, SQLNCLI. To get full support for the new data types, the SQL
Native Client must be used. The older OLE DB provider still works with the
new database version; some features of SQLXML, however, such as client-side
FOR XML, need SQLNCLI to work well with the XML data type. The service

provider has also been updated for SQL Server 2005; the updated one is called SQLXMLOLEDB4. The connection strings look like this:

SQLXML3
SQLXMLOLEDB provider:

```
Provider=SQLXMLOLEDB;
Data Provider=SQLOLEDB;
Server=srv;database=pubs;
Integrated Security=SSPI
```

ADO.NET managed classes:

```
Provider=SQLOLEDB;Server=srv;
database=pubs;Integrated Security=SSPI
```

SQLXML4
SQLXMLOLEDB provider:

```
Provider=SQLXMLOLEDB.4.0;
Data Provider=SQLNCLI;Server=srv;
database=pubs;Integrated Security=SSPI
```

ADO.NET managed classes:

```
Provider=SQLNCLI;Server=srv;
database=pubs;Integrated Security=SSPI
```

What this means in terms of installation is that to use all features of all SQLXML 4.0 to their fullest, you must also be sure that the SQL Native Client feature and the new SQLXMLOLEDB 4.0 provider are also installed. You can check for SQL Native Client in the Add and Remove Programs Control Panel applet. You can check for all the OLE DB providers by using the Data Links API. To do this graphically, first create a file with an extension of .udl. Double-click that file to open the Data Links API applet. The installed providers are listed on the Providers tab. If you have all the appropriate providers, you're on your way to being set up and ready to go.

The bulk load component works a little differently. The COM component itself has been updated, so there is a new version-dependent class, "SQLXMLBulkLoad.SQLXMLBulkload.4.0". This component can still use the SQLOLEDB provider, so its connection-string property looks like this:

```
"provider=SQLOLEDB;data source=srv;
database=pubs;integrated security=SSPI"
```

Note that both the SQLXMLOLEDB provider and the SQLXMLBulk-Load component use version-dependent COM PROGIDs, so you can install and run SQLXML 3.0 and SQLXML 4.0 side by side.

XML Stream and XML Column

SQL Server returns data from SELECT statements in columns and rows, known in the various data access APIs as Rowsets, Recordsets, Resultsets, or DataReaders. Each column in a Rowset must be a data type, and that data type must be known to SQL Server. In SQL Server 2000, there was no built-in XML data type, but XML data could be returned from in-database SQLXML functionality. This included but was not confined to the output from SELECT . . . FOR XML queries. Rather than specifying the column as data type NVARCHAR or NTEXT, SQL Server 2000 returned XML data through a different type of TDS packet: the stream. This stream can be easily integrated with ASP and ASP.NET because the Request and Response classes in each of these models use streams.

You've seen the stream, at least indirectly. When you issue a SELECT . . . FOR XML query in Query Analyzer or SQL Server Management Studio, you appear to receive a one-column rowset. The column has an interesting name, 'XML_F52E2B61-18A1-11d1-B105-00805F49916B'. This GUID is not a normal column name. It's an indicator to the underlying protocol to send the output as a stream instead of a Rowset. The SQLOLEDB provider can consume this stream through a COM object that implements the interface IStream. ADO (classic) implemented a special Stream class to encapsulate this functionality. Both SQLOLEDB and SQLXMLOLEDB providers also can stream commands as input. In OLE DB, the ICommand-Stream interface is used; in ADO, there is a CommandStream property on the Command object. The CommandStream is the basis for support of an additional query dialect in SQL Server: SQLXML (which is SQL statements embedded in XML wrapper elements). You can hook up the ASP or ASP.NET Request stream to feed the CommandStream.

ADO.NET supports the stream in two ways. The "vanilla" SQL Server data provider, System.Data.SqlClient, has a special method, ExecuteXmlReader, that can consume the stream. The XmlReader produced by this method can be used to populate the DataSet. The SqlXml managed classes have complete support for streaming the output of SELECT...FOR XML and also for streaming input. These classes make the appropriate calls to the underlying OLE DB provider.

In SQL Server 2005, however, there is a native XML data type. This means that SQL Server 2005 can send out columns and rows, with one or more rows being DBTYPE_XML. The way you accomplish this is to use the TYPE qualifier on SELECT FOR XML calls, like this:

```
SELECT * FROM authors FOR XML AUTO, TYPE
```

Bear in mind that even with this support in the server, you must still use an up-level API (like ADO.NET 2.0) to consume the XML column in the client. In addition, the TYPE qualifier does not work with all the variations of FOR XML—namely, not with the FOR XML EXPLICIT syntax. Unless you write a stored procedure or user-defined function that takes an XML data type as an input parameter, there is no additional support for using an XML data type as a CommandStream.

Data Type Support and SQLXML Functionality

SQLXML 4.0 contains some bug fixes, but the major change is support of the new SQL Server 2005 data types. Client-side functionality in SQLXM-LOLEDB 3.0 service provider doesn't recognize the XML data type, and the SQLOLEDB provider does not even support user-defined types in binary format. Let's illustrate this by using some simple tables and a ComplexNumber UDT that is similar to one of the SQL Server Engine Samples. The table definitions are shown in Listing 12-23.

LISTING 12-23: Tables with XML and UDT columns

```
CREATE TABLE ctab (
 id INT PRIMARY KEY,
 cnum complexnumber)
GO
INSERT ctab VALUES(1, '100:200i')
INSERT ctab VALUES(2, '5:6i')
GO
CREATE TABLE xmltab (
 id INT PRIMARY KEY,
 thexml XML)
GO
INSERT xmltab VALUES(1, '<root><person name="bob"/></root>')
INSERT xmltab VALUES(2, '<root><person name="mary"/></root>')
GO
```

We'll try out the functionality with a simple C# program. The program, shown in Listing 12-24, uses the `Microsoft.Data.SqlXml` library from either SQLXML 3.0 or SQLXML 4.0. Only the connection strings need be changed, as mentioned earlier.

LISTING 12-24: Program using XML stream

```csharp
using System;
using System.IO;
using Microsoft.Data.SqlXml;

public static void Main()
{
  // See connection string above...
  DoSqlXml(connString, "select * from ctab for xml nested");
  DoSqlXml(connString, "select * from xmltab for xml nested");
}

public static void DoSqlXml(connString string, cmdText string)
{
  SqlXmlCommand xc = new SqlXmlCommand(connString);
  xc.ClientSideXml = true;
  xc.CommandText = cmdText;
  Stream s = xc.ExecuteStream();
  s.Position = 0;
  StreamReader sr = new StreamReader(s);
  Console.WriteLine(sr.ReadToEnd());
}
```

Using the XML data type with SQLXML 3.0 yields a completely entitized string, as shown in Listing 12-25.

LISTING 12-25: Entitized XML

```
<xmltab id="1" thexml="&lt;root&gt;&lt;person
name=&quot;bob&quot;/&gt;&lt;/root&gt;"/>
<xmltab id="2" thexml="&lt;root&gt;&lt;person
name=&quot;mary&quot;/&gt;&lt;/root&gt;"/>
This entitized string would be difficult if not impossible to consume in a
vanilla XML client. Using SQLXML 4.0 yields the familiar XML serialized
form.
<xmltab id="1">
<thexml><root><person name="bob"/></root></thexml></xmltab>
<xmltab id="2">
<thexml><root><person name="mary"/></root></thexml></xmltab>
With a UDT input the results with SQLXML 3.0/SQLOLEDB provider are even
more startling:
<ctab id="1" cnum="dbobject/ctab[@id=&apos;1&apos;]/@cnum"/>
```

```
<ctab id="2" cnum="dbobject/ctab[@id=&apos;2&apos;]/@cnum"/>
```
With SQLXML 4.0, we get the binary representation of the UDT, as shown below. To get the XML form of the UDT, you must CAST or CONVERT to XML on the SERVER.
```
<ctab id="1" cnum="01C05900000000000001C06900000000000000C20000"/>
<ctab id="2" cnum="01C01400000000000001C018000000000000002C0000"/>
```

The XML data type is represented in mapping schemas as xs:Any elements, as shown in Listing 12-26.

LISTING 12-26: XML representation of UDT

```
<xsd:schema xmlns:xsd="http://www.w3.org/2001/XMLSchema"
  xmlns:sql="urn:schemas-microsoft-com:mapping-schema">
  <xsd:element name="xmltab" sql:relation="xmltab" >
    <xsd:complexType>
      <xsd:sequence>
        <xsd:element name="thexml" sql:field="thexml"
             sql:datatype="xml" type="xs:anyType"/>
      </xsd:sequence>
    </xsd:complexType>
    <xsd:attribute name="id" type="xs:int"/>
  </xsd:element>
</xsd:schema>
```

This makes them available in most SqlXml features that use mapping schemas—namely, updategrams—and SQL bulk load. You cannot use XPath template queries with mapping schemas to query into the XML data type column, however. To query an XML data type column, use the server-side XQuery support. Because XQuery is a superset of XPath, XPath queries will also work. CLR-based UDT are also supported, although there is no special support in mapping schemas for UDTs. They are used by declaring them as xsd:string columns and passing the binary representation. This works using mapping schemas for XPath queries or XML Bulk Load.

The SQLXML .NET Framework API

SQLXML 4.0 comes with a .NET Framework API that uses the .NET Framework System.IO.Stream object as input and output. The SqlXml support consists of a series of classes used to call the SQLXML OLE DB–based functionality. These classes are not a .NET Framework data provider as such, but they will be familiar to programmers who have worked with .NET Framework data providers like SqlClient. Table 12-1 lists the SqlXml managed classes and the major properties and methods on each class.

TABLE 12-1: SqlXml Managed Classes

Class	Method/Properties	Usage
SqlXmlCommand	CreateParameter ExecuteNonQuery ExecuteStream ExecuteToStream ExecuteXmlReader	ConnectionString specified as part of the SqlXmlCommand constructor. Parameters are accepted in string format.Execute methods output to stream or XmlReader.
	BasePath ClientSideXml CommandStream CommandText CommandType Namespaces OutputEncoding RootTag SchemaPath XSLPath	Client-side pre- and postprocessing. The BasePath, SchemaPath, and XSLPath are used for ancillary files. Command input can be stream- or text-based. Because FOR XML queries almost always produce XML fragments, a root element tag can be added.
SqlXmlCommandType	Diffgram SQL Template TemplateFile UpdateGram XPath	Different types of SQLXML commands. These include both queries and updates.
SqlXmlAdapter	Fill Update	Updates use diffgram format.
SqlXmlParameter	Name, Value	Note that the parameter has no data type specification.
SqlXmlException	ErrorStream	Stream- rather than collection-based.

A distinction should be made for clarity between this library, Microsoft. Data.SqlXml, and the System.Data.SqlXml library that we describe in *A First Look at SQL Server 2005 for Developers,* by Bob Beauchemin, Niels Berglund, and Dan Sullivan (Addison-Wesley, 2004). System.Data.SqlXml will not expose any public functionality in the .NET Framework 2.0 release. The Microsoft.Data.SqlXml library is an extension of SQLXML 3.0 functionality and encapsulates the OLE DB provider functionality. One thing to consider is that the XSLT processor used when you specify the XSLPath property of SqlXmlCommand is the processor in MSXML 6.0, not either of the processors in System.Xml.dll. If a specific feature of .NET Framework XSLT is required, you can easily feed the stream from SqlXmlCommand into these processors.

SQLXML Bulk Load Component

SQLXML Bulk Load is a COM component that uses SQLXML mapping schemas to permit loading large XML files in bulk. A new version of this component, SQLXMLBulkLoad4, can be used only with SQL Server 2005 databases because it makes use of the built-in XML data type in that release. It's been improved to support of decomposition into the XML and CLR UDT data type columns. Note that you can still use SQLOLEDB as the provider in the connection string for SQLXML Bulk Load. The program in Listing 12-27 will work using the XML data type with the mapping schema shown in Listing 12-28.

LISTING 12-27: SQLXML bulk loader

```
// STAThread attribute is required
[STAThread]
static void Main(string[] args)
{
  SQLXMLBULKLOADLib.SQLXMLBulkLoad4Class b = new
    SQLXMLBULKLOADLib.SQLXMLBulkLoad4Class();
  b.ConnectionString =
    "Provider=sqloledb;server=svr;database=pubs;integrated
security=SSPI";
  b.ErrorLogFile = "error.xml";
  b.KeepIdentity = false;
  b.Execute ("mapping_schema.xml","data.xml");
}
```

When using a UDT column, you must use the binary form of the XML; the SQLXMLBulkLoad component does not send a string value to

SQL Server, even though SQL Server can do an implicit conversion from string to UDT. The mapping_schema and data files are in Listing 12-28 and Listing 12-29.

LISTING 12-28: mapping_schema.xml

```
<xsd:schema xmlns:xsd="http://www.w3.org/2001/XMLSchema"
         xmlns:sql="urn:schemas-microsoft-com:mapping-schema">
     <xsd:element name="CTab"  sql:relation="CTab" >
          <xsd:complexType>
                <xsd:sequence>
                      <xsd:element name="id"
type="xsd:int"></xsd:element>
                      <xsd:element name="CNum"
type="xsd:string"></xsd:element>
                </xsd:sequence>
          </xsd:complexType>
     </xsd:element>
</xsd:schema>
```

LISTING 12-29: data.xml

```
<ROOT>
     <CTab>
          <id>1</id>
          <CNum>01C02400000000000001C02400000000000000480000</CNum>
     </CTab>
</ROOT>
```

One final enhancement is the use of the XML data type as an overflow column when you specify the SchemaGen option to generate a relational-database schema from the XML mapping schema. Listing 12-30 shows the use SchemaGen and Visual Basic Script.

LISTING 12-30: SchemaGen option

```
Dim objBL
Set objBL = CreateObject("SQLXMLBulkLoad.SQLXMLBulkload.4.0")
objBL.ConnectionString = "provider=SQLOLEDB;data source=localhost;
database=tempdb;integrated security=SSPI"
objBL.ErrorLogFile = "c:\error.log"
objBL.CheckConstraints=true
objBL.XMLFragment = True
objBL.SchemaGen = True
objBL.SGDropTables = True
objBL.Execute "SampleSchema.xml", "SampleXMLData.xml"
Set objBL = Nothing
```

Now there are at least three different ways to get XML inside the SQL Server database if you have SQL Server 2005:

* In-database decomposition using OpenXML
* In-database decomposition using XML nodes
* BULK INSERT using the new BULK OLE DB provider

So what is the best practice for deciding which functionality to use? All the scenarios presented for SQLXML 3.0 in SQL Server 2005 in the paper "XML Options in Microsoft SQL Server 2005," available on MSDN, are still valid when using SQLXML 4.0. If there is a lot of preprocessing of SQLXML, Bulk Load is preferred. SQLXML also makes it easier to code if you have diverse clients that provide XML in slightly different formats; you need to change the mapping schema, rather than the code. In-database loading and decomposition are preferred if you have enough processing power to accomplish this in the database, have homogeneous XML, or want to import individual XML files into rows in a table with an XML column. OpenXml is the decomposition method that is supported in SQL Server 2000, as well as SQL Server 2005. It has been slightly enhanced in SQL Server 2005 to support the XML data type, but because it creates an in-memory representation of an XML DOM, XML nodes, or client-side SQLXML, bulk copy is a better choice for large volumes of XML. You can even use the new SQL BULK INSERT provider to insert multiple XML documents into multiple rows in a table with an XML data type column, but these documents have to have a row separator in the file. There is also the possibility of using System.Data.Xml in a .NET Framework procedure or function if you need some special functionality that none of the components that come in the box provides.

Web Service and Other Web Support

SQLXML 3.0's IIS/ISAPI functionality, including Web Services, isn't included with SQLXML 4.0. If you used this functionality for anything but trivial demos, you probably wrote code that preprocessed or postprocessed the HTTP data stream. You can still use this code with SQL Server 2005, but for forward compatibility with future Web Service specifications, you'll probably want to switch to using ASP.NET and the .NET Framework

SqlXml managed classes. SQLXML 3.0 and 4.0 use version-dependent Class IDs, so you can even install them side by side as you're doing your conversion. In addition, in Intranet scenarios where you just want to communicate with the database using SOAP, the HTTP Endpoint support in SQL Server 2005 will serve your needs admirably. You can even pass the stream from IIS into SQL Server 2005's endpoints and integrate with future enhancements to the Service Oriented Architecture at the Web server level. The useful feature of HTTP endpoints is that the metadata for the SOAP operations is stored in the database using DDL rather than being stored in the Windows Registry, as in SQLXML 3.0. Listing 12-31 shows a simple HTTP endpoint definition for exposing a stored procedure as a Web Service.

LISTING 12-31: SQLXML 3.0 Web Service

```
CREATE ENDPOINT pubs_endpoint
STATE = STARTED
AS HTTP
(
      SITE = '*',
      PATH = '/pubs',
      AUTHENTICATION = (INTEGRATED),
      PORTS = (CLEAR)
)
FOR SOAP
(
  WEBMETHOD 'urn:www-develop-com:invoices'.'byroyalty'
  (
    name='pubs.dbo.byroyalty',
    SCHEMA = STANDARD
  ),
  BATCHES = ENABLED,
  WSDL = DEFAULT,
  DATABASE = 'pubs'
)
GO
```

The HTTP endpoints do not support SQLXML templates directly, as SQLXML 3.0 did, but you can write stored procedures exposed as Web Services in T-SQL or .NET Framework that do XML processing using XQuery or System.Data.Xml. You can even write custom WSDL for your Web Service to expand support to diverse groups of users. For more information on HTTP Endpoints, reference the papers "Overview of Native XML Web Services for Microsoft SQL Server 2005" and "Usage Scenarios for SQL Server

2005 Native Web Services," by Srik Raghavan and Brad Sarsfield, on the MSDN Web site.

The client-side processing component and mapping-schema architecture in SQLXML 3.0 have been enhanced for SQL Server 2005, and additional storage and decomposition facilities have been added both outside and inside the database. SQLXML 4.0 is not a complete rewrite of SQLXML 3.0, but an evolutionary enhancement. Programmers can continue to use the same programming model as they move toward ASP.NET and Web Services.

Where Are We?

SQL Server 2005 provides an alternative way to make a connection via a Web Service. The Web Service can provide the functionality that applications typically expect from a TDS connection, but with only the tools provided by most Web Service development environments. Web Service connections support authentication of the user in the same way that TDS connections do.

SQL Sever 2005 can generate a WSDL file that is compatible with virtually all development environments for Web Services. Visual Studio 2005 was designed with SQL Server 2005 in mind and can use the SQL Server 2005–specific information in the WSDL file.

SQL Server 2005 can host stored procedures, user-defined functions, and arbitrary SQL batches in a Web Service.

Web Services in SQL Server 2005 support functionality tightly bound to the Windows environment and much more loosely coupled functionally via industry-standard XML specifications.

■ 13 ■
SQL Server 2005 and Clients

W ITH THE ADVENT OF CLR user-defined types, as well as improved large value type data support, XML support, and other SQL Server engine features, comes enhancement of the client APIs. This chapter looks at the enhancements to the ADO.NET client libraries as well as the classic data access APIs—OLE DB, ADO, and ODBC—to support new SQL Server 2005 features.

SQL Native Client

SQL Server ships with support for four main data access APIs currently used in client-side programming:

- ADO.NET
- OLE DB and ADO
- ODBC
- JDBC

ADO.NET is the managed data access layer for the .NET Framework. If you're using the .NET Framework in your client-side code, the ADO.NET data provider, `System.Data.SqlClient`, is your best choice. It is more powerful and has better performance than using either the ADO.NET `OleDb` or `Odbc` bridge data providers with SQL Server. The `OleDb` and `Odbc` bridges were provided mostly for compatibility with those data sources for which a managed ADO.NET data provider doesn't exist. OLE DB is a data access API based on the Component Object Model (COM), and ODBC is a vendor-neutral set of APIs based on C-style calls. If you are not using the .NET Framework or Java for your client application, you're most likely using OLE DB or ODBC for data access. OLE DB and ODBC are still very much used inside the SQL Server 2005 database as well. SQL Server–linked servers are still configured using OLE DB providers, for example. Microsoft ships a JDBC driver for SQL Server 2005, but coverage of this driver is beyond the scope of this book.

If you are using ADO.NET, you must use the latest version of the .NET Framework, version 2.0, to use the cornucopia of new SQL Server 2005 features. That means you must deploy the .NET Framework 2.0 runtime to every Web server or client workstation that talks to SQL Server 2005. If you are using OLE DB or ODBC, you must use SQL Native Client to get at the new features. Older versions of all the APIs (ADO.NET 1.0 and 1.1, and the OLE DB provider and ODBC driver in MDAC) are still supported at the SQL Server 2000 level of functionality.

Support for the new features in SQL Server 2005 involved a refactoring of the client-side functionality for the traditional data access APIs and in removal of the dependency between ADO.NET and Microsoft Data Access Components (MDAC). In the OLE DB and ODBC data access arena, there is a new, separate client-side OLE DB provider and ODBC driver: SQL Native Client. If you want to use the new features of SQL Server 2005, such as multiple active resultsets or Query Notifications from OLE DB, ADO, or ODBC, you're going to need this new client stack.

SQL Native Client is meant to separate SQL Server's OLE DB provider, ODBC driver, and network library calls from the MDAC stack. Currently, the SQL Server OLE DB provider (SQLOLEDB) and ODBC driver (listed as SQL Server in the driver list) ship as part of MDAC. This provider and driver will continue to be supported at a pre–SQL Server 2005 level of functionality, but their functionality will not be upgraded. A new version of MDAC (called MDAC 9.0) was originally planned to support the new SQL Server 2005 functionality, but this didn't happen. Instead, the current components of MDAC have become part of the Windows family of operating systems, most likely along with the next operating system Service Pack. MDAC will change infrequently, and changes will not be tied to new SQL Server functionality. SQL Native Client will be versioned with new versions of SQL Server (starting at

SQL Server 2005), will ship with SQL Server, and can keep current with server improvements. If you've installed SQL Server 2005, you can see SQL Native Client in the Install and Remove Programs Control Panel applet.

When you've installed SQL Native Client, you should see a new OLE DB provider (SQLNCLI, listed as "SQL Native Client") and a new ODBC driver (listed as "SQL Native Client"). You need to use them instead of the older versions to get the SQL Server 2005–specific functionality. Note that they need to be coded into the connection string (OLE DB, ADO, or ODBC) or ODBC DSN. SQL Native Client does have a limitation—it does not run on Windows 9x (Windows 95 and 98) operating systems—so keep this in mind as you plan your upgrade.

If you're using ADO.NET's `SqlClient` data provider, it has been rearchitected so it doesn't rely on MDAC or SQL Native Client. The calls it makes to SQL Server over the network, which used to be supported through separate network libraries, use a facility known as SNI (SQL Server Network Interface), and this facility is separate from analogous SNI calls made in the SQL Native Client. That's good news, because you have to be concerned with only one data access piece instead of two, as Figure 13-1 shows.

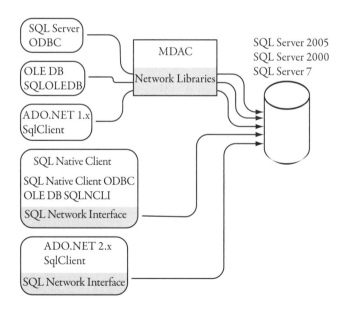

FIGURE 13-1: Network library functionality in ADO.NET 2.0 SqlClient and in SQL Native Client

Now that you are wondering what specific feature support you get by using SQL Native Client or ADO.NET 2.0, we'll just say these are the features covered in this chapter, namely:

- Support of the SQL Server 2005 data types
- Query Notifications
- Multiple active resultsets
- Password change for SQL logins
- Promotable transactions (ADO.NET only)
- Automatic client failover
- Support for the self-signed certificates generated by SQL Server 2005

As we discuss each feature, we'll begin with an exposition of the functionality in ADO.NET and conclude with a short description of where the functionality resides in the SQL Server Client APIs. ADO.NET does have better support and extended support in the API for certain new features.

For those of you who currently use ADO (classic ADO rather than ADO.NET), you may be worried because ADO itself (msado15.dll and friends) are part of MDAC, and we've just said that MDAC won't change for SQL Server 2005. ADO users can use the new features through the new OLE DB provider (SQLNCLI), because the new features have been exposed on this provider using special connection-string parameters or extended properties on the ADO `Connection` and `Command` object.

When you are converting an application to use the new provider or driver, you'll notice very few changes. SQL Native Client has been designed with backward compatibility in mind. As with any conversion, of course, you should retest your applications. One small difference in existing functionality that we noticed was that if you are using named parameters in OLE DB, the parameter names must be valid (must begin with an at sign). Using named parameters and incorrect SQL parameter names with SQLNCLI will cause an error; with SQLOLEDB, this is OK. You can also choose to use positional parameters and leave the names out, but if you do specify parameter names in SQLNCLI, they must be correct names. Another difference is that the SQLNCLI provider does not support all the client-side provider-specific functionality in SQLOLEDB—namely, support for the ICommandStream interface used with a small subset of the SQL Server 2000 XML functionality. This functionality has largely been superseded by the XML data type functionality in SQL Server 2005.

The new OLE DB provider does have two new features that are not in the SQLOLEDB provider. The first is that SQLNCLI implements support for asynchronous connections and asynchronous commands directly. This is accomplished by implementing the IDBAsyncStatus interface on the OLE DB Session and Command objects. SQL Server's OLE DB provider actually goes one step further and implements a provider-specific interface, ISSAsyncStatus, to provide more functionality in this area. For more information on using asynchronous connections and commands with OLE DB, consult "OLE DB Programmer's Reference" in the MSDN documentation, and SQL Server Books Online for SQL Server specifics. Note that this built-in asynchrony is not consumed by ADO; this library has its own way to implement asynchronous operations. It uses additional library threads instead of implementing the functionality in the network protocol. The SQL Native Client OLE DB provider also exposes an interface for programming bulk copy, IBCPSession, in addition to IRowset-FastLoad for memory-based bulk loading. In previous versions, programmatic bulk copy (BCP) functionality was available only through ODBC. There also are new implementations of ISQLServerErrorInfo to provide more comprehensive error information and ISSAbort to cancel executing SQL commands and batches.

New Data Types and Data Type Compatibility Mode

The change in SQL Server 2005 that has the most pervasive impact on the new provider and driver is the new data types—namely, the XML data type, CLR user-defined types, and large value types. If you simply convert existing programs by switching to the new SQL Native Client providers or ADO.NET 2.0 SqlClient data provider, and then use the new types in your SQL Server 2005 database, it's quite possible that parts of the program that inspect a rowset's column information, parameter information, or schema metadata may fail. To ease conversion, you can set the connection-string parameter setting DataTypeCompatibility=80 in OLE DB or Type System

`Version=SQL Server 2000` in ADO.NET. It's not yet supported for ODBC but due to be supported in the next SQL Server release. In this case, the new data types will be represented as their closest possible SQL Server 2000 data type. `VARCHAR(MAX)` may show up in metadata as `NTEXT`, for example. We'll have more to say on this in the discussion of new data type support for each of the types in question.

User-Defined Types and Relational Data Access APIs

SQL Server 2005 offers inside-the-database support for some new data types. Although basic support of the new `VARCHAR(MAX)` data types is straightforward, the user-defined types and the `XML` data type are complex types. Because we'd like to deal with the user-defined types and XML in its native form on the client as well as on the server, the client APIs need to be enhanced as well. In the book *Essential ADO.NET*, by Bob Beauchemin (Addison-Wesley, 2002), Bob speculated on the challenges of adding UDT support to the .NET Framework `DataSet`. We'll also discuss how this is supported with SQL Server 2005 UDTs.

Most client application programming interfaces designed for use with relational databases were not designed with complex-type features built in. The original database-independent library, ODBC, was tailored specifically around SQL:1992–style database operations. It was not updated when extended types were introduced into the SQL standard in SQL:1999. Each ODBC column binding was supposed to refer to an ODBC-defined data type; user-defined types were not recognized as ODBC types. The COM-based data access APIs, OLE DB and ADO, were designed with some thought given to UDTs; there is an OLE DB `DBTYPE_UDT`, and ADO maps this data type to its `adUserDefined` data type. `DBTYPE_UDT`, however, was meant to be used to bind to data as COM objects, binding the data by using the COM interface `IUnknown` or `IDispatch`.

Though ADO.NET was not designed with user-defined types in mind either, this is the client-side library that programmers using SQL Server 2005 are most likely to use. ADO.NET does contain rich support for mixing relational and XML data, however. Combined with the fact that user-defined types are actually .NET Framework types (classes and structures), this gives ADO.NET the tightest and richest integration with the new extended SQL Server type model.

Using .NET Framework UDTs in ADO.NET

When we deal with UDTs from clients in ADO.NET, we'll usually be storing them in tables or retrieving them from tables. The "instance" of the UDT is actually stored in the database, and we manipulate it in place. We can do this all from the client by using conversion from strings or through carefully thought-out mutator functions, regardless of the API. Listing 13-1 shows a simple example in ADO.NET.

> ■ **NOTE**
>
> Everywhere we use a connection string in an example program, we obtain it through a pseudocode method named `GetConnect-StringFromConfigFile`. It's not a good idea to hard-code connection strings in program code. You can either get them from your own location in a configuration file or, in ADO.NET 2.0, use the `Configura-tionManager.ConnectionStrings` collection that's provided in `System.Configuration.dll`.)

LISTING 13-1: Manipulating a UDT inside the server

```
/*
 assuming a UDT called LDim that has an "Inches" property
 and a table dbo.Tiles defined like this:
  CREATE TABLE dbo.Tiles(
    id      INTEGER,
    length LDim,
    width  LDim)
*/

string connect_string = GetConnectStringFromConfigFile();
SqlConnection conn = new SqlConnection(connect_string);
SqlCommand cmd = new SqlCommand();
cmd.Connection = conn;

conn.Open();
cmd.CommandText =
  "INSERT INTO dbo.Tiles VALUES(1, '10 ft, 8 in')";
int i;
i = cmd.ExecuteNonQuery();
cmd.CommandText =
  @"UPDATE dbo.Tiles
     SET Length.ToIn()
     WHERE id = 1";
i = cmd.ExecuteNonQuery();
cmd.Dispose(); conn.Dispose();
```

Note that in this example, we're using the LDim type only on the server, passing in string values to INSERT and integer values to UPDATE through the mutator. We don't have to have access to the LDim type code on the client at all.

It is possible to manipulate user-defined types from client code by using only SQL statements, stored procedures, and user-defined functions. Instances of user-defined types will not ordinarily be held in the database past the end of a SQL batch, however. If we want to manipulate the same instance of the UDT over multiple batches, we could store it in a SQL Server temporary table, but this would incur the overhead of serializing and deserializing the instance (from the temporary table) each time we access it.

New functionality in ADO.NET permits the use of UDT code in client programs as well as server programs. You can deploy the UDT code to each client as part of a program's installation process. You can early-bind to UDT code if you reference it in an application or use .NET Framework reflection to use late binding. You can also use UDTs as stored procedures or user-defined function parameters. Let's see how this would look in code.

Fetching UDT Data from a DataReader

In the preceding simple example, we did all the UDT manipulations in code on the server side. We didn't need the UDT on the client at all. But we could also change the statement to fetch the entire UDT over to the client via a SqlDataReader. The code would start by looking like Listing 13-2.

LISTING 13-2: Fetching a UDT through SqlDataReader; no compile-time reference

```
// Use the same Tiles table as in the first example.
string connect_string = GetConnectStringFromConfigFile();
SqlConnection conn = new SqlConnection(connect_string);
SqlCommand cmd = new SqlCommand();
cmd.Connection = conn;
conn.Open();

// get the entire LDim column
cmd.CommandText = "SELECT id, length FROM dbo.Tiles";
SqlDataReader rdr = cmd.ExecuteReader();
while (rdr.Read())
  {
    // rdr["Length"] contains an instance of a LDim class
    // easiest access, WriteLine calls ToString() implicitly
```

```
        Console.WriteLine("column 1 is {0}", rdr["Length"]);
    }
rdr.Close();
cmd.Dispose();
conn.Dispose();
```

The LDim class inside the DataReader can be used in a few different ways, but the bottom line is always the same. To manipulate the LDim— including the simplest method, which consists of returning a string representation of it—the code for the LDim class has to exist on the client. If you've not deployed it, the code exists only inside the SQL Server instance. When the attempt to load the LDim class using normal assembly loader mechanisms fails, the ADO.NET client code will throw an exception. Although the information in the TDS data stream is sufficient to "fill in" an instance of the LDim class that exists on the client, it is not sufficient to instantiate a LDim if the assembly does not exist on the client. It's more like an opaque binary blob. There is additional information in the TDS stream to identify the class name and the assembly version, however. The UDT assembly must be deployed into the global assembly cache (GAC) or available in the caller's assembly probing path, or instantiating it on the client will fail.

In addition to retrieving the information from the LDim class, you can create an instance of LDim directly for every row read through the DataReader by getting the value of the column and casting it to the correct type, as shown in Listing 13-3.

LISTING 13-3: Fetching a UDT through SqlDataReader; compile-time reference required

```
while (rdr.Read())
    {
    // rdr["length"] contains an instance of a LDim class
    // get a strongly typed instance
    LDim ld = (LDim)rdr["length"];
    }
```

Note that the big difference between using ToString and using the code in Listing 13-2 is that you must have an assembly containing the LDim class available at compile time as a reference. This method probably will be used most often because it lets you deal with the SQL Server CLR classes as though they were "normal" client classes, with special data access methods based on the fact that they can be persisted.

There are a few slight performance optimizations based on either dealing with the instance as a stream of bytes or using your own object serialization code. If you just want to pass the stream of bytes around without deserializing it—for example, to perform a kind of manual object replication—you can use GetBytes or GetSqlBytes to read the bytes as a binary stream. If you have implemented your own serialization using IBinarySerialize or want to hook the serialized form into a .NET Framework technology like remoting, you can pass the bytes around and deserialize them manually. Except in applications that need a very high degree of optimization, the small performance gain is not worth the increase in code complexity.

When you get an instance of a UDT through a DataReader using any of the methods shown earlier, it is not a reference to the data in the DataReader directly; you are making a copy. The instance data in the DataReader itself is read-only, but the data in the copy can be updated. When you update the data, accessing the data again from the DataReader will return the original data, not the changed data. Listing 13-4 shows an illustrative example.

LISTING 13-4: UDT retrieved is a copy of the UDT in the SqlDataReader

```
// SqlDataReader obtained from the previous code

LDim p1, p2;
rdr = cmd.ExecuteReader();
while (rdr.Read())
  {
    // rdr[1] contains an instance of a LDim class
    // p1 is a copy of rdr[1]
    p1 = (LDim)rdr[1];

    // attempting to update this will work
    p1.Inches = 1000;

    // retrieve the value in the DataReader again
    p2 = (LDim)rdr[1];
    // now p1 != p2
  }
```

This covers almost every case in which we'd want to access a UDT from a DataReader. But what if we were writing a generic access layer, had a library of types loaded, and wanted to know the type so that we could instantiate the correct strongly typed class at runtime? Or what if we wanted to be able to specify a UDT as a parameter in a parameterized query, stored procedure, or user-defined function?

The way to get information about a `DataReader`'s columns at runtime in ADO.NET is to use the method `SqlDataReader.GetSchemaTable`. This method has been extended to provide two UDT-specific pieces of information in ADO.NET 2.0: the .NET Framework class name and the name of the UDT in SQL Server. Note that the CREATE TYPE DDL statement does not mandate that the SQL Server type object name be the same as the .NET Framework class name. The "database name" of a UDT is the SQL Server object name (for example, `demo.dbo.LDim`), and the .NET Framework name is a string containing a four-part CLR type name, including assembly (for example, LDim, Dimension.dll, Version=1.0.0.0, Culture=neutral, PublicKeyToken=bac3c561934e089). GetSchemaTable returns a DataTable containing one row of information about each column in the resultset, and using it in our code would look like Listing 13-5.

LISTING 13-5: Getting metadata about a UDT on the client

```
SqlDataReader rdr = cmd.ExecuteReader();
DataTable t = rdr.GetSchemaTable();

// either of these print Dimensions.LDim,
// the .NET Framework class name
// prints byte[] if "Type System Version=SQL Server 2000"
Console.WriteLine(t.Rows[1]["DataType"]);
// prints SqlBinary if "Type System Version=SQL Server 2000"
Console.WriteLine(t.Rows[1]["ProviderSpecificDataType"]);

// this prints demo.dbo.LDim, SQL Server name for UDT
// prints varbinary if "Type System Version=SQL Server 2000"
Console.WriteLine(t.Rows[1]["DataTypeName"]);

// this prints 4-part assembly name,
// blank if "Type System Version=SQL Server 2000"
Console.WriteLine(t.Rows[1]["UdtAssemblyQualifiedName"]);
// Prints 21 (varbinary) if "Type System Version=SQL Server 2000"
// else prints 29
Console.WriteLine(t.Rows[1]["ProviderType"]);
// Always prints 29 (SQLCLR UDT)
Console.WriteLine(t.Rows[1]["NonVersionedProviderType"]);
```

A typical row in the `DataTable` of schema information would contain columns of information about the data. In other rowset metadata, although the `SqlDbType` is present, this does not completely describe the UDT, and the `SqlDbType` would be `SqlDbType.SqlUdt`. Using `GetSchemaTable` is the only API that permits getting rich UDT information. Note that the provider type and other information change when SQL Server 2000 client compatibility mode is used; in this case, the UDT appears as a byte array (`varbinary` in SQL Server).

We have a similar issue when we go to set the data type of a `SqlParameter`. Only `SqlDbType` is actually specified using the current implementation of `DbParameter` or `IDbParameter`. In addition to using `SqlDbType` for a UDT parameter, you need to specify the `SqlParameter.UdtTypeName` when using UDT parameters in a parameterized query.

Let's look at calling a user-defined function that adds two `LDim` instances together, returning another `LDim` instance as the result. Such a user-defined function, LDimAdd, is part of the LDim class itself. Refer to Chapter 5 for details.

Alternatively, the UDF could be defined in Transact-SQL (T-SQL) using the T-SQL definition of the type and the .NET Framework implementation of the `LDim` class, as shown in Listing 13-6.

LISTING 13-6: TSQL implementation of user-defined function that uses a UDT

```
--
-- T-SQL implementation of AddLDim
--
CREATE FUNCTION AddLDim2 (@a LDim, @b LDim)
RETURNS LDim
AS
BEGIN
 DECLARE @c LDim
 SET @c = '0 in' - set the units
 SET @c.Inches = @a.Inches + @b.Inches
 RETURN @c
END
GO
```

Because no data access is done in adding two `LDim`s together, it might be best to implement this operation either completely on the server side (call the `LDim` UDF from another UDF or a SQL statement) or all on the client side (instantiate two `LDim` objects and add them on the client) rather than calling from client to server, but we'll use this example to demonstrate call-ing a parameterized function from the client.

To invoke the UDF from the client, we'll need to instantiate a `SqlCommand` and add the parameters to its `ParametersCollection`, the `Parameters` property of the `SqlCommand`. The code would look like Listing 13-7.

LISTING 13-7: Using UDTs as parameters (naïve implementation)

```
string connect_string = GetConnectStringFromConfigFile();
SqlConnection conn = new SqlConnection(connect_string);
SqlCommand cmd = new SqlCommand("dbo.AddLDim", conn);
cmd.CommandType = CommandType.StoredProcedure;

// define two LDims to add
LDim p1 = LDim.Parse("2 ft");
LDim p2 = LDim.Parse("10 in");

// now, define the Parameters
// use the overload that takes a parameter name
// and type for the input parameters
cmd.Parameters.Add("@a", SqlDbType.Udt);
cmd.Parameters[0].Value = p1;
cmd.Parameters.Add("@b", SqlDbType.Udt);
cmd.Parameters[1].Value = p2;
// define the output parameters. This parameter need not be initialized
cmd.Parameters.Add("@c", SqlDbType.Udt);
cmd.Parameters[2].Direction = ParameterDirection.ReturnValue;
```

This code is incomplete because although the client is telling SQL Server that the Parameter contains a user-defined type, there is no indication of which user-defined type we're passing in! We need to specify the correct meta-data to SQL Server. This consists of the `UdtTypeName`—that is, the name that SQL Server uses to identify the type. This name need not be fully qualified, but we're doing this to make it clear which name is required. When SQL Server has the correct name, it can check to see that we're passing in the correct parameter type and then invoke the UDF. We specify the type name using the `SqlParameter` class. Our finished code would look like Listing 13-8.

LISTING 13-8: SQL Server data type must be used when using UDTs as parameters

```
// now, define the Parameters
// use the overload that takes a parameter name
// and type for the input parameters
cmd.Parameters.Add("@a", SqlDbType.Udt);
```

```
cmd.Parameters[0].UdtTypeName = "demo.dbo.LDim";
cmd.Parameters[0].Value = p1;
cmd.Parameters.Add("@b", SqlDbType.Udt);
cmd.Parameters[1].Value = p2;
cmd.Parameters[1].UdtTypeName = "demo.dbo.LDim ";

// define the output parameters. This parameter need not be initialized
cmd.Parameters.Add("@c", SqlDbType.Udt);
cmd.Parameters[2].UdtTypeName = "demo.dbo.LDim";
cmd.Parameters[2].Direction = ParameterDirection.ReturnValue;
```

Using .NET Framework UDTs in ODBC, OLE DB, and ADO Clients

The SQL Native Client OLE DB provider and ODBC driver have some special functionality with respect to the new UDT types, although none of these APIs can get .NET Framework–based UDTs as though they were COM objects. Even though there are facilities to build a COM-callable wrapper around any .NET Framework object, fetching these as COM objects is specifically unsupported by the SQLNCLI data provider. The metadata in the new providers and drivers can report on and consume rich data about these types, however.

Any database API will be able to get a string representation of these types. You'd do this by using ToString in the SQL SELECT statement and retrieving the data as a SQL_WVARCHAR or SQL_WLONGVARCHAR(ODBC) or DBTYPE_WSTR(OLE DB) data type. Alternatively, you can select the entire UDT column and get the binary representation as a SQL_VARBINARY or SQL_LONGVARBINARY type (ODBC) or DBTYPE_BYTES (OLE DB). Note that this could also return the XML representation if the UDT were converted to XML format on the server. The SQL statements to accomplish this are pretty straightforward and are shown in Listing 13-9.

LISTING 13-9: T-SQL code to access UDT; results obtained in ODBC

```
--
-- SQL statements to enable getting LDim
-- as a SQL_WVARCHAR/SQL_WLONGVARCHAR
--
SELECT id, length.ToString() AS dim_str
  FROM dbo.Tiles
GO
```

```
--
-- SQL statements to enable getting LDim
-- as a SQL_VARBINARY/SQL_LONGVARBINARY
--
SELECT id, length FROM dbo.Tiles
```

In all cases, you are required to reformat and use the string or binary form manually or find some way to reconstitute the data in the objects manually.

If the UDT supports public fields that are data types that SQL Server APIs support, you can use SQL statements or UDT accessor methods on the server to pull out the individual field values in a form that non–.NET Framework APIs can understand, and use SQL statements containing mutator methods on the UDT to update the values on the server. This works, as in the first ADO.NET example, because you are fetching and updating ordinary SQL types such as INTEGER or NVARCHAR, not using the UDT directly. In the case of the LDim data type mentioned earlier in this chapter, you can get the property representing dimension in inches as integers and update the fields directly or by using mutator methods on the UDT.

When you use the SQL Native Client driver or provider, you are able to see that the data type of a column or parameter is a UDT when the T-SQL statement specifies a UDT column or parameter. These APIs also provide additional metadata information for UDTs when using IDBSchemaRowset::GetSchemaRowset in OLE DB.

When using the SQL Native Client ODBC driver, you'll get the UDT as a new SQL Server–specific data type, SQL_SS_UDT. You can get four additional properties of the UDT using SQLDescribeCol. These are shown in Table 13-1.

In OLE DB and ADO, support is a bit richer. Using the SQLNCLI provider, the UDT is returned as DBTYPE_UDT. There is no additional metadata for columns in OLE DB by using IColumnInfo::GetColumnInfo, but analogous information to the ODBC information above is returned when you use IColumnsRowset::GetColumnsRowset. The four additional columns are shown in Table 13-2.

This data also appears as extended properties in ADO's Field Object Properties collection. In OLE DB and ADO, there is additional support for UDT parameters as well. This is exposed through a special interface,

TABLE 13-1: ODBC Metadata Columns for UDTs

SQL_CA_SS_UDT_CATALOG_NAME	UDT catalog name
SQL_CA_SS_UDT_SCHEMA_NAME	UDT schema name
SQL_CA_SS_UDT_TYPE_NAME	UDT type name
SQL_CA_SS_UDT_ASSEMBLY_TYPE_NAME	Qualified name of the UDT, including assembly version information

ISSCommandWithParameters, that extends IDBCommandWithParameters. The two methods, GetParameterProperties and SetParameterProperties, permit using a new OLE DB property set, DBPROPSET_SQLSERVER PARAMETERS, that exposes UDT catalog name, schema name, and name. These are also exposed in the extended properties collection of ADO's Parameter Object. In OLE DB and ADO, there is support in the DBSCHEMA_COLUMNS and DBSCHEMA_PROCEDURE_PARAMETERS for UDTs. There is also a special DBSCHEMA_SQL_USER_TYPES schema rowset that enumerates the UDTs that exist in a database, as well as DBSCHEMA_SQL_ ASSEMBLIES and DBSCHEMA_SQL_ASSEMBLY_DEPENDENCIES to obtain .NET Framework assembly information.

To summarize this, you can get information and set information about UDTs in ODBC, OLE DB, and ADO. There is even additional metadata in OLE DB. But you cannot manipulate and store UDTs directly without mixing .NET Framework code with your C++ code.

TABLE 13-2: OLE DB Metadata Columns for UDTs

DBCOLUMN_UDT_CATALOGNAME	UDT catalog name
DBCOLUMN_UDT_SCHEMANAME	UDT schema name
DBCOLUMN_UDT_NAME	UDT type name
DBCOLUMN_UDT_ASSEMBLY_TYPENAME	Qualified name of the UDT, including assembly version information

Supporting the XML Data Type on the Client

SQL Server 2005 includes a new native XML data type, described in Chapter 9. Although this type can be manipulated on the server, we'd like to manipulate it using the client-side data access APIs as well.

One method for using XML is to serialize it into a string of characters. The original specification for XML (Extensible Markup Language 1.0) is a description of "a class of data objects called XML documents" and is couched entirely in terms of this serialized form. In addition to being able to work with the serialized form as a string, you can simply consume XML by using XML APIs such as DOM (Document Object Model), SAX (Simple API for XML), or the .NET Framework's XmlReader. Both ADO (used in conjunction with MSXML) and ADO.NET provide a way to consume the XML database and use it in parameterized queries using both strings and XML APIs.

Using the XML Data Type in ADO.NET

There are two types of XML output that SQL Server 2005 can produce. The statement SELECT * FROM AUTHORS FOR XML AUTO produces a stream of XML, not a one-column, one-row rowset. This type of output is unchanged from SQL Server 2000. The XML stream output appears in SQL Server Query Analyzer as a one-column, one-row rowset only because of the limitations of the Query Analyzer tool. You can distinguish this stream from a "normal" column by its special unique identifier name, "XML_F52E2B61-18A1-11d1-B105-000805F49916B". This name is actually an indicator to the underlying TDS (that's Tabular Data Stream, SQL Server's network format) parser that the column should be streamed to the client rather than sent as an ordinary rowset would be. There is a special method, SqlCommand.ExecuteXml-Reader, to retrieve this special stream on the client. In SQL Server 2005, the SELECT . . . FOR XML dialect has been enhanced in many ways, discussed in detail in Chapter 9. To mention a few of them:

- SELECT . . . FOR XML can produce XML documents as well as XML fragments.
- You can prepend a standard XSD schema to the stream.
- You can produce an XML data type column in addition to the stream.

You get your first indication that XML is now a first-class relational database type by referencing the relational data type enumerations in ADO.NET 2.0. System.Data.DbType and System.Data.SqlDbType contain additional values for DbType.Xml and SqlDbType.Xml, respectively. There is also a new class in the System.Data.SqlTypes namespace, SqlXml. This class encapsulates an XmlReader class. We'll demonstrate by means of some simple code. Suppose that we have a SQL Server table that looks like this:

```
CREATE TABLE xmltest (
  id INT IDENTITY PRIMARY KEY,
  xmlcol XML)
```

You can access this table on the client using the ADO.NET 2.0 code in Listing 13-10.

LISTING 13-10: Accessing an XML data type column in ADO.NET

```
using System;
using System.Data;
using System.Data.SqlClient;
using System.Data.SqlTypes;
using System.Xml;

void GetXMLColumn() {
string connect_string = GetConnectStringFromConfigFile();
using (SqlConnection conn = new SqlConnection(connect_string))
using (SqlCommand cmd = new SqlCommand(
      "select * from xmltab", conn))
 {
  conn.Open();
  SqlDataReader rdr = cmd.ExecuteReader();
  DataTable t = rdr.GetSchemaTable();

  while (rdr.Read())
    {
      SqlXml sx = rdr.GetSqlXml(1);
      XmlReader xr = sx.CreateReader();
      xr.Read();
      Console.WriteLine(xr.ReadOuterXml());
    }
 }
}
```

The column metadata that is returned when we browse through the DataTable produced by GetSchemaTable correctly identifies the column:

```
ProviderType: 25 (25 = XML)
ProviderSpecificDataType: System.Data.SqlTypes.SqlXml
DataType: System.Xml.XmlReader
DataTypeName: [blank]
```

It looks like any other type that's built in to SQL Server. Note that the ".NET Framework type" of this column is XmlReader, and to the .NET Framework, it looks just like any XML that is loaded from a file or produced with the XmlDocument class. Using the XML data type column as a parameter in a stored procedure or parameterized statement in ADO.NET 2.0 is just as straightforward, as shown in Listing 13-11.

LISTING 13-11: Using an XML data type as a parameter in ADO.NET

```
using System;
using System.Data;
using System.Data.SqlClient;
using System.Data.SqlTypes;
using System.Xml;

void AddARow() {
string connect_string = GetConnectStringFromConfigFile();
using (SqlConnection conn = new SqlConnection(connect_string))
using (SqlCommand cmd = new SqlCommand(
        "INSERT xmltest(xmlcol) VALUES(@x)", conn))
 {
  conn.Open();
  cmd.Parameters.Add("@x", SqlDbType.Xml);

  // connect the parameter value to a file
  XmlReader xr = XmlReader.Create("somexml.xml");
  cmd.Parameters[0].Value = new SqlXml(xr);
  int i = cmd.ExecuteNonQuery();
 }
}
```

Getting the XML As XML or a String

Both of the methods in the preceding code use the SQL Server–specific data type in SqlTypes. When we use the more generic accessor method of SqlDataReader, GetValue(), the value is quite different. The column does not appear as an XmlReader but as a .NET Framework String class. Note that even though the metadata identifies the column's .NET Framework data type as XmlReader, you can't just cast the column to an XmlReader. Using any accessor but GetSqlXml() returns a string, as shown in Listing 13-12.

LISTING 13-12: The generic ADO.NET methods return XML column as a string

```
using System;
using System.Data;
using System.Data.SqlClient;
using System.Data.SqlTypes;
using System.Xml;

void GetXMLColumn2() {
string connect_string = GetConnectStringFromConfigFile();
using (SqlConnection conn = new SqlConnection(connect_string))
using (SqlCommand cmd = new SqlCommand(
        "select * from xmltest", conn))
 {
  conn.Open();
  SqlDataReader rdr = cmd.ExecuteReader();
  // prints "System.String"
  Console.WriteLine(rdr[1].GetType());

  // fails, invalid cast
  XmlReader xr = (XmlReader)rdr[1];

  // this works
  string s = (string)rdr[1];
 }
}
```

You can get the provider-specific field type information by using GetProviderSpecificFieldType or return an instance of the provider-specific value using GetProviderSpecificValue. In this case, you'll get the System.Sql.Types.SqlXml type, as shown in Listing 13-13.

LISTING 13-13: Getting the provider-specific data type, SqlXml

```
// System.Data.SqlTypes.SqlXml
Console.WriteLine(rdr.GetProviderSpecificFieldType(1));

// System.Data.SqlTypes.SqlXml
Object o = rdr.GetProviderSpecificValue(1);
Console.WriteLine(o.GetType());
```

SqlClient provides symmetric functionality for XML parameters; you can also use the String data type with these. Being able to pass in a string

(NVARCHAR) where an XML type is expected relies on the fact that SQL Server provides automatic conversion of VARCHAR or NVARCHAR to the XML data type. Note that this conversion can also happen on the client side, as shown in the following example. Passing either type to the stored procedure insert_xml will work. This is illustrated in Listing 13-14.

LISTING 13-14: Conversion of string to XML can occur client-side or server-side

```
-- T-SQL stored procedure definition
CREATE PROCEDURE insert_xml(@x XML)
AS
INSERT xmltest(xmlcol) VALUES(@x)

using System;
using System.Data;
using System.Data.SqlClient;

void InsertXMLFromClient() {
string connect_string = GetConnectStringFromConfigFile();
using (SqlConnection conn = new SqlConnection(connect_string))
using (SqlCommand cmd1 = new SqlCommand(
        "INSERT xmltab (xmlcol) VALUES(@x)", conn))
using (SqlCommand cmd2 = new SqlCommand(
        " insert_xml", conn))
 {
  string s = "<somedoc/>";

  conn.Open();

  // server-side conversion
  cmd1.Parameters.Add("@x", SqlDbType.NVarChar);
  cmd1.Parameters[0].Value = s;
  cmd1.ExecuteNonQuery();

  // client-side conversion works too
  cmd2.CommandType = CommandType.StoredProcedure;
  cmd2.Parameters.Add("@x", SqlDbType.Xml);
  cmd2.Parameters[0].Value = s;
  cmd2.ExecuteNonQuery();
 }
}
```

Documents, Fragments, and FOR XML Support

The XML data type in SQL Server 2005 supports both XML documents and XML document fragments. A fragment differs from a document in that fragments can contain multiple root elements and bare root elements. The T-SQL code in Listing 13-15 illustrates support for fragments.

LISTING 13-15: Storing an XML fragment into an XML data type column

```
CREATE TABLE xmltab (
  id INT IDENTITY PRIMARY KEY,
  xmlcol XML)
GO


-- insert a document
INSERT xmltab VALUES('<doc/>')
-- fragment, multiple root elements
INSERT xmltab VALUES('<doc/><doc/>')
-- fragment, bare text element
INSERT xmltab VALUES('Hello World')
-- even this fragment works
INSERT xmltab VALUES('<doc/>sometext')
```

XML fragments are also produced by SELECT ... FOR XML. The statement "SELECT job_id, min_lvl, max_lvl FROM jobs FOR XML AUTO" produces the following output. Note that there are multiple root elements:

```
<jobs job_id="1" min_lvl="10" max_lvl="10" />
<jobs job_id="2" min_lvl="200" max_lvl="250" />
<jobs job_id="3" min_lvl="175" max_lvl="225" />
<jobs job_id="4" min_lvl="175" max_lvl="250" />
<!- some jobs elements deleted for compactness ->
```

Both documents and fragments are supported using SqlXml. SqlXml's CreateReader method always creates an XmlReader that supports fragments by using the new XmlReaderSettings class, like this:

```
// pseudocode from SqlXml.CreateReader
    Stream stm = stm; // stream filled from column (code elided)
    XmlReaderSettings settings = new XmlReaderSettings();
    settings.ConformanceLevel = ConformanceLevel.Fragment;
    XmlReader xr = XmlReader.Create(
        stm, String.Empty, null, null, settings);
```

You can use XML fragments in input parameters if you construct your XmlReader the same way. Although fragment support is built in when using the SqlXml type, you need to be careful about handling an XmlReader that contains fragments. Be aware that calling XmlReader.GetOuterXml will provide only the first fragment; to position the XmlReader to get succeeding fragments, you must call XmlReader's Read method again. We'll demonstrate this later in this chapter.

T-SQL's "SELECT...FOR XML" produces a stream of XML by default rather than a one-column, one-row rowset. It also provided the XML in a binary format rather than XML's standard serialization. Because of the format differences, and also because "SELECT...FOR XML" always produced fragments, a special method was needed to consume it. The SqlClient data provider implements a provider-specific method, SqlCommand.ExecuteXmlReader, for this purpose. Using SQL Server 2000 and ADO 1.0/1.1, it's required to use ExecuteXmlReader to get the results of a FOR XML query unless you want to use some fairly ugly workarounds that require string concatenation. With SQL Server 2005's FOR XML enhancements and the support of XML as a data type, it's almost never necessary to use ExecuteXmlReader, but because a lot of legacy code used it, this method is supported and enhanced in ADO.NET 2.0. ExecuteXmlReader is the only way to guarantee full end-to-end streaming without buffering the result, however.

You can use ExecuteXmlReader to retrieve any stream from a FOR XML query, as in previous versions. In addition, this method supports retrieving an XML data type column produced by an ordinary SELECT statement. The only caveat is that when an ordinary SELECT statement returns more than one row, ExecuteXmlReader returns only the content of the first row. Listing 13-16 shows an example that illustrates this using the same table as in previous examples.

LISTING 13-16: Consuming XML documents and XML fragments on the client

```
using System;
using System.Data;
using System.Data.SqlClient;
using System.Data.SqlTypes;
using System.Xml;

void UseExecXmlReader() {
string connect_string = GetConnectStringFromConfigFile();
using (SqlConnection conn = new SqlConnection(connect_string))
using (SqlCommand cmd1 = new SqlCommand(
      "SELECT * FROM pubs..authors FOR XML AUTO,ROOT('root')", conn))
using (SqlCommand cmd2 = new SqlCommand(
      "SELECT * FROM pubs..authors FOR XML AUTO", conn))
using (SqlCommand cmd3 = new SqlCommand(
      "SELECT * FROM xmltab", conn))
```

```
  {
  conn.Open();
  // contains fragment
  XmlReader xr1 = cmd1.ExecuteXmlReader();
  // contains document
  XmlReader xr2 = cmd2.ExecuteXmlReader();
  // contains contents of first row in xmltab only
  XmlReader xr3 = cmd3.ExecuteXmlReader();
  // use XmlReaders, then
  xr1.Close(); xr2.Close(); xr3.Close();
  }
}
```

To finish the discussion of getting XML in ADO.NET 2.0, it's helpful to mention the lifetime of the XmlReader content in various usage scenarios. Investigating the lifetime of the XmlReader also helps you understand the buffering done by SqlClient and how to use this data for maximum performance. The XmlReader uses resources, and to free those resources, the Close or Dispose method should be called, just like with SqlConnection, SqlCommand, and SqlDataReader. In the case of reading XML columns through a SqlDataReader, there can be an XmlReader allocated for each row. Remember that the XmlReader is good only as long as that row is being read; the next call to SqlDataReader.Read() will invalidate the XmlReader's contents. In addition, to support moving backward through columns in the same row, the XmlReader's contents will be buffered in memory. You can use SqlCommand's CommandBehavior.SequentialAccess to optimize reading large data, but you must be more careful when using this access method. The XmlReader associated with a column must be completely consumed before moving to the next column in the rowset when using CommandBehavior.SequentialAccess; after moving to the next column, the XmlReader appears to be valid, but calling its Read method produces no data. When you are using ExecuteXmlReader or ExecuteScalar instead of ExecuteReader, you don't need to be aware of this behavior as much, but don't forget to Close/Dispose the XmlReader here, too.

Using the XML Data Type in ADO Classic

The only way to consume XML in ADO is to treat it as a string. This string can be used as input to either the DOM or the SAX APIs. When we bind an XML column in a Recordset as a string in ADO, we bind it using adBindVariant. Assuming that we have a table that contains an XML type column named xml_col, binding as a string looks like Listing 13-17.

LISTING 13-17: Using the XML data type in ADO, Visual Basic 6.0

```
Dim rs As New ADODB.Recordset
Dim connect_string as String
connect_string = GetConnectStringFromConfiguration
rs.Open "SELECT xml_col FROM xml_tab1", connect_string

' Prints 141 - XML
Debug.Print rs(0).Type

' adBindVariant is the default
' Deserializes as a String
Debug.Print rs(0)

' Load it into a DOM
Dim dom As MSXML2.DOMDocument40
dom.loadXML rs(0)
```

We can also use a string as input to a SAX Reader. Assuming that we define a SAX ContentHandler and ErrorHandler elsewhere, the same Recordset could be used as in Listing 13-18.

LISTING 13-18: Consuming XML in Visual Basic 6.0 through the SAX API

```
Dim rs As New ADODB.Recordset

Dim saxXMLReader As New SAXXMLReader40
Dim saxContentHandler As New clsSAXHandler
Dim saxErrorHandler As New clsSAXError

Dim connect_string as String
connect_string = GetConnectStringFromConfiguration
rs.Open "SELECT xml_col FROM xml_tab1", connect_string

' default binding as string
rs.Fields("xml_col").BindType = adBindVariant

' Load SAX Reader, hook up handlers, parse
Set saxXMLReader.contentHandler = saxContentHandler
Set saxXMLReader.errorHandler = saxErrorHandler
saxXMLReader.parse (rs.Fields("xml_col").Value)
```

You can use direct updating or parameterized updating through either strings or SAXXMLReader40. The code for updating through a `Recordset` and a SAXXMLReader40 would look like Listing 13-19.

LISTING 13-19: Updating an XML data type column using ADO and MSXML SAXXMLReader

```
Dim xmlStream as Stream
Dim saxXMLReader As New SAXXMLReader40

' populate the stream
Set saxXMLReader.InputStream = xmlStream

' Update the Recordset through the SAX Reader
Set rs.Fields("xml_col").Value = saxXMLReader
rs.Update
```

Both OLE DB and ODBC return the correct data type for XML (141) when you fetch or use an instance of it with the SQL Native Client provider or driver. When you fetch XML in any of the older APIs, it is fetched as a Unicode string type (SQL_WVARCHAR or DBTYPE_WSTR). In addition, you can stream XML input and output (which includes the byte-order marker) in OLE DB by using the OLE DB IStream interfaces. This would use XML as data type DBTYPE_UNKNOWN, which uses data accessed through a COM interface pointer (any pointer that derives from IUnknown—in this case, IStream). The latest provider and driver also return additional metadata about the XML data type, indicating the database, schema, and name of the associated XML Schema Collection if one is associated with the XML instance.

The additional XML Schema Collection metadata is analogous to the additional UDT information in these APIs. Table 13-3 and Table 13-4 list the ODBC and OLE DB metadata constants, respectively.

TABLE 13-3: ODBC Metadata for XML Data Type Column with an XML Schema Collection

SQL_CA_SS_XML_SCHEMACOLLECTION_CATALOG_NAME	Catalog name
SQL_CA_SS_XML_SCHEMACOLLECTION_SCHEMA_NAME	Schema name
SQL_CA_SS_XML_SCHEMACOLLECTION_ NAME	Object name

TABLE 13-4: OLE DB Metadata for XML Data Type Column with an XML Schema Collection

DBCOLUMN_SS_XML_SCHEMACOLLECTION_CATALOGNAME	Catalog name
DBCOLUMN _SS_XML_SCHEMACOLLECTION_SCHEMANAME	Schema name
DBCOLUMN _ SS_XML_SCHEMACOLLECTION_NAME	Object name

OLE DB's schema rowsets also contain a special schema rowset for XML SCHEMA COLLECTION metadata information with the symbolic name DBSCHEMA_XML_COLLECTIONS.

Supporting the Large Value Data Types on the Client

SQL Server 2005 introduces large value types: VARCHAR(MAX), NVARCHAR (MAX), and VARBINARY(MAX). These are new, distinct types that act somewhat like an ordinary VARCHAR/VARBINARY and somewhat like TEXT/IMAGE data type. As far as ADO.NET is concerned, the new large value types are more like long versions of the vanilla data type VARCHAR than they are like the old TEXT data type. This is evident in the metadata returned by the SqlDataReader's GetSchemaTable method. Table 13-5 lists a subset of the columns that GetSchemaTable returns.

When it comes to fetching the data through a SqlDataReader, you can use a variety of methods to use the large value types:

- GetChars/GetBytes—These methods get the value as a stream of Unicode characters or bytes.
- GetSqlChars/GetSqlBytes—These methods get the value as a stream of Unicode characters or bytes.
- GetSqlString/GetSqlBinary—These methods work like Get-SqlChars and GetSqlBytes, respectively, but they work by copying the contents rather than by providing a reference to it. Because of this behavior, it's not recommended to use these when memory is at a premium—for example, in a SQLCLR procedure.
- GetValue—This method gets the entire type into memory.

TABLE 13-5: Metadata Columns Returned from ADO.NET for Large Value Types

SQL Server DataType	DataType Name	ColumnSize	ProviderSpecific DataType	IsLong
varchar(8000)	varchar	8000	SqlString	False
varchar(max)	varchar	2147483647	SqlString	True
text	text	2147483647	SqlString	True

The SqlChars and SqlBytes data types have some additional properties—namely, IsNull and Buffer. SqlBytes have a Stream property that can be used like any other of the .NET Framework Stream classes. SqlChars is particularly useful when setting character-related properties such as Sort Options in a SQLCLR procedure.

Using any of the Get methods mentioned so far can fetch the large value type in user-defined chunks. This keeps from having to have enough memory on the client workstation to be able to hold the entire large value in memory at one time. For this buffering to work, you must use CommandBehavior.SequentialAccess with your SqlCommand. If you do not use this method, when you invoke SqlDataReader.Read, the entire row (including the entire large value type) is fetched into memory. Using GetValue will read the entire type into memory regardless of the setting of the Command-Behavior parameter. Using CommandBehavior.SequentialAccess also means that you must fetch the SqlDataReader's columns in ordinal order.

Listing 13-20 shows examples of ways to access a large value type column.

LISTING 13-20: Three ways to consume a large binary value type in ADO.NET

```
string s = GetConnectionStringFromConfigFile();
using (SqlConnection conn = new SqlConnection(s))
using (SqlCommand cmd1 = new SqlCommand(
 "select top(1) LargePhoto from Production.ProductPhoto", conn))
{
  conn.Open();
  SqlDataReader rdr1 =
    cmd1.ExecuteReader(CommandBehavior.SequentialAccess);
    rdr1.Read();

    int buffer_size = 1000;
```

```
    // gets reference to internal buffer (SQLCLR)
    SqlBytes sb = rdr1.GetSqlBytes(1);
    if (!sb.IsNull) {
      BinaryReader br = new BinaryReader(sb.Stream);
      byte[] buffer = new byte[buffer_size];
      int bytes_read;

      do {
        bytes_read = br.Read(buffer, 0, buffer_size);
        // do something with the buffer
      }
      while (bytes_read == buffer_size);
    }

    // makes a buffer-size copy into address space
    if (rdr1[1] != DBNull.Value)
    {
      byte[] buffer2 = new byte[buffer_size];
      long long_bytes_read; long dataIndex = 0;

      do {
       long_bytes_read = rdr1.GetBytes(
          1, dataIndex, buffer2, 0, buffer_size);
       dataIndex += long_bytes_read;
       // do something with the buffer
      }
      while (long_bytes_read == buffer_size);
    }

    // copy the whole thing into memory
    SqlBinary sbin = rdr1.GetSqlBinary(1);
    if (!sbin.IsNull) {
      byte[] bigbuffer = new byte[sbin.Length];
      bigbuffer = sbin.Value;
    }
}
```

Using the new data types with SqlParameter has some interesting
twists. When you use the new large value types with ADO.NET 2.0, the
parameter's data type DbType or SqlDbType should be set to SqlDbType.Var
Char, SqlDbType.NVarChar, or SqlDbType.VarBinary, respectively, rather
than SqlDbType.Text, SqlDbType.NText, and SqlDbType.Image. When
you use the SqlDbType.VarChar and friends with data longer than 8,000
bytes in previous releases, ADO.NET throws an error, because it cannot infer
the data type. You must specify the exact size of the data. In ADO.NET 2.0,
you still need to specify a size, but the size can be –1. The SqlClient data

provider will read as much data is in the stream (input parameter) or in the database (output parameter).

Even in ADO.NET 2.0, there is no way to stream in a long input parameter. Regardless of the method you use to push the data into the parameter, at some time in the statement execution, the entire value of the data will exist in memory on the client. This is also the case if `System.Data.SqlClient` is being used in process with .NET Framework procedural code. When you consume the large data types in `SqlDataReader` or as output parameters, using either of the bytewise/characterwise APIs can buffer the value in memory. If you are using `SqlDataReader`, you need to set `Command Behavior.SequentialAccess` in the `SqlCommand` instance. Setting this behavior requires you to consume each column in ordinal order. If you use `GetValue` or `GetValues`, the entire row (including the entire large value) is fetched into memory.

When you use ADO.NET 1.1, the "old" OLE DB provider or ODBC driver, or specify Data Type Version = SQL Server 2000" in the ADO.NET connection string, the large values look like and have the same behavior as the TEXT/NTEXT and IMAGE data types. This mostly affects the reported maximum size of the column in the metadata. Be careful, though, because the method T-SQL statements for fetching and updating large value types are different from the methods in T-SQL for dealing with `TEXT/NTEXT/VARBINARY`. Large value types are updated by using the `WRITE` mutator method rather than by using the `READTEXT`, `WRITETEXT`, and `UPDATETEXT` methods, as the large object types do.

When you use the new providers without the `DataTypeCompatibility` connection string parameter (that is, using the SQL Server 2005 behavior), the size of the large value types is reported as -1. In OLE DB, they appear as character or binary data types with the `ISLONG` flag set to true. In ODBC, they appear as `LONGVARCHAR`, `LONGWVARCHAR`, and `LONGVARBINARY`, as the `TEXT` and `IMAGE` data types do.

Query Notification Support

Any nontrivial relational database application is bound to have a lot of lookup tables. If you code graphic user interfaces as a specialty, you know these as the lists that populate the drop-down list boxes. We categorize lookup tables into two types: read-only tables and read-mostly tables. The difference is what can cause those tables to change. You can think of a table as read-only if it takes a staff meeting or user meeting to change them. A good example is a table that contains categories of the company's products. That one's not about to change until the company launches a new product or a company reorganization occurs. Read-mostly tables are lists that are relatively constant but can be changed by end users. These usually are presented in combo boxes rather than drop-down lists. An example of a read-mostly table would be a term-of-greeting table. Your application designers can always think of the most common ones, such as Ms., Mr., Mrs., and Dr., but there's always the user who has a title you've never thought of and wants to add it. As an example of how common this is, the last medium-size product we worked on had a nice third normal form relational database that contained 350 to 400 tables. We'd estimate that about 250 were read-only or read-mostly tables.

In the traditional Web application (which is the quintessential example of a three-tier application), you'd like to cache these types of tables as much as possible. This not only decreases the number of round trips to the database, but also decreases the query load on the database, making it more responsive for use cases like new orders. Read-only tables are easy to cache; you always keep the table in the cache and give a DBA a way to reload the cache on the rare occasion where she has to reload the table. Ideally, meetings that change the basic database structure and content are rare occurrences in your organization. Refreshing read-mostly lookup tables in a middle-tier cache is a bit more problematic. Refreshing the cache infrequently on a schedule doesn't produce the behavior you want; users don't see one another's changes immediately. A support person could add a new item using a different application or send an instant-messenger message to a friend who tries to use it, but the friend's list of choices doesn't include the new entry. Worse, if the second user tries to re-add the "missing list entry," he receives a database error indicating that the item already exists. Caching read-mostly tables usually isn't done if they have more than one "point of update" because of problems like this.

In the past, programmers have resorted to hand-crafted solutions using message queuing, triggers that write to files, or out-of-band protocols to notify the cache when someone outside the application has updated a read-mostly table. These "signaling" solutions merely notify the cache that a row has been added or changed, indicating that the cache must be refreshed. Notifying the cache about which specific row has changed or been added is a different problem; it's the province of distributed database and transactional or merge replication. In the low-overhead signaling solution, when the program gets a "cache invalid" message, it just refreshes the entire cache.

If you're using SQL Server 2005 and ADO.NET 2.0, there is now a signaling solution built into the SqlClient data provider and the database: Query Notifications. At last, there's a built-in, easy-to-use solution to this common problem! Query Notifications are also directly supported with a built-in feature in ASP.NET 2.0. The ASP.NET Cache class can be used to register for notifications, and the notifications can even be used in conjunction with the page and page-fragment caching that ASP.NET uses.

The infrastructure that accomplishes this useful function is split among SQL Server 2005's Query Engine, Service Broker, an internal ADO.NET notification listener mechanism, ADO.NET's SqlNotification and SqlDependency classes, and ASP.NET's Cache class. In brief, it works like this:

1. You can add a SqlNotification property to a new ASP.NET Cache entry or as a parameter on the OutputCache directive.

2. Each ADO.NET SqlCommand contains a property that represents a request for notification.

3. When the SqlCommand is executed, the presence of a Notification property causes a TDS packet that indicates a request for notification to be appended to the request.

4. SQL Server registers a subscription for the requested notification with its Service Broker and executes the command.

5. SQL Server watches the query results for anything that could cause the originally returned rowset to change. When a change occurs, a message is sent to a Service Broker service.

6. The Query Notification message sits in a Service Broker's service queue, available for processing.

7. You can use either a built-in listener or custom processing to process the message.

The ASP.NET `SqlCacheDependency` class and `OutputCache` directive use `SqlDependency` to use the automatic message-processing capability. ADO.NET clients that require more control can use `SqlNotificationRe-quest` and process the Service Broker queue manually, implementing whatever custom semantics they like.

Before proceeding, it's important to clarify that each `SqlNotification-Request` or `SqlDependency` gets a single notification message when the rowset changes. The message is identical whether the change is caused to a database INSERT, a DELETE statement that deletes one or more rows, or an UPDATE that updates one or more rows. The notification does not contain any information about which rows have changed or how many have changed. When the cache or user application receives the single change message, it has one choice: Refresh the entire rowset, and reregister for notification. You don't get multiple messages, and after the single message fires, the user's subscription in the database is gone. The Query Notification framework also works on the premise that it's better to be notified of more events than not to be notified at all. Notifications are sent not only when the rowset is changed, but also when a table that participates in the rowset is dropped or altered, when the database is recycled, or for other reasons. The cache or program's response is usually the same regardless: Refresh the cached data and reregister for notification.

Now that you've got the general semantics involved, we'll look at how this works in detail from three perspectives:

- How Query Notifications are implemented in SQL Server and how the optional listener works
- How `SqlClient`'s `SqlDependency` and `SqlNotificationRequest` work on the client/middle tier
- How ASP.NET 2.0 supports `SqlDependency`

Query Notifications in SQL Server 2005

At the server level, SQL Server handles queries from clients in batches. Each query (think of the query as the `SqlCommand.CommandText` property) can contain only one batch, although a batch can contain multiple T-SQL statements. A SqlCommand can also be used to execute a stored procedure or user-defined function, which can contain multiple T-SQL statements. In SQL Server 2005, a query from a client can also contain three additional pieces of information: the name of a Service Broker service to deliver notifications to, a notification identifier (which is a string), and a notification timeout. If these three pieces of information are present in the query request, and the request contains SELECT or EXECUTE statements, SQL Server will watch any rowsets produced by the query for changes made by other SQL Server sessions. If there are multiple rowsets produced—for example, in a stored procedure execution—SQL Server will watch all of the rowsets.

So what do we mean by *watching* rowsets, and how does SQL Server accomplish this? Detecting changes to a rowset is part of the SQL Server engine and uses a mechanism that has been around since SQL Server 2000: change detection for indexed VIEW synchronization. Query Notifications use a variation of this mechanism. In SQL Server 2000, Microsoft introduced the concept of indexed views. A view in SQL Server consists of a query against columns in one or more tables. A view has a name that can be used like a table name. For example:

```
CREATE VIEW WestCoastAuthors
AS
SELECT * FROM authors
  WHERE state IN ('CA', 'WA', 'OR')
```

Now you can use the view as though it were a table in a query:

```
SELECT au_id, au_lname FROM WestCoastAuthors
  WHERE au_lname LIKE 'S%'
```

Most programmers are familiar with views but may not be familiar with indexed views. In a nonindexed VIEW, the VIEW data is not stored in the database as a separate copy; each time the VIEW is used, the underlying query is executed. So in the example above, the query to get the WestCoast Authors rowset will be executed, and it will include a predicate to pull out the particular WestCoastAuthors that we want. An indexed view stores a copy of the data, so if we make WestCoastAuthors an indexed view, we have two copies of these authors' data. Now you can update the data through two paths, either through the indexed VIEW or through the original table. Therefore, SQL Server has to detect changes in both physical data stores to apply the changes to the other one. This change-detection mechanism is similar to the one that the engine uses when Query Notifications are used.

Because of the way change detection is implemented, not all `VIEW`s can be indexed. The limitations that apply to indexed views also apply to queries that can be used for Query Notifications. The `WestCoastAuthors` `VIEW`, for example, is not indexable the way it is written. To be indexable, the `VIEW` definition must use two-part names, name all the rowset columns explicitly, and use the `"WITH SCHEMABINDING"` option of `CREATE VIEW` to ensure that the underlying metadata that the view uses cannot be changed. So let's change the VIEW to be indexable:

```
CREATE VIEW WestCoastAuthors
WITH SCHEMABINDING
AS
SELECT au_id, au_lname, au_fname, address, city, state, zip, phone
  FROM dbo.authors
  WHERE state in ('CA', 'WA', 'OR')
```

Only queries that go by the indexed VIEW rules can be used with notifications. Note that although the same mechanism is used for determining whether the results of a query have changed, Query Notifications do not cause SQL Server to make a copy of the data, as indexed views do. There is a list of the rules for indexable views that is quite extensive; you can find it in SQL Server 2005 Books Online. If a query is submitted with a notification request, and it does not go by the rules, SQL Server immediately posts a notification with a reason "Invalid Query." But where does it post the notification?

SQL Server 2005 uses the Service Broker feature to post notifications. We discuss how Service Broker works in Chapter 11; the only special consideration for Query Notifications is that your `SERVICE` must use the built-in `CONTRACT` for Query Notifications. Its name is `http://schemas.microsoft.com/SQL/Notifications/PostQueryNotification`. The SQL DDL to define such a service would look like this:

```
CREATE QUEUE mynotificationqueue
CREATE SERVICE myservice ON QUEUE mynotificationqueue
([http://schemas.microsoft.com/SQL/Notifications/PostQueryNotification]
)
GO
```

Now you could use the `myservice SERVICE` as a destination in a Query Notification request. SQL Server sends a notification by sending a message to the `SERVICE`. You can use your own `SERVICE` or have ADO.NET create one for you on the fly. If you use your own `SERVICE`, you must write code to read the messages and process them. If you use the built-in listener facility, there is prewritten code that looks for the message. We'll come back to this later.

Because Query Notifications use Service Broker, there are some additional requirements. Service Broker must be enabled in the database where the notification query runs. If Service Broker is not enabled in the database you're using, you can enable it with DDL, like the following:

```
ALTER DATABASE pubs SET BROKER ENABLED
```

If you use ADO.NET's built-in listener, the user submitting the query must have the permission to subscribe to Query Notifications. This is done on a per-database basis. The following DDL would give the user `bob` permission to subscribe in the current database:

```
GRANT SUBSCRIBE QUERY NOTIFICATIONS TO bob
```

Using Query Notifications in OLE DB and ODBC

Query Notifications are supported when using SQL Native Client in OLE DB, ADO, and ODBC at the level of ADO.NET's `SqlNotificationRequest`—that is, there is no built-in listener in these APIs à la `SqlDependency` in ADO.NET. You set three properties, shown in Table 13-6, on the ODBC statement to enable Query Notifications in ODBC. In OLE DB, there are analogous properties that you set by using the `DBPROPSET_SS_ROWSET` property set of the OLE DB Command object. These properties, shown in Table 13-7, are exposed as extended properties in ADO.

TABLE 13-6: Notification Request Properties in ODBC

SQL_SOPT_SS_QUERYNOTIFICATION_TIMEOUT	Notification Timeout
SQL_SOPT_SS_QUERYNOTIFICATION_MSGTEXT	Notification Subscriber ID
SQL_SOPT_SS_QUERYNOTIFICATION_OPTIONS	Notification Service Broker Info

TABLE 13-7: Notification Request Properties in OLE DB and ADO

SSPROP_QP_NOTIFICATION_TIMEOUT	Notification Timeout
SSPROP_QP_NOTIFICATION_MSGTEXT	Notification Subscriber ID
SSPROP_QP_NOTIFICATION_OPTIONS	Notification Service Broker Info

Dispatching a Notification to an End User or Cache

So at this point, we've submitted the correct kind of query batch with a notification request to SQL Server. SQL Server has put a watch on the rowset, and when anyone changes the rowset, a message will be sent to the SERVICE of our choice. What now? You can write custom code that takes care of reading the messages and performing whatever logic you like when the notifications occur, or you can have the built-in listener take care of it for you. So let's look at the built-in listener. It's part of the SqlDependency class.

You must start the listener using a static Start method of the SqlDependency class. You specify a connection string and an optional Service Broker QUEUE. The listener opens a connection to the instance of SQL Server you specify. If you do not specify a QUEUE, the listener will create a SERVICE and a QUEUE for you. The SERVICE's name is SqlQueryNotificationSer-vice-[GUID]. Then the listener begins a Service Broker DIALOG to listen on that SERVICE using a WAIT FOR...RECEIVE statement. The SQL code executed by SqlDependency.Start using a default QUEUE is illustrated in Listing 13-21.[1]

LISTING 13-21: Code issued in SQL server during SqlDependency.Start

```
{GUID} = 5e15087f-7039-4f03-aeab-15063d38b004
{GUID2}= C0588F48-C503-DA11-AC11-0003FFAA155A

CREATE PROCEDURE [SqlQueryNotificationStoredProcedure-{GUID}]
AS
BEGIN
  IF (SELECT COUNT(*) AS numRows FROM sys.sysprocesses
```

---

1. Be aware of the fact that this is an internal implementation detail of the current ADO.NET 2.0 implementation and could change subtly in Service Packs.

```
    WHERE program_name='SqlQueryNotificationService-{GUID}') <= 0
    BEGIN
      BEGIN TRANSACTION;
      DROP SERVICE [SqlQueryNotificationService-{GUID}];
      DROP QUEUE [SqlQueryNotificationService-{GUID}];
      DROP PROCEDURE [SqlQueryNotificationStoredProcedure-{GUID}];
      COMMIT TRANSACTION;
    END
END

declare @p3 uniqueidentifier
set @p3='{GUID2}'

exec sp_executesql
 N'IF OBJECT_ID(''[SqlQueryNotificationService-{GUID}]'') IS NULL
   BEGIN
     CREATE QUEUE
      [SqlQueryNotificationService-{GUID}]
       WITH ACTIVATION
       (PROCEDURE_NAME=[SqlQueryNotificationStoredProcedure-{GUID}],
         MAX_QUEUE_READERS=1,
         EXECUTE AS OWNER);
   END;

IF
(SELECT COUNT(*) FROM SYS.SERVICES
  WHERE NAME=''[SqlQueryNotificationService-{GUID}]'') = 0
  BEGIN
    CREATE SERVICE [SqlQueryNotificationService-{GUID}]
      ON QUEUE [SqlQueryNotificationService-{GUID}]

([http://schemas.microsoft.com/SQL/Notifications/PostQueryNotification]
);
  END;

BEGIN DIALOG @dialog_handle
FROM SERVICE [SqlQueryNotificationService-{GUID}]
TO SERVICE ''SqlQueryNotificationService-{GUID}''',
   N'@dialog_handle uniqueidentifier output',
     @dialog_handle=@p3 output

select @p3

exec sp_executesql
N'BEGIN CONVERSATION TIMER (''{GUID2}'')
    TIMEOUT = 120;
  WAITFOR(RECEIVE TOP (1)
      message_type_name, conversation_handle,
      cast(message_body AS XML) as message_body from
        [SqlQueryNotificationService-{GUID}]),
```

```
        TIMEOUT @p2;',N'@p2 int',@p2=0

exec sp_executesql
N'WAITFOR(RECEIVE TOP (1)
        message_type_name,
        conversation_handle,
        cast(message_body AS XML) as message_body from
          [SqlQueryNotificationService-{GUID}]),
        TIMEOUT @p2;',N'@p2 int',@p2=60000
```

Calling `SqlDependency.Stop` shuts down the listener and deletes the SERVICE and QUEUE if they were created by the call to `SqlDependency.Start`. Each client that uses Query Notifications will have an open connection (and use a thread on SQL Server). One nice feature about being able to specify your own queue as well as your own connection string is that in a situation where every Web server in a large Web farm is listening on the same Query Notification, the queue can be on different physical machines. When configured this way, it limits the number of listener connections on any of the instances of SQL Server. The feature that enables this is Service Broker delivery. If you spread the listeners out like this, you are responsible for defining your own queue and also your own Service Broker routes. See Chapter 11 for more information on Service Broker and routing.

Using Query Notifications from a Database Client

Now that we know all the internal plumbing, let's write an ADO.NET client that uses it. Why all this explanation before we write some relatively simple client-side code? Although the code is relatively simple to write, you have to remember to go by the rules. The most common problems are submitting an invalid query for notifications and forgetting to set up the Service Broker and user permissions. This has caused frustration with this powerful feature, even giving some beta testers the impression that it wasn't working. A little prep work and research go a long way. Finally, it was good to do internals first, because we're going to specify properties like Service Broker SERVICEs or QUEUEs, and by now, you know what these terms refer to.

You can write a Query Notification client in ADO.NET as we'll be doing, use OLE DB, or even use the new HTTP Web Service client, but a point to remember is that Query Notifications are available only through client-side

code. You cannot use this feature with T-SQL directly or with SQLCLR procedural code that uses the `SqlClient` data provider to talk to SQL Server.

The `SqlClient` data provider contains two classes that you can use:
`SqlDependency` and `SqlNotificationRequest`. You use `SqlDependency`
when you want automatic notification using the dispatcher. You use `Sql-`
`NotificationRequest` when you want to process the notification messages
yourself. We'll look at an example of each one.

Using SqlDependency

The steps to use `SqlDependency` are simple. First, call the Start method to
initialize the listener. Then create a `SqlCommand` that contains the SQL
statements that you want Query Notifications for. Associate the `SqlCom-`
`mand` with a `SqlDependency`. Register an event handler for the `SqlDepen-`
`dency`'s OnChange event. Then execute the `SqlCommand`. You can process
the `DataReader`, close the `DataReader`, and even close the associated `Sql-`
`Connection`; you'll be notified by the listener when there is a change in
your rowset. Listing 13-22 shows the code.

LISTING 13-22: Using SqlDependency in ADO.NET

```
static void Main(string[] args)
{
  string connstring = GetConnectStringFromConfigFile();
  SqlDependency.Start(connstring);
  using (SqlConnection conn = new SqlConnection(connstring))
  using (SqlCommand cmd =
    // 2-part table names, no "SELECT * FROM ..."
    new SqlCommand("SELECT au_id, au_lname FROM dbo.authors", conn))
  {
   try
   {
     // create dependency associated with cmd
     SqlDependency depend = new SqlDependency(cmd);
     // register handler
     depend.OnChange += new OnChangeEventHandler(MyOnChange);

     conn.Open();
     SqlDataReader rdr = cmd.ExecuteReader();
     // process DataReader
     while (rdr.Read())
          Console.WriteLine(rdr[0]);
     rdr.Close();
     // Wait for invalidation to come through
     Console.WriteLine("Press Enter to continue");
```

```
     Console.ReadLine();
     SqlDependency.Stop(connstring);
  }
  catch (Exception e)
    { Console.WriteLine(e.Message); }
 }
}

static void MyOnChange(object caller, SqlNotificationEventArgs e)
{
  Console.WriteLine("result has changed");
  Console.WriteLine("Source " + e.Source);
  Console.WriteLine("Type " + e.Type);
  Console.WriteLine("Info " + e.Info);
}
```

You can write the same code in Visual Basic .NET, using the familiar WithEvents keyword along with the SqlDependency. Note that this program will get and process only a single OnChange event, no matter how many times the underlying results change. For any nontrivial usage, what we really want to do when we're notified is invalidate our cache. When the next user needs the result, we resubmit the command with a fresh notification and use its results to refresh the cache with the new data. If we take our code in Main() in the example above and move it to a routine named GetAndProcessData, our code might look something like Listing 13-23.

LISTING 13-23: Responding to the query notification

```
static void Main(string[] args)
{
    string connstring = GetConnectStringFromConfigFile();
    SqlDependency.Start(connstring);
    GetAndProcessData();
    UpdateCache();
    // wait for user to end program
    Console.WriteLine("Press Enter to continue");
    Console.ReadLine();
    SqlDependency.Stop(connstring);
}
static void MyOnChange(object caller, SqlNotificationEventArgs e)
{
    GetAndProcessData();
    UpdateCache();
}
```

We'll see in a few paragraphs that this is exactly what you can do in ASP.NET 2.0, using the ASP.NET `Cache` class as your data cache.

When you use `SqlDependency`, you can customize how the listener works and where the `SERVICE` that the listener is listening on resides, as mentioned earlier in the chapter. With the `SqlNotificationRequest`, we have even more control.

Using SqlNotificationRequest

Using `SqlNotificationRequest` is only a little bit more complex than `SqlDependency` on the setup side, but it's up to your program to process the messages. When you use `SqlDependency`, the notifications on the server will be sent to the `SqlQueryNotificationService` or `SERVICE` of your choice, and the listener will process the messages for you. With `SqlNotificationRequest`, you must process the messages yourself. Listing 13-24 shows a simple example of using `SqlNotificationRe-quest` and the `SERVICE` that we defined earlier.

LISTING 13-24: Using SqlNotificationRequest in ADO.NET code

```
class Class1
{
  static string connstring = null;
  static SqlConnection conn = null;
  SqlDataReader rdr = null;

  static void Main(string[] args)
  {
    connstring = GetConnectStringFromConfigFile();
    conn = new SqlConnection(connstring);
    Class1 c = new Class1();
    c.DoWork();
  }

  void DoWork()
  {
    conn.Open();
    rdr = GetJobs(2);
    if (rdr != null)
    {
      rdr.Close();
      WaitForChanges();
    }
```

```
    conn.Dispose();
}

public SqlDataReader GetJobs(int JobId)
{
  using (SqlCommand cmd = new SqlCommand(
      "SELECT job_id, job_desc FROM dbo.jobs WHERE job_id = @id",
      conn))
  {

  try
  {
    cmd.Parameters.AddWithValue("@id", JobId);
    SqlNotificationRequest not = new SqlNotificationRequest();
    not.UserData = (new Guid()).ToString();

    // this must be a service named myservice in the pubs database
    // associated with a queue called notificationqueue (see below)
    // service must go by QueryNotifications contract
    not.Options = "service=myservice;local database=pubs";
    not.Timeout = 0;
    // hook up the notification request
    cmd.Notification = not;

    rdr = cmd.ExecuteReader();
    while (rdr.Read())
        Console.WriteLine(rdr[0]);
         rdr.Close();
  }
  catch (Exception ex)
  { Console.WriteLine(ex.Message); }
  return rdr;
  }
}

public void WaitForChanges()
{
  // wait for notification to appear on the queue
  // then read it yourself
  using (SqlCommand cmd = new SqlCommand(
   "WAITFOR (RECEIVE CONVERT(xml,message_body) FROM myqueue)",
    conn))
  {
    object o = cmd.ExecuteScalar();
    // process the notification message however you like
    Console.WriteLine(o);
  }
}
```

The power (as well as the extra work) in using `SqlNotificationRe-`
`quest` is that you have to wait for and process the notification yourself, as
shown in Figure 13-2.

When you use the `SqlNotificationRequest`, you need not ever connect to the database again until you receive the notification. You don't really
need to wait around for the `SqlNotificationRequest`'s notification, either;
you can poll the queue every once in a while. Another use of `SqlNotifi-`
`cationRequest` might be to write a specialized application that may not
even be running when the notification is fired. When the application starts
up, it can connect to the queue and determine which results in its persistent
cache (from a previous application run) are now invalid.

Discussing applications that can wait around hours or days for a notification brings up the question "If there are no changes in the data, when
does the notification go away?" The only things that cause a notification
to go away (that is, be purged from the database's subscription tables) is
when the notification is fired or when it expires. Database administrators
who might be annoyed at having notification subscriptions hanging
around (because they use SQL resources and add overhead to queries and
updates) have a way to dispose of a notification manually in SQL Server.
First, you query one of SQL Server 2005's dynamic views and find the

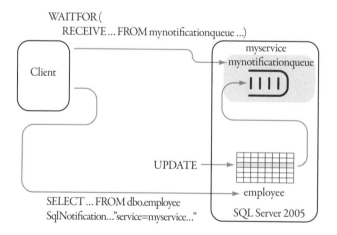

FIGURE 13-2: Using SqlNotification request

offending notification subscription; then you issue the command to get rid of it:

```
-- look at all subscriptions
SELECT * FROM sys.dm_qn_subscriptions

-- pick the ID of the subscription that you want, then
-- say it's ID = 42
KILL QUERY NOTIFICATION SUBSCRIPTION 42
```

We've seen how the internals of Query Notifications work; looked at the low-level implementation in OLE DB, ODBC, and ADO.NET's SqlNoti-ficationRequest' and shown how ADO.NET provides a built-in listener and client-notification mechanism through SqlDependency. ASP.NET 2.0 uses a level of abstraction above the SqlDependency to direct tie Query Notifications into the ASP.NET Cache class and its built-in page caching functionality. Let's look at this now.

Using SqlCacheDependency in ASP.NET
Query Notifications are also hooked up to the ASP.NET Cache class. In ASP.NET 2.0, the CacheDependency class can be subclassed, and SqlCache Dependency encapsulates the SqlDependency and behaves just like any other ASP.NET CacheDependency. SqlCacheDependency goes beyond SqlDependency in that it works whether you are using SQL Server 2005 or earlier versions of SQL Server. It's implemented completely differently for pre–SQL Server 2005 versions, of course.

When you use earlier versions of SQL Server, the SqlCacheDependency works by means of triggers on TABLEs that you want to watch. These triggers write rows to a different SQL Server table. Then this TABLE is polled. Which TABLEs are enabled for dependencies and the value of the polling interval are configurable. The details of the pre–SQL Server 2005 implementation are beyond the scope of this book; for more information, see the MSDN online article "Improved Caching in ASP.NET 2.0."

When you use SQL Server 2005, the SqlCacheDependency just encapsulates a SqlDependency instance similarly to the ADO.NET example shown above. Listing 13-25 shows a short code example that illustrates using SqlCacheDependency.

LISTING 13-25: Using SqlCacheDependency manually with the ASP.NET cache

```
// called from Page.Load
CreateSqlCacheDependency(SqlCommand cmd)
{
  SqlCacheDependency dep = new SqlCacheDepedency(cmd);
  Response.Cache.SetExpires(DateTime.Now.AddSeconds(60));
  Response.Cache.SetCacheability(HttpCacheability.Public);
  Response.Cache.SetValidUntilExpires(true);
  Response.AddCacheDependency(dep);
}
```

A nice ease-of-use feature is that SqlCacheDependency is even hooked into page or page-fragment caching. You can declaratively enable all the SqlCommands in a particular ASP.NET OutputCache directive. This uses the same SqlDependency for all the SqlCommands in the page and looks like this for a SQL Server 2005 database:

```
<%OutputCache SqlDependency="CommandNotification" ... %>
```

The general concept behind this, and how it affects the underlying database, is shown in Figure 13-3.

global.asax

```
void Application_Start(object sender, EventArgs e)
{
    System.Data.SqlClient.SqlDependency.Start(
    "server=Canopus5;…");
}
```

```
CREATE QUEUE [SqlQueryNotificationService-dca343…]…
CREATE SERVICE [SqlQueryNotificationService-dca353…]
    ON QUEUE [SqlQueryNotificationService-dca343…]…
```

	Service Name	Queue Name
1	SqlQueryNotificationService-dca34373-6c70-4424-8...	SqlQueryNotificationService-dca34373-6c70-4424-8...
2	http://schemas.microsoft.com/SQL/Notifications/Even...	EventNotificationErrorsQueue

default.aspx

```
<%@ Page Language="C#" AutoEventWireup="false"
CodeFile="Default.aspx.cs" Inherits="_Default" %>
<%@ OutputCache SqlDependency="CommandNotification"
Duration="10000" VaryByParam="None" %>
...
<asp:SqlDataSource ID="SqlDataSource1"
  runat="server"
  ConnectionString="server=Canopus5…"
  SelectCommand="select … from person.address">
</asp:SqlDataSource>
```

FIGURE 13-3: Using query notifications with the ASP.NET OutputCache directive

Note that `CommandNotification` is a keyword value that means "Use SQL Server 2005 and `SqlDependency`"; the syntax for this directive parameter is completely different when earlier versions of SQL Server are used. Also, the `CommandNotification` keyword value is enabled only when you are running ASP.NET 2.0 on specific operating system versions.

Eager Notifications

A design policy of SQL Server Query Notifications is that it is better to notify a client too often than to miss a notification. Although it's most often the case that you'll be notified when someone else has changed a row that invalidates your cache, that's not always the case. If the database is recycled by the DBA, for example, you'll get a notification. If any of the TABLEs in your query is ALTERed, DELETEd, or TRUNCATEd, you'll be notified. Because Query Notifications take up SQL Server resources, it is possible that if SQL Server is under severe-enough resource stress, it will start to remove Query Notifications from its internal tables; you'll get a notification on the client in this case as well. And because each notification request includes a timeout value, you'll be notified when your subscription times out.

If you are using `SqlDependency`, the dispatcher will wrap this information up in a `SqlNotificationEventArgs` instance. This class contains three properties—Info, Source, and Type—that will allow you to pinpoint what caused the notification. If you are using `SqlNotificationRequest`, the mes-sage_body field in the queued message contains an XML document that con-tains the same information, but you'll have to parse it out yourself with XPath or XQuery. Listing 13-26 shows an example of the XML document that was produced from the earlier ADO.NET `SqlNotificationRequest` example.

LISTING 13-26: Query notification message format

```
<qn:QueryNotification
xmlns:qn="http://schemas.microsoft.com/SQL/Notifications/QueryNotification"
 id="2" type="change" source="data" info="update"
 database_id="6" user_id="1">
<qn:Message>{CFD53DDB-A633-4490-95A8-8E837D771707}</qn:Message>
</qn:QueryNotification>
```

Note that although we produced this notification by changing the value of the job_desc column to `"new job"` in the row with job_id = 5, you'll never see this information in the message_body itself. This brings up a few final nuances of the notification process. The notification is only smart enough to know that a SQL statement altered something that could change your rowset. It is not smart enough to know that your UPDATE statement doesn't change the actual value in a row. Changing a row from `job_desc = "new job"` to `job_desc = "new job"` would cause a notification, for example. Also, because Query Notifications are asynchronous and are registered at the moment you execute the command or batch, it is possible to receive a notification before you finish reading the rowset. You can also get an immediate notification if you submit a query that does not conform to the rules; these are the rules for indexed views that we mentioned earlier.

When Not to Use Notifications

Because you now know how Query Notifications work, it's fairly straightforward to figure out where to use them: read-mostly lookup tables. Each notification rowset takes up resources in SQL Server; using them for read-only tables would be wasteful. In addition, you don't want to use them for ad hoc queries; there would be too many different rowsets being watched at the same time. A useful internal detail to know is that SQL Server folds together notification resources for parameterized queries that use different sets of parameters. Always using parameterized queries (as shown in the `SqlNotificationRequest` example above) will return more bang for your notifiable query buck. If you are worried after hearing this, bear in mind that this performance feature does not mean that you won't get the appropriate notifications. If user1 watches authors with `au_lname` from A–M, and user2 watches `au_lname` from N–Z, using the `au_lname` values as parameters, each user will get only the "right" notifications for his subset.

One last caution: When some folks think of notification applications, they envision a roomful of stockbrokers with changing market prices, each screen changing continuously. This is *absolutely* the wrong use of this feature, for two reasons:

- The rowsets are changing continuously, so the network may be flooded with Query Notifications and query refresh requests.
- If there are more than a trivial number of users, and they all watch the same data, each notification will cause many users to requery for the same results at the same time. This could flood SQL Server with many requests for the same data!

If you think you have programmers who might abuse this feature, you'll be happy to know that SQL Server provides information to allow DBAs to monitor this feature through dynamic management views (DMVs). In addition to the Service Broker–related system views and DMVs, there is a special DMV, `sys.dm_qn_subscriptions`, that lists information about the current subscriptions. Remember, it's always possible for SQL Server 2005 to decide that notifications are taking too many resources and start purging them itself.

Multiple Active Resultsets

SQL Server clients can fetch data from the server using two different semantics: server-side cursors; and forward-only, read-only, cursorless mode, also referred to as firehose mode. Although a single client connection can open multiple database cursors at the same time and fetch data from any of them, in SQL Server 2000 and earlier, only one cursorless-mode resultset could be active at a time. In addition, no other commands (such as a SQL UPDATE statement) could be issued while the cursorless rowset was active. Cursorless mode is the default behavior of all SQL Server database APIs when using resultsets, from DBLib to ADO.NET. Cursorless mode consumes fewer resources on the server, is the fastest mode for fetching data, and is the only mode to support processing multiple resultsets produced by a single batch of SQL statements. This mode reads rows in a forward-only, read-only fashion, however. Although multiple resultsets can be processed, the results must be read sequentially; you cannot interleave reads from the first and second resultset. This was due to the inner workings of the TDS protocol—the network protocol that SQL Server clients use.

In the SQL Server 2005 release, the SQL Server engine has been changed to permit multiple batches to be active simultaneously on a single connection. Because SQL Server batches can produce resultsets, this means that more than one cursorless-mode resultset can be read at the same time using the same connection. This feature was nicknamed MARS (multiple active resultsets). Although this feature is enabled on the server, the TDS protocol and client libraries had to be updated to permit clients to access this functionality. Figure 13-4 illustrates one way the functionality can be used.

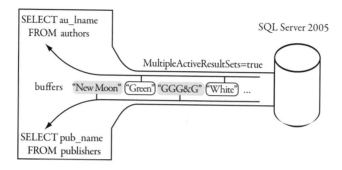

Figure 13-4: MARS multiplexes resultsets over the same connection.

In the past, database APIs dealt with the single-batch limitation in different ways. In ADO (classic), for example, the API made it appear that you could execute multiple simultaneous batches, as shown in Listing 13-27.

Listing 13-27: ADO will silently open a new connection for each new result

```
Dim conn as New ADODB.Connection
Dim rs1 as New ADODB.Recordset
Dim rs2 as New ADODB.Recordset

rs1.Open "SELECT * FROM authors", conn
rs2.Open "SELECT * FROM jobs", conn

' Note: This only reads as many rows
' as are in the shortest resultset
' rows from the longest resultset are dropped
While not rs1.EOF and not rs2.EOF
    Debug.Print rs1(0)
    Debug.Print rs2(0)
    rs1.MoveNext
    rs2.MoveNext
Wend

conn.Close
```

Although this gave the appearance of multiple active batches, it was accomplished by a little library sleight of hand. The OLE DB provider simply opened additional connections under the covers to service the additional request. Although this prevented runtime errors, a well-meaning programmer could accidentally use up connections if he wasn't aware of the way things worked. The code in Listing 13-28 will open a separate connection for every row in the loop that processes `Recordset rs1`.

LISTING 13-28: The hazard of automatically opening new connections

```
Dim conn as New ADODB.Connection
Dim rs1 as New ADODB.Recordset
Dim rs2 as New ADODB.Recordset

rs1.Open "SELECT * FROM authors", conn
While not rs1.EOF
   rs2.Open "SELECT * FROM titleauthor WHERE au_id = " & _
      rs1("au_id"), conn
   rs1.MoveNext
Wend
```

This behavior is controllable through a property on the OLE DB `Data Source` object, `"Multiple Connections=false"`. This property is also available through ADO as an extended property on the `Connection` object.

Although it annoyed programmers who weren't aware of how the protocol worked, ADO.NET's way of dealing with the pre–SQL Server 2005 limitation was an improvement over ADO. When you attempted to open multiple batches containing results using `SqlCommand.ExecuteReader`, a runtime error occurred. The error message was verbose but exactly described the situation: "There is already an open DataReader associated with this Command, which must be closed first." Programmers had to be careful to play by the rules.

Using MARS in ADO.NET 2.0

ADO.NET and other SQL Server APIs can use updated network library call to SNI—the SQL Server Networking Interface—to achieve true multiplexing of result batches on a single connection. Because this functionality is actually implemented on the server, it works only with a SQL Server 2005–release database, though OLE DB, ADO, and ODBC can take advantage of it, as well as ADO.NET. We'll look at the implementation in ADO.NET first, although this is the API where you'd be least likely to use it.

MARS is enabled by connection-string parameters when you are using the ADO.NET data provider in .NET Framework 2.0 and a SQL Server 2005 client. You must use the connection-string parameter `MultipleActiveRe-sultSets=true` to enable MARS support; the default value of this parameter is false.

Although you use the same `SqlConnection` instance with multiple resultsets, you must use different `SqlCommand` instances for each simultaneous resultset. The resultset is encapsulated by the `SqlDataReader` class, so you will have two `SqlDataReaders` as well. You can read from either `SqlDataReader`, although the behavior of `SqlDataReader` is still forward-only and read-only. Listing 13-29 shows a simple example.

LISTING 13-29: Using multiple active resultsets in ADO.NET

```
string connect_string = GetConnectStringFromConfigFile();
SqlConnection conn = new SqlConnection(
    connect_string += ";multipleactiveresultsets=true");
conn.Open();

SqlCommand cmd1 = new SqlCommand(
   "SELECT * FROM authors", conn);
SqlCommand cmd2 = new SqlCommand(
   "SELECT * FROM jobs", conn);

SqlDataReader rdr1 = cmd1.ExecuteReader ();

// second resultset, same connection
SqlDataReader rdr2 = cmd2.ExecuteReader ();

while
 ((rdr1.Read() == true && rdr2.Read() == true))
{
  // write first column of each resultset
  Console.WriteLine (rdr1[0]);
  Console.WriteLine (rdr2[0]);
}

// clean everything up
rdr1.Close(); rdr2.Close();
cmd1.Dispose(); cmd2.Dispose();
conn.Dispose();
```

Note also that each command can contain an entire batch of statements and return more than one resultset. The basic functionality of the cursorless-mode resultset has not changed, however, so these resultsets must be read in order. If, in the preceding example, the `CommandText` for cmd1 was SELECT * FROM authors;SELECT * FROM titles, we would read all the authors rows first, followed by the titles rows. This also does not change the fact that the stored-procedure output parameters are returned after all the resultsets, and the SqlDataReader must still be closed before the output parameters are available. See Chapter 3 of *Essential ADO.NET*, by Bob Beauchemin (Addison-Wesley, 2002), for details.

Although you can execute multiple batches in parallel over the same connection, parallel transactions over the same connection are not supported. The example in Listing 13-30 shows that the transaction is still scoped to the connection.

LISTING 13-30: Even with MARS, transactions are scoped to the connection, not the command

```
string connect_string = GetConnectStringFromConfigFile();
SqlConnection conn = new SqlConnection(connect_string);
conn.Open();

// one transaction
SqlTransaction tx1 = conn.BeginTransaction();

// this would fail
//SqlTransaction tx2 = conn.BeginTransaction();

SqlCommand cmd1 = new SqlCommand
  ("update_authors_and_getresults", conn, tx1);

// both SqlCommands must be enlisted
SqlCommand cmd2 = new SqlCommand(
  "update_authors_and_getresults", conn, tx1);
cmd1.CommandType = CommandType.StoredProcedure;
cmd2.CommandType = CommandType.StoredProcedure;

SqlDataReader rdr1 = cmd1.ExecuteReader();

// second resultset, same connection
SqlDataReader rdr2 = cmd2.ExecuteReader();

while
  ((rdr1.Read() == true && rdr2.Read() == true))
{
  // write first column of each resultset
  Console.WriteLine (rdr1[0]);
  Console.WriteLine (rdr2[0]);
}

// commit one transaction (both authors & jobs)
```

```
tx1.Commit();

// but you cannot roll back just one or the other,
// attempt to build second transaction failed
// tx2.Rollback();

// clean everything up
rdr1.Close(); rdr2.Close();
cmd1.Dispose(); cmd2.Dispose();
conn.Dispose();
```

Besides making things easier for the programmer, if multiple simultaneous operations need to be performed on the same connection, the MARS feature can be used in conjunction with the asynchronous execution feature, covered in Chapter 14, though this does not provide an overall performance improvement. MARS sessions do not execute in parallel but execute interleaved.

You should be careful using MARS, because if you execute two commands, the execution of the commands is not guaranteed to be in order. Also, do not use SQL statements that change the connection environment, such as the SQL "USE database" command. Because command execution in order of execution in the client is not guaranteed, there is the possibility that you could be changing database context at the "wrong" time. This could cause later commands to fail, as shown in Figure 13-5.

Because of the fact that the commands in multiple MARS sessions on the same connection are not guaranteed to be serialized, transaction Savepoints

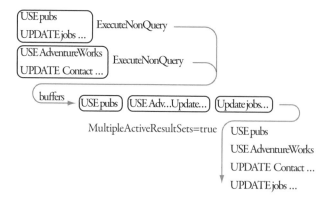

FIGURE 13-5: Command execution between sessions is not guaranteed to be serialized.

are not available when using MARS. In addition, transactions are scoped to the stored procedure or to the SQL batch when using MARS. If a transaction in a MARS session is not committed by the end of the stored procedure or SQL batch, the transaction will be rolled back automatically.

MARS in SQL Native Client

MARS support is also provided in the SQL Native Client driver and provider. You indicate that you want MARS support by using the connection-string name–value pair `"MARS Connection=True"`. You can also use an OLE DB property `SSPROP_INIT_MARSCONNECTION` or an ODBC connection option `SQL_COPT_SS_MARS_ENABLED`, but the connection-string method will most likely be more popular, as it can also be used in ADO.

New Transaction and Isolation Features in ADO.NET

Using the New Isolation Levels

In Chapter 7, we discuss one of the biggest enhancements to the SQL Server engine in SQL Server 2005: the ability to use versioning rather than locking to achieve user isolation inside a SQL Server transaction. This capability is also exposed in the client in a way analogous to that on the server, as a database capability and a new transaction isolation level. The code to accomplish this using `SqlClient` is straightforward, as shown in Listing 13-31.

LISTING 13-31: Using snapshot isolation level in ADO.NET

```
public void DoSnapshot()
  {
    string connstr = GetConnectStringFromConfigFile();
    SqlConnection conn = new SqlConnection(connstr);
    conn.Open();

    SqlCommand myCommand = conn.CreateCommand();
    SqlTransaction tx = null;

    // Start a local transaction.
    tx = conn.BeginTransaction(IsolationLevel.Snapshot);

    // Associate Command with Transaction
    SqlCommand cmd = new SqlCommand(
```

```
          "INSERT INTO jobs VALUES('new job', 100, 100)",
          conn, tx);

     try
     {
        // first insert
        cmd.ExecuteNonQuery();

        // second insert
        cmd.CommandText =
      "INSERT INTO jobs VALUES('Grand Poobah', 200, 200)",        cmd.Exe-
    cuteNonQuery();
        tx.Commit();
     }
     catch(Exception e) {
        try {
          tx.Rollback();
        }
        catch (SqlException ex) {
          // no-op catch, tx already rolled back
        }
     }
     finally {
        cmd.Dispose();
        conn.Dispose();
     }
  }
```

This is normal client-side local transaction code; the only thing that may look a little odd is that when you roll back a transaction from the client, you do so in a `try/catch` block and ignore the error that you catch. This is because the transaction may already have been rolled back inside the database; attempting to roll back a nonexistent transaction will cause an exception. You can safely catch and ignore the exception.

In OLE DB and ODBC, the code is just as simple, and there is an enumerated constant for the SNAPSHOT isolation level in the C++ include file `sqlncli.h` in addition to the standard transaction isolation levels in `transaction.h`. Because the ADO library itself has not been updated for SQL Server 2005, if you want to use the SNAPSHOT isolation level with ADO, you must use the hard-coded value for the transaction isolation level of SNAPSHOT, because there is no enumerated constant. You can also use SET TRANSACTION ISOLATION LEVEL SNAPSHOT as part of a command batch to achieve this isolation level in any version of any of the data access APIs.

The isolation level specifically named `IsolationLevel.Snapshot` is actually transaction-level snapshot. This is the only new named isolation level in SQL Server 2005. Using statement-level snapshot isolation is transparent from the client; you need only enable statement-level snapshot on the database and use `IsolationLevel.ReadCommitted`, which is the default. The behavior of `IsolationLevel.ReadCommitted` in SQL Server 2005 depends entirely on the setting in the database.

Promotable and Declarative Transactions

Microsoft Transaction Server (MTS) and its successors, COM+ and `System.EnterpriseServices`, popularized the concept of distributed transactions, for better or worse. These server- and object-based libraries permitted programmers to specify automatic transactions on a class or method level. Because the COM+ interceptor had no knowledge of which database the instance was going to use, or whether it was going to use a single database or multiple databases, COM+ always began a distributed transaction.

Distributed transactions are always slower than local transactions—sometimes, much slower. The network traffic that is generated when the distributed transaction coordinator (MSDTC) is involved is substantial. For an in-depth description of how distributed transactions work and how MTS/COM+ works, refer to *Transactional COM+*, by Tim Ewald (Addison-Wesley, 2001).

Promotable transactions is a feature that transparently promotes an existing local transaction to a distributed transaction automatically if you access any other transactional resource manager (including another connection to SQL Server) inside a transactional method. Promotion also works on a single SQL Server and any other transactional resource that supports it. This requires code both inside the SQL engine and in the client-side libraries but does not require the programmer to write additional program logic. It is designed for cases where the new `System. Transaction` library is used to manipulate transactions. Simply starting a transaction and using a command to access multiple instances of SQL Server will cause the transaction to be promoted automatically. Listing 13-32 shows a simple example that illustrates using the `TransactionScope` class.

LISTING 13-32: Using TransactionScope to obtain promotable transactions in ADO.NET

```
using (TransactionScope ts = new TransactionScope())
{
  SqlConnection conn1 = new SqlConnection(
    "server=.;integrated security=sspi;database=pubs");
  // start local tx if SQL 2005, distributed tx if not
  conn1.Open();
  SqlCommand cmd1 = new SqlCommand(
    "INSERT jobs VALUES('job1', 10, 10", conn1);
  cmd1.ExecuteNonQuery();

  SqlConnection conn2 = new SqlConnection(
    "server=other;integrated security=sspi;database=pubs");
  // promote to distributed tx if SQL 2005
  conn2.Open();
  SqlCommand cmd2 = new SqlCommand(
    "INSERT jobs VALUES('job2', 10, 10", conn2);
  cmd2.ExecuteNonQuery();

  ts.Complete();
  // dispose SqlCommands and SqlConnections here
} // commits transaction when TransactionStream.Dispose is called here
```

If you have used MTS or COM+ declarative transactions in the past, the same transaction composition functionality exists using System.Transactions and the TransactionScope. You can nest TransactionScope, for example. Inside a nested TransactionScope, you have the ability to use a composition option, TransactionScopeOption, that has the familiar (to MTS programmers) values Requires, RequiresNew, and Suppress. Programmers who attempt to use TransactionScope and promotable transactions, with the familiar MTS object composition pattern, may be surprised that even opening a second connection with exactly the same connection string will start a distributed transaction, even when SQL Server 2005 is the database. Listing 13-33 shows an example of this behavior.

Listing 13-33: Two identical connections produce a distributed transaction

```
using (TransactionScope ts = new TransactionScope())
{
  SqlConnection conn1 = new SqlConnection(
    "server=.;integrated security=sspi;database=pubs"))
  // start local tx if SQL 2005, distributed tx if not
  conn1.Open();
  SqlCommand cmd1 = new SqlCommand(
    "INSERT jobs VALUES('job1', 10, 10", conn1);
```

```
cmd1.ExecuteNonQuery();
// EXACT same connection string as the first one
// second connection always causes promotion to distributed tx
SqlConnection conn2 = new SqlConnection(
  "server=.;integrated security=sspi;database=pubs");
conn2.Open();
SqlCommand cmd2 = new SqlCommand(
   "INSERT jobs VALUES('job2', 10, 10", conn2);
cmd2.ExecuteNonQuery();
ts.Complete();
} // dispose SqlCommands and SqlConnections here
```

The new System.Transactions library is used for more than transaction promotion with SQL Server 2005. Because it does not require entries in the MTS/COM+ component catalog or require that .NET Framework classes be registered as COM classes, it probably will replace System.Enterpris-eServices eventually. In addition, the System.Transactions library will be used with the .NET Framework implementation of the Web Service standard WS-Transactions.

Changes Related to SQL Server 2005 Login

Password Change Support

SQL Server 2005 will expire passwords on SQL Server security accounts, just as the Windows 2003 security authority expires passwords on Windows accounts used by SQL Server. Because you use a SQL Server account only to log onto SQL Server, the SqlClient libraries provide a secure mechanism allowing a SQL Server account to change password during login.

When a SQL Server user with an expired password attempts to log in using ADO.NET, a SQL Server user with an expired password will receive an exception with a specific SQL Server state code. After catching the error, the program can prompt for a password (there is no standard "password expired" dialog box), and obtain a new password and the old password from the user. The program will use a static method on the SqlConnection class, ChangePassword, to change the password on SQL Server. The server validates the old password against the password in the connection string, and ensures that the new password is policy compliant, so you can't just put in a random string for the old password. Using the ChangePassword method looks something like Listing 13-34.

LISTING 13-34: Setting a password using ADO.NET ChangePassword

```
string connstring = GetConnectionString();
SqlConnection conn = new SqlConnection(connstring);
for(int i=0; i < 2; i++)
  {
  try
    {
      conn.Open();
      break;
    }
  catch(SqlException ex)
    {
      // 18487 = password expired
      // 18488 = must change password on first login
      if ((ex.Number == 18487) || (ex.Number == 18488))
        {
          // prompt the user for the new password
          string newpw = PromptPassword();
          // change it on SQL Server
          // note that the first parameter of ChangePassword
          // is a connection string containing the old password
          // not just the old password
          SqlConnection.ChangePassword(connstring, newpw);

          // fix connection string in config and SqlConnection instance
          // to include the new password

          // reattempt the login
        }
    }
  }
```

Note that you must define your own `PromptPassword` method and write program-specific code to change both the configuration file and the connection string currently being used to use the new password. It was a programmer inconvenience to hard-code connection strings containing passwords in programs in the past, because the source code needed to be changed if the administrator changed the password. With the advent of SQL Server password-expiration policies, connection strings containing passwords must be stored outside the program. Not only should they be stored in a configuration file, but the connection string should be encrypted to guard against unauthorized access through the configuration file.

In OLE DB, ADO, and ODBC, there is a special connection-string parameter, NewPassword, to permit setting the new password. Clients can watch for the 18486 and 18487 error numbers in these APIs, as in ADO.NET. The ability to change the password when it expires has been incorporated into the login dialog boxes in these APIs, when you use DBPROP_INIT_PROMPT in OLE DB ("Prompt" extended property on the ADO Connection object) or SQLDriverConnect with fDriverCompletion in ODBC.

Failover Support

When running against a SQL Server 2005 database, your SqlClient, OLE DB, ADO, or ODBC code can support automatic failover. This requires that the server use database mirroring[2] and that you know the network names of both the running server and the mirror. You enable this by specifying "Failover Partner=partner name" in the connection string. When the database fails over, any transaction in progress will be rolled back the next time you try to issue a command on the "failed" connection, but then the client will automatically connect to the failover partner server. Be aware of the fact that on failover, the transaction in progress will be rolled back, or the work in progress must be redone. In addition, the connection will be dropped and must be reopened. Listing 13-35 shows an example that uses this functionality.

LISTING 13-35: Using client failover with ADO.NET

```
// Connection string in program to show special parameters
using (SqlConnection conn = new SqlConnection(
    @"server=.\SQLDev01;failover partner=.\SQLDev02;
      integrated security=sspi;database=pubs"))
using (SqlCommand cmd = new SqlCommand())
{
  conn.Open();
  SqlTransaction tx = null;
  for (int i = 1; i < 101; i++)
  {
    try
    {
      // failover will close the connection, you have to reopen it
      // or put the conn.Open here
      // and remove it from before the tx = null line
```

---

2. The database mirroring feature in SQL Server 2005 was not officially supported when SQL Server 2005 shipped but can be enabled for testing by specifying trace flag 1400 as a startup option. It should be supported by H12006.

```
        if (conn.State == System.Data.ConnectionState.Closed)
          conn.Open();

        cmd.Connection = conn;
        tx = conn.BeginTransaction();
        cmd.Transaction = tx;
        cmd.CommandText = "insert jobs values('row " + i + "',10,10)";
        int numrows = cmd.ExecuteNonQuery();

        // stop at this line
        // then fail the master instance to test
        Console.WriteLine("row {0} added", i);
        tx.Commit();
        Console.WriteLine("transaction {0} committed", i);
      }
    catch (Exception e)
    {
        Console.WriteLine(e.Message);
        try
        {
          // this has to be in a try/catch block with no catch
          // because losing the master will cause a transaction
          // that cannot be committed on rolled back
          tx.Rollback();
        }
        catch { }
      }
  }
} // SqlConnection and SqlCommand disposed here
```

Encryption Support

SQL Server 2005 does not have a distinct multiprotocol library to support encrypted data connections, as SQL Server 2000 does. Instead, it will rely on having a certificate available, because SQL Server 2005 can always generate certificates internally, even if there are no certificates currently installed. If SQL Server must generate a certificate to use to negotiate a session key for data encryption, it will generate a self-signed certificate, for which SQL Server itself is the root certificate authority. If a company does not want to provision client certificates, each SqlClient connection can choose to trust the SQL Server self-signed certificate. A client indicates this by using TrustServerCertificate=true along with Encrypt=true in the connection string. If certificates are provisioned to both the server and clients, the TrustServerCertificate parameter is not necessary. Note that using `TrustServerCertificate=true` is subject to man-in-the-middle attacks—a common security attack vector.

Comparing the Client and Server Model for Stored Procedures

With the advent of procedural code that can be written using `System.Data.SqlClient` either on the client or server, the question has arisen when to use a series of textual SQL commands and when to encapsulate these commands into a .NET Framework method that can be executed on the client or transparently moved to the server and declared as a .NET Framework stored procedure. In addition, SQL Server 2005 adds UDTs into the mix, and allows complex types with properties and methods to execute either on the server or on the client. With so much functionality at any tier, what are the best coding practices and deployment techniques? We'll discuss this more in Chapter 17, but for now, let's mention stored procedures invoked from the client versus procedural code invoked on the server.

The SQL Server engine works best fetching and operating on its own data, managing execution plans, memory buffers, and data buffers. If you could do the same on the client, you would have replicated the database functionality à la XBase databases. If, however, you are going to perform operations that SQL Server doesn't support internally—say, processor-intensive operations—you could use the server to query and filter your data down to a small subset and then distribute processor-intensive operations to every client. These operations wouldn't necessarily need to involve traditional data management unless you are working with UDTs that need to be sorted and grouped and that don't support binary ordering. So in general, for data-intensive operations, stored procedures executed on the server with results returned to the client in a single round trip are still best.

Bear in mind that all the client functionality of the SqlClient data provider does not work inside SQLCLR stored procedures. Query Notifications and MARS are two examples; neither works when you are using SqlClient on the server. See Chapter 4 for a list of client- and server-specific SqlClient classes and methods.

Where Are We?

In this chapter, we've seen how the new SQL Server data types, especially UDTs and the XML type, affect the client libraries and cause us to rethink our coding models. Although ADO.NET has the richest support for the new nonrelational types, OLE DB and ADO (mostly because of COM interop and rich XML support) can take advantage of them as well. Because the authors of the SQL:1999 specification did not enhance SQL/CLI, the call language interface implemented by Microsoft and others as ODBC, this API has only cursory support for the new complex types.

In Chapter 14, we'll look at the plethora of other new features exposed through the ADO.NET APIs in the client tier. Some of these enhancements are SQL Server–specific but work with older versions of SQL Server; others are enhancements to the ADO.NET framework itself.

■ 14 ■
ADO.NET 2.0 and SqlClient

I N THIS CHAPTER, we round out the functionality enhancements for SQL Server clients and go into some general ADO.NET provider-model enhancements. All these enhancements are backward compatible—that is, they work with SQL Server 2000 and SQL Server 7 as well. We'll look at these enhancements using the ADO.NET SqlClient provider, though we'll point out where equivalent new functionality is available to other ADO.NET data providers or through other APIs.

Generic Coding with the ADO.NET 2.0 Base Classes and Factories

ADO.NET is a database-agnostic API. It is an API in which database vendors write plug-in data providers for their database à la OLE DB/ADO (providers), ODBC (drivers), or JDBC (drivers), rather than a database-specific set of functions like dbLib or a database-specific object model like OO4O (Oracle Objects for OLE). Predecessors of ADO.NET factored their providers into sets of interfaces, defined by a strict specification. Each OLE DB provider writer implemented a standard set of interfaces, although this could include required and optional interfaces. Required interfaces specified the lowest common denominator; optional interfaces were defined for advanced database/provider features. Although the OLE DB specification permitted providers to add new interfaces to encapsulate database-specific functionality, the library that programmers used with OLE DB providers, ADO, generally did not use those interfaces.

ADO.NET was designed from the beginning to allow the provider writer space to support database-specific features. Provider writers implemented a set of classes, such as a `Connection` class, `Command` class, and `DataReader` class. Because classes as well as interfaces are visible in the .NET Framework (in COM, in general only interfaces were visible to the programmer), ADO.NET provider writers implement a set of provider-specific classes, exposing generic functionality via interfaces and database-specific functions as class methods. Each provider writer implemented his own parallel hierarchy of classes. Table 14-1 shows the parallel class hierarchies for the SqlClient and the OracleClient data providers, as well as the interface implemented by both data providers. These interfaces are defined in the `System.Data` namespace.

In ADO.NET 1.0 and 1.1, programmers had two choices: They could code to the provider-specific classes, or they could code to the generic interfaces. If there was the possibility that the company database could change during the projected lifetime of the software, or if the product was a commercial package intended to support customers with different databases, they had to program with the generic interfaces. You can't "new" an interface, so most generic programs included code that accomplished the task of obtaining the original `IDbConnection` by calling "new" on the appropriate provider-specific class, as shown in Listing 14-1.

LISTING 14-1: Generic code using interfaces in ADO.NET 1.0 and 1.1

```
enum provider {sqlserver, oracle, oledb, odbc};
public IDbConnection GetConnectionInterface()
{
// determine provider from configuration
provider prov = GetProviderFromConfigFile();
IDbConnection conn = null;
switch (prov) {
  case provider.sqlserver:
    conn = new SqlConnection(); break;
  case provider.oracle:
    conn = new OracleConnection(); break;
 // add new providers as the application supports them
 }
return conn;
}
```

TABLE 14-1: Provider-Specific Classes and Generic Interfaces in ADO.NET 1.0/1.1

SqlClient Class	Oracle Class	Generic Interface
SqlConnection	OracleConnection	IDbConnection
SqlCommand	OracleCommand	IDbCommand
SqlDataReader	OracleDataReader	IDataReader/IDataRecord
SqlTransaction	OracleTransaction	IDbTransaction
SqlParameter	OracleParameter	IDbDataParameter
SqlParameterCollection	OracleParameterCollection	IDataParameterCollection
SqlDataAdapter	OracleDataAdapter	IDbDataAdapter

The GetProviderFromConfigFile method referred to above was hand-coded by each company, as was the mechanism for storing the provider information in the configuration file. In addition, vendors that supported multiple databases had to write vendor-specific code to allow the user or software programmer to choose which database to use at installation time.

ADO.NET 2.0 codifies configuration, setup, and generic coding with a prescribed set of base classes for providers to implement, connection-string setup and handling, and factory classes to standardize obtaining a provider-specific Connection, Command, and so on. These features make it easier for software companies that support running on the user's choice of database, as well as for programmers who think that the database might change (from Access to SQL Server, for example) during the lifetime of the project.

ADO.NET adds new features to the "base provider profile" with each release. Version 1.1 added a property to the DataReader to allow the programmer to determine whether the DataReader contained a nonzero number of rows (the HasRows property) without calling IDataReader.Read. Because interfaces are immutable, this property could not just be added to the IDataReader interface; this new property had to be added to each provider-specific class (SqlDataReader, OleDbDataReader, and so on). The usual way to use versioning with interfaces is to define a new interface. This new interface could either extend the original interface (IDataReader2 inherits from IDataReader and adds HasRows) or includes only the new functionality (IDataReaderNewStuff contains only HasRows).

Another way to version functionality is to use base classes. Although using base classes restricts the class inheritance model (each class can inherit from only a single base class in the .NET Framework), this is the preferred mechanism if you expect changes to your set of functionality in the future. Lots of new functionality is exposed in ADO.NET 2.0, and more changes are expected going forward, and so the model now uses base classes instead of interfaces. The ADO.NET 1.0/1.1 interfaces are retained for backward compatibility, however. To use our original example, ADO.NET 2.0 contains a `DbDataReader` class that includes a `HasRows` property. More properties, methods, and events can be added in the future. The only ADO.NET 1.0/1.1 provider class to be based on the base class concept was the `DataAdapter`; all provider-specific base classes, such as `SqlDataAdapter`, derived from `DbDataAdapter`, which derived from `DataAdapter`. The new ADO.NET provider base classes are listed in Table 14-2. These classes are defined in `System.Data.Common`. All new generic functionality is included in the base classes (but not the interfaces) in ADO.NET.

TABLE 14-2: Generic Base Classes and Generic Interfaces in ADO.NET 2.0

SqlClient Class	Base Class	Generic Interface
SqlConnection	DbConnection	IDbConnection
SqlCommand	DbCommand	IDbCommand
SqlDataReader	DbDataReader	IDataReader/IDataRecord
SqlTransaction	DbTransaction	IDbTransaction
SqlParameter	DbParameter	IDbDataParameter
SqlParameterCollection	DbParameterCollection	IDataParameterCollection
SqlDataAdapter	DbDataAdapter*	IDbDataAdapter
SqlCommandBuilder	DbCommandBuilder	no generic interface
SqlConnectionStringBuilder	DbConnectionStringBuilder	no generic interface
SqlPermission	DBDataPermission*	no generic interface

*These base classes existed in ADO.NET 1.0.

In addition to these "main" base classes, many new base classes were added in ADO.NET 2.0, including some that we'll be talking about later in this chapter. The provider base classes in ADO.NET are abstract, however, meaning that they can't be instantiated directly, either. Our interface-based code would change to the code shown in Listing 14-2.

LISTING 14-2: Adding new providers means changing code

```
enum provider {sqlserver, oracle, oledb, odbc};
public DbConnection GetConnectionBaseClass()
{
// determine provider from configuration
provider prov = GetProviderFromConfigFile();
DbConnection conn = null;
switch (prov) {
  case provider.sqlserver:
    conn = new SqlConnection(); break;
  case provider.oracle:
    conn = new OracleConnection(); break;
 // add new providers as the application supports them
 }
return conn;
}
```

That wouldn't be much of an improvement from a programmer-usability standpoint. Enter provider factories.

Provider Factories

Rather than rely on the case statements above, it would be nice to have a class that gave out a DbConnection, for example, based on instantiating the "correct" provider-specific connection. But how do you know whether to instantiate SqlConnection or OracleConnection? The solution is to use a Provider Factory class to give out the right type of concrete class. Each provider implements a provider factory class—for example, SqlProvider Factory, OracleProviderFactory, or OleDbProviderFactory. These classes all derive from DbProviderFactory and contain static (shared in Visual Basic .NET) methods to dole out creatable classes. Here's the list of DbProviderFactory's methods:

- CreateCommand
- CreateCommandBuilder

- `CreateConnection`

- `CreateConnectionStringBuilder`

- `CreateDataAdapter`

- `CreateDataSourceEnumerator`

- `CreateParameter`

- `CreatePermission`

- `CanCreateDataSourceEnumerator` (read-only property)

Note that we don't need a `CreateDbDataReader` class, for example, because `DbDataReader` isn't creatable directly with the "new" operator; it's always created via `DbCommand.ExecuteReader()`.

Each data provider that exposes a `DbProviderFactory`-based class registers configuration information in `machine.config`. This information can also be added to program-specific configuration files like `web.config`. A typical entry in `machine.config` for the SqlClient data provider looks like this:

```
<system.data>
 <DbProviderFactories>
<add name="SqlClient Data Provider"
 invariant="System.Data.SqlClient"
 description=".Net Framework Data Provider for SqlServer"
 type="System.Data.SqlClient.SqlClientFactory, System.Data,
  Version=2.0.0.0, Culture=neutral, PublicKeyToken=b77a5c561934e089" />
 <!-- other provider entries elided -->
 </DbProviderFactories>
</system.data>
```

Some of these attributes can be used for displaying a list of available data providers. One important attribute, from a programming point of view, is `invariant`—the provider-invariant name that can be passed as a string to the `DbProviderFactories` class, mentioned in the next paragraph.

The `DbProviderFactories` class, which you could think of as "a factory for factories," has static methods to accommodate choosing a provider and instantiating its `DbProviderFactory`. These methods are listed in Table 14-3.

The methods of `DbProviderFactories` could be used to produce a drop-down list box with a list of .NET Framework data providers (via `GetFactoryClasses`), let the user choose one, and instantiate the correct

TABLE 14-3: DbProviderFactories Methods

DbProviderFactories Method	Purpose
GetFactoryClasses()	Returns a DataTable of provider information from the information in machine.config
GetFactory(DataRow)	Returns the correct DbProviderFactory instance, given a DataRow from the DataTable produced by GetFactoryClasses
GetFactory(string)	Returns the correct DbProviderFactory instance, given a provider-invariant name string that identifies the provider

DbProviderFactory via GetFactory(DataRow), or just get the correct DbProviderFactory with a string. So now, if we choose to prompt the user for a provider to use, our code to select a provider and instantiate a DbConnection looks like Listing 14-3.

LISTING 14-3: Using the ProviderFactories class to obtain a ProviderFactory

```
public DbConnection GetConnectionBaseClass2()
{
DbProviderFactory f = GetProviderFactoryFromUserInput();
// call provider factory-specific CreateConnection
return f.CreateConnection();
}

public DbProviderFactory GetProviderFactoryFromUserInput()
{
DataTable t = DbProviderFactories.GetFactoryClasses();
int selected_row;
DataRow r;
// code elided,
// user selects a DataRow selected_row from DataTable t
r = t.Rows[selected_row];
return DbProviderFactories.GetFactory(r);
}
```

When we have the appropriate DbProviderFactory, we can instantiate any of the creatable classes that the provider supports; the DbConnection is just the most common example.

This takes care of allowing the user to configure a provider, but this is usually done once, during setup of a particular application. After setting up the database and choosing a database instance, this information should be stored in a user's config file, and it should be changed only if the company changes database products or if the location of the database instance changes (for example, the application moves from a test server to a production server). ADO.NET 2.0 accommodates both of these cases with built-in functionality; you don't have to roll your own.

Specifying Configuration Information

In addition to the `DbProviderFactories` section of configuration files, there are a standard config file location and APIs for manipulating connection-string information. This requires a little more handling than name–value pairs that you might expect. OLE DB/ADO, ODBC, and JDBC connection strings contain two discrete types of information: information identifying the provider/driver and name–value pairs of information describing how to connect to the provider. Here's a typical ADO (classic) connection string:

```
"provider=sqloledb;data source=mysvr;integrated security=sspi;initial
catalog=pubs"
```

When the Visual Basic 6.0 programmer codes the statement

```
Dim conn as New Connection
conn.Open connstr 'use the connection string defined above
```

the connection-string information is used by the OLE DB service components to:

- Search the Registry and load the correct provider (`CoCreateInstance` on the OLE DB data source class for the provider name specified)
- Create an ADO Connection instance that encapsulates the OLE DB `Data Source` (and `Session`) objects
- Return the correct ADO interface pointer (`_Connection`, in this case) to the program
- Call `Open()` on the ADO `_Connection` interface, which calls the underlying OLE DB provider code using OLE DB interfaces

ADO.NET database-specific connection strings do not contain provider information.[1] Programmers must decide which provider to use at program coding time or invent a mechanism to store that information. ADO.NET 2.0 connection configuration information takes care of this. A typical ADO.NET 2.0 connection string in an application configuration file looks like this

```
<configuration>
  <connectionStrings>
    <add name="Publications" providerName="System.Data.SqlClient"
      connectionString="Data Source=MyServer;Initial Catalog=pubs;
                        integrated security=SSPI" />
  </connectionStrings>
</configuration>
```

and contains a connection-string name and provider name, as well as the connection string itself.

This information is exposed through the ConnectionStringsSettings Collection collection class of ConnectionStringSettings. You can fetch a connection string by name and retrieve all the needed information with very little code. Using the connection-string information above, the generic DbConnection fetching program becomes the code shown in Listing 14-4.

LISTING 14-4: Getting a generic DbConnection

```
public DbConnection GetInitializedConnectionBaseClass()
{
DbConnection conn = null;
ConnectionStringSettings s =
  ConfigurationManager.ConnectionStrings["Publications"];
DbProviderFactory f = DbProviderFactories.GetFactory(
  s.ProviderName);
conn =  f.CreateConnection();
conn.ConnectionString = s.ConnectionString;
return conn;
}
```

Storing named connection-string information is just as easy using the ConnectionStringSettingsCollection class, as we'll see later in this chapter.

---

1. The OleDb and Odbc data providers in ADO.NET do, but this information is for the underlying OLE DB or ODBC layer.

Enumerating Data Sources and Building Connection Strings

So now, we can configure and load connection strings, and get a connection to the database using ADO.NET 2.0 in a completely provider-independent manner. But what if the database that you're connecting to changes? The DBAs have moved the data you're using from the "Publications" instance of SQL Server to the "Bookstore" instance, and you've received e-mail that your configuration should be changed. Although Microsoft System Management Server (SMS) or other automatic deployment could be used to automate the process of pushing the new configuration, a program could be written to list all the SQL Server databases on the network and allow you to reconfigure it yourself. ADO.NET 2.0 introduces Data Source Enumerator classes just for that purpose.

The ADO.NET data source enumerators derive from a common base class (of course): DbDataSourceEnumerator. You can retrieve the appropriate DbDataSourceEnumerator through the DbProviderFactory using the pattern described above. In addition, you can use SqlDataSource Enumerator's static property, named "Instance," to get an instance, like this: SqlDataSourceEnumerator en = SqlDataSourceEnumerator. Instance.

DbDataSourceEnumerator classes expose a single instance method, GetDataSources. If my database or data source changes, the code to change it would look like Listing 14-5.

LISTING 14-5: Using ADO.NET to change the data source in a connection string

```
public void ChangeDataSourceOrProvider()
{
// see this method in the example above
DbProviderFactory f = GetProviderFactoryFromUserInput();
// if our factory supports creating a DbConnection, return it.
if (f.CanCreateDataSourceEnumerator)
  {
    DbDataSourceEnumerator e = f.CreateDataSourceEnumerator();
    DataTable t = e.GetDataSources();
    // code elided, user chooses a Data Row selected_row
    int selected_row = 0;
    DataRow r = t.Rows["selected_row"];
    string dataSource = (string)r["ServerName"];
```

```
    if (r[InstanceName] != null)
      dataSource += ("\\" + r["InstanceName"]);
    // change "Pubs" connection string, this method is defined below
    RewriteConnectionStringAndUpdateConfigFile(f, dataSource, "Pubs");
  }
else
  Console.WriteLine("Source must be changed manually");
}
```

Note that this was fairly simple generic code, with the exception of the last RewriteConnectionStringAndUpdateConfigFile method. Because connection strings are name–value pairs, we'll have to do some string manipulation to ensure that we're replacing the right value. And what if not only the instance of the database changes, but also other connection-string parameters, such as the User ID or Initial Catalog (Database)? It would be nice to have a built-in class to help with this task. ADO.NET 2.0 provides just such a class: the generic base class `DbConnectionStringBuilder`.

In ADO.NET, connection strings are name–value pairs, as with other generic APIs. Unlike OLE DB and ODBC, ADO.NET does not mandate what those name keywords should be, though it is suggested that they follow the OLE DB conventions. The OleDb and Odbc bridge data providers each follow their own convention. Microsoft's `OracleClient` follows OLE DB convention, and SqlClient supports either keyword when the OLE DB and ODBC keywords differ. Table 14-4 contains some examples.

The `DbConnectionStringBuilder` is a base class for provider-specific connection-string builders. Because it cannot be guaranteed that an ADO. NET data provider supports a specific connection-string parameter, the `Db ConnectionStringBuilder` just keeps a dictionary of name–value pairs. All the ordinary collection methods are available, including a `GetKeys` and `GetValues` method to get the entire list from the dictionary. `DbConnectionStringBuilder` does support some specific properties to do with connection-string parameters, such as `ShouldSerialize` (the user may not want the password value serialized into a file, for example). You can get an instance of the generic `DbConnectionStringBuilder` through the `DbProviderFactory` class. Specific `ConnectionStringBuilder` classes have convenience properties, such as a `Data Source` property that refers to the database server to connect to. In general, the properties are data provider–specific, as the keywords are.

TABLE 14-4: Example Connection-String Parameters in SQL Server APIs

Meaning	Odbc	OleDb	SqlClient	OracleClient
Source to connect to Source	Server	Data Source	Server or Data Source	Server or Data
User	UID	User ID	UID or User ID	User ID
Password	PWD	Password	PWD or Password	Password
Is a Windows In login used?	Trusted_Connection	Integrated Security	Trusted_Connection or Integrated Security	Integrated Security
Database to con- nect to	Database	Initial Catalog	Database or Initial Catalog	N/A
Connection Pooling		OLE DB Services	Pooling	Pooling

To implement the `RewriteConnectionStringAndUpdateConfigFile` method mentioned earlier in this chapter, using the `DbConnectionStringBuilder` would look like Listing 14-6.

LISTING 14-6: Rewriting the connection string

```
public void RewriteConnectionStringAndUpdateConfigFile(
  DbProviderFactory f, string dataSource, string name)
{
Configuration config =
ConfigurationManager.OpenExeConfiguration(ConfigurationUserLevel.None);
   DbConnectionStringBuilder b = f.CreateConnectionStringBuilder();
b.ConnectionString =
config.ConnectionStrings.ConnectionStrings[name].ConnectionString;
if (b.ContainsKey("Data Source"))
  {
   b.Remove("Data Source");
   b.Add("Data Source", dataSource);

   // Update ConfigurationSettings connection string
   config.ConnectionStrings.ConnectionStrings[name].ConnectionString =
      b.ConnectionString;
   config.Save(ConfigurationSaveMode.Modified);
}
```

One last thing to mention about building connection strings: Both ODBC and OLE DB provide graphic editors for configuring connection information. The ODBC editor is contained in a Control Panel applet (Configure ODBC Data Sources). The OLE DB editor is invoked whenever a file with the extension `.udl` is double-clicked. In Visual Studio 2003, the OLE DB UDL editor is used to configure .NET Framework data providers; the connection strings for SqlClient must be postprocessed by Visual Studio itself. Visual Studio 2005 contains a graphic editor that uses the `DbConnectionStringBuilder` and `ProviderFactories` classes. To have a look at it, configure a new data source in Visual Studio .NET, using the Server Explorer window. It lists the .NET Framework data providers, not the OLE DB providers anymore! This component is not usable directly, but the `DbConnectionStringBuilder` class can easily be bound to the `PropertyGrid` control as a data source. There are also provider-specific subclasses of `DbConnectionStringBuilder` that expose provider-specific connection-string parameters.

Other Generic Coding Considerations

So now, using ADO.NET 2.0, common base classes, and factories, we can write almost completely generic code. Databases, however, by their very nature aren't completely generic. Programmers never have been able to write one program that will work on every database and have it perform the same on each one. One big example of this is that strategies that work well on client-server databases (like SQL Server and Oracle) wouldn't work as well on file-based data stores (like Access and FoxPro). As we programmers found out in the ADO era, porting between file-based and client-server (network-based) involves a little more than changing the provider and connection string.

Each data provider may support some properties, methods, and events that are not supported by other data providers. The premise behind the base classes is that they expose generic functionality; provider-specific functionality is exposed on the provider-specific classes. These extras are always available through casting using the cast syntax, `"as"` or `"is"` in C#, or the `CType` method in Visual Basic .NET. Here's an example of using the SqlConnection-specific method `RetrieveStatistics` from C# code:

```
public void GetStatsIfPossible(DbConnection conn)
{
  if (conn is SqlConnection)
    Hashtable h = ((SqlConnection)conn).RetrieveStatistics();
}
```

Another place where providers differ is in their usage of parameters in parameterized queries or stored procedures. In ADO.NET, data providers can support named parameters (the parameter name is significant; the order in which parameters are specified is irrelevant), positional parameters (the parameter order is significant; the name is irrelevant), or both. Sql-Client and Microsoft's OracleClient provider insist on named parameters; OleDb and Odbc use positional parameters. Another difference is parameter markers, if you are using parameterized queries. Each provider has its own idea of what the parameter marker should be. Table 14-5 contains a short list of differences, using the providers that ship with ADO.NET as an example. If you obtain providers from DataDirect Technologies or Oracle Corporation, these can differ.

Other differences are based on how the database's network protocol works. The network protocol defines the way that result packets are returned from database to client. SQL Server uses TDS (Tabular Data Stream) protocol, for example; Oracle uses TNS (transparent network substrate). Because of how the database and protocol work, versions of

TABLE 14-5: Parameter Styles and Parameter Markers in ADO.NET 2.0 Data Providers

Provider	Named/Positional	Parameter Marker
SqlClient	Named	@parmname
OracleClient	Named	:parmname (or parmname)
OleDb	Positional	?
Odbc	Positional	?

SQL Server prior to SQL Server 2005 can have only one active resultset (`DataReader`, in ADO.NET terms) at a time. SQL Server 2005 does not have this limitation; the feature that permits multiple active resultsets on a single connection is known as MARS. In SQL Server, output parameters are available only after resultsets are returned and the `DataReader` is closed. Oracle, on the other hand, returns resultsets from stored procedures as a special type of output parameter, `REFCURSOR`, and has different behaviors with respect to `DataReader`s and output parameters. Nothing is completely generic, although ADO.NET 2.0 provides a way to find out such provider-specific data through generic metadata information.

Schemas in ADO.NET 2.0

As we've mentioned, Visual Studio 2005 Server Explorer now uses a dialog box containing a list of .NET Framework data providers (rather than OLE DB providers) to prompt for connection information. When you decide on a connection string and add a Data Connection, each Data Connection also displays a tree of information about the database objects (such as tables, views, and stored procedures) visible directly through the connection. But where does this information come from? Is Visual Studio 2005 hard-coded to produce this information only for certain data providers, leaving you with an empty node if you write your own data provider or buy one from a third party? Not in Visual Studio 2005. All this good information is brought to you courtesy of the new Schema API in ADO.NET 2.0. We don't know whether this is exactly the way that Visual Studio 2005 does it, but Listing 14-7 shows code to get a list of tables in a database using the new APIs.

LISTING 14-7: Using GetSchema to get a list of tables

```
// uses a ADO.NET 2.0 named connection string in config file
// uses ADO.NET 2.0 ProviderFactory and base classes
public static void GetListOfTables(string connectstring_name)
{
  ConnectionStringSettings s =
    ConfigurationManager.ConnectionStrings[connectstring_name];
  DbProviderFactory f = DbProviderFactories.GetFactory(s.ProviderName);
  using (DbConnection conn = f.CreateConnection())
```

```
  {
    conn.ConnectionString = s.ConnectionString;
    conn.Open();

    DataTable t = conn.GetSchema("Tables");
    t.WriteXml("tables.xml");
  }
}
```

Who Needs Metadata, Anyway?

Metadata is part of every data access API. Although the primary consumers
of metadata are tools like Visual Studio 2005 or code generators like DeKlarit,
they're not the only users. Application package designers may allow end
users to customize an application by adding new tables or new columns to
existing tables. When end users change the database schema like this, a general-purpose query and modification tool can use metadata to include the
users' new tables in maintenance, backup, and other application functions
just as though they were built-in tables that shipped with the application.
Programmers can use metadata to write their own custom classes that derive
from System.Data.Common.DbCommandBuilder and build insert, update,
and delete commands for use with the DataSet. Builders of multidatabase
applications (that is, applications designed to run on the user's choice of
database) can use metadata to maintain a common codebase as much as possible, optimizing the data access code when needed.

It's better to expose the metadata through a generic metadata API than
to have each consumer use the database-specific API. That way, tool writers can maintain a more manageable codebase. Such an API must be very
flexible as well, because there are three obstacles to consider when writing
a generic API to expose metadata.

The metadata collections and information differ among databases.
Users of SQL Server might want to expose a collection of linked servers, for
example; Oracle users might be interested in information about Oracle
SEQUENCEs.

The underlying system tables in which common database metadata is
stored is different, not only in different database products, but also in different versions of the same database. SQL Server 2005, for example, exposes
its metadata using new metadata views under a sys schema, sys.tables,

whereas previous versions of SQL Server use metadata tables such as sysobjects to store the same data.

Different programs may want to expose different views of metadata. As an example, many programmers complain about long lists of tables in an Oracle database because most metadata APIs mix "system" tables with user tables. They'd like to have a short list that consists only of tables they defined.

Most database APIs approach this by providing a standard set of metadata that all providers must support and allowing provider writers to add new metadata tables. This is consistent with the approach taken by the ANSI SQL standard. The part of the standard that addresses this is the Schema Schemata (INFORMATION_SCHEMA and DEFINITION_SCHEMA), part 11. The ANSI SQL INFORMATION_SCHEMA defines a standard set of metadata views to be supported by a compliant database. But even the spec needs to have a way to address the points above. It states that "implementers are free to add additional tables to the INFORMATION_SCHEMA or additional columns to the predefined INFORMATION_SCHEMA tables."

As an example of a data access API consistent in concept with the ANSI SQL standard, OLE DB defined a series of metadata that it called "Schema Rowsets." It started with a predefined set that roughly followed the INFORMATION_SCHEMA and added OLE DB–specific columns to each one. ADO.NET 2.0 provides an even more powerful and flexible mechanism to expose metadata.

What Metadata Is Available?

ADO.NET 2.0 permits a provider writer to expose five different types of metadata. These main metadata *meta-collections* or *categories* are enumerated in the class `System.Data.Common.DbMetaDataCollectionNames`:

- MetaDataCollections—A list of metadata collections available.
- Restrictions—For each metadata collection, an array of qualifiers that can be used to restrict the scope of the schema information requested.
- DataSourceInformation—Information about the instance of the database the data provider references.

- DataTypes—A set of information about each data type the database supports.

- ReservedWords—Reserved words for that database's query language. Usually, *query language* equates to a SQL dialect.

Using `DbConnection.GetSchema`, however, these metadata categories are also considered to be metadata. What this means in terms of code is that these collections can be obtained like ordinary metadata, as shown in Listing 14-8.

LISTING 14-8 : Getting the restrictions on metadata for VIEWs

```
// gets information about database Views
Table t1 = conn.GetSchema("Views");
// gets information about collections exposed by this provider
// this includes the five "meta-collections" described above
Table t2 = conn.GetSchema(DbMetaDataCollectionNames.MetaDataCollections);
// gets information about the Restrictions meta-collection
Table t3 = conn.GetSchema(DbMetaDataCollectionNames.Restrictions);
// No argument overload is same as asking for MetaDataCollections
Table t4 = conn.GetSchema();
```

Some of the five metacollections deserve further explanation.

Restrictions can be used to limit the amount of metadata returned. If you are familiar with OLE DB or ADO, the term *restriction* means the same thing in those APIs. As an example, let's use the `MetaDataCollection` `"Columns"`—that is, the set of column names in tables. This collection can be used to get all the columns in all tables. The set of columns requested, however, can be restricted by database name, by owner/schema, or by table. Each metadata collection can have a different number of possible restrictions, and each restriction can have a default. Following along with our example, Listing 14-9 shows an XML representation of the restrictions for the `Columns` metadata.

LISTING 14-9: Restrictions on the columns collection (XML format)

```
<Restrictions>
  <CollectionName>Columns</CollectionName>
  <RestrictionName>Catalog</RestrictionName>
  <RestrictionDefault>table_catalog</RestrictionDefault>
  <RestrictionNumber>1</RestrictionNumber>
</Restrictions>
```

```
<Restrictions>
  <CollectionName>Columns</CollectionName>
  <RestrictionName>Owner</RestrictionName>
  <RestrictionDefault>table_schema</RestrictionDefault>
  <RestrictionNumber>2</RestrictionNumber>
</Restrictions>
<Restrictions>
  <CollectionName>Columns</CollectionName>
  <RestrictionName>Table</RestrictionName>
  <RestrictionDefault>table_name</RestrictionDefault>
  <RestrictionNumber>3</RestrictionNumber>
</Restrictions>
<Restrictions>
  <CollectionName>Columns</CollectionName>
  <RestrictionName>Column</RestrictionName>
  <RestrictionDefault>column_name</RestrictionDefault>
  <RestrictionNumber>4</RestrictionNumber>
</Restrictions>
```

Restrictions are specified using an overload of `DbConnection.`
`GetSchema`. The restrictions are specified as an array. You can specify an
array as large as the entire restrictions collections or a subset array, because
`RestrictionNumbers` usually progress from least restrictive to most
restrictive. Use a null value (not database NULL, but .NET Framework `null`;
Nothing in Visual Basic .NET) for restriction values you want to leave out.
Listing 14-10 shows an example of using restrictions.

LISTING 14-10: Using restrictions with GetSchema

```
// restriction string array
string[] res = new string[4];

// all columns, all tables owned by dbo
res[1] = "dbo";
DataTable t1 = conn.GetSchema("Columns", res);

// clear collection
for (int i = 0; i < 4; i++) res[i] = null;
// all columns, all tables named "authors", any owner/schema
res[2] = "authors";
DataTable t2 = conn.GetSchema("Columns", res);

// clear collection
for (int i = 0; i < 4; i++) res[i] = null;
// columns named au_lname
```

```
// all tables named "authors", any owner/schema
res[2] = "authors";  res[3] = "au_lname";
DataTable t3 = conn.GetSchema("Columns", res);

// clear collection
for (int i = 0; i < 4; i++) res[i] = null;
// columns named au_lname
// any tables, any owner/schema
res[3] = "name";
DataTable t4 = conn.GetSchema("Columns", res);
```

You need not specify the entire array of restrictions. In the case above, where you'd like to see only columns in tables owned by "dbo," you can specify an array with only two members instead of all four. Note also that specifying an empty string as a restriction is different from specifying a null (Nothing in Visual Basic .NET) value. You do not need to memorize the restrictions; you can always query for them, just as you can with any other collection. The Restrictions collection itself does not allow restrictions, but because the information is fetched into a Data Table, you can use a DataView to provide similar functionality, as shown in Listing 14-11.

LISTING 14-11: Fetching restriction metadata using GetSchema

```
DataTable tv = conn.GetSchema(DbMetaDataCollectionNames.Restrictions);
DataView v = tv.DefaultView;
// show restrictions on the "Columns" collection, sorted by number
v.RowFilter = "CollectionName = 'Columns'";
v.Sort = "RestrictionNumber";
for (int i = 0; i < tv.Count; i++)
  Console.WriteLine("{0} (default){1}",
    tv.Rows[i]["RestrictionName"],
    tv.Rows[i]["RestrictionDefault"]);
```

The DataSourceInformation collection provides information about the current instance of the database (data source) for query builders. Although this collection can contain anything the provider desires, in the Microsoft providers (SqlClient, OracleClient, OleDb, and Odbc), this collection contains similar information. Table 14-6 lists the information you get by default.

More than enough information to produce SQL for a particular database dialect, don't you think? There is just one more piece of information

TABLE 14-6: DataSourceInformation in Microsoft Providers

Value	Format/Meaning
CompositeIdentifierSeparatorPattern	Separator for multipart names (for example, the dot in pubs.dbo.authors)
DataSourceProductName	Database product name
GroupByBehavior	Enumeration, System.Data.Common. GroupByBehavior
IdentifierPattern	Regular expression string
IdentifierCase	Enumeration, System.Data.Common. IdentifierCase
OrderByColumnsInSelect	Boolean, should you ORDER BY the columns in a SELECT statement by default
ParameterMarkerFormat	Do parameter markers begin with a special character (for example, @ for T-SQL)?
ParameterMarkerPattern	Regular expression string, used to create parameters
ParameterNameMaxLength	Max length of a parameter
ParameterNamePattern	Regular expression string, used to create parameters
QuotedIdentifierPattern	Regular expression string, used to quote identifiers
QuotedIdentifierCase	Enumeration, `System.Data.Common. IdentifierCase`
StatementSeparatorPattern	Regular expression string
StringLiteralPattern	Regular expression string
SupportedJoinOperators	Enumeration, `System.Data.Common. SupportedJoinOperators`

we'd like, and that's whether the provider uses named parameters or positional parameters in parameterized queries. We mentioned named and positional parameters earlier in this chapter as two ways to write parameterized commands.

Customizing and Extending the Metadata

Now that we've seen the base metadata that is provided and can find our way around `DbConnection.GetSchema`, let's look at the ways that provider writers can customize metadata using a simple declarative format and how programmers can hook into that format. This discussion ties back to our original metadata complications: how to provide database-version-independent metadata and how to deal with the fact that different customers may want different views of the same metadata.

Provider writers can hard-code metadata logic directly into their providers, each provider-writer using a potentially different internal algorithm for obtaining similar metadata. This is the way it's been done in the past—for example, in implementing OLE DB's `ISchemaRowset` method. In ADO.NET 2.0, however, Microsoft's four shipping providers all use base classes in the `System.Data.ProviderBase` namespace, so they all implement schemas similarly. We'll use this implementation for exposition, hoping that major provider-writing players like DataDirect Technologies and other provider writers will use it too.

The base class for exposing metadata is `DbMetaDataFactory`. Each provider that implements a subclass of it uses an XML file to define its metadata fetching behavior. These files are embedded resources in `System.Data.dll` and `System.Data.OracleClient.dll`. You can look at the raw XML files by running `ildasm.exe` (the.NET Framework intermediate language utility) from the command line:

```
>ildasm.exe System.Data.dll /out:dummy.il
```

This produces the XML resource files as a side effect. The files we're looking for have names like `System.Data.SqlClient.SqlMetaData.xml`. You can safely throw away dummy.il.

Looking at the XML resource files produced from `ildasm` peels another layer off the onion. The file enumerates the collections that are supported and the information contained in each metacollection (through the schema), and appears to be the output of the `DataSet.WriteXml` method using the `DataSet.WriteXml(XmlWriteMode.WriteSchema)` overload. The most interesting bits are the `MinimumVersion/MaximumVersion` elements in all the metacollections except `DataSourceInformation` and the `Population Mechanism/PopulationString` subelements in the `MetaDataCollections` elements.

Using `MinimumVersion/MaximumVersion` allows the provider writer to specify which metadata queries to execute for different versions of the database. By using multiple elements for a single `MetaDataCollection`, you can make `GetSchema` act differently for different versions of the database. As an obvious example, you could use different versions for SQL Server 2005 than for previous versions of SQL Server. Listing 14-12 shows an example of using `MinimumVersion` from the SQL Server metadata resource `System.Data.SqlClient.SqlMetaData`.

LISTING 14-12: Metadata entry for data type XML in data types collection

```
<DataTypes>
<TypeName>xml</TypeName>
<ProviderDbType>25</ProviderDbType>
<ColumnSize>2147483647</ColumnSize>
<DataType>System.String</DataType>
<IsAutoIncrementable>false</IsAutoIncrementable>
<IsCaseSensitive>false</IsCaseSensitive>
<IsFixedLength>false</IsFixedLength>
<IsFixedPrecisionScale>false</IsFixedPrecisionScale>
<IsLong>true</IsLong>
<IsNullable>true</IsNullable>
<IsSearchable>true</IsSearchable>
<IsSearchableWithLike>false</IsSearchableWithLike>
<MinimumVersion>09.00.000.0</MinimumVersion>
<IsLiteralSupported>false</IsLiteralSupported>
</DataTypes>
```

This defines information about the SQL Server data type `XML`. The `MinimumVersion` indicates that this data type is available only when using SQL Server 2005. If you ask `SqlConnection.GetSchema` for a list of data types that the database supports, only SQL Server 2005 databases (SQL Server 2005 is actually version 9) will report that they support the `XML` data type.

For collections usually exposed by the INFORMATION_SCHEMA (such as Tables, Views, and Stored Procedures), `PopulationMechanism` and `PopulationString` cause the wheels to spin. There are three `PopulationMechanisms` used in this implementation: `DataTable`, `SQLCommand`, and `PrepareCollection`. `DataTable` is used to populate the metacollections. Using `DataTable` means that the information used to populate the collection is in the XML resource file itself. In each case, the `PopulationString` is the name of the `DataTable` produced when the XML resource file is loaded into a .NET Framework `DataSet`. `SQLCommand` means that the provider will use a `DbCommand` instance to issue the command against the database. If you look at one of the `PopulationStrings` of a collection produced by a `SQLCommand`, shown in Listing 14-13,

LISTING 14-13: Entry for databases (catalogs) in SQL Server MetaDataCollection

```
<MetaDataCollections>
    <CollectionName>Databases</CollectionName>
    <NumberOfRestrictions>1</NumberOfRestrictions>
    <NumberOfIdentifierParts>1</NumberOfIdentifierParts>
    <PopulationMechanism>SQLCommand</PopulationMechanism>
    <PopulationString>select name as database_name, dbid, crdate as
create_date from master..sysdatabases where name = {0}</PopulationString>
    </MetaDataCollections>
```

it's fairly easy to deduce that string substitution will be applied to the base query when restrictions are used in `DbConnection.GetSchema`. If no restrictions are specified, that predicate will effectively be stripped out of the query.

The provider writer can use a custom mechanism when the value of `PopulationMechanism` is `PrepareCommand`. There is a `PrepareCommand` method of `DbMetaDataFactory` that, if overridden by the provider writer, can be coded to use whatever custom semantics the provider chooses. This mechanism is used in SqlClient is to produce the `DataTypes` metacollection. The `SqlMetaDataFactory` subclass's implementation of `PrepareCommand` first reads the built-in data types supported by SQL Server from the `DataTable`, as with other metacollections, and then uses custom logic to add user-defined types to the collection if the database is SQL Server 2005. (See chapter 5 for information on UDTs.)

User Customization

In addition to the provider customization mechanism, there is a hook that allows programmers to customize schema information on a per-application basis! Before loading the embedded resource, `DbMetaDataFactory` will consult the application configuration file. Each Microsoft provider will look for an application configuration setting named after the provider itself (for example, `system.data.sqlclient`). In this setting element, you can add or remove name–value pairs. `DbMetaDataFactory` looks for a name `"MetaDataXml"`. The value corresponding to the special name is the name of a file. This is a simple filename; the file must exist in the `config` subdirectory of the location where .NET Framework is installed. This is the directory where `machine.config` and the security configuration settings files live. This file must contain the entire set of schema configuration information, not just the changes.

You can use this mechanism, for providers that support it, for many reasons. You could change the schema queries in the OracleClient provider to use the USER catalog views rather than the ALL catalog views, for example. Because the USER views don't contain information about internal database tables, the list of Tables, for example, will be much shorter and easier to work with. Another example might consist of coding out metadata XML files for all .NET Framework data providers that give you a consistent standard set of metadata—possibly one that corresponds exactly to the SQL-99 INFORMATION_SCHEMA views. This might be just right for your application.

As an example, suppose that we want to expose information about SQL Server Service Broker metadata collections in SQL Server 2005. These collections might include QUEUEs, SERVICEs, CONTRACTs, and MessageTypes. We would start with the embedded XML resource file and embellish it with information on our new collections. If the filename were SQLBrokerAware.xml, we would install the file, and our application configuration file would look like this:

```
<?xml version="1.0" encoding="utf-8" ?>
<configuration>
  <system.data.sqlclient>
    <settings>
      <add name="MetaDataXml" value="SQLBrokerAware.xml"></add>
    </settings>
  </system.data.sqlclient>
</configuration>
```

That's all there is to it. Using that setup, we could write code in which Service Broker metadata is part of the built-in metadata available to the client. The code might look for all the QUEUEs, as shown in Listing 14-14.

LISTING 14-14: Using customized metadata with GetSchema

```
using (SqlConnection conn = new SqlConnection(connstring))
{
  conn.Open();
  // this includes Service Broker metadata collections
  Table t =
conn.GetSchema(DbMetaDataCollectionNames.MetaDataCollections);
  // get all the queues in my database
  Table queues = conn.GetSchema("Queues");
}
```

Although this is a very powerful feature, it does have the capability to be abused. Remember that you'll need to distribute the metadata XML file with every application that uses it and persuade the System Administrator to install it in the config directory for you. Also remember that you'll need to maintain it with each new version of the provider that ships. Because one of the reasons for generic metadata APIs is to have consistent metadata across databases and applications, this feature should not be used gratuitously. Note that you cannot provide a custom implementation of Prepare Command at this time.

As a final remark on customization, you might have guessed that customization and resources would work differently with the bridge providers for OLE DB and ODBC. When you use these providers, a separate XML resource is provided for each OLE DB provider or ODBC driver you want to support. Microsoft built-in support includes its providers and drivers for SQL Server, Oracle, and Jet databases. If you want to specify your own providers or drivers, the name attribute used in adding/removing settings subelements would not be MetaDataXml, but instead would be [providershortname]:MetaDataXml. If you want your file to be the default for the OleDb or Odbc data provider, you can even specify a name of defaultMetaDataXml.

We'd also like to mention two other metadata extensions that are not exposed through DbConnection.GetSchema. The DbCommandBuilder includes two properties, `QuoteIdentifier` and `UnquoteIdentifier`, that permit you to customize identifiers in commands that the `CommandBuilder` builds. As an example, in SQL Server you can use double quotes (") or brackets ('[' and ']') to quote identifiers, depending on your session settings. Finally, the `DbDataReader`'s `GetSchemaTable` method is used to expose metadata about columns contained in a `DbDataReader` returned through the SQL `SELECT` statement. This metadata is similar in concept to, though not nearly as detailed as, the metadata exposed in the `DataTypes` metacollection.

Tracing Data Access

We've been missing a good generalized built-in trace facility for data access since ODBC Trace. OLE DB had many types of tracing; two that come to mind are the Visual Studio Analyzer–compatible instrumentation and ATL-TRACE (a trace macro for ATL OLE DB templates). The issue in OLE DB and MDAC was not that there was no trace, but that there were too many separate kinds of tracing, each tied to a different evaluation mechanism. It was difficult, if not impossible, to trace down into various layers of the data access stack and get one trace output.

ADO.NET 2.0 and SQL Native Client (a new OLE DB/ODBC/network library feature) contain a flexible, rich, built-in data trace facility. Microsoft has instrumented all four of its .NET Framework data providers (SqlClient, OracleClient, OleDb bridge, and Odbc bridge); the ADO.NET DataSet and friends; SQL Native Client OLE DB and ODBC provider/driver; and, to top it off, the SQL Server 2005 network libraries.

Tracepoints are already programmed into the .NET Framework and SNAC libraries. Using an IL disassembler like Reflector, you may already have noticed them. The first step is configuring things to allow you to get basic output. The basic steps for using tracing are:

1. Set up the data tracing DLL Registry entry, ETW providers, and WMI schemas.
2. Configure and run the trace itself.
3. Harvest the trace results as a comma-separated value file.

Don't worry if some of the acronyms, like ETW (Event Tracing for Windows) and WMI (Windows Management Instrumentation), are unfamiliar to you for now; we'll explain them later. Let's go over the steps one by one and then go back to a discussion of how they work.

Setting Up Data Tracing

First, you need to set up the trace DLL Registry entry. This step consists of running a Registry script or manually editing the Registry to hook up data tracing to its Event Tracing for Windows (ETW) provider. Currently, editing the Registry is the only way to accomplish this; in the future, there may be a Control Panel application or a configuration file mechanism. We'll have more to say about using this Registry key later; for now, let's just enable tracing for every data-related process on the machine:

1. Locate the Registry key HKLM\Software\Microsoft\BidInterface.
2. Add a subkey named Loader.
3. Add a new string value (under the Loader key):
   Name=":Path"Value="[Path to AdoNetDiag.dll]".

On my machine, the "Path to AdoNetDiag.dll" is `c:\Windows\ Microsoft.NET\Framework\v2.0.50727`. Also, note that the colon before Path in a Name key is significant. You can also customize this into a .reg file for future use.

Next, you must register data tracing's schema. The AdoNetDiag.dll you have just registered is a component that contains multiple ETW providers. You now need to register the ETW providers and their WMI schemas for the events that AdoNetDiag.dll exposes. You do this with a special-format schema file called a Managed Object Format (MOF) file and a utility named mofcomp. ADO.NET 2.0 provides a MOF file in the .NET Framework directory. At this writing, there is no SQL Native Client MOF file as part of the SQL Server installation. We provide one as part of the ancillary materials on the book's Web site. If you issue the command manually from the command line, it would look like this:

```
1>mofcomp adonetdiag.mof
1>mofcomp snac.mof
```

You can check that the providers are registered correctly by listing the ETW providers using the command

```
1> logman query providers
```

You should see the providers that you have registered, as well as other providers that come with the OS or other products. Note that each provider is identified by a GUID. Your provider list should look something like this:

```
Provider                          GUID
-----------------------------------------------------------------------
*System.Data.1                    {914ABDE2-171E-C600-3348-C514171DE148}
ACPI Driver Trace Provider        {dab01d4d-2d48-477d-b1c3-daad0ce6f06b}
Active Directory: Kerberos        {bba3add2-c229-4cdb-ae2b-57eb6966b0c4}
IIS: SSL Filter                   {1fbecc45-c060-4e7c-8a0e-0dbd6116181b}
IIS: WWW Server                   {3a2a4e84-4c21-4981-ae10-3fda0d9b0f83}
IIS: Active Server Pages (ASP)    {06b94d9a-b15e-456e-a4ef-37c984a2cb4b}
MSSQLSERVER Trace                 {2373A92B-1C1C-4E71-B494-5CA97F96AA19}
*MSDADIAG.ETW                     {8B98D3F2-3CC6-0B9C-6651-9649CCE5C752}
Local Security Authority (LSA)    {cc85922f-db41-11d2-9244-006008269001}
*System.Data.SNI.1                {C9996FA5-C06F-F20C-8A20-69B3BA392315}
*SQLNCLI.1                        {BA798F36-2325-EC5B-ECF8-76958A2AF9B5}
Windows Kernel Trace              {9e814aad-3204-11d2-9a82-006008a86939}
*System.Data.OracleClient.1       {DCD90923-4953-20C2-8708-01976FB15287}
*ADONETDIAG.ETW                   {8B98D3F2-3CC6-0B9C-6651-9649CCE5C752}
ASP.NET Events                    {AFF081FE-0247-4275-9C4E-021F3DC1DA35}
NTLM Security Protocol            {C92CF544-91B3-4dc0-8E11-C580339A0BF8}
IIS: WWW Isapi Extension          {a1c2040e-8840-4c31-ba11-9871031a19ea}
HTTP Service Trace                {dd5ef90a-6398-47a4-ad34-4dcecdef795f}
Spooler Trace Control             {94a984ef-f525-4bf1-be3c-ef374056a592}
```

We've changed the output a bit, adding an asterisk next to the providers that we care about. You can also check out the WMI schemas that were registered by using the WMI CIM Studio tool. You can find this tool on the MSDN Online Web site. The WMI schemas for data tracing are fairly simple; we'll talk about them later in the chapter.

Running the Trace

Running the trace consists of defining named traces and issuing ETW commands to use them using a utility named logman (log manager). The logman command looks like this:

```
@Logman start MyTrace -pf provfile -ct perf -o Out.etl -ets
```

This command file defines a single named trace instance (MyTrace) specifying all the providers that we just registered. The file provfile would contain a list of the providers that you want to trace in a special format. The contents of this file are

```
{7ACDCAC8-8947-F88A-E51A-24018F5129EF} 0x00000000  0    ADONETDIAG.ETW
{914ABDE2-171E-C600-3348-C514171DE148} 0x00000000  0    System.Data.1
{C9996FA5-C06F-F20C-8A20-69B3BA392315} 0x00000000  0    System.Data.SNI.1
{DCD90923-4953-20C2-8708-01976FB15287} 0x00000000  0
System.Data.OracleClient.1
{BA798F36-2325-EC5B-ECF8-76958A2AF9B5} 0x00000000  0    SQLNCLI.1
```

The lines include a GUID for each provider, provider options, and the provider's name (watch for line wrap). We'll say more about the provider options later.

Invoking logman in this manner writes all the events in a concise binary format to an event trace log file. These files have the extension .etl by convention. When you've turned it on, run the program that you want to trace. Turn off the trace by running the following command from the command line:

```
@Logman stop MyTrace -ets
```

You should see a file, about 150KB, named out.etl in the directory where you issued the command from. Because we've turned the trace providers on at each level of detail (ADO.NET providers, network calls, and responses from SQL Server, if it's running on the same machine), there will be a large amount of output. We'll look at ways to filter the output later. Note that bringing up Visual Studio 2005 to run the test program may generate extra trace events when, for example, Server Explorer runs data access code.

Harvest the Results As a CSV File

The out.etl file is not in a human-readable format unless you're one of those rare humans who like to read binary. ETW utilities include a basic formatter named tracerpt.exe to convert it to a comma-separated-value (CSV) file. To get the CSV file, run report.cmd, which issues the following command:

```
@TraceRPT /y Out.etl
```

This utility produces two files: summary.txt, a summary of the trace events captured in the session, and dumpfile.csv. These are the default filenames output by tracerpt; you can change them through command-line options. dumpfile.csv is the file containing the information you want. You can browse this file with Excel for now; later, you can do some further postprocessing, such as loading the data into SQL Server and querying it with SQL. Now you have your first trace. Let's have a look at the output.

Reading the Trace Output

The data tracing providers expose three major types of information: trace-point information and provider identity, event type, and thread and timing information. Specifically, the columns of information consist of:

- Event Name—The name of the data tracing event provider
- Event Type—TextW or TextA
- TID—Thread ID
- Clock-Time—Timestamp of the event
- Kernel (ms)—Number of milliseconds in kernel mode (CPU time)
- User (ms)—Number of milliseconds in user mode (CPU time)
- User Data—Detailed information about the tracepoint

Although WMI providers are permitted to expose complex schema, the data tracing providers expose only two simple event types: TextW and TextA. Many of the data tracing events are bracketing "begin" and "end" pairs, which make it easy to follow the nested API calls. TextW and TextA are used to achieve that bracketing. In the following trace, for example, the User Data field looks somewhat like this:

```
"enter_01 <comm.DbDataAdapter.Fill|API> 1#  dataSet"
"enter_02 <comm.DbDataAdapter.Fill|API> 1#  dataSet  startRecord
maxRecords  srcTable  command  behavior=16{ds.CommandBehavior}"
"<sc.SqlCommand.get_Connection|API> 1#"
"<sc.SqlCommand.get_Connection|API> 1#"
"enter_03 <sc.SqlConnection.Open|API> 1#"
"enter_04 <prov.DbConnectionBase.Open|API> 1#"
"enter_05 <SNIInitialize|API|SNI> pmo: 00000000{void}"
... many events deleted
```

```
"leave_05"
 "<sc.TdsParser.CreateSession|ADV> 1# created session 2"
 "<prov.DbConnectionFactory.CreatePooledConnection|RES|CPOOL> 1#  Pooled
database connection created."
 "leave_04"
 "leave_03"
```

It's fairly straightforward to see that the user program called `Data Adapter.Fill(DataSet)` itself called in a different overload of `Data Adapter.Fill`, which called into `SqlConnection.Open`, and so on. Each enter_nn event has a corresponding leave_nn event. In this example, you're even tracing the call into the underlying SNI (SQL Server networking interface) low-level protocol events. But what is that funny bracket format of the user data put out by the "mainstream" tracer, System.Data.1?

User Data and ADO.NET Tracing

As the name implies, the content and format of the user data field are entirely at the user's (in this case, trace provider's) discretion. Calls to `System. Data.dll` and `System.OracleClient.dll` go by a special format that can be easily decoded. Take the entry from the previous trace record sequence:

```
"enter_04 <prov.DbConnectionBase.Open|API> 1#"
```

This can be decoded to:

```
<namespace abbreviation.classname.methodname|type of call> parms
```

So the example above means that there is an API call to the `System. Data.ProviderBase,DbConnectionBase`'s `Open` method with a single parameter. The reason for using abbreviated namespaces is to keep the output smaller. The pound sign (#) after the parameter number indicates that this parameter is an object reference, with simple values or value types in the .NET Framework; the actual parameter value is shown.

Table 14-7 and Table 14-8 will help you decode the user data.

Configuring Which Applications Are Traced

Earlier, we mentioned configuring the `:Path` string value of the `Loader` Registry key. Manual configuration is needed only because data access tracing is in its infancy. Specifically, vendors that ship products built around

TABLE 14-7: Namespace Abbreviations Used in .NET Framework Tracepoints

Description	Abbreviation	Namespace
SqlClient managed provider	sc	System.Data.SqlClient
OleDb managed provider	oledb	System.Data.OleDb
Odbc managed provider	odbc	System.Data.Odbc
Oracle managed provider	ora	System.Data.OracleClient
DataSet/DataTable/Data*	ds	System.Data
Common code	comn	System.Data.Common
Provider base implementation classes	prov	System.Data.ProviderBase

data tracing should not depend on this key to be manually configurable in future releases; it will most likely be protected by an ACL (security access control list).

With that warning out of the way, configuring only the :Path value makes tracing available on all applications running on a given machine. If a programmer is running a SQL Server 2005 instance and a data access client on her machine, for example, turning on SNI tracing will trace SNI calls from both sides. That can generate some large output, although in certain use cases, this can be exactly the type of output you want. You can configure applications to be traced if there is no :Path value or to be excluded from tracing if there is a :Path value.

If there is no :Path value, only applications that are specifically configured will be traced. You can configure applications to be traceable by specifying a REG_SZ or REG_MULTISZ entry with the program name as the value name and the full path to AdoNetDiag.dll as the value. You can also configure an entire directory to be traceable by using the pathname and the * wildcard.

If there is a :Path value, you can restrict applications or applications in a specific directory from being traced by adding a REG_SZ or REG_MULTISZ entry and the value of : (single colon). Wildcards in the directory name are allowed. The name field containing the directory

TABLE 14-8: Call Types Used in .NET Framework Tracepoints

Abbreviation	Type of Call
API	Public API (method, property) is called
API|OLEDB	Code calls OLEDB component
API|ODBC	Code calls ODBC API
API|SNI	Code calls SNI
API|SYS	Code calls an OS (for example, Win32) function
ERR	Error
WARN	Warning
INFO	Information
RET	Return value, usually in the form of API|RET
THROW	A *new* exception is being thrown (not applicable to exceptions being rethrown)
CATCH	Code catches an exception
LIFETIME	Lifetime-related activity, such as AddRef/Release for COM objects
RES	Resources in general
RES|MEM	Memory allocation/free
RES|CPOOL	Connection pool activities
ADV	Advanced tracepoints

name (C:\Program Files\Microsoft SQL Server\MSSQL.1\MSSQL\Binn*) along with a : value would keep all programs in SQL Server's Binn directory (such as SQL Server, SQL Profiler, and so on) from showing up in a trace. If you're running SQL Server on the same machine as your application, this is what you want most often. Remember that configuring the Registry entries just names the data tracing provider DLL (at this point, there is only `AdoNetDiag.dll` to choose); it does not turn on the trace.

You can also configure which provider information is traced to which files and control what is traced to a certain extent. You can trace the output from all five providers to a single file or separate them into one file per provider. You do this by making up named traces using the logman utility. Here's an example that creates five traces:

```
logman create trace test1 -p System.Data.1
logman create trace test2 -p ADONETDIAG.ETW
logman create trace test3 -p System.Data.OracleClient.1
logman create trace test4 -p SQLNCLI.1
logman create trace test5 -p System.Data.SNI.1
```

In addition to using logman from the command line, you can use the graphic Microsoft Management Console snap-in, the "Snap-in for Performance Logs and Alerts," to configure, run, and stop the trace. Describing how to use the MMC snap-in is beyond the scope of this book.

You have some control over what is traced by manipulating the bits in logman's control.guid file. You need not even have a control.guid file if you use a single provider per trace and take defaults, as the previous examples show. To refresh your memory, here's a single line from control.guid:

```
{914ABDE2-171E-C600-3348-C514171DE148} 0x00000000  0    System.Data.1
```

This information in this line consists of the following:

```
Provider Guid - which ETW provider

Control Bits - 0x00000000 in this case

Control Value - 0 in this case

Provider Name - Required by ETW, but ignored by the provider internally
```

By setting bits in the "Control Bits" and "Control Value" fields, you have a macro-level mechanism for prefiltering the events. The valid values are

```
0x0002 Regular tracepoints
0x0004 Execution flow (function enter/leave)
0x0080 Advanced Output
```

There is also a bit that has special meaning to System.Data.1 only:

```
0x1000 Connection Pooling specific trace
```

The bits can be or'd together, of course. If 0x00000000 is specified, 0x00000006 is assumed. There are two possible nondefault values that can be set in the control value:

```
128 - Convert Unicode text to ASCII text (reduces etl file size)
64  - Disable tracing in this component
```

Note that setting these control bits does not provide a granular mechanism for configuring individual components; it is meant to make it easy to filter types of events without postprocessing the CSV file yourself.

Using Tracing to Debug a Parameter Binding Problem

Now that we've gone through a quick overview of tracing, we'd like to present a simple use case. We'd often use ODBC trace to do problem determination when an application would "eat" a rich error message and produce a polite but fairly information-free message. Such application code would look like Listing 14-15.

LISTING 14-15: Sample program that replaces the real error message with a polite message

```csharp
string s = GetConnectionStringFromConfigFile();
using (SqlConnection conn = new SqlConnection(s);
using (SqlCommand cmd = new SqlCommand(
  "select * from authors where au_id = @auid", conn))
{
  // the error is hardcoded here but could have come from suboptimal
  // editing in a graphic user interface
  cmd.Parameters.Add("@auid", SqlDbType.Int);
  cmd.Parameters[0].Value = 123456789;
  SqlDataReader rdr = null;
  try {
  // some code that could fail goes here
  conn.Open();
  rdr = cmd.ExecuteReader();
  while (rdr.Read())
    Console.WriteLine(rdr[0]);
  rdr.Close();
  }
  catch (Exception e) {
    MessageBox.Show("polite error message");
  }
}
```

In this case, the error was caused by a parameter type mismatch, and the person diagnosing the error might not have access to the source code of the program. Turning on the trace, we'll see output like Listing 14-16.

LISTING 14-16: Trace output used to diagnose the real error

```
"enter_01 <sc.SqlCommand.ExecuteReader|API> 1#"
 "<sc.SqlCommand.get_Connection|API> 1#"
 "<sc.SqlCommand.get_Connection|API> 1#"
 "<sc.TdsParser.CreateSession|ADV> 1# created session 3"
 "<sc.TdsParserSessionPool.CreateSession|ADV> 1# adding session 3 to
pool"
 "<sc.TdsParserSessionPool.GetSession|ADV> 1# using session 3"
 "<sc.TdsParser.GetSession|ADV> 1# getting session 3 from pool"
 "<sc.SqlCommand.ExecuteReader|INFO> 1#  Command executed as RPC."
 "<sc.SqlCommand.get_Connection|API> 1#"
 "leave_01"
 "enter_01 <sc.SqlDataReader.Read|API> 1#"
 "<sc.SqlError.SqlError|ERR> infoNumber=245  errorState=1
errorClass=16  errorMessage='Syntax error converting the varchar value
'123-45-6789' to a column of data type int.'  procedure=''  lineNumber=1"
 "leave_01"
```

Although the value in the trace doesn't match the value in our program (it comes from row 1 of the authors tables), this shows us directly that there is a parameter value mismatch. The sample and the trace file are provided in the code on the book's Web site. Note that the trace file is much more compact in this case because we're tracing only with the `System.Data.1` provider, so no network traffic trace is provided.

We've barely scratched the surface of uses for this complex and powerful feature. Some other possible uses are

- Investigating connection pooling activity
- Debugging network connection problems
- Integrating tracing into unit testing
- Performing comparative analysis of `DataSet` and `DataReader` calls to determine where `DataSet` is spending its time
- Feeding the information into a monitoring facility like MOM (Microsoft Operations Manager)

- Using data tracing in conjunction with the ASP.NET and other ETW providers
- Doing a combined data trace and SQL Server trace using SQL Server's ETW provider

Inside Data Tracing

You now have a cookbook way to set up, run, and interpret traces in the Microsoft data access stacks. But aside from issuing command-line scripts, what is going on?

Data tracing is based on a provider model itself. ADO.NET data providers and other data access code use standard APIs (which themselves use standard trace hooks) to feed trace information into the model, and in the future, multiple data trace providers may be built. Currently, only `AdoNetDiag` is available, but you could imagine data tracing consumers that would provide a prefiltering of events at a granular level or that use a different trace output system, such as `Output-DebugString` or output into SQL Server directly for ease in searching/querying. You could even hook data tracing up to the .NET Framework's `System.Diagnostics.Trace`.

Anyone can instrument his own code, but Microsoft has not yet released a data tracing provider specification to the public. Instead, ADO.NET 2.0 and SQL Native Client come with a prebuilt tracing provider using the ETW system. ETW is a high-performance tracing system that was introduced to implement kernel-level tracing for device driver writers. Following is a high-level explanation of ETW using data tracing as an example.

What Is ETW?

Event Tracing for Windows is meant to provide low-overhead tracing as compared with Windows Performance Monitor. ETW usually takes up no more than 5 percent of the CPU and can log up to 20,000 events per second. It's fast enough to enable tracing in real time. ETW uses a provider-based model; in this case, a *provider* is a system or application component that sends events to the event system. Some examples of event providers are Active Directory, IIS, and ASP.NET. The ADO.NET and SQL Native Client data traces register five ETW event providers:

```
System.Data.1 - ADO.NET providers and classes in System.Data.dll
System.Data.OracleClient - OracleClient provider in
System.OracleClient.dll
System.Data.SNI.1  - SNI from System.Data
SQLNCLI.1 - SQL Native Client providers and SNI from SQL Native Client
ADONETDIAG.ETW - provides events from the trace providers themselves
```

ETW provider logs yield a timestamp with each event. When you start the trace, you can specify a high-resolution timestamp or a low-resolution timestamp. In our traceon.cmd file, we've chosen a high-resolution timestamp using the -ct perf option. In the single-file scripts above, we've chosen the default (low-resolution) timestamp. ETW chooses high performance over ease of use. Formatting ETW traces with tracerpt.exe produces a cursory decoding. The format of the ETL file is documented, and the schemas for individual trace providers are recorded in WMI, so programmers are welcome to build their own specialized formatters. A nice feature of using ETW is that the trace that you produce can be used in conjunction with an ASP.NET trace or, for that matter, with a low-level OS kernel trace. All the events can be logged on a per-provider basis to a single file for correlation or to separate files. Information on ETW is available in the "Performance Best Practices at a Glance" whitepaper on the MSDN Web site.[2]

ETW output can be consumed by a variety of tools, and if none of the tools suits your specific needs, you can build your own. One example of such a consumer tool is logparser, which can consume not only output from ETW, but also from other outputs, such as IIS log files and Windows Event Logs. Then logparser lets you query your events using a SQL-like syntax. It is available as part of the IIS Resource Kit on MSDN.[3]

Asynchronous Support

The OLE DB specification contains an interface that providers can implement to enable asynchronously executing a command. If these operations took a long time, your program could do other work in the meantime, such

2. The current URL for the whitepaper is http://msdn.microsoft.com/ library/default.asp? url=/library/en-us/dnpag/html/scalenet-atglance.asp.
3. The IIS 6.0 Resource Kit that contains logparser is available at http://www.microsoft.com/ technet/prodtechnol/WindowsServer2003/Library/IIS/993a8a36-5761-448f-889e-9ae58d072c09.mspx.

as responding to events in the graphical user interface or showing a progress bar. Implementing these interfaces was optional, and the SQLOLEDB provider did not implement them in the protocol. With the advent of the new client network libraries, asynchronous operation can be achieved not only with SQL Server 2005, but also with SQL Server 7 and 2000. This support has been added to OLE DB, ADO, and ADO.NET; for exposition, we'll look at the ADO.NET implementation.

SqlClient uses the standard .NET Framework paradigm for asynchronous operations. In addition to the ordinary method for synchronous invocation—for example, SqlConnection.ExecuteReader—there is a pair of related methods, BeginExecuteReader and EndExecuteRead, for asynchronous invocation. BeginExecuteReader starts the operation and returns immediately to the caller. When the operation completes, you use EndExecute Reader to harvest the return code (or an error) and the results of the operation. As a reminder, every time you call any of the "Begin Execute" methods, the corresponding "EndExecute" method must be called; otherwise, memory may be leaked.

Asynchronous methods around SqlCommand.ExecuteReader, Execute XmlReader, and ExecuteNonQuery (but not ExecuteScalar) are provided. Listing 14-17 shows the equivalent code to execute a SQL UPDATE statement asynchronously and retrieve the number of rows affected by the UPDATE. To use the asynchronous methods, you must specify "Async=true" in the connection string. You should not specify this connection-string parameter if you do not use asynchronous methods, because the protocol change that implements asynchronous methods adds a little extra overhead when you use synchronous methods.

LISTING 14-17: Using asynchronous command execution

```
string connect_string = GetConnectStringFromConfigFile();
connect_string += ";Async=true";
SqlConnection conn = new SqlConnection(connect_string);
SqlCommand cmd = new SqlCommand
  ("UPDATE authors SET state='OR' WHERE state='CA'", conn);
try
{
  conn.Open();
  // Asynch command execution
  IAsyncResult ar = cmd.BeginExecuteNonQuery();
```

```
  while (!ar.IsCompleted)
  {
    Console.Write(".");
    Thread.Sleep(250);
  }

  // retrieve the results (or error) here
  int i = cmd.EndExecuteNonQuery(ar);
  Console.WriteLine("done, {0} rows affected", i);
}
catch (Exception e) {
  Console.WriteLine(e.Message);
  Console.WriteLine(e.StackTrace);
}
finally {
  cmd.Dispose();
  conn.Dispose();
}
```

Executing an asynchronous operation using `Begin` and `End` uses nonblocking overlapped I/O against the network. A thread from the .NET Framework AppDomain's thread pool is used only when the I/O completion notification is dispatched to the process and only if the user specified a callback. I/O completion handling happens in a private thread in the provider; the thread pool is used only if the user provided a callback.

A more useful paradigm than just busy-waiting in the code (which just adds complexity and thread switching to the program, slowing overall execution) is registering an event handler to be called when the operation completes. Listing 14-18 shows a simple example that illustrates using an event handler with an asynchronous command execution.

LISTING 14-18: Asynchronous execution with an event handler

```
public void UseEventHandler()
{
string connect_string = GetConnectStringFromConfigFile();
connect_string += ";Async=true";
SqlConnection conn = new SqlConnection(connect_string);

try
{
  SqlCommand cmd = new SqlCommand
  ("SELECT * FROM authors", conn);
```

```
  // Synchronous Open
  conn.Open();

  // Asynch command execution
  cmd.BeginExecuteReader(
    new AsyncCallback(GetResult,
    null,
    CommandBehavior.CloseConnection);
}
catch (Exception e) {
  Console.WriteLine(e.Message);
  Console.WriteLine(e.StackTrace);
}
finally {
  cmd.Dispose();
  conn.Dispose();
}
}

public void GetResult(IAsyncResult result)
{
  // harvest results (or error) here
  SqlDataReader rdr = result.EndExecuteReader(result);

  // use results to populate page
}
```

Bear in mind that most of the time, you use asynchronous execution to perform two or more operations at the same time. This is useful in two major scenarios. In one scenario, you might be doing multiple data gathering operations in parallel over the same connection to fill up multiple sets of controls in a graphical user interface. The other scenario consists of doing multiple long-running operations against two databases, which may be in faraway locations. In each case, you want to synchronize at a point when all operations are complete and then continue. Multiple WaitHandles (a .NET Framework synchronization primitive) can come in handy here. You start a few operations and call WaitHandle.WaitAll to wait until they all complete. Listing 14-19 shows an example that uses MARS to wait for two different resultsets on the same connection, though the multiple database code would look similar.

LISTING 14-19: Using multiple asynchronous commands and wait handles

```csharp
public void UseWaitHandles()
{
string connect_string1 = GetConnectStringFromConfigFile("server1");
connect_string1 += ";Async=true";
string connect_string2 = GetConnectStringFromConfigFile("server2");
connect_string2 += ";Async=true";
SqlConnection conn1 = new SqlConnection(connect_string1);
SqlConnection conn2 = new SqlConnection(connect_string2);

// execute these simultaneously
SqlCommand cmd1 = new SqlCommand("SELECT * FROM authors", conn1);
SqlCommand cmd2 = new SqlCommand("SELECT * FROM titles", conn2);

WaitHandle[2] handles = new WaitHandle[2];

try
{
  conn.Open();
  handles[0] = (cmd1.BeginExecuteReader()).AsyncWaitHandle;
  handles[1] = (cmd2.BeginExecuteReader()).AsyncWaitHandle;
  // wait for both commands to complete
  WaitHandle.WaitAll(handles);

  SqlDataReader rdr1 = cmd1.EndExecuteReader();
  SqlDataReader rdr2 = cmd2.EndExecuteReader();

  // process both readers
  // ...

  rdr1.Close(); rdr2.Close();
}
catch (Exception e) {
  Console.WriteLine(e.Message);
  Console.WriteLine(e.StackTrace);
}
finally {
  cmd1.Dispose(); cmd2.Dispose();
  conn1.Dispose(); conn2.Dispose();
}
}
```

You can also process multiple results when any one of the commands completes by using `WaitAny` instead of `WaitAll`. You might use this to make a graphical user interface more responsive.

Using asynchronous execution with multiple commands on the same connection, using MARS to multiplex the commands, may sound like a good idea. It isn't as nice as it sounds. The reason for this is that although you can return multiple rowsets using MARS and multiple asynchronous commands, only one command per connection is executing at the same time. So you don't get the performance advantage that you might expect, and you add unnecessary complexity to your application.

Although executing each method call asynchronously may sound like a good idea at first mention, don't use the asynchronous calls unless:

- You have an operation that you know will take a long time.
- You have something useful to do with that time.

In the first two examples, we were simply spinning and wasting processor time. As noted earlier, excessive thread switching will slow your application. In addition, be aware that when using the AppDomain's thread pool, you are almost guaranteed to get the completion (the end request) on a *different* thread from the one on which you issued the original call. Some .NET Framework classes, such as GUI controls that wrap Window Handles, are usable only on the thread that the Window Handle is stuck to. A better way to accomplish this when you're using Windows Forms is to use the `BackgroundWorker` class with a synchronous command. Information on the `BackgroundWorker` can be found in the .NET Framework 2.0 documentation.

One last scenario for asynchronous command execution is high-end ASP.NET applications, where it's easy to run out of threads in the ASP.NET thread pool; a very common cause for that is that all threads are blocked for I/O on database execution requests. A way of freeing those threads is to use asynchronous execution so that you can unwind the thread when the database command is sent, allowing ASP.NET to reuse the thread. This requires either the creation of an asynchronous request handler (.ashx page) or the use of the new asynchronous pages in ASP.NET 2.0.

Finally, remember that when you read a resultset through a `Data Reader`, SQL Server queues (and locks) a buffer's worth of data at a time on the server, waiting for you to fetch it. Waiting around before reading the results can cause excessive memory utilization and locking on the server, and can affect the throughput of your SQL Server instance. Use asynchronous operations wisely and correctly.

Bulk Import in SqlClient

There are several ways to import an array of rows into SQL Server. In SQL Server 2005, there is a .NET Framework API to SQL Server Integration Services (SSIS), the utility that replaced SQL Import/Export in SQL Server 7 and Data Transformation Services in SQL Server 2000; it provides a job scheduler and programmatic control over transformations, in addition to simple importing and exporting of data. The fastest way to import data, as long as the data to import is in a file, is to use the T-SQL BULK INSERT statement or the new BULK rowset provider, which we discuss in Chapter 7. This statement can be invoked from a .NET Framework program using the SqlCommand class and the BULK INSERT statement as command text.

Each data access API has exposed the bulk insert functionality as an extension to the base API. You can use the SQL Server BCP utility programmatically through ODBC or OLE DB. BCP is the command-line utility that has been around since the early days of SQL. It is a favorite of database administrators and programmers alike, consuming and producing text files in a variety of formats, including comma-separated values and fixed-length text. OLE DB exposed similar programmatic functionality by means of a custom interface and property set on SQLOLEDB's Session cotype implementation. The custom interface, IRowsetFastLoad, has functionality reminiscent of SQL Server's built-in BULK INSERT.

In ADO.NET 2.0, SqlClient follows ODBC, OLE DB, and DBLib, and exposes a programmatic API with IRowsetFastLoad-like functionality called SqlBulkCopy. The class can use rows from a DataTable in memory or be hooked up to a DataReader over the set of data to be inserted into the database. In the simplest case, you need only instantiate a SqlBulkCopy instance, set properties on it, and point the DataReader at it, using the WriteToServer method. Listing 14-20 shows a simple example that copies the jobs table in the SQL Server database to a nearly identically structured table named newjobs.

LISTING 14-20: Using SqlBulkCopy with a DataReader as input

```
string connect_string = GetConnectStringFromConfigFile();
SqlConnection conn = new SqlConnection(connect_string);


SqlCommand createcmd = new SqlCommand (
@"CREATE TABLE newjobs(
```

```
  job_id SMALLINT PRIMARY KEY,
  job_desc VARCHAR(30),
 min_lvl TINYINT,
 max_lvl TINYINT)",
conn);

SqlCommand cmd = new SqlCommand("SELECT * FROM jobs", conn);

conn.Open();
createcmd.ExecuteNonQuery();
SqlDataReader rdr = cmd.ExecuteReader();

// Copy the Data to SqlServer
string connect_string = GetConnectStringFromConfigFile();
SqlBulkCopy bcp = new SqlBulkCopy(connect_string);

bcp.DestinationTableName = "newjobs";
bcp.WriteToServer(rdr);
```

Importing rows is rarely that simple, however. You usually need to map fields in the source data to equivalent fields in the target table, perhaps doing some data type coercion along the way. SqlBulkCopyColumnMapping and its associated collection class, SqlBulkCopyColumnMappingCollection, are the classes you use to map source to target, as shown in Listing 14-21.

LISTING 14-21: Using SqlBulkCopy with ColumnMappings

```
// Retrieve data from the source server.

string src_connect_string = GetConnectStringFromConfigFile("src");
SqlConnection src = new SqlConnection(src_connect_string);
src.Open();
SqlCommand cmd = new SqlCommand("SELECT * FROM orders", src);
IDataReader srcrdr = cmd.ExecuteReader();

// Connect to target server.
string dest_connect_string = GetConnectStringFromConfigFile("dest");
SqlConnection dest = new SqlConnection(dest_connect_string);
dest.Open();

// open a bulk copy using the destination connection
SqlBulkCopy bcp = new SqlBulkCopy(dest);
{
    bcp.DestinationTableName = "order_history";

    // map the columns
    bcp.ColumnMappings.Add("orderid", "order_hist_id");
    bcp.ColumnMappings.Add("description", "order_hist_desc");
    bcp.ColumnMappings.Add("date", "order_hist_date");
```

```
    bcp.WriteToServer(srcrdr);
}
bcp.Close();
dest.Dispose();
srcrdr.Close();
cmd.Dispose(); src.Dispose();
```

In addition to these simple examples that use `IDataReader`, `SqlBulk-Copy` can use a `System.Data.DataTable` or an array of `DataRows` as input. `SqlBulkCopy` exposes properties that will look familiar to anyone who has used the BCP utility. `SqlBulkCopy` actually uses direct TDS calls to write to the destination. This shows up in SQL Profiler as a command called `"INSERT BULK"` regardless of the version of SQL Server used. This is because `Sql-BulkCopy` is using the same TDS protocol commands that BCP uses. Nevertheless, it may be useful to compare its options with the options of SQL Server's `BULK INSERT` command. A list of the properties and their equivalents in `BULK INSERT` is shown in Table 14-9. As an example of its usefulness,

TABLE 14-9: SqlBulkCopy and BCP Equivalents

SqlBulkCopy	BCP Option
`ColumnMappings collection`	FORMATFILE
`BatchSize`	BATCHSIZE
`BulkCopyTimeout`	No equivalent
`NotifyAfter`	No equivalent
`SqlRowsCopied event`	No equivalent
`SqlBulkCopyOptions.CheckConstraints`	CHECK_CONSTRAINTS
`SqlBulkCopyOptions.Default`	N/A
`SqlBulkCopyOptions.FireTriggers`	FIRE_TRIGGERS
`SqlBulkCopyOptions.KeepIdentity`	KEEPIDENTITY
`SqlBulkCopyOptions.KeepNulls`	KEEPNULLS
`SqlBulkCopyOptions.TableLock`	TABLOCK
`SqlBulkCopyOptions.UseInternalTransaction`	N/A

one high-performance way of importing a large number of rows is to implement a custom `IDataReader` and have `SqlBulkCopy` pull rows and push them into the server.

Client Statistics

The SQL Server ODBC driver enabled collection and reading of statistics on a per-connection basis via API calls. This has been added to the .NET Framework 2.0 version of SqlClient. This functionality exists mostly to enable client-side statistics display in SQL Server Management Studio, which is an ADO.NET application that, among other things, replaces Query Analyzer, an ODBC application. You can also use it in your own program to provide execution-time diagnostics.

Because collection of statistics adds overhead, statistics must be enabled on a per-connection basis. You enable statistics on a `SqlConnection` by setting its `StatisticsEnabled` property. In addition, the `SqlConnection` exposes methods to retrieve and reset statistics. Listing 14-22 is a simple example of statistics gathering, followed by the output statistics that are gathered (shown in Listing 14-23). Using the client statistics API should make profiling client-side data access much simpler.

LISTING 14-22: Statistics output from the previous program

```
static void Main(string[] args)
{
string connect_string = GetConnectStringFromConfigFile();
SqlConnection conn = new SqlConnection(connect_string);
conn.Open();

// Enable
conn.StatisticsEnabled = true;

// do some operations
//
SqlCommand cmd = new SqlCommand("select * from authors", conn);
SqlDataReader rdr = cmd.ExecuteReader();

Hashtable stats = (Hashtable)conn.RetrieveStatistics();

// process stats
IDictionaryEnumerator e = stats.GetEnumerator();
```

```
while (e.MoveNext())
    Console.WriteLine("{0} : {1}", e.Key, e.Value);

conn.ResetStatistics();

}
```

LISTING 14-23: Statistics output from the previous program

```
BytesReceived : 2207
SumResultSets : 0
ExecutionTime : 138
Transactions : 0
BuffersReceived : 1
CursorFetchTime : 0
IduRows : 0
CursorOpens : 0
PreparedExecs : 0
BytesSent : 72
SelectCount : 0
ServerRoundtrips : 1
CursorUsed : 0
CursorFetchCount : 0
ConnectionTime : 149
Prepares : 0
SelectRows : 0
UnpreparedExecs : 1
NetworkServerTime : 79
BuffersSent : 1
IduCount : 0
```

.NET Framework DataSet and SqlDataAdapter Enhancements

The easiest way to get a set of data from SQL Server back to the client that supports client-side updates and to flush updates back to the database is to use the ADO.NET `DataSet`. The `SqlDataAdapter` class consists of four `SqlCommand` instances: one each to SELECT, INSERT, UPDATE, and DELETE rows from SQL Server. `SqlDataAdapter.Fill` uses the `SqlData Adapter`'s `Select Command` to move rows from SQL Server to the `DataSet`. The data can be changed offline. The `DataSet.SqlData Adapter. Update` method uses the `InsertCommand`, `UpdateCommand`, and `Delete Command` `SqlCommand` instances to push updated data back to the database.

Insert/Update/ DeleteCommand can have a CommandText property that
refers to textual parameterized update commands or stored procedures.
Figure 14-1 shows a diagram of the SqlDataAdapter class. Listing 14-24
shows a short sample of code updating through a DataAdapter and a
DataSet. For more information on the DataAdapter, see Chapter 5 of
Essential ADO.NET, by Bob Beauchemin (Addison-Wesley, 2002).

LISTING 14-24: Updating through a SqlDataAdapter and DataSet

```
// Instantiate a SqlDataAdapter
string connect_string = GetConnectStringFromConfigFile();

SqlDataAdapter da = new SqlDataAdapter(
  "select * from authors", connect_string);

// command builder for default update commands
SqlCommandBuilder bld = new SqlCommandBuilder(da);
DataSet ds = new DataSet();
da.Fill(ds, "authors");

// update the fifth row, third column
ds.Tables[0].Rows[4][2] = "Bob";
// use the default update commands
da.Update(ds, "authors");
```

This is an example of a generalized update pattern involving Sql-
DataAdapter, DataSet, and SqlCommandBuilder. Note that in .NET

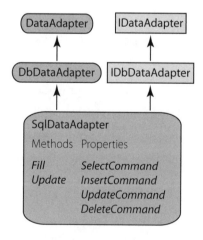

**FIGURE 14-1: Layout of the
SqlDataAdapter**

Framework 2.0, `SqlCommandBuilder` does not support generating commands that involve UDT or XML data type columns. UDT data type columns are not supported by Visual Studio 2005's strongly typed `DataSet` generation, either.

The `DataSet` is a disconnected cache. It consists of `DataTables` that contain `DataRows` and `DataColumns`, with semantics that mimic a relational database. `DataTables`, `DataRows`, and `DataColumns` are built over the .NET Framework `ArrayList` type; `ArrayList` is a .NET Framework collection class that implements a dynamic array. Rows can be selected in a `DataTable` using a SQL-like syntax known as data expression language. The `DataSet` can be marshaled as XML for use in Web Service scenarios. In ADO.NET 2.0, the `DataSet` can also be marshaled in a more compact binary format.

In ADO.NET 1.0 and 1.1, `DataColumns` in the `DataSet` were limited to a discreet set of .NET Framework types corresponding to the primitive types in a relational database. ADO.NET 2.0 extended this support to include the `SqlTypes` data types, including those added for SQL Server 2005. Figure 14-2 shows a list of the data types supported in version 2.0 of the `DataSet`.

Moving data from a database to the `DataSet` generally meant mapping a database data type to the closest-fit .NET Framework data type, mostly in the case of mapping SQL Server's DECIMAL type to .NET Framework's

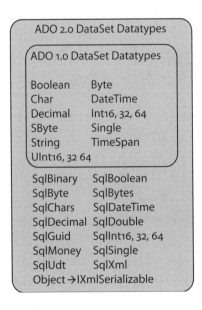

FIGURE 14-2: Supported types in the ADO.NET DataSet

`System.Decimal`. Although SQL Server's `DECIMAL` type can contain up to 38 digits of precision, .NET Framework's `System.Decimal` can hold only 28. In addition, supporting any other type (such as a SQL Server 2005 UDT) inside a `DataSet` did not throw an error and mostly worked but had some shortcomings:

- When the `DataSet` was serialized to `XML`, and the `DataColumn`'s type was not in the supported list, serialization was accomplished by calling `ToString()` on the type. Most types' `ToString()` method did not render the object as `XML`.
- There was no obvious corollary to `ToString()` to deserialize the `XML` on the other side. The `Parse` method is not required, so the `DataSet` couldn't rely on its being implemented by every class.
- Data expression language did not support column types other than the primitive, supported types.

These behaviors are described in detail in Chapters 6 and 7 of *Essential ADO.NET*.

In the SQL Server 2005 version of ADO.NET, this would present major problems for users of the `DataSet`. The data types that would cause problems would be UDTs and the `XML` data type.

The user-defined types would tend to be the most problematic, because a single `DataColumn` could contain multiple attributes (properties). Some new functionality in the `DataSet` takes care of this problem. The problem with the new non-UDT data types is resolved by support of new types in `System.Data.SqlTypes` and support of the SqlTypes family of classes in the `DataSet`. In addition, all the classes and structures that represent SQL Server data types in `System.Data.SqlTypes` are serializable. This means that they can be used in .NET Framework remoting scenarios or other places where `System.Runtime.Serialization` is used.

As mentioned earlier in this chapter, types other than the discrete set of types supported by the `DataSet` could always be pushed into a `DataSet`. There were a few problems with usability, however; most have been solved in ADO.NET 2.0. User-defined types are automatically serialized separately using `System.Xml.Serialization` rather than calling `ToString`. That obviates the necessity of implementing an `XML`-emitting `ToString()`

method and a constructor that takes a single `String` as an argument. In addition, the interface `System.Xml.Serialization.IXmlSerializable` has been surfaced (in .NET Framework 1.1, it was documented as "internal use only") as the way to implement custom serialization of an arbitrary class. `System.Data.SqlTypes.SqlDateTime` is one example of a class that implements `IXmlSerializable`. When the `DataSet` serializes itself into XML, if the classes contained in the underlying column implement `IXmlSerializable`, this implementation will be called.

One final piece of client-side disconnected model support needs to be mentioned. Although the `DataSet` supported (somewhat) `SqlTypes` as column values—and this would be helpful for the SQL DECIMAL value, for example—very few programmers used `SqlTypes` inside even a local `DataSet`, because there was no way to tell the `SqlDataAdapter` to use `SqlTypes` rather than .NET Framework basic types when `Fill` is called to fill the `DataSet`. In the new version of `SqlDataAdapter`, you can use the `ReturnProviderSpecificTypes` property to accomplish this. .NET Framework types inside the `DataSet` are still the default. In addition, a simplified but more ADO `Recordset`–like `DataSet`, the `SqlDbTable` class (this is not specific to SqlClient; all providers can implement a class that derives from `System.Data.DbTable`) can use strong types as well.

Finally, ADO.NET 2.0 contains changes to the `DataSet`'s updating semantics. In previous versions of ADO.NET, when the `DataSet` pushed a set of changed rows back to the database, it issued one update statement across the network at a time. In ADO.NET 2.0, SqlClient can batch multiple updates in a single network round trip by specifying `UpdateBatchSize` on the `SqlDataAdapter`. To support better a wide variety of optimistic concurrency scenarios, the `SqlCommandBuilder` now supports a variety of updated command generation options, and you specify them by using the `ConflictOption` property of the `DbCommandBuilder`. Your choices are now roughly equivalent to those in ADO classic. The conflict options are

- `CompareAllSearchableValues`—Generate a SQL UPDATE or DELETE statement with a WHERE clause that includes all columns in the query.
- `OverwriteChanges`—Generate a SQL UPDATE or DELETE statement with a WHERE clause that includes only the key.

- `CompareRowVersion`—Generate a SQL UPDATE or DELETE statement with a WHERE clause that includes only the TIMESTAMP column. The table must have a TIMESTAMP column if you choose this option.

See Chapter 5 of *Essential ADO.NET* for more information and a programmatic implementation for ADO.NET 1.0.

There are many more changes to the `DataSet` and related classes in ADO.NET 2.0, but a complete discussion of them is outside the scope of this book.

Where Are We?

In this chapter and in Chapter 13, we've covered many new features of the SQL Server client libraries. Some of the features are enabled by new server functionality and are available only when using SQL Server 2005 as the server. Table 14-10 shows where these features are available.

TABLE 14-10: SQL Server Version and Feature Availability

	SQL Server 7	SQL Server 2000	SQL Server 2005
`SqlClient`	X	X	X
MARS			X
`SqlNotificationRequest`			X
`SqlDependency`			X
`IsolationLevel.Snapshot`			X
Asynchronous commands	X	X	X
Bulk import	X	X	X
Password update			X
Statistics	X	X	X
Tracing	X	X	X

Support of the new data types, MARS, `SqlNotifications`, and SNAPSHOT isolation, depends on SQL Server 2005. Some features also depend on the new SQL client network library. Asynchronous invocation is an example of a network library–dependent feature that works against any version of SQL Server (7 and later). The network library enhancements are built into the .NET Framework 2.0 SqlClient provider, however. The rest of the features are enhancements to the ADO.NET API, including a tracing facility that is still in development at this writing. We covered the ones that are SQL Server–specific, including `SqlNotificationRequest` and `SqlDependency`, and the use of `System.Data.SqlTypes` inside the `DataSet`. Other data provider vendors, such as DataDirect Technologies, IBM, and Oracle Corporation, are also enhancing or have already enhanced their data providers to support the new features.

■ 15 ■
SQL Server Management Objects

Introduction

SQL Server Management Objects, known as SMO, is an object model for SQL Server and its configuration settings. SMO-based applications use .NET Framework languages to program against this in-memory object model rather than sending Transact-SQL (T-SQL) commands to SQL Server to do so. SMO makes it very straightforward to create applications that manage SQL Server because it encapsulates specific knowledge of each version of SQL Server and T-SQL in its object model.

SMO also provides some capabilities for managing other SQL Server applications, such as Analysis Services, Notification Services, and Reporting Services, but this chapter focuses on SQL Server itself—that is, the database engine, and specifically classes in the `Microsoft.SqlServer.Management.SMO` namespace, though this namespace covers only a portion of the capabilities of SMO.

In this chapter, a reference to SQL Server may mean an instance of the SQL Server database engine (sqlserver.exe) running as a service or the SQL Server product itself; context will differentiate the usage. "Use a SQL Server," for example, means to use an instance of sqlserver.exe loaded as a service.

SMO supports SQL Server 2000 and SQL Server 2005. A SMO-based application requires .NET Framework 2.0 on the machine running the SMO application. SMO is part client tool for SQL Server 2005 and part of the Feature Pack for Microsoft SQL Server 2005. It can be downloaded as a redistributable from http://www.msdn.com/sql. Browse to Downloads, Tools and Utilities page, and look for the SQL Server 2005 Feature Pack.

SMO views a machine that hosts SQL Server separately from SQL Server itself. A machine is represented by an instance of the `ManagedComputer` class, and a SQL Server is represented by an instance of the `Server` class. In this respect, SMO has two independent object models: one for a machine hosting some SQL Server applications and another for SQL Server. Figure 15-1 shows a `ManagedComputer` that hosts the various services we expect from SQL Server 2005: SQL Server itself, full-text search, and so on. A `Server`, on the other hand, represents a database engine that contains, among other things, databases.

ManagedComputer—that is, `Microsoft.SqlServer.Management.Smo.Wmi.ManagedComputer`—is used to manage the configuration of a machine with respect to the services provided by SQL Server. It can be used, for example, to enable or disable a SQL Server instance or to change its network configuration. SQL Server Configuration Manager, provided as part of the client tools for SQL Server, uses `ManagedComputer`, for example, to enable database engines and manage network configuration.

Server—that is, `Microsoft.SqlServer.Management.SMO.Server`—is used to manage an instance of SQL Server itself, a database engine. SMO looks at SQL Server as a collection of objects; each database, table, login, and so on is looked at as an object. SMO-based .NET Framework 2.0 applications program against these objects to add or remove databases, logins, tables, and so on.

The `ManagedComputer` object model is independent of the `Server` object model. The `ManagedComputer` object model cannot be used to obtain

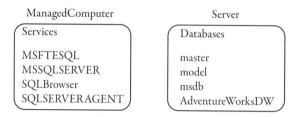

FIGURE 15-1: ManagedComputer and Server

a reference to an object in the Server object model and vice versa. Several other object models supported by SMO, such as a `Restore` object module, can be used to restore databases, `Backup` object model, and so on. This chapter will start by looking at the `Server` object model and later will look at the `ManagedComputer` object model.

Sqlservr.exe is the SQL Server application, and it runs as a Windows service. It is possible to run more than one copy of Sqlserver.exe, in which case each service has a different name. In any case, each copy is seen by SMO as a Server object. A SQL Server service may contain a number of databases, which in turn may contain multiple tables, and so on. Typically, the name of the service is the same as the name of the machine on which it is running. Figure 15-2 is a pictorial representation of an instance of SQL Server and its corresponding SMO object model in a client application.

The left side of Figure 15-2 shows a SQL Server (1) named Mfg_Svr, which contains a database (2) named Audit, which in turn contains a table (3) named Drops.

On the right side of Figure 15-2 is a code fragment of an application that is using SMO to manage SQL Server. The `Mfg_Svr Server` object (1) in the client application represents the instance of SQL Server. Note that the name of the server it represents, "Mfg_Svr," is the parameter that is passed into the `Server` constructor. The `Audit` object (2) represents the database named Audit, and the `Drops` object (3) represents the table named Drops. Each of these is accessed by its name in a corresponding collection of objects.

SMO can be used to write custom applications that manage SQL Server in any .NET Framework language and manage SQL Server directly through

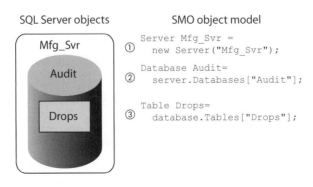

FIGURE 15-2: SMO object model

connections to SQL Server or to generate SQL scripts that can be applied to SQL Server at a later time. SQL Server Management Studio is an example of an application that uses SMO in its implementation. Another example is Visual Studio 2005, which uses SMO to implement its Server Explorer and database projects.

Why Use SMO?

SMO has no special access to SQL Server. A T-SQL script or an application written using ADO.NET, ODBC, or OLE DB can do any management operation that SMO can do. So why use SMO?

One of the compelling features of SMO is that all the tools and techniques used to develop .NET Framework applications work for SMO; after all, it is just a set of class definitions in some assemblies, just like any other library for .NET Framework. The application shown in Figure 15-2 refers to the instance of SQL Server by the symbolic name Mfg_Svr and accesses the Audit database by referring to the Audit object, the Drops table by referring to the Drops object, and so on. A SMO-based application can easily work with any database object in the same way that it works with any other object in the application.

A SMO-based application could be a custom GUI application that manages the access rights of employees in a corporate database. SMO is sometimes thought of as a DBA technology because it can be used to automate the administrative tasks done by DBAs. SMO, however, is useful for client-side and middle-tier application developers, too. Most of these applications need, or can be enhanced by the addition of, management features that can be used by non-DBAs, and using SMO is a straightforward way to do this.

An example would be a third-party application that managed maintenance data for machinery in a factory. An application like this might need the ability to add a new table to the database when a new kind of equipment is put into service. The maintenance personnel would define the attributes of a new kind of equipment in a dialog box that would use SMO to create a table for it.

The developer of this application could just use ADO.NET and T-SQL to add this kind of capability, but that would require, in general, knowledge of T-SQL, server configuration details, or even hundreds of system stored procedures in SQL Server. SMO encapsulates all that knowledge into its object model.

Figure 15-3 shows the C# code for a program to list databases in SQL Server on the console using ADO.NET.

The example in Figure 15-3 implements a simple task but does have a fair amount of ADO.NET overhead code just to get the names of the databases in an instance of SQL Server. The only parts that are really doing any work are the `SqlCommand` (1) and the `WriteLine` (2); the rest is just boilerplate. To construct `SqlCommand`, you need the specific knowledge that database names can be found in the sys.databases view, as well as the syntax and semantics of the T-SQL language; IntelliSense will give no hints on how to write a T-SQL query or on what tables and views are available to you.

Note that this program has a bug in it; it will not work if executed against an instance of SQL Server 2000. There is no sys.databases in this implementation of SQL Server. In general, programs like this need additional code to detect the version of SQL Server and then apply specific knowledge of those versions to the T-SQL code they contain.

```
static void Main(string[] args)
{
    SqlConnectionStringBuilder sb =
      new SqlConnectionStringBuilder();
    sb.DataSource = args[0];
    sb.IntegratedSecurity = true;
    SqlConnection conn =
    new SqlConnection(sb.ConnectionString);
    conn.Open();
①  SqlCommand cmd = new SqlCommand(
      @"SELECT database.name AS [Name] FROM
      master.sys.databases AS database
      ORDER BY [Name] ASC",conn);
    conn.Open();
    SqlDataReader rdr = cmd.ExecuteReader();
    while(rdr.Read())
    {
②      Console.WriteLine(rdr[0]);
    }
}
```

FIGURE 15-3: Listing databases with ADO.NET

Figure 15-4 shows the results of running the ADO.NET program that lists databases in SQL Server. The name of the SQL Server (1) is passed to the program on the command line; then the list (2) of databases found is sent to the console.

Figure 15-5 shows a program based on SMO that will produce the same results as the program in Figure 15-3.

Notice that the SMO program is much smaller and that the `foreach` (1) and `WriteLine` (2) make up almost the entire program. Everything is done using only techniques familiar to .NET Framework programmers. IntelliSense works for any of the classes in .NET Framework, so you always get a reminder of what the actual names of things are. In addition, this program will work when run against SQL Server 2000 or SQL Server 2005.

SMO can also be used in the upcoming Microsoft Command Shell, called Monad. Figure 15-6 shows a Monad interactive script that is the equivalent of the programs shown in Figure 15-3 and Figure 15-5. It starts by initializing the $server variable (1) with a SMO server object. Then it iterates (2) through all the databases in the server and prints out their names (3). Note that at this writing, Monad was available only as a beta; Microsoft had not announced anything about its specific availability. Search for "Monad" on http://www.msdn.com for more information about Monad.

Monad has its own kind of IntelliSense, as shown in Figure 15-7. The `get-member` cmdlet can display the members of any object. *cmdlets* are what Monad calls commands.

All the information that SMO provides is in the form of properties on objects, and all the functionality is accessed by methods on objects. This makes it fit in nicely with the languages used in .NET Framework.

Contrast the second two programs with the ADO.NET program in Figure 15-3. For ADO.NET, you need to know the T-SQL language and pretty much have in your head all the names of the database objects and stored procedures for each version of SQL Server to use ADO.NET. Things like Books Online, SQL Server Management Studio, and Enterprise Manager help in looking up names, syntax, and metadata, but they really don't integrate directly with the client/middle-tier language tools as SMO does.

Wow! IntelliSense, just one language to learn, and a familiar programming infrastructure at your service . . . why would anyone use ADO.NET?

FIGURE 15-4: Running ADOList
program

ADO vs. SMO

One of the classic problems of using an object model to represent a database is that the object model in memory is often much larger than the information you are trying to manage by using it. The ADO.NET program in Figure 15-3 brought back only the names of the databases, and it streamed them back at that, so at any instant, there really were only a couple of names in memory, not necessarily all of them. All things being equal, an ADO.NET program probably takes less space at runtime than a SMO program and likely runs faster.

In Figure 15-5, the line of code `Server = new Server(arg[0])` made an object that represented an entire SQL Server instance. The line of code `foreach(Database in server ...` made an object that represents a whole database. How big do you think these objects are?

The tradeoff is not quite as stark as it might seem, however. SMO is very aware of space problems that an object model in application memory can cause and makes sure that SMO minimizes its impact on the application that uses it and on SQL Server.

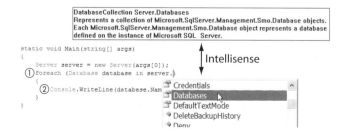

FIGURE 15-5: SMO program to list databases

```
Microsoft Command Shell (2)
MSH C:\temp> $SMO = "Microsoft.SqlServer.Management.Smo."
MSH C:\temp> $server = new-object ($SMO + 'server') ①
MSH C:\temp> foreach($database in $server.databases) { $database.name }
AdventureWorksDW      ②
master
model
msdb
Northwind  ③
pubs
Repairs
Scratch
tempdb
MSH C:\temp> _
```

FIGURE 15-6: Monad script to list databases

SMO has many features, such as partially loading object properties until needed, caching references to database objects rather than the objects themselves, and batching sequences of commands so that they can be done in a single round trip. All this can be controlled by the program that is using SMO.

By default, SMO will defer loading some information until you go to use it, but you can load all the properties for an object at the same time instead of doing a lazy load, if you want. Almost all this is completely transparent to the program using SMO. SMO is not your father's object model.

But in the end, ADO.NET can do anything that SMO can do, and a well-thought-out, purpose-built, and possibly rather complicated T-SQL batch executed via ADO.NET can almost always outperform the corresponding SMO operation. ADO.NET versus SMO is an application/database impact versus development/maintenance time tradeoff. An ADO.NET application will usually require more time and effort to develop and maintain than a corresponding SMO application, but it will have less negative impact on the application and database.

This is why SMO is used to create applications that manage SQL Server. These kinds of applications are not going to be used by hundreds, or thousands, or more users at the same time to do OLTP operations, so their

```
Microsoft Command Shell
MSH C:\temp> $server | get-member

      TypeName: Microsoft.SqlServer.Management.Smo.Server

Name                  MemberType Definition
----                  ---------- ----------
Alter                 Method     System.Void Alter()
AttachDatabase        Method     System.Void AttachDatabase(String
CompareUrn            Method     System.Int32 CompareUrn(Urn urn1,
DeleteBackupHistory   Method     System.Void DeleteBackupHistory(Da
Deny                  Method     System.Void Deny(ServerPermissionS
```

FIGURE 15-7: Monad IntelliSense

impact on the application itself or the database is not as important as the time it takes to develop and maintain them. The extra effort required to develop an ADO.NET solution is well worth it for updating an account in the general ledger by a typical OLTP application, but it really buys nothing for a typical management application.

SMO excels at applications that manage SQL Server. Unlike ADO.NET, it is not a general-purpose data access solution. It can be used only with SQL Server; it will not work with other databases, let alone other kinds of data stores. ADO.NET excels at applications that will be used by hundreds or thousands of users, or more, to store and retrieve data from SQL Server or other kinds of databases and data stores.

Object Model

SMO provides a rich object model that includes both SQL Server 2000 and SQL Server 2005. The object model for SQL Server contains many types of objects and includes a hierarchy composed principally of two kinds of objects: `SqlSmoObject` and `SmoCollectionBase` objects, with a single `Server` object, which is a `SqlSmoObject`, at its root. This hierarchy covers most of the objects developers are typically interested in, such as databases and tables.

Each object in the hierarchy has several properties, each of which describes something about the object or holds a reference to another `SqlSmoObject` or `SmoCollectionBase` object that extends the hierarchy further. Figure 15-8 diagrams a small part of the SMO hierarchy for a SQL Server.

The `Server` object in the middle of Figure 15-8 is a `SqlSmoObject` and shows three of its many properties: `Information`, `Databases`, and `State`.

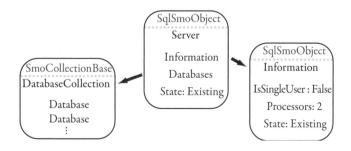

FIGURE 15-8: Basic SMO hierarchy

The root of the SMO object of the hierarchy we will be looking at is always a `Server` object. The `State` property describes something about the `Server` object itself—namely, whether it represents an existing instance of SQL Server. The `Information` and `Databases` properties refer to other objects that extend the hierarchy.

The Information object on the right side of Figure 15-8 is a SqlSmoObject and contains some properties that further describe the SQL Server instance.

The `DatabaseCollection` object on the left side of Figure 15-8 is a `SmoCollectionBaset`. It contains a collection of Database objects that represent the databases in the Server. Each `Database` object is itself a SqlSmoObject that further extends the hierarchy, and so on.

A full object model for even a small SQL Server is very large, easily containing hundreds or even thousands of objects. It is not possible to put such a diagram in this chapter or even on a good-sized wall, for that matter! An example program, with source, available from the Web site for this book, can be used to explore a SMO object model to get a better feeling for its composition.

Figure 15-9 shows the dialog box displayed by an example program, SMO Object Model Explorer program. It displays the object model in the form of a tree. Each branch of the tree is an object in the hierarchy. The

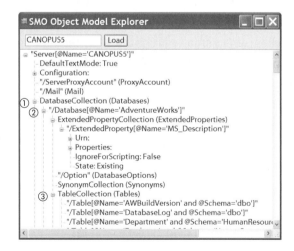

FIGURE 15-9: SMO object explorer

DatabaseCollection (1), for example, contains Database (2) objects, which in turn contain a TableCollection (3), and so on. Double-clicking a branch fills out its children, if it has any.

One of the differences between a SqlSmoObject and a SmoCollectionBase object is that a SqlSmoObject object has an Urn property, and a SmoCollectionBase object does not. The Urn object will be covered in detail later, but the Urn for a SqlSmoObject object uniquely identifies that object in SQL Server. The Urn can be used to access that object directly without drilling through the SMO hierarchy.

In the SMO Object Explorer, a SqlSmoObject object always has a quoted string displayed in its tree element. This string is the last part of the Urn for the object. The "/Database[@Name='AdventureWorks']" (2) in Figure 15-9 is an example of this. The ToolTip for an SqlSmoObject shows the full Urn value. Figure 15-10 shows the ToolTip for a Database in the DatabaseCollection of a Server.

We will take a short look at the SMO Object Explorer program, which uses several programming techniques used by SMO applications. It works by recursively using reflection to drill though the properties of an object, starting with the Server object. When it finds a property that is a subclass of a SqlSmoObject or SmoCollectionBase, or a few other selected types, it adds it to a tree control. A fragment of the code used to do this is shown in Figure 15-11.

First, to drill into the object hierarchy, the variable type (1) is set to the type of the current object. Each property (2) of the type is inspected (3) to see whether it derives from a SqlSmoObject or SmoCollectionBase object. If so, it is added to the tree (4). See the source for the SMO Object Explorer for a complete code listing.

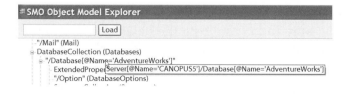

FIGURE 15-10: ToolTip for SqlSmoObject

```
①Type type = @object.GetType();
②foreach (PropertyInfo pi in type.GetProperties())
  {
    Type propertyType = pi.PropertyType;
    if (propertyType.IsSubclassOf(
        typeof(SqlSmoObject))
  ③ || propertyType.IsSubclassOf(
        typeof(SmoCollectionBase)))
  {
    Object propObject =
      pi.GetValue(this.@object, new object[] { });
    if (propObject != null)
    {
  ④   tn.Nodes.Add(MakeSmoNode(propObject, pi.Name));
  } } } }
```

FIGURE 15-11: Code for SMO object explorer

This chapter will not cover all the specific kinds of objects in the SMO object model. The core of the SMO object model is built around `SqlSmoObject` and `SmoCollectionBase` objects, as we have just seen. Use the SMO Object Explorer to drill into an instance of SQL Server to get a feeling for the richness of the SMO object model.

SMO Projects

SMO can be used in any kind of .NET Framework 2.0 application except for a SQL Server 2005 CLR application—that is, CLR code written to be run inside SQL Server 2005, though it is possible that this capability may be added in the future.

Several assemblies contain SMO classes, but applications that work with common database objects, such as databases and tables, will use the `Microsoft.SqlServer.Smo`, `Microsoft.SqlServer.Smo.Enum`, and `Microsoft.SqlServer.ConnectionInfo` assemblies. This section covers using Visual Studio 2005 to build a C# GUI application that is based on SMO.

To get things started and see the basics of how SMO is used, let's build a simple GUI application that lists the databases in an instance of SQL Server. Most of this section is about building a SMO-based GUI application using Visual Studio 2005. This application is a GUI version of the console applications shown in Figure 15-3, Figure 15-5, and Figure 15-6. This example goes through the steps of using Visual Studio 2005 to build a simple, SMO-based GUI application.

The UI for the application is shown in Figure 15-12. The application is called Database Lister, and the source code for it is available from http://www.pluralsight.com\dan\SQL2005Dev.htm.

To use the Database Lister application, you enter the name of an instance of SQL Server in the edit box (1) below the Instance Name label. When you click the List Databases button (2), the list box (3) below it shows the databases in the instance.

In this example, we are going to gloss over login issues to keep things focused on the SMO object model. Note that this application will log in to SQL Server 2005 with the credentials of the user running the applications. Later, we will discuss ways of controlling the identity used to log in to SQL Server 2005.

The Database Lister application is a Windows GUI app. We can create it easily by making a Visual Studio 2005 Windows project. This example is implemented in C#, but you could use any language supported by .NET Framework. The first thing that you do is use Visual Studio 2005 to start a Windows Project by opening Visual Studio, choosing File > New, and clicking Project (1), as shown in Figure 15-13.

Visual Studio 2005 will present a New Project dialog box, as shown in Figure 15-14, after you click Project. In this dialog box, you must name the

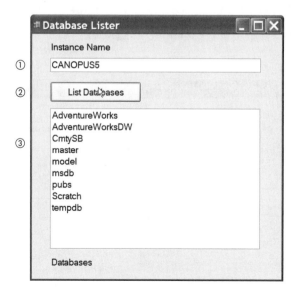

FIGURE 15-12: Database lister application

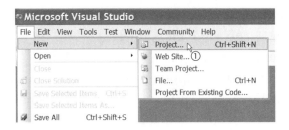

FIGURE 15-13: Starting a Windows project

solution that will contain your project (1), select the directory that will hold the solution (2), name your project (3), and then click Windows Application (4) in the Visual Studio installed templates.

SMO-based applications must have references to the appropriate SMO assemblies. This project, like most SMO projects, will need references to the `Microsoft.SqlServer.Smo` and `Microsoft.SqlServer.Connection-Info` assemblies; applications that use other features of SMO may need additional references. To do this, open Solution Explorer by choosing View Solution.

Next, open the Add Reference dialog box by clicking Add Reference, as shown in Figure 15-15.

In the Add Reference dialog box, shown in Figure 15-16, click `Microsoft.SqlServer.ConnectionInfo` (1) and `Microsoft.SqlServer.Smo` (2) while

FIGURE 15-14: Naming a Windows project

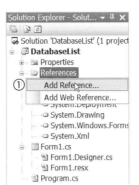

FIGURE 15-15: Adding assembly references

holding down the Ctrl key. Next, click the OK (3) button to add the assembly references.

Now you are ready to design the form. In this case, it is simple; just drop the appropriate controls on the form that Visual Studio 2005 presents to you, as shown in Figure 15-17. You should end up with the GUI shown in Figure 15-18.

All the work for this application happens when the List Databases button is clicked. To implement this, we must add a handler for the button click. The easy way to do this is to double-click the button (1) in the form for

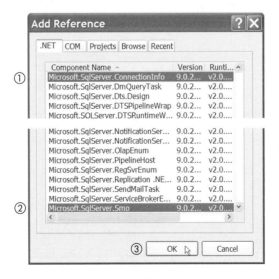

FIGURE 15-16: Selecting assembly reference

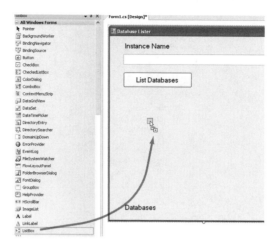

FIGURE 15-17: Adding a list box

the application, as shown in Figure 15-18. This will add the handler code and bring up a window where you can add your code.

Figure 15-19 shows the code for the button handler. The first thing this code has to do is clear (1) out the list box, named databaseList, that holds the database names.

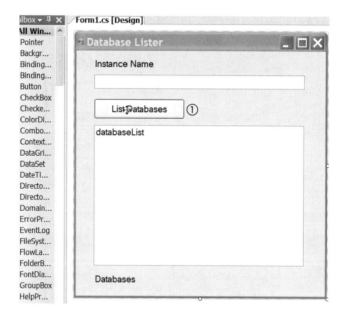

FIGURE 15-18: Form for database lister application

```
private void button1 _ Click(
   object sender, EventArgs e)
{
① databaseList.Items.Clear();
   Server server =
②    new Server(instanceName.Text);
③ foreach (Database database in
      server.Databases)
   {
   ④ databaseList.Items.Add(database.Name);
   }
}
```

FIGURE 15-19: Button handler

Next, make a `Server` object (2); this represents a SQL Server instance. The constructor for the `Server` object uses the name of the instance, which comes from the `instanceName` text box.

The `Server` object has a property named `Databases`, which you can iterate through using a C# `foreach` (3) statement and create a `Database` object for each database. When we have a `Database` object, we can easily add its name (4) to the list box.

It probably took more time for you to read how to create the Database Lister application than it will for you to build it. Although SMO is a fairly large object model, you will have Visual Studio 2005 IntelliSense to help you along the way, and most operations you will do with SMO will not require the use of T-SQL.

This brief introduction shows how SMO, Visual Studio 2005, Monad, or any other CLR-based programming language makes it very easy to implement custom management tools based on command-line, GUI, or scripting environments for SQL Server 2005.

Next, we will look at what makes up SMO. We will start by looking at what is needed to make a SMO application; then we will look at how SMO makes and manages connections to SQL Server. After that, we will look at the SMO object model and then generating scripts from SMO.

We won't be looking at all the details of all the SMO objects; there are close to 200 kinds. We will be looking at features that they have in common and the specific properties of a few.

Connections

Any application that uses SQL Server must make a connection to it first. SMO uses an instance of the `ServerConnection` class, from the `Microsoft.SqlServer.Management.Common` namespace, to make a connection to SQL Server. The `Server` objects in the previous examples made a `ServerConnection` as part of their construction.

The parameterless constructor for `ServerConnection` will make a connection to the default instance of SQL Server on the local machine. A connection to a specific instance of SQL Server is made by passing its name into the constructor for a `ServerConnection`. When the `ServerConnection` object has been constructed, a physical connection can be made by calling the `ServerConnection.Connect()` method. Later, we will see that in typical usage, `Connect()` is not called.

The first connection (1) made in Figure 15-20 is made to the default instance of SQL Server on the local machine. The second connection (2) is made to the default instance of SQL Server on the machine named `"CANOPUS5"`.

A connection made with ServerConnection is authenticated in one of three ways. The Windows credentials of the user who ran the program that made the connection are used by default. The second method of authentication is impersonating a Windows user, using his name and password, and the third method is using a SQL Server login name and password.

Default Windows Credentials Connection

First, we will look at using the Windows credentials of the user running a program who makes a connection. It is straightforward to do this, as shown in Figure 15-21. Start by constructing a new `ServerConnection` object

```
static void Main()
{
    ServerConnection local =
        new ServerConnection();
①  local.Connect();
    ServerConnection canopus5 =
        new ServerConnection("CANOPUS5");
②  canopus5.Connect();
}
```

FIGURE 15-20: Connecting to SQL Server

```
ServerConnection ServerConnection =
①new ServerConnection();
② ServerConnection.Connect();
```

FIGURE 15-21: Default connection

using the parameterless constructor and then execute the `Connect` (2)
method.

The behavior of the `Connect` method when called on a ServerConnection object built this way is the same as the `SqlCmd` utility, with no command-line switches or deprecated `osql` utility using just the `-E` command-
line switch; the connection is made to the default instance on the local
machine using the credentials of the person running the program. The sample
program `DefaultSMOConnection` uses this technique, and the code for it
is shown in Figure 15-22.

The DefaultSMOConnection program makes a connection object (1) and
then connects (2) to the server. The `ReadLine` method is used to stop the
program from terminating as soon as the connection is made so we can
observe the effect of the program on SQL Server.

Figure 15-23 shows a command shell that was stated using the `Runas`
utility with MiniDan's credentials. Note that user names, such as MiniDan,
are case insensitive, and some utilities will display them in lowercase. The
`DefaultSMOConnection` program is run (1) in that shell. The SQL Server
2005 Activity Monitor shows that the `DefaultSMOConnection` program
has done a login (2) as MiniDan on the Host CANOPUS5 (the local
machine) with an application name of ".Net SqlClient Data Provider." See
Books Online for information about running the SQL Server 2005 Activity
Monitor.

```
static void Main(string[] args)
{
    ServerConnection ServerConnection
①    = new ServerConnection();
②    serverConnection.Connect();
    Console.ReadLine();
}
```

FIGURE 15-22: DefaultSMOConnection program

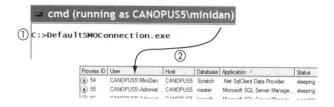

FIGURE 15-23: Using default connection

Using Runas

The machine being used to run the samples that illustrate `ServerConnection` has a couple of test Windows users on it. Specifically, it has Alice (1) and MiniDan (2), as shown in Figure 15-24. Both are ordinary users with no special privileges.

An easy way to run a program that has a particular user's identity is to start it with the `Runas` utility. The command shell is the utility `cmd.exe`, and starting it with a specific user's identity is shown in Figure 15-25.

The `Runas` (1) utility requires a `/user:` command-line switch with the user's name after it, followed by the name of the program to be run—in this case. `cmd`. It will prompt you for the user's password before it runs the program. After you have entered the user's password, `Runas` will start a command shell with the credentials of `/user:` and put the user's name in the title of the window for the shell. Echoing the USERNAME environment variable shows Alice's name (2). This is the technique used to run the following samples with a particular user's credentials and is also useful when you need to test your application with an identity other than your own.

Automatic Connection

`ServerConnection` has a method named `Connect`. Calling this method makes a connection to SQL Server. You are not required to call the

FIGURE 15-24: Windows test identities

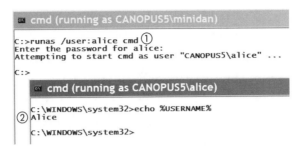

FIGURE 15-25: Using Runas utility

`ServerConnection.Connect` method to make a connection to SQL Server, and typically, it is not used. The connection will be opened automatically when you try to use the connection and it is not already open. If the connection is already open, calling the `Connect` method will not make another connection. If you do call `Connect`, it is important that you close the connection by calling `Disconnect`. If you do not call `Connect`, SMO will manage closing the connection for you.

Figure 15-26 shows a program that automatically connects to SQL Server. Construction of the `ServerConnection` (1) does not create a physical connection to SQL Server. Accessing the `ProcessID` property (2) requires connection to SQL Server, so the `ServerConnection` makes the connection and then uses it to get the `ProcessID` for the connection from SQL Server.

To see that the connection is not actually made until SMO needs information from the SQL Server, run the program shown in Figure 15-26 in the debugger. Put a breakpoint on the line that reads the `ProcessID` (1), as

```
static void Main(string[] args)
{
  ServerConnection serverConnection =
①   ServerConnection();
  Console.WriteLine(
②   serverConnection.ProcessID);
}
```

FIGURE 15-26: Automatic connection

shown in Figure 15-27; next, run to the breakpoint. Every connection to SQL Server 2005 is identified by a session id, which is listed in the SQL Server 2005 Activity Monitor as the Process ID. The ProcessID property of a connection returns this value. Use the SQL Server 2005 Activity Monitor to confirm that the connection (2) has not been made. Next, do a single step and then refresh the Activity Monitor. You will see that one connection (3) has been added to SQL Server and that the Process ID in the Activity Monitor is the same as the `ProcessID` property of the `ServerConnection`.

Windows Identity Impersonation

In the previous example, SMO just used the credentials of whoever happened to run the `DefaultConnection` program. Sometimes, we want to create the connection using some other Windows credentials.

Windows credentials are used for authentication when the `LoginSecure` property of the `ServerConnection` is true, which is its default value. When `LoginSecure` is true, the `ConnectAsUser` property determines whether the credentials of the user running the program or some other user's credentials are used to authenticate. The default value for `ConnectAsUser` is false and indicates that the credentials of the user running the program should be used.

When `ConnectAsUser` and `LoginSecure` are both true, the `ConnectAsUserName` and `ConnectAsUserPassword` properties of `Server Connection` are used to impersonate a Windows user when doing a login. The sample program `ImpersonateConnect` illustrates the use of these properties and is shown in Figure 15-28, where `ConnectAsUser` (1) is set to true.

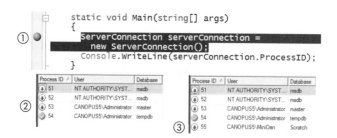

FIGURE 15-27: Connection upon property access

```
static void Main(string[] args)
{
  ServerConnection serverConnection
    = new ServerConnection();
  serverConnection.ConnectAsUser = true;
  serverConnection.ConnectAsUserName =
    args[0];
  serverConnection.ConnectAsUserPassword =
    args[1];
  serverConnection.Connect();
  Console.ReadLine();
}
```

FIGURE 15-28: ImpersonateConnect program

The result of running the ImpersonateConnect program is shown in Figure 15-29.

The ImpersonateConnect program is run in a shell that was started using the Runas utility and Alice's (1) credentials. The connection to SQL Server was made using MiniDan's (3) login. MiniDan's name and password (2) were passed to ImpersonateConnect on the command line.

Note that impersonating a Windows identity this way requires that the client application be running in the domain of the user or the domain that is trusted *by the user being impersonated*. In other words, you cannot use this technique to use Windows credentials to log in to SQL Server from a machine outside the domain, or trusted domain, in which the instance of SQL Server is running.

SQL Server Login

A ServerConnection will log in with a SQL Server log in when the LoginSecure property is false. It will log in using the Login and Password

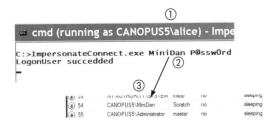

FIGURE 15-29: Impersonating Windows identity

properties of `ServerConnection`. The sample program `SQLConnect` illustrates the use of these properties and is shown in Figure 15-30.

The result of running the `SQLConnect` program is shown in Figure 15-31. In this example, Bob is a SQL Server login.

Alice (1) is running the `SQLConnect` program. Bob (2) is the login using the connection.

The `ServerConnect` object can also be constructed using a SQL login name and password. This is shown in Figure 15-32.

The password (1) can also be passed into the constructor as a `System.Security.SecureString`, and this is a much more secure practice. Note that building a SecureString from an ordinary string defeats its purpose. The `SecureString` should be built one character at a time, as the user types the password, not passed on the command line. Search MSDN for "secure-string application sample" for an example of how this is done.

Changing SQL Server Login Password

The password for the login using the connection can be changed if the login is a SQL Server login, but not if it is a Windows login. The `ChangePassword` method on the `ServerConnection` class is used to do this. An example of changing a password is shown in Figure 15-33.

The example shown in Figure 15-33 expects three strings to be passed in on the command line: a login, the password for the login, and the new password for the login.

The first argument is used to set the login name (1). The second argument (2) is used to set the password for the login. The third argument (3) is used

```
static void Main(string[] args)
{
    ServerConnection serverConnection =
        new ServerConnection();
    serverConnection.LoginSecure = false;
    serverConnection.Login = args[0];
    serverConnection.Password = args[1];
    serverConnection.Connect();
    Console.ReadLine();
}
```

FIGURE 15-30: SQLConnect program

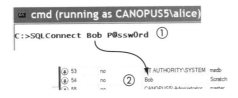

FIGURE 15-31: SQL Server login

to set the new password for the login. Note that this function, like the constructor for the `ServerConnection`, allows a `SecureString` to be used for the new password. The `ChangePassword` method can be used on an expired password.

Connection Management

SMO manages the physical connections a `ServerConnection` uses to connect to SQL Server. The management of connections is determined by connection properties of the `ServerConnection`, which are shown in Table 15-1.

By default, SMO uses pooled connections, but nonpooled connections have a more straightforward behavior, so we will look at them first.

SMO uses a single connection to an instance of SQL Server when Non-PooledConnection is true. None of the other connection properties has any meaning when NonPooledConnection is true. The connection to SQL Server is created when the ServerConnection.Connect method is called or when SMO needs a connection to SQL Server and none exists—for example, to retrieve some property of an object.

```
static void Main(string[] args)
{
    String name = "Bob";
①   String pwd = "P@ssw0rd";
    ServerConnection canopus5 =
        new ServerConnection(
        "CANOPUS5", name, pwd);
    canopus5.Connect();
}
```

FIGURE 15-32: SQL connection by constructor

```
static void Main(string[] args)
{
  ServerConnection serverConnection =
    new ServerConnection();
  serverConnection.LoginSecure = false;
① serverConnection.Login = args[0];
② serverConnection.Password = args[1];
  serverConnection.Connect();
③ serverConnection.ChangePassword(args[2]);
  Console.ReadLine();
}
```

FIGURE 15-33: Changing a password

The connection is maintained until the ServerConnection.Disconnect is called or the application using the connection terminates. Calls to ServerConnection.Connect are not counted—that is, a call to ServerConnection.Disconnect will terminate the connection regardless of the number of times ServerConnection.Connect has previously been called when NonPooledConnection is true.

The default value for ServerConnection.NonPooledConnection is false, which enables connection pooling. Also by default, the value of

TABLE 15-1: ServerConnection Connection Properties

Property	Description	Type
NonPooledConnection	Use of pooling	Boolean
MinPoolSize	Minimum number of threads in pool	Int32
MaxPoolSize	Maximum number of threads in pool	Int32
PooledConnectionLifetime	Lifetime of connection in seconds	Int32
AutoDisconnectMode	Controls ServerConnection. Disconnect when connections are pooled	Enum AutoDisconnectMode

`Server Connection.AutoDisconnectMode` is `AutoDisconnectionMode.`
`Disconnect IfPooled; ServerConnection.MinPoolSize` is 0; `MaxPool`
`Size` is 100; and `PooledConnectionLifetime` is 0. With these settings,
SMO completely controls connecting to and disconnecting from SQL
Server.

When connection pooling is enabled with the default property settings,
SMO will create a connection to SQL Server whenever it needs one up to the
limit specified by `ServerConnection.MaxPoolSize`. When no connection
exists, SMO will always create one when it needs to get information from
the SQL Server or `ServerConnection.Connect` is called.

When a connection already exists, sometimes SMO will create a new one
when it needs information from SQL Server or `ServerConnection.Con-`
`nect` is called. In no case will it create a new connection if `Server.Max-`
`PoolSize` connections already exist.

`ServerConnection.MinPoolSize` works in conjunction with `Pooled-`
`ConnectionLifetime`. Some connection-pooling mechanisms will immediately fill a pool to the minimum connection count when they start
running. SMO does not manage the connection pool in this way.

SMO creates connections as it needs them up to `ServerConnection.`
`MaxPoolSize` connections. When a connection is unused for longer than
`ServerConnection.PooledConnectionLifetime` seconds, it is disconnected if there are more than `ServerConnection.MinPoolSize` connections to SQL Server. This is the same pooled-connection behavior that is
found in ADO.NET.

When `ServerConnection.AutoDisconnectMode` is set to `AutoDis-`
`connectMode.NoAutoDisconnect`, SMO in effect calls `ServerConnec-`
`tion.Connection()` the first time it needs a connection and does not call
`ServerConnection.Disconnect`.

Server

The `Server` class from the `Microsoft.SqlServer.Management.Smo`
namespace represents an instance of the sqlservr.exe program, SQL Server.
A `Server` object is the root of the SMO object hierarchy for managing
SQL Server.

A `Server` object requires a connection to SQL Server, and it uses a `ServerConnection` object for this purpose. You saw in Figure 15-2 earlier in this chapter you can construct a `Server` object just by passing the name of an instance of SQL Server to its constructor. A `Server` can be constructed with its parameterless constructor, with the name of the SQL Server instance, or with a `ServerConnection`. When a `ServerConnection` is passed as a parameter, the `Server` object is constructed for the SQL Server on that connection. The first two constructors behave as though they were constructed with a `ServerConnection` that itself was constructed with the parameter passed into the Server constructor.

Regardless of how the `Server` object is constructed, a reference to the `ServerConnection` that it uses is held in `Server.Connection Context`.

Figure 15-34 shows a Server object created using a previously created `ServerConnection` object (1). The `Server.ConnectionContext` (2) returns the same `ServerConnection` that was used to construct it. Note that in typical usage, you would not create a `ServerConnection` and pass it to the `Server` constructor. This example just illustrates that a Server object always uses an underlying `ServerConnection` to connect to SQL Server.

Table 15-2 shows some of the properties of a `Server` object. It is beyond the scope of this of this introductory chapter on SMO to discuss these properties, but all are documented in Books Online in the description of the `ServerConnection` class.

```
    static void Main(string[] args)
    {
①   ServerConnection conn =
        new ServerConnection("CANOPUS5");
    Server canopus5 =
        new Server(conn);
②   ServerConnection conn2 =
        canopus5.ConnectionContext;
    }
```

FIGURE 15-34: Server constructed with ServerConnection

TABLE 15-2: Server Properties

Property	Class
ProxyAccount	ServerProxyAccount
Mail	SqlMail
Databases	DatabaseCollection
Endpoints	EndpointCollection
Languages	LanguageCollection
SystemMessages	SystemMessageCollection
UserDefinedMessages	UserDefinedMessageCollection
Credentials	CredentialCollection
Logins	LoginCollection
Roles	ServerRoleCollection
LinkedServers	LinkedServerCollection
SystemDataTypes	SystemDataTypeCollection
JobServer	JobServer
ServiceMasterKey	ServiceMasterKey
NotificationServices	NotificationServices
Settings	Settings
Information	Information
UserOptions	UserOptions
BackupDevices	BackupDeviceCollection
FullTextService	FullTextService
ActiveDirectory	ServerActiveDirectory
Triggers	ServerDdlTriggerCollection

SMO Objects

Objects from the SMO object model are created from classes that derive from `SqlSmoObject`. Each object is uniquely identified by a Uniform Resource Name (URN) and contains properties that hold references to its parent object and its children in the hierarchy.

All the objects in the hierarchy can be accessed through these references, sometimes by sequentially drilling through them, or directly accessed via the URN that identifies them.

All the objects have properties that describe them. These properties can be accessed either dynamically or statically.

Object Identity and URNs

The SMO object model identifies each `SqlSmoObject` in a SQL Server with a URN. A URN serves as a persistent, location-independent resource identifier. The formal definition of the syntax of a URN can be found in RFC 2141, "URN Syntax." The URN for a given object is in its `SqlSmoObject.Urn` property.

Having a URN for every object in SQL Server is a very useful feature. Given the URN for an object, you can retrieve it from a `Server` directly without having to traverse the object hierarchy. One thing that this means is that when you have a reference to a `SqlSmoObject`, you can remember its URN and then, in the future, retrieve it directly. Note that the URN is something that SMO uses; it is not a property of an instance of SQL Server itself.

URNs for `SqlSmoObjects` are significant, though URNs in general are not. That means that they are not arbitrarily created for an object, as a GUID might be, but are based on a formula that says the URN represents the path from the `Server` through the object hierarchy to the object. This means you can find an object in the SMO object hierarchy just by making its URN. Later, we will see how to use a URN to retrieve a `SqlSmoObject`, but first, we will look briefly at URNs.

The syntax for a URN breaks it into three parts: a scheme, a namespace identifier, and a namespace-specific string. The scheme for a URN is always urn: and is case insensitive. An example of a URN is shown in Figure 15-35. The namespace identifier is used to indicate how the namespace-specific string should be interpreted.

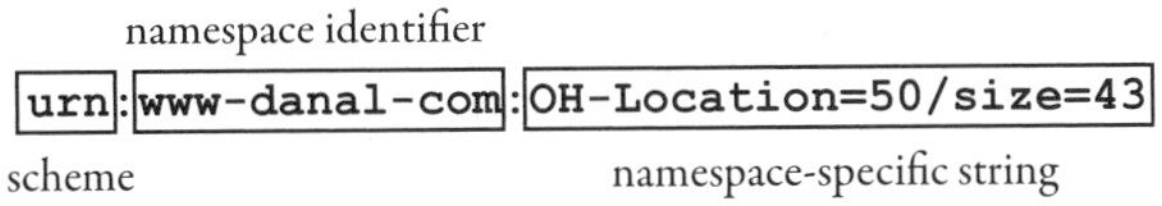

namespace identifier

$$\boxed{\texttt{urn}}:\boxed{\texttt{www-danal-com}}:\boxed{\texttt{OH-Location=50/size=43}}$$

scheme   namespace-specific string

FIGURE 15-35: URN format

The namespace identifier is something you can make up to keep track of things. Likewise, the namespace-specific string can be almost any format you want. In practice, you would use the namespace identifier to figure out how to interpret the namespace-specific string. There are other rules that a URN must follow; see RFC 2141 for all the details.

The `Server.GetSmoObject()` method can be used to access an object in SQL Server using its URN. If the object specified by the URN exists, `Server.GetSmoObject()` returns a reference to it; otherwise, it returns null. `Server.GetSmoObject()` accepts most properly formatted URNs but does not require them. It ignores everything in the URN except the namespace-specific string.

The namespace-specific string is an XPath location path that selects an object from an instance of SQL Server. The XPath recommendation defines the syntax of a location path and is located at http://www.w3.org/TR/XPath. In brief, an XPath location path consists of a number of location steps, each separated by a /. Each location step represents a level in the object hierarchy maintained by SMO.

Each location step in the XPath location path contains the name of a kind of SMO object in SQL Server and the name of that object. The namespace-specific string for the Authors table in the Pubs database on MySvr server, for example, would look like this: `Server[@Name='MySvr']/Database[@Name='Pubs']/Table[@Name='Authors']`

This XPath location path has three steps: `Server[@Name='MySvr']`, `Database[@Name='Pubs']`, and `Table[@Name='Authors']`.

In general XPath location paths ignore extra white space so the following namespace specific string would also identify the Authors table.

```
Server[@Name=''CANOPUS5']
/Database[@Name='Pubs']
/Table[@Name=''Authors']
```

There are a couple of places where XPath does not ignore white space. One is in names. The following would produce an error if used because of the space in `Ser ver`:

```
Ser ver[@Name='CANOPUS5']
/Database[@Name='Pubs']
/Table[@Name=''Authors ']
```

Another place that XPath does not ignore white space is in the value of an attribute. An *attribute* is a name that is prefixed with @, and its value, in quotes, comes after the = sign that follows its name. The following namespace-specific string identifies the "My Table" table in a database, not "MyTable"—that is, the space between "My" and "Table" must exist in the name of the object in the database:

```
Server[@Name='CANOPUS5']
/Database[@Name='Scratch']
/Table[@Name='My Table']
```

The fact that `Server.GetSmoObject()` ignores, for the most part, white space in XPath location path and preserves it in attribute values is very convenient. But technically, URNs are not allowed to contain white space, and `Server.GetSmoObject()` will not automatically unescape white space character codes. The following will look for the table `'My%20Table'`, not `'My Table'`, when passed to `Server.GetSmo Object()`:

```
Server[@Name='SVR1']
/Database[@Name='MyDB']
/Table[@Name='My%20Table']
```

If you are processing URNs from outside your control—that is, URNs that meet RFC 2141 but might contain escaped characters—you can use the `System.Web.HttpUtility.UrlDecode` method to convert the escaped characters to ones the SMO can handle. The C# code snippet below converts the `%20` in the URN into an actual space so that SMO can handle it. You can use this technique defensively, on any string, even if it doesn't have any escaped characters in it:

```
string urn = System.Web.HttpUtility.UrlDecode(
"Server[@Name='SVR1']/Database[@Name='My%20DB']");
```

So even though technically, a URN must have white space escaped, the URNs used by SMO may contain white space, and in general, SMO will not handle escaped white space as you might expect.

`Server.GetSmoObject()` will accept a complete URN as input, so the following will also identify the Authors table:

```
urn:www-danal-com:Server[@Name='CANOPUS5']
/Database[@Name='Pubs']
/Table[@Name='Authors']
```

SMO ignores the scheme and namespace identifier, and processes only the namespace-specific string. This means that URNs, as found in XML or HTML, can be used to identify SMO objects without any extra processing unless they contain escaped white space.

XPath calls `@Name` an attribute because it begins with the `@`, character and anything inside `[]` is a predicate that must be true. In the previous Pubs database examples, the effect of the step `Server[@Name='Canopus5']` is to return all the `Server` objects that have an attribute called `'Name'` whose value is `'MySvr'`. There is only one, of course. The next step, `/Database[@Name='Pubs']`, is asking for all the Database objects in the object found in the previous step whose name is `'Pubs'`. Again, of course, there is only one.

GetSmoObject

Every SMO object in a `Server` has a unique name. This name is the `SqlSmoObject.Urn` property. You can retrieve a SqlSmoObject by passing its SqlSmoObject.Urn to the `Server.GetSmoObject()` method. Note that the `@Name` attribute of the `Server` location step of the Urn is optional. If it is used, it must match the name of the `Server` that `SqlSmoObject` is being called on.

SQL Server 2005 supports schemas, and as a result, SQL Server objects may be contained in a schema other than dbo. For details on database schemas in SQL Server, see Chapter 6. The previous URN examples using the Authors table in the Pubs database ignored this fact to focus on the overall structure of a URN. An Object that is contained in a schema has a second attribute, `@Schema`, in its location step.

Extra attributes can be added to a predicate of a URN using the and operator. Figure 15-36 shows how to use the complete URN for the Authors table to access it directly.

```
static void Main(string[] args)
{
  Server local = new Server("CANOPUS5");
  Table Authors = (Table)local.GetSmoObject(
  new Urn(@"Server[@Name='CANOPUS5']
    /Database[@Name='pubs']
    ① /Table[@Name='Authors' and @Schema='dbo']"
  ));
}
```

FIGURE 15-36: Direct object access

The URN for the Authors table contains an @Schema attribute (1) that is passed as a parameter of the Server.GetSmoObject() method. It returns a reference to the Pubs table object if it exists; otherwise, it would return a null. When an @Schema attribute is not part of a step, the object is looked for in the default schema of the current user.

GetSmoObject() will also accept a string as an input parameter, which makes it very convenient to access an object directly via its URN.

Figure 15-37 accesses the same table as Figure 15-36 but does so by passing just the string value of the object's URN to GetSmoObject().

URN Retrieval Restriction

There is a restriction on using a URN to retrieve a database object: The URN must be from the Server on which the GetSmoObject is called. This means that the @Name attribute must correspond to the name of the Server. If the @Name for the Server is incorrect, GetSmoObject() will throw an exception. Also, it is permissible not to specify an @Name attribute for a Server. Note that the other steps in the URN require always require an @Name attribute.

```
static void Main(string[] args)
{
  Server local = new Server("CANOPUS5");
  Table Authors = (Table)local.GetSmoObject(
  ① @"Server[@Name='CANOPUS5']
    /Database[@Name='pubs']
    /Table[@Name='Authors' and @Schema='dbo']"
  );
}
```

FIGURE 15-37: Direct object access via string

The URN (1) in Figure 15-38 leaves out the @Name attribute. This means that GetSmoObject will return a reference to the Authors table on whatever server to which local happens to be connected. If the table does not exist on that server, it will return a null.

In some cases, it will be very convenient to leave out the @Name attribute for the Server locations step. In other cases—for example, when you want to document unambiguously a particular database object—it will be better to include the @Name attribute.

Figure 15-39 shows a program that uses a connection to the CANO-PUS5 instance of SQL Server and then attempts to use it to access an object in the PLUTO5 SQL Server instance (1) via its URN. The result is shown in Figure 15-40; an exception is thrown.

SMO Object Model

You can access any object in an instance of SQL Server either by using its URN or by drilling down to it starting with the Server object for the instance. This chapter won't go into the entire list of objects you can access using SMO; there are just too many for a single chapter. Refer to the Microsoft.SqlServer.Management.SMO namespace in Books Online for a comprehensive list of the object types used in the SMO object model. We will look at some specific features of a few objects that are representative of the many kinds of properties and features all SMO objects have.

Note that the names of many of the classes used by SMO are duplicated in other namespaces. All the classes we will be looking at come from the Microsoft.SqlServer.Management and related namespaces, not the Microsoft.AnalysisServices or Microsoft.ReportingServices namespace.

```
static void Main(string[] args)
{
  Server local = new Server();
  Table Authors = (Table)local.GetSmoObject(
①    @"Server
      /Database[@Name='pubs']
      /Table[@Name='Authors' and @Schema='dbo']"
  );
}
```

FIGURE 15-38: Default server

```
static void Main(string[] args)
{
  Server local = new Server("CANOPUS5");
  Table Authors = (Table)local.GetSmoObject(
①    @"Server[@Name='PLUTO5']
     /Database[@Name='pubs']
     /Table[@Name='Authors' and @Schema='dbo']"
  );
}
```

FIGURE 15-39: Using wrong server to get URN

We will start by looking at features that are common to all the objects in the SMO object model.

SMO Properties

All the objects in the SMO object model share several features because they derive from `SqlSmoObject`. One of the shared features is a `Properties` property, which is an enumeration of all the properties of the object.

Each property of the object is described by a `Property` object, which itself has eight properties, as shown in Table 15-3. All these properties are `System.Boolean` type except for the `Type` property, which is a `System.Type` and `Value`.

All the properties listed in the `SqlSmoObject.Properties` property have a corresponding property in the class definition of the object. The `Server` object, for example, has a property named `Instance Name`. There is a corresponding `Server.InstanceName` property of the `Server` class.

```
cmd (running as CANOPUS5\MiniDan)
C:>URN_Ident.exe
Unhandled Exception: Microsoft.SqlServer.Management.Smo.FailedOperationException
: Attempt to retrieve data for object failed for Server 'PLUTO5'. ---> Microsof
t.SqlServer.Management.Smo.SmoException: Invalid Urn filter on server level: fil
ter must be empty, or server attribute must be equal with the true server name.
   at Microsoft.SqlServer.Management.Smo.Server.CheckValidUrnServerLevel(XPathEx
pressionBlock xb)
   at Microsoft.SqlServer.Management.Smo.Server.GetSmoObjectRec(Urn urn)
   at Microsoft.SqlServer.Management.Smo.Server.GetSmoObjectRec(Urn urn)
   at Microsoft.SqlServer.Management.Smo.Server.GetSmoObject(Urn urn)
   --- End of inner exception stack trace ---
   at Microsoft.SqlServer.Management.Smo.Server.GetSmoObject(Urn urn)
   at URN_Ident.Program.Main(String[] args) in C:\Dan Docs\NewSql2005Book\SMO\Sa
mples\Server\URN_Ident\Program.cs:line 22
```

FIGURE 15-40: Exception due to mismatched server

TABLE 15-3: Properties of SqlSmoObject.Property

Property	Description
Dirty	The value in SQL Server may be different from the value in property if true.
Expensive	This property is considered to require a lot of resources to load if true.
IsNull	The value of this property is null if true.
Retrieved	The value of this property has been retrieved if true.
Readable	The property may be read if true.
Type	This returns the CLR type of property.
Value	This returns the value of the property.
Writable	This property may be written if true.

A property of a `SqlSmoObject` can be accessed dynamically in more than one way. `SqlSmoObject.Properties.Item` and `SqlSmoObject.GetPropertyObject` both access a property by its name or an ordinal.

Figure 15-41 shows an example that references properties dynamically and statically.

The program shown in Figure 15-41 accesses the "ActiveConnections" property of a Database. The indexer that represents the Items property (1)

```
static void Main(string[] args)
{
    Server local = new Server();
    Database database0 = local.Databases[0];
    Property property =
①     database0.Properties["ActiveConnections"];
    property =
②     database0.Properties.GetPropertyObject
        ("ActiveConnections");
    property =
③   database0.Properties.GetPropertyObject
        ("ActiveConnections", false);
④ int count = database0.ActiveConnections;
}
```

FIGURE 15-41: Using statically and dynamically referenced properties

is used to access the property and retrieve its value—that is, the returned value has its `PropertyRetrieved` property set to true.

Note that collections in SMO have a property named `Item` that typically is exposed in most languages as an indexer—the collection name with a `[]` suffix. So `Properties["ActiveConnections"]` (1) is actually using the `Item` property of the `Properties` property of `database0`.

The `GetPropertyObject()` method (2) is used to access the property and retrieve its value. A property is accessed without retrieving its value when `SqlProperty.GetPropertyObject` is called with a second parameter set to false (3). Last, the value of the property is retrieved when the corresponding instance property (4) is used.

Dynamically accessed properties also make it possible to write an application that displays the values of all the properties of an object without having to know the actual names of their corresponding instance fields. To do this, the properties of a `SqlSmoObject` are accessed by enumerating them from the `SqlSmoObject.Properties` property.

Figure 15-42 shows a method that will fill a Windows Forms ListBox named Properties with the names and values of the properties of a `SqlSmoObject`. The properties are enumerated by a `foreach` statement (1). The name (2) and value (3) of the property are added to the Properties ListBox.

This method does not have to know the names of the properties of the object at the time the code is written; it just enumerates each property and puts its name and value into a list box.

Each of the dialog boxes shown in Figure 15-43 uses the method in Figure 15-42 to fill the ListBox displayed in its window. The radio buttons

```
private void FillPropertyList(SqlSmoObject sso)
{
① foreach (Property property in sso.Properties)
    {
        Properties.Items.Add(
② property.Name + " = " +
③ property.Value);
    }
}
```

FIGURE 15-42: FillPropertyList for filling ListBox with properties dynamically

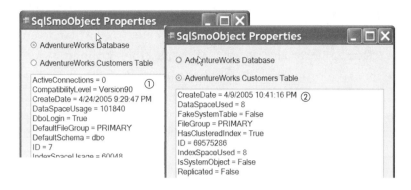

FIGURE 15-43: Program using dynamic properties

are used to choose the properties of either the AdventureWorks database (1) or the Customers table (2) from the AdventureWorks database. Note that the database has different properties from the table, and the FillPropertyList method determined that dynamically.

It is important to note that reading the Property.Value does not make SMO read the value from SQL Server. The meaning of Property.Value depends on the values of Property.Retrieved and Property.Dirty. If Property.Retrieved is false, Property.Value has no meaning. Table 15-4 summarizes the interpretation of Property.Value with respect to Property.Retrieved and Property.Dirty.

A property of a SqlSmoObject is categorized as expensive if Property.Expensive is true. Properties that are not expensive are read from SQL Server when the object they belong to is created. Expensive properties are not read from SQL Server by default. An expensive property is only

TABLE 15-4: Interpretation of Property.Value

Property.Value	Property.Retrieved	Property.Dirty
No meaning	false	false
No meaning	false	true
Reflects value read from SQL Server	true	false
Value has been changed since it was read from SQL Server	true	true

when it is explicitly accessed or the `Server.SetDefaultInit Field (true)` method on the server object has been called. Note that several over-loads of `SetDefaultInitField` allow a finer-grained selection of which expensive properties should be loaded when an object is created. Look for "Server.SetDefaultInitFields Method" in Books Online for more information.

SMO Parent Navigation

The SMO object hierarchy starts with the `Server` class. The object model is built out from the properties that derive from either `SqlSmoObject` or `SmoCollectionBase`. A `SqlSmoObject` property holds a child object, and an `AbstractCollectionBase` property holds a collection of child objects. Note that the complete class hierarchy for SMO is very large. This section concentrates on a small part of it to explain how navigation between objects works in SMO.

Every `SqlSmoObject`, except `Server`, has a `Parent` property. This prop-erty holds a reference to its parent and is of the same type as its parent. `Server.ServiceMasterKey`, for example, holds a reference to a `Service-MasterKey` object, which is a child of a `Server` object in the SMO object model. `ServiceMasterKey.Parent` is a reference to an object of type Server, its parent.

The `Parent` property of an object that is a member of a `SmoCollec-tionBase` object holds a reference to the object that holds the collection, not the `SmoCollectionBase` object itself. `Server.Databases`, for example, is a `SmoCollectionBase` object that holds `Database` objects. The `Data-base.Parent` property of a `Database` object holds a reference to a `Server` object, not the Database object.

Figure 15-44 shows a `Server` object that is holding a reference to a `ServiceMasterKey` and a collection of databases. Each of the databases in the collection holds a reference back to the `Server` object, not the `Data-bases` collection object. The `ServiceMasterKey` object is not a collection, and its `Parent` property, as expected, refers to the `Service` object that contains it.

Most of the SMO collection objects have an indexer associated with them that is used to access an object in a collection by ordinal or name. `Databases["AdventureWorks\"]`, for example, returns a reference to the

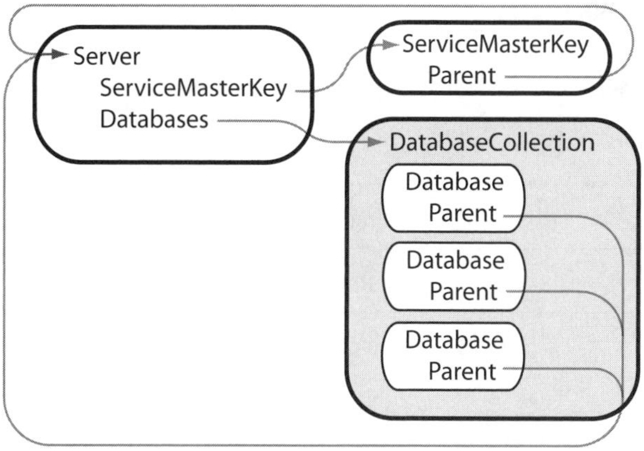

FIGURE 15-44: SMO parent

AdventureWorks database if the collection contains that database or a null otherwise.

The indexers for collections of objects that are contained in a schema have an optional extra parameter used to name the schema. If it is not specified, the default schema for the login used to make the connection to the server is used.

Figure 15-45 shows the use of collection indexers. Objects that are in the default schema for the user, such as the AdventureWorks database (1), are accessed by name in a collection. Objects that are contained in some other schema, such as the Customers (2) table in the AdventureWorks database, use both the name of the table and its schema. If only the name (3) of the table is used, the indexer will return a null unless the table is in the default schema for the current user.

```
static void Main(string[] args)
{
  Server local = new Server();
  Database AdventureWorks =
①   local.Databases["AdventureWorks"];
  Table customers =
②   AdventureWorks.Tables["Customer", "Sales"];
  Table customers2 =
③   AdventureWorks.Tables["Customer"];
}
```

FIGURE 15-45: Collection indexer

TABLE 15-5: SqlSmoState Values

SqlSmoState Value	Description
Creating	Being created.
Dropped	Being dropped.
Existing	Exists.
Pending	Object is in the process of being created so, for example, its Name and Parent fields might not yet be filled in.
ToBeDropped	Waiting to be dropped.

SMO State

SqlSmoObject.State reflects the state of an object in terms of its existence. The state of a SqlSmoObject is one of the values of the SqlSmoState enumeration. Table 15-5 shows the enumerated values of SqlSmoState.

Note that the SqlSmoObject.State property is used by GUI tools such as SQL Server Management Studio and Visual Studio 2005.

Create, Alter, and Drop

Most SqlSmoObjects have Create, Drop, and Alter methods that correspond to similarly named T-SQL statements. Some SqlSmoObjects, such as TableViewBase, are meant to be used as base classes for other SqlSmoObjects that implement these methods and do not have these methods. In other cases, such as Server, which has only the Alter method, some of these methods are not implemented because they do not make sense for that object. Objects from classes that implement ICreateable, IAlterable, or IDropable interfaces have corresponding Create, Alter, and Delete methods. You can look in Books Online to see which of these methods a particular class implements.

Because Create, Drop, and Alter don't make sense for all SqlSmoObjects, it is not possible for this class to specify them as virtual or abstract methods. SqlSmoObject does contain the implementation of these methods, however, in the protected methods CreateImpl, AlterImpl, and DropImpl.

Figure 15-46 shows the pseudocode for a typical `Create` method for a `SqlSmoObject`. In fact, the implementations of `Create`, `Drop`, and `Alter`, where they exist, merely delegate (1) their implementation to the corresponding Impl method in the base class.

It might seem strange that a concrete method in a base class implements the behavior of a derived class. Later, we will see that `SqlSmoObjects` can generate T-SQL scripts. The base class Impl methods use the derived class's ability to create this script to implement their behavior.

The general technique to use `Create`, `Drop`, and `Alter` is to get a reference to a SqlSmoObject and then call one of these methods as appropriate. The most straightforward example of this is the creation of a database.

Most SqlSmoObjects that implement `Create` also have a `Parent` property. A `Database.Parent`, for example, holds a reference to the `Server` that contains it. In addition, almost all `SqlSmoObject` that implement `Create` have a `Name` property; the few that don't, such as `UserDefinedMessage`, are identified by other means. In any case, a `Database` needs both a `Name` and a `Parent` before it can be created, as is typical of most `SqlSmoObjects`.

Figure 15-47 shows a program that creates a database in the CANOPUS5 server. First, the database is constructed, using the constructor (1) that allows both the `Parent` and `Name` to be passed in as parameters. Next, `Database.Create` (2) is called. Note that for all `SqlSmoObjects`, you will need a reference to a server to be able to `Create`, `Alter`, or `Drop` them.

`Alter` is used to change an existing `SqlSmoObject`. We might want to change the recovery model and disable Service Broker in the database created in Figure 15-47, for example.

To alter a database, you first must obtain a reference to its `SqlSmoObject`. Figure 15-48 shows database ScratchDB in server Canopus5 being altered. Using the URN and `SqlGetSmoObject` (1) is a very straightforward way to get a reference to an object that you need to alter. A `Database`

```
public void Create()
{
① base.CreateImpl();
}
```

FIGURE 15-46: Pseudocode for the implementation of Create

```
static void Main(string[] args)
{
   Server Canopus5 = new Server("CANOPUS5");
   Database ScratchDB =
①    new Database(Canopus5, "ScratchDB");
② ScratchDB.Create();
}
```

FIGURE 15-47: Database.Create

has several DatabaseOptions that can be altered (2). Change these options to the values you desire; then call Database.Alter to alter the actual database on the Server. Database.DatabaseOptions itself has an Alter method that could have also been used. In addition, these options could have been set before the database was created in Figure 15-47.

Dropping an object is done by getting a reference to an object and calling its Drop method. Figure 15-49 shows a database being dropped.

The details of Create, Alter, and Drop are different for each SqlSmoObject. As one last example, let's look at creating a database, adding a table with a primary key to it.

Figure 15-50 shows a program that creates a database using SMO. After it creates the database, it adds a table, Items (1), to it. Next, it adds a Serial Number column (2) to the table. The IsNullable property of the column is set to false because it is intended to be the primary key for the table. After the last column has been added to the table, the Create method is called on it.

```
static void Main(string[] args)
{
  Server Canopus5 = new Server("Canopus5");
  Database ScratchDB = (Database)
    Canopus5.GetSmoObject(
① @"Server/Database[@Name='ScratchDB']");
② ScratchDB.DatabaseOptions.RecoveryModel
     = RecoveryModel.Full;
  ScratchDB.DatabaseOptions.BrokerEnabled
     = false;
③ ScratchDB.Alter();
}
```

FIGURE 15-48: Altering a database

```
static void Main(string[] args)
{
    Server Canopus5 = new Server("CANOPUS5");
    Database ScratchDB = (Database)
      Canopus5.GetSmoObject(
      @"Server/Database[@Name='ScratchDB']");
    ScratchDB.Drop();
}
```

FIGURE 15-49: Dropping a database

Some more columns are created; then a primary key, PK_Items (3), is added to the table. An IndexedColumn is added (4) to the primary key to make Serial Number the primary key. Finally, the primary key is created.

Figure 15-51 shows the result of running the program shown in Figure 15-50. Notice that there is a ScratchDB5 database, and the Items table

```
    static void Main(string[] args)
    {
        Server Canopus5 = new Server("CANOPUS5");
        Database ScratchDB =
          new Database(Canopus5, "ScratchDB5");
        ScratchDB.Create();
①   Table Items = new Table(ScratchDB, "Items");
        Column SerialNumber = new Column(Items,
          "Serial Number", DataType.Int);
        SerialNumber.Nullable = false;
②   Items.Columns.Add(SerialNumber);
        Column value = new Column(Items,
          "Value", DataType.Money);
        Items.Columns.Add(value);
        Column name = new Column(Items,
          "Name", DataType.NVarChar(50));
        Items.Columns.Add(name);
        Items.Create();
③   Index primaryKey =
          new Index(Items, "PK _ Items");
        primaryKey.IndexKeyType =
          IndexKeyType.DriPrimaryKey;
        IndexedColumn ic =new IndexedColumn(
          primaryKey, "Serial Number");
④   primaryKey.IndexedColumns.Add(ic);
⑤   primaryKey.Create();
    }
```

FIGURE 15-50: Creating a database

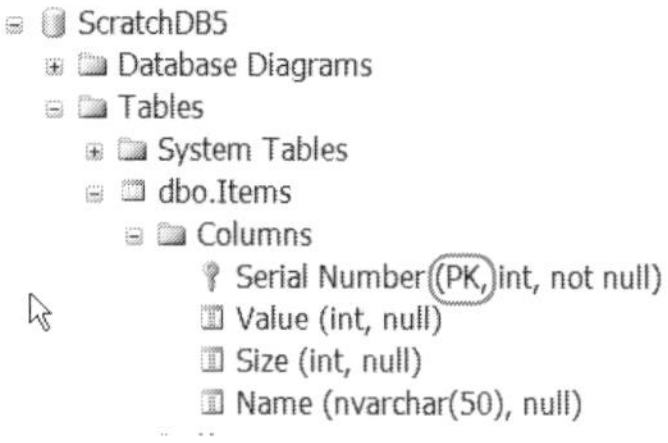

FIGURE 15-51: Database with
Table and Columns

has its Serial Number column as the primary key for the table. We decide
that we want to modify the database to remove the Size column and change
the Value column to be of type Money.

Figure 15-52 shows a program that removes the Size column of the Items
table and changes the type of the Value column to Money. Figure 15-53
shows the results of running the program shown in Figure 15-52.

Note that the previous examples that created database objects could
have been done without using URNs, but URNs are the topic of this section.

```
static void Main(string[] args)
{
   Server Canopus5 = new Server("CANOPUS5");
   Column dropMe = (Column)
     Canopus5.GetSmoObject(
     @"Server/Database[@Name='ScratchDB5']
     /Table[@Name='Items']
     /Column[@Name='Size']");
① dropMe.Drop();
   Column alterMe = (Column)
     Canopus5.GetSmoObject(
     @"Server/Database[@Name='ScratchDB5']
     /Table[@Name='Items']
     /Column[@Name='Value']");
② alterMe.DataType = DataType.Money;
③ alterMe.Alter();
   }
```

FIGURE 15-52: Changing a database

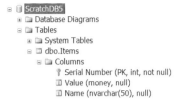

FIGURE 15-53: Database after changes

You can literally send an e-mail to someone with admin privileges for a database and say, unambiguously, "Delete column

```
Server[@Name='BigServer']/
Database[@Name='MyDatabase']/
Table[@Name='Accounts']/
Column[@Name='Region']."
```

Scripts

T-SQL scripts are used to create, change, and drop objects in SQL Server. SMO can be used to create these scripts. SMO can also manage object dependencies so that creates and drops are scripted in the correct order.

SMO objects have a `Script` method. This method is used to make a T-SQL script that can create or drop the corresponding object. By default, the Script method will make a script to create the object. The script is returned as a `StringCollection`. Note that `StringCollection` is in the `System.Collections.Specialized` namespace.

The `Script()` method (1) in Figure 15-54 builds a script to create the Customer table in the AdventureWorks database. It returns a `StringCollection` named script. The strings in script are enumerated using a `foreach` statement and printed to the console (2). The script it generates is shown in Figure 15-55.

A `ScriptingOptions` object passed into the `Script()` method determines how a script will be generated.

There are many scripting options available, far more than can be covered in this chapter. See Books Online for all of them.

Figure 15-56 creates a `ScriptingOptions` object (1), sets its `ScriptDrops` and `IncludeIfNotExists` properties to `true` (2), and then passes

```
static void Main(string[] args)
{
  Server local = new Server("CANOPUS5");
  Table customer = (Table)
    local.GetSmoObject(@"Server
    /Database[@Name='AdventureWorks']
    /Table[@Name='Customer'
    and @Schema='Sales']");
① StringCollection script = customer.Script();
  foreach (String s in script)
  {
②    Console.WriteLine(s);
  }
}
```

FIGURE 15-54: Scripting a table

it as an argument (3) to the `Script` method. The `Script` method generates the script shown in Figure 15-57 to drop the Customer table.

Most scripting tasks involve more than one object, and scripts that involve more than one object are sometimes large. A `Scripter` object can generate a script for a list of objects and can send the script directly to a file instead of a `StringCollection`.

A `Scripter` object requires a `Server` to generate a script. You can pass the `Server` in as a parameter to the `Scripter` constructor, as shown in Figure 15-58 (1), or set it into the `Server` property before you generate the script. A Scripter can script an array of SMO objects or URNs or an `UrnCollection` (2). To script directly to a file, the `Scripter.Options.FileName` and

```
SET ANSI_NULLS ON
SET QUOTED_IDENTIFIER ON
CREATE TABLE [Sales].[Customer](
  [CustomerID] [int] IDENTITY(1,1)
    NOT FOR REPLICATION NOT NULL,
  [TerritoryID] [int] NULL,
  [AccountNumber]  AS (isnull('AW'+
    [dbo].[ufnLeadingZeros]([CustomerID]),
    '')),
  [CustomerType] [nchar](1) COLLATE
    SQL_Latin1_General_CP1_CI_AS
    NOT NULL,
  [rowguid] [uniqueidentifier] ROWGUIDCOL
    NOT NULL,
  [ModifiedDate] [datetime] NOT NULL
) ON [PRIMARY]
```

FIGURE 15-55: Customer create script

```
static void Main(string[] args)
{
  Server local = new Server("CANOPUS5");
  Table customer = (Table)
    local.GetSmoObject(@"Server
    /Database[@Name='AdventureWorks']
    /Table[@Name='Customer'
    and @Schema='Sales']");
① ScriptingOptions sopts =
    new ScriptingOptions();
  sopts.ScriptDrops=true;
② sopts.IncludeIfNotExists=true;
③ script = customer.Script(sopts);
  foreach (String s in script)
  {
      Console.WriteLine(s);
  }
}
```

FIGURE 15-56: ScriptingOptions

ToFileOnly must be set (3). Note that these techniques can also be used for scripting individual objects.

The file named in FileName will be created and the script written into it when the Scripter.Script() method is called (4) unless the Scripter. Options.AppendToFile option is set to true. If it is true, the script will be appended to the file.

By default, the Scripter.Script() method will generate a script to create the objects. A drop script can be generated by setting the Scripter. Options.ScriptDrops property to true.

The script generated by the example shown in Figure 15-58 will script out the objects in the order in which they appear in the array or collection, as shown in Figure 15-59. The Customers table (1) is scripted out before the SalesTerritory table (2), as the Customers table comes before the SalesTerritory table in the Urn collection.

```
IF  EXISTS (SELECT * FROM
   sys.objects WHERE id =
   OBJECT_ID(N'[Sales].[Customer]') AND
   type in (N'U')
DROP TABLE [Sales].[Customer]
```

FIGURE 15-57: Customer drop script

```
static void Main(string[] args)
{
①Scripter scripter =
    new Scripter(new Server());
②UrnCollection urns = new UrnCollection();
 urns.Add(new Urn(@"Server
  /Database[@Name='AdventureWorks']
  /Table[@Name='Customer'
   and @Schema='Sales']"));
 urns.Add(new Urn(@"Server
  /Database[@Name='AdventureWorks']
  /Table[@Name='SalesTerritory'
   and @Schema='Sales']"));
③ scripter.Options.FileName=@"AW.sql";
  scripter.Options.ToFileOnly=true;
④ scripter.Script(urns);
}
```

FIGURE 15-58: Scripting multiple objects

Sometimes, an object has dependencies on another objects, and a script may want to take this into account. The Scripter manages these dependencies in a couple of ways.

First, the simplest way to handle dependencies is to set Scripter. Options.WithDependencies to true before calling the Script method. This makes a script that has the objects in the list in the proper order, according to whether a create or drop script is being built. In addition, it includes in the script all the dependent objects of the objects in the list.

Figure 15-60 shows the use of Scripter.WithDependencies (1). One of the side effects of Scripter.WithDependencies=true is that it scripts out all the dependent objects, in addition to getting objects in the correct order. This example scripts out the urnLeadingZeros user-defined function and an alias type named Name, in addition to the Customer and SalesTerritory tables.

Figure 15-61 shows the results produced by the code in Figure 15-60. The alias type Name (1) is scripted out before the SalesTerritory table because the SalesTerritory table has a column of type Name. The urnLeadingZeros

```
①CREATE TABLE [Sales].[Customer](
  [CustomerID] [int] IDENTITY(1,1)    GO
  ...
②CREATE TABLE [Sales].[SalesTerritory](
  [TerritoryID] [int] IDENTITY(1,1)
  NOT NULL,
```

FIGURE 15-59: Script to create objects

```
static void Main(string[] args)
{
  Scripter scripter =
   new Scripter(new Server());
  UrnCollection urns = new UrnCollection();
  urns.Add(new Urn(@"Server[@Name='CANOPUS5']
    /Database[@Name='AdventureWorks']
    /Table[@Name='Customer'
    and @Schema='Sales']"));
  urns.Add(new Urn(@"Server[@Name='CANOPUS5']
    /Database[@Name='AdventureWorks']
    /Table[@Name='SalesTerritory'
    and @Schema='Sales']"));
  scripter.Options.FileName=@"AW.sql";
① scripter.Options.WithDependencies = true;
  scripter.Options.ToFileOnly=true;
  scripter.Script(urns);
}
```

FIGURE 15-60: Scripting with dependencies

function (3) is scripted out before the Customer table because the Customer table has a computed column that uses this function.

In some cases, you want to get only the correct order for the objects in the script and want no additional objects in the script. The `Scripter.Filter CallbackFunction` lets you control which objects are output by the script when `Scripter.WithDependencies` is used.

The `FilterCallbackFunction` function is a delegate that is called once for each URN that is found by the Scripter in the process of determining all

```
① CREATE TYPE [dbo].[Name]
  FROM [nvarchar](50) NULL
  GO
  ...
  GO
② CREATE TABLE [Sales].[SalesTerritory](
  ...
  )
  GO
  ...
③ CREATE FUNCTION [dbo].[ufnLeadingZeros](
  @Value int
  )
  RETURNS varchar(8)
  ...
④ CREATE TABLE [Sales].[Customer](
```

FIGURE 15-61: Script with dependencies

the dependencies of the objects in the list for which it is generating a script. A return value of true from this function means filter it—that is, do not create a script for it.

Delegates are a feature of .NET Framework, and if you are not familiar with them, look for delegates and anonymous delegates in MSDN for more information. One way of thinking of a delegate is as a function with no name, defined in place where it is used. Figure 15-62 shows an anonymous delegate function (1) defined in place for the `Scripter.FilterCallbackFunction`. This delegate has a URN as an input parameter. Note that Urns is the UrnCollection defined at the beginning of the program. One of the useful features of an anonymous delegate is that it can refer to variables defined before it in the code. If the Urn passed into the anonymous delegate is not in the Urns, it returns `true` (2); otherwise, it returns `false` (3). When the `FilterCallbackFunction` returns `true`, it is saying to exclude this object from the script being produced. Figure 15-63 shows the script in dependency order.

Unlike the code shown in Figure 15-60, which scripts out dependent objects, the code in Figure 15-62 scripts out only the objects in the Urn collection.

```
static void Main(string[] args)
{
  Scripter scripter =
   new Scripter(new Server());
  UrnCollection urns = new UrnCollection();
  urns.Add(new Urn(@"Server[@Name='CANOPUS5']
    /Database[@Name='AdventureWorks']
    /Table[@Name='Customer'
    and @Schema='Sales']"));
  urns.Add(new Urn(@"Server[@Name='CANOPUS5']
    /Database[@Name='AdventureWorks']
    /Table[@Name='SalesTerritory'
    and @Schema='Sales']"));
  scripter.Options.FileName=@"AW.sql";
① scripter.FilterCallbackFunction =
    delegate(Urn urn)
    {
      if (urns.Contains(urn))
②      return false;
③      return true;
  };
  scripter.Options.WithDependencies = true;
  scripter.Options.ToFileOnly=true;
  scripter.Script(urns);
}
```

FIGURE 15-62: FilterCallback

```
① CREATE TABLE [Sales].[SalesTerritory](
     [TerritoryID] [int] IDENTITY(1,1)
     NOT NULL,
   GO
   ...
② CREATE TABLE [Sales].[Customer](
     [CustomerID] [int] IDENTITY(1,1)
```

FIGURE 15-63: Script in dependency order

Behind the scenes, the `Scripter` object is using a `DependencyTree` to figure out what is dependent on what. A `Scripter` can build a `DependencyTree` that defines all the dependencies that the objects in a list have with other objects. There are two kinds of `DependencyTrees`: `Dependency-Type.Parents` and `DependencyType.Children`. `DependencyType.Parents` defines all the dependencies that the objects in the list have on other objects. `DependencyType.Parents` is used to find the objects that must be created before the others in the list are created. Likewise, `Dependency-Type.Children` is used to find all the objects that must be dropped before other objects in the list can be dropped.

A `DependencyTree` is a tree of `DependencyTreeNodes`, where each `DependencyTreeNode` represents an object identified by its URN in the `DependencyTreeNode.Urn` property. The `DependencyTree` itself has an Urn property that represents the root object of the tree, if there is one; otherwise, `DependencyTree.Urn` is null.

A `DependencyTree` can be navigated using the `FirstChild` and `NextSibling` methods of a `DependencyTree` or `DependencyTreeNode` object.

Figure 15-64 shows an example of navigating a `DependencyTree` of type `DependencyType.Parents` depth first. The `TreeMember` method (1) takes a `DependencyTreeNode` from a `DependencyTree` and writes its URN to the console, prefaced by tabs that indicate its depth in the tree. If that `DependencyTreeNode` has children, it recursively calls the `TreeMember` function (2) on its first child. Then it calls the `TreeMember` function (3) on its next sibling, if it has one.

Figure 15-65 shows the result of running the example in Figure 15-64. The two tables from the `UrnCollection`, Customer (1) and SalesTerritory (4), are siblings at the top of the hierarchy. The user-defined type "Name" is repeated (3) as a child of the SalesTerritory table (2) that is a child of the

```
① static void TreeMember(
   DependencyTreeNode node, int depth) {
      string pad = new String('\t', depth);
      Console.WriteLine(pad + node.Urn);
      if (node.HasChildNodes)
      ② TreeMember(node.FirstChild, depth + 1);
      DependencyTreeNode next = node.NextSibling;
      if (next != null)
      ③ TreeMember(next, depth);
   }
   static void Main(string[] args) {
      UrnCollection urns = new UrnCollection();
      ...
      DependencyTree tree =
         scripter.DiscoverDependencies(
         urns, DependencyType.Parents);
      DependencyTreeNode n = tree.FirstChild;
   ④ TreeMember(n, 0);
   }
```

FIGURE 15-64: Depth first dependency tree

Customer table and as a child of the SalesTerritory table (2) that is a sibling of the Customer table.

Operations performed on SQL Server through SMO objects can also be scripted. A `ServerConnection` has a `CapturedSql` property that can be used to capture SQL commands issued by `SqlSmoObjects` to SQL Server.

A script for commands is captured in the `ServerConnection.Captured Sql` property whenever the `ServerConnection.SqlExecutionModes` property is equal to `SqlExecutionModes.CaptureSql` or `SqlExecution Modes. ExecuteAndCaptureSql`. In the latter case, and when Server Connection. SqlExecutionModes is equal to `ServerConnection.SqlExecutionModes. ExecuteSql`, the SQL commands are also executed.

Figure 15-66 shows a program that uses SMO to capture SQL. It sets the `SqlExecutionModes` property (1) of the `ServerConnection` to `CaptureSql`.

```
tree
① Table[@Name='Customer']
   ② Table[@Name='SalesTerritory']
      ③ UserDefinedDataType[@Name='Name' ]
      UserDefinedFunction[@Name='ufnLeadingZeros']
   ④ Table[@Name='SalesTerritory']
      UserDefinedDataType[@Name='Name']
```

FIGURE 15-65: Dependency tree

```
static void Main(string[] args)
{
    Server Canopus5 = new Server("CANOPUS5");
    Canopus5.ConnectionContext.
①    SqlExecutionModes
        = SqlExecutionModes.CaptureSql;
    Column dropMe = (Column)
        Canopus5.GetSmoObject(
        @"Server/Database[@Name='ScratchDB5']
        /Table[@Name='Items']
        /Column[@Name='Size']");
    dropMe.Drop();
    Column alterMe = (Column)
        Canopus5.GetSmoObject(
        @"Server/Database[@Name='ScratchDB5']
        /Table[@Name='Items']
        /Column[@Name='Value']");
    alterMe.DataType = DataType.Money;
    alterMe.Alter();
    foreach (String s in
② Canopus5.ConnectionContext.CapturedSql.Text)
    {
        Console.WriteLine(s);
    }
}
```

FIGURE 15-66: Capturing SQL

It uses the same code that was used in Figure 15-52 to change the columns in the Items table of the ScratchDB5 database. When this program is executed, however, nothing in the ScratchDB5 database is changed; instead, the script to perform those changes is output to the console.

Figure 15-67 shows the script that is output to the console by the program shown in Figure 15-66.

Configuration Management

The ManagedComputer class, in the namespace Microsoft.SqlServer.Management.Smo.Wmi, provides ways to manage those configuration settings of SQL Server that cannot be managed by T-SQL. An example of this is the network protocols used by SQL Server. These kinds of things typically are

```
USE [ScratchDB5]
ALTER TABLE [dbo].[Items] DROP COLUMN [Size]
USE [master]
USE [ScratchDB5]
ALTER TABLE [dbo].[Items] ALTER COLUMN [Value]
 [money] NULL
USE [master]
```

FIGURE 15-67: Results of CaptureSql

configured by Registry settings that may be machine or operating system dependent.

These configurations are meant to be managed through Windows Management Instrumentation (WMI). WMI exposes these configurations as data in a Common Information Model (CIM) repository. The data in this repository reflects the current configuration of SQL Server, and changes to the data in the repository cause the underlying configuration to change. WMI encapsulates all the machine and operating system dependent details in this way.

Using ManagedComputer is as straightforward as using a SqlSmoObject. Figure 15-68 shows a program that enumerates the network client protocols configured for SQL Server. First, it creates a ManagedComputer (1) by passing the name of the machine as a parameter to its constructor. Next, it uses foreach (2) to enumerate the client protocols available. Then it writes out to the console (3) the names of the protocols it found. The results of running this program are shown in Figure 15-69.

```
static void Main(string[] args)
{
    ManagedComputer Canopus5 =
①     new ManagedComputer("Canopus5");
    foreach (ClientProtocol p in
②     Canopus5.ClientProtocols)
    {
③     Console.WriteLine(p.Name);
    }
}
```

FIGURE 15-68: Enumerating client protocols

```
np
sm
tcp
via
```

FIGURE 15-69: Client protocols
on CANOPUS5

ManagedComputer is really just a facade in front of WMI, and it uses
WMI to manage the data in the CIM repository. Any access to the CIM
repository has to be strictly controlled, of course. ManagedComputer does
not log in to SQL Server; the CIM is part of Windows, and access to it is pro-
tected by Windows security. By default, ManagedComputer will use the
Windows identity of the person running the code that constructs it to access
WMI. A second and third parameter can be passed into the constructor for
ManagedComputer: the name and password of the identity that Managed-
Computer should use to access WMI.

ManagedComputer lets you manage, among other things, the network
protocols that SQL Server can use; the SQL Server services that are hosted
on the machine, such as the database engine or analysis engine, and the network connections each service uses.

Figure 15-70 shows a program that blocks all client network protocols
(1) and all SQL Server services (2) on the Canopus5 machine.

```
static void Main(string[] args)
{
  ManagedComputer Canopus5 =
    new ManagedComputer("Canopus5");
  foreach (ClientProtocol p in
    Canopus5.ClientProtocols)
  {
①   p.IsEnabled = false;
  }
  foreach (Service s in Canopus5.Services)
  {
②   s.Stop();
  }
}
```

FIGURE 15-70: Managing services

Where Are We?

SMO is a class library that is ideally suited to applications that manage SQL Server. Although at first glance, it seems made for DBA-type applications, in fact, it is useful for all applications that need SQL Server management facilities.

SMO integrates tightly with Visual Studio 2005 and presents a programming model that is identical to other tools for Visual Studio 2005, including full support of IntelliSense. It abstracts SQL Server so that in general, knowledge of SQL Server's database schemas or the T-SQL language is almost never necessary.

SMO efficiently manages its object model to minimize any negative impact it might have on an application or SQL Server. Expensive to load properties are not loaded until needed; operations that can be combined into a single round trip are.

SMO can produce T-SQL scripts to manage SQL Server. The scripts can take into account dependences and can trace operations used to manage SQL Server.

∎ 16 ∎
Notification Services

N OTIFICATION SERVICES IS another example of how SQL Server becomes a more visible part of a multitier, service-based application architecture. This chapter is a brief introduction to Notification Services.

What Is SQL Server Notification Services?

SQL Server Notification Services was originally released in the summer of 2002 as a licensed part of SQL Server 2000. It shipped as an MSI file that you downloaded from the Microsoft Web site, similar to the way improvements to SQLXML support were available as "Web releases." When installed, SQL Server Notification Services did not change the internals of `sqlservr.exe`; neither were the services loaded in SQL Server's process. It was not integrated into the SQL Server 2000 installation process but provided its own install and a command-line utility called `NSControl` to deploy and administer the service on the target computers.

SQL Server Notification Services (we'll abbreviate this as SQLNS from now on, for brevity) consists of an engine, which usually runs as part of an executable process (`NSService.exe`), and a framework for building a specific type of application, notification applications. Like SQL Server's Analysis Services and Service Broker, it extends your application coding reach, and it moves SQL Server and related services toward being an integrated platform for scalable application systems. Unlike with Service Broker, you do not code DDL for Notification Services or store its metadata inside

SQL Server catalogs, though when you generate an SQLNS application, its metadata is stored in SQL Server databases. SQLNS is, in SQL Server 2005, one of the series of application-enabling services that ship "in the box." When you install SQL Server 2005, one of the first installation screens provides a choice of installing one or more of the following:

- SQL Server Database
- Analysis Services
- Notification Services
- Reporting Services
- SQL Server Integration Services
- Documentation and Samples

That is because these services work in concert to provide pieces of a service-oriented architecture for building data-centric applications. In SQL Server 2005, you can install, control, and monitor SQLNS applications from SQL Server Management Studio, along with SQL Server itself. SQLNS application coding is not integrated into the SQL Server Management Studio environment, though you can use C++ makefile projects in Visual Studio to group the components in a Notification Services application and run the appropriate application generation utilities. You can also use Visual Studio 2005's XML editor with schema validation to provide validation and IntelliSense when editing the SQLNS XML configuration files.

There are a few key enhancements to SQL Server Notification Services in SQL Server 2005, some of which we have already alluded to:

- Notification Services installation is integrated into SQL Server installation.
- There is a new management interface for NSControl operations in SQL Server Management Studio.
- There are managed APIs for configuration, application generation, and application management known as Notification Management Objects (NMO).
- There is a new built-in provider for Analysis Services data.
- You can use a Notification Services instance using an existing database, or it can use its own separate databases.

- You can run the Notification Services engine as part of your own service program.
- You can use condition actions in Notification Services applications. A condition action provides the ability to have a subscriber-defined WHERE clause for a Transact-SQL (T-SQL) match rule.
- The application-dependent Notify function has been replaced with SQL INSERT INTO...SELECT syntax to improve security and scalability.
- There is 64-bit support for scale-up.
- Vacuuming performance improvements have been made.
- Object model reflection enhancements for subscription objects have been added to support subscriber-defined match rules.

Notification Applications

Almost everyone has been affected by notification applications in daily life. When you receive a daily weather forecast through your cell phone or PDA, when you're notified that your upgrade to first class has been granted on the way to the airport, and when you receive traffic reports over instant messenger at the office so you can more effectively plan your route home, you are interacting with notification applications. From a consumer point of view, notification applications consist of two pieces:

- You subscribe to receive notifications based on certain criteria through a subscription application, often over the Web.
- You receive notifications through the communication vehicle of your choice. Some popular choices are messaging products, cell phones, and e-mail.

Some examples of existing Notification Services applications and scenarios are the following:

- Financial services—Receiving and reacting to personal portfolio changes and current market conditions
- Travel and hospitality—Flight arrivals, schedule changes
- Electronic commerce—Search criteria, buying and selling
- Monitoring business data

- Alerting the appropriate person or system when action is required
- Defining the events that occur in a line-of-business application
- Tracking critical company data
- Numeric data reaching a threshold
- Focusing on key performance indicators
- Coexisting with and broadening existing monitoring—Going beyond the console to devices like cell phones
- Keeping employees informed—Updates to projects, timely research, alerts to actions that may be required

The SQL Server Notification Services architecture abstracts event, subscription, and notification data into classes using XML within two configuration files built by the application developer. The application generation process generates database tables and procedures based on application-specific data. It abstracts the mechanism for providing events, formatting notifications, and delivering notifications into a provider model. The SQLNS product comes with some providers built in; other providers come with related products; and if none of the providers meets your needs, you can build your own using managed code and optionally a COM wrapper API.

As an application developer, you must define the following:

- Incoming events that may provide the fodder for your notifications
- What types of notifications your users will be allowed to sign up for
- A subscription application, so users can sign up
- Pieces of information (data) that will make up your notification
- An algorithm for matching the existing subscriptions with incoming events (or other data to be queried) to produce notifications
- The format of the notification on different delivery vehicles (devices)

Through this short description, you can see that notification applications are publish–subscribe applications. The SQLNS feature gives you all the tools you need to build the applications, SQLNS provides a service process that runs the Notification Services engine, or you can use your host engine in your own application. The engine service process can be scaled to run as multiple pieces on multiple machines as well. SQLNS uses SQL Server to store its metadata and state data (SQL Server is mandatory, although it can integrate with outside data in other DBMS products and with Analysis Services) and also uses SQL Server stored procedures and T-SQL statements to affect its matching rules. Figure 16-1 shows an overview of the SQLNS application architecture.

This diagram shows that some parts of Notification Services are provided for you; some follow an extensible provider-based architecture; and you must code some yourself. Subscriptions enter the system through a custom subscription management application (1), which can be written using a Notification Services subscription object model. This object model contains subscriber, subscription, and subscriber device classes (among others) and stores its data in the database (2). Events enter the system through event providers (3) and are stored in the database in batches. A SQLNS component known as the *generator* executes T-SQL match rules, which generate notifications from events and subscriptions (4). Another component, known as the *distributor,* formats the notifications (using formatters) and delivers them to the ultimate destination (5).

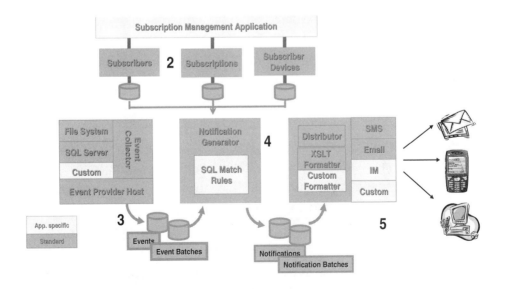

FIGURE 16-1: An overview of SQL Server Notification Services

Components of SQL Server Notification Services

When you choose to install SQL Server Notification Services, all its components install in a separate subdirectory of the SQL Server installation directory. You can see that there are very few discrete components:

- NSService.exe—Instances of Notification Services run as Windows services, using this program as the executable to run. Notification Services instances should not be confused with SQL Server instances.

- Microsoft.SQLServer.NotificationServices.dll—NSService. exe loads this .NET Framework assembly, which contains the code for SQLNS, the built-in providers, and components that you call to insert and retrieve data in the SQLNS tables when building subscription applications.

- Microsoft.SQLServer.NotificationServices.Rules.dll—This .NET Framework assembly contains the additional components that you use in subscription applications to program subscription-specific conditions for user-defined event conditions.

- Microsoft.SqlServer.SMO.dll—This .NET Framework assembly includes (as part of SQL Server Management Objects) the NMO.

- NSControl.exe—This utility program generates the SQL Server databases and database objects that the Windows service program and your subscription application use. The application also maintains metadata about Notification Services instances (instances of NSService.exe) that is stored in the Registry. You can also use NSControl.exe to enable and disable parts of your SQLNS application, provide status information, and detect the version(s) of Notification Services installed.

- *XML schemas*—When generating Notification Services applications, you specify the information in XML control files. NSControl.exe uses these schemas to validate your XML control files before it uses them to store metadata inside SQL Server database tables.

- *Sample applications*—SQLNS comes with a series of sample applications that you can use as a starting point to build your own applications or try out various SQLNS features. These applications come with C++ makefile projects and test data. Visual C++ must be installed for you to use these projects.

- *Providers*—As mentioned earlier in the chapter, what makes SQLNS extensible is the provider model for event providers, formatters, and delivery protocol providers.

Here's a list of built-in providers at this writing, providers in development, and the interface you would implement to build your own.

These are the **event providers:**

- *File Watcher event provider*—Built-in provider that watches for files to be dropped into a directory on the file system. Files must be in XML format, and you must write an XML schema that the SQLXML bulk loader (from SQLXML 3.0) will use to load the events into the event classes.
- *SQL Server event provider*—Built-in provider that runs the SQL statement of your choice at an interval you configure to determine whether rows in a SQL Server table have changed or merit that an event be submitted. Note that SQL Server–linked server connections are used; this data could be in a non-SQL Server database.
- *Analysis Services event provider*—New for SQL Server 2005, this will produce events based on Multidimensional Expressions (MDX), such as those used for key performance indicators.
- *SQLNS stored procedures*—You can use SQLNS-defined stored procedures, which are generated on a per–event class basis, to insert batches of events. This is not an event provider in itself but is an alternative way to generate event batches.
- `IEventProvider` *and* `IScheduledEventProvider`—You can write classes that implement one or the other of these interfaces to produce a custom provider.

These are the **content formatters:**

- *XML/XSLT formatter*—This built-in provider formats notifications into XML and then passes them through the XSLT transform that you specify.

- `IContentFormatter`—You can write classes that implement this interface to produce a custom provider.

These are the **delivery protocol providers:**

- *SMTP*—This built-in delivery provider delivers notifications using any SMTP-compliant mail server.
- *File*—This built-in delivery provider writes notifications to the file of your choice and is used mostly for debugging applications.
- `IDeliveryProtocol`—You can write classes that implement this interface to produce a custom provider.
- *HTTP*—You can write classes that implement `IHttpProtocol-Provider`. SQLNS comes with a class, `HttpExtension`, that encapsulates sending through HTTP. It's simpler to implement this interface if your custom protocol provider uses HTTP.
- *Microsoft Alerts provider*—This provider comes with the .NET Alerts 6.0 toolkit and is used to send notifications to the Microsoft Alerts service. From there, Microsoft Alerts can deliver them to instant messenger, e-mail, or SMS-compliant cell phones. Providers for older versions of the .NET Framework Alerts toolkit are also available.
- *SMS providers*—There are providers to send notifications to cell phones through the major commercial SMS aggregators.
- *Third-party products*—There are third-party products, released or in development, for fax delivery, SMS, and the BlackBerry Server.

When you start up a Notification Services instance, the command that is run is `NSService.exe`. If your instance is called StockTrader, for example, the whole command line actually looks like this:

```
[fullpath to NSService]\NSService.exe "StockTraderInstance"
```

When `NSService.exe` starts up, it reads that command-line parameter and looks for an application called StockTraderInstance in the Registry (SQLNS keeps a list of all of its instances as Registry subkeys of `HKLM\Software\Microsoft\Microsoft SQL Server\Services\Notification Services\Instances`). One parameter of this subkey holds the location of the SQL Server where the metadata for this instance is stored. It will connect to that instance of SQL Server, using integrated security or an SQL Server user ID and password, and read the metadata it needs to control the instance. This metadata includes information such as:

- What event, subscription, and notification classes are defined.
- Which providers should be loaded, including custom providers.
- Parameters for the service's generator and distributor subsystems. (We'll discuss the intricacies of these systems later in this chapter.)

We should mention a couple of details before we go on. First, multiple instances of SQLNS can run on a single machine, much as multiple instances of SQL Server itself can run on a single machine. A single instance of `NSService.exe` can run a single Notification Services application or more than one application. We'll define applications in more detail later, but we'll mention here that each application has its own application database separate from the instance database. Usually, one instance means one set of subscribers, because subscribers and subscriber delivery vehicles (known as subscriber devices) are stored in tables in the instance database. Subscriptions (to an application), events, and notifications are stored in the application database. This is shown in Figure 16-2.

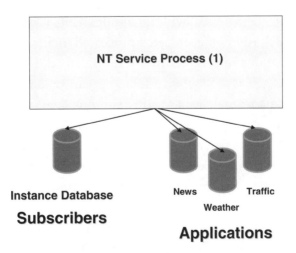

FIGURE 16-2: One application per instance versus multiple applications per instance

Finally, the generator and distributor subsystems can be spread across multiple machines. Each machine would run its own instance of `NSService.exe`, and the SQLNS work would be split among multiple machines. This is similar in concept to running federated SQL Servers. This is an advanced deployment concept not explained in detail in this chapter.

Notification Applications Design Patterns

Notification applications follow a few common patterns. The first distinction between application types is the distinction between event-driven subscriptions and scheduled subscriptions. To use an application that reports weather information to a cell phone, as an example, if we are interested in receiving a Portland, Oregon, weather forecast each day at 8 a.m., this is a scheduled notification. If we're interested in receiving notification when the temperature in Portland, Oregon, goes below 10 degrees, however, this is an event-driven notification. This difference demonstrates the different types of subscriptions and how the generator process handles event-based and schedule-based subscriptions in SQLNS.

With an event-driven notification pattern, events are written into event tables on a fairly continuous basis, as configured by the application administrator. Every so often, the SQLNS generator wakes up and looks for batches of events to process. It will run the algorithm (written in T-SQL and known as a match rule) for each batch processed, matching current events against subscriptions to produce notifications. In addition, each time the generator wakes up, it will obtain all the scheduled subscriptions that are due at that time and match these subscriptions against data to produce notifications. The data used in generating event-driven notifications typically is the raw event batches themselves. The data used in generating scheduled subscriptions is kept in history tables, known as *chronicle tables*. There are two flavors of chronicle tables: event chronicles and subscription chronicles.

A few refinements of these patterns are useful in making the notifications more meaningful to the consumer. Another variation of the scheduled subscription is the trend-based subscription. In this subscription type, we don't want to retrieve static information on a schedule (such as the weather forecast at a certain time), but a historical trend, such as the highest and lowest temperature of the day. This is accomplished by adding functionality to the T-SQL statement that updates the event chronicle table, known as the chronicle rule.

A second refinement might be based on the fact that we want to know when the temperature in Portland goes below 10 degrees at most once a day. Although temperature-change events are reported every 5 minutes, we don't want to be reminded every 5 minutes once the temperature goes below 10 degrees! This is known as duplicate removal and is accomplished by keeping historical subscription data known as subscription chronicle files.

Notification Services Delivery Features

Digest delivery is an option that makes for a better consumer experience. Let's say we subscribe to a stock subscription service that notifies us by e-mail when the stocks of our choice reach a certain threshold. We're interested in ten different stocks. If four of them go over the threshold price that we've set at the same time, we don't want to get four individual messages but a single message that has notifications about the four stocks. This is known as digest delivery.

One final feature is used not to enhance the consumer experience but to make the notification formatting (and possibly delivery) more efficient. If 1,000 people each register to receive the weather forecast for Portland by cell phone, and the notification message is the same for each user, the formatter doesn't need to format the same message 1,000 times. In addition, a Microsoft Alerts–based application that delivers cell phone messages may accept a single message with 1,000 different destinations. Producing a single message for multiple users and delivering it through a list is known as multicast delivery.

Terms Used in Notification Services

Notification Services uses quite a few overloaded terms—that is, terms that you might be familiar with in a different context with a different meaning. Before we go any further, we should define the vocabulary we're using and what these terms mean in a SQL Server Notification Services environment:

- *Events*—Events are external items that trigger notifications. In our example, it is changes of stock prices. The events can come from a variety of sources: stock-ticker feeds, changes of rows in database tables, news feeds, file directory changes, and so on. Event providers capture events and store them in the appropriate data-base tables. To improve scalability, SQLNS processes events in batches.

- *Subscribers*—Subscribers are the end users of the application. Sub-scribers are not exclusive to a specific SQLNS application but can be shared among applications. A subscriber can have a locale specified (language and possibly dialect) and a time zone.

- *Devices*—Devices are what the notifications are delivered to (e-mail, cell phones, Web Services). A subscriber can have several subscriber devices.

- *Subscriptions*—The subscriptions define what events a subscriber wants to be notified of. Depending on the events, a single application may use one or more subscription styles.

- *Chronicle tables*—Chronicle tables are used to store event history. The chronicle tables are useful for the different subscription styles men-tioned earlier.

- *Generator*—The notification pipeline consists of the event processor, the generator, and the distributor. The generator runs T-SQL match rules to generate notifications.

- *Distributor*—The distributor's job is to format and distribute notifications.

- *Quantum*—Both the generator and the distributor fire every so often; that duration is defined in seconds. This is known as the *quantum*.

- *Formatters*—Formatters are used to shape the raw notification data into a format the subscriber and the device understand. This can be based on device, locale, or both.

- *Delivery channels*—The delivery channel is the logical delivery mecha-nism, and a delivery channel targets one or several devices. It is mapped to delivery parameters: server name, user ID, and so on. Delivery channels are also mapped to delivery protocols—however, not in a one-to-one relation. Several delivery channels can use the same protocol.

- *Delivery protocols*—The delivery protocol is the physical delivery mechanism. Typical protocols are SMTP and HTTP.

Designing, Coding, and Generating a Notification Services Application

Because much of the application infrastructure is provided in the box in SQLNS applications, planning the application will be much more involved than designing or coding the applications. Following are two lists of steps that outline the process.

Planning Steps

1. Decide which notifications to expose:
   - One or many notification classes
   - Scheduled or event-driven subscriptions
   - Digest (consolidated) or individual notifications
   - Whether many subscribers will get the same notification
2. Tie notifications to subscriptions:
   - Category of notifications versus categories of subscriptions
   - Locale-driven notifications
   - Items of subscriber information used to personalize
3. Decide how events cause notifications:
   - Which criteria must be specified (SQL JOIN rules)
   - Whether users should be able to specify their own WHERE clauses for rules (known as condition actions)
   - Whether notifications are event-driven or scheduled
   - What history needs to be kept using chronicles or other supplemental data tables
4. Decide where subscribers and subscriptions come from:
   - Existing applications (for example, an existing line-of-business application or extracted from an Active Directory hierarchy)
   - Specially written Web application

5. Pick your providers:
   - Event provider(s)
   - Content formatter
   - Delivery protocol(s)—one per delivery channel

Coding Steps

1. Code your instance and application definition files:
   - Decide where you will store event schema files if using the File Watcher event provider.
   - Decide on a directory to watch for files of events to arrive if using the File Watcher event provider.
   - Decide where you will store XSLT transforms for formatting if using the XSLT formatter.
   - Code these locations into your application definition files or using NMO.
   - Code event, subscription, and notification classes in the application definition files or using NMO.
   - Code subscription rules in the application definition files or using NMO. These can be event rules, scheduled rules, and condition actions.
   - Code information needed for delivery formatting and locations.
   - Code machine locations where the SQL Server holding the databases will live, along with locations for the generator and the distributor.
   - Code generator quantum duration and other generator and distributor behavior parameters.
   - Code a schedule for the vacuum utility, which will run every so often to dispose of stale data.
2. Code your subscription management application:
   - It may be written in ASP.NET, ASP, or any tool that supports .NET Framework or COM-based components.
   - It will use the subscription application object model in the SQLNS DLL.
3. Code your event XML schemas if using the File Watcher event provider.
4. Code your XSLT transforms, one for each combination of locale and device supported.

Application Generation Steps

1. Use SQL Server Management Studio or NMO, or run `NSControl` `Create` to create the instance and application databases.

2. Use SQL Server Management Studio or NMO, or run `NSControl` `Register` to create the Registry entries and the Windows service process.

3. Use SQL Server Management Studio or NMO, or run `NSControl` to start (or stop) the various services used for the Notification Services instance and applications.

Some of these steps may refer to terms that haven't been discussed in detail yet. We'll delve into the details in our sample application.

A Sample Notification Application

The rest of this chapter consists of a series of tutorials that show developing a sample Notification Services application step by step. We begin with the minimalist application to keep from printing many pages of large configuration files and add functionality to the application incrementally, so you can see the changes to the minimalist configuration needed to implement different application functionality. On the way, we'll discuss the options available in an SQLNS application by looking at the options of the control file XML elements. The step-by-step application code and the final application are available as part of the samples on the book's Web site.

Imagine for a moment that you are a developer for a stock trading application. Apart from letting the clients enter trades over the Web, the clients should also be notified when certain stocks reach a specified price (the client has specified the price). The stock prices come in through a feed from a vendor of financial information. The prices are fed into tables in a SQL Server. As soon as the prices change, the application should notify the client if the price matches the preset price. Figure 16-3 shows what it looks like.

This example is one pattern: an event-driven notification application matching stock code and price from the event feed, with the stock code and

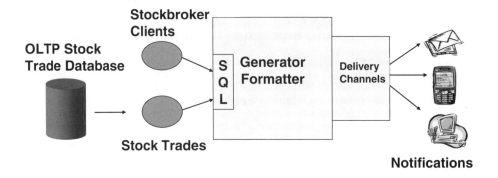

Figure 16-3: Financial application

a trigger price specified in the subscription. In addition, the customer may want to be notified at a certain time of the highest or lowest price at which a particular stock has traded at during a trading day. The same application now contains two kinds of notification patterns: event-driven notifications and scheduled notifications.

Instance and Application Configuration Files

In Notification Services, one instance of the notification server service can consist of one or more applications. As we mentioned earlier, the instance database[1] holds the subscriber information and control tables. The various application databases store the information specific to the application (stock, news, weather) and control tables. In SQL Server 2005 Notification Services, you can also choose to use an existing database. When you use an existing database, special schemas (not the dbo schema) are used as containers for the instance and application tables. We mentioned earlier that the instance is responsible for collecting events and so on. You may be asking yourself how the instance knows about the applications. The answer to this is the configuration files, which exist for both the instance and the applications.

---

1. Although SQLNS produces two separate databases for its objects by default, SQL Server 2005 also permits two separate schemas in the same database. This chapter will refer to these as separate databases hereafter.

These configuration files define the state and behavior of instances and applications. The configuration files are in XML format and are schema based. In SQL Server 2005, the schema for both the instance configuration file and the application configuration file can be located in the SQL Server directory under `\90\NotificationServices\<version>\XML Schemas\`. The schema for the instance file is called `ConfigurationFileSchema.xsd`, and the application schema is named `ApplicationDefinitionFileSchema.xsd`.

The instance configuration file contains control information and lists the applications. The application configuration file lists the applications schema and the actions. Now let's focus more closely on these two files, starting with the instance file.

Instance Configuration File

The instance configuration file describes a single instance of Notification Services. It holds metadata information about the applications that the instance hosts. The metadata information for applications consists of the application name, base directory path, and name of the application configuration file. The configuration file also contains metadata about the instance, database server, delivery protocols, and delivery channels.

A sample instance configuration file is shown in Listing 16-1. The file contains only the required sections and elements for a valid instance configuration file.

LISTING 16-1: Instance configuration file

```
<?xml version="1.0" encoding="utf-8" ?>
<NotificationServicesInstance
xmlns="http://www.microsoft.com/MicrosoftNotificationServices/
ConfigurationFileSchema">

<InstanceName>Stock</InstanceName>
<SqlServerSystem>SERVNB02</SqlServerSystem>

<Applications>
    <Application>
          <ApplicationName>StockPrice</ApplicationName>
        <BaseDirectoryPath>
      C:\MyPath
   </BaseDirectoryPath>
          <ApplicationDefinitionFilePath>
      appADF.xml
```

```
    </ApplicationDefinitionFilePath>
      </Application>
</Applications>

<DeliveryChannels>
      <DeliveryChannel>
            <DeliveryChannelName>FileChannel</DeliveryChannelName>
            <ProtocolName>File</ProtocolName>
      </DeliveryChannel>
</DeliveryChannels>

</NotificationServicesInstance>
```

When you inspect the file in Listing 16-1, you can see the metadata entries for the instance, as follows:

- InstanceName—The logical name for the instance of the Notification Services
- SqlServerSystem—The name of a SQL Server instance that hosts the instance database and its application databases
- DeliveryChannels—Contains <DeliveryChannel> nodes that describe all the delivery channels used by all applications hosted by the instance (more about delivery channels later in this chapter)

In the file, you can also see the metadata for one particular application. It is contained within an <Application> node under the <Applications> section:

- ApplicationName—Is the logical name of the application. It must be unique within the configuration file.
- BaseDirectoryPath—Is the application directory path. It is used to locate files specific to the application. These files typically are XML and XSLT files.
- ApplicationDefinitionFilePath—Is the name of, and optionally the path to, the application definition file (ADF).

As we mentioned before, the file in Listing 16-1 contains the bare minimum of information. You'll probably want to include more information in your configuration file, and SQL Server Books Online lists the complete set of elements and nodes available. You may want to enter version information through the `<Version>` node, for example. If you create custom delivery protocols, you register them with `<Protocol>` nodes in the `<Protocols>` section.

You could also do this by using NMO in SQL Server 2005. Here's a short equivalent example in NMO:

```
using System;
using Microsoft.SqlServer.Management.SMO;
using Microsoft.SqlServer.Management.NMO;

public static void Main()
{
Server theServer = new Server();

// create the SQLNS Instance
Instance theInstance =
  new Instance(theServer.NotificationServices, "MyInstanceName");
theInstance.DatabaseName = "SERVNB02";
theInstance.Name = "Stock";

// Add in the FileChannel
DeliveryChannel fileChannel =
  new DeliveryChannel(theInstance, "FileChannel");
fileChannel.ProtocolName = "File";

DeliveryChannelArgument fileNameArg =
  new DeliveryChannelArgument(fileChannel, "FileName");
fileNameArg.Value = @"c:\FileNotifications.txt";

fileChannel.DeliveryChannelArguments.Add(fileNameArg);
theInstance.DeliveryChannels.Add(fileChannel);

// Call another method to construct the Application
Application theApp = ConfigureApp(theInstance, "StockPrice");
theInstance.Applications.Add(theApp);
}
```

When you look at the configuration file in Listing 16-1, you may notice that all information is hard-coded into the file. For a production system, this is not ideal. For this reason, both the instance configuration file and the application configuration file have a `<ParameterDefaults>` node containing one or more `<Parameter>` nodes. The parameters are symbolic names appearing as name–value pairs. The application configuration file can inherit parameters from the instance file. Listing 16-2 shows an example of the configuration file in Listing 16-1 using parameters.

LISTING 16-2: Configuration file using parameters

```xml
<?xml version="1.0" encoding="utf-8" ?>
<NotificationServicesInstance
xmlns="http://www.microsoft.com/MicrosoftNotificationServices/
ConfigurationFileSchema">

<ParameterDefaults>
   <Parameter>
      <Name>Instance</Name>
      <Value>Stock</Value>
   </Parameter>
   <Parameter>
      <Name>DBSystem</Name>
      <Value>%COMPUTERNAME%</Value>
   </Parameter>
   <Parameter>
      <Name>BasePath</Name>
      <Value>C:\MyPath</Value>
   </Parameter>
   <Parameter>
      <Name>AppName</Name>
      <Value>StockPrice</Value>
   </Parameter>
</ParameterDefaults>

<InstanceName>%Instance%</InstanceName>
<SqlServerSystem>%DBSystem%</SqlServerSystem>

<Applications>
     <Application>
           <ApplicationName>%AppName%</ApplicationName>
        <BaseDirectoryPath>
      %BasePath%
    </BaseDirectoryPath>
           <ApplicationDefinitionFilePath>
      appADF.xml
    </ApplicationDefinitionFilePath>
    <Parameters>
                  <Parameter>
                        <Name>_App_</Name>
                        <Value>%AppName%</Value>
                  </Parameter>
                  <Parameter>
                        <Name>_NSHost_</Name>
                        <Value>%COMPUTERNAME%</Value>
                  </Parameter>
            </Parameters>
     </Application>
</Applications>
```

```
<DeliveryChannels>
      <DeliveryChannel>
            <DeliveryChannelName>FileChannel</DeliveryChannelName>
            <ProtocolName>File</ProtocolName>
      </DeliveryChannel>
</DeliveryChannels>

</NotificationServicesInstance>
```

Compare the file in Listing 16-2 with the one in Listing 16-1, and you'll see that we have a `<ParameterDefaults>` section, where we define different variables that are used farther down in the file. Within the `<Application>` section, we have a `<Parameters>` section, where we redefine some of the variables and give them new names. These names are inherited by the application configuration file.

You should also notice that we use systemwide environment variables— for example, `%COMPUTERNAME%`. We are not restricted to system environment variables, but we can set up our own variables in scripts and use the scripts when we build the SQLNS applications. This is very useful if you use Visual Studio 2005 to build your applications.[2]

By now, you may be asking yourself how we go about building databases, tables, and stored procedures from the configuration files. To build these items, you run the executable `NSControl.exe` and give it the name of your instance configuration file. We'll cover this topic later in the chapter. First, we need to look at the configuration file for the application: the application definition file.

Application Definition File

The ADF stores all metadata about a particular SQLNS application. The file must conform to the schema in the `ApplicationDefinition-FileSchema.xsd` schema. Also, the nodes and elements in the file must be provided in the same order as in the schema. Listing 16-3 shows a minimal ADF file.

---

2. At this writing, native Visual Studio projects for Notification Services don't exist. To build SQLNS applications, you use VC++ makefile projects. These projects allow you to run predefined build scripts.

LISTING 16-3: Minimal ADF file

```xml
<?xml version="1.0" encoding="utf-8" ?>
<Application xmlns="http://www.microsoft.com/
MicrosoftNotificationServices/ApplicationDefinitionFileSchema">

<SubscriptionClasses>
  <SubscriptionClass>
    <SubscriptionClassName></SubscriptionClassName>
    <Schema>
      <Field>
        <FieldName></FieldName>
        <FieldType></FieldType>
      </Field>
    </Schema>
  </SubscriptionClass>
</SubscriptionClasses>

<NotificationClasses>
  <NotificationClass>
    <NotificationClassName></NotificationClassName>
    <Schema>
    </Schema>
    <ContentFormatter>
      <ClassName></ClassName>
    </ContentFormatter>
  </NotificationClass>
</NotificationClasses>

<Generator>
  <SystemName></SystemName>
</Generator>

<Distributors>
  <Distributor>
    <SystemName></SystemName>
  </Distributor>
</Distributors>

</Application>
```

The ADF file has four required nodes:

- `SubscriptionClasses`—This is used to define the subscription classes you use in your application. The classes are defined by a name and a schema. The schema indicates what fields of data you store for the subscription and what the data type of each field is.

Optionally, you can define attributes for the fields. These attributes are SQL Server field attributes, such as nullability and default values.

- `NotificationClasses`—This is used to define the classes your application uses for notifications. As with subscription classes, you enter a name and a schema. In addition to the subscription class, you need to define what formatter is used to format the content of a notification.

- `Generator`—The generator manages the rule processing for the application. This node holds information about what system runs the process. You specify how often the `Generator` runs (`Quantum-Duration`) as a separate element at the same level at the `Generator` element, not as a child of the `Generator` element. Optionally, you can set how many operating system threads the generator can use. Read more about this in Books Online.

- `Distributor`—The distributor manages formatting and delivery of notifications. The node allows you to specify what systems run the distributor and, optionally, the thread pool size and how often the distributor runs (the `QuantumDuration`).

We mentioned before that the file in Listing 16-3 contains the minimal requirements. Although you can write an SQLNS application without defining `EventClasses`, `EventClasses` are also part of most applications. Later in this chapter, we will cover the required nodes in more detail, as well as what more we need to create a fully functional application.

Listing 16-4 shows an ADF file for our stock price application meeting the minimum requirements. The file is based on the file in Listing 16-3 and the instance configuration file in Listing 16-2. Notice how the parameters defined in the file in Listing 16-2 are used in the ADF file.

LISTING 16-4: ADF file for the stock price application

```
<?xml version="1.0" encoding="utf-8" ?>
<Application xmlns="http://www.microsoft.com/
MicrosoftNotificationServices/ApplicationDefinitionFileSchema">

<SubscriptionClasses>
  <SubscriptionClass>
    <SubscriptionClassName>
      %_App_%Subscriptions
```

```
    </SubscriptionClassName>
    <Schema>
      <Field>
        <FieldName>StockSymbol</FieldName>
        <FieldType>varchar(10)</FieldType>
      </Field>
    </Schema>
  </SubscriptionClass>
</SubscriptionClasses>

<NotificationClasses>
  <NotificationClass>
    <NotificationClassName>
      %_App_%Notifications
    </NotificationClassName>
    <Schema/>
    <ContentFormatter>
      <ClassName>XsltFormatter</ClassName>
    </ContentFormatter>
  </NotificationClass>
</NotificationClasses>

<Generator>
  <SystemName>%_NSHost_%</SystemName>
</Generator>

<Distributors>
  <Distributor>
    <SystemName>%_NSHost_%</SystemName>
  </Distributor>
</Distributors>

</Application>
```

We can read from the file in Listing 16-4 that we have one subscription class and that we store only one field of data for the subscription. That field is called StockSymbol (although technically, other helpful fields, like DeviceName, should be stored). To format the notifications, we use the XsltFormatter, which comes out of the box with the SQLNS framework. Finally, the local system generates and distributes the notifications.

Having the files in Listings 16-2 and 16-4, we can now build the stock price Notification Services application. The NSControl.exe tool is used for this.

NSControl

NSControl is a tool for administering SQLNS. You use it to deploy, configure, monitor, and control SQLNS instances and applications. It is run from the command prompt, and Table 16-1 presents the available commands. SQL Server Books Online covers these commands and their syntax in detail.

You use the `Create` command to create your new SQLNS instance. The syntax for `NSControl Create` follows:

TABLE 16-1: Commands for NSControl

Command	Description
Create	Creates a new instance of Notification Services
Delete	Deletes an existing instance of Notification Services
Disable	Disables the specified Notification Services components
DisplayArgumentKey	Displays the key used to encrypt delivery channel and event provider arguments
Enable	Enables the specified Notification Services components
ListVersions	Displays information about the installed versions and registered instances of Notification Services
Register	Registers an instance of Notification Services
Status	Displays the current enabled or disabled status of instances and applications
Unregister	Unregisters an instance of Notification Services
Update	Updates an existing instance of Notification Services
Upgrade	Upgrades an instance from Standard Edition to Enterprise Edition or to a newer version of Notification Services

```
nscontrol create
    [-help] |
    -in configuration_filename
    [-sqlusername login_ID  -sqlpassword password]
    [-argumentkey key]
    [parameter_name=value [,...n] ]
    [-nologo]
```

Here is a description of the arguments:

- -help—Displays the command syntax.
- -in configuration_filename—The pathname and filename of the instance configuration file. The path is not required if the file is in the current directory.
- -sqlusername login_ID—If you are using SQL Server authentication to log in to SQL Server, this is the SQL Server login ID. Best practice, however, is to use Microsoft Windows authentication to log in to SQL Server. In that case, do not use the -sqlusername and -sqlpassword arguments.
- -sqlpassword password—The password for the -sqlusername login ID.
- -argumentkey key—The value used to encrypt the delivery channel and event provider arguments that are stored in Notification Services databases.
- parameter_name=value—A name–value pair used to pass parameters to the configuration file from the command line.
- -nologo—Suppresses the product and version statement that appears when you run an NSControl command.

Now that you know the syntax for NSControl Create, it is time to compile the application. You need two XML files: appConfig1.xml and appADF1.xml. They represent the files in Listings 16-2 and 16-4, and you can use these two files to create your application. Copy them to a directory on your hard drive, and change the BasePath parameter in the appConfig1.xml file to the directory you copied the files to. Before you can run the NSControl Create command, you need to make sure that NSControl.exe is on the path. Alternatively, you can run NSControl Create with a fully qualified path.

The following code creates an SQLNS instance together with the stock price application. It is run from the directory where the configuration files are. It assumes that the NSControl exists on the path, and it uses integrated security to log on to SQL Server:

```
NSControl Create -in appConfig1.xml
```

When you run this, you will see something like this in your Command window:

```
Microsoft Notification Services Control Utility (Enterprise) 9.0.242
Copyright (C) Microsoft Corporation 2004. All rights reserved.

Creating instance
Stock

Creating application
Application name: StockPrice

Create successful.
```

If you now log on to the SQL Server that is defined in the DBSystem parameter, you can see two new databases: the instance database, named StockNSMain, and the application database, called StockStockPrice. You should *never* alter the data in these databases directly, but it's helpful to have a look at what's inside them at this point.

So far, the databases do not contain that much application data. The instance database has a table called NSApplicationNames, which consists of one record: the StockPrice application. Notice, however, that in the instance database, there are tables for time zones. These tables make it really easy to create time zone–aware applications. The application database does not have that much more interesting information, either. You can see the notification and subscription classes in the NSNotificationClasses and NSSubscriptionClasses tables. Although EventClasses aren't technically required, most applications will use one or more event classes and event providers. We'll add them next.

Events

Events can come from a multitude of sources, and they are the occurrences that cause notifications. The events are processed by *event providers*, which send the event data to the application, where it is inserted into the event table.

We discussed the built-in providers and customization hooks available at the beginning of the chapter. Apart from standard and customized event providers, SQLNS also differentiates between hosted and nonhosted (independent) event providers. Hosted event providers run inside SQLNS, and they either run continuously or fire based on a schedule. The schedule for a hosted scheduled provider is defined in the ADF file for the application. The hosted providers are controlled by a component in Notification Services, the event provider host. An independent event provider runs as an external application, and it submits events according to its own schedule.

Events in SQLNS are handled in batches in order to improve performance. Let's assume that the event provider picks up three events since it last fired. The provider can create a batch with a batch ID and insert each event into the event table together with the batch ID. The events are processed by the generator the next time the generator fires. This allows the generator to compare multiple events with subscriptions at one time, instead of doing it on an event-by-event basis. This is done because it gives good scalability for the tradeoff of real-time processing. If a little latency is allowed, it scales to huge numbers.

Event Classes

To catch the events you are interested in, you have to define what events to accept. This is accomplished by using event classes and event class definitions in the ADF file. Listing 16-5 shows the required elements and nodes for one event class definition.

LISTING 16-5: Event class definition in the ADF file

```
<EventClasses>
  <EventClass>
    <EventClassName></EventClassName>
    <Schema>
      <Field>
        <FieldName></FieldName>
        <FieldType></FieldType>
```

```
            </Field>
          </Schema>
        </EventClass>
    </EventClasses>
```

You can see that it looks very much like the definition for the subscription class and notification class in Listing 16-4. Both the `EventClass` node and the `Schema` node support quite a few optional nodes and elements, and they are listed in Books Online.

In our stock price example, we are interested in the stock code (MSFT, IBM, and so on), the exchange the stock trades on, and the price.[3] Listing 16-6 shows how the event class definition looks in our stock price application. Notice that there are a couple of nonrequired elements in the file: the `FieldTypeMods` element, to set attributes on the fields in SQL Server, and the `IndexSqlSchema` node, where in the `SqlStatement` you create indexes on the table.

LISTING 16-6: Event class definition in the ADF file

```
<?xml version="1.0" encoding="utf-8" ?>
<Application xmlns="http://www.microsoft.com/
MicrosoftNotificationServices/ApplicationDefinitionFileSchema">

<EventClasses>
  <EventClass>
    <EventClassName>StockEvt</EventClassName>
    <Schema>
      <Field>
        <FieldName>StockCode</FieldName>
        <FieldType>varchar(10)</FieldType>
        <FieldTypeMods>not null</FieldTypeMods>
      </Field>
      <Field>
        <FieldName>ExchangeCode</FieldName>
        <FieldType>varchar(15)</FieldType>
        <FieldTypeMods>not null</FieldTypeMods>
      </Field>
      <Field>
        <FieldName>Price</FieldName>
        <FieldType>decimal(18,5)</FieldType>
        <FieldTypeMods>not null</FieldTypeMods>
      </Field>
```

---

3. A stock can trade on different exchanges and not necessarily for the same price. For simplicity, we assume that all exchanges trade in the same currency.

```
      </Schema>
      <IndexSqlSchema>
        <SqlStatement>
          Create Index StockStockIndex on StockEvt
          (StockCode, ExchangeCode)
        </SqlStatement>
        <SqlStatement>
          Create Index StockStockIndex2 on StockEvt
        (ExchangeCode)</SqlStatement>
      </IndexSqlSchema>
    </EventClass>
</EventClasses>

<SubscriptionClasses>
  <!-Rest of file omitted
  ...


</Application>
```

There is still something missing from the ADF file in Listing 16-6: the information about what event provider to use. Remember that earlier, we discussed hosted versus independent providers? Initially, we will use an independent provider to collect the events.

Event providers are entered and named in the ADF file. They are located under the <Providers> node. This node contains <HostedProvider> and <NonHostedProvider> nodes. First, as we mentioned earlier, we'll use a nonhosted provider. Although some event providers need to be entered in the ADF to provide supporting information, others (like nonhosted providers) are entered mostly for internal documentation. We add to the ADF file in Listing 16-6 the <Providers> node, as shown in Listing 16-7. Notice that the <Providers> node needs to be placed after the <Notifica-tionClasses> node but before the <Generator> node.

LISTING 16-7: Providers node in the ADF file

```
</NotificationClasses>

<Providers>
      <NonHostedProvider>
            <ProviderName>SqlStockEvents</ProviderName>
      </NonHostedProvider>
</Providers>

  <Generator>
```

With these updates to the ADF file, the SQLNS application can be updated. For updates, the NSControl Update command is used, according to the following syntax:

```
nscontrol update
    [-help] |
    -in configuration_filename
    [-verbose]
    [-force]
    [-sqlusername login_id -sqlpassword password]
    [-argumentkey key]
    [parameter_name=value [,...n] ]
    [-nologo]
```

The Update command looks almost like the Create command. The only differences are the verbose and force flags. The verbose flag displays the information that has changed in the configuration file and the ADF file as it is found. The force flag forces the update to proceed without prompting for approval after displaying the actions that will occur. To set up the event classes in the SQLNS application, you run NSControl Update against the configuration file and the changed ADF file.[4] Running NSControl Update -in appConfig2.xml causes some changes to the application database:

- Additional tables have been created: NSCurrentStockEvtEvent-Batches, NSCurrentStockEvtEvents, NSStockEvtEventBatches, and NSStockEvtEvents. As the names of the tables indicate, they are used to store event and event batch information.
- Data has been inserted into the NSEventClasses and NSEvent-Fields tables.
- Among the new stored procedures are procedures for writing events and event batches.

In the ADF file, we indicated that we would use a nonhosted provider, and we gave it the name SqlStockEvents. With a nonhosted provider, the

---

4. On the book's Web site of samples, you will find the updated configuration file, appConfig2.xml, and the new ADF file, appADF2.xml, with the Notification Services samples.

only element that needs to be defined is the name of the provider. We will see how the name is used when events are submitted through the SQLNS stored procedures.

Event Stored Procedures

These are the stored procedures that have been created to write events to the database:

- NSBeginEventBatch<EventClassName>—Creates a new event batch and returns an ID for the batch.

- NSEventWrite<EventClassName>—Submits one event to the events table for the event. The NSBeginEventBatch<EventClassName> must be run first to obtain the batch ID.

- NSEventFlushBatch<EventClassName>—Closes the batch and marks it complete. When the batch is marked complete, the generator can process the events.

- NsEventSubmitBatch<EventClassName>—The previous procedures in this list are used mostly to write to the event table when the event is a single event from an outside source. When the events to collect are multiple entries in a database, we use this procedure, which allows us to specify a query to retrieve a batch of events to collect.

In this stage of our application, we are submitting only single events, so we start the event collecting process by starting a batch. We do this by using the NSBeginEventBatch<EventClassName> procedure. The syntax follows:

```
NSEventBeginBatchEventClassName
  [@ProviderName =] 'event_provider_name',
  [@EventBatchId =] event_batch_variable OUTPUT
```

The EventClassName is picked from the EventClassName element in the EventClass node. The procedure takes a provider name as the input parameter. This has to be the same name that appears in the ProviderName element. It returns a batch ID as the output parameter.

The batch ID is used in the NSEventWrite<EventClassName> stored procedure. This procedure also uses the event class name. The syntax looks like this:

```
NSEventWriteEventClassName
   [@EventBatchId =] event_batch_ID ,
   [@event_class_field_name =] event_class_field_value [, ...n]
```

The `@EventBatchId` parameter is the parameter received from the `NSEventBeginBatch` procedure. Name–value pairs follow the batch ID parameter. These name–value pairs correspond to the `FieldName` element in the `EventClass` node and its value. In the stock price database, the signature for the procedure looks like this:

```
NSEventWriteStockEvt
     @EventBatchId    bigint,
     @StockCode varchar(10) = NULL,
     @ExchangeCode varchar(15) = NULL,
     @Price decimal(18,5) = NULL
```

You close the batch with the `NSEventFlushBatch<EventClassName>` procedure when the event is submitted. This procedure takes the batch ID and, optionally, the number of events submitted as parameters:

```
NSEventFlushBatchEventClassName
     [@EventBatchId =] event_batch_ID
     [, [@EventCount =] number_of_events]
```

The code to create an event is shown in Listing 16-8. Because the application has just been created (and updated), it needs to be enabled and registered first. `NSControl` is used for this, and the syntax is

```
NSControl Enable -name instancename -server servername
```

where `-name` is the Notification Services instance name, and `-server` is the name of the server where the instance is installed.

LISTING 16-8: Code to create an event

```
DECLARE @ProviderName varchar(255)
DECLARE @EventBatchId bigint
DECLARE @EventCount bigint
DECLARE @RicCode varchar(6)
DECLARE @ExchangeCode varchar(6)
DECLARE @Price float(10)
DECLARE @EventClassName varchar(255)

SET @ProviderName = 'SqlStockEvents'
EXECUTE NSEventBeginBatchStockEvt @ProviderName,
                                  @EventBatchId OUTPUT
```

```
SET @RicCode = 'MSFT'
SET @ExchangeCode = 'NYSE'
SET @Price = 53.33
EXECUTE NSEventWriteStockEvt @EventBatchId,
                            @RicCode,
                            @ExchangeCode, @Price

SET @EventCount = 1
EXECUTE NSEventFlushBatchStockEvt @EventBatchId, @EventCount
```

To view information about the batch and the events in the batch, we can use a stored procedure named NSEventBatchDetails. The syntax for the procedure follows:

```
NSEventBatchDetails
    [@EventClassName =] 'event_class_name' ,
    [@EventBatchId =] event_batch_id
```

It takes the name of the event class and the ID of the batch you want the information about, and it produces two resultsets. The first resultset contains general information about the batch, such as the provider, how many events are in the batch, when the batch started, when it ended, and the total collection time in milliseconds. The second resultset contains information about the individual events in the batch: the event ID and the individual event fields of the event. Apart from getting information about batches and events, there are stored procedures for information about event providers and event classes:

- NSDiagnosticEventClass—This procedure produces information about event collection and processing of events by the application.
- NSDiagnosticEventProvider—This procedure contains information about the events collected through a specified event provider.

Event Providers

We started this whole section about events by discussing event providers. We also mentioned briefly the event providers that are part of the SQLNS framework: the File Watcher event provider and the SQL Server event provider. Now let's take a close look at them, starting with the File Watcher event provider (FS).

The File Watcher event provider monitors a directory. The provider fires when an XML file is added to the directory. It reads the content of the file into memory and writes the event data to the event table. Internally, the provider uses the `FileSystemWatcher` class from the .NET Framework. It is being run as a hosted nonscheduled provider, and it is set up in the ADF with these three mandatory arguments in addition to the provider name, class name, and system name:

- `WatchDirectory`—Full path and name of the directory that the event provider monitors
- `EventClassName`—Name of the event class that defines the events
- `SchemaFile`—Full path to a SQL-annotated schema file that describes the schema for the events

Listing 16-9 shows the provider part of the stock price application's ADF file when we have added the FS as a hosted provider.

LISTING 16-9: ADF file with hosted file system watcher provider

```xml
<Providers>
  <HostedProvider>
    <ProviderName>StockEP</ProviderName>
    <ClassName>FileSystemWatcherProvider</ClassName>
    <SystemName>%_NSHost_%</SystemName>
    <Arguments>
      <Argument>
        <Name>WatchDirectory</Name>
        <Value>%_BasePath_%\Test\Events</Value>
      </Argument>
      <Argument>
        <Name>SchemaFile</Name>
        <Value>%_BasePath_%\EventsSchema.xsd</Value>
      </Argument>
      <Argument>
        <Name>EventClassName</Name>
        <Value>StockEvt</Value>
      </Argument>
    </Arguments>
  </HostedProvider>
  <NonHostedProvider>
    <ProviderName>SqlStockEvents</ProviderName>
  </NonHostedProvider>
</Providers>
```

The provider is named `StockEP`; the class name has to be `FileSys-temWatcherProvider`; and the system name refers to the `_NSHost_` parameter. In the arguments node, we point the directory to watch to the `\Test\Events` directory underneath the base directory. The schema is located in the `EventsSchema.xsd` file in the base directory and is shown in Listing 16-10. Finally, we tell the provider that the event class to collect events for is the `StockEvt` class.

LISTING 16-10: Schema for the stock price events

```
<xsd:schema xmlns:xsd="http://www.w3.org/2001/XMLSchema"
   xmlns:sql="urn:schemas-microsoft-com:mapping-schema">
  <xsd:element name="event" sql:relation="StockEvt">
    <xsd:complexType>
      <xsd:sequence>
        <xsd:element name="StockCode" type="xsd:string"/>
        <xsd:element name="ExchangeCode" type="xsd:string"/>
        <xsd:element name="Price" type="xsd:decimal" />
      </xsd:sequence>
    </xsd:complexType>
  </xsd:element>
</xsd:schema>
```

`NSControl Update` can now be run again against the configuration file. The configuration file's `ApplicationDefinitionFilePath` element needs to point to an ADF file containing the `Providers` section in Listing 16-9. Notice, however, that the `_BasePath_` parameter is not defined at the application level. It needs to be defined first either in the configuration file or in the ADF file. We leave it up to you to figure out how to do it (or you can look in the `appConfig3.xml` and `appADF3.xml` files in the book's Web site samples). Before any updates can take place, the instance needs to be disabled. Use `NSControl Disable` to do this with a `-name` parameter and a `-server` parameter. These parameters are the same as those used for `NSControl Enable`. After the update has taken place, run `NScontrol Enable` again, as you did before you submitted events to the application in Listing 16-8.

The FS provider is a hosted provider and, as such, runs under the SQLNS service. So far, we haven't registered the service, but we have run SQLNS in nonservice mode. Unless we start the service, several parts of SQLNS won't run. Among them are the generator of events and notifications and the distributor of notifications.

To register the instance, we use NSControl Register with the name of the instance; the name of the server SQLNS runs on; and the -service argument, which registers this instance of SQLNS as a Windows service. It looks like this from the command line:

```
NSControl Register -name instance-name -server server-name -service
```

Notice that the previous command does not start the service explicitly. It needs to be started from Start > Administrative Tools > Services. The name of the service is NS$ followed by the instance name. Therefore, if the instance name is Stock, the service name is NS$Stock.

When the instance is registered and the service is started, the FS is ready to look for events in the watch directory. When a new file with an .xml extension is placed in the watch directory, the FS loads the file into memory. Then it uses an SQLNS EventLoader object to write the event information into the event table. When the batch has been processed and closed, the XML source file is renamed to indicate that it has been processed. The new filename is the original filename, to which the date and time of its processing are appended. A counter value is also appended to differentiate files processed at the same time, as well as a .done extension. If FS could not process the file, it will be renamed as described earlier, but with an .err extension. In the Notification Services sample code on the book's Web site is an XML file, EventsData.xml, that can be used to test the FS provider.

The second provider that is part of the SQLNS framework is the SQL Server event provider (SEP). This provider uses a user-defined query to query a database table for events. After retrieving the events, it uses the SQLNS event stored procedures to write the events to the event table. Queries can be defined to do pre- and postprocessing of the data. As opposed to the FS provider, the SEP runs as a scheduled provider, and the developer of the SQLNS application needs to define the schedule under which it should be run.

Listing 16-11 shows an example of an entry for the SQL Server event provider in the ADF file. By now, you should be familiar with the schema of the file, so let's look at what is new in it. There is a <Schedule> node that has two children elements: the <StartTime> and the <Interval>. The <StartTime> element is optional and defines at what time the provider should start running after the application has been set up. The <Interval>

defines at what interval it should run. The <Interval> in Listing 16-11 indicates that the provider runs every minute (60 seconds).

LISTING 16-11: ADF file with an entry for a scheduled SQL Server event provider

```
<Providers>
  <HostedProvider>
    <ProviderName>SQLStockPrice</ProviderName>
    <ClassName>SQLProvider</ClassName>
    <SystemName>%_NSHOST_%</SystemName>
    <Schedule>
      <StartTime>15:00:00</StartTime>
      <Interval>P0DT00H00M60S</Interval>
    </Schedule>
    <Arguments>
      <Argument>
        <Name>EventsQuery</Name>
        <Value>SELECT StockSymbol, StockPrice
              FROM StockPriceTable</Value>
      </Argument>
      <Argument>
        <Name>EventClassName</Name>
        <Value>StockEvents</Value>
      </Argument>
    </Arguments>
  </HostedProvider>
</Providers>
```

The format of the <Interval> entry is according to the XML duration data type. This data type is defined as P0DT00H00M00S, which specifies the interval as follows:

- P—Defines the duration data type
- 0D—Number of days
- T—Defines the time portion of the type
- 00H—Number of hours
- 00M—Number of minutes
- 00S—Number of seconds

The <Arguments> node has two children nodes. One defines the query to run, through the EventsQuery name; this is a required entry. The other argument is the EventClassName, which also is required. There is a possible third, optional argument, PostQuery, that defines a query to run after the events have been collected.

Chronicles

We have seen in this events section how events are collected. The model for events collection is based on the presumption that each event can cause a notification. They will not necessarily do that, but potentially, they can. For a scenario where the user is interested only in being notified at a certain time, regardless of whether an event occurred at that time, the model does not work that well. These are some possible scenarios:

- The user wants to get a traffic report at a certain time.
- The user wants to see the highest price of a particular stock during the day.
- The user wants to see historical event information.

To accomplish this, SQLNS uses chronicle tables and chronicle rules to store event data from event batches. Chronicle tables are defined in the `/EventClasses/EventClass/Chronicles` section of the ADF file, as Listing 16-12 shows.

LISTING 16-12: Chronicle table creation in the ADF file

```
<EventClass>
  <!-- other EventClass elements -->
  <Chronicles>
    <Chronicle>
        <ChronicleName>StockEvtChron</ChronicleName>
        <SqlSchema>
          <SqlStatement>
            -- drop table before creating it
            IF EXISTS(SELECT name FROM sys.tables
            WHERE name = 'StockEvtChron')
             DROP TABLE dbo.StockEvtChron
            CREATE TABLE StockEvtChron (
              [StockCode] nvarchar(6),
          [ExchangeCode] nvarchar(6),
              [StockPrice]    decimal(18,5))
          </SqlStatement>
        </SqlSchema>
      </Chronicle>
  </Chronicles>
  <!-- other EventClass elements -->
</EventClass>
```

The chronicle tables are populated from the corresponding event class through chronicle rules. The rules are defined by SQL statements, and they can be defined in two places: in the <ChronicleRule> node of an event class or in the <EventRules> node of a subscription class. The decision where to place the rules depends on when the chronicle data should be affected. If the data is to be affected before notifications are generated, the rule should be defined in the <ChronicleRule>. If the chronicle data should be affected after the notifications have been generated, the rule should be placed in the <EventRules> node. The following code shows a chronicle rule that updates entries in the chronicle table if the price in the events table is greater than the price in the chronicle table. Notice that the developer of the ADF file has to use the entity references of the greater-than (>) and less-than (<) signs because those are reserved characters in XML:

```
<EventClass>
  <!--  other EventClass elements -->
  <ChronicleRule>
      <RuleName>StockEventsChronRule</RuleName>
          <Action>
            -- Update value in the chronicle
            UPDATE   StockEvtChron
              SET    StockPrice = e.StockPrice
              FROM   StockEvt e
         JOIN StockEventsChron c
              ON e.StockCode = c.StockCode
          AND e.ExchangeCode = c.ExchangeCode
          WHERE   e.StockPrice &gt; c.StockPrice
          </Action>
          </ChronicleRule>
  <Chronicles>...</Chronicles>
</EventClass>
```

Events and chronicles are not interesting in themselves; we need some-one to be interested in the events. In other words, we need subscribers and subscriptions.

Subscribers and Subscriptions

To send subscriptions, the SQLNS needs information about the following:

- Who to send information to—The subscribers
- What information to send—The subscriptions
- What devices the information should be sent to—The devices

The setup of this is done through using subscription management objects in SQLNS. Information about the subscribers and their devices is stored in the SQLNS instance database, whereas information about subscriptions is stored in the SQLNS application database. The developer of the SQLNS application also needs to define information about subscriptions in the ADF file by subscription classes and device information in the configuration file (see Listing 16-1 or 16-2, where there is an entry for a `<DeliveryChannel>`).

Figure 16-4 tries to give a graphical illustration of how subscription information is entered through a subscription management application. The subscription management application uses the management objects to create subscriber information in the instance database and subscription information in the application database.

In Figure 16-4, you can see references to various objects (subscriber, subscription, and devices). These objects are part of the SQLNS management

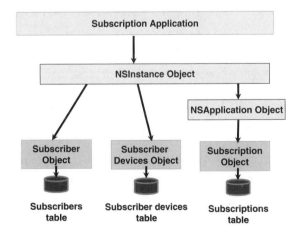

FIGURE 16-4: Subscription management

objects mentioned earlier, and for subscription management, we specifi-cally use the objects in the following list:

- `NSInstance`—Represents a specific SQLNS instance. Several Notifica-tion Services classes require a reference to this object to be initialized.
- `Subscriber`—Represents a Notification Services subscriber. Sub-scriptions and subscriber devices in the Notification Services system are associated with a subscriber by means of the subscriber ID.
- `SubscriberDevice`—Represents a device belonging to a subscriber that can be used to receive notifications.
- `NSApplication`—Represents a specific SQLNS application. As with the `NSInstance`, many SQLNS classes require a reference to this class.
- `Subscription`—Represents a single subscription within an SQLNS application.

All these classes live in the `Microsoft.SqlServer.NotificationSer-vices` namespace, and they are the main classes for developing subscription applications. These are not the only classes available for subscription man-agement, however; there are classes for enumeration/information of sub-scribers, devices, subscriptions, and so on. The `NotificationServices` namespace is not just for subscription management; it contains all the SQLNS classes and interfaces. All the classes in the `NotificationServices` namespace are written in managed code, but they also have COM wrappers, so they can be used from COM automation languages. In addition to the classes related to instances, applications, and subscription management in general, the namespace holds classes and interfaces related to the following:

- Submitting events to the Notification Services system
- Developing custom Notification Services components

Looking at Figure 16-4, we can see the steps to create subscription man-agement applications: create subscribers, create devices, and finally create subscriptions. Before the subscriptions can be created, the subscriptions schema needs to be defined in the ADF file through `SubscriptionClasses`.

Subscription Classes

One or more subscription classes in the ADF file decide the types of sub-scriptions that the SQLNS application accepts. A subscription class generally holds information about the device, information about the event, and what constitutes an event. You can add further information, such as locale. SQLNS use some subscription fields automatically for formatting and delivery. Examples of such fields are the subscriber ID and the device name, which are used by the formatter and the delivery mechanism; the formatter uses the locale field.

An example of an ADF file with a subscription class is shown in Listing 16-13. Perusing the code in Listing 16-13, we see that there are subscription fields defined for the device, the locale, the event information, and at what point an event triggers. The subscription class also has an SQL statement for dropping and creating indexes on the subscription table.

LISTING 16-13: Subscription class information in the ADF file

```
<SubscriptionClasses>
  <SubscriptionClass>
    <SubscriptionClassName>
      %_App_%Subscriptions
    </SubscriptionClassName>
    <Schema>
      <Field>
        <FieldName>DeviceName</FieldName>
        <FieldType>varchar(255)</FieldType>
        <FieldTypeMods>not null</FieldTypeMods>
      </Field>
      <Field>
        <FieldName>SubLocale</FieldName>
        <FieldType>varchar(10)</FieldType>
        <FieldTypeMods>not null</FieldTypeMods>
      </Field>
      <Field>
        <FieldName>StockCode</FieldName>
        <FieldType>varchar(15)</FieldType>
        <FieldTypeMods>not null</FieldTypeMods>
      </Field>
      <Field>
        <FieldName>ExchangeCode</FieldName>
        <FieldType>varchar(15)</FieldType>
        <FieldTypeMods>not null</FieldTypeMods>
      </Field>
      <Field>
        <FieldName>TriggerVal</FieldName>
        <FieldType>decimal(18, 5)</FieldType>
        <FieldTypeMods>not null</FieldTypeMods>
      </Field>
    </Schema>
    <IndexSqlSchema>
```

```
<SqlStatement>
  IF EXISTS (SELECT name FROM sys.indexes
  WHERE name = &apos;StockSubIndex&apos;)
  DROP INDEX %_App_%Subscriptions.StockSubIndex
</SqlStatement>
<SqlStatement>
  CREATE INDEX StockSubIndex
  ON %_App_%Subscriptions (SubscriberID)
</SqlStatement>
  </IndexSqlSchema>
  </SubscriptionClass>
</SubscriptionClasses>
```

For event-driven subscriptions, the subscription class also needs to define event rules. The event rules define how notifications are generated for the subscriptions. These rules are executed each time a new event batch is processed. The event rules are entered in the `EventRules` node in the subscription class; we cover more about event rules in the section about notifications. For schedule-driven notifications, the rules are created in a `ScheduledRules` section in the ADF file.

The ADF file can now be updated with the section in Listing 16-13. To update the application database, disable the SQLNS instance, run `NSControl Update`, and then enable the instance again.

Now let's look at the users of the subscription class: the subscribers and their subscriptions.

Subscribers

Subscribers are instance specific and are added to the instance database. The main class for subscribers is the `Subscriber` class mentioned earlier, which has methods for adding and deleting subscribers to the instance. From the `Subscriber` class, you can also get information about what subscriptions a particular subscriber has.

Listing 16-14 shows an example of a managed console application used for adding subscribers to an instance. In a production application, it is unlikely that a console application would be used. Instead, the application probably would be an ASP.NET WebForms application. With the support for COM, it could also be an ASP application. Notice the `using` statement for the `Microsoft.SqlServer.NotificationServices` namespace. When compiling, the application needs a reference to the `microsoft.sqlserver.`

notificationservices.dll file, which can be found in the C:\Program
Files\Microsoft SQL Server\90\NotificationServices\<version>\
bin directory. The code shows how we first create an instance of the NSInstance class. The NSInstance class has an overloaded constructor where
one constructor method takes the instance name as a parameter and initializes the SQLNS instance. If the constructor method that does not take an
instance name as a parameter is used, the instance can be set by a property.
In that case, the SQLNS instance needs to be initialized separately by the
Initialize method.

Then the instance is used as a constructor parameter for the initialization
of the Subscriber class. The ID of the subscriber is set on the SubscriberId
property, and Add is called.

LISTING 16-14: Code to add subscriber

```
using System;
using Microsoft.SqlServer.NotificationServices;

class nssub {
     static void Main(string[] args) {
    string subId = "NielsB";
    string inst = "Stock";
    AddSubscriber(inst, subId);
     }

static void AddSubscriber(string inst, string subId) {
    NSInstance nsInst = new NSInstance(inst);
    Subscriber sub = new Subscriber(nsInst);
    sub.SubscriberId = subId;
    try {
      sub.Add();
    }
    catch(Exception e) {
      Console.WriteLine(e.Message);
    }
  }
}
```

After successful completion of the methods, there will be an entry in the
NSSubcribers table in the instance database. After subscribers have been
added, devices need to be added, to define on what devices a subscriber can
receive notifications. A device is tied to a delivery channel, which is tied to a
delivery protocol. We haven't yet discussed delivery channels or protocols
much; they are covered later in this chapter. For now, what we need to

remember is that the SQLNS framework comes with a couple of predefined delivery protocols. You may remember that in the configuration file in Listing 16-2, we defined a delivery channel named `FileChannel`, which used the file protocol. The file protocol is one of the predefined protocols in the SQLNS framework. It is mainly used for debugging, and we will use it for the time being until we discuss delivery channels and protocols in greater detail later on.

The reason we go on about this is that when we define the devices, we also need to define the delivery channel to use, as the code in Listing 16-15 shows. Be aware that there is a FOREIGN KEY CONSTRAINT between the `NSDeliveryChannels` table and the `NSSubscribersDevices` table on the `DeliveryChannelName` columns. In other words, you need to make sure that the `DeliveryChannelName` property on the `SubscriberDevice` instance exists in the `NSDeliveryChannels` table. The records in the `NSDeliveryChannels` table depend on what has been entered in the configuration file under the `<DeliveryChannels>` node.

LISTING 16-15: Adding a subscriber device

```
static void AddSubscriberDevice(string inst, string subId) {
    NSInstance nsInst = new NSInstance(inst);
    SubscriberDevice dev = new SubscriberDevice(nsInst);
    dev.DeliveryChannelName = "FileChannel";
    dev.DeviceAddress = "";
    dev.DeviceName = "FileDevice";
    dev.DeviceTypeName = "File";
    dev.SubscriberId = subId;
    try {
      dev.Add();
    }
    catch(Exception e) {
      Console.WriteLine(e.Message);
    }

  }
}
```

The code in Listing 16-15 shows the following properties on the `SubscriberDevice` class:

- `DeliveryChannelName`—The name of the delivery channel used by the device
- `DeviceAddress`—The address of the device

- `DeviceName`—The name of the device
- `DeviceTypeName`—The name of the device type that describes the subscriber device
- `SubscriberId`—The ID of the subscriber

Subscriptions

The subscriptions node defines what information each subscriber gets and on what device he gets them. The class to use to add subscriptions is the `Subscription` class. This class has methods to add and delete subscriptions for a specific subscriber, as well as methods and properties to get and set information about the subscription record.

The code in Listing 16-16 shows how the `Subscription` class is used to add a subscription for an existing subscriber. The `NSInstance` class is instantiated first, followed by the `NSApplication` class. The constructor of the application class takes the instance and the name of the application we want to instantiate as constructor parameters. The `Subscription` class is created with the instance and the name of the subscription class. The subscription class name is needed because there can be several subscription classes in the application. Now the `Subscription` class can be used, and we call the `SetFieldValue` on the class. `SetFieldValue` is a method that takes a name–value pair as separate parameters. The name parameter corresponds to a subscription field in the aforementioned subscription class, and the value part sets the value of that field. From the code, you can see how we set the device the subscriber wants the notifications on, what locale to format the notifications with, the event information (`StockCode` and `ExchangeCode`), and when to trigger a notification (`TriggerVal`). We set the `SubscriberId` property to indicate who this subscription is for, and finally, we call `Add`.

LISTING 16-16: Adding a subscription

```
static void AddSubscription(string inst, string appName, string subId)
{
  NSInstance nsInst = new NSInstance(inst);

  //create an instance of the NSApplication class
  NSApplication app = new
             NSApplication(nsInst, appName);

  Subscription sub =
             new Subscription(app, "StockPriceSubscriptions");
```

```
//set the value of the fields
//in the subscription record
sub.SetFieldValue("DeviceName", "FileDevice");
sub.SetFieldValue("SubLocale", "en-US");
sub.SetFieldValue("StockCode", "SUNW");
sub.SetFieldValue("ExchangeCode", "NASDAQ");
sub.SetFieldValue("TriggerVal", 7);
sub.SubscriberId = subId;
try {
  sub.Add();
}
catch(Exception e){
  Console.WriteLine(e.Message);

}

}
```

The code in Listing 16-16 inserts the subscription information into the NS<SubscriptionClassName>Subscriptions table. The SQLNS framework, based on the schema in the subscription class, creates this table. The table is used when the framework generates notifications.

To allow subscribers to specify their own conditions in SQL Server 2005, condition actions were introduced. Condition actions are specified in the ADF but also must be specified (or entered by the user) as part of a subscription. The Subscription class now contains two additional fields, Condition and RuleName, that are used to specify the user-defined conditions. The Condition class is actually an abstract base class, and there are several subclasses that allow you to specify a single condition or a complex tree structure of conditions. These subclasses include

- ConditionTree
  - AndCondition, OrCondition
- LeafCondition
  - BetweenLeafCondition
  - BooleanLeafCondition
  - IsNullLeafCondition
  - LinkLeafCondition
  - SimpleLeafCondition
- NotCondition

If, for example, I wanted to allow the user-defined conditions instead of always looking for stock prices greater than a certain amount, I would change my user-interface and reprogram the `AddSubscription` method to use subclasses of Condition based on the user's input.

Notifications

Notifications are generated by finding matching information in event and subscription tables by joining those tables. The notification data is the event information that meets the subscription requirements, plus any additional information the developer wants to include. The data to include in a notification is defined in one of several notification classes in the ADF file. Information required in the notification class are the event data, what content formatter to use for the notifications, what delivery protocols this notification class uses, and how long notifications should be re-sent before being deemed out of date. In addition to this information, the notification class can define whether the notification class uses the following:

- Digest delivery—Digest delivery groups all notifications to one subscriber during one notification generation and sends them as one notification.
- Notification batch size—Normally, the generator creates one batch per firing. This setting defines how many notifications should be included in one batch. If this is set, the generator breaks the batch into smaller sizes that meet the set size.
- Multicast delivery—Notifications that share identical data and are in the same distributor work item are formatted once and sent to all subscribers.

Listing 16-17 shows one `NotificationClass`, which defines the data in a notification. The class uses the XSLT formatter, and the file protocol is used to send the notifications. There is an expiration time of two hours. If a notification has not been sent successfully after two hours, the notification is considered to be out of date.

LISTING 16-17: Notification class in the ADF file

```
<NotificationClasses>
  <NotificationClass>
    <NotificationClassName>%_App_%Notifications</NotificationClassName>
    <Schema>
      <Fields>
        <Field>
          <FieldName>StockCode</FieldName>
          <FieldType>varchar(15)</FieldType>
        </Field>
        <Field>
          <FieldName>ExchangeCode</FieldName>
          <FieldType>varchar(15)</FieldType>
        </Field>
        <Field>
          <FieldName>Price</FieldName>
          <FieldType>decimal(18, 5)</FieldType>
        </Field>
      </Fields>
    </Schema>
    <ContentFormatter>
      <ClassName>XsltFormatter</ClassName>
    </ContentFormatter>
    <Protocols>
      <Protocol>
        <ProtocolName>File</ProtocolName>
      </Protocol>
    </Protocols>
    <ExpirationAge>PT2H</ExpirationAge>
  </NotificationClass>
</NotificationClasses>
```

Running `NSControl Update` updates the `NS<NotificationClassName>
Notifications` table with the fields from the notification class. In addition, it alters a SQL Server user-defined function (UDF), which was originally created when `NSControl Create` ran.

Remember that in the discussions about subscription classes earlier in this chapter, we mentioned that we needed event generation rules to generate notifications. *Event rules* are SQL queries defining the contents of a notification and what constitutes a notification. When a notification is created, the raw data is inserted into the notifications table, and the only way that can happen in an SQLNS application is through the notification function. In other words, the SQL query for the event generation rule needs to use the function in some way.

In pre–SQL Server 2005 versions of SQLNS, this was accomplished by executing an SQLNS-generated UDF in the SQL query, sending in the necessary parameters. The parameters to the UDF were based on the fields defined in the notification class schema plus some generic parameters. The notify function looked somewhat like this:

```
StockPriceNotificationsNotify(@SubscriberId NVARCHAR(255),
  @DeviceName NVARCHAR(255), @SubscriberLocale NVARCHAR(10),
  @StockCode varchar(15), @ExchangeCode varchar(15),
  @Price decimal(18, 5))
```

One change in SQLNS between pre–SQL Server 2005 versions and the SQL Server 2005 version is the replacement of the notify function with an INSERT INTO / SELECT statement. This is an optimization, because in previous versions, the notify function had to be executed for each notification; the new mechanism is executed only once and is an optimizable T-SQL JOIN. In addition, you can add information from tables other than the subscription table and the event and event chronicle tables. This makes the notification generation mechanism more extensible.

Notice that the first columns in the INSERT statement are subscriber ID, device, and locale. These always need to be included, because the framework uses this information when generating and formatting the notifications. In addition to these fields, event data and other subscription data can be included.

Listing 16-18 shows the EventRules entry needed in the subscription class. In the event rule, we send in to the function the ID of the subscriber, the device, and the locale. This information is taken from the subscription table. The event information used are the stock code, the exchange code, and the price, all of which come from the event table. Finally, it is matched on the stock code and exchange code, and we want only data where the price is greater than the trigger value set in the subscription table. The EventRule also indicates in the EventClassName element which event it is for.

LISTING 16-18: Event rule

```
</Schema>
  <EventRules>
    <EventRule>
      <RuleName>EvtRule</RuleName>
      <Action>
      INSERT INTO %_App_%Notifications(
```

```
        SubscriberId, DeviceName,
        SubscriberLocale, RicCode,
        ExchangeCode, Price)
    SELECT s.SubscriberId, s.DeviceName, s.SubLocale,
        e.RicCode, e.ExchangeCode, e.Price
    FROM StockEvt e, %_App_%Subscriptions s
    WHERE e.RicCode = s.RicCode
        AND e.ExchangeCode = s.ExchangeCode
        AND e.Price &gt; s.TriggerVal
    </Action>
    <EventClassName>StockEvt</EventClassName>
  </EventRule>
 </EventRules>
<!-- Index schema information follows -->
<IndexSqlSchema/>
```

Note that in the EventRule element above, we are defining a specific condition to look for: stock prices greater than a user-specified amount. But what if some users want to be notified if prices are less than a certain amount? We would need to write another event rule. Perhaps some users would like to be notified only when two stock prices go above a certain amount as an indication of a market trend? Over time, this would lead to a proliferation of event rules, each of which would be run separately. In SQL Server 2005, there is support for user-specified conditions. Having a series of user-specified conditions may not be as efficient as a single event rule, but depending on how complex the user-specifications can get, it may be more efficient than having a plethora of separate event rules, as shown in Listing 16-19.

LISTING 16-19: Condition action

```
</Schema>
  <EventRules>
    <EventRule>
      <RuleName>StockCondition</RuleName>
        <ConditionAction>
            <SqlLogin>LowPrivLogin</SqlLogin>
            <SqlUser>LowPrivUser</SqlUser>
            <InputName>StockEvt</InputName>
            <InputSchema>StockTraderApp</InputSchema>
            <SqlExpression>INSERT INTO %_App_%Notifications(
                SubscriberId, DeviceName,
                SubscriberLocale, RicCode,
              ExchangeCode, Price)
              SELECT r.[Subscription.SubscriberId],
```

```
                    r.[Subscription.DeviceName],
                    r.[Subscription.SubLocale],
                    r.[Input.RicCode], r.[Input.ExchangeCode],
                    r.[Input.Price]
              FROM   [StockTraderApp].StockCondition AS r
            </SqlExpression>
          </ConditionAction>
      <EventClassName>StockEvt</EventClassName>
    </EventRule>
  </EventRules>
```

Note that because the evaluation of user-defined rules involves dynamic SQL, the condition action evaluation should run as a low-privileged user. In addition, when constructing your subscription management application, you should never allow users to key in freeform expressions to be evaluated, but only to select expressions from a well-defined list in a drop-down list box.

In addition to writing the notifications to the notifications table, the notification function participates in creating notification batches. When the function is called for the first time during firing of a rule, the system creates a new notification batch record. All the notifications that the function creates are part of this batch unless a batch size has been defined, in which case multiple batches would be generated. When the batches are closed, the notifications are ready for formatting and distribution.

Distributor and Formatters

The part of the SQLNS framework that is responsible for both formatting and distributing notifications is the distributor. The distributor runs continuously and partitions the batches ready for distribution into smaller work items. This allows the system to take advantage of parallel processing, whereas multiple distributors can run in parallel and/or a single distributor can process multiple work items in parallel.

Part of the processing of the work items is formatting the notification data. The distributor is responsible for the formatting and routes the notifications to a content formatter.

The content formatter is a managed class that implements the ICon-tentFormatter interface. The developer of an SQLNS application does not have to develop a customized formatter but can use the XSLT formatter that is part of the SQLNS framework. The XSLT formatter allows you to specify an XSL transform to be applied to the raw notification data. This XSL transform makes all the formatting changes that are required to prepare the notification data for display. The XSL transform does not have to be the same for a given notification class. The transform can be different, depending on locale and device.

The XSLT formatter reads the transform from a directory and creates an intermediate XML document in memory. This XML document contains the notification data. Then it applies the XSL transform to the document, and the result is the final formatted notification. The directory that the formatter reads the transform from is based upon whether the formatting is dependent on locale or device. Each type of device and locale supported should have an individual transform file placed in its own directory.

To define the XSLT formatter, an entry in the ADF file is needed in the `NotificationClass` section under the `ContentFormatter` node. Listing 16-20 shows the necessary entries in the ADF file for the XSLT formatter. The name of the class that is used for formatting is defined in the `ClassName` node. For a custom formatter, the assembly name needs to be defined, as well in an `AssemblyName` element. Following the `ClassName` comes the `Arguments` section, with one or more `Argument` nodes. When the XSLT formatter is used, the base directory needs to be defined, as well as the name of the transform file.

LISTING 16-20: Content formatter information in the ADF file

```
</Schema>
<!--Schema information above -->
  <ContentFormatter>
    <ClassName>XsltFormatter</ClassName>
    <Arguments>
      <Argument>
        <Name>XsltBaseDirectoryPath</Name>
        <Value>%_BaseDirectoryPath_%</Value>
      </Argument>
      <Argument>
        <Name>XsltFileName</Name>
        <Value>NoOp.xslt</Value>
      </Argument>
    </Arguments>
  </ContentFormatter>
<!-- Protocol information below -->
<Protocols>
```

The NoOp.xslt transform file in Listing 16-20 is a transform that comes with the sample applications of the framework. It is mostly used for debugging, and it outputs the raw notification data XML format. A slightly more functional transform is shown in the following code snippet:

```
<?xml version="1.0" encoding="UTF-8" ?>
<xsl:stylesheet version="1.0"
xmlns:xsl="http://www.w3.org/1999/XSL/Transform">

<xsl:template match="notifications">
    <html>
        <body>
            <xsl:apply-templates/>
            <i>Thank you for using StockTrader and
        SQL Server Notification Services.</i><br/><br/>
    </body>
    </html>
    </xsl:template>

    <xsl:template match="notification">
        <b><xsl:value-of select="StockCode" /></b>
        at
        <b><xsl:value-of select="ExchangeCode" /></b>
        is trading at: $
        <b><xsl:value-of select="Price" /></b>
        <br/><br/>
    </xsl:template>

</xsl:stylesheet>
```

The XSLT transform matches the notifications and the notifications' elements. The `<xsl:apply-templates/>` creates the header of the notification, and the `<xsl:value-of  select=""/>` produces the body information. When the notifications are formatted, they are handed to the delivery channels and protocols for delivery to the subscribers.

Delivery

Formatted notifications are distributed through delivery channels to delivery services. Delivery channels are an abstraction consisting of two concrete parts: the delivery protocol and the configuring/addressing information necessary to identify an endpoint. It is the protocol's responsibility to assemble formatted notifications into protocol packets that are sent through an external delivery system such as Simple Mail Transfer Protocol (SMTP).

The configuring/addressing information allows interaction with the delivery channel by including non–application-specific information. This information can be what gateway to use, authentication information, and so on. It is the distributor's job to figure out what delivery channel should handle a notification by looking at the device targeted for the notification (remember that device information is part of a notification record). By looking at the device record in the subscriber devices table, the distributor determines which delivery channel to use. From there, the distributor decides on the protocol to use by looking up the channel in the delivery channels table and matching the channel with the protocol.

Delivery Protocols

Delivery protocols are one concrete part of delivery channels, and several channels can use the same protocol. The protocols used can be custom-developed protocols or either of the two protocols that are part of the framework:

- File—Writes text data to a file specified in the configuration file
- SMTP—Creates and routes messages through SMTP mail systems

Information about delivery channels and protocols is located in both the application configuration file and the ADF file. For the file protocol, the only thing that needs to be added to the configuration file in Listing 16-2 is an entry for what file the output should be written to. The following code shows the relevant part of the configuration file:

```
<DeliveryChannels>
  <DeliveryChannel>
    <DeliveryChannelName>FileChannel</DeliveryChannelName>
    <ProtocolName>File</ProtocolName>
    <Arguments>
      <Argument>
        <Name>FileName</Name>
        <Value>%BasePath%\Notif\StockNotification.txt</Value>
      </Argument>
    </Arguments>
  </DeliveryChannel>
</DeliveryChannels>
```

In the `Argument` node is an argument called `FileName`, which points to the actual file that receives the output. That is the only required argument for the file protocol. An additional, optional argument named `Encoding` defines what encoding to use in the output file. By default, this is `utf-8`. Every protocol used needs an entry in the `Protocols` section in each of the notification classes using that particular protocol. For the file protocol, the only entry needed is the `ProtocolName`, and it must be `File`. Listing 16-17 shows an example of this. Other protocols may need specific information in the header of a notification, and for this purpose, you use the `Fields` section with `Field` nodes (more about this later). Each protocol can also have different execution settings: the interval between retries for a failed delivery, how many times a delivery can fail before an error is reported in the event log, and so on. This information is recorded in the `Protocol\ProtocolExecutionSettings` node.

Arguably, the file protocol is a "bare minimum" protocol, used mostly for debugging. The developer uses the file protocol to make sure that notifications are generated, formatted, and distributed as expected. For a production application, another protocol would be used, such as the SMTP protocol, which sends notifications to any SMTP mail system for delivery.

For SQLNS to be set up to work with the SMTP protocol, the entry in the configuration file's `DeliveryChannel` section should point to the actual SMTP server used. As with the file protocol, the encoding style can also be specified, as the following code snippet from a configuration file shows:

```
<DeliveryChannels>
    <DeliveryChannel>
        <DeliveryChannelName>EmailChannel</DeliveryChannelName>
        <ProtocolName>SMTP</ProtocolName>
        <Arguments>
            <Argument>
                <Name>SmtpServer</Name>
                <Value>SERVNB01</Value>
            </Argument>
            <Argument>
                <Name>BodyEncoding</Name>
                <Value>utf-16</Value>
            </Argument>
        </Arguments>
    </DeliveryChannel>
</DeliveryChannels>
```

Notice that the argument name for the encoding type is different between the file protocol (`Encoding`) and the SMTP protocol (`BodyEncoding`). The `ProtocolName` element must be `SMTP` for the SMTP protocol.

Compared with the file protocol, the SMTP protocol needs some more entries in the `/NotificationClasses/NotificationClass/Protocols/Protocol` section of the ADF file. The additional entries are the protocol fields we mentioned earlier. The use of protocol fields is to specify protocol-specific header information, such as `Subject` for an e-mail message. Protocol fields are named expressions that operate on raw notification data and subscriber information, and they are defined as `FieldReference` elements or `SqlExpression` elements in the ADF file's `Fields` node of the `/NotificationClasses/NotificationClass/Protocols/Protocol` section. A `FieldReference` element references fields in the `NotificationClass/Schema/Fields`, whereas a `SqlExpression` refers to arbitrary T-SQL expressions. An example of `SqlExpression` fields is shown in Listing 16-21. It shows the fields that the SMTP protocol uses. There are three required fields: `Subject`, `From`, and `To`. It also has two optional fields: `Priority` and `BodyFormat`. Listing 16-21 also shows how arbitrary string constants can be used from the `SqlExpression` element, by enclosing the constant in apostrophes. The apostrophes are defined by their entity reference, `&apos;`.

LISTING 16-21: SMTP protocol defined in the ADF file

```
<Protocols>
 <Protocol>
    <ProtocolName>SMTP</ProtocolName>
    <Fields>
      <Field>
        <FieldName>Subject</FieldName>
        <SqlExpression>
          &apos;Stock Notification: &apos;+
          CONVERT(varchar(30), GetDate())
        </SqlExpression>
      </Field>
      <Field>
        <FieldName>From</FieldName>
        <SqlExpression>
          &apos;tradingroom@dmgs.com&apos;
        </SqlExpression>
      </Field>
      <Field>
        <FieldName>To</FieldName>
```

```
      <SqlExpression>DeviceAddress</SqlExpression>
    </Field>
    <Field>
      <FieldName>Priority</FieldName>
      <SqlExpression>&apos;Normal&apos;</SqlExpression>
    </Field>
    <Field>
      <FieldName>BodyFormat</FieldName>
      <SqlExpression>&apos;html&apos;</SqlExpression>
    </Field>
  </Fields>
 </Protocol>
</Protocols>
```

Customization

In the last part of this section about delivery, we want to mention briefly that when existing protocols do not meet the requirements for the application, customized delivery protocols can be developed and used. Examples of custom protocols are protocols for MSMQ and Microsoft Instant Messenger. To develop a custom delivery protocol, developers need to implement one of two interfaces from the `Microsoft.SqlServer.NotificationServices` namespace:

- `IHttpProtocolProvider`—This interface makes it easy to create an HTTP-based protocol. All HTTP-related functionality already exists, so developers only have to provide the code for formatting the envelope and processing responses.
- `IDeliveryProtocol`—Developers can use this interface for non–HTTP-based protocols or where more flexibility is required from the `IHttpProtocolProvider`.

When a custom protocol is developed, it needs to be defined in the `Protocols` section of the configuration file, with information about the protocol name, the class name, and what assembly the class can be found in. Also, a delivery channel that uses the protocol needs to be defined in the `DeliveryChannels` node of the configuration file.

Customization is beyond the scope of this chapter; for more information, look in SQL Server Books Online.

Where Are We?

SQL Server Notification Services is a platform for developing and deploying applications that generate and send notifications to users. It uses Windows services and SQL Server as the foundation for the framework. A series of commercial applications that uses .NET Alerts (most use it in conjunction with Notification Services) is available for subscribers at http://www.microsoft.com/alerts.

■ 17 ■

Wrap-Up: Service-Oriented Database Applications

S QL SERVER 2005 is more than just a new version of SQL Server. It is the integration of relational data and XML data in a way that makes it easier to build secure, reliable, and scalable applications that are easily maintained. Features are geared to support both scale-up and scale-out, and work without application servers or in conjunction with them. In addition, the new features more tightly integrate the data to the kinds of service-oriented distributed applications we are building today and will be building tomorrow.

Lots of New Features: How to Use Them

SQL Server 2005 contains an amazing number of new features. We've covered most of them in previous chapters but haven't even touched on the new features for administration and replication, in Reporting Services, in Analysis Services, and in SQL Server Integration Services (SSIS), including .NET Framework–based libraries for everything. We've concentrated on developer topics.

SQL Server core functionality is enhanced with each new release. There are a great number of enhancements based on making SQL Server more secure and reliable. These enhancements include database user and schema separation, improved SQL Server user password handling, new encryption functions and secret storage, system metadata view security, and an in-database managed-code programming model. All these enhancements have been implemented while retaining a high level of reliability and security. This functionality melds well with the declarative model of SQL, implemented with procedural enhancements through Transact-SQL (T-SQL).

An entire new concurrency model that uses versioning instead of locking has been introduced. For those developers who have had difficulty porting or converting their applications to SQL Server because of the differences between locking-based and versioning-based concurrency, the new model goes a long way toward removing this obstacle.

T-SQL and SQL have also been improved, not only with new system-defined functions and new SQL extensions, but also by adding T-SQL exception handling. Whether you use T-SQL or in-database .NET Framework procedures; client-side ADO.NET and the SqlClient data provider; a COM-based API-like OLE DB or ADO; or ODBC, the SQL-92 standard database API, you should always be using statements that are written in SQL to invoke set-based, data-related functionality. SQL is still your way of processing set-based data, but beyond the set, there is a different story.

Data Models, Programming, and SQL Server

The new functionality in SQL Server 2005 gives us many choices for storing, processing, programming, performing calculations on, and sharing data. In large part because of the ease of sharing data over a well-known protocol, HTTP, in a few well-known formats, the concept of the remote application server—historically used only in monolithic systems—has become a "commodity" way of programming. The application server (and middle tier in the ANSI-SPARC three-tier architecture) has been popularized as the Web server. In addition, over time, three programming and data-related trends have become entrenched:

- Data is stored in databases based on the relational model in most cases.
- XML is used to eliminate architectural dependencies on data representation. It has its own data model for storing text-heavy data (where intrinsic ordering matters) and document replicas.
- Application programmers design and program using object-oriented concepts.

SQL Server 2005 and the libraries in .NET Framework 2.0 give programmers a lot of choices for which paradigm can be used and how it can be programmed. Here are a few examples, for purists of each paradigm.

Relational data can be stored in SQL Server; it's SQL Server's native format. It can be accessed through an object-oriented layer based loosely on the SQL-CLI (command language interface) known as ADO.NET, through OLE DB, or through ODBC (the most well-known implementation of SQL-CLI) directly through a proprietary protocol, Tabular Data Stream (TDS).

XML data can be stored in SQL Server directly. It can be validated on the server because XML schemas are stored in the server. It can be indexed to make XQuery language queries against it perform efficiently, or it can be searched based on their text content with full-text search. XML and relational data can be joined in a single query. Relational data can also be exposed as XML through T-SQL extensions, and XML messages can be marshaled using HTTP and Web Services for interoperability or using SQL Server Service Broker for the asynchrony and reliability that HTTP lacks.

Any Functionality at Any Tier

The most interesting thing (and the scariest, for those of us who want homogeneous, cut-and-paste solutions) is that this functionality can be deployed across any tier. Using SQL Server and .NET Framework 2.0 library code names, here are some of the ways you can deploy if you divide the world into client, middle tier, and database. Big caveat: These methods are technically possible, but their use, as always, is dictated by the needs of the system.

Here's what you can accomplish on the database alone:

- You can store XML data in SQL Server using the XML data type.
- You can query relational data in SQL Server as XML using SELECT ... FOR XML and store it using the xml.nodes method, OpenXml, or XML Bulk Insert in T-SQL.
- You can write .NET Framework programs that use System.Xml inside SQL Server to query XML or convert relational data to XML.
- You can produce XML in a stored procedure and transport it using HTTP instead of TDS using HTTP ENDPOINTs.

- You can transport binary, text, or XML through asynchronous messaging using Service Broker.
- You can extend SQL Server's scalar type system with user-defined types (UDTs).
- You can use ADO.NET using `System.Data.SqlClient` classes inside .NET Framework programs that run inside SQL Server.
- If you don't use the managed environment, you can still use extended stored procedures written in any unmanaged (unsafe) language and access data using ODBC or OLE DB.
- You can manipulate the data entirely with T-SQL stored procedures and user-defined functions.

Here's what you can accomplish on the middle tier or client:

- You can fetch and program against any type of data from SQL Server with ADO.NET (SqlClient), OLE DB and ADO, or ODBC.
- You can retrieve data through HTTP or TDS.
- You can work with extended scalar types from SQL Server as though they are .NET Framework types.
- You can bind data directly in relational form, as collections of objects or as XML trees, to graphical user interface components for either Web-based, interoperable consumption (ASP.NET, middle tier) or rich window user-interface consumption (Windows Forms, client).
- You can deploy, through SQL Server Express, an instance of SQL Server containing Service Broker on every client workstation for the ultimate in asynchronous, reliable transaction processing.

SQL Server 2005 and the .NET Framework base class library APIs have accomplished the integration of different models and data.

What Are the Best Practices?

With so many choices, the question that always arises is "What are best practices when the new technological functionality is factored into the equation?" We've always had a hard time with the concept of best practices because of the underlying implication that domain problems can fit into neat categories. They can't. It's like saying to an architect, "It's only a building; just build one just like the one you built last year." Although certain pieces can be prefabricated, the overall structure and look-and-feel depend on the landscape and aesthetics. We can't start to count the number of hours we've spent in meetings listening to software developers argue over "elegant" versus "ugly" designs or technological politics. Any software project must balance the concepts of ease of construction, time constraints, maintainability, and user responsiveness. Our favorite software development story is about a manager who writes the following on the whiteboard at a user/programmer architecture meeting:

Choose Any Two:
- Good
- Fast
- Cheap

During the years when SQL Server 2005 was being developed and applications were being developed and/or enhanced to use the feature set (a good example of this is the "Project REAL" information on the Microsoft Web site at http://www.microsoft.com/sql/solutions/bi/projectreal.mspx), a set of best uses for the new features became clear. Here is an outline of some uses and best practices for each feature, roughly following the book topic order. If the reason for the suggestions here aren't intuitively obvious from the compact descriptions, refer to the book topic for more details.

SQLCLR safety
- Avoid UNSAFE assemblies if at all possible. If you consider them, understand the repercussions of using UNSAFE.
- Use only base class libraries on the approved list.

SQL and procedural code (T-SQL and SQLCLR)
- Use single SQL statements if at all possible, as opposed to procedural code.
- Use T-SQL for data access.

- Use SQLCLR for:
  - computation.
  - business logic.
  - base class library built-ins such as regular expressions.
  - string manipulation.
  - user-defined functions.
  - anything you would use an extended stored procedure for in SQL Server 2000.
- If your procedure contains both data access and business logic, benchmark and test a SQLCLR alternative to your existing T-SQL procedure. The results may surprise you.

SQLCLR versus client-side and middle-tier programming

- Consider using the middle tier as a scale-out strategy. Procedures implemented within the SQLCLR can easily be moved to the middle or client tier.
- Keep the amount of data that must be shipped over the network in mind.

Using `SqlTypes` or .NET Framework primitive types in SQLCLR code

- UDFs should return null on null input.
- Stored procedures should use `SqlTypes` if nullability is a concern.
- `SqlTypes` are especially useful for `DECIMAL` parameters.

Using Visual Studio 2005 automatic deployment

- Use auto-deploy as a convenience during testing if your company standards permit it.
- Don't forget the limitation of auto-deploy: no ALTER ASSEMBLY.

Custom SQLCLR attributes

- Don't use `DataAccess/SystemDataAccessKind.Read` unless you intend data access.
- Use `SqlFacet` for UDT method return values.
- Your `IsPrecise/IsDeterministic` *must* be accurate.

In-process data access

- Do not replicate cursors in CLR.
- Use pipelining in table-valued UDFs (user-defined functions) or returned resultsets if results don't come from database data.
- Keep the amount of code executed during impersonation small.

UDTs

- Use these only for custom scalars.
- One possible use is data types used for conversion (for example, time duration).
- Remember to mark mutator methods as such using the `IsMutator` property of the `SqlMethod` attribute.
- Remember the 8,000-byte limit on UDT state.
- Be aware of issues with:
    - the UDT `IsNull` method.
    - SQL Server Management Studio display of NULL UDTs.
- Use Format.Native if at all possible.
- Use regular expressions in your Parse method to make it robust.
- Implement binary input checking.

User-defined aggregates

- Use these for convenience aggregates used in many places in your application.
- Remember the 8,000-byte limit.
- Custom specific functions written in T-SQL usually are faster than a generalized user-defined aggregate.
- There is no guarantee of ordering in this release of SQL Server; don't use `IsInvariantToOrder=false`.

Security

- Turn on features only when using them.
- Don't use DBO schema if possible.
- Schema should be owned by roles.
- Use `EXECUTE AS` for temporary privilege shift.
- Grant as few permissions as possible.
- Use `VIEW DEFINITION` permission sparingly.
- Use encryption only when needed.
- `DecryptByKeyAutoCert` simplifies key opening and closing.
- Use `ORIGINAL_LOGIN` or event for auditing.

Engine

- Prefer the new `MAX` data types to the deprecated `TEXT`, `NTEXT`, and `IMAGE`.
- Do not use `VARCHAR(MAX)` for every `VARCHAR`.

- Remember that VARCHAR(MAX) and NVARCHAR(MAX) are different data types from VARCHAR(n) and NVARCHAR(n).
- Don't assume that all built-in character functions support more than 8,000 bytes.
- Don't turn on Snapshot Isolation unless you intend to use it.
- Use DDL TRIGGERs to allow cancellation of the triggered operation.
- Use EVENT NOTIFICATIONS if you need:
  - asynchronous triggers.
  - business logic in triggered code.
  - events not supported by DDL TRIGGERs.
- Windows Management Instrumentation (WMI) is a bit faster than Event Notifications for trace events but not as configurable.
- Keep statement-level recompiles in mind as you design your stored procedures; some design limitations in previous versions may be lifted.
- Use query hints only as a last resort.
- Use plan guides unless hints are one-offs.
- Capture plans of existing queries in XML format for plan forcing if things change.

T-SQL
- Prefer TRY/CATCH over @@ERROR.
- Prefer CTEs when using resultset more than once in a single SQL statement.
- Rewrite custom hierarchical code to recursive CTEs.
- Prefer EXCEPT and INTERSECT to equivalent T-SQL code if database transparency is an issue.
- Use TOP UPDATE/DELETE instead of SET ROWCOUNT.
- Prefer OUTPUT when DML produces more than one output variable that you want to return to the client.
- Use the ROW_NUMBER function for paging a large rowset.

XML
- Use the correct data type choice.
- Relational—most often, for traditional application.
- XML
  - if order matters.
  - to save replicas of service requests.

- with ragged hierarchies.
- with semistructured data.
- with markup data.
- Prefer storing many small XML documents to one big document for best performance.
- Use MAX data types instead of the XML data type:
  - to maintain full-fidelity XML schemas.
  - to maintain lexical integrity of XML if, for example, you are storing data to use in an XML editor application.
- In hybrid XML-relational designs:
  - hoist often-used properties to computed columns.
  - use decomposition/composition between XML and relational.
- Use XML schemas only if you need validation; there is extra overhead.
- Use consistent workarounds for XML schema limitations
  - change lax to skip in xsd:Any productions.
- Use BULK provider to get XML from file.
  - SINGLE_BLOB is preferred over SINGLE_CLOB/NCLOB unless encoding matters.

XQuery
- Use indexing unless you don't often query your XML.
  - The primary XML index is almost a requirement if doing lots of querying.
  - Use secondary XML indexes if needed for your use cases à la relational index strategies.
  - DROP/REBUILD indexes for mass inserts.
- Remember repercussions of strong type checking.
- Schemas ease singleton issues and type checking but don't provide much performance gain for queries.
- Use sql:variable to make up for lack of XQuery variables.
- Use T-SQL loops to make up for one-node limit in XML modify method.
- Remember that XML modify is a mutator; using it with NULLs causes an error.

Service Broker

- Service Broker is
  - a replacement for transactional MSMQ applications, not all MSMQ applications.
  - a scale-out facilitator.
  - a more robust Web Services implementation.
  - a replacement for tables used as queues.
- Service Broker is not
  - platform independent.
  - WS-* compliant.
  - a built-in workflow engine; Service Broker CONTRACTs are not workflow.
- Use Service Broker on a SQL Express instance on clients for robust broker client input.
- Turn off XML schema validation of messages if not required.
- Use specific routes rather than rely on wildcard routes.
- Use activation procedures even on initiators; they can receive End-Dialog and Error messages.
- Consider XML messages to avoid CAST on RECEIVE.
- Consider XML messages even for text to avoid encoding issues.

Web Services

- Use them in a SQL Server instance with data to communicate with legacy systems.
- Use them in a SQL Server instance without having data in that instance to pipeline input from outside the firewall to Service Broker application.
- Use a custom WSDL generator procedure for strong typing of Web Service output.

Clients

- SQL Native Client
  - Use the new providers in SQL Native Client after testing existing applications.
  - The new providers are needed only for new SQL Server 2005 features.
  - SQL Native Client must be deployed to every client where it is used.

- SQL Native Client is not supported on Windows 9x clients.
- Not all netlibs are supported.
- Use version 8.0 data types for backward compatibility.
- ADO.NET 2.0
  - is backward compatible with older versions of ADO.NET.
  - is needed only for new SQL Server 2005 features.
  - requires .NET Framework 2.0 on every client or middle tier.
- UDTs and clients
  - UDTs should be used as .NET Framework objects if using ADO.NET, but beware that some Visual Studio 2005 components, such as the typed `DataSet` generator, don't support them.
  - UDTs should be used as string or XML format if using OLE DB, ODBC, or JDBC.
- XML
  - Use as string or as `SqlXml` class if using ADO.NET.
  - Use as string or stream (OLE DB only) if not using ADO.NET.
  - In XML processing, client versus server:
    - Validation always happens on the server.
    - Validating on the client may save database round trips.
  - Use XQuery on the server to cut down network traffic.
  - XML should be on database for management robustness.
- Large data on file system versus database:
  - Putting large data on the database may allow management robustness.
  - Data APIs allow streamed output but not streamed input of large data.

New SQL Server client features
- Don't use MARS for cursor behavior.
- Remember that serialized multiple-rowset access is not guaranteed with MARS.
- Query Notifications
  - Don't use for dynamic data.
  - Don't use for many subscribers.
  - Use parameterized queries.
  - Realize that you can get notifications for reasons other than "rowset changed."

- Wrap in cache sync for ASP.NET.
- Use cache initialization on multiple SQL Express instances for Web Farms.
- `System.Transactions`
  - Remember that default isolation level is serializable.
  - Promotion happens with a second instance of "same" connection.
  - Transactions using `System.Transactions` are not composed with "outer transaction" with in proc ADO.NET.

ADO.NET 2.0

- Use connection strings in configuration files.
- Use the "using" language construct for Connections and Commands.
- Remember that databases aren't generic, even though data access is in ADO.NET 2.0.
- Generic access is needed only if supporting more than one database or changing databases is anticipated.
- In asynchronous commands:
  - Only one statement executes at a time per connection.
  - Gratuitous multithreading slows things.
  - The asynchronous command should be used to implement a data access progress bar.
  - Asynchronous commands are useful for accessing multiple data sources in parallel.
  - Asynchronous commands are not useful for Windows Forms; use the `AsyncWorker` class instead.
  - Don't use asynchronous keyword in connection string if you don't use it.
- Prefer `BULK INSERT` on host over BulkCopy (or BCP).
- Prefer the `SqlBulkCopy` class for nonfile bulk insert.

SMO

- Get only the properties you need; libraries enforce this.
- Prefer SMO to ADO.NET schemas for SQL Server (only).
- Use singletons (or XPath) rather than collections for metadata access.

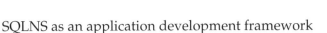

SQLNS as an application development framework

- Use if you have a large numbers of events and many consumers.
- Use SQLAgent or SQLMail if you don't have large numbers of events and many consumers.
- Prefer SQLNS over writing your own notification application.
- Use SQLNS in an existing database if you have a likely candidate database.
- Prototype your applications using SQL statements and the file provider before adding providers.
- Use multicast if all notifications are the same.
- Use Reporting Services for rich notification formatting.
- Don't use user filters if you have a discrete set of related event types.

Toward a Service-Oriented Database Architecture

Since the time that we went from monolithic mainframe computers to distributed systems, some of the main challenges of software programmers have revolved around locality of reference and speed of transport. That is, if all the software is not in one place, and we don't have a direct wire to the user, it matters not only how fast things go inside the computer, but also how long it takes to get the data from here to there and how many round trips we make. If we have the world's fastest supercomputer that can do calculations at near light speed, but if it takes five calls to access it and one second per call, why use it if our personal computer can calculate the same result in two seconds?

Many of the choices we've shown are locality-of-reference choices. Whether it's useful to transform columns and rows to objects on the server or middle tier depends on how many round trips are made and how long they take—or how powerful the server hardware is on the machine that's running the database. Whether they should be transformed to objects at all is based on the premise that object-oriented design saves money in development and maintainability.

Another big consideration is interoperability. It's more a consideration for applications used for sales and marketing that must have the widest possible reach. It certainly makes it easier to add new business partners if your company is not large enough to dictate the terms of intercompany communication. XML is the technology used today to ease interoperability. Because of its structured nature and strong typing, it's a great improvement over the comma-separated text files of the past. The same features make it a choice for marshaling data to unlike platforms.

As an overly simplistic generalization, for a line-of business application, we'd start with the following:

- Data stored in SQL Server in relational format
- XML used for database replicas, as a transport format, and for inter-operability
- Object-oriented programming concepts used on the client

It's actually better and more scalable to divide out the data into categories and determine best configuration based on data usage, concurrency requirements, caching/replications, and the requirement to share the data with business partners (the outside world). But that's beyond our current focus. This is with line-of-business online transaction processing (OLTP) applications; applications that store, index, and query documents would be designed differently.

Relational databases have been around for more than 20 years. They are a known quantity. Most programmers whom we've run into know SQL; the rest at least know what it is. There are domains in which user-defined types are very useful, such as time sequence, spatial data, and multimedia data. In addition, we may achieve synergies in terms of code reuse and programmer productivity by storing objects—the same objects we use on the middle and client tiers—in the database. In the current implementation of UDTs, however, unless the UDT is binary ordered, any SELECT type of operation must fetch the object's binary representation from disk, materialize it, and in turn operate on it. That's the equivalent of a query without an optimizable search argument, a non-SARGable query.

XML data storage and query are in their infancy. It is interesting that except for full-text applications, the preferred/fastest way to store XML documents is to decompose the data. It sounds rather relational—data decomposition, that is. XQuery has a lot of promise, just as SQL had a lot of promise (but was slow) in 1980. It will be interesting to see what happens when vendors have a few years to optimize XQuery processors.

Inside the database, using a managed environment for procedures that extend the capabilities of T-SQL in domain-specific ways is a big improvement over having every programmer use a low-level, type-unsafe language. The idea of .NET Framework stored procedures replacing extended stored procedures—for those who can't wait for Microsoft to produce everything they want as extensions to T-SQL or as system-defined functions—is an appealing one. Likewise, until T-SQL stored procedures can be compiled, processor-intensive calculations that should be done in the server should use compiled .NET Framework code. Data-intensive routines probably should still be done in T-SQL until access through the .NET Framework data provider in the database catches up, but the fact that there is an in-database provider makes it a more difficult decision.

Object-oriented programming concepts are here to stay. Whether you like a thin veneer of object orientation over a traditional data API, à la ADO.NET, or want to treat your data as objects, ignoring the underlying persistence format, you'll be programming with objects in your middle tier and client tier. If you're a fan of relating objects to databases, a new language integrated query model (LINQ) is in development at Microsoft at this writing. It features an extensible common metaquery language that can be implemented over relational databases (DLINQ) or XML data (XLINQ). Direct data binding, both to the `DataSet` and to the `XPathDocument`, makes using ADO.NET or `System.Xml` without having to change your data into domain-specific classes more viable. After all, the two most ubiquitous user interface paradigms are the grid (columns and rows) and the tree (data-centric XML). If you have a lot of domain-specific logic, it makes sense to use a domain-specific object model. Object-oriented programming used on the middle tier (many times, just a Web server), combined with its optimizations and possibly used in conjunction with asynchronous client notifications where real-time cache coherency is required, is a viable middle-tier model. XML-relational mapping, combined with an XML-data-centric, object-oriented, .NET Framework programming language, is a possibility looming on the horizon. Such an XML-data-centric language would make storing XML in its native format more appealing as well.

Interoperability among computer hardware and software vendors has been a problem since the second computer vendor appeared. Each vendor used slightly different hardware, and software was built to take advantage of the byte-order and floating-point-number format for speed. In addition, these differences sifted up into network protocols. To transmit fewer bytes in vendor-specific format using proprietary protocols is a laudable goal. As computers and networks have gotten faster, the search for the universal format and protocol (at the expense of speed and packet size) has quickened. Distributed systems, including current distributed object systems and remote procedure protocols, have always used binary. DCOM/RPC and IIOP are both binary based. Common XML-based formats are supplanting legacy comma-separated-text data exchange formats and TCP/IP network protocols. For maximum interoperability, you can marshal data between unlike platforms in XML format. Even when XML is used as a format and protocol, however, there are still cases of "multiple standards" that are chances for mismatch. Two of the current examples are the competing ebXML and SOAP protocols and document-literal versus RPC-encoded Web Service message format.

For the best chance at interoperability today, you can expose your data through Web Services. Whether the XML packets are served out of the database directly (making the database a combined storage system and application server) or from a separate application server (such as IIS or COM+) depends on your network configuration. If you know that all your users will have the SQL Server client libraries installed (they have been installed on every Windows-family OS machine for a while), TDS is still your best choice. All the APIs, such as ADO.NET, OLE DB, and ODBC, use TDS.

The Database As Part of the Platform

With SQL Server 2005, some new features integrate the database into the application development platform. SQL Server Notification Services, in addition to being an application framework, enables easier integration between the "home office" and mobile devices. SQL Server Service Broker brings asynchronous messaging—including reliable in-order delivery of complex domain-specific multimessage exchanges, client notifications, and messaging in XML format—into the database server. In addition, direct storage of XML and user-defined types mean that processing can be moved closer to the server.

HTTP endpoints make SQL Server a SOAP server for database data and HTTP-based Web Services as well. Reporting Services allow you to store and generate reports directly inside the database. Support of user-defined types and the possible support of a stream-based/file-based data type in the future enable SQL Server to become a multimedia server as well, and stream support means that SQL Server is becoming more integrated with the Windows file system. Look for more integration of file system, database storage, and query technologies in the future.

The Windows platform consists of operating systems for server, user, and mobile devices, with integrated graphical user interfaces; tools for consumers, office workers, and programmers; and an underlying development environment to permit building applications. Software vendors seem to be moving toward high-level, safe, intermediate language and execution engine–based APIs to allow their software architectures to adapt quickly to different hardware environments, like the plethora of mobile devices. In addition, there is a trend to ubiquitous information, available anywhere, either through a central repository or sent to the appropriate user at her desk or mobile device, but secure, administered, backed up, and internally consistent at the same time. SQL Server 2005 is a central adapter and facilitator as the platform evolves.

A

.NET Framework 101

by Niels Berglund

The .NET Framework is the latest component platform from Microsoft and probably is one of the biggest changes for software developers since the move from the 16-bit MS-DOS platform to the 32-bit Windows NT platform.

This appendix gives a brief introduction to the .NET Framework and the CLR for those of you who haven't done any development using the .NET Framework.

The Common Language Runtime

One of the biggest changes in the .NET Framework is that there is an execution engine: the CLR (Common Language Runtime), which handles many of the tasks you had to do previously. The runtime is responsible for (among other things):

- Memory management
- Lifetime management (garbage collection)
- Field layout
- Thread management
- Type safety
- IO management

These are things that you, as a developer, had to handle before the CLR and the .NET Framework, and there were errors in the applications you wrote if you did not handle them correctly. You are giving up control ideally to become more productive and ensure that your coding is less error prone.

This situation, in which you as a developer give up control, is very much like when you went from MS-DOS to Windows NT. In MS-DOS, you were used to handling physical memory and dealing with interrupts. You gave up control over this in favor of virtual memory and threads. Now you give up control over memory management, among other things, in favor of using types. A type is declared as a class; later in this appendix, we cover how to create them.

Figure A-1 shows a simplified picture of the new programming model, and as you see, your code now executes inside the CLR.

Having the code execute inside the CLR raises an interesting question: What do I do if I want to code against Windows, databases, or anything else outside the CLR? Most of the resources we know and use in our applications are outside the CLR.

You can access the underlying platform features from your application; Microsoft has put down a lot of work on making it possible to interoperate between managed and native code. Microsoft discourages this, however, and ships with the CLR a family of runtime libraries that provides a

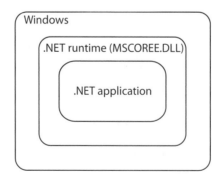

FIGURE A-1: The CLR programming model

language-neutral way to write Web programs, database access programs, XML programs, and Windows programs. Most of these libraries/routines reside in a DLL, `mscorlib.dll`, that also contains the metadata for the CLR type system. The runtime is an environment that is being initialized by various host environments: It is being *hosted*. Windows in itself acts as a host; ASP.NET acts as a host; and yes, SQL Server Yukon acts as a host.

What makes it possible to host the runtime from native code is a COM DLL, `mscoree.dll`. This DLL exposes several API functions that are used to initialize and host the CLR. But `mscoree.dll` is just a thin layer over the runtime. As soon as it is initialized, it loads either `mscorwks.dll` or `mscorsvr.dll`, dependent on certain rules. These two DLLs are the "real" runtime, and we discuss them in more detail in Chapter 2. Because `mscoree.dll` is needed by every .NET Framework application, you do not need to link to it explicitly, but the .NET Framework compilers reference it implicitly as well as `mscorlib.dll`.

Development Languages

As opposed to other, competing frameworks, the CLR allows you to choose what development language you want to use. The only requirement is that the language has a compiler that produces CLR executables. This also means that the features of the CLR are available to all languages. If the CLR allows implementation inheritance (which it does), for example, all languages can use that feature. Therefore, the choice of which development language to use can be based on what you feel comfortable with, not what restrictions the language puts on you. Microsoft ships compilers for five languages together with the CLR:

- C# (C-Sharp)
- Viusal Basic .NET
- MC++ (Managed C++)
- J Script
- MSIL (Microsoft Intermediate Language)

Compilers for other development languages also are available, ranging from Python to COBOL.

Looking at the list of languages above, you may wonder what MSIL (IL) is. IL is the CLR's assembly language. It turns out that when you compile your code, the code is not compiled to machine code but, as you can see in Figure A-2, to IL code, which can be seen as interpreted code.

Does this mean, then, that when your CLR application executes, it executes interpreted code? No, because when you run the application, the IL code will be compiled into machine code as needed through the Just-in-Time Compiler (JIT Compiler, also called JITter). After the application has been loaded, it is the JITter's responsibility to compile the IL code to machine code (native CPU instructions) when a function is first executed. The native code is saved, and for each subsequent time that particular function is called, the native code is executed without the JITter's being called. From a performance perspective, there is a slight delay for the first call into a particular function, whereas subsequent calls are executed at optimal speed.

Because most applications execute the same methods repeatedly, the performance hit is not significant. If you are worried about this, you can use a specific tool in the .NET Framework SDK: the NGen.exe, which compiles the IL code directly into native code.

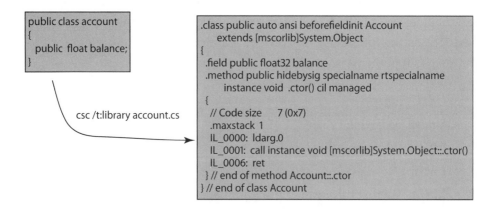

FIGURE A-2: Compilation of code into IL

Assemblies and Modules

When you read about the .NET Framework and the CLR, you are certain to come across the term *assembly*. Before we can define what an assembly is, we need to discuss briefly another term in the CLR: the *module*.

Modules

Programs written for the CLR reside in modules. A CLR module is a byte stream, typically stored as a file in the local file system or on a Web server. CLR modules contain code, metadata, and resources. The module's metadata describes the types defined in the module, including names, inheritance relationships, method signatures, and dependency information. The module's resources consist of static read-only data such as strings, bitmaps, and other aspects of the program that are not stored as executable code.

The compilers in .NET Framework translate source code into CLR modules. The compilers accept a common set of command-line switches to control which kind of module to produce. You normally choose between producing an executable (EXE) or a library module (DLL). Listing A-1 shows how to use the C# compiler from the command line. The first uncommented line of code creates an EXE, and the next uncommented code line creates a DLL. In both cases, the source-code file is called source.cs. It is the /target: switch that decides whether you want an EXE or a DLL. In Visual Studio .NET, you make the same decision by choosing an executable or a class library as the project type.

LISTING A-1: Compiling from command line

```
//compiling an EXE
csc /target:exe source.cs

//compiling a dll
csc /target:library source.cs
```

Table A-1 shows what choices you have when deciding what you want to compile your C# application into.

Notice that you can not compile netmodules from Visual Studio .NET. You have to do it from the command line.

In previous component model technologies, you had various ways of investigating the metadata of your component. In COM, you used the

TABLE A-1: Target Switches

Target	Type of Module	Visual Studio Choice
exe	Console Application Executable	Console Application
winexe	Windows Forms Executable	Windows Forms
library	Class Library (DLL)	Class Library
module	netmodule*	N/A

*Discussing netmodules is beyond the scope of what we cover in this appendix. For a complete overview of assemblies versus modules, we recommend *Essential .NET, Volume 1, The Common Language Runtime*, by Don Box (Addison-Wesley, 2003).

OLEView.EXE to get type information, and for non-COM components, you probably used DUMPBIN.EXE. In the .NET Framework, you have various tools if you want to inspect a module or assembly.

One such tool is ILDasm.EXE, which ships with the .NET Framework SDK. ILDasm stands for Intermediate Language Disassembler, and you use ILDasm to view the metadata and disassembled code of your application in a hierarchical tree view.

Figure A-3 shows the metadata for a component, which consists of a class called Person. Notice that you can see both private members and public members of the class. The figure also shows a method called SaySomething.

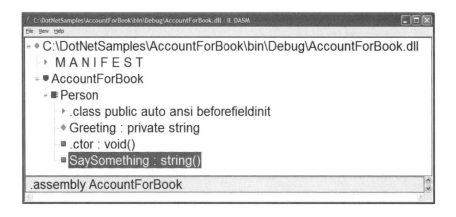

FIGURE A-3: Screenshot of ILDasm

As you can see, the method is fully disassembled, and the code you see is the compiled IL code.

ILDasm is extremely useful, and we urge you to get to know it, as it will help you when you develop applications, as well as understand what code from other developers does.

Assemblies

An *assembly* is the essential building block of your application and consists of a collection of modules. You can think of an assembly as being the logical EXE or DLL. The assembly is also the fundamental unit for deployment and is used to package, load, distribute, and version CLR modules. The assembly consists of one or more modules, and the most common scenario is that your assembly has only one module. This is what you get when you compile a Visual Studio .NET Framework project.

The main difference between a module and an assembly (between .net-module and EXE/DLL) is that in an assembly, exactly one module holds not only the metadata for the particular module, but also a manifest. The manifest is metadata with information about what types the assembly consists of and in what files those types can be found. The module containing the assembly manifest will also have a list of externally referenced assemblies. This list consists of the dependencies of every module in the assembly, not just the dependencies of the current module.

In Listing A-2, you can see the manifest for the component we showed the ILDasm for in Figure A-2. Notice that the only externally referenced assembly is mscorlib.dll.

LISTING A-2: Manifest for component

```
.assembly extern mscorlib
{
  .publickeytoken = (B7 7A 5C 56 19 34 E0 89 )
  //  .z\V.4..
  .ver 1:0:5000:0
}
.assembly account
{
  // --- The following custom attribute is added automatically, do not
uncomment -------
  //   .custom instance void
[mscorlib]System.Diagnostics.DebuggableAttribute::.ctor(bool,
  //
```

```
bool) = ( 01 00 00 01 00 00 )
   .hash algorithm 0x00008004
   .ver 0:0:0:0
}
.module account.dll
// MVID: {6802C533-1DBF-4E78-A61E-9B883723E40B}
.imagebase 0x00400000
.subsystem 0x00000003
.file alignment 512
.corflags 0x00000001
// Image base: 0x06cf0000
```

In Listing A-2, you can also see the version number for the actual component, as well as the version number for the referenced `mscorlib.dll`.
In the next section, we'll discuss assembly names and versioning.

Assembly Names and Versions

If you have a COM background, you probably remember that your components were uniquely identified by a Globally Unique Identifier (GUID). In the
.NET Framework, Microsoft has done away with the GUIDs, and assemblies
are identified by a four-part name. When the assembly is loaded by the runtime, this name is used to find the correct component. The name consists of:

- Friendly name
- Locale
- Developer
- Version

The `Name` property of the assembly name corresponds to the underlying filename of the assembly manifest without any extension, and this is the
only part of the assembly name that is not optional. The name is needed in
simple scenarios to locate the correct component at load time. When building an assembly, this part of the assembly name is selected by your compiler automatically based on the target filename. Although strictly
speaking, the `Name` of the assembly does not need to match the underlying
filename, keeping the two in sync makes the job of the assembly resolver
(and system administrators) much simpler.

Assembly names can contain a `CultureInfo` (locale) that identifies the spoken language and country code that the component has been developed for.

An assembly name can contain a public key (token) that identifies the developer of the component. An assembly reference may use either the full 128-byte public key or the 8-byte public key token. The public key (token) is used to resolve filename collisions between organizations, allowing components with the same name to coexist in memory and on disk. This is if each component originates from a different developer, each of which is guaranteed to have a unique public key. When you give your components a public key, you give them a strong name.

All assembly names have a four-part version number (`Version`) of the form `Major.Minor.Build.Revision`. If you do not set this version number explicitly, its default value will be 0.0.0.0. The version number is set at build time using a custom attribute in the source code or using a command-line switch. The runtime is doing a version check during the loading of the respective assemblies, which means you can differentiate between two assemblies with the same name and publisher based upon version number. Notice that we said "name and publisher." *Publisher* is the keyword here, as the runtime makes this version check only for strongly named assemblies.

The CLR Type System

The CLR is all about types, and some people go as far as to say that the CLR was developed to rectify previous models' shortcomings with regard to type and type information. Be that as it may, types are essential in the CLR, and there is a formal specification describing how to define types and how the types should behave. This formal specification is known as the Common Type System (CTS).

The CTS specifies, among other things:

- What members a type can contain
- The visibility of types and members
- How types are inherited, virtual functions, and so on

The CTS also specifies that all types within the CLR have to derive from a predefined type, which acts as the root of the type system. This type is `System.Object`, and because this type is the root, any member in the CLR can be assigned to variables of `System.Object`. This also means that every member in a class has a minimum set of behaviors (inherited from System.Object). Table A-2 shows the members of System.Object and what they do.

Because the CLR has a defined type system with System.Object as root, the runtime can make sure that the code we write is type safe. Figure A-4 illustrates the CLR type system. Notice that the type system is logically divided into two subsystems: reference types and value types.

Programming languages in general have a set of built-in types, referred to as simple or primitive types. Normally, they are int, float, bool, char, and so on. You find in the CLR a rich set of these types, which Listing A-3 illustrates.

LISTING A-3: Types in the CLR type system

```
struct Point
{
    bool outside;
    int X;
    int Y;
    float density;
}
```

In Figure A-4, you see some boxes that illustrate various user-defined types based on the primitive types. In the following section, we cover how to create these user-defined types.

TABLE A-2: Members of System.Object

Member	Description
Equals	Checks whether two instances of an object are equals
GetHashCode	Obtains the hash code for an object
GetType	Gets the type of the instance of an object
ReferenceEquals	Compares whether the instances of an object are the same instance
ToString	Gets a string representation of the current state of an object instance
Finalize	Allows an object to do cleanup before garbage collection
MemberwiseClone	Creates a bitwise copy of an instance

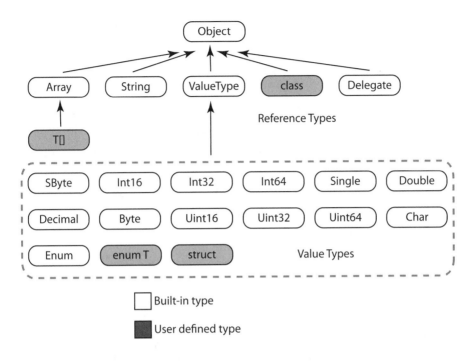

FIGURE A-4: The CLR type system

Classes and Types

When you create a type in the CLR, you ultimately derive from System. Object, System.ValueType, or System.Enum. Suppose that you want to create a new reference type called Person. The C# code for that would look something like Listing A-4. Because it is required that you ultimately derive from System.Object, however, you can write your code as shown in Listing A-5.

LISTING A-4: Create person class by explicitly deriving from System.Object

```
class Person : System.Object {

}
```

LISTING A-5: Create person class by implicitly deriving from System.Object

```
class Person {

}
```

You indicate that you want to inherit from a type by using the colon after your class name, followed by the type you want to derive from: `class YourType : TypeToDeriveFrom`.

Looking at the code in Listing A-4, you may think that to create a value type, you would write code something like `class MyValueType : System.ValueType`. That is not the case if you code in C#, Visual Basic .NET, or some of the other programming languages in the CLR. The programming languages use their own concepts of types: class, interfaces, structures, enumerations, and so on. The runtime sees these ultimately as type definitions, and it distinguishes among the various types based on base class or attributes in the metadata.

When you use C#, you indicate what kind of type you want to create by using the syntax in Table A-3.

The keyword `struct` may be somewhat misleading when creating a value type, and you may believe that the value type is only a data structure, nothing more. That is not the case at all; a value type can have fields, methods, properties and so on, exactly like a class. The value type can also support interfaces.

Visibility

When you create your types, you may want to decide how they should be accessible and whether they should be visible to the outside world. For this reason (as we mentioned earlier), the CTS defines rules for visibility and access to types, as well as members within a type. You decide what visibility and access you want by using access modifiers. These access modifiers are

TABLE A-3: Syntax for Type Definitions in C#

Syntax	Kind of Type
`public class MyClass {}`	Reference Type
`public struct MyValueType {}`	Value Type
`public interface MyInterface {}`	Interface
`public enum MyEnum {}`	Enumeration
`public delegate void MyDelegate {}`	Delegate

TABLE A-4: Access Modifiers

	C#	Visual Basic .NET	Visibility
Type	public	Public	Everywhere
	internal (default)	Private (default)	Inside declaring assembly
Member	public	Public (default for methods)	Everywhere
	internal	Friend	Inside declaring assembly
	protected	Protected	Inside declaring type and subtypes
	protected internal	Protected Friend	Inside declaring type and subtypes, or other types inside declaring assembly
	private (default)	Private (default for fields)	Inside declaring type

keywords that you mark your type or member with. Table A-4 shows the access modifiers for both types, as well as members. We cover type members later in this appendix.

Listing A-6 shows some code that uses these access modifiers.

LISTING A-6: C# Code making use of access modifiers

```
public class Person {   //this class is visible to anyone

    private int    age;     //this is private
    string         name;    //this is also private
    public  string address; //this field is visible to anyone

    //this method is visible from anywhere inside the assembly
    internal void DoSomethingInternally() {}

    //this method is visible from anywhere
    public void DoSomethingPublicly() {}

    //this method is visible only within the type
    //as the default is private
    void DoSomethingPrivately() {}
}
```

Instances

You access your types through instance variables. In Listing A-7, we see that the type system is divided into reference types and value types.

A reference type variable contains the memory address of the particular object it refers to and is not the actual type instance. Before a reference type variable can be used, it must be initialized to point to a valid object. Value types, on the other hand, are the instances themselves, not references. This means that a value type variable is useful immediately upon declaration.

In C#, you initialize reference type by using the new keyword, which will be translated into an IL newobj instruction. The corresponding keyword in Visual Basic .NET is New. The code in Listing A-6 shows how you initialize a reference type and a value type.

LISTING A-7: Initialization of reference types and value types

```csharp
class RefPerson {
    public int age;
    public string name;
}

struct ValPerson {
  public int age;
  public string name;
}

class App {

    static void Main(string[] args) {
    //initilize the reference type
    RefPerson p = new RefPerson();
    p.age = 33;

    //initialize the value type
    ValPerson vp;
    vp.age = 33;

    //the following code will not compile as it is a reference type
    //there will be an error: 'Use of unassigned local variable 'p1''
    //RefPerson p1;
    //p1.age = 33;
  }
}
```

Notice that we get an error when we try to use an instance of the reference type without having initialized it with new. A value type can be initialized using new as well. The difference from a reference type is that the IL instruction will be initobj instead of newobj. Listing A-8 shows how a value type is initialized with the new keyword.

LISTING A-8: Initialize a value type with new

```
//the definition for RefPerson and ValPerson is the same as in
//   A-6
class App {

     static void Main(string[] args) {
    //initilize the reference type
    RefPerson rp = new RefPerson();
    rp.age = 33;

    //get a new variable for RefPerson
    RefPerson rp1 = rp;
    rp1.age = 35;

    //here you will see the same age (35) for both rp as well as rp1
    System.Console.WriteLine("Reference Types:\nrp's age is:
    {0}\nrp1's age is: {1}", rp.age, rp1.age);

    //initialize the value type
    ValPerson vp = new ValPerson();
    vp.age = 33;

    //get a new variable for ValPerson
    ValPerson vp1 = vp;
    vp1.age = 35;

    //vp's age is 33, vp1's age is 35
    System.Console.WriteLine("\nValue Types:\nvp's age is:
    {0}\nvp1's age is: {1}", vp.age, vp1.age);
      }
}
```

Listing A-8 also shows how assignment of variables works differently depending on the type. For reference types, the assignment results in a duplicate variable pointing to the same address space as the first. Subsequently, when you change the state from one variable, that change is visible through the second variable as well.

The assignment for a value type results in a copy of the instance, which is completely unrelated to the first instance. Any change of state from one variable does not affect the other.

The main differences between reference types and value types are

- Reference types inherit from `System.Object` or a type that in its root of the inheritance chain has `System.Object`. A value type inherits from either `System.ValueType` or `System.Enum`[1] and from those two types only. In other words, you can derive from a reference type but not from a value type.
- A reference type is created on the garbage-collected heap, whereas a value type normally is created on the stack. A value type can be allocated on the heap, however. This happens when the value type is a member of a reference type, for example.
- Another difference is that a reference type always is accessed via a strongly typed reference. A value type, on the other hand, can be accessed directly or via a reference.

From the perspective of the developer, there is not much difference between a reference type and a value type. A value type can have fields, methods, properties and so on, exactly like a reference type.

Namespaces

When you develop your projects, the likelihood that you will have types related to one another is fairly big. These types may be located in different assemblies, for example, and you want to group them. You accomplish this by using namespaces.

Namespaces provide a way to group types logically. You use them both within your application to organize your types and in an external organization system. When you look through the helper libraries in the CLR, you find that namespaces are used everywhere. An example is the `System.Data` namespace, which defines types that have to do with data access. It is further

---

1. `System.ValueType` derives from `System.Object`, and `System.Enum` derives from `System.ValueType`.

divided into namespaces for certain providers, such as the System.Data.
SqlClient namespace and the System.Data.OleDb namespace.

You indicate that your type(s) belong to a namespace by using the
Namespace keyword, as the code in Listing A-9 shows.

LISTING A-9: Creating a namespace

```
namespace People {
  public class Person {

  }
  public class Instructor {

  }
}

public class Calculator {

}
```

In the code in Listing A-9, the Person and Instructor class both
belong to the People namespace. The Calculator class, however, does not
belong to any namespace.

The CLR has no knowledge about namespaces and sees the Person type in
Listing A-9 as being of the type People.Person. Subsequently, when you want
to create an instance of this type, you create an instance of People.Person.

With namespaces, the code to create an instance of a type can become
fairly verbose, as the code in Listing A-10 shows. Therefore, most compilers
have mechanisms to make it easier for the programmer and reduce the typing the programmer has to do. Listing A-11 shows how the C# developer
can use the using directive.

LISTING A-10: Explicitly typing full type names

```
public class DataStuff {

  public void Main() {
    //from the compiler's perspective as well as the CLR the type
    //is the full name including namespace
    System.Data.SqlClient.SqlConnection conn;
    conn = new System.Data.SqlClient.SqlConnection();
    //code to connect etc follows but not shown
  }
}
```

LISTING A-11: Use of the using directive in C#

```
using System.Data.SqlClient;

public class DataStuff {

  public void Main() {

    SqlConnection conn;
    conn = new SqlConnection();
    //code to connect etc follows but not shown
  }
}
```

The directive for the Visual Basic .NET developer is `Imports` instead of `using`.

Members of Types

For a type to be useful, it has to contain something. This something is member declarations, which describe the state or behavior of the type. The CLR supports six types of members; you can see them and their definitions in Table A-5.

TABLE A-5: Type Members

Member	Definition
Fields	Data storage that can be read from or written to.
Methods	Code that performs operations on the type; also called functions.
Constructors	Special kind of method that is executed when the type is instantiated. A constructor can have parameters.
Properties	A special type of method that allows fieldlike syntax for setting or getting values of the state of the type.
Events	Allows a type to send notifications to a listening type or object.
Types	A type can have nested types within it.

Listing A-12 shows code for a type containing the six members.

LISTING A-12: A type with members

```
using System;

class MyType {
  //field
  int _age;
  //field
  public string name;

  //constructor
  public MyType() {
    name = "Jim";
  }

  //method
  public void SayHello() {
    Console.WriteLine("hello");
  }

  //property
  public int Age {
    set { _age = value;}
    get {return _age;}
  }

  //this event doesn't do anything
  public event EventHandler MyEvent;

  //nested type
  class NestedType {
    //some members
  }
}
```

Each member in a type is of a certain data type. The data type can be some of the built-in types or a type that the developer has defined. Methods and properties may not necessarily have a particular return type. You declare this in C# with the keyword `void`. In Visual Basic .NET, you declare the method as a `Sub`.

Notice that the event MyEvent is not fully functional, as it is not implemented through any methods. We do not intend to cover events in this appendix; see *Essential .NET, Volume 1, The Common Language Runtime*, by Don Box, for a full coverage of events.

Fields and Properties

In Listing A-12, we have declared two fields: _age and name. _age is private, and name is public. Declaring a field as public is not considered to be good coding practice, as you should not allow direct access to the state of a type. Instead, fields should be accessed through properties. The property Age is an example of this.

Members can either be static members or instance members. The difference is that a static member is part of the type, whereas an instance member is part of the object. A popular definition of static members is that they are global. Static members are accessed by the syntax: type.member, as opposed to the instance member, which is accessed through variable.member.

As we mentioned in Table A-5 earlier in this chapter, a property is a special type of method that allows fieldlike syntax to retrieve or set state values. To the CLR, a property is a binding of a name to one or two method declarations, one of which is the "getter" and the other of which is the "setter." A property also has a type, which applies to the return type of the "getter" method and the last parameter to the "setter" method.

In C#, you define a property as a special method that consists of a get part and a set part. Listing A-13 shows the code for a class with a property called Name. You make the property read-only by omitting the set part. For a write-only property, you omit the get part.

LISTING A-13: Property declaration

```
public class Person {

   string _name;

   public string Name {
      set { _name = value;}
      get {return _name;}
   }
}
```

Note that when you assign a value to a property, the value is passed in through an intrinsic parameter called value. Listing A-14 shows how to access the Name property in Person.

LISTING A-14: Accessing a property

```
public class App {

  string _name;

  static void Main() {
    Person p = new Person();

    //set the property this uses the value parameter
    p.Name = "Jim";

    //get the property
    System.Console.WriteLine(p.Name);
  }
}
```

Parameters and Methods

When you pass parameters to a method, the method's declaration determines whether the parameters will be passed by reference or by value. Passing parameters by value (the default) results in the method's getting its own private copy of the parameter values. If the parameter is a value type, the method gets its own private copy of the instance. If the parameter is a reference type, it is the reference that is passed by value. The object the reference points to is not copied. Rather, both the caller and method wind up with private references to a shared object.

When the parameters are passed by reference, the method gets a managed pointer pointing back to the caller's variables. Any changes the method makes to the value type or the reference type will be visible to the caller. Furthermore, if the method overwrites an object reference parameter to redirect it to another object in memory, this change affects the caller's variable as well. In C#, you indicate that you want to pass a parameter by reference by using the ref or out modifier. Listing A-15 shows a method that takes three parameters and how it is called. When you pass parameters by reference, you need to indicate that in the calling code with the ref or out modifier.

LISTING A-15: Parameter passing

```
public class Person {

  public int DoSomething(int x, ref string y, out int z) {
    //do something
    z = 100;
    //return a value
    return 99;
```

```
    }
}

public class App {
    static void Main() {
        int a = 99;
        string b = "Jim";
        int c;
        Person p = new Person();
        p.DoSomething(a, ref b, out c);
    }
}
```

The difference between the `ref` and `out` modifiers is that the `out` marked variable does not need to be initialized before calling. Subsequently, it cannot be used in the method before it has been assigned a value from within the method.

Memory Management

Memory is allocated on the heap/stack by creating an instance of a type. The allocation is handled by the runtime, and the developer does not need to care explicitly about memory management, field layout, and so on. The same is true of reclaiming memory. The CLR is wholly responsible for reclaiming (deallocating) memory. Memory management is one of the primary benefits of the CLR's managed execution mode. So how does the CLR know when to reclaim memory?

When an object is created, the CLR tracks the reference to this object (and all other objects referenced in the system). Because the CLR has this knowledge about the object references, it also knows when an object is no longer referenced. The memory allocated for the object can be reclaimed at this stage. The memory reclamation is done through garbage collection. Doing garbage collection affects performance. Because of this, garbage collection does not necessarily happen as soon as the object is no longer referenced. Instead, the CLR performs garbage collection when certain resource thresholds are exceeded.

Normally, the developer does not care about garbage collection, but if he wants explicit control, the `System.GC` class exposes the garbage collector programmatically. The `Collect` method tells the CLR to perform garbage collection as soon as the method is called. Be aware, however, that calling `GC.Collect` frequently can have a negative impact on performance.

Finalization and Destructors

Generally, the objects do not need to know when they are garbage-collected. Objects referenced by the one that is garbage-collected will themselves be collected as part of the normal garbage-collection run. Sometimes, however, there may be situations where an object holds references to resources that will not be garbage-collected or references to scarce resources. Examples are file handles, database connections, and so on. In a situation like that, the object may want to get a notification saying that it is about to be collected.

This can be achieved by something called object finalization. System.Object exposes Finalize, which is a method that can be overridden in derived types. Finalization, however, is a technique that adds complexity. Because of this, you cannot implement Finalize directly in C#. Instead, you implement a destructor, which causes the compiler to emit your destructor code inside a Finalize method. Listing A-15 shows this. The compiler also makes sure that the Finalize method in your base class is called. As you see in Listing A-16, the destructor looks like a constructor, but it is prepended with ~.

LISTING A-16: Use of destructor

```
public class Person {
   //other methods not shown

   ~Person() {
     //call your cleanup code
     CleanUp();
   }

   void CleanUp() {
     //code to free scarce resources

   }
}
```

One thing to bear in mind about finalizers is that the Finalize method may be called long after the object has been identified by the garbage collector. When the garbage collector tries to reclaim an object that has a finalizer, the reclamation is postponed until the finalizer can be called. Rather than reclaim the memory, the garbage collector puts the object onto a specific finalization queue. A dedicated garbage-collector thread eventually will call the object's finalizer, and when the finalizer has completed execution, the object's memory is available for reclamation.

Disposing

If your objects have scarce resources, finalization may not be ideal, based on the discussion in the preceding paragraph. Because of this, Microsoft has introduced a standard idiom in the CLR that provides an explicit method and that can be called when the user is done with the object. The method is Dispose, and it is part of the System.IDisposable interface. In fact, it is the only method in that interface.

Implementing this interface indicates that the specific class requires explicit cleanup. It also indicates that it is the client programmer's responsibility to invoke the IDisposable.Dispose method as soon as the referenced object is no longer needed. Listing A-17 shows a class that implements the IDisposable interface. Listing A-18 shows a client using the class in Listing A-16.

LISTING A-17: Implementing IDisposable

```
using System;
public class Person :IDisposable {
  //other methods not shown

  ~Person() {
    //call your cleanup code
    CleanUp();
  }

  void CleanUp() {
    //code to free scarce resources
  }

  public void Dispose() {
    GC.SuppressFinalize(this);
    CleanUp();
  }
}
```

You may wonder what the GC.SuppressFinalize(this) call does. As the Dispose method probably performs the same operations as your finalizer, you may not want the finalizer to run. The GC.SuppressFinalize (this) tells the runtime not to run the finalizer.

LISTING A-18: Using an IDisposable class

```
class App {
  static void Main() {
    Person per = new Person();

    try {
      //do something with per
    }

    finally {
      per.Dispose();
    }
  }
}
```

As a C# developer, you have the opportunity to let the compiler call `Dispose` automatically. The `using` statement (this is different from `using` for namespaces) does this. It allows the developer to declare one or more variables whose `IDisposable.Dispose` method will be called automatically. Listing A-19 shows client code utilizing `using`.

LISTING A-19: C# using

```
class App {
  static void Main() {
    using(Person per = new Person()) {
      //do something with per
    } //Dispose is called here
  }
}
```

B

SQL Server Management Studio

Introduction

SQL Server Management Studio, SSMS for short, is a GUI application that is used by database administrators and developers alike to interact with SQL Server, Analysis Services, Integration Services, Reporting Services, SQL Server Mobile, and SQL Express. This appendix focuses on features used by developers working with SQL Server.

For developers, SSMS revolves around projects used to build queries and managing databases that will run those queries. The queries themselves may end up being run as stand-alone scripts or as commands executed by ADO.NET in client and middle-tier applications.

The main screen of SSMS, shown in Figure B-1, is configurable. Figure B-1 shows a typical configuration a developer might use. The Database Object Explorer (1) is on the left; it is used to explore and build the databases, tables, and other objects that make up an instance of SQL Server, and provides utility similar to that provided by Enterprise Manager in SQL Server 2000. The Query window (2) is in the center top; it is used to try out queries and shows their results in the Results (3) window at the center bottom. It serves the same purpose Query Analyzer did in previous versions of SQL Server. The Solution Explorer (4), at the right of the screen, holds projects that themselves hold connections to databases, SQL Scripts, and miscellaneous files.

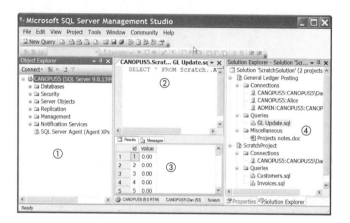

FIGURE B-1: SSMS main screen

In this appendix, we will look at working with SSMS solutions and projects, ad hoc queries, creating and managing connections to databases, and using and creating script templates.

Solutions and Projects

The main development element of SSMS is the project. A *project* consists of a collection of connections, a collection of Transact-SQL (T-SQL) scripts, and a collection of miscellaneous files. Ad hoc queries are stand-alone queries that are not part of a project.

SSMS is based on the same framework as Visual Studio 2005 and incorporates a development idiom that has been part of Visual Studio since it first shipped. A developer works on a project, which is just a collection of files that the developer feels belong together. Projects are grouped into a solution so they can be worked on together.

The same project can belong to multiple solutions. The idea is that a solution represents a number of projects that are related in some ad hoc way. One project might contain scripts that manage an accounting application, for example; another project might contain scripts that set up the accounting application; and yet another project might contain scripts that test the accounting application. A different solution might have the project with the accounting application in it and an application that managed inventory. Projects are put into solutions for the convenience of the developer.

SSMS visually displays solutions and projects as a tree. Later in this appendix, we will be looking at building solutions. Figure B-2 shows a typical SSMS solution. At the top of the tree is the name (1) of the solution—in this case, ScratchSolution. It contains two projects below it: the General Ledger Posting project (2) and the ScratchProject. A project consists of Connections (3), Queries (4), and Miscellaneous files (5).

The connections are used to keep track of the instances of SQL Server you typically connect to. Queries are the SQL script files the developer is working on. Miscellaneous files keep track of the other odds and ends typically associated with a project.

Configuration

SSMS can be configured to suit your tastes. When it is first installed, it is configured to open a connection to the local instance of SQL Server and display summary information about it. Figure B-3 shows SSMS opened with a summary view.

To change the configuration of SSMS, choose Tools > Options, as shown in Figure B-4.

FIGURE B-2: SSMS solution

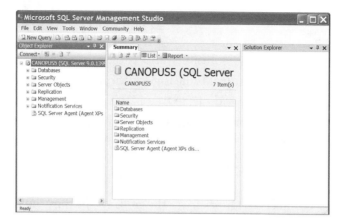

FIGURE B-3: Summary of local instance of SQL Server

The Options command will bring up the Options dialog box, shown in Figure B-5. Use the tree (1) on the left side of the dialog box to select the options you want to configure. You can experiment with the various options to see what they do, but they let you control everything from enabling word wrap in editors to what phrase you want to use as a batch separator. If you want to keep the overhead associated with opening SSMS to a minimum, select Environment Layout/Open Empty Environment (2). Then SSMS will not try to connect to the local instance of SQL Server when it starts.

With Environment Layout set to Open Empty Environment, SSMS will open more quickly and look like Figure B-6.

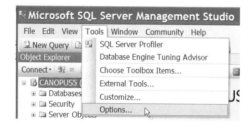

FIGURE B-4: Configuration options

FIGURE B-5: Options dialog box

Making a Solution/Project

There is no way to make an empty solution as there is in Visual Studio 2005; you must create a project, and that will create a solution that contains it. To make a new project, choose File > New > Project, as shown in Figure B-7.

The Project command will bring up the New Project dialog box, shown in Figure B-8. In this dialog box, select the SQL Server Scripts templates (1). Fill in a name for the project (2), a directory (3) to store it, and a name for the solution (4). Leave the Create Directory for Solution checkbox checked. This will create a new directory for the solution and make the project part of it.

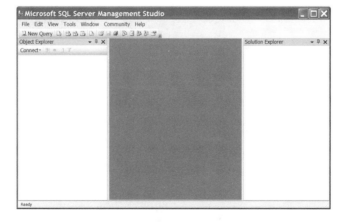

FIGURE B-6: Empty environment

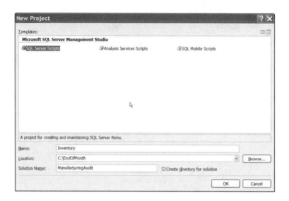

FIGURE B-7: Making new project and solution

Figure B-9 shows how the Solution Explorer tree looks for a new project.

The New Project dialog box will create two new directories, as shown in Figure B-10. One will have the name of the solution (1), and the other will be its child and have the name of the project (2). The solution is in a file with an .ssmssln (short for SSMS Solution) extension (3). The project is in a file with a .ssmssqlproj extension (4).

Adding a Connection

When you have created a project, it's probably best to add connections to it first. Connections allow you to create new queries without having

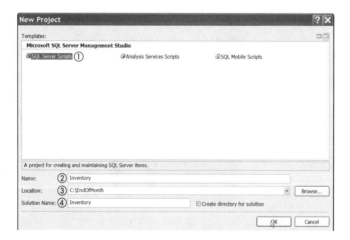

FIGURE B-8: New project dialog box

FIGURE B-9: New project

to type connection information. You can make connections with a Windows identity or a SQL login. You add a connection by right-clicking the Connections folder in the Solution Explorer tree, as shown in Figure B-11.

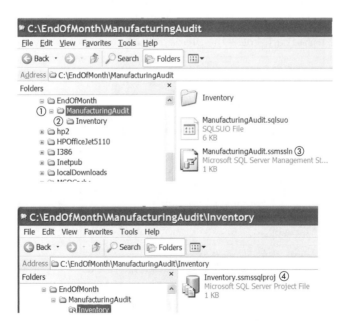

FIGURE B-10: Directories and files for new project

FIGURE B-11: Making new
connection

The New Connection command will bring up the Connect to Server dialog box, shown in Figure B-12. From this dialog box, you can select (1) Windows or SQL Server authentication. The Options button (2) allows you to pick the default database to use after the connection is made.

Connections are displayed (1) in the Solution Explorer tree, as shown in Figure B-13. Note that connections that use Windows authentication will authenticate with the identity that is running SSMS, not necessarily the identity that created the connection for the project.

Connections have properties, some of which you can change, as shown in Figure B-14. You can access the properties of a connection by right-clicking

FIGURE B-12: Connect to server
dialog box

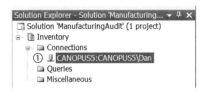

FIGURE B-13: Connection in tree.

the connection itself. Note that you cannot change the SQL Server instance for the connection, but you can change the execution and login timeouts, as well as the initial database for the connection.

Adding a Query

Queries, or SQL scripts, are added to a project through the New Query command in a connection's context menu, as shown in Figure B-15. Note that you bring up the context menu by right-clicking the connection.

Clicking the New Query command will add a query, as shown in Figure B-16. The query will be named automatically, but you can change the name after it has been added by right-clicking the query in the Solution Explorer tree.

FIGURE B-14: Connection properties

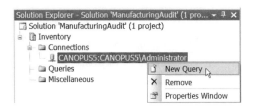

FIGURE B-15: Adding query

Note the query was opened according to the connection properties, including the initial database.

The connection a query is using can be disconnected or changed by right-clicking the background of the query, as shown in Figure B-17.

The query window acts the same way that a similar window in Query Profiler did; you can type a query and then execute it by pressing the F5 key. If nothing in the query window is highlighted, everything in the query window is executed; otherwise, only the text that is highlighted is executed. The results appear in the results window below the query window, as shown in Figure B-18. The results window can be toggled on and off by pressing Ctrl+R.

The query window has a GUI query designer similar to one in Access and Visual Studio 2005. The query designer can be used to design a single SELECT, UPDATE, INSERT, or DELETE statement. You can access the query designer by right-clicking the query window, as shown in Figure B-19. Note that the menu that appears also gives access to other tools for queries.

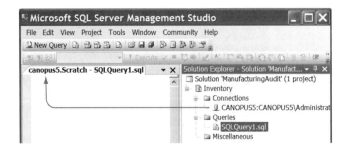

FIGURE B-16: New query

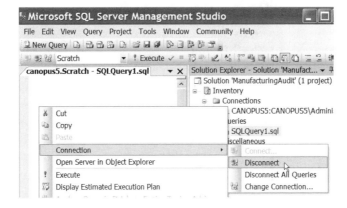

FIGURE B-17: Changing query connection

If something is selected in the query window, as it is in Figure B-19, the query designer will be initialized with that expression when it is opened. If nothing is selected, the query designer will open ready to design a query from scratch.

The Design Query in Editor command brings up the Query Designer dialog box, shown in Figure B-20. This designer is documented in Books Online; look for "Query Designer" in the index. We will look at a few features of it.

The Query Designer is divided into three parts. The tables (1) that will be used in the query appear in the top window. The criterion (2) for what

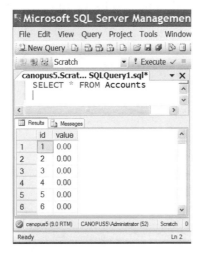

FIGURE B-18: Query results

FIGURE B-19: Selecting query
designer

columns are returned, sorting, and so on appear in the middle windows.
The text form of the query (3) appears in the bottom window. These windows are synchronized—that is, a change in one window will be updated
automatically in the others.

Several of the tools for making queries are available by right-clicking the
background of the query windows, as shown in Figure B-21. Group By (1)
can be added and the type query can be changed (2)—for example, to an
INSERT. You can also add tables (3) to the query.

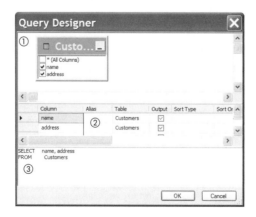

FIGURE B-20: Query designer

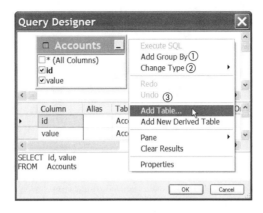

FIGURE B-21: Adding table

Choosing the Add Table command brings up the Add Table dialog box, shown in Figure B-22. From this dialog box, you can add tables, views, and so on to the query. Note that the objects shown in the list box come from the connection for the query.

When a table is added to the query designer, as shown in Figure B-23, it is joined to the other tables in the query based on the same column names. The join itself (1) is shown as a line between the tables. Right-clicking this line brings up a dialog box that allows you to adjust the characteristics of the join or delete the join. Any columns selected (2) in the table will be

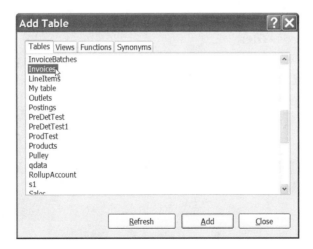

FIGURE B-22: Add table dialog box

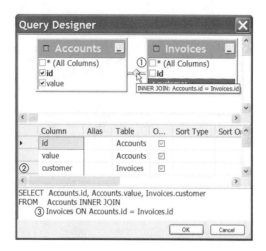

FIGURE B-23: Table added to query designer

shown in the center window. The table itself will appear in the text (3) form of the query.

Clicking the OK button in the query designer inserts the query into the query window, as shown in Figure B-24, with the entire query selected.

The query window will allow you to edit queries and execute them, but it does not provide the debug capabilities that were available in Query Analyzer. You can debug queries, however—that is, single-step through the T-SQL—from Server Explorer in Visual Studio 2005.

Adding Miscellaneous Files

Miscellaneous files are added to a project by right-clicking the project name in the Solution Explorer tree and then selecting Add > Existing Item, as shown in Figure B-25.

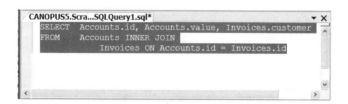

FIGURE B-24: Selected query

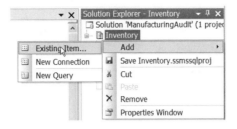

FIGURE B-25: Adding miscellaneous file

The file you select with the Existing Item command will appear in the Miscellaneous folder of the project, as shown in Figure B-26. Note that if the file you select to add has an .sql extension, it will be added to the Queries folder, not the Miscellaneous folder.

Templates

Many queries are similar except for a few object names or terms—for example creating the skeleton of a new Service Broker application. SSMS includes a large selection of templates that will do most of the "busywork" part of a query for you; you just fill in a few values in a dialog box, and it fills in the rest. You can also add your own templates. You use Template Explorer to select and manage templates. You bring up Template Explorer by choosing View > Template Explore, as shown in Figure B-27.

Template Explorer is a tree. Templates are kept track of in folders, and some of these folders contain folders themselves, as shown in Figure B-28.

FIGURE B-26: Excel spreadsheet added to project

FIGURE B-27: Selecting template explorer

To use a template in a query, drag and drop it into a query window, as shown in Figure B-29.

The template will be dropped into the window and selected, as shown in Figure B-30. Notice that some parts of it have a comma-separated list of names inside angle brackets (< >). Each of these is a template parameter that you will fill in through a dialog box.

To fill in the template parameters, choose Query > Specify Values for Template Parameters, as shown in Figure B-31.

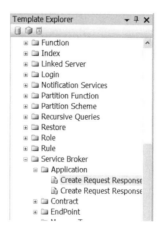

FIGURE B-28: Template explorer

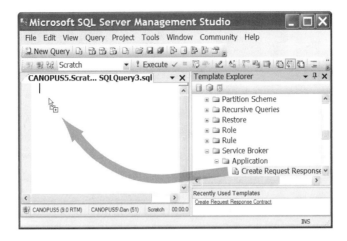

FIGURE B-29: Dragging in template

The Specify Values for Template Parameters command will bring up the Specify Values for Template Parameters dialog box, shown in Figure B-32. Each line in the dialog box contains the name of the parameter, what the type of the parameter is, and a default value for that parameter. You can type a new value over the default value to change it. Note that the type specified for the parameter is only a hint, in that it will not check whether what you type is in fact the type that was specified.

Clicking OK in the Specify Values for Template Parameters dialog box will fill in all the parameters in the template, as shown in Figure B-33. This template contains several items, including the stored procedure

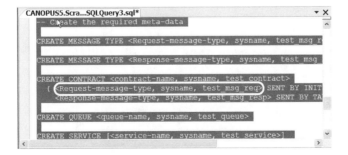

FIGURE B-30: Dropped template

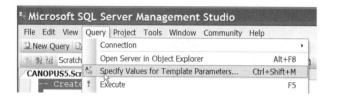

FIGURE B-31: Specify values for template parameters command

named MyProc. This stored procedure was filled in, in multiple places, from the input in Figure B-32. When you have inserted the values, in general, you cannot insert them again unless immediately after inserting the values, you use the undo feature, by pressing Ctrl+Z or choosing Edit > Undo. Note that the inserts are done individually, so it may take several undos to get the original template back.

You can create your own templates. Right-clicking any folder in Template Explorer will allow you to add a folder or a template to Template Explorer, as shown in Figure B-34.

Choosing New > Template will add a new template to the folder, as shown in Figure B-35. The template will be named automatically, but you can change the name by right-clicking it.

A template is just text sprinkled with parameters in angle brackets, as we saw in Figure B-30. To edit the new query, right-click it and choose the

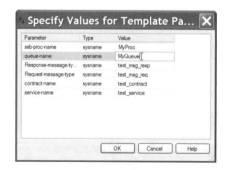

FIGURE B-32: Filling in template parameters

```
CANOPUS5.Scra...SQLQuery3.sql*                              ▾ ✕

--  Create the stored procedure

if exists (select * from dbo.sysobjects
    where id = object_id(N'[dbo].[MyProc]') and OBJECTPROPERTY(
drop procedure [dbo].[MyProc]
GO
SET ANSI_NULLS OFF
go                                  I
SET QUOTED_IDENTIFIER OFF
go

CREATE PROCEDURE [dbo].[MyProc]
    AS declare @message_body nvarchar(MAX)

    declare @message_type int
    declare @dialog uniqueidentifier



while (1 = 1)
begin
   begin transaction
```

FIGURE B-33: Script with parameters filled in

Edit command, as shown in Figure B-36. This will open a query window in which you can type your template. Choosing File > Save or pressing Ctrl+S will save the template.

Templates are fairly straightforward to create. The Specify Values for Template Parameters dialog box, shown in Figure B-32 earlier in this chapter, does a simple copy and replace. Figure B-37 shows a simple template. Everywhere, there are three comma-separated strings enclosed in angle brackets in the template; they are mapped to the three columns in the Template Parameters dialog box.

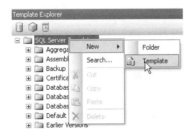

FIGURE B-34: Adding a new template

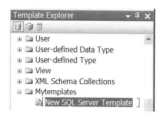

FIGURE B-35: Template added to tree

The same name can appear in more than one template parameter, as shown in Figure B-38. The parameter name "table" is used twice. The Type and Value columns of the Template Parameters dialog box will be filled out according to the first appearance of the parameter in the template. Note that the second table parameter has two commas in it; even though the Type and Value descriptions from this template parameter are ignored by the Template Parameters dialog box, empty values must be used, or the whole template parameter will be ignored.

The result of using the same parameter name more than once is shown in Figure B-39.

Templates are a very powerful and straightforward way to encapsulate coding techniques. It is important to keep in mind that they use a simple copy-and-replace mechanism and do no syntax or other checks. Note that the resulting query shown in Figure B-39 is syntactically incorrect. You cannot

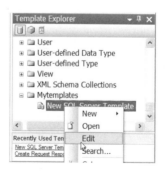

FIGURE B-36: Selecting a template to edit

```
/*
Test Query
*/
SELECT <col1, sysname, Locations>
FROM <table, a customer table, [Big Customer]>
```

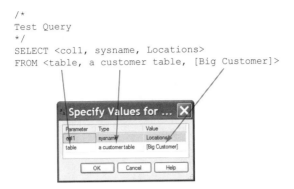

FIGURE B-37: Template parameter mapping

```
/*
Test Query
*/
SELECT <col1, sysname, Locations>
FROM <table, a customer table, [Big Customer]>
JOIN <table,,>
```

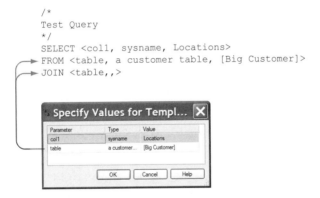

FIGURE B-38: Parameter name used twice

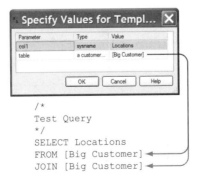

```
/*
Test Query
*/
SELECT Locations
FROM [Big Customer]
JOIN [Big Customer]
```

FIGURE B-39: Result of using same
parameter name twice

check the syntax of a template directly; the angle brackets in the template will always produce a syntax error. You must use your template to create a query and then check the results to be sure that they are syntactically correct. Even then, because a template is just a simple copy-and-replace mechanism, it is possible for users of a template to enter values that produce syntactically incorrect results.

Object Explorer

SSMS includes an Object Explorer that can be used to view and maintain the many objects used by SQL Server 2005. You access it by choosing View > Object Explorer, as shown in Figure B-40.

Object Explorer can be used to explore any of the services provided by SQL Server 2005. Choose Connect > *Service Name* to make a connection, as shown in Figure B-41. This will bring up a connection dialog box. You cannot explore any objects or services your identity or login does not have rights to access, of course.

Object Explorer shows a tree for each SQL Server 2005 service it has a connection to. Figure B-42 shows a tree for a connection to a database engine. Note that the tree is just a hierarchy of all the objects in the SQL Sever 2005 instance that the connection has access rights to.

Figure B-43 shows some of the typical objects than can be explored. Notice that things such as stored procedures are in the Programmability folder.

Objects can be scripted, created, and used from Object Explorer. These functions are available by right-clicking an object or a folder. Figure B-44 shows the menus that are accessed by right-clicking a stored procedure object. The right side of the figure shows the result of choosing Script Stored Procedure As > Create To > New Query Editor Window. You can

FIGURE B-40: Object explorer command

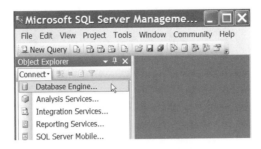

FIGURE B-41: Service-Connection menu

edit this script and then execute it to change the definition of the stored procedure.

The Script Stored Procedure As command shown in Figure B-44 is used to execute a stored procedure and brings up the Execute Procedure dialog box, shown in Figure B-45. Clicking the OK button in this dialog box after entering the values for the parameters as appropriate will produce the results of executing the stored procedure in a query window similar to that shown in Figure B-18 earlier in this chapter.

Object Explorer can be used in conjunction with the Summary window. You can bring up the Summary window by pressing the F7 key or choosing View > Summary. The Summary window will expand what you have selected in Object Explorer, as shown in Figure B-46. Object Explorer will allow you to select only a single object for scripting. The Summary window will let you select multiple objects for scripting.

Figure B-47 shows multiple objects in the Summary window selected for scripting.

FIGURE B-42: Explorer tree

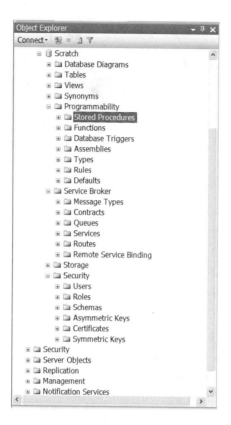

FIGURE B-43: Typical objects

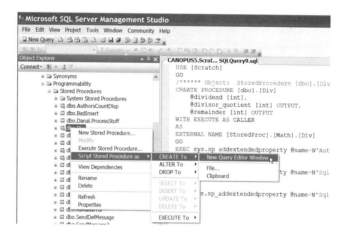

FIGURE B-44: Object menu

FIGURE B-45: Executing a stored procedure

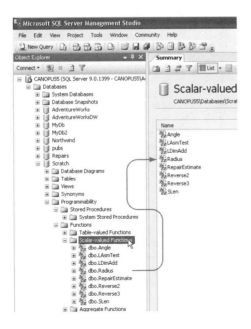

FIGURE B-46: Summary window

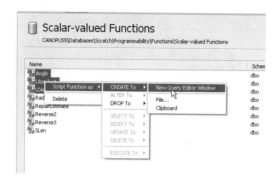

FIGURE B-47: Scripting multiple objects

Enterprise Manager in SQL Server 2000 had a similar capability and also allowed the stored procedure to be debugged—that is, executed one expression at a time. SSMS does not have this capability, but Visual Studio 2005 does.

SSMS provides different capabilities for different objects; you can right-click an object or folder to find these capabilities.

▪C▪
Visual Studio 2005 Integration: SQL Server Projects

THROUGHOUT THE BOOK, everything we have done can be accomplished with nothing more than the command line, a text editor, the command-line compilers, and the command-line utilities that ship with SQL Server 2005. Most developers today, however, are accustomed to using productivity-enhancing development tools—code editors with IntelliSense, tools to define database schemas, and so on. In fact, Microsoft is renowned for its development tools and Integrated Development Environments (IDEs).

Visual Studio 2005

The primary development tool for the great majority of developers working with SQL Server 2005 is Visual Studio 2005. Visual Studio has always had solid integration with SQL Server; with the 2005 releases of SQL Server and Visual Studio, the integration is enhanced by an order of magnitude. Attempting to describe all the integration points among the products would comprise an entire book by itself. In this book, we'll enumerate most of the integration points and cover one feature in depth: Visual Studio 2005 SQLCLR projects (known as SQL Server Projects).

Some of the Visual Studio 2005 integration is in the SQL Server 2005 tool set. SQL Server Business Intelligence Development Studio is installed with SQL Server, and if Visual Studio 2005 itself is installed on the same machine, the two products will be integrated. SQL Server Business Intelligence Development Studio exposes the following new project types:

- Analysis Services Project
- Import Analysis Services 9.0 Database
- Integration Services Project
- Report Server Project Wizard
- Report Model Project
- Report Server Project

SQL Server Management Studio itself, which is covered in Appendix B, has a Visual Studio 2005 "look and feel" and is built from the same basic framework (it is referred to as an *appid* of Visual Studio), although it is a stand-alone tool. Visual Studio 2005 Solutions (collections of Projects) cannot include SQL Server Management Studio Projects, and vice versa.

The Visual Studio 2005 product itself (and the comprehensive Visual Studio Team System) contains quite a few integration points with SQL Server 2005 on its own. These include:

- SQL Server Projects for the C#, Visual Basic .NET, and Managed C++ languages.
- Server Explorer.
- Database Projects for SQL Server.
- Designers that work with Toolbox components in Visual Web Designer Projects, Windows Forms Projects, and other projects.
- An XML editor with IntelliSense. If the appropriate XML schemas are referenced, it includes XML schema–based IntelliSense and schema validation.
- An XML Schema editor and an XML Schema inference tool that infers an XML Schema from an XML document.
- An XSLT editor and debugger.
- A SQL Server Extended Stored Procedure Project for C++.

Although database application development projects usually include many of these features, coverage of all these project types is beyond the scope of this book. In general, these projects must support SQL Server 2000 and 7.0 in addition to SQL Server 2005. Visual Studio Database projects include a few enhancements for SQL Server 2005, such as support for database synonyms. The graphic query designer, however, always creates SQL statements using one-part object names at this writing. Because SQL Server 2005 separates users and schemas, this means that you need to hand-edit the queries after generation or that every object must be resolvable using one-part names. Database Projects, in conjunction with Server Explorer, provide support for creation, source control, maintenance, and debugging of the following Transact-SQL (T-SQL) objects:

- Tables
- Views
- Stored Procedures
- Triggers
- T-SQL Scripts

The bulk of this appendix describes the support in Visual Studio 2005 for developing, deploying, and debugging SQL Server 2005 objects written in .NET Framework languages. This is the SQL Server Project project type for managed programming languages and works in conjunction with Server Explorer. In addition, you can always use the Class Library project type, but this project type will not expose automatic deployment or integrated debugging. Custom attributes in the code enable the automatic deployment feature.

Visual Studio 2005 has some new project types for C#, Visual Basic .NET, and Managed C++: the SQL Server Project. You use this kind of project to create CLR functions, stored procedures, triggers, user-defined types, and user-defined aggregates. Figure C-1 shows how to create a new project in Visual Studio 2005.

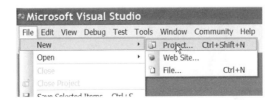

FIGURE C-1: Choosing to create a new project

Choosing New > Project will bring up the New Project dialog box, shown in Figure C-2. Note that in this figure, a C#/Database project has been selected and the mouse is ready to click SQL Server Project. Below the Visual Basic .NET and Managed C++ entry in the tree on the right is a similar entry.

At the bottom of the dialog box, you can select your project and solution names, as well as the directory where you want them to reside.

Clicking the OK button in the New Project dialog box will bring up the Add Database Reference dialog box, shown in Figure C-3. Use this dialog box to select a database to deploy the code you are going to write to.

The Add Database Reference dialog box includes a list of the current data connections that you have configured through Server Explorer. You can also add a reference by clicking the Add New Reference button, which presents the New Database Reference dialog box. This is the same dialog box you'd work with if you added a new data connection in Server Explorer, with the exception that the Microsoft SQL Server (SqlClient) data provider is already selected.

If you add a new reference, a corresponding data connection will be added to Server Explorer.

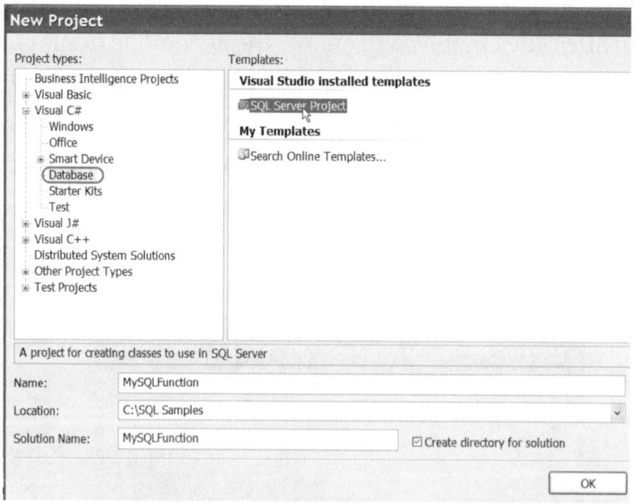

FIGURE C-2: C# database project

FIGURE C-3: Add database reference

After you choose a database reference, Visual Studio 2005 will create a project. Its appearance is configurable. If Server Explorer and Solution Explorer are not visible, as they are in Figure C-4, choose View > Server Explorer and View > Solution Explorer, respectively, to display them. This figure shows Server Explorer on the left.

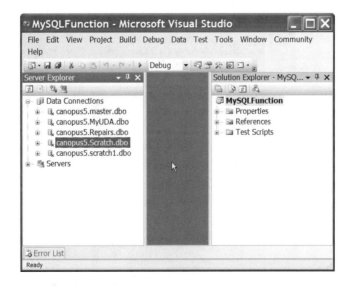

FIGURE C-4: Server and solution explorers

Debugging must be enabled on the data connection. You can enable it by right-clicking, in Server Explorer, the connection you want to do debugging on, as shown in Figure C-5.

Keep in mind that by enabling debugging, you will affect the other users of that instance of SQL Server 2005.

Now that we have chosen the database reference, the setup of the project is completed. The project consists of three folders: Properties, References, and Test Scripts, as shown in Figure C-6. The Properties folder contains an AssemblyInfo.cs module that contains the suggested attributes for the assembly. The References folder contains the commonly used reference assemblies, `System.dll`, `System.Data.dll`, and `System.Xml.dll`.

Before writing any code, you need to add a new item, which you can do by right-clicking the project name in Solution Explorer. Adding a new item presents a selection of adding a user-defined function, user-defined type, user-defined aggregate, user-defined stored procedure, or user-defined trigger. Figure C-7 shows a user-defined function being added to the project.

In Figure C-7, we choose the User-Defined Function template, which we give the name Math. That produces a source file called `Math.cs`, containing a partial public class, `UserDefinedFunctions`, and a static public function, `Math`. Visual Studio 2005 creates a skeleton that you can add code to, as shown in Figure C-8.

FIGURE C-5: Enabling debugging

FIGURE C-6: Solution
explorer in a C# SQL
Server project

Custom Attributes and Automatic Deployment

SQL Server projects differ from Class Library projects in a few ways:

- There is an extra tab named Database in the Properties page.
- The Add Reference dialog box produces a different choice of libraries to use.
- The Build menu contains a Deploy command.
- There is a Test Scripts folder.

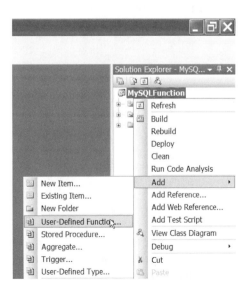

FIGURE C-7: Adding user-defined function

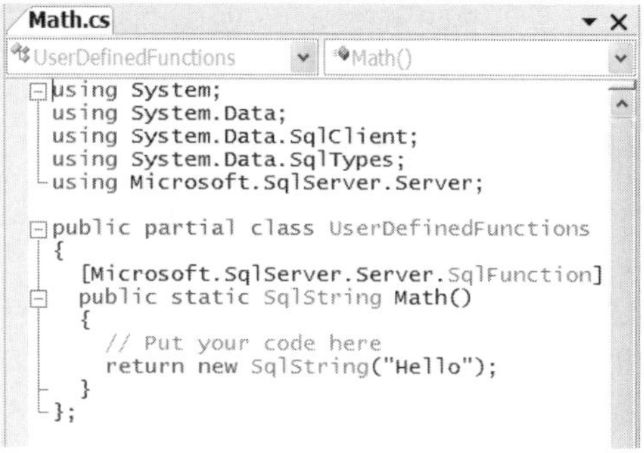

FIGURE C-8: Code skeleton

We'll discuss the Add Reference difference first. In Chapter 2 (SQLCLR) and Chapter 6 (Security), we expounded on the fact that only a subset of the .NET Framework class libraries is "approved" for loading into SQL Server. Only these assemblies appear in the Add Reference dialog box.[1] In addition, assemblies that have already been catalogued in the database appear in the list.

Automatic Deployment

When you choose Build > Deploy, Visual Studio 2005 will build SQL Server DDL statements, connect to the database that you specified when creating the project, and submit the DDL to SQL Server. Depending on which type of SQL Server objects your project contains, the DDL statements include

- CREATE ASSEMBLY
- ALTER ASSEMBLY with ADD FILE option
- DROP ASSEMBLY
- CREATE/DROP PROCEDURE
- CREATE/DROP FUNCTION

---

1. At this writing, one of the libraries on the approved list, System.Configuration.dll, did not appear in the list of libraries to reference. This makes it difficult to add a reference to this assembly.

- CREATE/DROP TRIGGER
- CREATE/DROP TYPE
- CREATE/DROP AGGREGATE

Note that Visual Studio 2005's automatic deployment does not, for safety reasons, support ALTER ASSEMBLY except to add files. Automatically deploying the project will use ALTER ASSEMBLY only to add files related to the assembly. All source-code files are added; this gives the DBA the ability to reconstruct the assembly if necessary. Visual Studio 2005 also deploys the debug symbol files (.pdb files), which are required for debugging inside SQL Server. If any database objects reference the items in the assembly or reference the assembly itself, automatic deployment will fail, with a generic error message. References that can cause an automatic deployment to fail include use of a user-defined type as a column in a table or a user-defined function specified in the definition of a computed column.

The exact DDL statements used are based on the project properties and custom attributes on the code. In the Database tab, you can specify whether the PERMISSION_SET clause of CREATE ASSEMBLY should be Safe, External (EXTERNAL_ACCESS in DDL), or Unsafe. Safe is the default for a project, as it is the default in SQL Server. CREATE ASSEMBLY works with the assembly_bits option rather than using the assembly file. This alleviates permission problems. The connection string of the data connection indicates which SQL Server principal will be used, and this principal must have the appropriate permission in SQL Server, as discussed in Chapter 2. The Output window indicates which assemblies and files were deployed but not which objects, such as stored procedures and triggers, were deployed or the exact DDL generated by automatic deployment. To view the automatic-deployment DDL, you must use a SQL Profiler trace. You can also query the database after the fact.

When you add a new SQLCLR item to your SQL Server Project, you'll notice that your class or method is decorated with a custom attribute. The attribute is different for each type of item. These attributes live in the Microsoft.SqlServer.Server namespace in System.Data.dll, and a C# using statement is included so that the short class name can be used in the code. Table C-1 shows a list of custom attributes.

TABLE C-1: Custom Attributes on SQLCLR Items

Attribute	On Method or Class	Defines
SqlProcedure	Method	Stored procedure
SqlFunction	Method	User-defined function
SqlTrigger	Method	Trigger
SqlUserDefinedType	Class	User-defined type
SqlUserDefinedAggregate	Class	User-defined aggregate

All these attributes are used for automatic deployment—that is, creating SQL DDL statements when the Deploy command is selected. Some of the attributes are used only for automatic deployment. If you do not use automatic deployment, these attributes are not required. Some of the attributes are used both for deployment and to indicate behaviors of the code to SQL Server. In Chapter 3, for example, we discussed the SqlFunction attribute and how you use this attribute to inform SQL Server about how the function behaved. Each attribute is used for automatic deployment, and each attribute has different properties that are used to construct the deployment DDL.

Data Types and SqlFacet

When using automatic deployment, the data type of the SQL Server parameter or return code that should be specified in the DDL statement is inferred from the type of the .NET Framework method parameter or return code. The mapping of data types to SQL Server types follows the same rules that the SqlClient data provider uses. See Books Online for a complete list and Chapter 3 for an explanation of, and the repercussions of, using SqlTypes instead of "vanilla" .NET Framework data types in method declarations. When you are using automatic deployment of procedures and functions, there are three places where the SQL Server type system requires more accuracy than type inference provides. The .NET Framework System.String class does not specify a maximum length, as the SQL Server does. Also, .NET Framework System.String does not have the capability to require a string to be a fixed length—that is, to specify the difference between the VARCHAR and CHAR data types. If you use String or SqlString in the declaration of a user-defined function or stored procedure, NVARCHAR(4000) is always used at automatic deployment. The final limitation is that the .NET Framework System.Decimal data type is a variable precision and scale data type. You cannot specify the precision and scale of a DECIMAL data type when your procedure or function is defined in SQL Server. SQL Server's DECIMAL data type is a fixed precision and scale data type. The default value of DECIMAL(18,0) is always used.

The SqlFacet attribute is a custom attribute that allows you to overcome these limitations. It can be used on fields, properties, return values, and parameters. This attribute can be used with all the SQLCLR objects where it makes sense—that is, stored procedures, user-defined functions, user-defined types, and user-defined aggregates. When the methods have been deployed, the behavior in SQL Server follows the ordinary conversion and truncation rules of T-SQL.

Table C-2 shows the fields on each of the custom attributes that are used for deployment, their meaning, and whether the attribute is used only for deployment.

Executing and Debugging the Code

To test the code, we can always execute the procedure or function created in the database from inside SQL Server Management Studio. It would be nice if this could also happen from inside Visual Studio 2005, however, and this is where the Test Scripts folder comes in. The Test Scripts folder contains one script, Test.sql, when a project is created. This is the SQL script that will be executed if you choose Debug > Start or press F5. You can add more test scripts to the folder. You can execute any script by right-clicking the script and choosing the Debug Script command. You can also make any script the default debugging script.

If you open the Test.sql file, you'll see that it contains a series of commented SQL statements. You can uncomment the statement that looks similar to the item you are testing or write test code from scratch. Using the Test Scripts folder enables you to keep your SQLCLR source code and the scripts you use to test it in the same project location. When you are debugging SQLCLR procedures in Visual Studio 2005, the procedure output appears in the Output window.

TABLE C-2: Custom Attributes Properties on SQLCLR Items

Attribute	Deployment Only?	Property	Defines
SqlFacet	Yes	IsNullable	Nullability of parameter.
		IsFixedLength	If true for a string parameter, NCHAR will be generated. False (the default) generates NVARCHAR.
		MaxSize	Size of a string (NCHAR or NVARCHAR) parameter. A value of -1 generates a "MAX" data type parameter; a value of 0 generates the default length (4000).
		Precision	Precision for decimal parameters.
		Scale	Scale for decimal parameters.
SqlProcedure	Yes	Name	Name of procedure in SQL Server.
SqlFunction	No	Name	Name of function in SQL Server.
		FillRowMethodName	Name of the method that will be defined as the table valued function in SQL Server (table-valued functions only).
		TableDefinition	Defines the table in the SQL DDL RETURNS clause (table-value functions only).
SqlTrigger	Yes	Name	Name of trigger in SQL Server.
		Target	Table or View specified in the SQL DDL "ON" clause in CREATE TRIGGER for DML triggers. In DDL triggers, this is either Database or Server.

TABLE C-2: Custom Attributes Properties on SQLCLR Items (*Continued*)

Attribute	Deployment Only?	Property	Defines
		Event	The event specified in the SQL DDL "FOR" clause of CREATE TRIGGER.
`SqlUserDefined Type`	No	Name	Name of type in SQL Server.
`SqlUserDefin-edAggregate`	No	Name	Name of aggregate in SQL Server.

It is not necessary to run the project from inside Visual Studio 2005 to debug the CLR code. If the debug symbols of the CLR assembly have been loaded into SQL Server, the procedure or function can be executed from inside SQL Server and stepped through in the Visual Studio .NET debugger. To make this work, you need to attach the debugger to the SQL Server process by following these steps. You must have additional permissions on the machine where SQL Server is installed for this to work, and it's useful mostly when you're debugging an instance of SQL Server installed on your own desktop.

1. Choose Debug > Attach to Process.
2. In the Attach to Process dialog box, choose the `sqlservr.exe` process, as shown in Figure C-9.
3. Make sure that the Show Processes from All Users checkbox is checked.
4. Set breakpoints in the CLR source file.
5. Execute the T-SQL code.

You can also use Visual Studio 2005 to debug T-SQL procedures and functions. To accomplish this directly, in Server Explorer, right-click the procedure or function you want to debug, and choose Step into Stored Procedure or Step into Function.

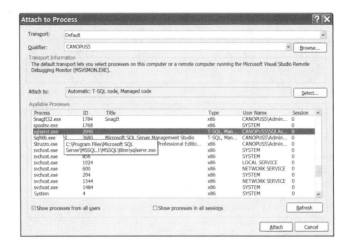

FIGURE C-9: Attach to process dialog box

Visual Studio 2005 gives you the facilities to integrate programming, testing, and debugging SQL Server 2005 code whether that code is written in T-SQL or SQLCLR. Your in-server development can take advantage of the same rich developer environment that you are used to if you use databases in client-side code. You can even have a Solution that consists of one or more Database Projects, one or more SQL Server Projects for SQLCLR code, and one or more client code projects. The integrated debugger even works when you step from client code into T-SQL or SQLCLR code, step through the code, and step back into client code. This provides complete coverage for both server and client development.

References

ANSI/ISO/IEC International Standard (IS). Database Language SQL. 1992, 1999, 2003.

Beauchemin, Bob, with Chris Sells. *Essential ADO.NET.* Boston: Addison-Wesley, 2002.

Beauchemin, Bob. "XML Indexes in SQL Server 2005." http://msdn.microsoft.com/library/default.asp?url=/library/en-us/dnsql90/html/xmlindexes.asp.

Beauchemin, Bob. "XML in Yukon: New Version Showcases Native XML Type and Advanced Data Handling." *MSDN Magazine*, February 2004.

Box, Don. *Essential .NET Volume 1 The Common Language Runtime.* Boston: Addison-Wesley, 2003.

Brundage, Michael. *XQuery: The XML Query Language.* Boston: Addison-Wesley, 2004.

Date, C. J., and Hugh Darwin. *An Introduction to Database Systems.* 6th ed. Boston: Addison-Wesley, 2001.

Ewald, Tim. *Transactional COM+.* Boston: Addison-Wesley, 2001.

Gulutzan, Peter, and Trudy Pelzer. *SQL-99 Complete, Really.* Lawrence, Kansas: R&D Books, 1999.

Henderson, Ken. *The Guru's Guide to SQL Server Architecture and Internals.* Boston: Addison-Wesley, 2004.

Katz, Howard, ed. *XQuery from the Experts.* Boston: Addison-Wesley, 2003.

Melton, Jim. *Advanced SQL:1999: Understanding Object-Relational and Other Advanced Features.* San Francisco: Morgan Kaufmann, 2001.

Melton, Jim, and Alan Simon. *SQL:1999: Understanding Relational Language Components.* San Francisco: Morgan Kaufmann, 2001.

Microsoft OLE DB 2.0 Programmer's Reference and *Data Access SDK.* Redmond, Washington: Microsoft Press, 1998.

Pal, Shankar, et al. "XQuery Indexes in a Relational Database System." http://www.vldb2005.org/program/paper/thu/p1175-pal.pdf.

Pratschner, Steven. *Customizing the Microsoft .NET Framework Common Language Runtime.* Redmond, Washington: Microsoft Press, 2005.

Walther, Steven. "Improved Caching in ASP.NET 2.0." *MSDN Online.* http://msdn.microsoft.com/library/default.asp?url=/library/en-us/dnvs05/html/CachingNT2.asp.

W3C XQuery Specifications. http://www.w3c.org/XML/Query#specs.

Index

Y

Microsoft .NET Development Series

.NET Framework Standard Library Annotated Reference
Volume 1: Base Class Library and Extended Numerics Library

Brad Abrams

0321154894

.NET Framework Standard Library Annotated Reference
Volume 2: Networking Library, Reflection Library and XML Library

Brad Abrams
Tamara Abrams

0321194454

.NET Web Services
Architecture and Implementation

Keith Ballinger

0321113594

A First Look at SQL Server 2005 for Developers

Bob Beauchemin
Niels Berglund
Dan Sullivan

0321180593

Visual Studio Tools for Office
Using C# with Excel, Word, Outlook, and InfoPath

Eric Carter
Eric Lippert

0321334884

Visual Studio Tools for Office
Using Visual Basic 2005 with Excel, Word, Outlook, and InfoPath

Eric Carter
Eric Lippert

0321411757

Graphics Programming with GDI+

Mahesh Chand

0321160770

Framework Design Guidelines
Conventions, Idioms, and Patterns for Reusable .NET Libraries

Krzysztof Cwalina
Brad Abrams

0321246756

Enterprise Services with the .NET Framework
Developing Distributed Business Solutions with .NET Enterprise Services

Christian Nagel

032124673X

Data Binding with Windows Forms 2.0
Programming Smart Client Data Applications with .NET

Brian Noyes

032126892X

Essential ASP.NET
with Examples in C#

Fritz Onion

0201760401

Windows Forms Programming in Visual Basic .NET

Chris Sells
Justin Gehtland

0321125193

The Visual Basic .NET Programming Language

Paul Vick

0321169514

Essential .NET
Volume 1
The Common Language Runtime

Don Box
with Chris Sells

0201734117

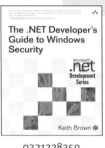

The .NET Developer's Guide to Windows Security

Keith Brown

0321228359

The C# Programming Language

Anders Hejlsberg
Scott Wiltamuth
Peter Golde

0321154916

ADO.NET and System.Xml v. 2.0
The Beta Version

Alex Homer
Dave Sussman
Mark Fussell

0321247124

ASP.NET v. 2.0–
The Beta Version

Alex Homer
Dave Sussman
Rob Howard

0321257278

Common Language Infrastructure Annotated Standard

James S. Miller
Susann Ragsdale

0321154932

Essential ASP.NET
with Examples in Visual Basic .NET

Fritz Onion

0201760398

Building Applications and Components with Visual Basic .NET

Ted Pattison
with Dr. Joe Hummel

0201734958

eXtreme .NET
Introducing eXtreme Programming Techniques to .NET Developers

Dr. Neil Roodyn

0321303636

Windows Forms Programming in C#

Chris Sells

0321116208

Programming in the .NET Environment

Damien Watkins
Mark Hammond
Brad Abrams

0201770180

Pragmatic ADO.NET
Data Access for the Internet World

Shawn Wildermuth

0201745682

.NET Compact Framework Programming with C#

Paul Yao
David Durant

0321174038

.NET Compact Framework Programming with Visual Basic .NET

Paul Yao
David Durant

0321174046

For more information go to www.awprofessional.com/msdotnetserie

Register Your Book

at www.awprofessional.com/register

You may be eligible to receive:
- Advance notice of forthcoming editions of the book
- Related book recommendations
- Chapter excerpts and supplements of forthcoming titles
- Information about special contests and promotions throughout the year
- Notices and reminders about author appearances, tradeshows, and online chats with special guests

Contact us

If you are interested in writing a book or reviewing manuscripts prior to publication, please write to us at:

Editorial Department
Addison-Wesley Professional
75 Arlington Street, Suite 300
Boston, MA 02116 USA
Email: AWPro@aw.com

Visit us on the Web: http://www.awprofessional.com

BOOKS ONLINE

ENABLED

THIS BOOK IS SAFARI ENABLED

INCLUDES FREE 45-DAY ACCESS TO THE ONLINE EDITION

The Safari® Enabled icon on the cover of your favorite technology book means the book is available through Safari Bookshelf. When you buy this book, you get free access to the online edition for 45 days.

Safari Bookshelf is an electronic reference library that lets you easily search thousands of technical books, find code samples, download chapters, and access technical information whenever and wherever you need it.

TO GAIN 45-DAY SAFARI ENABLED ACCESS TO THIS BOOK:

- Go to **http://www.awprofessional.com/safarienabled**

- Complete the brief registration form

- Enter the coupon code found in the front of this book on the "Copyright" page

Addison
Wesley